TO RAISE AND DISCIPLINE AN ARMY

TO RAISE AND
DISCIPLINE AN ARMY

Major General Enoch Crowder, the Judge Advocate
General's Office, and the Realignment of Civil
and Military Relations in World War I

JOSHUA E. KASTENBERG

NIU PRESS/DEKALB

Northern Illinois University Press, DeKalb 60115
© 2017 by Northern Illinois University Press

26 25 24 23 22 21 20 19 18 17   1 2 3 4 5
978-0-87580-754-6 (cloth)
978-1-60909-213-9 (e-book)
Book and cover design by Yuni Dorr

Library of Congress Cataloging-in-Publication Data
Names: Kastenberg, Joshua E., 1967- author.
Title: To raise and discipline an army : Major General Enoch Crowder, the Judge
    Advocate General's Office and the realignment of civil and military relations in
    World War I / Joshua Kastenberg.
Other titles: Major General Enoch Crowder, the Judge Advocate General's Office
    and the realignment of civil and military relations in World War I
Description: First edition. | DeKalb, IL : NIU Press, [2017] | Includes bibliographical
    references and index.
Identifiers: LCCN 2017001163 (print) | LCCN 2017004509 (ebook) | ISBN
    9780875807546 (cloth : alk. paper) | ISBN 9781609092139 (e-book)
Subjects: LCSH: Crowder, E. H. (Enoch Herbert), 1859-1932. | Judge Advocates—
    United States—Biography. | United States. Army. Office of the Judge Advocate
    General—Biography. | Civil-military relations—United States—History—20th
    century. | World War, 1914-1918—Law and legislation—United States.
Classification: LCC KF373.C728 K37 2017 (print) | LCC KF373.C728 (ebook) |
    DDC 343.73/0143—dc23
LC record available at https://lccn.loc.gov/2017001163

Contents

Preface   vii

INTRODUCTION   3

1 ENOCH CROWDER AND THE WILSON PRESIDENCY   11

2 STAFFING AND DIRECTING THE JUDGE ADVOCATE
GENERAL'S DEPARTMENT: DUTIES AND DISCIPLINE   40

3 THE CONSCRIPTING AND TRAINING
OF A DISCIPLINED FORCE   93

4 JUDGE ADVOCATES IN THE AEF   150

5 INTERNATIONAL LAW AND ADMINISTRATIVE
DUTIES IN WAR AND AFTER THE ARMISTICE   198

6 POLITICAL OVERSIGHT OF MILITARY DISCIPLINE   250

7 COURTS-MARTIAL, CONCERNS OVER
SUBVERSION, AND CONSCIENTIOUS OBJECTION   300

8 COURTS-MARTIAL AND DISCIPLINE
CONTROVERSY: 1918–1920   352

CONCLUSION: RETURN TO NORMALCY
AND A FORGOTTEN HISTORY   408

Bibliography   425
Notes   437
Index   485

Preface

The First World War began over a century ago, among a European populace imbued by nationalism but also shaped by political, social, and economic movements including socialism, anarchism, women's suffrage, and new religious sects. Empires that had lasted for centuries, such as the Habsburg (also called Austria-Hungary), the Ottoman, and Russian were still globally influential even if their power was weakened by the rise of the German Empire and the United States. Of course, Great Britain had maintained its power through the industrial age and the acquisition of vast overseas territories, and although France had been defeated in the 1870–1871 war against Prussia and its German state allies, it too had wealth and military power. While the United States did not enter the war in 1914, its population encountered the same political and social movements found in Europe. Indeed, in the fifty years prior to the war, European political refugees and revolutionaries came to the United States, as did millions of immigrants from areas such as Italy and Eastern Europe where revolutionary movements had taken root. In 1917, when the US government did declare war on Germany and side with Britain, France, Belgium, Italy, Japan, China, and Romania against Germany, Austria-Hungary, Bulgaria, and the Ottoman Empire, the United States was not unanimously "united" in support of the war. And the president who sought a declaration of war from Congress, Woodrow Wilson, only reluctantly did so. But once he did, he assumed the mantle of power with an authority not seen since Abraham Lincoln's presidency. Put another way, in 1928 Wilson's predecessor William Howard Taft opined to a British friend, "he hated war, and yet he loved the power which the President necessarily must be given in time of war, and he exercised it *con amore*." Since 1918, but particularly beginning in the late 1950s and accelerating during the Vietnam Conflict, historians have rightfully viewed the period between 1917 and 1920 as a time of vastly diminished individual rights. It was also a period in which the traditional subservience of the military to the three branches of the civilian government came into question.[1]

This book attempts to address the phenomena of how a very small US Army was shaped into a massive and disciplined instrument of war, and it attempts to explain how, in the process, the civil and military construct was altered. But it does so with the approach that the change occurred as a result of the efforts of a diverse grouping of lawyers, some of whom were military professionals before the war, although most were not. Indeed, most were part of the legal fabric of the nation, including professors from Columbia's and Harvard's law schools, trial judges from Kansas and Nebraska, and prosecuting attorneys from Wisconsin and California. In a sense, this study is premised on the idea that both vast changes in the law and the unprecedented enforcement of the law occurred "from the ground up." In this light, I hope that this book contributes to studies of civil and military relations, political science, and legal and military history.

While all of the errors in this book are mine, I recognize that it would not have been written at all but for the support I have had from friends, as well as from the dedicated librarians and archivists at the Library of Congress's manuscript division. I also visited the archives of most of the collections cited in this book. All of the individuals associated with these archives were extremely helpful. I must point out that, Professor Gordon Hylton, Colonels Adam Oler and Kate Oler, Colonel (retired) Fred Borch, Colonel (retired) Don Christensen, Colonel Robert Preston, Colonel Joe Dene, Colonel Mark Allred, and my very good friend (and hopefully future colonel) Erin Lai, also provided insight and the needed encouragement to get this book finished.

By the time this book is in print, I will have been retired from active duty as a commissioned officer in the United States Air Force. I served in uniform for twenty-two years, and the last five years I had the privilege of serving as a military trial judge who had the duty to ensure that the due process rights of service-members who were prosecuted for various crimes were assiduously protected. This was a difficult but rewarding duty, and I encountered dozens of diligent and ethical officers who were assigned as prosecutors and defense counsel. I also served alongside some very bright judges. Prior to my judicial tenure, I spent over a year in Iraq, where I advised commanders on the legal constraints of military operations, including intelligence collection and targeting. I also worked with truly exceptional (and indeed, intellectually inspirational) British and Australian service-members and Iraqi judges and prosecutors.

In World War I, men brought into the army as judge advocates tended to be older and already established in the legal profession. In our modern times, women and men in the army, air force, marine corps, navy, and coast guard Judge Advocate General's Corps enter into active duty at a much younger age. They and their enlisted paralegals are both diverse and extraordinary. I believe it is important to note that there are women and men in critical leadership positions within the US military. This is the way it should be. The military cannot succeed in its mission of defending the nation if it is not fully inclusive not only of gender but of gender identity. That is, the composition of the military has to be diverse, but it also has to embrace its diversity as a moral necessity. As an aside, albeit an important one, inclusivity in the military's legal arm began in World War I on the insistence of its highest officer, Major General Enoch Crowder.

In the early 1990's I was a graduate student and one of my favorite professors, who taught urban history called "discovering the undiscovered history" his passion. This effort requires travel and meeting unique and wonderful people along the way. After my two children, this process of discovery is one of my central passions as well. However, I dedicated my first two books to my children and I hope that they will forgive me for dedicating this book to one of my oldest friends, my "big" brother, Andrew E. Kastenberg. In life, there are unpaid debts and sometimes these debts are not known to the person owed. Andy has protectively been in my corner for almost fifty years, he has supported me in a number of ways, from camping on beaches in the Greek Islands and wandering through historic Turkey to climbing mountains in the Sierra Nevada above the tree line, all the while listening to my rambling and often sophomoric observations about humanity. He has reminded me to believe in myself, and when unfortunate circumstances threaten to suffocate a passion, if the passion was worth anything, to fight for it. This dedication is the best way that I know of to tell him that as his brother and friend, I love him.

TO RAISE AND DISCIPLINE AN ARMY

INTRODUCTION

WHEN, ON APRIL 2, 1917, President Woodrow Wilson urged Congress to recognize that a state of war existed between the German Empire and the United States, the US Army numbered less than 150,000 soldiers. As of that date, of all male civilians in the United States who would soon become amenable to military service, military jurisdiction reached less than 1 percent. By 1919 over 24 million American citizens and residents were potentially subject to the military's jurisdiction. Because the nation's population was slightly over 100 million, a significant percentage of its residents was immediately affected by a change in legal status: from citizen to service-member or possible service-member. The effect of an expansive military jurisdiction extended to family members as well as churches, industries, and political organizations. On July 1, 1917, the military's jurisdiction reached all males who received a "draft order," and at war's end, almost four million males served in the army. That is, many of these men were subject to prosecution in the army's courts—known as courts-martial—not only for violations of common offenses but also for infractions against military laws and regulations. These numbers alone evidence that the United States' entry into the war resulted in a massive shift in civil and military relations. Traditionally the army had been small and, with the exception of the Civil War, wholly subservient to the federal government's three branches. The army had, with the exception of militia matters, also remained outside of state government functions.

From April 1917 through the end of 1921, the army conducted over 31,000 general courts-martial, the most severe of the military's criminal trials somewhat equating to felony trials, and almost three-quarters of these resulted in a conviction. A general court-martial could, in addition to sentencing a soldier to death or to years in prison, also punish a convicted soldier with a dishonorable discharge. (Officers in such trials could be "dismissed," which, under the law, was equivalent to a dishonorable discharge.) During this same period, the army conducted over 300,000 lesser trials known as special courts-martial and summary courts-martial. These trials were analogous to those in misdemeanor and ordinance courts and could not sentence a soldier to a dishonorable discharge. Special courts-martial could sentence enlisted soldiers to a year in prison and reduce them to the lowest enlisted rank, and summary courts-martial could reduce junior enlisted soldiers in rank and confine them to a stockade for thirty days. Convictions in all of these courts created a permanent federal record, but there was no true means of appeal through the federal courts.

As of September 1, 1917, the army was issuing dishonorable discharges to soldiers at the rate of over one hundred per week, a number that the judge advocate general, the War Department's chief legal officer, considered appallingly high. While not all general courts-martial convictions resulted in a dishonorable discharge, those soldiers who were dishonorably discharged faced a permanent social stigma and were blocked from receiving any veterans' benefits. Put another way, between 1917 and 1920, the War Department added over 24,000 convicted felons to the United States' population. Although courts-martial were one indication of the military establishment's influence in American society, in several other respects, the military establishment expanded into the commercial, social, and political life of the nation as well as the civil liberties of its people.[1]

The nation's founders believed that standing armies were a menace to liberty, and in times of peace, few Americans were expected to serve in the army. From 1868 to 1897, the army's authorized strength was approximately 25,000 soldiers. The army's sized peaked at slightly more than 100,000 soldiers during the Spanish-American War and Philippine Insurrection, but after 1903, its numbers dwindled to half that size. Prior to 1916, the army was smaller than the armies of Belgium, the Netherlands, Portugal, or Spain. Yet the United States' population was larger than that of all these countries combined, and not only did its geography stretch across an entire continent, it also governed Alaska, the Hawaiian Islands, Guam, the Philippines, Cuba, and Puerto Rico. From the founding of the nation forward, the US government expected that its foreign interests would be safeguarded by the nation's naval forces, and if the need arose for an expanded land force, the nation could rely on state militias, many of which had become the National Guard by 1916. But reliance on state militia had not always occurred without resistance. During the War of 1812, Federalist-dominated northern state governments undermined the necessary unity to confront Great Britain by limiting the use of their state militias. And while, during the Spanish-American War and Philippine Insurrection, state militia forces augmented the regular army with little impediment from state governments, state governors were able to exercise a great deal of control over their respective militia forces in a manner that no longer exists.[2]

Until Theodore Roosevelt's presidency, state militia forces were not federalized in the modern sense because governors were able to effect terms of enlistment, control training, and commission officers without federal interference. State governments could exert influence on military discipline in two other respects prior to 1903. Between 1870 and 1903, when the militia forces were federalized, Congress had ensured through various statutes that courts-martial of militia soldiers were composed of militia officers. State governors also had the ability to pardon or annul the courts-martial convictions and sentences of militia soldiers. In 1902 the Supreme Court, in *McClaughery v. Deming*, upheld this construct against a War Department challenge. By World War I, there was no longer any statutory protection to ensure that militia officers would sit in judgment of militia soldiers in courts-martial, and state governors could no longer overturn courts-martial convictions.[3]

The army's discipline was administered by the Judge Advocate General's Office. Technically the term *office* meant the office that the judge advocate general occupied in Washington, DC, and the term *Judge Advocate General's Department*, referred to the staff department that supervised all judge advocates regardless of where the individual judge advocate was located. By 1914, the War Department, Congress, and the nation's newspapers interchangeably used the terms *office* and *department* so that the distinction between the two became blurred. At the time the war in Europe erupted, the Judge Advocate General's Office numbered twelve officers and one clerk, but it stood equal in authority to the Army's Engineer, Ordnance, and Quartermaster Departments and that of the surgeon general. From 1868 until 1897, the Judge Advocate General's Office numbered no more than six judge advocates, and after the Spanish-American War, the office grew to twelve. By 1919 more than four hundred judge advocates would be assigned to the Judge Advocate General's Office. Many of these men would be at the forefront of the alteration of civil and military relations.[4]

Neither the judge advocate general nor his staff regularly prosecuted courts-martial. Judge advocates assigned to the various geographic departments ranging from the Philippines to the Department of the Atlantic at Governors Island, New York, sometimes prosecuted courts-martial, but usually they too delegated these duties to "line officers" who had some legal training. These line officers served on an ad hoc basis, and after short tours as a trial judge advocate, they would return to their infantry, artillery, cavalry, or engineering duties. This practice was developed following the War of 1812 and given further shape by the War Department after 1865. In World War I the army directly commissioned officers as judge advocates and placed these men at the headquarters of the divisions, corps, and larger commands such as the Services of Supply. An American division numbered over twenty thousand soldiers and, in addition to its judge advocate, a division often had two or three assistant judge advocates. The assistant judge advocates occasionally served as prosecutors, but they too mainly reviewed records of trial, as well as answered constitutional law, contracting, and law of war questions from their respective commands. In May 1918 Captain Bernard Gorfinkle, the Twenty-Sixth Division's first assistant judge advocate, wrote to his mother the following apt description: "I see that the procedure is properly conducted. The trial judge advocate is a Major Regular. Do not be confused in this. My office is the Division Judge Advocate. We are not supposed to try cases. They put me in to see that the rules are properly complied with." In 1919 Lieutenant Colonel Hugh W. Ogden, a prominent Boston attorney and the Forty-Second—or "Rainbow"—Division's judge advocate, informed that city's bar association that "ordinarily, the divisional judge advocate does not try cases because as the commander's legal advisor he could not sit in judgment of his own trials."[5]

There is an important demarcation as to the authority of the judge advocate general prior to 1950. No judge advocate had the legal power to reverse a court-martial, even when the court-martial was glaringly bereft of due process. Instead, a judge advocate had a duty to advise a general in command of a geographic department or division, the secretary of war, or the president, that a court-martial should either be approved or denied, or that clemency should be granted in the form of reducing a sentence. A judge advocate's legal review of a court-martial might read similarly to an appellate brief or judicial decision, but the legal review was advice and nothing more. Nonetheless, as advice, the legal review could be compelling, and usually a commanding general, secretary of war, or president followed it. However, even when the secretary of war or president determined the opposite of the judge advocate general's advice, a court-martialed soldier was unlikely to find any relief from either Congress or the federal courts. In *Ex Parte Mason*, the Supreme Court in 1881 implicitly determined, in bypassing an issue decided by a lower court, that the judge advocate general's advice not only was not binding on the Executive Branch but also was a privileged communication of which the federal courts could take no cognizance. Private John A. Mason, a prison guard, had been court-martialed for attempting to kill Charles Guiteau after Guiteau was arrested for assassinating President James Garfield. Mason argued to the federal courts that his court-martial should be overturned because President Chester Arthur refused to follow the judge advocate general's advice to disapprove the conviction and sentence. *Ex Parte Mason* contributed to the Judge Advocate General's Office's leaders' assumption that the powers of the judge advocate general were limited to advising the secretary of war and general officers and did not extend to overturning courts-martial convictions and sentences.[6]

On March 31, 1913, Henry A. Stimson on his last day as secretary of war reported to his successor, Lindley M. Garrison, that "the Judge Advocate General's Office had thirteen employees of which ten are commissioned officers." Stimson further advised Garrison that the judge advocate general's duties included, in addition to reviewing courts-martial records and recommending whether to approve the findings or sentences, giving legal advice on a variety of civil matters including the governance of the Indian Territories, the administration of national parks, equipment and supply purchases, contracting issues, and claims made against the War Department. Stimson also noted that the office was responsible for reviewing proposed legislation and advising on the need for additional laws and orders as well as on promotions, officer seniority, and the command authorities of the various military departments. Stimson could have added that occasionally judge advocates defended the government in the federal courts, including the Supreme Court. In 1863 Brigadier General Joseph Holt, the judge advocate general of the army during the Civil War, represented the Executive Branch in the Supreme Court while defending the army's arrest and military trial of a former congressman in *Ex Parte Vallandigham*. During the fifty years following that decision, it was not uncommon to see a judge advocate's name as the government representative in a federal court decision. For instance, Major Asa Bird Gardner, a judge advocate, drafted the government's brief and argued to the Supreme Court in *Ex Parte Mason*, and Lieutenant Colonel Enoch Crowder, who headed the Judge Advocate General's Office in World War I, argued and lost *McClaughery v. Deming*. What Stimson also inadvertently omitted from his memorandum to Garrison was that the judge advocate general not only served as an advisor to the president, commanding general, and secretary of war, he also frequently interacted with other cabinet secretaries, federal judges, Congress, and state governments.[7]

To this day, there is no published study on how the Judge Advocate General's Office participated in the United States' war efforts, took part in shaping the nation's strategy for victory over Germany, oversaw conscription, or worked to prevent a recurrence of war in the four years after the Armistice. There has never been a study on courts-martial in the World War I army, or even a treatise limited to military trials in the American Expeditionary Forces during that conflict. Likewise, there is no study published in either English or French on the legal interaction between the American Expeditionary Forces and their Allied counterparts. A study of each of these areas will contribute to a greater understanding of civil-military relations during a time of crisis a century ago, and of how that crisis influences the current status of civil-military relations. A study of these areas also enables a better understanding of the suppression of individual rights in World War II and the Cold War, as well as responses, both internal and external to the government, that led to the eventual recognition of the existence of broader individual and civil rights. Additionally, although military historians of the so-called "Great War" have occasionally referenced the Judge Advocate General's Office, most of their studies only passingly refer to courts-martial, and a smaller number of publications reference the interaction between the Allies on important legal matters such as jurisdiction and liability for damages to property and injuries to people. As an example, in 2014 David Woodward authored *The American Army and the First World War*, a treatise heralded as "the definitive history of the American Army in World War I." But there is only one comment on courts-martial and no mention of a "gentleman's agreement" between the War Department and the Allies that maintained the United States Army's exclusive jurisdiction over Americans in both France and the United Kingdom. As a result of this agreement, which Crowder effectuated, neither a French nor British civil or military court could be used to prosecute an American soldier accused of a crime committed against one of their nationals. Certainly, Professor Woodward's book is focused on a very broad subject and not on the alteration of civil-military relations during the period 1917 to 1920, and this observation of his book is not a criticism of an alleged weakness in an otherwise expansive scholarly publication. Rather, it is brought up as an example of an aspect missing from the studies of the United States during the war.[8]

As detailed throughout this treatise, the judge advocate general served as an informal advisor to more than one Supreme Court justice. Judge advocates drafted the first-ever national insurance policy, which Congress passed into law. Judge advocates also convinced Congress to temporarily usurp the full jurisdiction of state courts in delaying civil actions against citizens brought into the army. Army officers, including several judge advocates, would, during the conflict, serve as food inspectors, port officials, road and bridge inspectors, and adjuncts to law enforcement, and undertake a variety of other roles in which the army had never taken part. Congress enabled the War Department to set price controls on certain commodities, commandeer railroads, and enact regulations binding civilians against selling alcohol near military installations. The War Department was also able to limit the distribution of newspapers and pamphlets near military bases. Violations of these regulations were prosecutable in the federal courts, and in some instances, in state courts. Often judge advocates assisted federal prosecutors in cases involving violations of these regulations. Customarily in American history, Congress had enacted criminal statutes and did not defer to agencies in the Executive Branch to do so. But in 1917, Congress did empower the War Department—the cabinet agency that controlled the army—to regulate much of American life.

In order to best present how the Judge Advocate General's Office took a prominent role in altering the nation's civil-military construct, both a chronological and thematic analysis are necessary, not only because of the short duration of the nation's involvement in the war but also because of the complexity of the office's actions undertaken within the War Department, toward Congress, and with the Judicial Branch. These actions included convincing Congress that it could constitutionally empower the War Department with the authority to regulate the distances from installations within which brothels and other "houses of ill repute" could be prohibited, and then arguing to the federal courts that the War Department had the authority to criminalize violations of such rules. Prior to 1917, with the exception of the "Mann Act," the regulation of prostitution, like so many other types of commerce—moral or otherwise—was strictly a state matter. In 1919 the Supreme Court upheld the War Department's authority to regulate prostitution within the United States.[9]

Expanding the study of civil-military relations is always a worthwhile endeavor that is often written about in history and political science books, editorials, polemics, and law reviews. From the outset, it must be noted that an impressive cross section of the nation's lawyers who served as judge advocates during World War I, either by being attached to the Judge Advocate General's Office or in the field as acting judge advocates assigned to brigades, divisions, and corps, later went on to prominent legal and governmental careers that shaped the nation's laws and political construct. Their number included future Supreme Court justices Felix Frankfurter, Frank Murphy, and Sherman Minton, and Elijah Barrett Prettyman, who became an influential judge on the Court of Appeals for the District of Columbia, as well as dozens of others who achieved postwar prominence in the legal profession, Congress, and state governments. For instance, Guy Despard Goff, the son of a US senator, left his position as US attorney for Wisconsin to serve as a judge advocate, and after the war, he replaced his father in the Senate. Likewise, Burnett Chiperfield left his congressional seat to assist in the administration of the army's discipline and then returned to Congress. Many of these men understood that their actions would influence the governance of the national defense for decades after the conflict ended. In World War I, Major General Enoch H. Crowder served as the judge advocate general of the army.

What follows is not a biography of Crowder, though he has a central role in this treatise, but rather a study of how he led four hundred judge advocates not only to administer the discipline of the army but also to oversee conscription, and in certain aspects, to police the national population. Neither Crowder nor the judge advocates intended to create a permanent alteration in civil and military relations. Indeed, they were sometimes reluctant and often cautious in inserting the army into traditional areas of civil governance. Although they did take part in some of the more draconian intrusions into civil and political rights in American history, they did so with the belief that their actions were necessary to succeed against Germany and that nation's allies, the Austro-Hungarian Empire, the Ottoman Empire, and Bulgaria.

1

ENOCH CROWDER AND THE WILSON PRESIDENCY

UNLIKE DOZENS OF GENERAL OFFICERS during the Civil War and World War II, whose names have been kept in the nation's memory by veterans, politicians, newsmen, and ultimately historians, few of the army's World War I generals are remembered today. Other than John J. "Black Jack" Pershing, who commanded the American Expeditionary Forces, one is hard pressed to find the names of corps and division commanders, let alone full-length biographies. The Judge Advocate General's Department is no different in this context. General Holt, the Civil War judge advocate general who, in addition to arguing before the Supreme Court on the legitimacy of expanded military jurisdiction in wartime, presided over the trial of Mary Surratt and clashed with President Andrew Johnson, has a modern full-length biography, and several other studies focus on him. But Crowder is seldom mentioned today, even in biographies of President Woodrow Wilson. Arguably, Crowder's wartime responsibilities were more extensive than Holt's. His prewar duties encompassed what today includes not only those of the Judge Advocate General's Corps, but also that of the modern-day civilian general counsel who serves as the legal advisor to the secretary of the army. After the United States' entry into the war against Germany, Wilson appointed Crowder as the director of the nation's first-ever selective service program in a position titled provost marshal of the United States. Holt did not oversee the Civil War's state-run conscription programs or serve as a provost marshal. On Secretary of War Newton Baker's insistence, Crowder also retained full authority as judge advocate general of the army. Because Crowder staffed the Selective Service Agency with commissioned judge advocates, studies of conscription and of the Judge Advocate General's Office are necessarily intertwined.[1]

During World War II, David Lockmiller, a North Carolina historian, authored a biography of Crowder, but fewer than three hundred libraries now possess it. In the past decade, Colonel Frederic Borch, a retired judge advocate and army historian, published a biographical article on Crowder as well. Both works present a good timeline of the broader aspects of Crowder's military career. However, neither Lockmiller nor Borch intended a study of the full range of duties Crowder undertook, his impact on the shaping of the nation's military laws, or the conduct of the Judge Advocate General's Office during the First World War. With the exception of Lockmiller and Borch, the few historians or legal scholars who mention Crowder do so in colorful and sometimes quite uncomplimentary terms. "Crowder was a bony, vile tempered bachelor whose hobby was work and whose creed was efficiency," penned Merion and Susie Hinds in 1997. In 2004 noted military historian Edward M. Coffman in his *Frontier Regulars* called Crowder an "outstanding bureaucrat," but two decades earlier in a biography of Army Chief of Staff Peyton C. March, Coffman referred to Crowder as "this vinegary Missourian." In between these two books, Coffman complimented Crowder as a "prodigious and efficient worker." In 1992 legal historian Jonathan Lurie, in *Arming Military Justice: The Origins of the United States Court of Military Appeals, 1775–1990*, presented the first—and perhaps only—dispassionate detailed analysis on the origins of the modern Court of Appeals for the Armed Forces. He characterized Crowder as driven and externally humorless, which appears to be what Crowder's contemporaries thought of him. Some of Crowder's peers had little positive to say for him. General George Wilcox McIver, the chief of the Militia Bureau from 1915 to 1917, wrote in his autobiography in 1945 that Crowder was a "very ambitious man, greedy for power and authority." Likewise, General Peyton March, the army's chief of staff for much of the war, disparaged Crowder. On the other hand, Felix Frankfurter, who served at the Judge Advocate General's Office during the war, later lauded Crowder for his intelligence and work ethic.[2]

Crowder was born on April 11, 1859, in Grundy County, Missouri, roughly thirty miles from Pershing's birthplace. The two men had a similar upbringing, not only in that they came from parents of limited means, but also in that both excelled in their rural schools and both taught in public schools before attending the United States Military Academy. Crowder matriculated at the academy in 1877, four years prior to Pershing. At that time, General John McAlister Schofield was the academy's superintendent, and midway through Crowder's education, General O. O. Howard replaced Schofield. Both Schofield and Howard were Civil War veterans who had led large masses of soldiers in battle, and following the war, each would shape aspects of army discipline. Schofield influenced military discipline throughout the late nineteenth century by advocating for statutory reforms for courts-martial and the establishment of a military prison, while Howard unsuccessfully tried to open the army to the possibility of African American officers. During Crowder's time at the academy, he was exposed to both Schofield's view of an "enlightened military discipline" and the military establishment's attempts to preclude the commissioning of black officers despite Howard's efforts. It does not appear that Crowder ever openly advocated for the commissioning of African American officers, but he also did not take part in hazing or other actions to stifle the efforts of African Americans aspiring to become commissioned officers. Neither his official memoranda nor personal correspondences indicate that he viewed African American soldiers as a separate class to be judged by different standards. One incident, which perhaps provides some insight into his view on race, was his opposition to Theodore Roosevelt's summary dismissal of 167 African American soldiers after the so-called "Brownsville Raid." Crowder conceded that Roosevelt had the presidential authority to dismiss the soldiers but argued that to do so after the soldiers had been exonerated by an army investigation denied them due process. In 1917 Crowder pushed the War Department to commission the army's first-ever African American judge advocate. He also, on one occasion, informed Baker that he did not oppose hiring a female attorney for his office.[3]

Crowder's first assignment was to Texas, where he patrolled the border with Mexico, and in his free time he studied law. As Texas was a frontier state with no formal state bar examination, he became a licensed attorney by satisfying a local judge of his competence in law through a written test. In 1884 Crowder transferred to Jefferson Barracks, Missouri, and he resumed his legal study, this time under the tutelage of Thomas Crittenden, a Civil War veteran and former state governor. Jefferson Barracks was one of the army's posts used for the basic training of new soldiers. In the late nineteenth century, the army's basic training regimen was a mere thirty days, and the majority of recruits came from the lower economic echelons of American society, with a large proportion of immigrants. Crowder's experience of supervising basic training later influenced his decision to endorse conscription, and it shaped his view on military discipline to push for certain reforms while maintaining an austere command-driven court system. In the midst of his law studies under Crittenden, the War Department ordered Crowder to return to Texas, where he led cavalry patrols against Apache Indians. Led by Geronimo, for several years the Apaches had effectively waged guerilla warfare against both Mexico and the United States. In late 1886 Geronimo and his fighters surrendered and Crowder returned once more to Jefferson Barracks.[4]

While in Missouri, Crowder also took on additional employment as a professor of military science at the University of Missouri, and he obtained a law degree from its law school. In 1889 he attached to the Eighth Cavalry and was sent to the Dakota Territory to take part in the final campaign against the Sioux Indians. To get to the Dakota Territory, the regiment traversed from its Missouri and New Mexico outposts to the Canadian border. Crowder took part in the long march but did not see fighting against the Sioux, and shortly after the conclusion of hostilities he was assigned as the acting judge advocate to the Department of the Platte. In 1890 he suffered a debilitating head injury that caused painful headaches for the rest of his life.[5]

From his time as an acting judge advocate to his service at the Department of the Platte, Captain Crowder learned that a judge advocate's interaction with civil authorities could draw the secretary of war's interest if not the president's or Congress's. On March 31, 1896, Secretary of War Daniel Lamont ordered Crowder to explain why he had advised the commander of Fort Robinson, Nebraska, to refuse to comply with an arrest warrant for a lieutenant assigned to the post. A local sheriff had accused the lieutenant of violating Nebraska law by selling beer without a state license. Crowder reported to Lamont that because the lieutenant was ordered to control the fort's post store, and the beer sales from the store had been approved by Stephen Elkins, Lamont's predecessor, as well as by General Schofield, the issue was simply a matter of the lieutenant following orders. Crowder also concluded that since the post store was on "a military reservation and therefore an instrumentality of the federal government," a state could not regulate it. This incident appears unremarkable at first glance, but Lamont's inquiry occurred as a result of Senator William V. Allen's complaint to the War Department. Crowder then informed Lamont that the sheriff was a part owner of a town saloon as well as a member of an association of saloon owners that had been formed in Nebraska and the Dakotas for the purpose of forcing the army's post stores to elevate their prices so that soldiers would purchase alcohol at the local saloons rather than on post.[6]

Following Crowder's explanation to Lamont, the army's judge advocate general, G. Norman Lieber, questioned Crowder as to why he believed that a post-exchange store could be considered an instrumentality of the United States because, although Crowder's view may have reflected the prevailing belief in the War Department, no statute articulated that a post store was such an instrumentality. Crowder likely anticipated Lieber's query. He responded that he had consulted with Oliver P. Shiras, the United States District Court judge for the District of Iowa, and Shiras accepted his position that a post store was such a federal instrumentality. That Shiras, a former judge advocate in the

Civil War and a cousin of a sitting Supreme Court justice, might have been biased toward the War Department was of no concern to Crowder. What did matter to him was that his response pleased Lieber, who in turn supported his transfer into the Judge Advocate General's Office. In 1896 the War Department approved Crowder's permanent transfer to the Judge Advocate General's Office with a promotion to major. He was thirty-six years old, and more importantly, had been the sole officer selected from more than fifty officers who applied. His supporters included the former secretary of war, Redfield Proctor; Senator Francis Marion Cockrell of Missouri; Nebraska territorial delegate Experience Estabrook; Henry Clay Caldwell, a federal judge serving on the Court of Appeals for the Eighth Circuit; Generals John C. Bates, Wesley Merritt, and Thomas Ruger; and Colonels Elwell Otis and Milton Moore, the commandant of the Missouri National Guard.[7]

In 1898 the War Department sent Crowder to the Philippine Islands to serve as judge advocate to Major General Merritt. Although Merritt quickly returned to the United States, Crowder remained in the islands and reported first to Major General Otis and then to Major General Arthur MacArthur. Otis, a Harvard-educated lawyer, became thoroughly impressed with Crowder and expanded his duties beyond reviewing courts-martial and advising on contractual obligations. At Otis's direction, Crowder also undertook a study of Spanish court records, became president of the Board of Claims, and was appointed as an associate justice to the Philippine Supreme Court.[8]

The Philippine Insurrection, which has been superbly written about in Brian Linn's *The Philippine War, 1899–1902*, was a watershed for several officers, Crowder included. The army's senior commanders such as Otis, MacArthur, and Merritt had their military beginnings in the Civil War, but they commanded men who were born after that conflict. When senior officers retired or were relieved, the younger generation of officers, who had waited over a decade to gain promotion to captain, advanced up through the field grade ranks of major, lieutenant colonel, and colonel. Some officers, such as Pershing, jumped rapidly from captain to general. The Philippines experience taught Crowder that communications and well-defined lines of command and control were essential to a modern military. In one instance, a line officer waited for Crowder's approval to order soldiers to attack Emilio Aguinaldo's forces, and Crowder had to explain to the officer that as a judge advocate assigned to the staff, he had no authority to approve such an order. It had simply been the case that Crowder was the senior officer in the area and the line officer assumed Crowder had the authority to command troops.[9]

Crowder's judge advocate duties in the Philippines were, on one level, similar to his duties at the Department of the Platte. For instance, he reviewed over six hundred courts-martial and oversaw the terms of various War Department contracts. Yet there were unique aspects to his Philippine tenure: had he not been stationed in the Philippines, he would not likely have advanced to become judge advocate general. During his service on the Philippine Supreme Court, he proved his intellectual prowess by authoring the protectorate's criminal procedural code. In 1900 MacArthur, who by this time commanded all forces in the Philippines, promoted Crowder to be his military secretary and legal advisor. As such, Crowder served as a de facto general counsel and attorney general to the military government. Although William Howard Taft, President William McKinley's civilian representative and eventual governor general of the Philippines, clashed with MacArthur, he too became friends with Crowder and frequently sought Crowder's advice. While Crowder's lifelong relationship to Taft was important to his advancement, during his time in the Philippines he also befriended John Bassett Moore, one of the nation's leading internal law experts and a frequent counsel to the State Department and delegate to various international tribunals.[10]

Early on, it became apparent to Taft not only that Crowder was a superb lawyer but also that they had similar political views. Crowder likewise took an interest in Taft's advancement. In 1901 he expressed to Taft his hope that Theodore Roosevelt would offer Taft a cabinet post. The following year, when Roosevelt ordered Taft to travel to Rome and meet with Vatican officials to negotiate a purchase of papal properties, as well as explain to the Holy See how the US government would protect the rights of Catholics in the Philippines, Taft, in turn, asked a willing Crowder to accompany him. One of the benefits to having Crowder on the mission was that the United States' military leadership in the Philippines worried that the local churches could stoke rebellion by asserting claims that the army had unlawfully taken over its property. Crowder realized that affirmative "renunciation to title" by the Vatican would minimize this possibility, and he was able to obtain the renunciation statement. The purchase of Vatican—sometimes referred to as friars'—lands resulted in over 30,000 Philippine citizens becoming small landholders. In an era when property rights were considered the entry into participation in government and the paramount right of a citizen, Taft and Crowder believed that the creation of 30,000 landholders was an important step toward creating an indigenous representative government. In a later instance, Taft turned to Crowder to defuse a political controversy. During a campaign speech in 1908, Taft lauded Ulysses Grant but noted that he had resigned from the army in 1854 to avoid a court-martial. In his autobiography Grant claimed to have resigned his commission to support his wife and two children. Grant's son took offense at Taft's statement, but Crowder conducted the necessary research to prove Taft's statements were correct, and the younger Grant withdrew his complaint.[11]

There is one apparent instance from Crowder's career in the Philippines that would run afoul of the law of war as this body of law had developed since 1861. During the Civil War, the War Department issued General Order 100, which served as the first codified law of war in US military history, and the code remained in effect throughout Crowder's career. In 1900 he recommended against court-martialing a Private Putnam of the Twentieth Kansas Volunteers. After a battle at Caloocan, Putnam murdered two defenseless prisoners of war, and an acting inspector general wanted him court-martialed for murder. Crowder advised both Otis and MacArthur against a court-martial, even though he conceded a "terrible crime, had been committed with no justification." Crowder also acknowledged that Putnam's conduct was not isolated, and if he were prosecuted, it was "probable that facts would develop implicating many others." Though he recognized that Putnam's superiors who were in a position to stop the murders were even more liable for the crime than Putnam himself, a desire to protect the superiors was not the reason why Crowder later claimed he was reticent to hold Putnam accountable. "Caloocan was one of the initial fights of the insurrection, and I was impressed with the view that the publicity incident to a trial for this unlawful killing would result in giving information to the insurgent leaders that we failed to accord to insurgent prisoners of war, the protection to which they were entitled under the laws of war," he informed Secretary of War Elihu Root. "This would lead to acts of reprisal in the event that any of our soldiers would be captured by insurgents in subsequent fights." Moreover, Crowder, like Otis, MacArthur, and even Taft, believed that General Order 100 applied only when an opposing force adhered to the laws of war. On the other hand, Crowder approved the courts-martial of General Jacob Smith and Major Littleton Waller for war crimes.[12]

In 1901 Crowder returned to the United States and was promoted over three senior officers to become deputy judge advocate general. In this posting he reported to Major General George Breckenridge Davis, one of the last Civil War veterans on active duty. Davis had enlisted in the First Massachusetts Volunteer Cavalry in 1861 at the age of sixteen. Following the war, and despite being a commissioned lieutenant, he attended the United States Military Academy and was formally commissioned into the army. In 1871 he was assigned to the Fifth Cavalry and served in the Wyoming and Arizona Territories, and in 1874 he returned to the academy as a Spanish professor. Davis became acquainted with Crowder during this time, though the historic record is sparse as to whether the two men remained in contact. After a brief tenure at the academy, Davis returned to the western frontier, but again in 1883 he returned to the academy to become a professor of law. In 1888 Davis was transferred to Washington, DC, to serve at the Judge Advocate General's Department, and it was not until this time that he attended law school, earning an LLB from the Columbian Law School—the predecessor to the George Washington University Law School—by taking classes at night. He was a prolific writer in both law and history, and in 1901 he replaced Lieber as judge advocate general of the army.[13]

In 1903 Secretary of War Root initiated a wide-sweeping set of army reforms, and during this time he appointed Crowder as a deputy chief of staff with the task of analyzing the impact of pending reorganization legislation on the military establishment, as well as strategically analyzing the placement of troops, methods of training, and use of the new National Guard forces. Much of Crowder's duties were nonlegal, and Root thought so highly of him that he later lobbied Woodrow Wilson to permit Crowder to remain as judge advocate general for the rest of his life. In 1904 Root assigned Crowder to observe the Japanese Imperial Army in the Russo-Japanese War. The importance of this duty cannot be overstated. The US Army had not fought in a truly large-scale modern war against a well-equipped adversary since 1865, and the last opportunity to observe such an event had occurred in the war France fought against Prussia and Prussia's German allies in 1870–1871. But even that conflict did not involve the logistical hurdles that both Russia and Japan faced in 1904. The Japanese military's superior strategy and tactics in fighting a much larger Russian opponent, and its soldiers' adherence to a rigid disciplinary code, provided Crowder with a compelling example of the necessity of a disciplined army in modern war.[14]

After returning to the United States to resume his judge advocate duties, Crowder was sent by Secretary of War Taft to Cuba for almost three years to perform duties similar to those he had undertaken in the Philippines. In 1909 Crowder began a study of the European military disciplinary systems, and two years later Taft nominated him to become judge advocate general of the army. Although Crowder frequently advocated for the Congress to maintain the army's disciplinary system, he was concerned with due process. Crowder showed his independent jurisprudence in 1912 when he lobbied Congress to alter the Civil War–era desertion laws. Since 1863 a convicted deserter could potentially lose his citizenship. During the Civil War, Secretary of War Stanton and Secretary of War Holt successfully lobbied Congress to couple the loss of citizenship with desertion. They, along with congressional Republicans, were convinced that proslavery and prosecession copperheads influenced desertion through propaganda, and therefore the loss of citizenship was justified.

Although the Supreme Court determined in 1957 that a constitutional prohibition against the loss of citizenship existed, Crowder did not believe the Eighth Amendment prohibited the loss of citizenship in wartime in all cases. He did, however, argue that the loss of citizenship in peacetime as a penalty for desertion was excessive and unfair, and in wartime the loss of citizenship should only be permissible if it occurred with the intention of aiding an enemy. In 1915 Wilson showed his satisfaction with Crowder and reappointed him as judge advocate general, and as previously noted, in 1917 Wilson appointed him provost marshal in charge of the nation's conscription program.[15]

Crowder's initial confirmation as judge advocate general occurred without any vocal opposition from either inside or outside the military establishment. Prior to the war, John Callan O'Laughlin, the editor of the *Army-Navy Journal*, an influential newspaper that reported on matters related to the armed services, supported Crowder's nomination to become judge advocate general and publicized the endorsements of dozens of other supporters for Crowder. Several congressmen openly endorsed Crowder's nomination as well. John Bassett Moore, who at the time was a professor at Columbia's law school as well as the government's special representative to Chile, advocated to Congress for Crowder's quick confirmation. Likewise, in 1915 there was no visible opposition to Crowder's renomination.[16]

Crowder's jurisprudence appears to have been progressive in the sense that he was open to the expansion of insanity as a defense, believed that shell-shock was a real malady, and accepted that the federal and state governments had a positive regulatory duty to safeguard the public's health. Beginning in 1909 he worked to reform the army's prisons so that soldiers who committed military offenses such as desertion were rehabilitated for further service rather than simply confined and punished. In 1914, when the army established a disciplinary barracks at Fort Leavenworth, Crowder could be partly credited with its creation. He insisted that in stateside training camps, soldiers suspected of mental deficiencies be psychologically examined before trial to ensure that only persons responsible for their acts could be convicted. On the other hand, he staunchly fought to protect the Executive Branch's traditional governance of military discipline, and his view of the First Amendment's guarantee of freedom of speech ultimately aligned with Taft's conservatism. By 1915 Crowder was a keen advocate of preparedness, and in the two years prior to the United States' entry into the war, he conceived of how millions of citizens might be conscripted and then formed into a disciplined United States Army.[17]

Although Crowder was concerned at the prospect of subversion and espionage during World War I, he advised against suspecting soldiers based solely on their religion or ethnic heritage. He worried that anti-Catholicism and anti-Semitism could cause soldiers to be accused of disloyalty. As the nation's provost marshal, he determined not to classify draftees on the basis of religion so as not to place soldiers under suspicion of antiwar or socialist affiliation. When Supreme Court Justice Louis Brandeis asked Crowder for information on the numbers of Jews serving in the army, indicating that he had already obtained similar information from the British and French governments, Crowder explained that he "purposely refrained" from classifying soldiers by their religion to prevent discrimination in the ranks. Brandeis found Crowder's insistence on this point commendable. During the war, particularly as challenges to selective service and other war measures came to the Supreme Court, Brandeis informed Wilson's confidant, "Colonel" Edward House, that Crowder deserved the high esteem that other staff officers such as General George Goethals held for him.[18]

Of all Crowder's contributions to the War Department prior to 1917, three were to have a profound impact on how the Judge Advocate General's Office functioned during the war. In 1914 he initiated a program to send a few handpicked officers to law schools. For instance, Lieutenant Cassius M. Dowell, a cavalry officer, was selected to attend George Washington University's law school, and Lieutenant Hugh S. Johnson was picked to attend the University of California's law school. Both of these men graduated with high honors. Crowder also encouraged officers already serving on his staff such as John A. Hull, Edward Kreger, and Blanton Winship to augment their legal training by taking courses at George Washington University. In 1916 Crowder actively campaigned to add some of the nation's leading legal minds to his staff as reservists. As covered in detail in the next chapter, Harvard professors Eugene Wambaugh and Felix Frankfurter, and John Henry Wigmore, the dean of the Northwestern University Law School, joined the Judge Advocate General's Office as reserve officers. That Crowder established ties to the legal academy would later be a factor in shielding the army's disciplinary systems from reform efforts.

His second contribution was that in 1916, Congress adopted his draft Articles of War into law with little modification. Crowder had labored on revising the 1874 Articles of War for four years, and while in retrospect the revised laws might largely appear to mirror the previous Articles of War, he was able to remove archaic aspects of the old articles such as rules about mandatory attendance at religious services. Most importantly, Crowder testified that the army had conducted too many general courts-martial for minor offenses, and he intended for a new Articles of War to reduce the numbers of severe sentences for petty offenses by lowering the maximum allowable punishments.

Crowder insisted on retaining a commander's authority over courts-martial and other aspects of military discipline. That is, he believed that commanding officers rather than judge advocates should determine when to convene a court-martial as well as whether to approve of the results of such trials. He was, as he informed Pershing in 1915, enormously proud of the draft articles but frustrated with the legislative process.[19]

Crowder's third contribution was his adherence to *Ex Parte Milligan*, one of the Supreme Court's more important civil liberties decisions in history. During the Civil War, the Judge Advocate General's Department oversaw the military trials of well over four thousand civilians. Some of these military trials were prosecutions of persons who committed the common law offenses of larceny, murder, or fraud. Other trials involved law of war offenses such as murdering Union soldiers or dynamiting railroad tracks. A smaller number of trials arose as a result of civilians publicly criticizing Lincoln, the war, and the abolition of slavery. Dozens of northerners were prosecuted in military trials when the state and federal courts—often referred to as civil courts—were fully functioning. *Milligan* arose from one such trial, and while the defendants, who were Indiana residents, clearly intended an armed uprising in Indianapolis in support of the Confederacy, the Lincoln administration bypassed the civil courts in favor of a military trial. The defendants appealed to the Supreme Court, which determined by a five to four vote that under no condition could a military trial constitutionally be used to prosecute a citizen in a state where the civil courts fully functioned. Crowder not only believed *Milligan* to be correctly decided, he sought to prevent the encroachment of military authority over civilian law enforcement functions in many circumstances, with the exception of civilians ordered to report for military service. However, he did not always succeed in keeping the army out of traditional civilian regulation and law enforcement functions.[20]

There is one final comment on Crowder that is essential to understand how the Judge Advocate General's Office operated in World War I. In addition to his experiences as a cavalry officer, his service as an observer of the Russo-Japanese War, his keen mind, and his understanding of military law, one of Crowder's chief assets in serving as a wartime judge advocate general was that while this position was inherently political, and could—as had occurred under Holt in the Civil War—become visibly so, Crowder appears to have had no political ambition. He was reactive to political forces, rather than proactive. In 1913, at Garrison's behest, Crowder drafted an order prohibiting political activities in the officer corps. Garrison was concerned that the officer corps had increasingly become politicized in reaction to the first Democrat administration in sixteen years. Officers belonging to a Philippine veterans' organization known as the

Carabao Club had publicly disparaged Secretary of State William Jennings Bryan. Crowder enthusiastically drafted a formal reprimand for Garrison to issue to these officers. Shortly after Garrison issued the reprimand, he tasked Crowder with investigating General William Gorgas, the surgeon general of the army, after Gorgas was accused of publicly opposing the repeal of Panama Canal tolls. Garrison also ordered Crowder to investigate a lieutenant accused of assisting a Republican political candidate for Congress. Crowder confirmed that both instances occurred and advised Garrison to reprimand both officers. At no time did Crowder inject party favoritism into his duties. When, in 1919, Taft urged him to consider running for office or supporting the Republican presidential nominee, he responded that he had no interest in either and that politics were "all Greek" to him. Crowder believed he had a duty to be responsive to Congress, but not to shape policies outside of selective service or the army's internal military discipline. Notably, in 1917 he demurred from giving Postmaster General Albert Burleson advice on newspaper censorship in the mails, and in 1918 he informed Burleson that he would not permit the sharing of information on persons suspected of subversion with the American Protective League, a private organization formed to combat antiwar movements. In 1913 he advised Stimson against assigning a cavalry regiment to guard a suffrage parade in New York because he worried about the War Department sanctioning a political activity. Crowder's reasoning stemmed from his belief that the army had to remain outside of politics.[21]

Because the army and the National Guard were subject to the direction of the federal and state governments, Crowder took part in some of the pressing domestic events of his time, even if on the periphery. In 1913 West Virginia court-martialed civilians whom the state governor deemed to have threatened the state's safety. The civilians were pro-union laborers, some of whom were affiliated with the Industrial Workers of the World (IWW). The West Virginia civil courts functioned throughout the state, and though conservative politicians, mine owners, and railroad executives feared that the IWW planned for a national rebellion, there was little reason to resort to state military trials when the state's civil courts functioned. Crowder took a keen interest in the outcome of the civilians' state court-martial convictions, and he regularly corresponded with Lieutenant Colonel George Wallace, the state's judge advocate general. Crowder questioned Wallace as to whether a governor could abridge the rights of civilians to a jury and defense counsel simply through a declaration of emergency. Although Crowder conceded that the individuals prosecuted in the state's courts-martial might have been dangerous, he did not agree that state military jurisdiction was necessary and argued to Wallace that it created an "unwise precedent." Yet Crowder understood that Wallace's analysis on the governor's authority under the state constitution, coupled with the fact that state military trials were not prohibited by either *Milligan* or the express language of the Fourteenth Amendment, would likely be upheld by the state supreme court. In 1916 Crowder provided guidance to a number of state governments on how to enforce the 1903 "Dick Law" through the courts-martial of National Guard troops who refused to submit to military authority when called into federal service. Named after Congressman Charles Dick, among its many provisions the law extended the army's court-martial jurisdiction over guardsmen who refused to be federalized. Prior to the passage of the law, national guardsmen who refused to be federalized could only be prosecuted in state courts-martial, state courts, or a United States District Court. Crowder informed Wallace, who had become the National Guard's judge advocate on the Mexican border, that the courts-martial of guardsmen would serve as a "test case" in the event conscripted citizens refused to submit to their orders to report to training should the United States enter into the war in Europe.[22]

Once the United States entered the war against Germany, Crowder made it known he wanted to obtain a field command and fight overseas. But he was unsuccessful in convincing Secretary of War Newton D. Baker to reassign him to a brigade or division. Baker simply believed that Crowder was needed more in Washington, DC, than at the front, and although Pershing would have accepted Crowder for a divisional or perhaps corps command, there were more physically fit officers to fill those positions. Both Baker and Pershing believed that there were not enough officers with Crowder's intelligence and foresight to oversee conscription. At times this decision embittered Crowder. On August 15, 1917, he asked General Tasker Bliss, the army's acting chief of staff, to withdraw his name from consideration to lead a parade of recently drafted men through New York City. "This place properly belongs to one of those officers whom the Secretary has selected for command rank in the New National Army and would most appropriately not be bestowed on one whom he has so recently relatively pronounced unfit for such rank," he concluded.[23]

Although Crowder had sent Baker a similar, albeit less angry letter, and had asked Bliss not to share his letter to Baker, Bliss did so. Baker assured Bliss that Crowder was a "brilliant and sane officer," but he could not fathom why Crowder would believe that a line command would be a promotion over being both provost marshal and judge advocate general. Baker informed Bliss that he had publicly and privately lauded Crowder and would reluctantly assign another general officer to head the parade. "I do not know whether this is the sort of matter that you and General Crowder are likely to discuss," Baker also noted to Bliss, "but if it does come up, I feel sure you will not leave him under any doubt, if one has been bred of his disappointment, that I entertain for him feelings of respect and gratitude which are wholly unaffected by any other sentiment than regret that, in the middle of his most brilliant performance, he finds himself grieved about this or any other personal matter." In June 1918, as the American Expeditionary Forces prepared to launch their first large-scale offensive at St. Mihiel, Pershing told Crowder that while he understood why he wanted to serve in France, his work with Baker was "far more valuable to the country than anything else you could do."[24]

Pershing and Crowder had developed a friendship dating to their Philippine service. In 1911 Pershing noted to Crowder that he was pleased that Taft had nominated him to replace Davis as judge advocate general. For reasons that are absent from the historic record, Pershing believed that the Judge Advocate General's Office suffered a poor reputation at the time and that Crowder was the one officer who could resurrect it in the War Department's esteem. Three years later while lauding Crowder's efforts at revising the Articles of War, Pershing claimed that Crowder's reputation was such that Congress should consider the revisions in light of Crowder's reputation rather than debating the substance of the changes from the old code. During the war, Crowder provided Pershing with information from the War Department, including the fact that Baker was fully confident in his command over the American Expeditionary Forces even when the French government argued that he had acted too slowly in getting Americans into the front lines.[25]

The opposite of Pershing, Peyton March, who became the chief of staff of the army after Bliss departed to Europe, was Crowder's chief antagonist in the War Department during World War I. For decades prior to 1918, the War Department staffs and bureaus had worked independently of the army's commanding general, and despite the efforts of commanding generals such as William Sherman and John McAlister Schofield, this staff independence continued in some measure. The Judge Advocate General's Office would naturally exert its independence from the army's chief of staff, even in times of war, because of the nature of the sweeping legal work of the department and the fact that its officers, much like those in the surgeon general's staff, came from a regulated profession. Seven months before the declaration of war, Crowder advised Baker that under a 1903 law establishing the General Staff, the chief of staff only had general supervision over the staffs and bureaus and could not dictate their advice to the secretary of war. On one occasion Major General Hugh Lennox Scott opposed Crowder's advice and became "disturbed" when Baker sided with Crowder. During the war, March attempted to force both the Judge Advocate General's Office and the office of the provost marshal general to yield to his complete authority. In late 1917

March appealed to Baker to grant him clear power over Crowder, but after hearing the arguments of both officers, Baker sided with Crowder. March and Crowder had compelling arguments for and against staff independence. March advocated for a unity of command that is essential in wartime, and Crowder sought to preserve the profession of law for legal experts, arguing that just as the army would not send an infantry officer to supervise a bridge construction, which was essentially an engineer's duty, it should not permit a nonlawyer to command the army's legal office. Crowder's feud with March became vocal enough to cause concern at the American Expeditionary Forces headquarters over whether enough soldiers could be transported to France in time to launch full-scale American offensives against the German Army.[26]

WILSON, CROWDER, AND THE POLITICAL AND MILITARY ENVIRONMENT

Military policy and war-making is, in the United States, influenced by a wide range of political forces beginning with the basic fact that elites within the three independent branches of government may have vastly differing views on the training, recruitment, and placement of forces as well as the mass production and purchase of armaments and other materiel. In World War I, Congress was divided into several camps on the fairness of courts-martial, the Espionage Act, and the need for national conscription. The Judge Advocate General's Office had to be both cognizant of and responsive to the members of all three branches as well as to other political entities. Although the Judge Advocate General's Office was first and foremost responsible to Wilson and Baker, even state governments and representatives of national organizations could seek to influence the army's discipline, particularly in regard to conscription.

Whatever the motivations of individual legislators, governors, and other political entities were in asserting their influence into the courts-martial and conscription processes, it cannot be ignored that in addition to the traditional fears of a standing army, there was a belief that an unchecked presidential authority in courts-martial could likewise pose a menace to civil liberties. In 1951 constitutional law scholar Clinton Rossiter pointed out that because "the president is the fountainhead of military justice," courts-martial were central to Executive Branch primacy. Although Rossiter penned this observation at the height of the Cold War, with the United States engaged in an ongoing war against communist forces in Korea and a military that numbered in the millions, the importance of courts-martial to the Executive Branch was well understood in 1917. President Wilson certainly desired a strong Executive Branch, but partly as a result of his southern heritage, he also distrusted a large standing army. One of Wilson's closest confidants, Senator John Sharp Williams of Mississippi, urged in 1915 that while the construction of a large navy was essential to the national defense, a large standing army was "both objectionable and a waste of money" since no foreign nation could invade the United States. "Let the modern critics laugh at it as much as they please, a large standing army is always a menace to free institutions, both directly and indirectly—always indirectly, and at critical periods directly," Williams claimed. "The liberties of no people, as far as I have read, have never been threatened by an efficient navy." Wilson responded to Williams that he was "in accord with the principles you lay down and I hope very confidently that we can agree upon the method of realizing them." Another of Wilson's supporters, Senator Willard Saulsbury of Delaware, likewise informed Wilson that while he too supported a large navy, the nation could defend itself without a large standing army, "and certainly without conscription." Until July 1916, Wilson agreed with Saulsbury, and he informed the senator that he opposed a forced federal military service. As a lawyer and constitutional scholar, Wilson viewed courts-martial with skepticism not only as to the procedural fairness of such trials, but also, in a broader sense, as to whether the expansive use of courts-martial could serve ends that were dangerous to democracy. Thomas R. Marshall, the nation's vice president, likewise distrusted courts-martial and urged Wilson to consider that expansive military jurisdiction "would ultimately result in the destruction of the government."[27]

When, on April 6, 1917, Congress voted on whether to declare war against Germany, eighty-six senators voted in favor of doing so, but six voted against and eight abstained. In the House of Representatives, 379 voted to declare war, while fifty voted against and nine did not vote at all. Those legislators who voted against declaring war did so for differing reasons, including sincere isolationist ideologies, the belief that the Central powers and the British, French, and Russians were equally culpable in violating international law, and in the case of one congressman who was the sole member of the Socialist Party, the argument that common working Americans would suffer, while financiers and industrialists would reap large profits. Other representatives agreed that war profiteering was one of the many reasons not to go to war. These beliefs existed in organized labor and antiwar movements as well. Unlike in World War II where only one representative and no senators voted against declaring war, political support for the nation entering the war in 1917 was widespread but hardly close to unanimous. The Judge Advocate General's Office would have to interact with and respond to congressmen across the political spectrum, from the most ardent supporters of preparedness and war against Germany, to powerful senators such as Republicans George W. Norris of Nebraska and Robert La Follette of Wisconsin, who voted against war. One of the other aspects of military discipline was that a number of legislators distrusted courts-martial, regardless of whether they voted for war or not. In December 1919, Norris wrote, "the private soldier has, in my judgment, been unmercifully treated in many, many, cases. Court-martials have shown that men seem to be devoid not only of justice, but of human mercy." Other congressmen would share in these sentiments, but as long as the war persisted, and as long as the threat of the war reigniting was believed exist, they would be in the minority.[28]

Another political aspect of the Judge Advocate General's Office had to do with both of the nation's two surviving former presidents. Roosevelt and Taft alike took an active interest in the administration of the military laws throughout the war. Taft provided suggestions to the Judge Advocate General's Office on prisoner of war exchanges modeled after the Union-Confederate agreements during the Civil War. He also backed Wilson's quest for a League of Nations and sought out Crowder's opinion on how treaty commitments might affect the War Department. Roosevelt, having campaigned for the union vote in 1912, changed his position on labor rights and argued that the use of the military for strikebreaking in the mining and manufacturing industries was necessary. He also lobbied Crowder to support his idea of a volunteer division, but Crowder rebuffed him because he considered the former president too old and uneducated in modern warfare to command soldiers. From time to time, Roosevelt contacted the Judge Advocate General's Office to inquire on a variety of matters and make other suggestions, such as sending Leonard Wood, the controversial former chief of staff, to Europe. Crowder was well aware that in 1916 Roosevelt had called Wilson "feckless," and that one year later Roosevelt accused Wilson of being "timid, utterly cold and selfish, and without a particle of understanding the meaning of honor" in reaction to the president's denial of establishing a volunteer division the next year. He was also aware of Wood's public political alignment with Roosevelt. In June 1918, when Wood asked for Crowder's support to obtain a field command, Crowder demurred, noting that Baker's and Pershing's decision to keep Wood from the front was final.[29]

A third influence on the legal administration of the War Department, and particularly that of the army's discipline, had to do with the rise of political and social movements out of the industrial revolution, some of which transcended the nation's borders. In the four decades prior to World War I there was an increase in labor upheaval, resulting from the growth of socialism and anarchism as political movements. Regardless of the horrific labor conditions and income disparities that gave rise to anarchism, socialism, and communism, the military establishment had come to fear the influence of "radical" political movements. Historically, war machines succeed or fail based on their discipline, and by the time the United States entered the conflict, the leaders of each of the Allied governments believed that the needed discipline was undermined by "radical" elements. In 1917 the Bolshevik Revolution in Russia exacerbated such fears in the leadership of the British, French, Belgian, Italian, and American militaries.[30]

Anarchists and persons affiliated with leftist organizations assassinated Czar Alexander II of Russia in 1881, President Marie Carnot of France in 1894, King Umberto I of Italy in 1900, and President William McKinley in 1901 and attempted to kill a number of other statesmen, industrialists, and bankers. In 1910 three men who were members of a union affiliate of the IWW bombed the *Los Angeles Times*, killing over a dozen workers, and in 1916 an anarchist was believed to have bombed a "Preparedness Day" parade in San Francisco. From 1875 on, strikes had become increasingly violent in the mining, steel, garment, and food processing industries. The violence was shared by the strikers on one side, and the private security companies and enforcement of so-called "law and order" and "right to work laws" on the other. In 1917 Crowder and much of the army's leadership feared that German espionage agents would work in tandem with the IWW and radical socialist groups to weaken the public's confidence in conscription and foster army-wide mutinies. Even though the German government was opposed to organizations such as the IWW, and the IWW's leadership as well as that of socialist and Bolshevik groups was clearly anti-Hohenzollern, Crowder and others believed that "subversives" and Germans allied to undermine the army's discipline.[31]

In spite of these fears, Crowder initially tried to minimize the War Department's intrusion into the nation's civil construct. This was not an easy goal to accomplish, and Crowder was confronted by problems he had not imagined would arise. Two weeks before Wilson asked Congress to declare war on Germany, Crowder drafted an order for Baker to issue to the army's geographic commanders enabling the army to arrest civilians caught committing crimes against the military. Crowder urged Baker to add that commanding officers had to differentiate between ordinary crimes and crimes against the army, and not intrude into local police matters. Baker, in turn, advised Wilson that he would instruct the army's geographic and divisional commanders to cooperate with local authorities. That this discussion occurred two weeks before the United States entered the war highlights not only that the Judge Advocate General's Office was already in the process of preparing for an inevitable alteration in civil-military relations, but also that it had already planned to minimize the military's intrusion into society.[32]

Despite Crowder's intent to limit the military from overtaking the federal government's as well as local governments' civil functions, on seemingly minor wartime problems he could not always find a means to preserve the civilian laws. For instance, in 1917 a German pharmaceutical firm held a patent for the production of Salvarsan, a drug used to treat syphilis. Crowder informed the surgeon general that the necessities of war could negate the patent, and the pharmaceutical firm could later claim damages, but the War Department itself was entitled to produce the drug. After Mississippi senator James Vardaman, an opponent of the declaration of war, warned the surgeon general that the production of the drug was unlawful, Crowder obtained Senator John Sharp Williams's assurance that the Senate would not protest against the production of this essential drug. Likewise Congressman Edwin Yates Webb, the chairman of the House of Representatives Judiciary Committee who had campaigned against going to war in 1917, opposed the enlargement of the army out of a fear that it would supplant the civil government and encroach on individual liberties, and only reluctantly sided with the majority of the vote in going to war, informed Crowder that he believed the War Department was free to ignore patent protections as necessary to ensure victory.[33]

Another instance of the alteration of civil-military relations occurred early in the war regarding river commerce. For several years, transport corporations using the Allegheny River had attempted to have bridges spanning the river in Pittsburgh heightened so that greater amounts of cargo could be stocked on barges. Allegheny County residents opposed having to pay taxes for new construction, and the shipping companies and taxpayers each claimed the other party was responsible. Moreover, Pittsburgh's manufacturing and smelting corporations were opposed to elevating the bridges because to do so would disrupt railway shipments. Instead, the management of these corporations insisted on the construction of new bridges. On April 2, 1917, Baker ordered the bridges elevated without regard to who would pay, and on April 6, he ordered Allegheny County to rapidly accomplish this. That afternoon Senator Philander Knox urged President Wilson to revoke Baker's order on the basis that it violated the Constitution's recognition that only state governments and not the War Department possessed this type of authority. It is difficult to imagine that Baker gave his order much thought—the surviving documentary record on his decisional process is sparse—because during the two weeks prior to the war, the General Staff brought thousands of matters to his attention, and Crowder's de facto wartime deputy, Brigadier General Samuel Ansell, advised him that the War Department had the authority to issue such orders. Baker did respond to Knox that his predecessors, including Taft, had wanted the bridges raised based on the chief of engineer's assessment. Although ultimately Baker delayed the order's implementation, his issuance of it evidences a mindset that the War Department had expansive authority during wartime. After all, none of Baker's predecessors had issued such an order.[34]

Drug patents and bridges were, in reality, nominal issues compared to three proposals to extend military jurisdiction over citizens. When Congress first considered enacting a law to prosecute espionage, spying, and sedition, Senator George Earle Chamberlain, an Oregon Democrat, tried to attach a section to the draft espionage bill that would enable the army to prosecute civilians accused of spying in courts-martial. In addition to arguing that spying for an enemy nation was a law of war offense, Chamberlain articulated his trust in courts-martial. Although extending military jurisdiction over civilians, if permitted, would have given Crowder tremendous power, he opposed Chamberlain. Ultimately Chamberlain's attempt to expand military jurisdiction failed to win over the Senate Judiciary Committee and ironically, in 1919 he would allege that courts-martial violated due process. However, he was not the only prominent government official to push for an expanded military jurisdiction.[35]

In early 1917 Assistant Attorney General Charles Warren pushed for legislation to create military commissions' trials of civilians suspected of violating the 1917 Espionage Act, similar to the Civil War trial of Mary Surratt and others alleged to have conspired to assassinate President Lincoln. Warren acted independently of Attorney General Thomas Watts Gregory, but once the proposal became known, it resulted in a political uproar that caused Warren to resign from the government. Drawing on the Union's Civil War experience, Warren wanted to prevent pro-German or other subversive elements from disrupting conscription or sabotaging the defense industry. As 1917 drew to a close, the Senate considered Warren's draft bill which, if enacted, would empower the president to use the military to prosecute civilians who obstructed the war effort as well as spies and saboteurs. Introduced as Senate Bill 4364 or "a Bill to subject to trial by courts-martial persons who endanger the good discipline, order, movements, health, safety, or successful operations of the land or naval forces of the United States by acting as spies in time of war and for other purposes," the bill was never voted on by the House of Representatives. Warren admitted to North Carolina senator Lee Slater Overman that he did not have the president's sanction to introduce the bill. "Speaking personally and not officially in any way for the Department of Justice, I have been convinced that the only effective way of dealing with enemy activities in this country was by the military under the Military Law," he argued. "I do not believe that war can be effectively carried on by the criminal courts." While this bill would have empowered the Judge Advocate General's Office to a degree that equaled its Civil War authority, Crowder vehemently opposed it. Likewise, Wilson and Gregory did not endorse Warren's proposed legislation, but the fact that Crowder—who would have personally achieved tremendous power had it passed into law—also argued against it, evidenced his constitutional view in support of a military subservient to the civil government.[36]

In spite of Warren's failure to expand military jurisdiction over civilians, there was a secondary effort to increase the War Department's authority in the United States. In October 1918, Attorney General Gregory informally proposed to a skeptical Baker that Washington, DC, could be declared a war zone. Crowder and Ansell advised against doing so, arguing that without an imminent threat, the declaration of a war zone would undermine the military's subordination to the civil government and usurp the constitutional authorities of Congress. *Milligan* and the Civil War experience was partly the driving force for Crowder's opposition to an expanded military presence in the capital, but he also believed that an overarching military presence there would, in addition to undermining the Constitution, provide propaganda fodder for antiwar movements and socialist and anarchist leaders. Crowder was also aware of past judicial advice on the government's use of the military as a police force.[37]

In 1889 Associate Justice Stephen J. Field informed General Nelson A. Miles that the army should not be used to police a strike at a mine. Field even added that it was inappropriate for the army to safeguard a Supreme Court justice, just as it was wrong to have the army serve as a domestic police force. Field had survived an assassination attempt, and Miles had simply offered the service of a cavalry company to protect him. Having sided with the majority in *Milligan*, Field made it clear to Miles that the army had to be subordinate to the civil government in both fact and appearance. During the Pullman Strike in 1894, Miles and Secretary of War Daniel Lamont concluded that only a minimal use of the regular army was "lawfully acceptable." In their discussion, Miles alluded to the earlier guidance Field had given. Considering that Miles, a conservative reactionary who spoke publicly about the dangers of socialism and anarchism, eschewed an expanded military jurisdiction during violent public strikes, it should not be surprising that the War Department would do likewise in World War I. During the war, Crowder informed Baker about Field's prior advice to Miles.[38]

TOTAL WAR, MILITARY LAW, AND THE WILSON ADMINISTRATION

In spite of attempts to prepare the United States for war, neither the government nor the population was ready to fully enter the conflict, with perhaps the exception of the navy. There was, to be sure, a terrible carnage in the Civil War, but the geographic scope of World War I ranged from France through the Middle East, into Iran, Russia, and the Pacific. Battles had also taken place in Africa as well as China. During the Civil War, the Army of the Potomac, the Union's largest fielded force, seldom exceeded 120,000 soldiers, and the Union army barely surpassed 400,000 soldiers in total. France, with a population of slightly more than 40 million citizens, fielded an army of over three million at its peak size, and suffered between 1,300,000 and 1,700,000 deaths. As horrific as Civil War battles were, none came close to the carnage on the Western Front. On the single day of July 1, 1916, over twenty thousand British, Canadian, and Newfoundlandian soldiers were killed and over forty thousand injured. In the four years of war, the British Isles alone lost over 700,000 killed, and with the addition of imperial troops the British Empire lost over one million. The British dominion of Canada, with a 1914 population of 7,890,000, mobilized over 600,000 soldiers, and suffered 67,000 killed and over 150,000 injured. Unlike in the Civil War in which the northern states' economy was nowhere fully harnessed to fight a "total war" as defined by the twentieth-century definition of that term, the British and French societies and their economies were fully enveloped by the war, and had it lasted through 1919, the United States was headed in that direction. Until Wilson believed it to be otherwise inevitable, he opposed being a part of this conflict.[39]

Although Wilson was a scholar of politics and law, he had little direct knowledge of the military's disciplinary construct. Perhaps with the exception of Grover Cleveland, he was the least likely of all post–Civil War presidents to have an appreciation of military law. After all, Taft had been a secretary of war and a federal appeals judge, and Roosevelt an assistant secretary of the navy and Spanish-American War veteran. McKinley had fought in the Civil War, as had Benjamin Harrison, James Garfield, Rutherford Hayes and, of course, Ulysses Grant. Grover Cleveland, the first post–Civil War Democrat, had avoided service in the Civil War, but in the first of his two nonconsecutive terms the small frontier army fought a number of Indian engagements, and in his second term the army took part in policing labor agitation. Even Chester Arthur, who replaced the assassinated Garfield in 1881, had a modicum of Civil War military experience when he served as a New York state quartermaster. Wilson's first secretary of war, Lindley Garrison, likewise had no prior experience with the military, though like Wilson he was a legal scholar. One of Wilson's early biographers characterized Garrison as being "ill at ease in his sudden plunge into a strange environment." Like Wilson, Garrison did not initially trust courts-martial. His replacement, Newton Baker, proved to be a superb administrator, but he too had little military experience and initially worried that courts-martial lacked due process. Indeed, Clarence H. Cramer, one of the first biographers of Baker, wrote that Wilson's appointment of Baker, given his pacifist and prewar antimilitary sentiments, may have been a political calculation in line with Wilson's reelection slogan, "He kept us out of war."[40]

Prior to World War I, court-martialed and other aggrieved soldiers not only regularly petitioned congressmen but also presidents and secretaries of war. Perhaps, as a result of his busy schedule, but also perhaps because of his general disinterest in the subject matter, Wilson had his personal secretary Joseph Tumulty screen most correspondence from soldiers and veterans. Often, Tumulty concluded that a soldier's complaint was of minor importance to the war effort, and he did not share it with Wilson. As with Wilson, Garrison, and Baker, Tumulty had no prior experience with the military, and his initial impressions of military discipline were that it was inherently conservative and did not possess the prevailing standards of due process. Tumulty was a young thirty-three-year-old secretary with a political familiarity limited to New Jersey. However, Wilson's, Garrison's, Baker's and, Tumulty's views on military affairs, including its disciplinary mechanisms, would change.[41]

Early in Wilson's presidency, Tumulty inquired whether the army might release a private named Louis A. Salmons from his prison sentence after the army had court-martialed him for disobedience of orders. Salmons enlisted in the army as a minor and without his parents' permission and therefore had fraudulently enlisted. Tumulty opined that because Salmons was too young to have enlisted in the first place, he could hardly be held responsible for whatever minor infractions he committed, and therefore the War Department should simply restore Salmons to civilian status without any record of a dishonorable discharge. Because Crowder was in Cuba at the time of the appeal, his acting deputy, Major Blanton Winship, responded to a shocked Tumulty that "the War Department customarily exercises the right to retain and punish for fraudulent enlistment." Winship then countered that not only should Salmons's court-martial stand, he would recommend a second court-martial for the fraudulent enlistment. After all, Winship concluded, by lying about his age, Salmons had wasted army resources. Tumulty found Winship's response appalling and took Salmons's appeal to Wilson in the hopes that the president would grant some form of clemency. In early 1914 Wilson ordered Salmons released to the care of his parents.[42]

More infuriating to Tumulty than Winship's response over Salmons's appeal was the case of Private Clarence L. George, who was court-martialed after writing an inflammatory letter to Secretary of War Garrison that criticized the command at Fort Leavenworth. While serving a two-year sentence, George communicated with the Washington-based Newspaper Press Association and the *Chicago Tribune*, and the commander of the military prison determined his letters, once made public, constituted disrespect to superior officers. Tumulty was convinced that George had suffered an injustice, and in January 1914 he urged Wilson to intercede with Garrison. Tumulty conceded that "after seven years in the Army, George acquired the habit of using intoxicants and was absent without leave some six times within a year," but "he had reenlisted three times and enjoyed good ratings."[43]

Wilson, in turn, had Garrison order a second review of the court-martial, and after reading Crowder's advice to commute George's sentence, the president determined to order the army to restore George to duty and give him all back pay. Crowder then informed Wilson that only Congress or the Court of Claims could restore George's back pay, a law which Wilson responded served only to deny wronged soldiers of their full rights. At the end of the month, the president of the Connecticut Life Insurance Company, who was also a corporate lawyer, took up George's cause. In the end, Wilson pardoned Private George, the Newspaper Press Association headlined Tumulty as aiding a wronged soldier, and the Court of Claims ordered the army to remunerate the soldier.[44]

After his first year as secretary of war, Garrison increasingly sided with the Judge Advocate General's Office, and on occasion, he disagreed with Crowder's recommendations for clemency to aggrieved soldiers. In 1914 the army court-martialed Captain Edgar F. Miller, a doctor who had served for two years in the Philippines. Miller had returned to a stateside posting, and he was either suffering from alcoholism or having an unusual reaction to antimalarial drugs. He regularly failed to show up for duty, and he became incoherent while on duty. To compound his difficulties, Miller was a surgeon, and according to the court-martial's findings, his patients went unattended. The court-martial sentenced him to a dismissal and two years in prison. Medical personnel at Walter Reed General Hospital were divided as to whether Miller was criminally responsible for his conduct. Crowder believed that Miller's conduct resulted from a combination of a tropical disease and a neurological reaction to medication. To Crowder, this was enough doubt to recommend to Garrison that the court-martial not be approved or, at a minimum, to release Miller from prison. Assistant Chief of Staff Bliss pushed Garrison to approve the findings and sentence with the argument that disapproving the court-martial would set a precedent that ultimately undermined discipline. Garrison disagreed with Crowder on granting clemency and determined to approve the court-martial verdict and sentence.[45]

CONCLUSION

One of the governing principles of military operations is that a disciplined force is more likely to prevail over a less disciplined adversary. The Prussian victory over Austria in 1866, the Prussian-German victory over France in 1870–1871, and the Japanese victory over Russia in 1905 were a reminder that discipline had to be an inherent part of an army's governance. Of course, an ill-equipped, outnumbered, or badly led yet otherwise disciplined force might be defeated nonetheless, but discipline was an essential part of the industrial age mass forces. When the United States entered World War I, its army was small and untested for modern war, and it was unknown whether conscripts could be made to fight in an overseas war once confronted by the horrors of trench fighting, poison gas, increased machine gun rates of fire, and larger and larger artillery calibers that were unheard of in prior conflicts. By the summer of 1917 the French and British armies had seen devolution from discipline to mutiny, and the German war machine appeared ascendant, particularly as fighting on the Eastern Front drew to a close with Russia's collapse. Some of the political forces that undermined the British and French war effort were present in the United States as well.

In April 1917, the army's organization was divided into six geographic departments (referred to as divisions prior to 1917) in which each department commander had the authority to convene general courts-martial. These six departments were titled "Northeastern," "Eastern," "Southeastern," "Central," "Southern," and "Western." Outside of the United States, the three generals commanding the army's forces in the Philippines, the Panama Canal Zone, and "Hawaii Territory" had an authority similar to that of their counterparts in the United States. Each geographic division contained various regiments in a structure that had developed out of the post–Civil War army and somewhat mirrored that of the pre–World War I British Army. Once the United States entered the war, this basic construct remained, but the units that trained in the United States went over to France in a different type of unit known as a division, which Pershing called the "square division." A division was the smallest unit in an army that contained artillery, transport, infantry, signal forces, hospitals, and supply units needed to sustain an independent action. An American division numbered between 24,000 and 28,000 soldiers, making it almost twice the size of its British and French counterparts. The large size of the American division resulted partly from the lack of trained professional officers. Each division was assigned one judge advocate and between three and six assistant judge advocates who were responsible for a number of different duties, including the selection of trial judge advocates to prosecute

courts-martial and appointment of defense counsel for soldiers accused of
crimes. The American divisions that went to France in late 1917 and 1918 were
composed of men from all parts of the country, whose beliefs ranged across a
broad political and religious spectrum, and who were rapidly subjected to the
demands of military discipline.[46]

Ultimately, the United States fielded a highly disciplined expeditionary
force of some two million soldiers in Europe, and this force contributed
to Germany's defeat as well as that of its ally Austria. Regardless of the
disagreements between Pershing and the Allied generals and political leaders,
by August 1918, an American army was fully capable of sustained fighting
against the German war machine. The Judge Advocate General's Office
contributed to this accomplishment. However, following the war, when courts-
martial and other aspects of military discipline were attacked as an odious
system that was antithetical to the American principles of fair trials, a process
was set in motion in which courts-martial were analyzed as a separate part of
the military history of that conflict, and usually unfavorably so. Sometimes
this occurred for good reason. World War I courts-martial, like their Civil
War predecessors and World War II progeny, were at times encumbered by
a lack of due process, even in comparison to the standard federal criminal
trials of their respective times. Moreover, World War I generals were often
portrayed as distant, aloof, ready to sacrifice huge numbers of men as cannon
fodder to gain a few yards of territory from the enemy, and therefore naturally
unconcerned with the results of courts-martial.[47]

Even without the inclusion of the multifaceted other duties of the Judge
Advocate General's Office, the study of courts-martial it conducted during
World War I presents a complex history deserving of analytic treatment for
several reasons. A study of the Judge Advocate General's Office adds not
only to the nation's military history, it also adds to its political, legal, and
social history. For the purposes of this study, the history of World War I is
not simply the years 1914 to 1918. The War Department's leadership and
Wilson assumed that war could flare up again after the Armistice. Specifically,
Crowder believed that even with the defeat of the Central powers in late
1918, the war could quickly renew through either a revived Germany or a
revolutionary alliance between Central European communists, German
Spartacists, and Russian Bolsheviks. As a result, the span of this study extends
from 1914 to 1922.[48]

Secondly, the Judge Advocate General's Office was staffed by a large
number of progressives who considered that the government had a
positive regulatory duty to protect society from unscrupulous people and
corporations. During the Civil War, Holt recruited judge advocates who

were staunchly abolitionist and driven to defeat both the Confederacy and "the enemy from within." Beginning in 1916, Crowder sought to commission judge advocates with a legal jurisprudence that ranged across the political spectrum. The variety of jurisprudential ideology and diversity of backgrounds prevented a push for trials based solely on deterrence and at the expense of fairness. Even among the more conservative professional officers serving as judge advocates, there was a desire to create a disciplined reliable force without resorting to "kangaroo courts" or the arbitrary application of discipline. On July 5, 1918, a general court-martial at Fort DuPont, Delaware, convicted Sergeant Stephan Hansen of engaging in "buccal coitus" with a male civilian and sentenced him to be dishonorably discharged and serve two years in confinement. On September 21, 1918, a general court-martial convicted Bugler Fredrick Keyser of "unlawfully carnally abusing a fourteen year old girl" and sentenced him to eight years in prison and a dishonorable discharge. In both instances, Colonel Frank L. Dodds, the judge advocate for the Eastern Department, recommended to Major General Franklin Bell to disapprove the findings and sentences because the judge advocate prosecuting each case had impermissibly permitted hearsay evidence to be used against the accused soldiers, and in the case of Hansen, the judge advocate unfairly appealed to the passions of the tribunal in his closing argument. Given the homosexual nature of Hansen's acts, it is, in retrospect, surprising that he would be shown any leniency. Yet Bell followed Dodds's advice.[49]

In the American Expeditionary Forces, the desire for fair trials balanced against the army's disciplinary needs was also evident in the work of the judge advocates. On July 9, 1918, General Walter Bethel, the American Expeditionary Forces judge advocate who directly reported to Pershing, noted to the fielded judge advocates:

> It has been observed that some Judge Advocates in making their recommendations to their commanding general, accept the finding of the court without question, no matter how inconclusive or insufficient the evidence. While the finding of the court is entitled to great weight, reviewing authorities in the past have never regarded themselves as bound by such finding and have not hesitated to disapprove sentences on account of the insufficiency of the evidence; and Judge Advocates should not hesitate to comment upon the weakness or the evidence of the impropriety of the sentence, to the end that the reviewing authority may be properly advised as to what he should do in his disposition of the case. A Judge Advocate who does not do this seriously neglects his duty, not only to the United States, but to his commanding general.[50]

On July 17, 1918, Lieutenant Colonel H. H. Morrow, who served at the Judge Advocate General's Office, compiled a list of errors found in records of trial occurring in a one-month period at the various stateside camps and posts. Morrow pointed out that in twenty instances, a judge advocate failed to inform an accused soldier of the right not to testify or to make an unsworn statement to the court-martial; on twelve occasions, a court-martial was informed of a sentence limitation that exceeded a legally permissible sentence; dozens of records of trial had been improperly authenticated; witnesses had failed to be sworn; and in thirty-seven instances, the government had failed to place any evidence in the record that the accused soldier was subject to the army's jurisdiction in the first place. That these errors occurred while the United States had been at war for fourteen months and the army was in the process of shipping hundreds of thousands of soldiers to France to take part in the enormous offensive operations against Germany offended Crowder. After learning of Morrow's review, Crowder explained to his staff that the army would fall apart if its soldiers believed that courts-martial were slipshod.[51]

While the judge advocates serving in higher echelon commands such as the Judge Advocate General's Office and the American Expeditionary Forces headquarters noted hundreds of errors, the judge advocates assigned to the division and corps staffs were often careful in their reviews of the thousands of special and general courts-martial records of trials. Although providing two examples may appear nothing more than anecdotal, thousands of records located within the National Archives and Records Administration mirror such examples. On March 4, 1919, the Seventh Division court-martialed Corporal Julius Urbon for disobeying a lawful order. Major Joseph W. Bartlett, the division's judge advocate, advised the divisional commander Major General Edmund Wittenmyer that Urbon's confession was involuntarily obtained, and Wittenmyer reversed the court-martial's finding of guilty. One month earlier Bartlett prevailed on Wittenmyer to grant clemency to a Private Homer Stevens, a deserter who failed to make the transport to France out of fear of serving in the war. Wittenmyer overturned the court-martial conviction after the soldier came to France and volunteered to serve in dangerous nighttime reconnaissance patrols.[52]

A similar result played out in the Thirty-Sixth Division on April 11, 1919. On October 10, 1918, Bugler Ernest Meier abandoned his post while his "company was engaged with the enemy" in the Meuse-Argonne. The prosecuting judge advocate did not introduce the unit's muster rolls into evidence, but the court-martial's presiding officer obtained these rolls along with "other inadmissible evidence." In all likelihood the fact that witnesses testified that Meier had run away from his peers in the direction of the rear with a frightened expression and that he informed some of his peers that he was petrified would have been enough to find him guilty of desertion. But the divisional judge advocate, Major Victor E. Ruehl, advised the divisional commander to overturn the finding of guilty for desertion, approve only a finding of unauthorized absence, and commute the sentence of a dishonorable discharge and five-year term of imprisonment to six months' confinement and a return to the ranks. Instead, the divisional commander reduced the sentence to one year in confinement but then held the sentence in abeyance and returned Meir to the ranks.[53]

2

STAFFING AND DIRECTING THE JUDGE ADVOCATE
GENERAL'S DEPARTMENT: DUTIES AND DISCIPLINE

ON JUNE 7, 1917, GENERAL Pershing expressed his dissatisfaction with the discipline of the various staff bureaus to General Tasker Bliss, the acting chief of staff of the army. One of Pershing's more poignant complaints was that in spite of an obvious need for secrecy, an Ordnance Bureau officer sent a telegram listing the name of the vessel that Pershing and his headquarters staff had sailed in to Britain, as well as the date of its departure. The telegram was marked confidential, but all of the information in it was in unencrypted English. To remedy the lack of secrecy, Bliss turned to Crowder to draft a regulation requiring all confidential communications to be written in cipher. German naval intelligence ultimately had no knowledge of Pershing's travels, but the fact that two years earlier a German submarine sunk a vessel carrying Lord Horatio Herbert Kitchener, Britain's war minister, was a reminder of the importance of secrecy. Prior to 1914, Kitchener had been a military hero of various colonial wars, and although there is no evidence German naval intelligence knew of his travel, at the time of his death the Allied forces did not know the full extent of German intelligence.[1]

It was nothing unusual for the Judge Advocate General's Office to draft an order, but the nature of this particular order indicated that even professional officers at the War Department had not fully comprehended that the nation had entered into a modern "total war." In light of the British intercept of the so-called "Zimmerman Telegram," which partly led to the nation's entering the war, the casualness of professional officers is surprising. A turn-of-the-century "total war" was not simply predicated on the numbers of fielded soldiers and the mass industrial production of military materiel. A "total war" meant harnessing the nation's finance and commerce, achieving industrial stability, and convincing the majority of the nation's citizenry of the justness of the war's costs, including limits on individual rights. Moreover, for the first time since Reconstruction, the War Department assumed responsibilities that affected the lives of everyday Americans, and these responsibilities included the enforcement of the selective service laws through courts-martial, something that had never before occurred.[2]

Although Crowder had determined to try to maintain as apolitical a staff office as possible, he was unable to do so. The sweeping duties of the Judge Advocate General's Office, which were soon to encroach on the civil life of the nation, made it impossible to run a staff office free from the nation's politics. Legislators, state governors, and both federal and state judges lobbied Crowder and his wartime deputy, Brigadier General Samuel Tilden Ansell, to have the War Department commission hundreds of "by-name" lawyers. For instance, Congressman Henry De La Warr Flood, who advanced the resolution declaring war on Germany through the House of Representatives, applied for a judge advocate commission and supported his cousin Jonathan Flood's application as well. Crowder offered Flood his support, but Secretary of War Newton Baker convinced Flood that he was needed in Congress. Even with Senator Oscar Underwood's and Representative Carter Glass's support, Jonathan Flood was unable to obtain a commission until late in the war. Although Crowder favored applicants with prior military experience, he took pains to ensure that successful applicants without a military background had substantial government experience. He gave state judges, legislators, and federal and state prosecutors precedence over other civilian applicants. Crowder hoped that the selection of prominent attorneys with ties to both political parties would not only result in greater trust in the War Department's administration of courts-martial but also would improve its overall wartime conduct. Perhaps because it was well known that Crowder's career had progressed as a result of President Taft's help, congressional Republicans expected that Crowder would favor their nominees for judge advocate commissions. But he did not do so, and in September 1918, Senator Joseph Frelinghuysen, a New Jersey Republican, complained to Ansell that Crowder had become "a sop to Tumulty." Ansell defended Crowder, responding that not only was Frelinghuysen in error, but "Crowder did not regard Tumulty as one of the best sources of professional information, from which this office has endeavored to inform its judgment as to the lawyers best qualified for service in this department."[3]

Another politicizing aspect had to do with the judge advocate general's relationship to the army's chief of staff. Since the end of the Civil War, there was an argument internal to the army over the independence of the staff bureaus and departments. The staff departments and bureaus tended to function without full regard to the chief of staff. Beginning with General William Tecumseh Sherman's ascension as commanding general, efforts were made to curtail staff independence because this independence eroded unity of command and resulted in misallocated War Department personnel and resources. Despite Sherman's and his successors' efforts, a degree of staff independence remained in 1917. As a member of the staff, the judge advocate general was technically subservient to the chief of staff, but because the judge advocate general was often tasked to directly communicate to the president and Congress, the chief of staff could only hope to be informed of these communications rather than influence them. Crowder's predecessor, General George Davis, was known to anger the chief of staff for failing to consult with him prior to meeting with President Roosevelt. Shortly after the United States' declaration of war on Germany, General Hugh Lennox Scott, the army's aged chief of staff, made it clear to the staff and bureau chiefs, and the surgeon general and judge advocate general, that they had to work with a singular purpose and coordinate all activities so that the chief of staff could, along with the secretary of war, enable a clear unified war effort. During the war Crowder clashed with Scott's eventual replacement, General Peyton March, over whether the Judge Advocate General's Office was required to be wholly subservient to the chief of staff.[4]

A third politicizing aspect had to do with Congress's reliance on the Judge Advocate General's Office. During the war, the Judge Advocate General's Office drafted legislation for Congress to include patent protections as well as protection against patent infringement claims, War Risk Insurance, civil protections for soldiers, and the Selective Service Act. All of these duties had the potential to politicize the Judge Advocate General's Office because of the national, state, and commercial interests affected. Crowder recognized that the successful implementation and management of each of these functions ultimately rested on both congressional and public acceptance of the army's disciplinary enforcement. This was because an erosion of the public trust in courts-martial could lead to an erosion of trust in the other functions, and in particular, conscription. While a later chapter analyzes congressional oversight of courts-martial and the army's other governing aspects, it is of foremost importance to understand how courts-martial operated and how the Judge Advocate General's Office influenced the shaping of the nation's military laws prior to the war as a matter of context.

PHILOSOPHIES OF DISCIPLINE IN THE ARMY: JUDGE ADVOCATES AND GENERALS

If, in 1917, the nation's citizenry was generally unfamiliar with the mechanics and rules governing courts-martial, the prevailing views of the army's senior officers regarding military discipline were wholly alien. In 1917 civilians, to include President Wilson and his cabinet chiefs, likely did not know the full extent of the views of the army's senior general officers regarding courts-martial and other disciplinary enforcement. Even under the most ardent "right to work" or "freedom of contract scheme," civilians could quit their employment. To do so in the military was called desertion, and a simple failure to show up to work on time could constitute absence without leave (AWOL). Under the Articles of War, offenses such as desertion, cowardice, straggling, "misbehavior before the enemy," or mutiny in a time of war could result in a death sentence. Moreover, AWOL could result in imprisonment for five years. In civilian employment an employee's arguing with a supervisor might be a basis for a firing, but in the army it could result in a court-martial. And freedom of speech was significantly curtailed under the Articles of War, even by pre-1920 standards. Although senior officers believed this was necessary to maintain discipline in the ranks, civilians in the early twentieth century might find this system ludicrous. On October 19, 1917, Major General Thomas Barry, the commanding general of the Central Department, approved Private Frank J. Gaffney's conviction and sentence to five years in prison and a dishonorable discharge. While in a mess hall, Gaffney called his regimental commander a "son of a bitch" and threatened a lieutenant.[5]

The gulf in understanding courts-martial between the views of military commanders and the general public was also increased because military-type offenses such as desertion in peacetime were generally treated far more leniently prior to 1917 than in the period between April 1917 and January 1920. On October 20, 1915, the army court-martialed Private George N. Henwood for deserting his coastal artillery battery in New York. This was Henwood's third conviction, and the prior two convictions were for being AWOL. The last court-martial sentenced Henwood to six months in confinement, but he had been reenlisted in the army. Three weeks earlier, the army court-martialed Private Charles H. Clark for deserting from the Mexican border, an important assignment at the time. Despite the fact that Clark had deserted once before and been confined for three months, the court-martial sentenced him to only one year in confinement. But the commanding general permitted Clark to reenlist as a matter of clemency. In contrast, courts-martial for desertion from the American Expeditionary Forces often resulted in sentences of five years or more with dishonorable discharges as well. Crowder, however, did not advocate for the imposition of a disciplinary system that was devoid of any leniency. On September 22, 1917, he convinced Baker to have the adjutant general send out a memorandum reminding all divisional commanders that a sentence of a dishonorable discharge should only be approved when an offender no longer "had the capacity for further military service."[6]

The disciplinary philosophies of the army's senior officers were partly a product of their own experiences. In 1902 the army court-martialed Captain John Leonard Hines for "committing cruelty and maltreatment" against a private under his command. During a barracks inspection on Jolo Island in the Philippines, Hines discovered that a Private Peter Pinneo possessed a number of stolen jewelry items belonging not only to senior officers, but also to Philippine prisoners in army custody. Hines concluded that Pinneo had not acted alone, and during an interrogation in which Pinneo asserted no knowledge of the offenses, Hines ordered Pinneo "tied up by his wrists to the ceiling, with his toes on the ground, and kept in this position of constraint for a few, not more than three minutes." When questioned about his conduct, Hines admitted to tying Pinneo up in this manner twice. Hines considered that his actions were "required by the exigencies of the occasion" and "for the protection of the lives and property of the people at the post." For reasons that are now unclear, Hines's court-martial was held at Governors Island, New York. The court-martial agreed with Hines's assessment of necessity and acquitted him. Samuel Ansell, at the time a captain, served as the trial judge advocate—a duty further explained below—agreed that "Hines offered a sound defense for his actions against Pinneo," and urged the court-martial to acquit Hines. Ansell also noted to the court-martial that Pinneo had pleaded guilty to larceny in a different court-martial, and therefore Hines had solved a crime. Ansell's conduct, by analogy to a civilian criminal trial, was of a prosecutor arguing to a jury to acquit a defendant. But in military trials, Ansell's conduct was commensurate with his duties and therefore not entirely unheard of. Undoubtedly Hines believed himself vindicated and his methods of interrogation justified. He went on to serve as a divisional and then corps commander in the American Expeditionary Forces, and in 1924 he became the army's chief of staff. He would also, in 1919, try to inform a Senate subcommittee that Ansell was "the basest hypocrite."[7]

Pershing, Crowder, and other senior American military leaders were acutely aware that in 1915 British discipline was superb, so that their forces did not crumble after experiencing the first instance of a poison gas barrage. Nor did French discipline collapse in the first two years of the war, including during the horrific defensive operations at Verdun. But in 1917 the strain of the war had affected both Allied forces. In the spring of 1917, General Robert Nivelle, the French Army's newest commanding general, ordered a general offensive against the German lines in the Chemin des Dames. Within one week, almost thirty thousand French soldiers were killed and over 100,000 were wounded. For an army that had survived the German offensive at Verdun months earlier with horrific casualties, Nivelle's failed offensive was ruinous to morale. Whole regiments in the French Army mutinied and refused to "go over the top." Hastily formed soldiers' unions also tried to make demands on senior officers. In the fall of 1917, British soldiers openly rioted at the port of Etaples. In January 1919, British soldiers in Folkestone and Dover refused to board ships headed for France. Moreover, senior American Army officers also knew that in the war's closing months, German sailors influenced by communist and socialist organizations engaged in a wholesale mutiny in Kiel and made it impossible for the German fleet to conduct operations. By September 1918, a growing number of German soldiers refused to attack Allied positions.[8]

As regressive as American generals could seem in enforcing discipline, they tended to be more progressive than their Allied counterparts. On July 20, 1917, Pershing, along with Colonel James G. Harbord and Captain George Patton, met Field Marshal Douglas Haig, the commander of the British Expeditionary Forces, for the first time. During their meeting they observed that a British court-martial had sentenced a "Tommie," as British soldiers were called, to death for the crime of cowardice. The British court-martial, known as a "field court-martial," was conducted in a trial akin to an American summary court-martial. But in an American summary court-martial, the maximum sentence a soldier could receive was thirty days in confinement, reduction in enlisted rank, and a fine. The British military laws enabled a field court-martial for charges of cowardice, mutiny, or desertion, and if a soldier were sentenced to death, a British Army commander could approve the execution within twenty-four hours. As there were five British armies on the Western Front, six senior officers (to include Haig) had the authority to approve executions, and there was no requirement for a verbatim record of trial in which a condemned soldier could appeal on the basis of a legal error. The "Tommie" in question was executed the morning after Pershing departed Haig's headquarters. During the war, over three thousand British soldiers were sentenced to death, as were over two thousand French soldiers, and over four thousand Italian soldiers, all for military crimes such as desertion, mutiny, or "subversion." In several instances, the Allied armies permitted summary executions. Although many of the soldiers originally sentenced to death were ultimately granted clemency in the reduction of their sentences to terms of imprisonment, British, French, Belgian, and Italian courts-martial, in comparison to their American counterpart, were often bereft of due process.[9]

In the American Expeditionary Forces, few death sentences were carried out. Before April 5, 1917, there was an influence internal to the army against the broad use of capital punishment. In the late nineteenth century, Major General G. Norman Lieber, while serving as judge advocate general, informed Congress that he believed the peacetime army no longer required capital punishment as a disciplinary measure. Shortly after, Lieutenant General John McAlister Schofield, the army's commanding general, informed Congress he agreed with Lieber. Despite Lieber's testimony, Congress maintained the possibility of the death penalty under the Articles of War, but the reviewing judge advocates tended to cite Lieber's position in their reviews of general courts-martial. Although the Forty-Eighth Article of War empowered Pershing to approve executions for the crimes of rape, murder, spying, or mutiny, as a result of a War Department order captioned as General Order 7, beginning in late 1917, Baker and Wilson had the authority to override him, and the order required Pershing as well as all stateside generals in command of the army's geographic departments to seek Baker's permission prior to carrying out any execution. In reality, even without General Order 7, Pershing would have had great difficulty in quickly ordering executions because soldiers had a de facto right of appeal to the secretary of war, and as a result, he normally would have had to wait for several days to see if there would be a commutation from the president or War Department. With the addition of General Order 7, the secretary of war's silence could not be taken as a waiver for Pershing to proceed to order the execution. General Order 7 became significant for a reason other than the War Department's notion of due process. Crowder ordered Major E. G. Davis, a judge advocate assigned to the Judge Advocate General's Office, to draft General Order 7 for Baker's signature over Ansell's objection. Although Ansell opposed the order because he considered it only a "half measure" to address deficiencies in courts-martial, his objection would resurface, to be used against him after the war during a contentious debate over the fairness of courts-martial.[10]

Senior commanders from Pershing on down were unhappy with the prospect of having lesser disciplinary authority than their British and French counterparts. General Hunter Liggett, who commanded the First Corps prior to assuming command over the First Army, argued that "while the majority of soldiers were reliable and law-abiding, too many miscreants escaped the right punishment." Liggett was concerned that soldiers who committed atrocious crimes ranging from desertion to murder "escaped the harshest punishments." He later complained that "the American Army had not been long in France before the power of enforcing the death penalty, no matter how flagrant the crime, was made subject to the approval of Washington, and that was rarely given." Harbord agreed with Liggett and placed the blame for laxity in discipline on "our authorities at home." He later lamented, "one regrets to admit it, but the American Expeditionary Forces furnished quite a number of military crimes for which death was the just penalty, if discipline was to be maintained, but the offender escaped it."[11]

While many of the judge advocates assigned to the staff and at the American Expeditionary Forces headquarters in 1917 had experience fighting against Indians, or the Spanish Army in Cuba, or guerilla forces in the Philippines or in Mexico, or had observed the highly disciplined Japanese Army in their war against Russia, they understood that some recognition of civil and individual rights was essential to discipline. That is, they believed that military justice was a two-edged sword. The British disciplinary model would have undermined domestic support for the war. Too lax a system of enforcement would create what Liggett pointed out was the Union army's weakness at the beginning of the Civil War: "a well-intentioned mob." Crowder and his judge advocates, as this study stresses throughout, served as a check on senior career officers who endorsed aspects of the British model of harshness. Crowder, in response to Pershing's lobbying for greater authority over courts-martial, countered to Baker that "American public opinion would be less patient with summary execution than that" of the Allies." But the judge advocates also served as a bulwark against "civilizing" military justice. In essence, they enabled a "middle ground" in which soldiers could be held accountable and discipline enforced, but without completely undermining the public's confidence in military justice by wholly ignoring traditional rights. One such example of this middle ground was that in early 1918, Crowder convinced Pershing to issue General Order 56, which emphasized sending accused service-members, whenever possible, to special courts-martial instead of general courts-martial. Given that the maximum sentence limitation of a special court-martial was one year in confinement and a reduction to the lowest enlisted grade, many of the trials, which might have resulted in severe sentences of a year or more, were dealt with in trials akin to misdemeanor courts.[12]

JUDGE ADVOCATE GENERAL'S DUTIES: COURTS-MARTIAL, AND CIVIL AND INTERNATIONAL LAW

In 1917 the Judge Advocate General's Office was divided into "sections" and "divisions" responsible for the War Department's various legal matters,

which ranged from constitutional interpretations of the army's position in
the nation, to the governance of national parks. Judge advocates were also
assigned to the Council of National Defense as well as national industrial
boards and legislative committees. Although the military justice division was
the largest and perhaps most well known of the divisions, a brief description
of the other aspects of the staff office illustrates the broad sweep of the judge
advocate general's responsibilities.

In 1915 an administrative law division was created to resolve matters ranging from the recognition of foreign marriages to the legality of an officer campaigning on behalf of a politician running for office. A War Risk Insurance
division, legislation division, accounts, claims and contracting division, civil
administration and insular affairs division, constitutional division, and even a
maritime division were part of the Judge Advocate General's Office. In October 1917, the War Risk Insurance Bureau—which had been created in 1914
as part of the Treasury Department to protect maritime commerce—became
responsible to the Judge Advocate General's Office's War Risk Insurance division for determinations issued on behalf of claimants. Although Congress
unanimously expanded the War Risk Insurance law to financially protect the
families of servicemen who died or were injured, some insurance corporations opposed the law because it foreclosed the possibility of tremendous corporate profits. Not only did the War Risk Insurance division examine claims
prior to transfer of its decisions to the Treasury Department, judge advocates
also investigated allegations made by soldiers that the Treasury Department failed to abide by the division's decisions. As to the maritime division,
Crowder believed that since over a million men and tremendous tonnages of
army materiel were to be shipped to France on War Department contracted
vessels, judge advocates were required to master admiralty law, a traditional
naval expertise. As an example of how the maritime division functioned,
when on August 15, 1918, a German submarine torpedoed and sank the War
Department contracted cargo vessel SS *Montanan*, the vessel's owners filed a
demand against the War Department to compensate for the loss. Colonel Herbert A. White, who headed the maritime division, advised Baker that the War
Department was not required to repay the company for the loss because the
vessel's master, who was employed by the corporation, abandoned ship while
the ship still had the ability to steam into Le Havre, France.[13]

Since the nation's founding, a number of officers had taken a scholarly
interest in the laws of war and other aspects of international law, and in 1916
Crowder created a separate international law division to advise on such matters. At any given time prior to the war, a judge advocate was expected to
be an advisor to the War Department and the president on "all insular and

foreign matters." Although the term "insular matters" has not been used in the last fifty years, it referred to the governance of all US overseas territories. Following the Spanish-American War, Crowder's predecessors regularly conferred with Secretary of War Elihu Root on law enforcement and the civil and criminal courts in Cuba, Puerto Rico, and the Philippines.

Because the War Department partially governed the Philippines, Puerto Rico, Cuba, and Guam, the secretary of state often turned to the Judge Advocate General's Office for guidance. Presidents Roosevelt and Taft and their respective secretaries of state relied on Crowder and his subordinates to draft legislation as well as recommend civilians to staff the various judicial functions in these territories. Moreover, judge advocates represented the governments of the Philippines, Cuba, and Puerto Rico before the federal courts of appeal and the United States Supreme Court. As a result, by the time Wilson became president, Crowder and his subordinates had a strong reputation as international law experts as well as an expertise in constitutional law. The State Department's reliance on Crowder did not change with William Jennings Bryan's appointment, despite Bryan's antimilitarism, and it continued after Robert Lansing replaced Bryan.[14]

The Judge Advocate General's Office also authored proposed legislation for the secretary of war to convey to Congress. One of the issues that became important on the eve of the war was whether retired officers who were recalled to duty would be eligible for promotion, and how a recall might affect retirement pay. The statutes governing the effect of recalls to active duty on military retirements were unclear regarding promotion eligibility and retirement compensation, and General Scott turned to Crowder to author a proposed law clarifying that recalled officers were entitled to compete for promotion. Crowder also had a role in the drafting of antialcohol statutes near military installations as well as statutes restricting the shipment of private firearms during the war.[15]

In order to focus conscripted soldiers' attention on their training and deployment to France, Crowder turned to Colonel George S. Wallace, a West Virginia National Guard judge advocate, to draft a proposed law that prohibited state courts from proceeding with civil suits against soldiers. Wallace penned a bill that became known as the Soldiers and Sailors Civil Relief Act, which prioritized military necessity in wartime over a state's fundamental authority to enforce its jurisdiction. The law permitted state and municipal governments to bring suit against their citizens, but importantly, it delayed a bank, corporation, landowner, or civilian from suing a soldier as long as the soldier was on duty. That Wallace—a coal corporation and banking lawyer who took part in West Virginia's suppression of strikers—drafted the bill is only one of its remarkable aspects. Interestingly, Wallace wanted the law to extend to protect the properties of the spouses of soldiers that predated a marriage, but Congress was not willing to extend the protective law that far. Yet Congress unanimously passed the protection from state lawsuits into law. Another remarkable aspect to the law was that during the Civil War, Lincoln had asked the states to enforce a similar prohibition, but there was no federal usurpation of state jurisdiction over civil suits. In 1918 Crowder informed the judge advocates that he expected them to vigorously advocate for soldiers' rights under this act.[16]

Baker and Crowder believed that while all of the broad legal matters handled by the Judge Advocate General's Office were critical to the war effort, military justice remained at the forefront of the office's duties. Since the first continental army of the War for Independence, a unique body of laws titled the Articles of War had governed courts-martial and other aspects of military discipline, such as boards of inquiry and procedures for the investigation of allegations of wrongdoing by superior officers. Although the American Articles of War dated to 1775, these were adopted wholesale from the British Army and, in turn, the British military laws dated to the seventeenth-century Swedish code of King Gustavus Adolphus. In 1805 President Thomas Jefferson asked Congress to draft an American code and the following year it did so, though much of the American code remained British in nature. The 1806 Articles of War were still in effect during the Civil War. In 1874 a new Articles of War came into being, in part to bring the laws closer to federal criminal practice, and in part because the Judge Advocate General's Department's leadership determined that aspects of the British, French, and Prussian military codes were worthy of incorporation, particularly in light of the growth in acceptance of a universal law of war and Prussia's success in its war against the Habsburg Empire in 1866 and against France in 1870–1871. The rapidity and decisiveness of the Prussian-German victories shocked military policy makers, and General Holt wanted to ensure that the Articles of War were both predictable and streamlined.[17]

In 1916 Congress enacted a new Articles of War with the principal purpose of further incorporating greater due process than under the old code. The 1916 code was essentially Crowder's creation, though he had the support of several congressmen, including Senator Francis E. Warren and Congressman Frank Lester Greene, both of whom chaired the respective committees responsible for the passage of the articles. In July 1916 Greene informed Crowder that Oregon senator George Earle Chamberlain could also be relied on to "stifle any opposition to the revised Articles." Ironically, Chamberlain would later attack Crowder as "an autocrat who oversaw a despotic system." This is an important point because in authoring the draft of the new Articles, Crowder maintained the principle that military discipline would remain wholly within the military establishment and subject to the authority of the secretary of war and the commanders of the various geographic departments and corps, divisions, and brigades. Crowder disavowed any intention to increase the authority of the Judge Advocate General's Office, which he believed served only in an advisory capacity. Nonetheless, there remained in effect a Civil War statute that further clarified the judge advocate general's duties. This statute, titled Section 1199, governed military jurisdiction, which included jurisdiction over veterans in receipt of retirement or disability pay, and it used the words "receive, revise, and cause to be recorded the proceedings." However, no judge advocate until World War I ever publicly advocated that the Judge Advocate General's Office had the authority to overturn a court-martial, and the term *revise* simply became synonymous with the term *advise*. Likewise, the term *revisory authority* simply meant the authority to advise.[18]

World War I–era courts-martial had similarities to civilian criminal trials in that a soldier on trial, referred to as "the accused," had to be placed on clear notice of the existence of a prohibited conduct through the codification of a crime covering that conduct. And the trial judge advocate was required to prove the alleged offense beyond a reasonable doubt in order to achieve a conviction (often referred to as a finding of guilt). Common law rules of evidence applied to courts-martial as well, and by 1914 an accused service-member was entitled to be represented by "counsel" in general courts-martial. Prior to 1963, a person accused of a felony and prosecuted in state felony trials was not constitutionally entitled to the assistance of counsel. That is, the person accused of a crime had to procure counsel or, if lacking the means to do so, go into trial without legal representation. Although a soldier prosecuted in a general court-martial had the right to counsel, there was no requirement that the "counsel" was a lawyer, and most of the time, infantry, cavalry, artillery, and engineering officers defended accused soldiers. As the army increased in size after April 1917, the majority of soldiers prosecuted in general courts-martial were defended by officers who had been attorneys in their civilian lives. Similar to federal criminal trials, courts-martial employed rules of "professional responsibility" to prevent the trial judge advocate from surprising an accused with evidence that the accused soldier had not been made aware of prior to trial.[19]

In some respects, a court-martial was more progressive than a state trial. The right against self-incrimination was enforced in courts-martial, but a similar enforcement was not required in state criminal trials until after World War II. In a court-martial, the trial judge advocate was prohibited from asking "degrading questions." Similar protections did not exist in many states. Under the rules for courts-martial, race and religion could not be used as a basis for declaring a witness incompetent to testify. In several states race and religion were used to exclude witnesses. Of course, such "color-blind" rules could not overcome innate prejudices, but at least there was a rule preventing the exclusion of an African American witness testifying against a white soldier. All courts-martial were supposed to begin with the judge advocate advising an accused soldier of his basic rights, including the right against self-incrimination. General courts-martial were preserved through the creation of verbatim transcripts, but most states did not require the production of a verbatim transcript in felony trials. Often a general court-martial would end in the early afternoon so that a stenographer could finish the transcript by the next morning. And officers serving on courts-martial were supposed to agree on the accuracy of the transcript by the time the trial ended. An omission from a verbatim record of trial could result in a de facto acquittal. For instance, on April 17, 1917, the army court-martialed Private Philip Merwin, an Illinois national guardsman called into active duty, for the murder of a civilian named Frederick Studer after Merwin shot and killed Studer. At the time of the shooting, Studer was unarmed but he had verbally threatened Merwin. Merwin testified in his own defense, and it appears that the court-martial voted to convict him of manslaughter instead of murder. Merwin was sentenced to a dishonorable discharge and five years in prison. However, the trial record failed to include a guilty finding, and since neither the trial judge advocate nor the court president was able to clarify the omission, Major General Barry, the Central Department's commanding general, "acquitted" Merwin, who went on to be commissioned as a second lieutenant, serve in the trenches, and be honorably discharged in 1920. Three decades before Merwin's conviction, the Supreme Court in *Runkle v. United States* had earlier reversed a court-martial under similar circumstances. It is unlikely that in a civilian trial Merwin's conviction would have been overturned, because without a verbatim transcript, a court of appeals could only look to the defendant's claims.[20]

There was an oddity with the composition of general and special courts-martial that placed a tremendous responsibility on the trial judge advocate to ensure that the laws and procedures governing the rights of the accused soldier were adhered to. Notwithstanding the means by which Hines extracted a confession, Ansell's conduct in Hines's court-martial is reasonably explained by the nature of a trial judge advocate's duties. Concern over prosecutorial misconduct is found in both British and American military law texts, and trial judge advocates were instructed to protect the rights of accused soldiers. For instance, in 1813, in his *Principles and Practice of Naval and Military Courts-Martial*, John McArthur, a British military law scholar, penned, "though a judge advocate may be considered in the light of a prosecutor for the crown, it does not from thence follow that he is to deny reasonable assistance to the prisoner in his defence, either in point of law or justice." Notably, McArthur went so far as to argue that prosecutors should not "impose novel legal arguments on a court-martial," or in other words, not misguide a court-martial. Likewise, Captain R. M. Hughes, a British Army officer, wrote in 1845 that because a court-martial was "a truth seeking function," a "judge advocate must produce without partiality or favor to either party, all evidence that tends to elicit the truth." American military law adopted McArthur's and Hughes's positions on the professional requirements on judge advocates. Of course, without a defense counsel or judge, a court-martial functioned on trust rather than on the protections of an adversarial system with a neutral arbiter. On the other hand, it was not until 1935 that the Supreme Court determined that a prosecutor's ethical lapses in court could be a basis for overturning a conviction.[21]

There were significant due process deficits in courts-martial as well. Under the Articles of War, there was no requirement for unanimity in courts-martial, and a two-thirds vote was all that was required to assign guilt or sentence a soldier to death. A simple majority was required for lesser sentences. Although unanimity has never been held to be a constitutional requirement in state criminal trials, by 1900 most of the states and all federal criminal trials required unanimity to achieve a verdict of guilt. Panels of officers, rather than a jury of one's peers, adjudged the guilt or innocence of an accused. Until 1948 enlisted soldiers were prohibited from serving on courts-martial. There was little to stop a commander from "stacking" a court-martial with officers who were predisposed to convict the accused soldier. Additionally, officers serving on courts-martial could ask questions of witnesses as well as have evidence produced that neither the judge advocate nor the accused had presented. As a significant due process matter, the Fifth Amendment requirement for a grand jury did not apply to courts-martial. And until 1968, courts-martial possessed no judge, and the ranking officer on the panel was entrusted with considerable power that no juror would possess in a state or federal trial.

Until World War I, in most instances an accused soldier was not defended by a counsel in the true sense of what the word *counsel* implied. This was because a trial judge advocate was tasked with a threefold duty. A trial judge advocate served as a prosecutor and a legal advisor to the court-martial and was also required to present exculpatory evidence on behalf of an accused and protect the accused's rights. Such a triple duty today would be wholly at odds with the professional standards of legal practice, but at the time, officers serving as trial judge advocates were considered to be honorable servants of the law. This is why Ansell believed it necessary to argue for Hines's acquittal in 1902. Assignment as a trial judge advocate was perceived as a career-enhancing duty for junior officers. A court-martial verdict might not be made available for days or weeks after the panel of officers determined the guilt or innocence of an accused or the sentence. General courts-martial records were sealed and forwarded to the commanding officer, who convened the court-martial, and then forwarded through a command chain to the secretary of war for final approval before the announcement of the verdict or sentence. Finally, and perhaps most troubling from a civilian perspective, was that it was possible in some limited instances for a commanding general to not approve an acquittal and instead reopen the court-martial to consider new evidence. In all likelihood, a state or federal court of appeals would prevent such an occurrence as a violation of protections against double jeopardy. But Congress's justification in enabling a commander's authority to this degree was that because the court-martial had not yet announced its verdict, there was no double jeopardy. During the war, at least one federal judge reviewed an appeal that challenged the constitutionality of a statute authorizing a commander to reopen a court-martial that had voted for an acquittal to consider new evidence. In January 1918, David C. Westenhaver, the United States District Court judge for the Northern District of Ohio, informed Baker that while he considered the authority to "reopen a case after a jury's vote was unprecedented, he conceded that as a matter of military discipline such an authority was necessary."[22]

In 1812 the Supreme Court, in *United States v. Hudson and Goodwin*, determined that when Congress created a criminal statute, the statute had to clearly place a person on notice that an act was prohibited and carried with it a punishment. The military was exempt from this decision though not through any specific grant from the Court. The Articles of War contained a general article, derisively known as "the devil's article," which prohibited "disorders" that "undermined discipline," without stating what the "disorders" were. The prosecution simply had to prove that the "disorder" undermined discipline. Some "disorders" such as brawling were evident crimes that the public could understand, but others, such as a disheveled uniform or a perceived slight to a sergeant, were not so obvious. In 1916 Crowder reaffirmed the importance of this article to a receptive Senate Military Affairs Committee chaired by Senator Chamberlain. There was an even broader set of prohibitions on officers. Commissioned officers have historically been held to a higher standard of conduct due to the importance of their command responsibilities and the fact that the president is responsible for issuing the commission. This is why there was an offense in the Articles of War captioned as "conduct unbecoming an officer and gentleman." To this day, the offense of "conduct unbecoming an officer and gentleman" does not specifically enumerate prohibited conduct, though beginning in 1950, it contained a nonexclusive list of examples. The offense criminalizes repugnant but otherwise legal conduct, if the officer's repugnant conduct degrades the status of the officer or the military. For instance, in 1917 a court-martial sentenced a lieutenant to a dismissal for "registering at a hotel with a woman who was not his wife," the woman being married to a fellow officer. The commanding general who convened the court-martial recommended to Baker to exercise clemency and restore the lieutenant to the rank, and the secretary of the treasury penned a letter asking President Wilson to do so, but Ansell successfully prevailed on Baker and Wilson on the basis of "general principles of officer-ship" to approve the dismissal.[23]

One other significant civilian right absent from courts-martial was the right of appeal against a finding of guilt or a sentence. Until 1950 no military appellate court existed, and the federal courts were reticent to review courts-martial as much, if not more, than they were to grant appeals from state criminal trials. In *Dynes v. Hoover*, the Supreme Court articulated a doctrine that the federal courts would leave to the Executive Branch the governance and oversight of courts-martial. Only the president, the secretary of war, or the general who convened a general court-martial had the authority to disapprove (the term for "overturn"), a general court-martial conviction or reduce a sentence. Following the Civil War, more than one commentator advocated for the establishment of a specialized appellate court, but Congress never acted on these suggestions. The secretary of war and the president, as well as the commanding generals who convened courts-martial, served as the appellate authority. Without fixed legal rules that were enforceable in courts of appeal, courts-martial were derided as "kangaroo courts." Indeed, several scholars in the years following the Civil War presented courts-martial as arbitrary and harsh in comparison to federal criminal trials.[24]

The term *court-martial* necessitates a further explanation, because there were three types of courts-martial during World War I. The most severe of these, the general court-martial, could adjudge a sentence of death if the nature of the charge or the accused soldier's conduct warranted it. Moreover, regardless of the severity of the charge, all officers accused of violating an article of war were prosecuted in general courts-martial. Only commanding generals of armies and geographic divisions, and corps and division commanders, had the authority to convene general courts-martial. A general court-martial required a minimum of five officers sitting in judgment, in addition to the trial judge advocate, to establish jurisdiction. The 1806 Articles of War stated that thirteen officers constituted an appropriate maximum ceiling, and this number had been carried over into the 1916 Articles. Whenever a court-martial proceeded with fewer than thirteen officers, the trial judge advocate and commanding general were supposed to explain why necessity resulted in a smaller number. However, even when there was a failure to explain the lesser number, the Supreme Court in 1921 unanimously determined that this failure was not appealable to the federal courts.[25]

In some cases, a commander might first convene a court of inquiry to determine whether to proceed to general court-martial. Courts of inquiry were conducted similar to courts-martial, except that the panel of officers sitting on the inquiry merely recommended a course of action to the secretary of war or a ranking general. Typically three officers sat on courts of inquiry, but this number was not mandated. Moreover, not all courts of inquiry were conducted for the purpose of deciding whether to proceed to a court-martial. Some courts of inquiry were conducted to investigate a matter in dispute, such as when an officer claimed to have been libeled by being wrongfully removed from command. For instance, in 1880 a former Civil War cavalry general, Gouvenor K. Warren, demanded and obtained a court of inquiry to prove that General Philip Sheridan's reports on his inefficiency in 1865 were in error.[26]

Below the general court-martial was the special court-martial, which had amalgamated regimental and garrison courts-martial into a trial akin to a misdemeanor-type trial. This lesser court-martial required only a regimental or garrison commander—usually at the rank of colonel—to charge an offense. Unlike a general court-martial, the maximum sentence a special court-martial could adjudge was capped at twelve months' confinement and forfeitures of pay not to exceed one year in addition to the loss of rank. Because a "lesser court" did not possess the sentencing authority to dishonorably discharge enlisted soldiers, neither a defense counsel nor detailed judge advocate review was deemed necessary. Special courts-martial consisted of three officers serving in the same regiment or garrison as the accused. Instead of a stenographer creating a verbatim transcript, the junior officer had the additional duty of serving as "recorder" and prepared a summary of the proceeding. Of significance, a special court-martial was not normally a basis for removing a soldier from the army.[27]

Finally, the lowest type of court, the summary court-martial, could sentence an accused soldier to no more than thirty days of hard labor and confinement. This type of trial only required one officer, and summary courts-martial convictions, like those of special courts-martial, were not considered to be a basis for terminating a military career. In and of themselves, such trials were simply a means to address minor disciplinary infractions, with one exception. A summary court-martial conviction could always be provided as evidence in a later general court-martial for the purpose of increasing the sentence of a convicted soldier. It was not uncommon, however, for a soldier to have at least one summary court-martial conviction. For instance, in 1902 Lieutenant Blanton Winship, the acting judge advocate for the First Separate Brigade in the Philippines, advised that Private Edward L. Leavering's four summary court-martial convictions should not negate the convening authority restoring him to duty following his general court-martial conviction for being drunk on duty and assaulting a sergeant.[28]

Traditionally, the Judge Advocate General's Office reviewed general courts-martial records to determine whether a particular trial was conducted in compliance with the Articles of War or other basic principles of law. In 1884 Colonel William Winthrop, the deputy judge advocate general, authored an influential military law treatise titled *Military Law*, in which he pointed out that judge advocates only possessed the authority to review records of trial and advise a commanding general or secretary of war as to whether a court-martial was properly conducted. This was, at the time, a correct statement of the law, albeit one that Ansell later challenged. Although Winthrop noted that courts-martial were an instrument of ensuring discipline solely within the provenance of the Executive Branch, he admonished judge advocates that because of the judicial nature of courts-martial, the fundamental rights of soldiers had to be preserved. Such rights included having an impartial panel, applying common evidentiary rules, and ensuring the enforcement of prevailing prosecutorial and judicial ethics. Winthrop noted, moreover, that military law had to be blind to race and religious faith in its application. *Military Law* was first published in 1884, and then in 1895 it was expanded and retitled *Military Law and Precedents*. Both books were replete with scholarly cross references to American and European military laws as well as rules of evidence and even corresponding state courts of appeal decisions.[29]

In 1865 and in intervening periods after, Winthrop and other judge advocates published a *Digest of Opinions of the Judge Advocate General*, which was designed to enable uniformity in legal interpretation throughout the army's forts and garrisons. After Winthrop retired in 1895, two officers, Captain William E. Birkhimer and General Davis, authored texts on military law. Birkhimer argued that Winthrop had "written too much" and wrongly adopted aspects of intellectual interpretation into the law such as what Oliver Wendell Holmes had advocated. In essence Birkhimer lobbied to have the military law be viewed as a rigid code, much as the British code was interpreted in 1914. Birkhimer appears to have been influenced by a "codification movement" in American law, which had originated decades earlier. Had Birkhimer prevailed over Winthrop, it is likely that Congress would have significantly reformed courts-martial in 1919. Davis, like Winthrop, was a Civil War veteran, and his *Military Laws of the United States*, published in 1911, in many respects mirrored Winthrop's work.[30]

Perhaps because as early as 1872 the Supreme Court recognized Winthrop as the nation's leading military legal scholar, *Military Law and Precedents* practically governed courts-martial until the Uniform Code of Military Justice came into existence in 1950, though the federal judiciary continues to cite Winthrop's work to the present day. The use of *Military Law and Precedents* became a contested facet of World War I courts-martial, in particular because Ansell objected to the limited advisory roles of the Judge Advocate General's Office. While Winthrop championed the fair application of evidentiary rules, ethical canons, and strict adherence to protecting an accused soldier's rights, he did not advocate for creating a mirror of federal criminal trials or courts of appeal. Crowder, Ansell, and all of the other commissioned judge advocates were innately familiar with Winthrop's treatise, as were many of the army's regular commissioned officers, since the treatise was a required text at the United States Military Academy.[31]

Because reviews of courts-martial were conducted in a quasi-appeal manner, often judge advocates cited legal principles found in a combination of federal and state case law as well as learned treatises. Some of these treatises, which originally applied to the British Army, were quite old by 1917. For instance, Alexander Tytler's *An Essay on Military Law and the Practice of Courts-Martial* and John McArthur's *Principles and Practice of Naval and Military Courts-Martial* were late eighteenth-century British texts but were still occasionally used for describing offenses such as mutiny and conduct unbecoming an officer and gentleman. Early nineteenth-century American texts such as Alexander Macomb's *The Practice of Courts-Martial*, William Chetwood DeHart's *Observations on Military Law and the Constitution, and Practice of Courts-Martial*, and John O'Brien's *A Treatise of Military Law and the Practice of Courts Martial* were also still in occasional use. However, both the *Digest* and Winthrop's treatise remained the two most used authorities.[32]

Traditionally a court-martialed soldier had little hope of successfully appealing a conviction to the federal courts. By the mid-nineteenth century, the federal judiciary determined that for the purposes of appellate review, courts-martial were akin to state criminal trials, and the Supreme Court created a restrictive jurisdictional test to grant an appeal. Known as the habeas test, it said that for an aggrieved court-martialed soldier to gain access to the federal courts, there had to be proof that a court-martial possessed no jurisdiction over the soldier. A civilian such as Lambdin Milligan could succeed in an appeal of a sentence assessed by a military trial. A member of the state militia called into the federal service might also succeed in an appeal under certain conditions, such as an instance prior to 1903 where a court-martial panel was composed of regular officers instead of militia officers. But gross injustices arising from evidentiary defects or other due process challenges were hardly a means for challenging courts-martial in the federal courts until World War II, and in reality, not reliably so until 1954 beginning with Chief Justice Earl Warren's tenure on the Supreme Court.[33]

It was not the case that the federal judges were uninterested in the fairness of military trials, or that the federal judiciary universally believed that the War Department was entitled to ignore due process as it pleased. In 1864 at the height of the Civil War, Attorney General Edward Bates issued an opinion to the War and Naval Departments that "courts-martial sit to pass upon the most sacred questions of human rights that are ever placed on trial in a court of justice, rights which, in the very nature of things, can neither be exposed to danger, nor subjected to the uncontrolled will of any man, but which must be adjudged according to law." Attorney generals' opinions have been held to be binding on the Executive Branch, but these opinions were seldom enforceable in the courts. Yet Bates's opinion became a part of a judicial lexicon that lasted well beyond the Civil War.

In 1887 the Supreme Court, in *Runkle v. United States*, incorporated Bates's opinion into its decision, and this reminded the War Department that the judiciary expected courts-martial to adhere to the prevailing laws. In *Runkle*, the Supreme Court restored a dismissed officer into retirement because neither the War Department nor the attorney general had proof in the form of a transcript or presidential order that President Ulysses Grant had approved Major Runkle's dismissal, which had been adjudged by a court-martial almost a decade earlier. Congress had required the War Department to maintain courts-martial records and presidential orders. The Court did not rule on the fairness of the court-martial. Rather, it reminded the War Department that as long as it maintained the full record of a court-martial and possessed jurisdiction over the accused, the federal courts would not intervene in the military's discipline. In Runkle's case there were missing records, and the government could no longer prove that Runkle's dismissal comported with the procedural laws governing courts-martial. In 1907 in *Grafton v. United States*, a decision further analyzed in chapter 8, the Supreme Court determined that the Constitution's prohibition against double jeopardy protected service-members from being prosecuted in the federal courts after an acquittal in a court-martial for the same offense. That is, the Court determined in Grafton that if a solder was acquitted in a court-martial, he could not be prosecuted in any type of federal court, including overseas consular courts, for the same offense. But decisions such as *Grafton* and *Runkle* were the exceptions to the judiciary's reluctance to review appeals from courts-martial, and the federal judiciary continuously placed responsibility for the fairness of courts-martial on the Executive Branch.[34]

Prior to the Civil War, Congress enabled aggrieved soldiers to seek redress through the United States Court of Claims, but that court could not jurisdictionally overturn a court-martial. Instead, the claims court could award back pay if its judges concluded that a court-martial conviction was wrongly decided. For instance, in General David Swaim's appeal, the Court of Claims conceded that President Chester Arthur's conduct in influencing the court-martial was highly unusual, but that it could not use Arthur's intrusive influence into the trial as a basis for overturning the verdict, and the Supreme Court agreed. While serving as judge advocate general, Swaim defrauded the government and lied to Secretary of War Robert Todd Lincoln about contracting irregularities as well as the source of his enlarged bank accounts. Both Lincoln and Arthur were appalled at the court-martial's lenient sentence, which consigned Swaim to be relieved of duties for twelve years. Under this sentence, Swaim would ultimately collect a deferred retirement. Arthur thrice ordered the court-martial to reconvene and reassess its sentence, clearly indicating that he believed the first two sentences were too forgiving, but the Court of Claims determined it did not have jurisdiction over the matter. Today Arthur's conduct would be appropriately prohibited as "unlawful command influence" because he attempted to use his position as commander in chief to influence the court-martial to increase the sentence. Like Swaim, many aggrieved service-members sought awards of back pay through the claims court, but even when they prevailed, the Supreme Court could reverse. In 1891 in *United States v. Page*, the Supreme Court reversed a Claims Court decision awarding back pay and retirement status to an officer who had been dismissed in a court-martial a decade and a half earlier. The government's preparation for this case may have actually been the first contact between Taft and Crowder. At the time Taft served as solicitor general and Crowder was the Department of the Platte's judge advocate. The aggrieved former officer resided in Crowder's department, and it appears that Crowder conducted the initial deposition in the appeal.[35]

One of the other unique features of military law was that often a court-martialed officer would unsuccessfully appeal to the federal courts on multiple occasions spanning many years. Two appeals that Crowder took part in illustrate how former officers could remain at the forefront of the War Department for decades after a court-martial. In 1875 the city government officials of Gallipolis, Ohio, petitioned President Ulysses Grant to appoint Oberlin Carter to the United States Military Academy as "a cadet at large." Carter's supporters also included future president Rutherford Hayes and Senator John Sherman, the author of the nation's first antimonopoly law and the brother of General William Tecumseh Sherman. Five years later, Carter graduated first in his class from the academy.[36]

Carter was a gifted engineering officer, and the War Department placed him in charge of the disbursement of funds for improvements to the Savannah, Georgia, harbor. However, he ran afoul of the War Department over his control of the funds. Carter entered into contracts with civilians who had intentionally overcharged the government, and Secretary of War Russell Alger was convinced that Carter masterminded an embezzlement scheme. In 1898 the army charged Carter with sixteen offenses ranging from larceny to conduct unbecoming an officer and gentleman. A court-martial held at Governors Island, New York, found him guilty of all of the offenses and sentenced him to a dismissal, a $5,000 fine, and imprisonment for five years. President William McKinley approved four convictions out of the sixteen, but he did not alter the sentence. McKinley was not required to reduce the sentence, but on the advice of the attorney general, he concluded that the sixteen convictions were duplicative. (In modern legal language, the sixteen convictions were "multiplicious" and therefore violated the prohibition against double jeopardy.) Interestingly, General Norman Lieber advised McKinley that the sixteen convictions should be left intact.[37]

One year after his trial, Carter appealed to the United States District Court for New York, and failing to obtain any habeas relief from that court, he appealed to the Court of Appeals for the Second Circuit. Carter argued that his court-martial was deprived of jurisdiction because the sentences were improperly aggregated and the court-martial failed to follow evidentiary procedures. Whatever the merits of those appeals, he also correctly argued that his alleged civilian coactors had fled to Canada, and as a result, he was unable to present them to the court-martial as the real "guilty party." One year after his court-martial, the Canadian government extradited the civilians back to the United States, but Carter was unable to secure a retrial. In essence, Carter sought to convince the appellate court that he had been denied the Sixth Amendment right to present exculpatory evidence that he was an unknowing victim of nefarious civilians. In following the traditional restrictive habeas test, the appeals court determined that since the court-martial was properly constituted and had lawful jurisdiction over Carter, he could not obtain relief. After being transferred to the army's penitentiary at Fort Leavenworth, Carter appealed to the United States District Court for Kansas. Again, this court, in applying the restrictive habeas test, granted Carter no relief.

In 1902 Carter's appeal came before the Supreme Court. In a decision authored by Chief Justice Melville Fuller, the justices determined that the army had lawful jurisdiction over Carter, and by implication, that the sentence aggregation was lawful. The Court also determined that the fact that Carter had been convicted of both a substantive offense of embezzling funds as well as a military offense of conduct unbecoming an officer did not violate double jeopardy. In reviewing the test of restrictive habeas jurisdiction, Fuller placed into the middle of the Court's decision the following observation on that test: "Its application would seem to be essential to the maintenance of that discipline which renders the army efficient in war and morally progressive in peace, and which is secured by the military code and the decisions of the military courts." While Fuller was not a military veteran, Justices John Harlan and Edward Douglass White were, and they agreed with the outcome.[38]

For the next three decades, Carter unsuccessfully tried to have his court-martial decision reversed. In 1937 he once more appealed to the Court of Appeals for the District of Columbia, asserting that the presiding officer in his court-martial hated him and conspired with the judge advocate to direct the court-martial to a guilty finding. Carter also alleged that although the attorney general advised McKinley against approving the court-martial findings and sentence, the president ignored this advice, and finally, that in the absence of a court of appeals, there was no real mechanism to challenge the true defects of the trial. The appellate court recognized that Carter's appeal contained allegations that, if true, could have undermined the fairness of his court-martial, but since the court-martial possessed jurisdiction over both Carter and the offenses, the federal courts did not possess the jurisdiction to consider the merits of the appeal. That year, the Supreme Court agreed, and Carter was heard from no more, although Justice Frankfurter would later refer to him as an "unfortunate officer."[39]

Another example illustrating the difficulties a soldier had in obtaining relief was the appeal of Captain George A. Armes. In 1883 the secretary of war retired Captain Armes after twenty-three years of military service. Represented by Charles Ewing, a Civil War veteran and relative of William Sherman, Armes unsuccessfully contested his forced retirement in the federal courts. Armes was a colorful officer who repeatedly insulted General Schofield. A native Virginian, Armes refused to join the Confederacy and enlisted in the Union army as a private. In December 1864 he was promoted to major "for gallantry." When the war ended he was demoted to lieutenant along with thousands of his officer peers. Armes had "fought with distinction" during the Indian Wars, and eventually was promoted to captain. But he was also thrice court-martialed, dismissed twice, and reinstated by two presidents. One court-martial occurred as a result of Armes assaulting Pennsylvania governor James A. Beaver during Benjamin Harrison's inauguration. The court-martial records indicate that Armes was intoxicated and had no reason for the assault. Beaver, a Civil War veteran whose leg was amputated after being wounded outside of Petersburg in 1865, demanded Armes be court-martialed. Harrison reinstated Armes into the army, but the reasons for Harrison's actions are now unknown. In 1889 the *New York Times* headlined Armes as "a lucky officer" after President Grover Cleveland reinstated his commission following a second court-martial. At the turn of the century, Armes authored a book titled *Ups and Downs of an Army Officer*, in which he criticized the military justice system and fashioned himself as a victim of several senior officers. The book highlighted his long history of feuding with Schofield and portrayed Swaim as a victim of an unfair trial. Schofield had served as the ranking officer in Swaim's court-martial, and he took offense at Armes's characterization of the trial.[40]

A decade after he was forced into retirement and was working as a civilian, Armes wrote a personal letter to Schofield and damned him for causing his forced retirement. Armes also accused Schofield of "manufacturing false evidence" against him and then conspiring to "ruin and disgrace him." At the time Armes delivered the letter, Schofield was not only the army's commanding general, he was also temporarily acting as secretary of war. The letter enraged him, and he ordered a staff officer named Colonel H.W. Closson to arrest Armes with the intent of charging him under the Articles of War for "gross insubordination." After his arrest, Armes convinced a federal judge to release him from confinement, but the judge did not divest the army of court-martial jurisdiction. Schofield then charged Armes with conduct to the prejudice of good order and discipline, and conduct unbecoming an officer and gentleman. The law regarding military jurisdiction was fairly well settled by this time, and even though Armes had not donned a uniform for twelve years at the time of his offense, he remained subject to the army's orders as long as he was in receipt of retirement pay. To defuse any public criticism of the army's jurisdiction, the secretary of war issued a nationwide statement that because retired officers could be recalled to active duty, they had to remain subject to the Articles of War.[41]

To this end, Armes appealed the army's assertion of its jurisdiction to the Court of Appeals for the District of Columbia, which then, as now, was considered the nation's second-most important court. The government counterappealed against the district judge, who ordered Armes freed from confinement. Armes's best argument against a court-martial was that as a matter of equity, his offenses did not merit a recall to active duty and certainly not an arrest. Instead, Armes argued a legal technicality. The Articles of War required the army to serve charges within eight days of an arrest, but it had not done so. On the other hand, this rule applied to soldiers in confinement, and Armes was no longer under arrest. In what became captioned as *Closson v. United States ex. rel. Armes*, the appellate court determined that Schofield and the War Department had acted lawfully and could proceed with the court-martial. Armes's case continued to generate wide-sweeping publicity. On October 3, 1895, General Lieber personally drafted two charges against Armes, including conduct unbecoming an officer and gentleman.[42]

Judge Martin Ferdinand Morris wrote the appellate decision, essentially siding with the War Department against Armes. Morris's role in the decision is worthy of mention because at the same time he served as a federal judge, he was also the dean of the Columbian Law School, the predecessor to George Washington University's law school, and he taught law to several army officers assigned to the Judge Advocate General's Office. He began the appellate decision with a clear indication that the law was not on Armes's side: "This case is not that of a civilian ruthlessly imprisoned by arbitrary military authority. The appellee is an officer of the army of the United States, entitled to wear its uniform and to draw pay as such, and by express provision of the statute law of the United States for the government of the army, made subject to the rules and Articles of War and to trial by court-martial for any infraction of those articles." As to the lawfulness of the arrest and imprisonment before trial, Morris and his judicial peers conceded that lesser measures could have sufficed in Armes's particular case, but because of the "exigencies of military service," a commanding officer had the right to immediately place an offender such as Armes under arrest. When Schofield retired in 1896, his successor, General Nelson A. Miles, determined that it was best for the charges against Armes to lapse, and even though the army did not court-martial Armes, he continued to seek redress through the courts. However, Armes also remained in the news due to other misconduct, including being held in contempt by a district court for his refusal to pay alimony in 1899 and then moving to Canada to avoid that court's jurisdictional reach.[43]

In 1914, after a subcommittee investigation determined that he had been unjustly retired, the House of Representatives recommended that Armes be reinstated into the army and then retired as a colonel. Crowder and Garrison opposed any reinstatement; both men believed that Armes had lied to Congress. To put an end to Armes's attempts for reinstatement into the army, Crowder lobbied Senator Morris Sheppard of Texas. Crowder was able to prove to Sheppard that on one occasion Armes had gone so far as to forge Schofield's signature on a letter to the War Department. Garrison and Crowder also informed Sheppard that the War Department had received a typewritten letter purporting to be from the Senate Agricultural Committee, but in reality it was a forgery, and since Sheppard chaired this committee, he could hold Armes in contempt. The "letter" demanded a reinvestigation of Armes's claims against Schofield. Crowder discerned that the number and detail of the questions in the letter were far more numerous than usually found in an ordinary legislative inquiry. "I could not properly answer the questions as framed, as their obvious purpose is an improper one," Crowder noted to Sheppard. "I doubt that you will find any copy of this letter in your files and if not, I will be pleased to show it to you." Once Sheppard confirmed that the letter was a fake, he ceased supporting Armes, but determined "not to waste the Senate's time with a contempt investigation." For reasons that are now as unclear as President Harrison's earlier actions, in 1916 Baker reinstated Armes and permitted him to retire once more at the rank of major.[44]

THE EXPERIENCE OF MILITARY DISCIPLINE IN OVERSEAS CONFLICTS

In the three decades before the United States' entry into the war in Europe, judge advocates had overseen courts-martial in Cuba, the Philippines, Guam, and Mexico. The application of international law to the United States Army had also been a part of a judge advocate's advisory duties. But of all the overseas expeditions or occupations undertaken by the War Department, the China Relief Expedition of 1900–1901 is perhaps the closest example that the Judge Advocate General's Office could have used to prepare for World War I. The army's performance in China influenced Crowder to argue that universal conscription was necessary to defeat Germany and the other Central powers. The expeditionary force sent to China was the first American force to fight alongside foreign armies with which it would later align, particularly those of Britain, France, Italy, and Japan. Because Crowder served as the judge advocate to the Philippine headquarters, he was responsible for supervising the judge advocate attached to the China Relief Expedition, and he prevailed on General Arthur MacArthur to select Captain Grote Hutcheson to serve as the expedition's judge advocate.[45]

In November 1900, as the army in the Philippines assembled forces for the expedition, Hutcheson advised MacArthur that it would be impracticable to permit a sergeant in the Fifteenth Infantry and a Ninth Infantry bugler to transit to China in light of their pending courts-martial for desertion and larceny. MacArthur agreed, and the expedition sailed without replacements for the two soldiers. Perhaps more troubling to Colonel Emerson Liscum, the advance force's commander, and General Adna Chaffee, the expedition's overall commander, was that fifty-seven other soldiers assigned to the Ninth Infantry and Sixth Cavalry regiments were also unable to join the expedition because they too had been found guilty of various offenses in special courts-martial and were serving terms in prison as a result. Equally problematic was that in the two months prior to embarking, 285 soldiers had been prosecuted in summary courts-martial, and while all of these soldiers were able to serve in the expedition, many had lost rank and pay as a result of their sentences.[46]

Once in Peking, the expedition conducted two significant courts-martial. The first of these involved a soldier who was found guilty of rape and sentenced to five years in prison as well as a dishonorable discharge but then escaped from custody and disappeared. The deputy acting judge advocate, Lieutenant Herbert A. White, asked Crowder whether the soldier could be tried in absentia for desertion. Crowder responded that "while the Articles of War permitted trial in *absentia*, this was not favored." The second court-martial arose from the murder of a Chinese civilian. Private Fredrick Hamilton had been found guilty of "murder without provocation," and the court-martial had sentenced him to five years in prison. White conveyed to Crowder his concern that because the Articles of War stated that the sentence of a court-martial for murder should approximate the civil laws of a state or territory in which the crime had occurred, and since the laws of China required a sentence of death, the court-martial sentence violated the Articles of War. Adding complexity to the issue was that the Treaty of Tientsin signed between the United States, Great Britain, Russia, France, and China in 1858 required the United States to consider Chinese sentencing law when a crime was committed against a Chinese national. Crowder responded that ordinarily White's analysis would be correct, but the treaty itself was suspended in times of war or insurrection, and therefore the sentence had to stand as adjudged. In 1913 White was selected for a judge advocate commission after Crowder rated him as the top candidate out of seventy applicants.[47]

On April 24, 1901, Hutcheson informed Crowder that 271 soldiers, to include five officers, had been sent to a debarkation area to await a trial by general courts-martial. Of these cases, twenty-seven resulted in acquittals. For an expeditionary force that numbered fewer than 2,500 soldiers and marines, the loss of 10 percent of the soldiers to courts-martial indicates that military discipline remained a paramount concern in a war zone. Policing the local population under American control also became an important feature. On April 21, 1901, Hutcheson informed Crowder that he had observed the Chinese Criminal Court of Justice sentence nine civilians who had committed "robbery by violence, against Americans to death by beheading."[48]

Writing to Crowder in late 1901, Hutcheson noted that one of the reasons for the large number of courts-martial was that the Chinese people had become ingrained with a culture of respecting military authority, and the army's undisciplined soldiers and junior officers had taken advantage of the civilian population. He added that "perhaps the most pronounced cause of the number of trials held, is due, to an element in the class of men in our ranks which represents a very low and irresponsible order of our home population, who stop at nothing, and can be properly controlled only by the most forceful modes of punishment." Yet Hutcheson also observed that the summary methods of punishment in foreign armies were an anathema to principles of justice. In 1916 Crowder referenced the China Relief Expedition when he testified to Congress that conscription was necessary to bring greater numbers of "law-abiding Americans" into the army.[49]

In one other sense, the judge advocate experience in China portended some of the unusual aspects of military discipline that arose both in the American Expeditionary Forces as well as in the post-Armistice occupations of the Rhineland and in Murmansk and Port Arthur, Russia. Although the small American forces in China operated independently of Allied command, there were instances where courts-martial required inter-Allied diplomacy and language translation. On November 24, 1900, French officers arrested four American soldiers after a Chinese storekeeper accused them of stealing watches and money. Some of the watches and money were found in the soldiers' pockets, and under questioning by a French officer and an Italian diplomat, the soldiers admitted to the theft. On December 7, 1900, Hutcheson informed General Chafee that "Privates Ellis, Kelley, Mitchell, and Moan" had been found guilty and sentenced to a year in prison. Also, Private Ellis had falsely claimed to the French officer that his name was "Jere'c-zeh," and that he was from Alsace. To accomplish the trial, translation was required in French, Mandarin, Italian, and German. Because the Habsburg Austrian ambassador was appointed to explain the court-martial to the Chinese empress, German transcription became necessary. Hutcheson concluded his memorandum by stressing that no clemency ought to be considered for any of the soldiers because they had committed their offenses during a time in which strict discipline was required to assure the population of the United States' good intentions. Chafee and Crowder concurred with Hutcheson's advice.[50]

PERSONNEL

The judge advocates Crowder supervised in April 1917 were far too few in number to carry out the important and wide-ranging duties that were about

to consume his staff office. In 1914 the Judge Advocate General's Office, in
order of seniority, consisted of Colonels George M. Dunn and John A. Hull;
Lieutenant Colonels Frank L. Dodds, John B. Porter, and Lewis E. Goodier;
and Majors Henry M. Morrow, Walter A. Bethel, Blanton B. Winship, Beverly
A. Read, Edward A. Kreger, Samuel T. Ansell, and Hebert A. White. These officers came into the army by various means, but each became a judge advocate
through a competitive War Department selection board process. A selection
board consisted of general officers who reviewed dozens of applicants and
then recommended candidates to the secretary of war. The judge advocate
general presided over the board and had considerable input into the selection
of judge advocate commissions, but his support did not guarantee a candidate
a judge advocate commission. Likewise, a chief of staff's endorsement of a candidate did not guarantee a judge advocate commission. For instance, in 1913
Major General Franklin Bell angrily wrote to Crowder that not a single officer
he had endorsed was selected for a judge advocate commission. Crowder, for
his part, responded that the officers Bell supported were not of the quality of
the officers ultimately selected. In theory, a secretary of war could select any
person for a judge advocate commission and disregard the selection board's
recommendations altogether. Of course, the president was the final arbiter
of the judge advocate selection process if he chose to intervene. Both James
Abrams Garfield and William McKinley had commissioned judge advocates
from civilian life, and Garfield had also nominated Swaim, who had been his
aide during the Civil War, to be commissioned judge advocate general ahead
of eight judge advocates.[51]

Success in obtaining a commission often required the backing of senior
officers, congressmen, or influential citizens, though such a strong backing
might not be enough. For instance, in 1903 Clarence M. Condon, a Medal of
Honor recipient from the Philippine Insurrection, applied for a judge advocate commission but did not succeed. Although backed by Congressmen Gilbert N. Haugen, Benjamin P. Birsall, E. C. Burleigh, and John A. T. Hull—who
was able to secure his son a judge advocate commission—as well as Secretary
of Agriculture James Wilson and Secretary of the Treasury Leslie Mortimer
Shaw, Condon's record was not enough to overcome Blanton Winship's application. It was not the case that the judge advocate general favored Winship,
though Crowder had commended Winship on a prior occasion. Rather, Secretary of War Elihu Root was impressed with Winship's acting judge advocate
tenure in the Philippines as well as the fact that unlike Condon, Winship had
already earned a law degree.[52]

George M. Dunn, the most senior officer next to Crowder, who was to serve
as judge advocate to the Southern and Northeastern Departments during

most of the war, was commissioned into the army in 1886 from the United States Military Academy. His military service mirrored Crowder's in that he fought in the closing campaigns against the Apache and participated in the last campaign against the Sioux. Dunn transferred into the Judge Advocate General's Department in 1897 and served in Cuba and then the Philippines. In 1906 he was stationed at the Presidio in San Francisco during the destructive earthquake that leveled the city and caused roughly three thousand deaths. Dunn achieved some acclaim in the War Department for his role in overseeing housing construction and directing soldiers to control looting. Like Crowder, Dunn was wedded to Winthrop's military jurisprudence. However, shortly after the United States' entry into the war, Dunn infuriated Crowder and Baker over his role in the courts-martial and executions of African American soldiers in Texas, as well as his promising Theodore Roosevelt that he would lobby the War Department to permit the former president to create a volunteer division. In the war's final days Dunn transferred to the Northeastern Department in Boston, where he further angered Crowder by claiming that Bolsheviks had encouraged African American laborers to strike and riot. In 1919 Crowder asked Major General Clarence Edwards, the department's commander, to force Dunn to retire, and he punctuated his request by calling Dunn "a meagre legal acumen."[53]

Although Colonel John Adley Hull, a University of Iowa Law School graduate, had supporters within the War Department, Crowder never approved of him, in part because Hull had come into the army and ultimately into the Judge Advocate General's Office through his father's influence. Hull's father, John Albert Tiffin Hull, had fought in the Civil War and served in Congress from 1891 to 1910, including as chairman of the House Committee on Military Affairs. The elder Hull secured his son a judge advocate commission in the Iowa National Guard, and during the Spanish-American War the elder Hull secured for his son a regular army judge advocate commission. Thus Hull did not come through one of the army's combat branches as had Crowder and several other judge advocates. In 1908 a rumor permeated the War Department that Congressman Hull tried to have Crowder transferred to the Adjutant General's Department to enable his son to be next in line for promotion to judge advocate general, and although Colonel Hull denied the truth of the rumor, Crowder suspected him from that point forward. In February 1911 Crowder complained to John Bassett Moore that Hull was unable to handle all of his responsibilities at Governors Island, and he objected to Moore including Hull in an international law committee. Another reason why Crowder did not approve of Hull had to do with the fact that General Rufus Shafter, a Civil War, Indian War, and Cuba veteran, was Hull's other benefactor. Crowder justifiably believed that Shafter was incompetent and had arbitrarily court-martialed junior officers to include the army's first African American officer, Henry Ossian Flipper. In 1926 Crowder wrote to Pershing that he could not understand why any general officer "took a fancy" to Hull. "Hull never decided a legal question except by throwing the dice. He is not a lawyer and will never be one, and yet with senior years he stands in the way of a proper recognition of Kreger," Crowder complained.[54]

During the war, Hull was assigned as the judge advocate to the Services of Supply, where he worked under General James Harbord. Throughout the conflict Hull remained a colonel while Bethel, Kreger, and Ansell were brevetted brigadier general. However, at war's end, Hull retained his rank while the three younger officers reverted to lieutenant colonel. The Services of Supply was a unique command charged with the duty of training soldiers in France before they entered the front lines. The command was also responsible for constructing railway networks across France, transporting men and materiel to the front, and contracting with the Allies. When, in 1919, Crowder was slated to retire, Harbord attempted to have Pershing lobby the secretary of war and the president to have Hull promoted to judge advocate general, going so far as to write Pershing that Hull was "much quicker, sounder, and brighter, than General Bethel who had served as the American Expeditionary Force's judge advocate." Pershing sided with Crowder and disagreed with Harbord on his assessment of both Hull and Bethel.[55]

For reasons that are absent from Crowder's correspondences as well as the Judge Advocate General's Office records, neither John B. Porter, Lewis Goodier, or Frank L. Dodds was selected for overseas duties. Each of these men was first commissioned into the infantry. Additionally, each served in the Philippines. Goodier enlisted in the army during the Spanish-American War after earning his law degree from Yale University. He was commissioned in 1900, served as a lieutenant in the Philippines, and served as an acting judge advocate for six months in Manila. In 1904 he obtained a judge advocate commission and served in the Western Department in San Francisco through the end of 1917, and as the Northeastern Department's judge advocate in Boston afterward. Porter came into the army in an almost identical manner. He enlisted as a private following his attainment of a law degree from Georgetown University, was commissioned as a lieutenant in 1900, and then was commissioned as a judge advocate one year after Goodier. During the war Porter remained at the Judge Advocate General's Office.[56]

In 1901 General George Davis recommended that Frank L. Dodds join the Judge Advocate General's Office. Born in 1854 in Pennsylvania, and two years older than Crowder, Dodds was commissioned into the infantry in 1886 after graduating from the United States Military Academy. Although he was commissioned into the infantry, Dodd's first assignment was as a history professor where he served under William Winthrop's supervision. Dodds fought in Cuba and then the Philippines, but he medically retired from the army in 1902. After Dodds retired, he attended the University of Pennsylvania's law school and then worked for the state attorney general. However, in 1914, with Crowder's help, he was able to rejoin the army. During the war, Dodds served as the Eastern Department's judge advocate at Governors Island.[57]

Henry M. Morrow graduated from the University of Michigan in 1883 and then its law school in 1888. Instead of pursuing a law career, he commissioned into the state militia in 1889, and then in 1890 he commissioned into the army as an infantry officer. He served in the Spanish-American War and for a brief time in the Philippines, where he gained Davis's approval. In 1902 he was commissioned as a judge advocate. The following year Morrow was assigned as a judge advocate to the Department of California. In 1914 he was assigned to the Southern Department and two years later to Washington, DC. During World War I, he remained with Crowder and Ansell at the Judge Advocate General's Office.[58]

Next to Crowder and Ansell, Walter Augustus Bethel was arguably the most influential judge advocate during the war. He was born in Ohio in 1866 and attended the United States Military Academy. In 1889 he was commissioned into the artillery and stationed in North Dakota. In 1903 he transferred into the Judge Advocate General's Department, and from there served as the judge advocate to the Department of Alaska, in the Philippines, and in California. In 1892 while stationed in Georgia, he earned a bachelor of law degree from the Atlanta Law School, which operated as a night school. Two years later, while stationed at Governors Island, he earned a master in laws from Columbia University's law school. Following his graduation he tutored law and briefly taught first-year law student Harlan Fiske Stone.[59]

In 1915 Bethel served as a professor of law at the United States Military Academy, and while he was there, Crowder ordered him to update *Military Law and Precedents*. Crowder believed that Winthrop's work had continued vitality, but he wanted to ensure that a proper analysis of the 1916 Articles of War would be incorporated into the revised text. For unknown reasons, Bethel had not succeeded in a revision by the outbreak of war, and Crowder came to believe that he was incapable of an intellectual challenge. When Crowder tried to prevent Hull from becoming judge advocate general in 1923, he also urged Pershing to favor Kreger over Bethel.[60]

Although Beverly A. Read was a politically connected officer, there are only a few documents detailing his wartime duties. Read was born in Texas in 1870, and his father-in-law, Hernando de Soto Money, was a long-serving congressman from Missouri. Moreover, Read was a cousin of both Mississippi governor James Vardaman and Texas senator Charles Culberson. Read was educated at the University of Texas, and after earning a degree in history, he graduated from its law school. He commissioned as a cavalry officer in 1898 in the Texas National Guard but obtained a regular commission in early 1901. President McKinley, two months before his assassination, personally selected Read for a judge advocate commission. Like many of the other officers, Read served in the Philippines as a judge advocate. Although he embarked for France as the First Division's judge advocate, he only stayed there for six weeks. For most of World War I, he served in Washington, DC, as the head of the legislative military justice divisions.[61]

Blanton Winship, the First Army's judge advocate from July 6, 1918, to October 5, 1918, graduated from Mercer University in Georgia in 1889 and earned a law degree from the University of Georgia in 1893. It was not until the United States declared war on Spain in 1897 that Winship was commissioned into the First Georgia militia as an infantry officer. Two years later he was commissioned as a regular officer and served under General Leonard Wood in Cuba. Winship gained Secretary of War Root's attention while serving as the acting judge advocate to the Department of the Lakes. Winship developed the army's first formal exchange program with Canadian judge advocates, and he invited Root to speak to the first meeting between the two groups of judge advocates. On November 19, 1903, Root and Wood asked President Roosevelt to permanently appoint Winship to the Judge Advocate General's Department.[62]

Winship's prewar service included teaching law at the army's Service School at Fort Leavenworth. He also served as a temporary judge advocate to a detached brigade in the Northern Philippines for a year beginning in October 1901. This duty enabled him to apply the law of war to military discipline. On March 14, 1902, he oversaw two general courts-martial of soldiers accused of rape. After the courts-martial determined the soldiers were guilty, Winship advised General MacArthur to deny clemency, arguing that "offenders of this crime not only committed a heinous crime, they also undermined the Army's ability to pacify the population." One of Winship's unusual contributions during World War I was his assumption of temporary command over two infantry regiments in the Argonne Forest. Baker awarded him the Silver Star in recognition of his combat heroism. Winship was almost prevented from going to France at all. In early 1917 Crowder became livid at both Winship and Wood after learning that Winship complained to Wood that Crowder had excluded him from joining Pershing's vessel to France, and since it was possible that he would be denied a judge advocate posting in the American Expeditionary Force, he asked Wood to intercede in obtaining for him command of an infantry regiment. Crowder had, in fact, intended for Winship to serve as Kreger's deputy in France, and informed Wood that although he considered Wood a personal friend, his "interference in the Judge Advocate General's Office's decisions was unwelcome."[63]

Edward Albert Kreger was born to German immigrant parents in Iowa in 1868, graduating from Iowa State College in 1890 and then the University of Iowa's law school in 1893. His father, William Kreger, served in the Union army from 1861 until 1866 and fought at the Battle of Gettysburg. Edward Kreger was active in the Grand Army of the Republic organization with his father, but until the Spanish-American War, this seems to be the only military activity he was involved in. From 1891 until 1897 he was employed as a high school principal and then a district superintendent of the Manilla, Iowa Schools. In 1898 he commissioned into the Fifty-Second Iowa Infantry and fought in the Philippines. In January 1901 he presided over a military commission and then led a patrol in Mindanao, where he came under Major Robert Bullard's command. The next year, after being awarded a distinguished service cross he earned a regular commission, but it was Bullard who assisted him in obtaining the necessary letters of support from higher ranking officers to successfully compete for the commission. Bullard informed General Arthur MacArthur that of the two regiments of volunteers he commanded, he had "no better officer than Kreger." In 1907 Kreger was posted as an infantry officer in Cuba, and while stationed there he assisted Crowder in drafting the island's election laws. The following year he was commissioned as a judge advocate and sent to Denver. In 1928 Pershing recommended to the secretary of war that Kreger become judge advocate general. In his recommendation Pershing noted that he had first met Kreger in Mindanao when Kreger was an infantry lieutenant and had developed a reputation of "sound judgment and general efficiency."[64]

Of all the judge advocates assigned to the Judge Advocate General's Office in 1914, Samuel Tilden Ansell would gain the most notoriety. Several judge advocates were actually senior to Ansell, and although he served, as a result of his temporary promotion to brigadier general, as the senior ranking judge advocate—or de facto acting judge advocate general— Crowder maintained overall control of the Judge Advocate General's Office. The majority of wartime Judge Advocate General's Office correspondence now housed at the National Archives and Records Administration bears Crowder's signature, not Ansell's. Nonetheless, Ansell was placed into a position that enabled him to develop policy and interact with the Legislative and Judicial Branches. Professor Jonathan Lurie in his *Arming Military Justice* correctly recognized that Crowder at one point favored Ansell over other judge advocates, but Professor Lurie did not reveal to his readers the depth of Crowder's early esteem for his deputy.[65]

In June 1913 Crowder informed General Bell that Ansell was a more worthy selection than any of Bell's nominees and went so far as to compare Ansell to Elihu Root. "In Ansell I have a man of such transcendent ability in law as would make him formidable in the civil practice in any court, state or federal." In 1910 Crowder wrote to Pershing that Ansell was "with the exception of Edward Kreger, fully ahead of the best men in the service." In February 1917 Crowder sought Senator Francis E. Warren's support to modify an appropriation bill to provide the Judge Advocate General's Department with higher ranks so that Ansell would be promoted to lieutenant colonel. In 1911 Crowder assigned Ansell to study the difficulties of irregular warfare in Cuba and the Philippines, as well as the guerilla warfare encountered by the British Army during the Boer War, and then draft a modification of General Order 100. That order, which formed the basis for the modern codification of the law of war, was authored in the Civil War by noted legal scholar Francis Lieber with the expectation that American soldiers would adhere to it or face a court-martial. But Crowder believed that the order, which had served military discipline well, required some modification because neither the Philippine insurrectionists, nor the Boer guerillas who fought against Britain, respected codes limiting the effects of warfare to the narrowest population. He entrusted Ansell to travel to the United Kingdom and India to study the British application of the laws of war so that the American application of such laws did not differ from its Anglo counterpart.[66]

Ansell was born in 1875 in North Carolina and commissioned into the army after graduating from the United States Military Academy in 1899. Immediately after his commissioning he was assigned to the Philippines. While stationed in North Carolina in 1902, he earned a law degree from the University of North Carolina, and he ably served as an infantry officer. During two tours of duty in the Philippines, he was appointed as an acting judge advocate, and in this position he impressed Crowder with his work ethic and intelligence. After his return to the United States, he studied law at Harvard University without earning an advanced degree, but he impressed the law faculty, including Frankfurter.[67]

Although in 1914 Crowder considered Ansell one of his most capable officers, Ansell did not always succeed in his legal endeavors. In 1909 he represented, in an appeal to the Supreme Court, an officer who had been convicted in a federal court for embezzlement against the government. For now unknown reasons the US attorney prosecuted the officer rather than the War Department. It appears that Judge Advocate General Davis permitted

Ansell to represent the officer as a pro bono—or without pay— attorney, because the officer's interests were contrary to those of the government. Ansell argued that the officer had the right to be tried in a court-martial instead of a federal court and that Congress had unconstitutionally delegated to the state legislatures the authority to "bootstrap" state sentences for federal crimes. In 1898 Congress affixed the punishment for the crimes of larceny and embezzlement that occurred on federal reservations such as military bases, to the state sentencing statute in which the crime was committed. This law applied to federal courts but not courts-martial. In the officer's appeal to the United States District Court, Judge Learned Hand, who was to become one of the leading American jurists in the first half of the twentieth century, credited Ansell with ingenuity in bringing the appeal forward but then articulated that the appeal was "metaphysical" and "based on a naïvely nonsensical and fatuously verbal argument which could only mislead the court." In less strident language, the Supreme Court agreed. In 1910, when Ansell asked Hand for a letter of recommendation to place into his application for a judge advocate commission, Hand agreed to write one, but with one caveat. While Hand recognized that Ansell was an "intelligent and vigorous attorney," he added that "the principal criticism which [Hand] could make upon your presentation of the case was that you were inclined to overelaborate details."[68]

Well before the schism between Crowder and Ansell, there were high-ranking officers who did not approve of Ansell's performance as the senior judge advocate at the Judge Advocate General's Office. Bliss accused Ansell of making promises to personal friends who were retired officers, recalling them to active duty and then manipulating the secretary of war into believing the recalls were necessary. In one instance involving the recall of a Lieutenant Robert K. Spiller, Bliss and the adjutant general, General H. P. McCain, complained to General Scott that it would be unwise to permit Ansell, or any other staff officer assigned to an "acting capacity," to communicate directly with the secretary of war and bypass the adjutant general in determining whether the recall was necessary. Bliss was also furious that Ansell had not informed Crowder of his advice to Baker, and he surmised that there were enough judge advocates attached to the state guard units to fill in at the Judge Advocate General's Office. Equally importantly, Ansell had bypassed the normal chain of command for determining a retired officer's fitness to be recalled. Crowder was not angry with Ansell on this issue, but he had to remind Ansell that he, and not Ansell, retained authority over the Judge Advocate General's Office. Bliss may have detected, before Crowder did so, that Ansell believed he was the acting judge advocate general.[69]

Ansell angered Bliss and McCain further when they discovered that on August 16, 1917, he had sought out Senator John Sharp Williams's assistance in getting Spiller appointed. Spiller had been retired for a medical disability in 1908 after a decade as an infantry officer, and he had never been a judge advocate. He had served in the infantry in the Spanish-American War in Cuba, and following his retirement he attended the University of Virginia's Law School. Virginia governor H. C. Stuart endorsed his efforts to obtain a reserve commission, as did the president of the Norfolk and Western Railway Company. Senator Williams also endorsed Spiller, and given Williams's relationship with President Wilson, Spiller had an advantage over other applicants. But it was Ansell who enabled Spiller's application to bypass Crowder, McCain, Scott, and Bliss and convince Baker to appoint Spiller as a reserve officer. Not surprisingly, Spiller became one of Ansell's adherents during the dispute with Crowder in 1919.[70]

There would be another motive for Spiller to side with Ansell in his dispute with Crowder. During the war, Spiller served as General Leonard Wood's judge advocate at Camp Funston, Kansas. In June 1918, muckraking journalist Upton Sinclair informed Wilson and Baker that Wood had permitted conscientious objectors to be beaten and starved. Spiller assured Crowder that Sinclair's allegations were meritless and that five judge advocates in his office had thoroughly investigated Sinclair's claims. Moreover, Spiller agreed with Wood's assessment that prisoners who had been forced into showers, force-fed, and court-martialed in dirty uniforms were not religious conscientious objectors but rather socialists and Bolshevik sympathizers who advocated mutiny. When Crowder learned in December 1918 that Spiller's report was false, he summarily moved to dismiss Spiller from the army as "a disgrace to the Judge Advocate General's Department." However, Crowder did not succeed in summarily forcing Spiller out of the army.[71]

In October 1917 Ansell lobbied Baker to issue a War Department order stretching from the trenches in France to the duty stations in Hong Kong and the Philippines that prohibited the consumption of alcohol at any time. It was true, as Ansell pointed out, that Secretary of the Navy Josephus Daniels had issued a similar order prohibiting alcohol consumption aboard vessels, and this order served the purpose of focusing sailors on their duties. Baker was lukewarm to Ansell's idea and sought Crowder's guidance. Crowder responded that such an order would undermine the very discipline Ansell professed required the prohibition. Bliss also joined with Crowder and countered that Ansell's suggested order would create hundreds of unnecessary courts-martial in France alone. Although Baker sided with Crowder and Bliss in this matter, Ansell did not relent in his pursuit to ban alcohol from soldiers wherever possible. At the end of October, he tried to lobby Baker to reach an agreement with Attorney General Thomas Watts Gregory to enforce liquor prohibition at debarkation ports. Without turning to Bliss or Crowder, Baker responded that he felt it unwise to meddle in the Justice Department's responsibilities.[72]

TRANSFERS IN 1916

On September 11, 1916, Crowder sent Pershing a confidential assessment of his efforts to enlarge the Judge Advocate General's Office. Congress had enabled an expansion of the office from thirteen to thirty-one officers. Over one hundred officers applied for the vacant positions. Crowder's assessment was written in the form of a memorandum for the secretary of war, but he first wanted Pershing's private impressions of his design for an expansion of the staff office. Crowder informed Pershing that he opposed recruiting civilians without past military experience. This had only occurred once since Chester Arthur's presidency, and Crowder believed that regular army officers had to be given precedence. However, he also noted that "while there were a considerable number of officers who had studied law in civil life, some possessed only very moderate ability." Crowder also forwarded to Pershing a list of forty-two names of officers who he believed could perform well as judge advocates. What is remarkable about Pershing's role in the expansion of the Judge Advocate General's Office is that there was no indication that he would lead the largest expeditionary force in American military history to date, or that he would later become chief of staff. Indeed, the American general thought most likely to command an expeditionary force to France was Frederick Funston, but Funston died in February 1917.[73]

Included in Crowder's list were several officers who ultimately served as judge advocates during the war. Crowder acknowledged that Pershing favored Captain Arthur Winton Brown and Lieutenant Hugh S. Johnson, and Bliss supported Captain Kyle Rucker, who would later become the judge advocate of the American forces in Germany. Other officers whom Pershing recommended included lieutenants Wiley Howell, Cassius Dowell, James A. Gallogly, Allen W. Gullion, and Edward C. McNeil. While all of these officers were over thirty-two years of age, Brown and Rucker were already over forty. Howell was commissioned from the enlisted ranks in 1897 and later attended Georgetown University's law school. During much of the war he served as a judge advocate attached to the intelligence chief of the American Expeditionary Forces. Gullion was commissioned into the infantry after he graduated from the United States Military Academy in 1905 and served in the Philippines from late 1905

until 1908. While stationed in Lexington, Kentucky, he attended the University
of Kentucky's law school and graduated in 1914. He came to Pershing's attention in early 1916 while leading patrols along the Mexican border.[74]

Gallogly was commissioned from the United States Military Academy
in 1907 and assigned to the Coast Artillery. While stationed in Atlanta, he
attended law school at night and was admitted to the Georgia Bar in 1910.
The following year he was appointed as a temporary judge advocate in Florida,
and after being selected to join the Judge Advocate General's Department in
1916, he was sent to Hawaii. In 1917 he trained in North Carolina, and in
April 1918 he was assigned as the Third Division's judge advocate and took
part in the fighting at Chateau Thierry. On August 6 he was reassigned as the
First Corps judge advocate. Dowell would later become known for defending
Nazi saboteurs in American military trials and in a Supreme Court appeal
during World War II. He enlisted in the army in 1902 and obtained a commission in 1904. Prior to his enlistment he earned a law degree at the Columbian
Law School. He proved himself a capable officer and judge advocate, and had,
in General Clarence Edwards, a benefactor. By war's end he was convinced
that there were over a million pro-Bolshevik radicals in the United States and
several thousand in the army, and he claimed that if Ansell prevailed in the
court-martial controversy, he would have enabled a widespread Bolshevik
infiltration into the army.[75]

In 1915 Henry Morrow wrote that McNeil had "shown fitness for duty in
the Judge Advocate General's Department" after observing him prosecute
courts-martial at Governors Island. The following year Crowder agreed that
McNeil was "fit to become a judge advocate" but dryly commented that he was
only an average law student at Columbia University. What Crowder perhaps
missed was that while McNeil graduated in the middle of his class, Dean Harlan Fisk Stone conveyed to Winship that McNeil was his top constitutional law
student. Also, while at Columbia, McNeil impressed Professor John Bassett
Moore, who at the time was one of the leading scholars of international law in
the world. Moore too would inform Crowder of his high opinion of McNeil.[76]

Arthur Winton Brown was born in Iowa in 1873, enlisted in the Utah militia for the Spanish-American War, and obtained his commission in 1899 while
serving in the Philippines. He was brought into the Judge Advocate General's
Office in 1916. In 1897 Cornell University awarded Brown an LLB degree,
which led to his appointment as a temporary judge advocate both during
the Philippine Insurrection and later. During his time in the Philippines he
caught General Norman Lieber's attention, and in 1912 Brown was sent to
Cornell University's law school, where he obtained his graduate law degree in
two years. In 1914 he landed with the army in Veracruz, and General Funston

turned to him not only to oversee courts-martial but also to establish a temporary legal system administered by the War Department in Mexico. Funston pushed for Brown to be permanently assigned to the Judge Advocate General's Office in 1916. Funston was not alone in having enthusiasm for Brown. Colonel Hull recommended Brown to Crowder as well, calling him "a man of sound judgment."[77]

Historian David Lockmiller once commented that Hugh Johnson, a regular army officer who attended law school at the University of California, Berkeley, was Crowder's favorite judge advocate. Lockmiller overstated Crowder's enthusiasm, because Kreger always remained Crowder's favored judge advocate, but in August 1917 Crowder noted to Bliss that in his "forty years of service, no officer of the Army has challenged and held my attention as this officer has." In the same letter, Crowder credited Johnson with "possessing zeal, industry, and genius." A week after sending Bliss his impressions of Johnson, Crowder lobbied Pershing to take Johnson to France and used the same ebullient language that he had penned in his letter to Bliss. There were reasons to admire Johnson. In 1914 he enrolled in the University of California's law school, squeezed a three-year course of study into eighteen months, and graduated with top honors in his class. The university's president, Benjamin Ide Wheeler, selected Johnson to give the commencement speech and communicated to Crowder that because Johnson had developed a reputation among the faculty for his brilliance, the faculty wanted Johnson to return as a professor.[78]

When Johnson graduated from Berkeley in 1916 he expected to take a leave of absence, but Crowder convinced him to forgo it and join in the punitive expedition against Pancho Villa as Pershing's judge advocate. "The order to Mexico filled my cup to overflowing. I know that it may be possibly only an opportunity for active service, but I cannot help thinking it will be a far wider opportunity," Johnson wrote to Crowder. "It may be that my absence from military work and my lack of experience in a judge advocate's office may handicap me but I shall overcome that handicap if I can." Pershing would inform Crowder that Johnson had "impressed him with his endurance and clearness in providing legal guidance."[79]

For much of the war Johnson assisted Crowder in the administration of selective service, including the extension of military jurisdiction over citizens who refused to comply with an induction order. Additionally, Johnson, along with Frankfurter, was seconded to wealthy financier and Wilson confidant Bernard Baruch at the War Industries Board. While Crowder understood that service in the American Expeditionary Forces was likely to catapult younger officers to higher rank after the war ended, he valued Johnson's intellect and believed he could properly advise Baruch on the legal issues attendant to the government's authority to set prices. At war's end, Baruch lauded Johnson's efforts and the two men remained in close contact until Johnson's death in 1943.[80]

THE JUDGE ADVOCATE RESERVE CORPS: CROWDER'S CREATION

At the same time Crowder lobbied to increase the number of commissioned judge advocates, he also developed a reserve plan to augment the Judge Advocate General's Office. One of the reasons for this plan was that he foresaw difficulties with national conscription. Unlike his oversight of regular army judge advocate expansion, for the commissioning of reserve officers Crowder favored prominence in the legal academy over prior military service. Under Crowder's reserve judge advocate plan, reserve judge advocates would attach to the Judge Advocate General's Office and serve tours of duty in Washington, DC, for a fixed number of days per year. Crowder assumed that at least one month per year would be the minimum days of service, but if war occurred the reserve judge advocates would be called into federal service for the duration of the conflict. More importantly, Crowder was convinced that if war came and conscription with it, in order to withstand political scrutiny the administration of military justice had to be accomplished by the nation's foremost legal minds. In June 1916 Congress legislated Crowder's plan into law and he began to recruit attorneys. In early 1916 he informed Garrison of his desire to add Felix Frankfurter, James Brown Scott, Joseph Wheless, Eugene Wambaugh, Nathan MacChesney, and John Henry Wigmore if his plan became law.[81]

Wambaugh was the first and oldest of the reserve judge advocates whom Crowder recruited. Born in 1856 in Ohio, he attended Harvard for both his undergraduate and law degrees. He also taught law at the University of Iowa and at Harvard. By 1915 he had advised the State Department on international law and neutrality, and he published a nationally used constitutional law treatise. Wambaugh remained in Washington, DC, during the war, and after the Armistice he was instrumental in persuading Baker to authorize a comprehensive study of foreign military justice systems. On Wambaugh's advice, Crowder contemporaneously recruited Wheless, a gifted lawyer whose credentials were almost the opposite of Wambaugh's. Wheless was born in 1868 and by 1915 was a noted scholar in international law. He published treatises on the laws of Argentina and Mexico. In 1898 he published an annotated treatise on the laws of Tennessee as well. By 1916 he was also well known as a leading scholar and practitioner of atheism who publicly denied the existence of any creator. Unlike the other reserve judge advocates, Wheless never attended college and was self-taught in the law. He too impressed Crowder with his intellect, and Wigmore endorsed him.[82]

When Congress authorized an expanded reserves in June 1916, Crowder wrote to Harvard professor Felix Frankfurter, "I am going to assume that you have the desire to serve your country in a real emergency and that you may wish to avail yourself of this opportunity to place yourself in the position to do so." Crowder feared Wilson and Baker would pressure him to retire as a result of supporting Garrison in 1916, but Frankfurter assured him this was not the case. Frankfurter, who perhaps more than any other Supreme Court justice influenced the nation's military establishment, had already lobbied Baker—a fellow progressive with whom he had worked since 1910—to safeguard Crowder's position. Born in 1882 in Vienna, Austria, and a practicing Jew, Frankfurter was an unlikely but beneficial officer to be recruited into the reserves. He began his legal career after graduating from Harvard by working for Henry Stimson when Stimson served as a United States attorney for the Southern District of New York. In 1911 Stimson brought Frankfurter into the War Department as the solicitor for the Bureau of Insular Affairs. It was in this position that Frankfurter first met Crowder. After Frankfurter obtained a reserve commission, he orchestrated a meeting between Crowder and Brandeis to discuss how to create a "constitutionally sound conscription program." In the Civil War, northern disgust with the conscription program, which enabled wealthy citizens a means for avoiding military service, contributed to riots in New York City and other areas. This did not occur in World War I, in part because both Crowder and Frankfurter designed the draft law to minimize any effect of economic disparities. Shortly after Wilson's declaration of war, Frankfurter impressed on Crowder the importance of not placing American soldiers under British or French command, fearing that constitutional challenges to conscription by soldiers serving under foreign commands would be entertained by the federal judiciary. In late April 1917, the British general staff recommended to General Hugh Scott and Baker that Americans training under British supervision in Britain or France should be subject to the British military code. Frankfurter quickly drafted a memorandum for Crowder to oppose the British recommendation, which neither Wilson nor Congress would have tolerated at any rate.[83]

Frankfurter's wartime focus was not military justice. He was instrumental in trying to keep the War Department neutral in labor disputes, and although today this is all but required, in 1916–1918 it was not so. To this end, he regularly reported to Wilson and Baker rather than Crowder or Ansell. How Frankfurter was brought into his role in settling labor disputes and advising on other industrial matters had to do with Bernard Baruch. In 1917 Baruch prevailed on Baker to appoint Frankfurter to the War Industries Board. Frankfurter also served as a "minister without portfolio" to Crowder. He opposed Assistant Attorney General Charles Warren's draft legislation to empower the Executive Branch to create military trials for citizens accused of hampering the war effort. Frankfurter adamantly argued that military trials of civilians were unconstitutional in light of *Ex Parte Milligan*, and even if constitutional, a poor reflection on President Wilson's stated democratic ideals.[84]

One of the aspects not covered in Lockmiller's biography on Crowder or Colonel Borch's biographical sketch of Crowder is that Frankfurter brought Crowder into regular discussions with Justices Holmes and Brandeis two years prior to the Supreme Court's review of selective service appeals. It is unsurprising that the Court would uphold selective service as a constitutional function of government, but that the court unanimously ruled without a dissent from Brandeis or Holmes may be partly attributable to Frankfurter's serving as an intermediary between Brandeis and Crowder. On February 23, 1916, Crowder wrote to Frankfurter that while he initially distrusted Brandeis and thought him nothing more than a "labor propagandist," he now considered him "preeminently a man to prepare the way and in this regard, a kind of John the Baptist." Another interesting aspect of Frankfurter's relationship with Crowder is that Taft warned Crowder against becoming involved with either Frankfurter or Brandeis. Taft's antipathy toward Frankfurter in 1917 was such that he tried to have Root intervene to exclude Frankfurter from Crowder's headquarters staff. However, Stimson thought very highly of Frankfurter, and although he also owed his political advancement to Taft, he prevailed on Crowder to keep Frankfurter. One month before Congress declared war on Germany, Holmes congratulated Frankfurter for "breaking his career" by entering the army, and he wanted to be kept informed of the War Department's plans for war. Frankfurter obliged Holmes on this request.[85]

Although Crowder could not have truly foreseen that Frankfurter would rise to become an influential long-serving Supreme Court justice, he certainly knew that bringing John Henry Wigmore, the dean of the Northwestern University Law School, into the Judge Advocate General's Office would raise the office's standing in both Congress and in the academic community. Wigmore was a well-known legal scholar, particularly on the law of evidence and Japanese law, and he corresponded with Justice Holmes on these subjects beginning in 1899 when Holmes was still serving on the Supreme Judicial Court of Massachusetts. When, at the beginning of his presidency, Wilson mulled over the possibility of a federal minimum wage for certain occupations, he sought out Wigmore's advice, and from 1913 on, Wigmore served as an informal advisor to Wilson. Like Frankfurter, Wigmore also had a close relationship with Brandeis, and the two men corresponded on foreign policy as well as evidentiary issues prior to the war.[86]

Born in 1863 in San Francisco to working-class immigrant parents, Wigmore earned both undergraduate and law degrees from Harvard University. Following graduation he went to Japan to teach Anglo-American law at Keio University and became fluent in Japanese. When Northwestern University established a law school in 1895, the university's president, on Holmes's advice, recruited Wigmore to the faculty. In 1901 the university's trustees elevated Wigmore to the deanship. Crowder first encountered Wigmore in 1913 because Northwestern University's law school was selected as one of the nation's six law schools to educate army officers under a government-funded program. Two years later Crowder asked Wigmore to provide an assessment of the law department at the United States Military Academy, and Wigmore suggested maintaining Winthrop's treatise as a mandatory text for all cadets, but he added that the academy's faculty "were out of touch with the body of modern schools in the various universities." Interestingly, Bethel began a correspondence with Wigmore well before Crowder. In 1899 while Bethel was on recruiting duties in Chicago, he attended Wigmore's law lectures. In 1916 Blanton Winship began a correspondence with Wigmore and his protégé Roscoe Pound over the applicability of judicially created federal evidence rules to courts-martial. Thus it was unsurprising that Crowder asked Wigmore to apply for a reserve commission.[87]

By 1916 one of the issues Crowder was concerned with was whether Winthrop's *Military Law* treatise remained "sound law" for courts-martial, or if another text was required. Crowder preferred to maintain Winthrop's treatise "without encountering the criticism of the Legislative Branch to which body we must report annually." Wigmore responded to Crowder that Winthrop's work remained usable and had been noted as a learned treatise by the Supreme Court, which "should give confidence to its continued use." He also informed Crowder that in the event Congress were to adopt a system of appeals similar to the federal construct, as Ansell would later propose, he would refuse to have any part of such a development. During and after the war, Crowder approached Wigmore for assistance in drafting legislation such as a new Cuban constitution and for countering Ansell's criticisms. Wigmore also shared Crowder's opinion of Hull, and in 1925 Wigmore informed Hull that his attempts to restudy courts-martial procedure were a waste of time. In 1940 Wigmore informed Lockmiller that Crowder deserved to have a biography published in order to "give a full account, of his contributions to the nation."[88]

When Crowder recruited Johns Hopkins University professor James Brown Scott, Scott had already gained a reputation as one of the nation's foremost international law scholars. Born in Canada in 1866, Scott earned his bachelor's degree at Harvard in 1890 and master's degree the following year. In 1894 he earned a doctor of laws degree from the University of Heidelberg, making him the only judge advocate to have studied law in Germany. In 1897 he established a law practice in Los Angeles, founded the Los Angeles Law School—which eventually became the University of Southern California School of Law— and joined the California Seventh Regiment during the Spanish-American War. He may have come to Crowder's notice during this time because he advised President McKinley on Philippine legal matters, but there is no evidence the two men met. From 1899 until 1903 he was the dean of the University of Illinois Law School and then a professor of law at Columbia University. Early in his career, Scott espoused an internationalist approach to American foreign policy, and through his extensive writings he came to Elihu Root's attention. Root hired him as a special advisor to the State Department in 1905, and although after a year in government employment he returned to academia, teaching at both George Washington University and Johns Hopkins University, he was frequently appointed as a special advisor to the State Department. In 1905, when Scott applied for admission to the New York Bar, the chief justice of California's supreme court provided an affidavit attesting to his stature in California as the state's "top legal mind."[89]

Most importantly, in 1907 Scott assisted General George Breckenridge Davis in representing the United States at the Second Hague Conference. In 1913 Scott, Crowder, and Root studied Ansell's analysis of General Order 100 and concluded that it remained consistent with the contemporary principles of international law. The following year, Scott was elected chairman of the Carnegie Endowment for International Law. Secretary of State Bryan and the State Department's general counsel Robert Lansing relied on Scott's advice for maintaining the United States' neutrality following the assassination of Franz Ferdinand in 1914. Scott recommended the creation of a joint committee between Bryan and Lansing and Secretary of the Navy Josephus Daniels to enforce American neutrality, and utilization of the proper means for interning belligerent sailors who remained in US jurisdiction. In August 1914 Lansing informed former attorney general Richard Olney that Scott, "whose abilities in law are unsurpassed, was necessary for employment as a special advisor in relation to international questions which are at present before this office." In June 1915 Crowder asked Scott whether his duties in assisting Secretary of State Bryan in establishing a permanent arbitration court would make it impossible to be commissioned as a reserve officer should an opportunity arise. On March 21, 1917, Crowder asked Stimson to pressure Scott to accept a reserve commission, claiming that Scott's addition would only be surpassed if Stimson himself were to join. Scott accepted a reserve commission one week later and not only assisted Crowder in drafting the nation's selective service laws but foresaw the later judicial appeals that would arise from challenges to conscription and drafted model legal briefs that were later incorporated into the solicitor general's brief to the Supreme Court. Throughout the war, Scott also served as a liaison between the State Department and the Judge Advocate General's Office. At war's end, Crowder intended for Scott to represent the War Department in any peace negotiations with Germany.[90]

Recruited in November 1916, Nathan MacChesney was the president of the Illinois State Bar and a former state attorney general. Crowder had a special reason for seeking MacChesney's commission. In 1914 a lieutenant colonel in the Ohio National Guard Inspector General's Office sued the state governor after the governor complied with a War Department order that limited the rank of state inspector general to lieutenant colonel. Ostensibly Lieutenant Colonel Daniel Stearns, the aggrieved officer, believed that he should attain higher rank and that the proper enforcement remedy was the federal courts. MacChesney successfully represented the state of Ohio in the Supreme Court, which decided that Stearns had failed to state a legal cause in the first place, with the understanding that even if Stearns had a legitimate grievance, the federal courts would not provide him a remedy. Moreover, the Court also implicitly determined that the secretary of war possessed the authority to govern the composition of the state national guards. Another reason for Crowder's interest in MacChesney was that Wigmore insisted on his commission.[91]

In January 1917 Joshua Reuben Clark Jr., who had served as solicitor for the Department of State and represented the United States in claims against Great Britain, accepted a reserve commission. He too played a role in the administration of selective service. Clark had earlier served as general counsel for the Cuban government, and it was during that time that he first met Crowder. Although Clark was an influential attorney in Republican circles, he had a close relationship to Robert Lansing. Clark was also a confidant and advisor of Pennsylvania senator Philander Knox. A conservative Republican, Knox earlier served as Taft's secretary of state and McKinley's attorney general. When American forces landed in Tampico, Mexico, in 1914, Clark advised Knox that Wilson was within his lawful authority to seize the Mexican city. In addition to administering conscription, Clark advised Baker on international law and law of war matters.[92]

Neither Crowder nor Baker was concerned with the age of some of the attorneys recruited for reserve commissions. Fifty-eight-year-old William

Call, who had served as a civilian clerk for Crowder before becoming the War Department's solicitor in 1913, was commissioned in early 1917. Several of the reserve judge advocates, including George S. Wallace, George P. Whitsett, Victor Ruehl, and Thomas Hamer, had served in National Guard units during the Spanish-American War or in the Philippines campaigns. The fifty-year-old George Wallace, who is covered in greater detail in the following chapter, served in the West Virginia National Guard as well as on the Mexican border. George Pentzer Whitsett was born near Crowder's Missouri birthplace in 1865. He graduated from the University of Missouri and earned a degree in history, and then a law degree from the University of Michigan. In 1899 he was commissioned into the Missouri National Guard and served in the Philippines. Ruehl served in the Hospital Corps during the Philippine Insurrection and then attended Indiana University's law school. From 1907 until the start of the war he taught law in New Jersey and edited the *Corpus Juris*, the nation's leading legal encyclopedia. In 1914 the state attorney general employed him. Attorney General Gregory recommended Ruehl to Ansell, and after obtaining a judge advocate commission Ruehl was shipped to France and had the good fortune to befriend Captain Harry S. Truman. Hamer, like Whitsett, Wallace, and Ruehl, served in the Philippines, but he came to Crowder's attention after the Battle of Caloocan when Crowder investigated the shooting of prisoners and advised against taking action against the offenders. In 1901 Crowder recommended to MacArthur that Hamer be appointed to the Philippine Supreme Court. Born in Illinois in 1864, Hamer attended Bloomington Law School, a predecessor to the modern Chicago Kent Law School, and then moved to Idaho where he served as a county attorney and in the state legislature. In 1908 Hamer was elected to Congress as a Republican but was not reelected to a second term.[93]

    In early 1917 Frederick Gilbert Bauer, Edwin Davis, Charles Beecher Warren, and Hugh Aiken Bayne were commissioned as reserve judge advocates. Bauer was born in Massachusetts and graduated summa cum laude from Harvard University Law School in 1903. He obtained a National Guard commission in 1910 and served on the Mexican border. Edwin Davis was commissioned in the army in 1900 after graduating from the United States Military Academy, and he served in the Philippines. In 1910 the War Department retired him for medical reasons, but he persistently tried to return to the army. Between 1910 and 1917 he was elected to the Idaho state legislature and then served as the state's assistant attorney general. Charles Beecher Warren represented the United States in international tribunals involving claims made against Britain over fishing rights. Charles Evans Hughes, Elihu Root, and James Brown Scott recommended Warren to Crowder. Notably,

Warren had detractors, including a Detroit judge who claimed to Wilson and Baker that Warren was an "active representative of the sugar trust and bitter in his criticisms of the President." This was not enough to prevent Baker from supporting Warren's commission, where he proved to be a critical participant in the administration of selective service and other matters of military law. Although Wallace had crafted the Soldiers and Sailors Civil Relief Act, Crowder routinely turned to Warren to inform all state governors that the state governments could not abridge the act.[94]

Of the others, Hugh Bayne came from a prominent southern military family. His grandfather John Gale was Alabama's governor prior to the Civil War, and Bayne was also related to General Josiah Gorgas, the Confederate army's ordnance chief during the Civil War. Bayne's father served in the Confederate army and following the war moved his family to New Orleans to establish a law practice there. Bayne grew up on his family's landholdings in Louisiana, Alabama, and Georgia, graduated from Yale University in 1892 and then from Tulane University's law school two years later. Prior to college, both Gorgas and former Supreme Court justice John Archibald Campbell, who had served as the Confederacy's assistant secretary of war, tutored Bayne. He also studied for a year in Rouen, France, and another year in Germany. After graduating from Tulane's law school, Bayne joined the Strong and Cadwalader law firm in New York. Between 1901 and the nation's entry into the war, he represented the city of Florence, Italy, as well as members of the Italian nobility in the United States District Court for Southern New York over an art ownership dispute. He also represented two German chemical manufacturers and traveled to Bremen on several occasions. In one appeal before the federal circuit court, Bayne represented a German-owned sugar refinery against Charles Evans Hughes and Harlan Stone, and he impressed both men. Hughes and Stone, along with Cornelius Vanderbilt, later recommended Bayne to Crowder. Bayne also represented the War Department in a land dispute with New York and then obtained a National Guard commission in 1915, which also made him a likely candidate for a reserve commission. However, Judge Learned Hand was Bayne's most vocal supporter. Hand and Bayne had been friends since 1902, and the two men often stayed at each other's homes.[95]

Of all the judge advocates, Burnett M. Chiperfield was the most connected to the Legislative Branch. A native of Illinois, he was admitted to the bar in 1891 and employed as a county prosecutor for four years before being elected to the state legislature in 1896. In 1898 he was commissioned into the Illinois National Guard and served for a year in the Philippines. In 1914 he was elected to Congress as a Republican, where he served a single term before joining the Judge Advocate General's Office. Once Chiperfield was commissioned,

Crowder relied on him to serve as a deputy provost marshal general, and in that capacity he assisted in administering selective service as well as the military's jurisdiction over inductees. Chiperfield's assignment to this position was fortuitous since he was well known in the House of Representatives and trusted by his Republican peers.[96]

For the first half of the United States' involvement in the war, Chiperfield was assigned to the Judge Advocate General's Office, but in April 1918 he traveled to France and became the Thirty-Third Division's judge advocate. On April 29, 1919, MacChesney reported to Crowder that of all the divisions he investigated, the Thirty-Third had the fewest courts-martial errors, and commensurately, the fact that it had the fewest severe sentences of any of the divisions investigated was a credit to Chiperfield rather than a detraction. MacChesney went so far as to recommend to Crowder that the division's disciplinary record would defeat Ansell's criticisms. After the Armistice, Chiperfield remained in France as the judge advocate to the Third Corps under General Hines. In April 1919, when Chiperfield was slated to return to the United States, Hines asked Bethel for Chiperfield to be reassigned to the American Forces in Germany command.[97]

CONCLUSION: THE JUDGE ADVOCATE GENERAL'S OFFICE AND A CONTROVERSY'S ORIGINS

Prior to the nation's entry into the war, Crowder oversaw the creation of an enlarged Judge Advocate General's Office not only to administer the army's discipline but also to provide confidence to Congress, the Judicial Branch, the legal academy, and the public that military justice and the legal oversight of the War Department's other duties, which were inevitably to reach into the population's daily lives, would be conducted with regard to protecting citizens' rights. He understood that if the nation were to become involved in a worldwide conflict, because of the army's alien legal system, the War Department would have to commission some of the top minds within the army's officer corps as well as recruit the nation's leading academics. He also reached out to his personal friend General Pershing to select army officers for judge advocate commissions, which ultimately led to Pershing and his subordinates more confidently relying on the judge advocates sent to the American Expeditionary Force during the war. However, while Pershing and his subordinate commanders largely entrusted oversight of discipline to the judge advocates, as did the majority of senior generals in the United States, dissension in the Judge Advocate General's Office became apparent by November 1917.

In August 1917 Baker approved of Ansell taking over the duties of the judge advocate general without a commensurate appointment as acting judge advocate general. As a brevet brigadier general, Ansell was the senior judge advocate in the Judge Advocate General's Office and was responsible for its internal functions. But without a formal appointment with the title of acting judge advocate general, Ansell could not assign judge advocates to divisions or develop legislation or establish regulations cementing international law to military affairs. Moreover, he could not fully represent the office to the chief of staff. Within weeks of his brevet, Ansell informed Baker that judge advocates had the authority to modify the findings and sentences of courts-martial. His claim was based on Section 1199, the Civil War statute that used the word *revise* to describe a particular duty regarding courts-martial. Several judge advocates assigned to the military justice division initially supported Ansell's position, including Herbert White, George Wallace, and Guy D. Goff, a former United States attorney and the son of a senator. However, most of these judge advocates cautioned Ansell that congressional action would be required to expand the meaning of "revise." For instance, Wambaugh drafted a proposed statute to establish a military court of appeals known as a "national military court," and he also favored an expanded use of the judge advocate revisory responsibility to include altering sentences. But he informed Ansell that Congress should quickly enact changes rather than have Baker assume a power existed, because Congress might interpret a unilateral action on Baker's part as giving to the president more authority than Congress had originally intended. Ansell also sought from Baker greater personal authority over the Judge Advocate General's Office, as though he were judge advocate general in both name and fact. Ultimately Ansell was unsuccessful in convincing Baker about the need for the Judge Advocate General's Office to exert greater authority over courts-martial or to permit him to exercise the full authority of a judge advocate general.[98]

Ansell's initial concerns arose as a result of a series of courts-martial captioned as the "Texas Mutiny cases." While training at Fort Bliss, Texas, several sergeants were accused of minor infractions. After a summary court-martial adjudged the sergeants guilty, they were restricted to their quarters. They refused to drill or perform other duties while in restriction, because they believed that army regulations prevented them from performing military duties. After a commanding officer charged the sergeants with mutiny, the men were prosecuted in general courts-martial, convicted, and then harshly sentenced. On October 30, Ansell attempted to assert the expanded revisory authority he had advocated, and he set aside the convictions and sentences of the sergeants. However, he did not date the order of setting aside the convictions until November 8. Problematic to Ansell's dating was that on November 3, Ansell informed Crowder that he was unable to function as an "acting" judge advocate general without the full authority vested in the judge advocate general, and Crowder advised Ansell that he did not object to his asking Baker for an official appointment as acting judge advocate general. Crowder did not, however, join Ansell in requesting his formal appointment as acting judge advocate general. On November 6, Ansell informed the chief of staff that Crowder supported his official appointment as acting judge advocate general and provided the chief of staff with a draft general order to that effect. The adjutant general signed the order but never published it to the army. Baker, on Crowder's advice, also ultimately restored the sergeants to the army, but, as Ansell argued, there is a difference between restoration and a reversal of a conviction.[99]

On November 10, 1917, Ansell gave Baker a memorandum insisting that Section 1199 empowered the judge advocate general to reverse the findings of the courts-martial. He then followed his own memorandum and ordered the sergeants returned to duty. In doing so, he seems not to have considered that his actions trumped the determination of a higher ranking officer without a specific statutory grant to do so. Following Crowder's advice, as well as the chief of staff's and inspector general's opposition to Ansell's assertion of a new authority, Baker reversed Ansell's order. Ansell urged Baker to consider that if the Judge Advocate General's Office were authorized to modify or overturn convictions and sentences, many injustices, such as wrongful convictions of mutiny, could be quickly reversed. Ansell also pleaded with Crowder to acknowledge that the Judge Advocate General's Office had taken too passive a role in the administration of courts-martial, and as a result the chief of staff's oversight would render military trials less than a judicial proceeding. While Crowder was sympathetic to some of Ansell's points, including the fact that the Judge Advocate General's Office had taken too passive a role in the oversight of courts-martial, he advised Baker against adopting a broader definition of "revise." Baker sided with Crowder and decided that "revise" only equated to "advise." However, Baker and Crowder established a division within the Judge Advocate General's Office to review records of trial and recommend disapproving the findings or sentences to Baker based on both law and equity. Ansell's actions of asserting his authority likely contributed to Baker's determination not to vest him with the full authorities of the judge advocate general, and on November 17 Baker rescinded the unpublished order appointing Ansell as acting judge advocate general.[100]

On December 20, 1917, Ansell drafted Baker a second memorandum further explaining why it was essential for the War Department to adopt the position that the judge advocate general had the authority to overturn courts-martial convictions and reduce sentences. Ansell stressed that because of the numbers of injustices that were coming to the Judge Advocate General's Office's attention, this authority became necessary. Once more, Crowder opposed Ansell on Ansell's assertion that there was a need for an expanded revisory authority. Crowder asserted that the secretary of war could reverse injustices through the existing system. Ansell, for his part, informed Baker that he regretted Crowder opposed him and sided with the chief of staff and inspector general, because in the past Crowder had advocated for progressive changes in the military laws. Baker once more sided with Crowder on this point, though he noted that he found it "impossible not to admit the earnestness and eloquence with which General Ansell presents his views." However, in response to a horrific injustice that resulted in the execution of several African American soldiers—described in the next chapter—Baker issued a general order captioned as General Order 169 that forbade any sentence of execution being carried out until the record of trial was published and the judge advocate general reviewed the record for legal sufficiency. Ansell believed that this order, along with the order captioned as General Order 7, was a "half-measure" that avoided the fundamental issue of due process. Without greater judge advocate oversight, he urged, a court-martial was less than a judicial function. Crowder continually countered that Ansell's proposals went too far and would undermine a commander's necessary authority over the forces under his command. It was true, he conceded, that Congress could expand the definition of "revise" to include the authority to overturn. But he opposed seeking this change from Congress and cautioned that it would weaken the president's direct oversight over military discipline and therefore unconstitutionally undermine the commander in chief authority of the presidency.[101]

Crowder, as Professor Lurie points out, found several aspects of Ansell's arguments meritorious, but he did not agree with extending the revisory authority to the degree that Ansell urged. Instead, he proposed that Congress make it clear that the president had the statutory authority to overturn courts-martial in their entirety and also that the president could delegate this authority to the secretary of war. In early 1918 the Judge Advocate General's Office conveyed a memorandum for Baker to sign and transmit to Senator Chamberlain and Congressman Stanley Dent, the military affairs committee chairmen in the Senate and House. Neither Chamberlain nor Dent held hearings on Baker's proposed bill, and so Congress never acted on it.[102]

During the war Crowder, Ansell, and other judge advocates attached to the Judge Advocate General's Office discovered repeated errors in the prosecution and processing of general courts-martial. In September 1918 Crowder

determined that some of these errors had occurred with enough regular-
ity to warrant a widespread response. Instead of just issuing directives and
memoranda to the field, he determined it necessary to publish advice in the
Army-Navy Journal, the leading newspaper dedicated to military affairs. Several divisional commanders had permitted capital offenses to be prosecuted
in summary and special courts-martial. The Articles of War required capital
offenses to be tried in general courts-martial. When commanders and judge
advocates ignored this requirement, it resulted in a situation where soldiers
charged with murder, mutiny, and sedition would face no more than a year in
prison if found guilty, or if tried in a summary court-martial, no more than
thirty days. Crowder pointed out that eighteen courts-martial in the Southern
Department were conducted in violation of the Articles of War on this basis.
However, the soldiers could hardly complain since they had benefited from a
windfall in having a significantly reduced sentence cap. Another serious error
was that several base commanders, who were not in command of a division,
had convened general courts-martial when their authority extended only to
convene special courts-martial. Crowder pointed out that soldiers who had
been convicted and sentenced in such trials had to be freed since the general
courts-martial did not possess jurisdiction.[103]

   As Professor Lurie notes in his analysis of the creation and functions of
the Court of Military Appeals, until the Armistice, the disagreement between
Crowder and Ansell was merely academic. Missing from Lurie's analysis is that
in February 1918, Crowder encouraged Baker to have Ansell travel to Europe
to study the courts-martial system in Britain, France, and Belgium and advise
whether the War Department might adopt any Allied courts-martial practices he found commendable. Also missing from Lurie's study is that Crowder
consulted with Solicitor General John Davis and Attorney General Thomas
Gregory prior to responding to Ansell's November and December memoran-
dums, and Baker was well aware that these senior Justice Department officials
agreed with Crowder. Additionally, in spite of Ansell's concerns, judge advocates reviewing courts-martial could, and often did, recommend overturning
courts-martial, restoring a convicted soldier or officer to the ranks, or reducing a sentence as a matter of clemency to a commanding general, the secretary
of war, or the president; and courts-martial were often reversed or modified by
generals and the secretary of war. Beginning in December 1918, the brief facts
as detailed above would form the basis for an explosive controversy involving
the War Department, Congress, and the legal academy. The controversy would
be widely reported alongside Wilson's attempts to have the United States join
the League of Nations, the passage of the Volstead Act, labor strikes, the Bolshevik takeover of Russia, and women's suffrage.[104]

3

THE CONSCRIPTING AND TRAINING

OF A DISCIPLINED FORCE

ON MAY 18, 1917, PRESIDENT Wilson signed into law the United States' first conscription mandate of the twentieth century and, in reality, the country's first true national draft. Known as the Selective Draft Act of 1917, the law required all men between the ages of eighteen and thirty years to register with the federal government. Civilians, rather than military officers, manned local draft boards, and state governors and legislatures had a prominent role in the selection of citizens to staff the boards. But the boards operated under federal law, and the Executive Branch appointed the members of the boards. Unlike the Civil War draft, there were no state quotas, substitutions, or commutations. The 1917 law was remarkable in several other respects. Great Britain, the power most similar to the United States, had avoided conscription until 1916, but when conscription became law, it was one of the reasons for the fall of Prime Minister Herbert Asquith's government. Canada, an internally self-governing British dominion, avoided universal conscription altogether. Mandatory military service in the United States was considered to be a risky endeavor because it not only compelled male citizens to potentially forfeit their lives, it also forced this part of the population to surrender certain basic constitutional freedoms such as freedom of speech, freedom of assembly, and the right to jury trial. Conscription was also thought to require the extension of court-martial jurisdiction over civilians ordered into military service. In the United States, the history of conscription gave pause to its supporters, including Crowder. While mandatory military service had its early advocates such as Martin Van Buren in the War of 1812, the federal government did not pursue it, and no less an icon of American politics and law than Daniel

Webster vehemently argued that mandatory military service was an anathema to freedom. During the Civil War, conscription led to draft riots and the murder of federal officers.[1]

In 1915 General William Harding Carter analyzed the Civil War conscription experience and concluded that "the failure of execution of the conscription or draft act during the Civil War makes it most unlikely that the principle of compulsory service will ever be acceptable to our people, unless the very existence of the Republican institutions shall be at stake." Carter, a Civil War, frontier, and Spanish-American War veteran, misjudged the nation's willingness to conscript its citizens for a foreign war, but clearly the 1863 Draft Riots influenced the military establishment's strategic thinking in preparing for a pending war in Europe. Crowder believed that conscription was inherently constitutional, but he understood that the Civil War draft, with its multitude of exemptions and payoffs, was not a model for a modern conscription program.[2]

In one respect, the Supreme Court unintentionally made military conscription appear to Crowder to be more likely sustainable against a challenge in federal court. In 1905 the justices decided in *Jacobson v. Massachusetts* that a state could mandate vaccinations against diseases that had the potential to threaten the health of the state's population. Placed within the decision is a statement that a citizen could be compelled "to take his place in the ranks of the army of his country, risk the chance of being shot down in its defense." In 1916 the justices decided in *Butler v. Perry* that the Thirteenth Amendment, which outlawed peonage and slavery, did not apply to a state's mandated conscription of civil labor as long as it applied to all males. Like *Jacobson, Butler* was not a military compulsion case, but Crowder and many preparedness adherents believed it stood for the proposition that citizens could constitutionally be compelled to perform labor for the public good, even if the labor was dangerous.[3]

Despite *Jacobson* and *Butler*, Crowder could not be fully confident that selective service would pass legislative muster. On February 26, 1917, Wilson asked Congress to approve the arming of American flagged merchant ships, but a few senators, led by Robert La Follette, George Norris, and Robert Hardwick (a Georgia Democrat), filibustered to defeat the bill. The filibuster worried Crowder because he believed that congressional resistance to subjecting sea-going civilians to risk, might translate into a groundswell against compelled military service. Moreover, powerful politicians such as James "Champ" Clark, the Speaker of the House of Representatives, vigorously opposed selective service, even though he supported the declaration of war. Although a Democrat, Clark echoed the sentiments of many midwesterners who argued that an enlarged army was a means to open foreign markets to American business investment at the expense of working-class citizens. In 1916 Congressman George Huddleston, an Alabama Democrat who ultimately voted to declare war on Germany, campaigned on a promise never to support conscription. In January 1917, he accused Crowder and other preparedness advocates of "enabling the creation of a military satrapy." Congressman Stanley Hubert Dent, the chairman of the House Military Affairs Committee, refused to endorse conscription, even though he voted to declare war on Germany. In 1915 Senator Willard Saulsbury of Delaware informed a Society of Friends Convention that while he believed that Germany had made war plans against the United States, a strong navy and a volunteer militia was sufficient to defend the nation and would not cause militarism to take root. Saulsbury also noted that he conveyed his views to "a willing" Wilson. Southern legislators such as Claude Kitchin, the majority leader of the House of Representatives and chairman of the powerful Ways and Means Committee, not only opposed a large standing army and voted against declaring war but also wanted to prohibit the conscription and training of African Americans. Clark's and Kitchin's opposition enabled socialists to proclaim that it was not only their political party that had determined conscription to be unconstitutional.[4]

CROWDER AND THE ADMINISTRATION OF SELECTIVE SERVICE

One day after Congress declared war on Germany, Secretary of War Baker delivered a Selective Service bill to the House Military Affairs Committee. Shortly afterward, the Senate received the same draft bill. Baker also informed a small number of legislators that he intended for Crowder to be the selective service director in a position titled provost marshal of the United States. Crowder did not set out to become the chief administrator of conscription, and throughout the war he told Baker, Bliss, and Pershing that he desired to exercise a divisional command rather than to possess the vast authority of both judge advocate general and provost marshal of the United States. Nonetheless, because of his past interaction with Congress and the confidence that many legislators had in him, he was a worthy candidate to serve as the provost marshal for the nation at large. How Wilson and Baker concluded that Crowder was the right officer to head the Provost Marshal's Office can be adduced from Crowder's participation in the creation of the Selective Service Program. In late 1916, Crowder worked with the small staff at the Army War College to develop a national conscription plan and then led his judge advocate staff to draft the administration's proposed conscription legislation for Congress. By the time Congress declared war on Germany, Crowder was intimately familiar with how the War Department intended the program to function. As a result, conscription and the Judge Advocate General's Office were, in reality, intertwined as a singular function. By January 1, 1918, there were seventy-two judge advocates assigned to the Provost Marshal's Office. Of the almost four million soldiers in the army in November 1918, well over two million were conscripts.[5]

A recent Woodrow Wilson biographer credited the president for the creation and passage of a universal conscription program, and this biographer is by no means alone. Certainly, as commander in chief, Wilson was the final arbiter of any conscription bill sent to Congress, but crediting Wilson for the design and implementation of the draft oversells his role. It also ignores the efforts of senior officers in the War Department, and in particular, the judge advocate general. Baker may have unintentionally caused Crowder's role in the origins of the World War I draft to be minimized when, in 1932, he recalled that during a conversation with Crowder, the judge advocate general claimed that conscription was "not in harmony with the spirit of the people." Quoting Baker, Professor Edward Coffman, a distinguished military historian, leaves his readers with an impression that Crowder opposed a universal draft. To the contrary, shortly after Baker was confirmed as secretary of war, Crowder presented him with a confidential assessment supporting not only universal conscription but also the creation of a formal committee to "coordinate the various industrial and scientific forces of the United States with the military and naval defense forces." Baker enthusiastically endorsed Crowder's ideas on conscription and the intergovernment committee and forwarded them to Secretary of the Navy Josephus Daniels. Moreover, in March 1917, Crowder informed Henry A. Stimson of his reasons for endorsing conscription. Crowder believed that if the nation were to rely on volunteers and state militia to build an army of one million soldiers, it would take a year to provide uniforms and weapons and two and one-half years to get the army trained and sent over to France. By then Germany would have overrun France, with the battlefront moving into the United Kingdom. However, Crowder deduced that conscription would enable the mass fielding and training of an army within a year's time. On March 23, 1917, "Colonel" Edward House, Wilson's confidant, wrote to Baker that while he believed a volunteer army was a viable option, Crowder did not, and he noted that Crowder's position that "universal obligation to military service is the only theory which satisfies the requirements of democracy" had become accepted by the War Department's bureau chiefs.[6]

In July 1917, David Kinley, the president of the University of Illinois, wrote to Baker that the reason for the success of the nation's conscription laws was solely creditable to Crowder and that he should be promoted to lieutenant general. At the same time, Lieutenant Colonel Hugh Johnson, one of Crowder's judge advocates who assisted in the implementation of selective service, proclaimed to Congress "that from the very beginning, General Crowder has been the architect and the genius of [selective service] enforcement." Kinley and Johnson overstated Crowder's role, but their claims evidenced that Crowder enthusiastically supported conscription. So too did the newly elected congressman Everett Sanders who, in a Flag Day address in Indiana on June 14, 1918, lauded Crowder with being the reason that no draft riots occurred. In 1987 Professor John Whiteclay Chambers II concluded, in his comprehensive study on the history of modern conscription, *To Raise an Army: The Draft Comes to Modern America*, that Crowder, more than any other individual, created the modern American Selective Service System. One of the minor points not found in Chambers's study is that at least in some instances, congressmen were confident in the soundness of conscription owing to the fact that Crowder authored the conscription laws. While it is true that Crowder worried throughout the war that the population would begin to oppose conscription if the army suffered high casualties or the public perceived military discipline to be arbitrary and unfair, he vigorously implemented the draft.[7]

In actuality, Crowder's role in developing conscription predated Wilson's second term. In early 1915 he wrote a memorandum to Secretary of War Garrison that the National Guard was an unreliable and ill-disciplined organization. Later that year Garrison reported to Congress his assessment of the War Department's lack of readiness to commit its forces to a large-scale war. He proposed the creation of a 250,000-man federalized reserve force that could, if called upon, expand the army without relying on the state governors to mobilize the National Guard in a timely manner. Under Garrison's plan, the National Guard would only be federalized if the reserve forces were not strong enough for the purpose under which they had been mobilized. Crowder assisted Garrison in formulating a federalized reserve force, but he encouraged Garrison to seek a half-million-man reserve army. While speaking to a large audience in New York City in January 1916, Garrison echoed Crowder's earlier letter to him, stating that "the nation cannot possibly have any military system worthy of name based upon forty-eight separate armies, operating under forty-eight separate authorities, raised, officered, and trained by forty-eight separate commanders in chief." State governors and the National Guard lobby opposed Garrison, arguing that the creation of a reserve force would diminish the National Guard's importance. Garrison's plan failed, not only because of state opposition but also because Wilson did not advocate for it. Instead, Wilson campaigned on preserving American neutrality, and prior to the 1916 presidential election he accepted Garrison's resignation.[8]

Despite Garrison's resignation, there was, at the Executive Branch, recognition of the weaknesses in the state militia system. State militia units were extensively used during the Spanish-American War and the Philippine Insurrection, and they contributed to the victories in both conflicts, but neither the Spanish military nor the Philippine Insurrectionists were the equivalent of the German Army. By 1916 there was a consensus among the War Department's senior officers and the staff of the Judge Advocate General's Office that the nation fielded a poorly disciplined force in the Spanish-American War and Philippine Insurrection. These same officers also feared that state governors who opposed the declaration of war against Germany could hamper the federalization of their state militia. Because of the political strength of the National Guard, questions in Congress arose as to whether the president could order guardsmen into the federal service for overseas duties without the acquiescence of a state governor. Such questions led regular army officers and advocates of conscription to further doubt the National Guard's reliability. In 1916 Major George van Horn Moseley, a regular officer attached to the Pennsylvania National Guard during its service on the Mexican border, recorded in his diary that he informed the War Department that guardsmen required six months of intensive army training to become reliable simply for arriving as intact units at a battlefield.[9]

Beginning in 1915, the War Department sponsored summer military training camps for volunteer citizens as part of what became known as the "Preparedness Movement" or "Plattsburgh Movement." This movement, which gained traction after the German sinking of the passenger liner RMS *Lusitania* on May 7, 1915, had a precursor dating to 1911. General Leonard Wood sponsored summer military camps at universities while he served as the army's chief of staff beginning in 1910. In the summer of 1915, Wood and a number of former generals, along with wealthy citizens such as William Randolph Hearst and Bernard Baruch, pushed to expand voluntary summer military training as a matter of preparing the nation for war. In early 1916 Wood established a thirty-day training regimen at the Plattsburgh Barracks in New York and other locations. Over ten thousand citizens enrolled in camps similar to the one established at Plattsburgh in the summer of 1916. For the most part Crowder supported these efforts, and although the army's jurisdiction did not extend to the volunteers, he wanted the Plattsburgh volunteers to adopt a military disciplinary scheme with judge advocate involvement. At this time, Crowder and Baruch established a friendly relationship, and from 1917 on, Crowder ensured that Baruch, who became a special emissary to various national and international commissions, would have a judge advocate on his staff to advise him on military matters.[10]

At the same time that Wood advocated preparedness, he also took part in the creation of the National Association for Universal Military Training. This organization's members included retired generals such as former chief of staff General Samuel B. M. Young, politicians, and wealthy citizens. Wood presciently urged that universal conscription was necessary to prepare the United States Army to fight its likely enemies, either Germany or Japan. He influenced the association to lobby for a strengthened national defense, which included increasing the size of the army through conscription. Senator George Chamberlain, an influential legislator from Oregon, who later became an outspoken critic of the War Department and in 1919 publicly demeaned Crowder, was one of the association's more ardent members. In 1916 he introduced a draft bill to enable a large increase in the size of the National Guard as well as establish a universal military training regimen, but his bill failed to pass through the Senate, largely because the War Department reported that the limited training time permitted in the bill would not be sufficient to create a modern army. Elihu Root was also a member, and he regularly corresponded with Crowder on conscription as well as the need for a federalized draft and enlargement of the army. Crowder believed that because of the prohibition against political activity, he could not openly advise the association, though he privately discussed his agreement with the association's positions on conscription and preparedness with Root and Stimson. Root, in turn, informed Young that Crowder supported universal military training and relayed that Crowder had stated that "The vast change in the way of carrying on war which has occurred within a very few years has created a situation in which it is perfectly plain that no country can be ready to defend her independence against foreign aggression except by universal military training and a resulting universal readiness for military service." In reality, Crowder had been arguing these points since the China Relief Expedition.[11]

Crowder also frequently discussed military readiness with former president William Howard Taft. Both men studied the Civil War era draft, which placed the onus on the states to fulfill a quota allotment and also enabled wealthy Americans the ability to purchase their way out of military service. Taft and Crowder agreed that exemptions from mandatory service should be minimal in number and based only on family requirements, the nation's economic needs of prosecuting the war, or religious opposition to war. Both men also opposed the creation of volunteer regiments such as had occurred in the Spanish-American War as well as the use of state militia units such as the army had relied on in the Philippines. To Taft, any call for volunteer regiments would come "at great expense, with no training that ultimately inured to the benefit of the Army." Crowder agreed with Taft and on February 6, 1917, he and the former president lobbied Baker to ensure that conscription would be locally administered but federally overseen.[12]

In April 1917, Crowder openly backed Baker's opposition to the creation of volunteer divisions such as those advocated by Theodore Roosevelt. In an effort to curb potential congressional support for Roosevelt, Crowder argued to Stimson of the necessity to intervene with congressional Republicans to side with the administration. Stimson became, in effect, a private lobbyist against Roosevelt and urged Republicans that selective service could only be fully supportable in the long term if Roosevelt were thwarted. Additionally, Crowder prevailed on Stimson to privately convey to Roosevelt's backers that if the former president were permitted to raise divisions of untrained volunteers, not only would selective service be undermined, the disciplined German Army would crush the volunteers and public support for the war would end.[13]

On January 26, 1916, Crowder testified to the House Committee on Military Affairs that the Judge Advocate General's Department required an increase of seven additional permanent officers from the thirteen he presently had. He rationalized that an increase in the size of the army would necessarily increase the numbers of general courts-martial requiring review. However, his testimony was rapidly diverted to the issue of conscription, and he focused Congress's attention on the work of General Emory Upton, a Civil War veteran who had advocated for a federal army modeled somewhat after the Prussian military system of regulars, reserves, and retired reserves. Upton was not particularly influential in his lifetime and he committed suicide in 1881, but Elihu Root incorporated Upton's studies, particularly his book titled *Military Policy of the United States*, into the army reform programs following the Spanish-American War. Although Crowder was not an Upton adherent, he pointed out to Congress that Upton had intelligently analyzed the Civil War draft's flaws and Congress should take cognizance of his writings.[14]

Although he was aware that influential legislators such as Chamberlain had advocated for a sizeable increase in the National Guard, Crowder cautioned the committee that legislation enabling a president to federalize the state militias was not without pitfalls. He pointed out that the primary weakness of Chamberlain's draft bill was that it did not directly empower the president to commit the National Guard to an overseas war. Moreover, Crowder cautioned Congress that because the Constitution reserved to the states the authority to train their respective militias and commission officers, and Chamberlain's draft bill did not address this issue, the draft bill would not enable the creation of a fully disciplined force. He cited *Houston v. Moore*, a post—War of 1812

Supreme Court decision that he claimed stood for the proposition that in the absence of legislation, the Constitution favored the state governors' assertions over the control of their militias. He then urged that Congress needed to pass legislation empowering the War Department to assume greater authority over the commissioning and training of militia officers. Crowder also worried that while the National Guard could be federalized for the duration of a war, the residual state militia forces that had not become part of the National Guard would have to be directly conscripted. However, he believed that state governors would resist losing control over their internal militia forces. As to conscription itself, he advised Congress that while "I recognize it can be tyrannically used, I do not think it can be unconstitutionally used." Most important in undermining a thesis that Crowder opposed conscription, he argued that conscription would reduce desertion rates. "Soldiers are a transitory class," he testified, "they do not come generally from established homes," and as a result "were likely to desert." On the other hand, he claimed that "if conscripts were brought into the military from all walks of life, very few would desert from the Army under the fear of returning home in disgrace." When one congressman asked him to compare the army's desertion rate to those of European armies, Crowder responded that the German and French armies were manned by conscripts and desertion was a minor problem for these armies. He once more added that conscription in the United States Army would cause desertion to largely disappear, before concluding that "foreign countries draw into the ranks of their armies a large percentage of men who have homes to return to, and who therefore cannot afford to desert."[15]

The interests of the state governors in preserving their authority over National Guard units created difficulties for the War Department's goal of creating a national army. To this end, in late 1916 Crowder turned to Majors James Brown Scott and Samuel Pepper, a Michigan National Guard judge advocate, to reinforce the president's authority to control all state guard forces once called into federal service, including the promotion and fitness of officers as well as the placement of guard units. Scott, in turn, drafted an impressive memorandum for Baker and Wilson to consider, while Pepper corresponded with midwestern congressmen over the need to give the Executive Branch full control over the guard without having to extend conscription over guardsmen for overseas service, once they were called into duty. Crowder delivered Scott's memorandum to Attorney General Gregory and Solicitor General Davis as well. Although Scott's legal analysis centered on the Constitution's "commander in chief" authorities, he also conveyed, for the first discernable time, that once a citizen was called into service, the citizen fell under the War Department's jurisdiction. Until this moment, Crowder seems not to have considered that courts-martial could be used to prosecute conscripted citizens who refused induction into the army.[16]

Shortly before the declaration of war, Major Chiperfield advised Crowder to inform Baker and Wilson that conscription was best left to a civilian agency, and preferably that the establishment of draft boards would occur as a state function responsible to the federal government. Chiperfield believed that the federal courts, and in particular the Supreme Court, would be more accepting of a Selective Service program that was not wholly militarily administered and would therefore not be viewed as the military's elevation over civilian government. Crowder agreed and added that the Court's jurisprudence since *Milligan*, coupled with Justice Stephen Field's advice to General Miles three decades earlier, made a civilian-administered conscription program necessary to withstand scrutiny.[17]

Also prior to Congress's vote to declare war on Germany, Crowder lobbied key Southern Democrats to support selective service because he realized that several of their legislative peers would likely oppose the nation's entry into the war. In 1916 Crowder obtained Congressman Asbury Francis Lever's support for conscription. A South Carolina congressman, Lever was an important ally to Wilson because several other Southern Democrats, to include Senators James Vardaman and Benjamin Tillman, opposed not only the concept of a standing army but also the empowerment of the Executive Branch. In 1917 Lever spearheaded the passage of a law empowering the Executive Branch to regulate domestic food production and shipment. Named the Lever Act, this regulation also enabled, over the objections of distillers and brewers, the president's ability to prevent the manufacture and shipment of liquor during the war. In late March 1917, Crowder asked Lever to pressure Tillman to support a national conscription program, regardless of whether the army drafted African Americans. Tillman, one of the United States' more outspoken racist demagogues, had opposed the United States' imperial expansion into the Philippines and Cuba, as well as the war with Spain, and he believed that the acquisition of overseas territories through military conquest would lead to a despotic military-oriented government in the United States. While Tillman was absent from the vote to declare war, he grudgingly supported the declaration, and within a week of the nation entering the war, Lever convinced Tillman on the need to support conscription as a democratic response. Although Tillman opposed "arming negroes," he went so far as to respond to Lever that the failure of Southern Democrats to embrace Crowder's conscription bill "would hearten Germany too much," and that Lever was free to share this message with other legislators. Vardaman, a virulent racist demagogue equal to Tillman in his attacks on minorities, had also worked to disenfranchise

African Americans. He had not only voted against the declaration of war, he had earlier opposed preparedness and the "Armed Ship Bill" and feuded with John Sharp Williams, Mississippi's other senator. He also had publicly supported Irish independence and claimed that the British had violated international law to a degree equal to Germany. Lever was unsuccessful in getting Vardaman to support Crowder.[18]

Although throughout 1916 and the first three months of 1917, Crowder and several judge advocates attached to the headquarters office labored to author the Selective Service Act, prior to their presenting the draft law to Baker and Wilson, Solicitor General John Davis proofread it and made two minor suggestions to the wording of the exemption categories regarding farmers and religious faiths. One of the aspects of the history of selective service that neither Professor John Chambers nor other scholars seem to have analyzed was the role of Solicitor General Davis in influencing military law during World War I. Davis became an ally to Crowder during the 1919 congressional dispute over courts-martial reform, but the two men barely knew each other prior to the declaration of war, even though Davis had served two terms in Congress during Crowder's tenure as judge advocate general. However, Colonel George Wallace had known Davis for several years through their West Virginia Democratic Party association. After Guy D. Goff, another West Virginian, joined the Judge Advocate General's Office in May 1918, Davis freely communicated to Crowder through Goff as well. Davis would ultimately argue successfully to the Supreme Court on the constitutionality of conscription.[19]

After Baker presented the draft bill to Congress, Representative Julius Kahn, a California Republican, became the House of Representatives' manager for the bill, and he conveyed to Crowder that he would not permit the draft bill to be altered. Kahn was selected by the House Military Affairs Committee after the committee's chairman, Stanley Dent, informed his congressional peers that he continued to oppose conscription. To Crowder, Kahn's assurance of fighting against any alterations to the draft bill was important because during Baker's testimony, Congressman Harry Hull, an Iowa Republican, notified Baker and Crowder that the Military Affairs Committee was likely to change certain provisions. Kahn had come to Crowder's attention as a potential ally in late December 1916. While serving as the Republican minority leader on the House Military Affairs Committee, Kahn showed his understanding of modern warfare and interest in the ability of the army to fight in Europe. He was particularly concerned with the army's small number of airplanes. Moreover, he agreed with Crowder's testimony that only a national conscription program could field a disciplined army within a year.[20]

As chair of the Senate's Military Affairs Committee, Chamberlain was instrumental in the passage of Crowder's draft bill through the Senate. Although he and Crowder had bickered over various matters since Chamberlain became a senator in 1908, in terms of bringing mass conscription into law, the two men were aligned, with the exception of Chamberlain wanting to permit the formation of volunteer units. Chamberlain became a source of trouble to the War Department as the war progressed, but until the Armistice he endorsed conscription. In 1912 he assisted in swaying Oregon's delegates to the Democratic convention over to Wilson, and he traveled to California to campaign for Wilson and against House Speaker Clark's potential insurgent campaign in 1916. As early as 1916, Democrats such as Alton B. Parker, who in 1904 lost to Theodore Roosevelt, considered him the leading advocate for military preparedness in the Senate. He enthusiastically offered to raise a volunteer regiment in Oregon in February 1917 as a matter of preparedness, and in May 1917 he commended Crowder to the chief of staff. Yet he also distrusted War Department bureaucracy, and on one occasion, he excoriated the surgeon general for failing to investigate whether the death of a soldier was due to an army doctor's negligence. On receipt of the draft Selective Service bill on April 11, Chamberlain announced it to the Senate as constitutional and necessary to the war effort. However, the Senate added a provision that mandated the creation of a volunteer division, and Senator Thomas Martin, a Virginia Democrat, insisted on an amendment that ensured that within four months of Germany's surrender, all conscripted soldiers would be honorably discharged. While Baker and Crowder objected to this provision, Crowder was able to convince Chamberlain to modify Martin's amendment so that the War Department would comply only inasmuch as transport was available.[21]

Two weeks later, on April 28, the House voted for national conscription by a margin of 397 to 24. One hundred ninety-three Democrats and 201 Republicans voted in favor of conscription, while fourteen Democrats, eight Republicans, and the Socialist Party representative voted against. More importantly to Crowder, the House, led by Kahn, also eliminated the creation of mandatory volunteer divisions as well as an aspect of the Senate bill that would have permitted a draft only after the volunteer numbers were found not to have met the needs of a national army. On January 20, 1918, Crowder conveyed the first provost marshal report to Congress, and he gave Chamberlain a signed copy, which read: "In grateful acknowledgement of the leadership in placing the Selective Service Law on the Statute Books and his political courage in standing for the principles of obligatory service." In June 1918 Chamberlain lauded Crowder to Baker for having the courage to rebuff the "money interests from

gaining exemptions." One month later, Chamberlain attempted to introduce a bill that would elevate Crowder to the rank of lieutenant general, going
as far as to lobby Wigmore to convince Crowder to support the bill. Crowder
demurred, however, answering Chamberlain that he did not deserve a wartime promotion.[22]

On Crowder's design, the Selective Draft Act created three categories of
men who refused to comply with it. Men who failed to register for conscription came to be identified as "slackers." Registering for conscription and being
conscripted were two different matters, because it was possible to register and
never be ordered to serve. Men who refused to appear before a local induction
board became classified as "delinquents." Again, this class of persons was not
yet necessarily compelled to be inducted into the army, because they could
apply for exemption or conscientious objector status or be determined as
medically or morally unfit. Finally, men whom the local boards had ordered
to be inducted into the army, but who had refused to comply with the order,
were classified as deserters and subject to the Articles of War. Crowder had
wanted to extend military jurisdiction over all categories, but during the war,
only men in "delinquent" and deserter categories could be court-martialed.
The Justice Department prosecuted thousands of "slackers" in federal court,
and together the Justice and War Departments, along with state and local law
enforcement, conducted mass arrests known as "slacker raids."[23]

Although Crowder, with limited exception, disapproved of alterations
to the conscription law, there was at least one occasion when Congress
determined that the nation's economic interests required modification to
the law over his strenuous objection. In March 1918, Congress enabled
the commanding officers of training cantonments to approve furloughing
soldiers for agricultural purposes, such as seeding and harvesting.
Crowder informed Congressman Henry Flood, the author of the bill, that
he thought this was an unwise idea, but Congress nonetheless enacted the
statutory change. On other matters Crowder prevailed. On June 25, 1918,
Congressman William Mason of Illinois introduced an amendment to the
Selective Draft Act that enabled inducted citizens to opt out of serving
outside of the United States and its territories. Crowder initially feared
the passage of this act because the Supreme Court had not specifically
addressed the constitutionality of mandatory overseas service coupled
with the draft. He turned to Congressman Cordell Hull, a junior Democrat from Tennessee, to defeat the bill. Hull represented a district in which
at least half of the constituents opposed the draft, to include Alvin C.
York, a future war hero. Nonetheless, Hull spoke to several members of
Congress, and Mason's bill failed to achieve a majority vote. However, if

Hull believed that Crowder was indebted to him for his assistance, any personal debts would not be repaid by favoring challenges to exemption denials. Following the defeat of Mason's bill, Hull contacted Crowder to intervene on behalf of two citizens, but Crowder responded that the citizens had to appeal to the state board.[24]

Once selective service became law and Crowder was appointed to oversee the nation's conscription program, he understood that in order for the law to survive constitutional scrutiny, not only must it enable conscientious objection based on a narrow religious objection to all war, but also the War Department would have to ensure that deferments were not liberally granted for personal or political reasons. He turned to Major Charles Beecher Warren to monitor the state boards for this reason. At times Baker became flustered with Crowder and Warren for their thoroughness and on one occasion commented to Wilson that the two officers produced legal advice of a "glacial character" and promised that he would protect the president from the volume of legal correspondence the two officers generated. Almost from the start Warren uncovered that several local boards departed from the selective service laws, ignored War Department circulars, and arbitrarily denied or granted conscientious objector classifications. Warren discerned that in North Dakota, Minnesota, and Nebraska, local boards had automatically given conscientious objectors a dissenting vote to enable a right of appeal through the state boards and then make it more possible for a federal court to grant jurisdiction over a challenge. When an applicant applied for conscientious objection, a local board composed of three officials voted on the question of exemption from service. But if one board member dissented, the applicant had the right to appeal to a state board. With Crowder's permission, Warren informed officials in all three states that the practice of guaranteeing an appeal through a dissenting vote was illegal.[25]

Crowder also believed that selective service had to be fairly applied so as not to provide anecdotal reasons for a federal court to find conscription unconstitutional such as liberally exempting wealthy citizens. To this end, he had Hugh Johnson work with Bernard Baruch to isolate essential industries from conscription based on the status of workers rather than family ownership or investor status. He also obtained both Taft's and Roosevelt's assurances of their support for limiting exemptions. Perhaps unnoticed at the time as well as by later historians is the fact that Crowder brought judge advocates into the Provost Marshal's Office who had represented unions prior to the war. For instance, Joseph Fairbanks, a 1906 Harvard Law School graduate, represented the American Federal of Labor in 1912, served on the War Department's Board of Contract Adjustment after the war, and was assigned to the Provost

Marshal's Office as a judge advocate. Crowder also assigned Major Alfred Craven, a former New York prosecutor who had earlier tried to convict sweatshop owners, to review appeals from exemption denials. Additionally, until he was shipped to France, Major Jasper Brinton, a Pennsylvania attorney who campaigned to end child labor, served as a judge advocate examining exemption appeals at the Provost Marshal's Office.[26]

A typical appeal from a denial of exemption based on privilege came to the provost marshal through a congressional inquiry. In August 1918, one of Virginia's leading bankers lobbied Congressman Carter Glass to obtain an exemption for his son, because he had named his son to become the president of the Farmers and Merchants Bank. Crowder had Warren and Craven draft an answer and then replied to Glass that a future promotion as a bank president was no different from a future promotion as a bank cashier and therefore there was no basis for exemption. Crowder added, at Craven's behest, that in Britain the bank cashiers at the Bank of London had formed their own battalion, who were known as a "Pals' Battalion" and "went off into the trenches." Crowder omitted from his response to Glass the fact that many of the men in this "Pals' Battalion" were killed at the Battle of the Somme in July 1916, leading to a shortage of trained cashiers.[27]

In August 1917, Henry Ford approached Major Warren to obtain an exemption for his son Edsel Ford. Warren responded by sending the elder Ford a copy of the exemption laws and War Department regulations and then informed Ford that his son would not receive special consideration from the provost marshal. Three months later, Crowder directly resisted the elder Ford's efforts to exempt Edsel from military service. The younger Ford did not claim conscientious objection, but rather, his father argued that his presence at the Ford Motor Company was essential to that corporation's contribution to the nation's war efforts. Ford had previously advocated peace and nonintervention, and Crowder understood that Ford's political standing and wealth placed him in a position of influence unlike the majority of citizens. "I have no willingness to interfere with its normal course of decision," Crowder noted to Baker, before adding that if either the secretary of war or president acted favorably to Ford, the decision "ought to be backed up by an entirely uncolored and unclouded consideration of it on its merits." Crowder then concluded that Henry Ford had advanced no argument for his son beyond that of being in a privileged position in American society. Ultimately Edsel Ford was exempted from military service, but this occurred over Warren's and Crowder's objections.[28]

While Crowder suspected Ford's commitment to the war was not based on anything more than the ability to win government contracts, he treated

Walter Lippman, an influential journalist and confidant of Frankfurter, no differently than he treated Ford. In July 1917 Lippman asked Crowder for help in obtaining an exemption and explained that he wanted to go to the front and favorably report on the war. Lippman assured Crowder of his willingness to face the dangers of war and Crowder did not doubt Lippman's sincerity, but he countered that despite Baker's support for the exemption, Lippman was required to appear for his induction and medical examination, and he could not "weigh in on the exemption." In 1918 Lippman was ultimately commissioned as an officer and served in France.[29]

In August 1918 Crowder received a letter from Lucien Knapp, New York's Selective Service chairman, accusing Congressman Charles Caldwell of inserting the Tammany Hall political machine into the registration boards in New York City. A number of newspaper articles reported on Caldwell's political favors, and Crowder was convinced that corruption in the administration of the draft in New York City was occurring. However, he advised Lieutenant Colonel Roscoe Conkling, a judge advocate and son of New York's former senator, not to endorse Knapp's letter. Instead, Crowder informed Attorney General Gregory of Caldwell's conduct. The next month, managers employed by the Ford Motor Company alleged to Senator Chamberlain that Michigan's draft boards were staffed by former Buick officials who unfairly targeted Ford employees. Crowder bristled at Chamberlain's acceptance of Ford's complaints, but again he forwarded the complaints to the attorney general, believing that at a minimum there had to be an investigation.[30]

Although Senator Robert La Follette opposed conscription and voted against the Selective Draft Act, he approved of Crowder's oversight of Selective Service. In early 1918, La Follette asked Crowder for advice regarding his son Phillip's exemption, but he assured Crowder that he did not want Phillip's exemption to be expedited. Crowder did review the exemption application but informed La Follette that a grant was unlikely. Crowder overlooked La Follette's opposition to the war, in part because his other son ultimately was commissioned as an infantry officer and served in France, and also because he and the senator worked well together on other military legislation such as War Risk Insurance. Moreover, one of the differences in La Follette's approach to conscription from that of the IWW's was that the senator never encouraged citizens to avoid conscription. For instance, on August 20, 1917, he acknowledged to a Mr. D. C. Wolfe that while "the constitutionality of the draft law, particularly for service abroad, such as now contemplated ... has never been passed upon by the Supreme Court," he advised Wolfe that "until the law was declared unconstitutional every citizen should obey its provisions." La Follette had this letter forwarded to Crowder. When, in February 1918, the Senate Committee on Privileges and Elections investigated whether La Follette should be removed from office, Crowder informed Senator Atlee Pomerene, the committee's chair, that La Follette had not obstructed the nation's war efforts.[31]

Major Samuel Pepper, a National Guard judge advocate from Michigan who arrived in a training encampment at Fort Bliss early in the war, pointed out to Crowder one of the other early problems with selective service. Military officers and federal marshals received bounties for bringing conscripted civilians who refused to be inducted into training camps. Civilians who had not achieved conscientious objector status and refused induction were considered deserters and therefore became amenable to trial by court-martial. But a number of young men with dual nationalities posed a problem for international relations. It was (and is) a violation of international law to force a foreign national, including a person who has lived and worked in the United States for several years, into military service. Most of the dual nationality claims came from citizens residing in the border states who professed ties to both Mexico and the United States. In his diary in October, Pepper wrote of this problem:

> One of the questions which bothers us these days is the status of the so-called deserters from the draft-men who have been called up but failed to appear. Under General Crowder's construction of the law, these men are deserters. Down here in Texas the most numerous class of such deserters is the Mexican and most of them are alien. The officers bring them in every day as deserters and claim a $50.00 reward. I have examined many of them to see if they want to serve. I ask them if they want to serve but none do. They have the right to apply for exemption as aliens. Today I recommended to General Haan that he wire General Crowder to cancel the offer of reward for Mexican deserters. It is a mistake to force aliens into the Army, and a mistake to treat them as deserters.[32]

Haan conveyed Pepper's concerns to Crowder, and Crowder responded by notifying draft boards and Attorney General Gregory that the War Department needed to establish a policy to refuse bounty payments for the arrest of civilians who claimed loyalty to Mexico. But he also asked Gregory to consider deporting all persons to Mexico who claimed this loyalty as well. However, in this instance, Crowder neglected to inform Secretary of State Lansing of his deportation advice, and Lansing disagreed on the wisdom of forced deportations because it assumed the Mexican government recognized such persons as Mexican citizens. Lansing pointed out that several men had

been shuttled back and forth across the border at Del Rio and Ciudad Acuna
and although they claimed Mexican citizenship, the Mexican government did
not recognize them as citizens.[33]

From July 1917 through the Armistice, Crowder turned to Major Charles
Warren to answer the hundreds of questions from state governors, congressmen, and local boards regarding exemptions. Warren also had to repeatedly
warn state officials from violating the law. In December 1917, the governors
of Michigan, Illinois, Ohio, and Wisconsin sought to have all "Great Lakes
pilots and mariners" deferred from having to report to training for a year's
time so that retired pilots could train replacements. While from an economic standpoint the request for deferral made sense, Warren advised the
governors that no deferrals for this class of person would be authorized.
Concurrently, he informed California's and Nevada's local boards that they
did not have the legal authority to turn away or try to dissuade teachers
from voluntarily enlisting. Two months later he informed South Carolina's
governor that the War Department would not "turn away negroes only on
account of their race," and "it was illegal for state officials to do so." Warren
also had to caution governors that they did not have the authority to promise pay rates for former guardsmen who were called from retirement into
the army or to pardon registrants who refused induction and were then
classified as deserters. In January 1918, Secretary of the Navy Daniels forwarded complaints from midwestern governors against Crowder to Baker
for not granting enough deferments for farmer-laborers. In this instance
Baker rebuffed Daniels, indicating that he had full confidence in Crowder
as provost marshal.[34]

While conscription created a set of legal challenges that the nation had
never before confronted, unique issues of a disciplinary nature arose from the
National Guard's incorporation into the federal service. On April 10, 1917, Senator Thomas Walsh cabled Crowder a question on the status of two National
Guard soldiers who had previously lied about their youth to be enlisted in the
state military. Both soldiers were shortly to be enrolled into the army and were
enthusiastic about the prospect of fighting in the war, but neither was of legal
age to be formally enlisted. The Montana governor had, through an executive
order, permitted the young men to remain in the state service and pardoned
them from any criminal liability for their lie. Walsh sought out Crowder's
assistance in permitting the two young men to continue in the army without
liability. While Crowder appreciated the young men's zeal as well as Walsh's
efforts, he could not condone a knowing breach of the Articles of War and
advised Walsh that the youths could be prosecuted for fraudulent enlistment.
Ultimately the youths were not court-martialed and they returned to their

homes, but this instance surely gave Walsh pause for concern on the welfare of his state's militia.[35]

Odd questions came to Crowder as well. In one instance he assigned Major Lewis Call to travel to Alabama and argue to a district court that the War Department did not have the authority to order a state court to reverse the conviction of a convict serving in prison so that the convict could appear for registration. In another matter he had to respond to the secretary of labor's query about a conscripted soldier who had previously served in the German Army and had been court-martialed by that army in 1912. The former soldier had complied with his induction order and was willing to serve in the US military but feared that if he were captured by the Germans, he would be summarily executed. Crowder assigned Craven to draft an exemption order so that the former German soldier could enlist in the navy.[36]

In January 1918 Crowder was unable to assist Congressman Wallace White of Maine in two matters. White's first request was to ascertain if an eighteen-year-old willing to be conscripted into the army could have his naturalization expedited. The eighteen-year-old, John McLoughlin, was born in Germany but had been adopted and brought to Maine by Irish parents, who themselves had never been naturalized and did not support the war. Crowder responded to White that although he considered McLoughlin a British subject, the German government could likewise assert McLoughlin was a German citizen since he had never been given British citizenship. Moreover, he advised that because "mere residence in the United States does not change nationality," it would violate international law in regard to Germany, as well as a treaty with Britain, to conscript McLoughlin. The second instance on which Crowder was unable to assist White arose from a refusal of the Maine board to accept the application from a resident named Andrew Farrah. Like McLoughlin, Farrah was willing to be conscripted, but he was born in Syria and served in the Ottoman Army during the 1915–1916 Battle of Gallipoli. His real name was Andrew Farrah el-Cassis, and he initially failed to inform the draft board that he had altered his name. Crowder determined that, as a subject of the Ottoman Empire who had served in the Ottoman Army, el-Cassis was not eligible for military service through conscription. In a similar instance, a retired Danish Army colonel living in New York insisted on being permitted to register for the draft with his "adoptive country" and demanded that Crowder permit him to volunteer to enlist in the army, even though the retired officer was past fifty years of age. The Danish embassy confirmed to Crowder the identity and age of the former officer, as well as its enthusiasm for the man joining the army. But in this instance, the Dane was quickly made a citizen and entered the army as a "top" sergeant.[37]

In August 1917, former congressman Thomas Watson, a Georgia Democrat but an opponent of Wilson, represented a constituent who challenged the constitutionality of conscription in the United States District Court for the district of Georgia. Judge Emory Speer, a former Confederate officer who fought against Sherman's forces in Atlanta, rejected Watson's argument that conscription was a form of slavery and therefore prohibited by the Thirteenth Amendment. Watson's argument was amusing to Crowder from the standpoint that on numerous occasions, the former congressman decried Reconstruction and argued that the emancipation of slaves violated the Constitution's prohibition against the seizure of property without compensation. Moreover, Watson was a demagogic racist, but his client was an African American conscript. Unsurprisingly, Speer did not agree with Watson, but perhaps now forgotten in this episode is the fact that Crowder had ordered Colonel Herbert A. White to represent the government in this case. Crowder insisted to Attorney General Gregory that as conscription was a War Department function, his office was best suited to defend it.[38]

NATIONAL GUARD JUDGE ADVOCATES AND THE ENLARGEMENT AND DISCIPLINING OF THE ARMY

If there were widespread worries about the National Guard's abilities to fight a modern war against Germany, Crowder was confident in the abilities of several National Guard judge advocates, even when he had disagreed with their past advice on martial law. Similar to his recruitment of civilians into a reserve judge advocate force, Crowder recruited several experienced National Guard judge advocates both prior to and immediately after the United States' entry into the war. He believed that while not all of the state judge advocates were suitable for judge advocate duties at either the Judge Advocate General's Office or in the combat divisions or corps, those who were suitable were preferable to recently commissioned officers with no prior military experience. Several state guardsmen had served as judge advocates in the Spanish-American War, in the Philippines, or on the Mexican border. Others had the unusual experience of advising state governors on the extension of martial law, to include extending state military jurisdiction over civilians. Before 1917 strike suppression and large-scale police duties were a common experience for National Guard judge advocates. Some judge advocates advised on martial law and the establishment of military courts during labor upheavals such as the 1915 strikes in Ludlow, Colorado. Likewise, during a period of intense labor agitation in Montana in 1915, the state judge advocate served as a summary

court officer in Silver Bow County for misdemeanor offenses and then organized military commissions for felonies under state and federal law.[39]

Although the National Guard's judge advocates' varied experiences in
policing strikes were not without controversy, Crowder believed that experience in civil-military relations was an important qualifier for active service,
not only because of challenges to conscription, but also because he understood that the IWW and socialist opposition to the war could result in the
army being tasked to conduct police duties. Yet he was also aware that a number of congressmen had opposed the use of the National Guard to contain
labor strife through the usurpation of the state civil laws. The experience of
West Virginia's state judge advocate, Lieutenant Colonel George Wallace, provided Crowder an example as to how controversial the use of the National
Guard in strike duties could become. In 1916 Wallace testified to a Senate
committee that, in his opinion, the state governor had the authority to impose
martial law against the IWW, even when the National Guard worked in concert with private law enforcement agencies employed by coal mining corporations that had infiltrated miners' unionization meetings and taken armed
action against the miners.[40]

Wallace was the first National Guard judge advocate Crowder brought
into federal service. He was born in 1871 in Greenwood, Virginia, attended
the University of Virginia for an undergraduate degree, and then earned a
law degree at West Virginia University. In 1897 he was commissioned into
the state militia and fought in Cuba against the Spanish Army as an infantry
officer. The following year he served in the Philippines as a judge advocate
alongside Crowder. Wallace became involved in state politics by campaigning
for conservative Democrat candidates, and the governor appointed him as
the state's judge advocate in 1902. In late 1915 Wallace left West Virginia to
become the judge advocate for all National Guard regiments called into duty
on the Mexican border.[41]

Wallace's role in strike suppression, however, was what brought him to
Crowder's attention. From 1912 on, he regularly corresponded with Crowder
on the subject of state martial law. During a virulent coalfield strike, Wallace
had argued for the maximum extension of state military jurisdiction over civilians in areas of labor unrest, to include trials of civilians by state courts-martial. Under the West Virginia constitution, military trials did not include the
right to have defense counsel, the right to subpoena witnesses favorable to the
defense, or the right to have a trial by jury. In 1912 Wallace prosecuted Mary
Harris "Mother" Jones along with other strikers, and he later defended to the
state supreme court Governor William E. Glasscock's order to quash a socialist
newspaper during the 1916 "Paint Creek" strike. Wallace described his duty to

Bethel: "A later case, reported under the style of *Hatfield et al v. Graham*, 73 W.Va., 759, grew out of the Governor's suppressing a socialist newspaper and he was later sued for damages, and, as I explained to you in a personal conversation, I filed several pleas setting out the fact that there was no malice in the governor's action, and that he was acting as the executive head of the State government." Thus Wallace believed that the suppression of newspapers did not violate the Constitution when the suppression occurred under the order of a state governor who first had declared an emergency. During the war, Wallace, more than Crowder, supported both Postmaster General Burleson's efforts to censor the mails and the Justice Department's prosecutions of citizens who publicly opposed the draft.[42]

In 1916 Wallace attempted to resign his militia commission in order to accept a reserve army commission. However, as late as January 1917, Glasscock tried to prevent Wallace from leaving the state because he considered him invaluable "in the suppression of labor radicals." In late 1916 Crowder assigned Wallace to assist Wigmore in updating Winthrop's *Military Law and Precedents* after Bethel had failed to accomplish this duty. Although Wallace was initially assigned to Washington, DC, in October 1918, he transferred to the American Expeditionary Forces. As previously noted, before Wallace left for France he drafted a proposed law to shield conscripted soldiers from being sued until the cessation of hostilities. In what became the predecessor of the current Soldiers and Sailors Civil Relief Act, when Wallace's draft became law, conscripted soldiers became protected from losing their homes and property in their absence through court judgments.[43]

In 1916, when the Senate investigated the imposition of military law in West Virginia, Senator William Borah objected to Wallace's argument that Governor Glasscock's decision to impose martial law and prosecute Marry Harris "Mother" Jones and over hundred companion strikers in military commissions was constitutional. To be sure, the state supreme court backed the governor, but it sidestepped *Milligan*. Borah and Senator John Sharp Williams were especially offended that Wallace claimed that the laws of war permitted the state National Guard to prosecute civilians even when the civil courts fully functioned. Problematic to Wallace's assertion was that, notwithstanding the Civil War, the law of war was never thought to apply to citizens in peacetime, and even the most violent labor strikes could not be considered "war." Not only were Borah and Williams opposed to the military trials of civilians, the secretary of the American Society of Military Law opposed the state militia arrests and trials as well. While Crowder remained publicly silent on state military trials, Ansell lauded Wallace for his performance before the state supreme court and informed him that his legal analysis should not be confined to West Virginia, concluding, "it is certainly unwise to permit such a reservoir of information to go unrevealed."[44]

Not all of the state judge advocates shared Wallace's opinions on martial law. Michigan's judge advocate, Major Samuel Pepper, advised Governor Chase Osborn during that state's copper mining strikes in 1912 that state military trials were unconstitutional in light of *Milligan*. Pepper also opposed permitting private security companies to assume police status alongside the National Guard. In 1913 he authored a treatise on state military authorities during periods of labor unrest. While Ansell sided with Wallace, Bethel lauded Pepper and forwarded the treatise to each state guard judge advocate. Pepper served in the American Expeditionary Forces as the Thirty-Second Division's judge advocate from August 1917 through the end of the war and as the Fifth Corps judge advocate in France from the Armistice through the end of 1919.[45]

In several respects Pepper was precisely the type of judge advocate Crowder had in mind for the army's wartime expansion. Born in 1877 in Ontario, Canada, Pepper emigrated to Port Huron, Michigan, and then studied law at the University of Michigan. He enlisted in the guard in 1905 and was commissioned as a judge advocate in 1908. Four years later he became the state's assistant attorney general, and he was instrumental in leading the state guard to break a strike in the copper fields without resorting to military trials of civilians. Instead, he recommended that judge advocates and officers assist local district attorneys to prosecute the cases in civil court. Pepper, moreover, was not a controversial officer.[46]

Pepper's other state guard work included challenging a state trial judge's finding of contempt against a militia officer who refused to perform jury duty in a trial where a striker was a defendant and the officer had been involved in his arrest. The state laws required guardsmen to avoid jury duty during state emergencies, and because the governor had not declared an end to the emergency, this law was still in effect. Pepper prevailed in the Michigan Supreme Court over the trial judge. In 1911 he lobbied Congress to accelerate the path to citizenship for guardsmen who served during statewide emergencies, but he was unable to convince enough congressmen to pass his proposed law through a committee. As a precursor to the modern Uniformed Services Employment and Reemployment Rights Act, in 1912 Pepper also attempted to broaden the state laws to protect guardsmen who were called into military service from being fired by their employers. To do so, he initiated a lawsuit against an industrial bakery that fired its workers who were called into state service.[47]

In 1916 Pepper, like Wallace, served as a judge advocate on the Mexican border. During this duty, he prosecuted his first court-martial, a trial of a colonel.

The colonel, a veteran of several Indian campaigns, was charged with dereliction of duty and conduct unbecoming an officer and gentleman. Although Pepper had drafted charges against guardsmen in Michigan, in his eight years as a judge advocate he had never prosecuted a court-martial. Pepper recorded in his diary that he felt woefully short on his knowledge of courts-martial procedure and was unsurprised that the court-martial ended in an acquittal. The acquittal, however, did not offend him because he was sympathetic to the colonel, "a gray-haired veteran of the Indian Wars and the war with Spain." One aspect of his guard service that he found troubling stemmed from the killing of an unarmed African American soldier by a Texas Ranger. Pepper ensured that all of the military witnesses to the event were present at the state trial, but the trial judge, whom Pepper accused of "being in cahoots with the rangers," dismissed the case on the grounds of self-defense.[48]

Pepper corresponded with Wallace and Crowder during his prosecution of Michigan guardsmen in courts-martial who refused to muster into their state units for Mexican border service. Crowder was intensely interested in the outcome of these trials, and he wanted to find a test case to see if national conscription would survive judicial scrutiny. In 1824 in *Martin v. Mott*, the Supreme Court determined that the New York governor possessed the constitutional authority to order the state militia to duty in response to a presidential declaration of an emergency. Even through Michigan's governor, Woodbridge Ferris, had ordered the men into service, his act of doing so followed President Wilson's order for the guard to muster into service to patrol the border. The guardsmen first unsuccessfully appealed to the state courts under a writ of habeas, and then attempted to appeal directly to Chief Justice Edward Douglass White to prohibit the government from shipping them to the border. They failed in this endeavor, but because Chief Justice White acted alone in delaying the guardsmen a hearing, his decision did not preclude a federal appeal. "It is possible that these cases may be a land-mark in our constitutional history," Wallace noted to Ansell. "Our congressional lawyers are making all sorts of assertions as to what can or cannot be done, and I should like to see the case go to the Supreme Court." The guardsmen were found guilty of failing to obey a lawful order and sentenced to terms in prison as well as dishonorable discharges, and their appeals to the federal court failed to achieve them any relief. Chief Justice White's denial to the appealing guardsmen gave further confidence to Crowder that the federal judiciary would determine conscription to be constitutional.[49]

Because of Crowder's preference for National Guard judge advocates to federalize into the Judge Advocate General's Office, some of the fielded judge advocates were quite old, even by the army's prewar standards. For instance,

Major Charles C. Teare was born in Illinois in 1857 and commissioned from the United States Military Academy in 1883. He resigned from the army in 1888, practiced law in Minnesota, and served in the state national guard until 1893. He came back on guard duty during the Spanish-American War but then resigned his commission once that conflict ended. Prior to 1917, Teare served two terms as the St. Louis County prosecutor. On January 21, 1918, he was commissioned as a major and assigned to the Fourth Division as its judge advocate. After the Armistice, he remained on active duty as part of the occupying forces in Trier, Germany, and finally returned to his civilian law practice in Duluth in 1920. While serving in the Fourth Division, he took part in both the St. Michel and Meuse-Argonne battles. When he departed for France, he was sixty years old.[50]

For the duration of the Twenty-Seventh Division's time in France, forty-nine-year-old Major James L. Kincaid served as its judge advocate. Kincaid had been the New York National Guard's judge advocate prior to the war. From 1908 until 1917 he was employed in the New York Attorney General's Office. In 1914 while he was a lieutenant, he was assigned to the guard as a cavalry officer. He had also served at the same rank in the Spanish-American War, evidencing the slowness of promotion in the National Guard. When Kincaid left for France he was over the age of fifty. In 1909 Henry Stiness, who would become the Forty-First Division's judge advocate at the age of sixty, lobbied the Rhode Island legislature to provide funds for the defense of indigent persons accused of crimes. That same year, the Rhode Island National Guard listed him as a signals officer who had served in the war with Spain at the rank of lieutenant. Born in 1857, Stiness was the same age as Crowder. His older brother, Walter Stiness, was a Rhode Island congressman who conveyed to Baker that Rhode Island was barely represented in the War Department. Stiness remained in France through the end of 1919 but transferred as the Fourth Division's judge advocate after Teare was moved up to the Second Corps staff. In May 1918 Bethel complimented Stiness for his efficiency.[51]

Although many National Guard judge advocates had served in the Philippines and on the Mexican border, their experience with courts-martial and other aspects of military discipline was limited. When, on February 16, 1918, Major Edwin McNeil, a regular officer, was ordered to France, General Henry Allen, the Ninetieth Division's commander, wrote to Crowder that while McNeil's replacement, Major Charles Cresson, was "experienced in the law and helpful in matters concerning arrests under the vice clauses of the selective draft act, he has not much experience in courts-martial practice." Prior to 1916, Cresson was a United States attorney and his Texas National Guard service was as a cavalry officer. He had become a National

Guard judge advocate in 1916 but had never seen a court-martial. Allen wanted an officer thoroughly familiar with the army's disciplinary needs and did not "believe Cresson fit the bill." Crowder informed Allen that his division would have to "make due with Cresson." Crowder had, in fact, recommended to Baker that Cresson be brought onto active duty and assigned to the Ninetieth Division because of his ties to Texas law enforcement. Lieutenant Colonel Herbert A. White, a judge advocate assigned to the Judge Advocate General's Office, and Senator Morris Sheppard had lobbied Baker for Cresson as well. In comparison to other state judge advocates, Cresson was a youthful forty-two years old.[52]

The incorporation of National Guard judge advocates into the army had other benefits in regard to civil-military relations. When the War Department curtailed the consumption of alcohol by prohibiting the sale of it to soldiers, it impacted civilian communities both in their economies and in law enforcement. There was a sound basis for prohibiting alcohol sales to soldiers. Drunkenness undermined discipline and brought on disease, and after Crowder and other officers testified as to its effects, Congress barred the sale of alcohol to uniformed soldiers. Since all soldiers in training were required to wear their uniforms off post, in theory, none of the soldiers should have been able to purchase alcohol. Nonetheless, a profitable black market arose near training installations. On January 2, 1918, Major McNeil reported to Crowder that the division's policy of giving leniency to soldiers who informed on black market liquor sales was beneficial to the division's discipline. He also reported that the Bureau of Investigation—the predecessor to the Federal Bureau of Investigation—and the division's command had planted soldiers along San Antonio's streets to capture "bootleggers." This operation achieved the desired results. "The Federal District Court is now in session and the docket contains over four hundred liquor cases," McNeil reported. "Judge Duval West is giving sentences of three months to all who plead guilty to selling liquor to soldiers. It is understood that he will give six months to those who are convicted after pleading not guilty." McNeil seemed not to have worried about the post–Civil War *Posse Comitatus* act, which prohibited the army from serving in a law enforcement capacity unless there was a national emergency such as an insurrection. His lack of worry had to do with the fact that Cresson was well known to the local community and had prosecuted several cases in front of Judge West.[53]

In addition to enabling the prosecution of civilians who took part in the alcohol and prostitution black markets, judge advocates were involved in ensuring food safety, which likewise affected civil-military relations. At the same time McNeil reported on law enforcement operations against bootlegging and prostitution, he reported to Crowder that Cresson was instrumental in the "destroying of over two tons of turkey, chicken, ox-hearts, and livers that were unfit for human consumption." Importantly, the army had yet to bid on, or pay for, the delivery of these items, which had been placed in a corporation's cold-storage facility. Nonetheless, because "there was a high probability that the unfit food would have ended up in Army messes," Cresson directed the US marshal to destroy the carcasses. Prior to the war, it was unlikely the federal government would have intervened in the sale of rotten foodstuffs. But as a result of the army's experience during the Spanish-American War, where thousands of soldiers became sick after consuming spoiled canned meat, McNeil and Cresson were proactive in the food's destruction. McNeil informed Crowder that Cresson also advised General Allen that the War Department should refuse to pay for the destroyed meat.[54]

THE JUDGE ADVOCATE'S AD HOC COMMISSIONING AND TRAINING EXPERIENCE

By January 1918, over five thousand citizens applied to obtain a judge advocate's commission, and the War Department could only select roughly three hundred applicants out of this pool. Obtaining a judge advocate commission was a difficult endeavor for interested citizens, and many applicants had political backing. For instance, George C. Wing, the son of a distinguished state judge, attended Brown University as well as Harvard's law school and had the backing of Maine's governor and Congressman Wallace White. He had also represented Maine before the Supreme Court as a temporary state solicitor. But he was not selected as a result of his young age of twenty-seven. Charles M. Seward, the grandson of Secretary of State William Henry Seward, had the backing of Georgia Senator M. Hoke Smith, but Seward could not overcome the fact that he had only been admitted to the bar in 1916. Senator Claude Augustus Swanson of Virginia was unsuccessful at obtaining a judge advocate commission for George L. Browning, one of Virginia's more prominent attorneys, a part-time state solicitor and future state supreme court justice. Supreme Court Justice Willis Van Devanter asked Crowder to not only favor his son Winslow but also the applications of two men named Homer Guerrey and Charles Frailey. Both Guerrey and Frailey had argued appeals before the Supreme Court. Van Devanter only partly succeeded with Crowder. Winslow had only graduated from law school in 1916, and was commissioned into the artillery after Crowder recommended him to Pershing, while Frailey became a judge advocate attached to the Fourth Division and then to the American

Expeditionary Forces headquarters. Guerrey prosecuted selective service violations in the United States, but as a civilian. In 1917 Congressman Tillman tried to push Crowder to have Brewton A. Hayne, a California attorney, commissioned as a judge advocate. Born in 1860 in South Carolina, Hayne was a graduate of the University of California and practiced law in San Francisco. He had letters of support from the California Supreme Court, but he believed that Tillman could make a difference in his favor. Hayne's grandfather, Robert Y. Hayne, had been South Carolina's governor during the 1833 Nullification crisis, and Tillman argued to Crowder that Governor Hayne was "heroic," suggesting that the "heroism" was hereditary. However, Crowder was not impressed with Tillman's endorsement or Hayne's application. In August 1918, Virginia Senator Carter Glass, one of Crowder's more ardent supporters, informed a Virginia trial judge who sought Glass's support to become a judge advocate that "the War Department bitterly resents any attempt to manage such military details," in response to the judge's request.[55]

Although Samuel MacKay Wilson, the Seventy-Seventh Division's judge advocate, was one of the first civilians commissioned as a judge advocate, he was also one of the least likely to be accepted into the army because he was largely deaf and had to use a large hearing aid and observe mouth movements. Born in 1871 in Louisville, Kentucky, to one of the city's leading religious leaders, Wilson was educated at Centre College, Kentucky, and transferred to Williams College in Massachusetts. Following his graduation from Williams, he returned to Centre College to study law and also studied in a local judge's office. Admitted to the bar in 1894, between 1903 and 1908 he served as a county commissioner, which entitled him to be referred to as "Judge Wilson." He also served as an ad hoc circuit judge between 1910 and 1917. Wilson came to the attention of his state's governing elite while defending former Kentucky secretary of state Caleb Powell. Powell had been accused of complicity in the murder of the state governor, and Wilson obtained an acquittal. In addition to a vibrant legal practice and his part-time judicial duties, Wilson taught law at Transylvania University and was employed as a title company's general counsel. He was also an influential citizen in Lexington and Frankfort. He served as the secretary of the Lexington Orphan Asylum, held posts in several societies including as a director for a school for blind children, and was the president of the Kentucky chapter of the Sons of the Revolution. He was also the chairman of the Battle of New Orleans Centennial Commission, and he advised the Navy League of the United States, a private organization dedicated to building a fleet to rival the Royal Navy. Justice Brandeis not only knew of Samuel Wilson's reputation, he wrote a letter of support for his application for a commission.[56]

Ultimately Wilson was quickly able to obtain a judge advocate commission for a number of reasons that other applicants were not fortunate to have. Major General J. Franklin Bell, the army's chief of staff from 1906 to 1910, was his first cousin, and the two men corresponded frequently even though Bell was fourteen years older than Wilson. In the last decade of the nineteenth century when Bell served as a temporary judge advocate at Fort Apache, Arizona, he sought Wilson's advice on evidentiary rules and federal jurisdiction. In 1898 Bell informed Wilson that he would call on him "when several vacancies occur in the regular corps of judge advocates," and then advised Wilson to "make [himself] solid with politicians so that I can secure one of those appointments." In 1901 Bell needed Wilson for a significant reason. While in the Philippines, Bell was promoted to the rank of brigadier general, but he was also accused of both causing and condoning war crimes. He asked a willing Wilson to help craft a written defense of his conduct, and Wilson delved into the law of war to do so. Bell's career not only survived the allegations, he faced no congressional opposition when nominated as chief of staff. In May 1914 Wilson ebulliently informed Bell that while he was "a Woodrow Wilson man" and believed the president would be elected to a second term, he also wanted to manage Bell's political future because "every American War has made a President." Two years later Bell asked Wilson to help him gain the president's attention so that he could be assigned to command all forces on the Mexican border. In light of the close relationship between Wilson and Bell, it is unsurprising that Bell penned a letter of endorsement on behalf of his cousin to President Wilson on April 5, 1917, or that several other senior officers endorsed Samuel Wilson's application for a judge advocate commission.[57]

In addition to Bell's support, there were other reasons for Samuel Wilson's success in obtaining a judge advocate commission. By 1910 he had become a prominent Democrat in his state and advised Kentucky's congressmen on labor conditions. Although he was a Democrat, his defense of Caleb Powell, a Republican, won him support from leaders of both parties. As Europe descended into war in 1914, Wilson corresponded with Solicitor General Davis not only on conditions in the Kentucky and West Virginia coalfields but also for Davis's impressions as to how long the conflict in Europe was likely to last and how neutrality would affect commercial laws. Wilson also informally advised Attorney General Gregory on the international law of neutrality in regard to coal shipments to France. On August 10, 1916, he traveled to Plattsburg, New York, to participate in General Leonard Wood's training encampment.[58]

In February 1917, Wilson spoke to "a group of several hundred citizens" at the Kentucky Rotary Club and advocated for universal military training.

He concluded his speech by calling Henry Ford a "sissy." Two days after the declaration of war, Wilson telegraphed President Wilson asking for his support to obtain a commission. He noted that his younger brother, a doctor and National Guard officer, was commissioned major and ordered to France as a medical observer. Two weeks after the declaration of war, Wilson penned a letter for the Navy League to endorse compulsory military training for all able males. On April 10, 1917, Senator Ollie James praised Wilson to Baker as Kentucky's best candidate for a judge advocate commission.[59]

On May 1, 1917, Wilson left for Plattsburg Barracks, New York, to train once more as an officer, but he was not yet a judge advocate. He had to forward dozens of pending civilian court cases and clients to his fellow attorneys in Lexington, but in a spirit of patriotism, some of his peers took on his clients without expectation of compensation. In early June, Colonel Frank Dodds informed Wilson that Crowder, after reviewing his application, commented that there were "more than two thousand applications for about thirty appointments and that as the list of applications contains many prominent lawyers, he fears the prospect of getting your deafness waived is rather unfavorable." But in July Wilson's application included letters of endorsement from Attorney General Gregory, Solicitor General Davis, General Bell, both of Kentucky's senators, three congressmen, and the governor, as well as three other generals and eighteen other officers. This was enough support for a judge advocate commission. Not all political leaders were happy with the appointment, however. On September 1, 1917, John Flood complained to his uncle, Congressman Flood, "Samuel Wilson has just been commissioned Major in the Judge Ad. Genl's Dept. He is a splendid lawyer, but deaf as a post and I know his commission was secured largely through political influence."[60]

John Philip Clayton Boynton Hill provides another example of a successful applicant, albeit one with unique prior National Guard service. Hill was born in Annapolis, Maryland, in 1879, was educated at Johns Hopkins University, and earned his law degree at Harvard in 1903. Although he remained in Boston to work in a law firm, the next year he returned to Annapolis to lead a citywide campaign against an amendment to the state constitution that, if passed, would disenfranchise all African American voters. It was known as the "Poe Amendment" after its author, former state attorney general John Prentiss Poe, and state Democrats sought to use it to imitate the removal of African Americans in Mississippi and South Carolina from any political influence. Maryland's African American voters teamed with Republicans in Baltimore and Annapolis to defeat the amendment. The same year that Hill led an anti-Poe organization, he also joined the Maryland National Guard, took part in joint guard maneuvers at Manassas, and was commissioned as a lieutenant. In 1909 he successfully led another organization against an attempt to disenfranchise African American voters. This time, the amendment would only allow persons to vote if their grandfathers had been permitted to vote at the age of eighteen. Very few African Americans in Maryland would have qualified to vote in state elections under this proposed amendment. Hill campaigned against "permitting the defeated confederacy and slave power to return to Maryland." In 1910 he was promoted major and appointed judge advocate for Maryland. That same year, President Taft also named him United States attorney for Maryland. Although the Senate confirmed Hill, the Democrat-dominated Maryland Bar bitterly opposed the nomination as a result of his championing of civil rights for African Americans.[61]

In 1913 President Wilson, on Attorney General Gregory's advice, decided to leave Hill in office, and for two years Hill prosecuted a number of political corruption and tax fraud cases. He unsuccessfully ran for mayor of Baltimore in 1915, hoping that the African American vote would be enough to overcome Democrat opposition. The following year he campaigned for Charles Evans Hughes against Wilson. As the state guard's judge advocate he oversaw multimillion dollar contracts for the improvement of Maryland's coastal defenses. In 1916 he attended the Republican National Convention and then left his Baltimore law practice to serve as the Fifteenth Division's judge advocate on the Mexican border. Although his legal duties with the state national guard and service on the Mexican border coupled with his five years as a federal prosecutor favorably impressed Crowder, Hill had another quality that was not only lacking in the National Guard: most regular army officers did not possess Hill's knowledge of the German military.[62]

In addition to Hill's legal practice and guard duties, he undertook a vigorous study of the German Army and foreign and military policies. Between 1904 and 1916 he published four essays on the German Army. Most notably, in 1909 the German government permitted him to spend two weeks with the German XI Army Corps during its maneuver training in the Harz Mountains, and the Maryland National Guard funded his travel. Hill not only learned of German military tactics from several German officers who obtained high rank during World War I, including Colonel Erich Ludendorff, he also interviewed Field Marshal William Leopold Colmar Freiherr Von der Goltz, an aged veteran of Prussia's wars with Austria in 1866 and France in 1870. The German government attached Von der Goltz to the Ottoman Army in 1892 and he had written extensively on the Turkish military. More impressive than his military experience was the fact that Von der Goltz was also one of Germany's leading military theorists and was instrumental in the German Army's modernization and enforcement of discipline. Some of Von der Goltz's works—particularly his analysis of the Franco-Prussian War—became mandatory reading at the Army War College. Called out of retirement in 1914, Von der Goltz commanded a Turkish army in Mesopotamia, but his influence in the German Army on the Western Front remained throughout the war. In addition to observing the German Army, Hill advocated for universal military training in 1913 as a means for not only making a large cohesive army possible but also for creating a society in which ethnic barriers and crime rates were lowered.[63]

Wartime service in any capacity was likely to be beneficial to citizens with political or judicial aspirations. Notwithstanding the patriotic impulses of applicants, given that the Judge Advocate General's Office had frequent access to President Wilson's cabinet as well as Congress, appointment as a judge advocate could translate into important government jobs or further political careers at the war's conclusion. Of the over five thousand lawyers who applied for judge advocate commissions prior to the Armistice, only forty-eight were directly commissioned as judge advocates from civilian life with no prior military experience. Other applicants who were initially denied judge advocate commissions were first commissioned into the infantry, artillery, cavalry transportation, or quartermaster branches, and then after serving as trial judge advocates were commissioned into the Judge Advocate General's Department.[64]

Mendel Smith presents an example of a successful applicant who was initially denied a commission. The day after Congress declared war on Germany, Smith, who was at the time a South Carolina trial judge, offered to resign his judicial post and enlist in the army. He was born in 1870 and educated at the Citadel and at the University of Virginia's law school. He entered state politics and was elected to the state legislature, where he became Speaker of the South Carolina House of Representatives. He unsuccessfully ran for governor in 1908. In 1909 the governor appointed him as judge of the Fifth Judicial District. Prior to 1917 his sole military experience had been as an officer in a state militia unit known as the "Kershaw Guards." This unit was not part of the National Guard and therefore was not subject to overseas service. After he failed to gain a judge advocate commission, he tried for an infantry commission. Between April and October 1917, he failed to obtain an infantry, cavalry, or engineer commission as a result of his age and medical condition. Although Smith wanted to be a judge advocate, he was persistent in his efforts to enter the army, and he ultimately accepted a commission with the rank of captain in the Quartermaster Corps. However, Congressman J. Williard Ragsdale, the chairman of the Committee on Foreign Affairs and a personal friend, advised him to reapply for a judge advocate commission. So too did Smith's political opponent, Senator Tillman.[65]

On October 16, 1917, Smith once more applied for a judge advocate commission. As a well-known state trial judge, he had political connections commensurate to Samuel Wilson's. In addition to Ragsdale, Senator Ellison Smith, Congressman Asbury Francis Lever, and Governor Richard Manning endorsed Smith's application to Crowder. By the time of Smith's application, Crowder had turned the duties of responding to applicants to Colonel White, who noted to Senator Smith that although over 250 prominent attorneys and members of the bar had applied for commissions, Mendel Smith's application "would be given the most favorable consideration." Finally, Smith, at the age of forty-seven, was directly commissioned as a judge advocate with the rank of major. On July 23 Governor Manning further lobbied Crowder to ensure that Smith would be transferred to the American Expeditionary Forces. In October 1918, Crowder assigned Smith to Camp Meade, Maryland, and while this assignment did not get him to France, it enabled his family to move on post. Smith's son was enlisted as a sergeant and became his legal secretary.[66]

The example of John H. Flood proved how difficult it became to obtain a judge advocate appointment. A cousin of Henry Flood, the influential senator who authored the Senate's resolution declaring war on Germany, John Flood had not only his cousin's support but also that of Senator Oscar Underwood of Alabama and Virginia representative Carter Glass. Nonetheless, Flood's application was rejected in October 1917. In response, Senator Flood obtained an interview with Colonel White, who informed him that John Flood's "application was very meagre" and "the Judge Advocate General's Office wants endorsements from the Kentucky Judges, both state and federal, and from the bar." John Flood accepted a commission into the artillery, but like Smith, he continued to apply to a judge advocate commission. As of January 1918, Senator Flood was unable to convince Crowder to create a special opening for his cousin, in spite of the support of six congressmen. On March 6, 1918, however, after receiving a favorable report from the Kentucky Supreme Court to Baker, the Judge Advocate General's Office offered John Flood a commission.[67]

Cleon N. Berntheizel, a Pennsylvania state legislator, is another example of a successful applicant. Born in 1874 in Lancaster County, Pennsylvania, Berntheizel attended the Dickinson Law School. He served as a district attorney from 1904 to 1913 and then was elected to the state house of representatives. After his legislative service he returned to his district attorney duties. He was also a National Guard officer assigned to the state adjutant general's office, and he provided legal advice during labor upheavals. He briefly served on the Mexican border. Both Senator Philander Knox and Congressman William Griest recommended him to Crowder. Because the Twenty-Eighth Division was manned primarily by National Guard soldiers from Pennsylvania, it is unsurprising that having accepted a judge advocate commission, on July 23, 1917, he became that division's judge advocate. From the start of his service on the border in 1916, he clashed with Major George van Horn Moseley. In September 1916, Moseley recorded in his diary, "Colonel Smith and Major Berntheizel went east today, the latter, our J.A., is totally useless." Moseley, a virulent anti-Semite who was given to anti-immigration rhetoric, likely disliked Berntheizel because, as he recorded in his diary, he "suspected him to be a jew." Moseley's wartime letters and diary entries also evidenced a visceral dislike of the Democratic Party, and Moseley believed Berntheizel was also a progressive Democrat.[68]

A small number of applicants, who had unsuccessfully tried to be commissioned judge advocate prior to the war, applied after the declaration of war, probably assuming that they would be given priority. At the same time Germany's armies crossed into France in August 1914, Senator Thomas Walsh of Montana impressed on Crowder the "merits" of a Lieutenant Paul C. Raborg, a National Guard officer. Walsh noted that Raborg had graduated from the University of Illinois and practiced before the Montana Supreme Court. Crowder assured Walsh that Raborg would be given favorable attention by a board to select officers for entry into the Judge Advocate General's Office, but made no promises beyond this. Raborg was not selected either in 1914 or in 1916. In May 1917 Raborg applied for a judge advocate commission once more. Again he was not selected, though he was later noted for his bravery in commanding a tank battalion in 1918.[69]

In early 1918 James Harrison Wilson, a retired brigadier general and veteran of both the Civil War and the Spanish-American War, lobbied Crowder to commission Mortimer L. Schiff, the son of the wealthy financier Jacob Schiff. Wilson and the elder Schiff, "the great Jewish Banker of New York," had been longtime friends, and Wilson had already lobbied Secretary of the Treasury McAdoo to support the younger Schiff. However, on Frankfurter's advice, Crowder informed James Wilson that he could be of no service to Schiff. In 1916 Crowder rebuffed Wilson on the application of a John Percy Nields who, at the time, was sitting as the US attorney in Delaware. Instead, Crowder obtained a position in the ordnance corps for Nields, and in 1930 President Herbert Hoover appointed Nields as a federal judge. Crowder concluded that Nields lacked the temperament necessary to succeed as a judge advocate.[70]

Crowder likewise determined that he could not support two candidates whom former president Theodore Roosevelt recommended for judge advocate commissions. One of the applicants lacked the experience Crowder believed necessary, and the other suffered significant medical problems. Brandeis lobbied Crowder to endorse William Rand, a prominent New York attorney and Harvard Law graduate, for a judge advocate commission. After Crowder interviewed Rand, and then sent Rand to Winship for a second interview, both officers informed him that they lacked the authority to commission Rand into the Judge Advocate General's Office, but the secretary of war did have such authority. Crowder promised Rand that he would intercede with Baker, but for reasons that are no longer known, Rand did not become a judge advocate until early 1919. However, he would perform an important task of being part of a board of judge advocates to review court-martial appeals.[71]

Several attorneys bypassed Crowder and appealed directly to Baker or Wilson. Otis B. Drake, a one-time clerk to the Court of Appeals for the District of Columbia, corresponded with Baker to obtain a judge advocate commission and had the support of the judges on the court to that end. Drake, however, was almost blind and could not be accepted. To Crowder's consternation, Joseph Tumulty encouraged Max Steuer, one of the most effective attorneys in American history, to apply for a commission, promising that President Wilson would support the appointment. In 1911 Steuer successfully defended the owners of the Triangle Shirtwaist Company, but Crowder was convinced that "Steuer's commission would not aid in unifying the nation's population." He surmised that working-class laborers who were being conscripted might be swayed by the socialist claim that World War I was a "bankers' and merchants' war" if Steuer became a judge advocate.[72]

Although service as a trial judge advocate became a "proving ground" for applicants seeking a judge advocate commission, neither Crowder nor Ansell was directly involved in the selection of trial judge advocates attached to brigades and divisions. The duty of appointing trial judge advocates fell to the divisional commanders, who were supposed to act on the advice of their commissioned judge advocate. Future Supreme Court justice Frank Murphy, and Elijah Barrett Prettyman, a future judge on the Court of Appeals for the District of Columbia, are two examples of how the selection process worked.

Murphy was born in 1890, graduated from the University of Michigan in 1912, and then earned a law degree at that university's law school in 1914. Between 1914 and 1917 he worked in private practice, though he represented Detroit on civil matters in the state courts. Commissioned into the army in 1917 as an infantry officer, Lieutenant Murphy quickly experienced the military's justice system as a trial judge advocate. While in training at Fort Sheridan he defended a lieutenant charged with manslaughter after the lieutenant accidentally killed a sergeant at a rifle range. Before he headed to France in August 1917, his first officer efficiency report read, "fine mind, thorough, will make an excellent officer." Although he trained as an infantry officer, his commander recognized his legal talents and appointed him brigade judge advocate. In this capacity, Murphy assisted the US attorney in prosecuting a civilian quartermaster in a United States District Court for theft, and following this trial he prosecuted the civilian's coactor, a captain, in a court-martial. Both men were found guilty, and the court-martial sentenced the captain to twenty years at hard labor. The *New York Times* reported on the trials, bringing Murphy briefly into a national spotlight. While defending another soldier in a court-martial, Murphy offended several senior officers with his closing argument: "This case is brought to trial only as a result of the gross and wanton negligence on the part of those who investigated the case." After this trial resulted in an acquittal, Murphy was prevented from serving as a judge advocate again. The divisional adjutant informed Murphy that his conduct in the trial "made it apparent" that he could not function both as a lawyer and officer, and then added, "in order that you may not be in the future subject to conditions which may cause you to forget that you are now an officer of the army, you are directed not to appear before any court-martial." As Murphy's biographer Sidney Fine noted, his wartime experience shaped his future judicial career, particularly as it applied to claims of Executive Branch authority in wartime. In appeals arising from assertions of military authority over individual or civil rights, Murphy was more likely to side with individual and civil rights than any other justice during his Supreme Court tenure. On the other hand, after his removal from judge advocate duties, Murphy not only remained in the army but was promoted to captain and then major. In 1921 he informed the adjutant general that he considered it his duty "to remain affiliated with the army through the reserve corps."[73]

Elijah Barrett Prettyman was born in 1891 in Lexington, Virginia, earned a law degree at Georgetown University in 1915, and became a lawyer in Hopewell, Virginia. He was commissioned into the army in 1917 as an artillery captain. He was also assigned as a temporary or ad hoc judge advocate for extended periods during his military service. Prettyman was initially ebullient at the prospect of his chances to see combat. In his diary entry of April 17, 1918, he penned, "I wonder if Kaiser Wilhelm Hohenzollern would be quite easy in his mind if he could see 2,000,000 Americans between 21 and 31 years old in perfect health, clothed, and fed and all at play. I imagine he would be more disturbed than he would be at the reserve army of the allies on his front!" Although Prettyman wanted to serve in combat, at least half of his service was as a brigade judge advocate.[74]

While in training in Texas, he oversaw a dozen general courts-martial, of which six were for drunkenness, five for sleeping on post, and one for refusing to obey a lawful order. He advised his brigade commander to overturn one of the convictions. The soldier was charged with refusing to obey a lawful order and disrespect for a superior officer. A company commander named Lieutenant Louis E. Lanborn had ordered a diminutive Private George E. Naylor to "box a much larger and healthier soldier" in an unauthorized boxing tournament. In Prettyman's description, Naylor "slouched up to Lanborn and said the words, can't you get someone else to box, I am sick." Lanborn mockingly responded, "It seems to me that the thing that is the matter with you instead of being sick is that there is something wrong with your backbone." To this, Naylor retorted, "Go ahead, God damn you! Smile all you damn please, you seem to get such a hell of fun out of it." Although Prettyman advised the divisional commander that the order to box was unlawful since a surgeon had, in fact, placed Naylor on "the sick list," he conceded that Naylor's later statement was contemptuous. However, he urged that the three-year sentence to imprisonment was overly severe and should be reduced to a reprimand because "Lanborn had goaded a sick and diminutive Naylor to fight for his personal entertainment." Prettyman's additional argument to the divisional commander was that if officers could freely violate the limits of their authority, such as Lanborn had done, then the authority of general officers would be diminished in the trenches. Naylor was returned to the ranks and Lanborn reprimanded.[75]

A small number of officers became judge advocates in the American Expeditionary Forces after specifically being rejected in the United States. Bernard Gorfinkle, a former sergeant in the Massachusetts National Guard, was commissioned as a cavalry officer on August 10, 1917. He was born in 1899 in Boston to Reform Jewish parents, graduated from Boston University with an LLB in 1911, and opened a general legal practice. In 1913 he enlisted in the state militia and quickly attained the rank of corporal. In 1916 he was promoted to sergeant and served for a two-month period on the Mexican border in a cavalry unit. By November 1916 he had returned home to his law practice, promising his mother that if the United States entered the war against Germany, the army's regulars would go over to France, but he was unlikely to do so because the guard would take over patrol duties on the border with Mexico. However, in January 1917 he learned that Crowder had recruited prominent attorneys into the Judge Advocate General's Office and was impressed that Frankfurter was among the first officers brought in.[76]

The next month, Gorfinkle applied for a reserve judge advocate commission, but his application was not given favorable consideration, and indeed, the Adjutant General's Office appears to have misplaced it for over a month. Undeterred, Gorfinkle obtained letters of recommendation from the US attorney for Massachusetts, Boston's city attorney, local judges, Governor Samuel

McCall, and Congressman James Gallivan. In spite of these recommendations, the army commissioned him as an artillery supply officer. But Gorfinkle persisted in his desire to obtain a judge advocate commission and volunteered to serve as a trial judge advocate at "every opportunity." In July 1917 he competed in a division-wide moot court and prevailed over all of his competitors, and he served as a trial judge advocate in twenty-eight courts-martial. Like Frank Murphy, he defended an officer accused of theft and conduct unbecoming an officer and gentleman in a general court-martial and won an acquittal. From August 1 until being shipped to France in late September 1917, Gorfinkle was assigned as the division's summary court officer. "I therefore sit as a judge over criminal cases that might arise in camp and it is considered a very important job," he said, before adding in Yiddish, "Oi Yoi vill ich enriebben day goyem!" Despite his successes, when he shipped to France, he did so as an artillery supply officer. However, he persisted and for reasons that are noted in the following chapter, by November 1917 he served at a divisional staff as an assistant judge advocate.[77]

A smaller number of trial judge advocates were chosen from the ranks and then commissioned as officers. Leon Adler, a Baltimore attorney, enlisted in late 1917 and was sent to training at Camp Hancock, Georgia, and Fort Meade, Maryland, to become a signals soldier. Had Adler been trained as a commissioned officer, he would have been deprived of an enlisted military experience that ultimately helped him gain an understanding of the rigors of military life. He recorded that on January 9, 1918, he "spent a strenuous day with shovel in hand in training in Macon Georgia," but as the day closed the army promoted him to sergeant. On April 18, the army sent him to Pittsburgh to train as an ordnance specialist, and on May 1, 1918, transferred him back to Camp Hancock, Georgia. His diary entry, "Reverted back to a private due to Army loss of my records," appears to have been a resigned recognition of shortcomings in the War Department's bureaucracy.

During the month of May 1918, Adler "bunked with Privates Allen, France, Newkirk, Grady, and Siebert, all college graduates and a great bunch of fellows"; he dug ditches—he wondered whether the army would use him for anything other than digging; spent a week on "Kitchen Patrol duty"; "ate three rotten meals"; and investigated two suicides. On May 12, he hopefully recorded: "After a couple of hours of drill we get to class and go straight through until 8 o'clock. I am going to stop taking baths and be connected with personal affairs. I may be mistaken but it seems to be intensifying. I am still swiping cigarette butts and drinking bad coffee." At the beginning of June, he counted twenty-five lawyers who were enlisted as privates in his training brigade, all on "fatigue duty." On August 20, he reported to an officers' training camp at Fort

Meade, and while waiting for the formal training to begin, he was assigned to serve as a trial judge advocate on seven general courts-martial, including one manslaughter charge. Mendel Smith supervised him in these duties. The army promoted Adler to first lieutenant on November 1, 1918, and he was ordered to "ship out to France in January 1919." Had the war continued, he would have been assigned as a signals officer, but also he would have likely been commissioned as a judge advocate in the Eighteenth Division, assisting Mendel Smith. Instead, he was commissioned as a judge advocate on December 29, 1918, but demobilized two months later. For a citizen who had graduated from the University of Maryland's law school and practiced real estate law for six years, the opportunity to conduct military criminal trials was as unique an experience as was his basic training. Had the war never come, Adler would likely have been content to draft wills and estate protections for Baltimore's gentry. But in his own estimation, he "took responsibility to ensure that the soldiers accused of crimes in the seven courts-martial were fully prepared to defend their trials." Adler's caseload at Camp Meade was a microcosm of the total number of summary and special courts-martial in the Eighteenth Division. On November 1, 1918, Smith reported to the commanding general of the division that the two brigades assigned to the camp had, in the prior month, conducted sixteen general courts-martial, eighteen special courts-martial, and over three hundred summary courts-martial, which was the largest number of summary courts-martial trials in the division for any month since the war began.[78]

THE DISCIPLINING OF A CONSCRIPTED ARMY: MAY 1917–JUNE 1918

The new judge advocates who reported to the stateside training camps—called cantonments—began an experience that had no previous analog. In the Civil War, the formal training of soldiers could occur in as little as thirty days, and this abbreviated training remained the norm until after the Spanish American War. In World War I, the divisional-sized training in Texas, Kentucky, Georgia, Tennessee, and New York took months to accomplish, and when units of soldiers transited to France, their training continued. Judge advocates assigned to the National Guard became instrumental in the disciplining of whole divisions, which numbered on average over 25,000 soldiers. In some instances, recently commissioned judge advocates who weeks earlier were engaged in civilian practice became responsible for oversight of military discipline as well as sophisticated contracting and property law problems. Even some of the career judge advocates had difficulty adjusting to the army's rapid enlargement. In late December 1917 Colonel George Dunn advised

Major General John Ruckman, the commanding general of the Southern Department, that soldiers sentenced to short terms of confinement were exempt from drilling. Ruckman, in turn, shared Dunn's advice with other departmental commanders. Crowder excoriated Dunn after learning of his advice. It was true, Crowder conceded, that old army regulations had permitted exemption from drill for prisoners. But new regulations specifically mandated that prisoners "sentenced for minor offenses" continue to train with their units "in order that the man-power involved may be saved to the country and not be frittered away through confinement and detachment from training and service," Crowder lectured Dunn.[79]

Samuel Wilson's experience was likely typical of the early judge advocates involved in training. The Seventy-Seventh Division was ordered into existence on June 15, 1917, with its training to occur at Camp Upton, New York. On August 27, Major General J. Franklin Bell, the former chief of staff of the army, assumed command over the division, and over the next three days, Wilson and 1,500 fellow junior officers arrived. On September 10, the first drafted soldiers were brought into camp, and by October 17, there were 27,000 soldiers in training. The majority of these soldiers were from New York and New England. (In all, 58,000 men would pass through Camp Upton by war's end.) From October until early April when the division sailed for France, soldiers trained in infantry techniques, gas warfare, and basic military drill. On November 1, the division's judge advocate, Lieutenant Colonel Marian Howze, was assigned as General Bell's operations officer, and Wilson became the division's judge advocate. Between October 1, 1917, and April 1, 1918, the Seventy-Seventh Division conducted dozens of general and hundreds of special courts-martial ranging from murder and desertion to petty larceny. Wilson served as trial counsel on eight general courts-martial and reviewed over two hundred other trials. He also provided advice on protecting soldiers from civilian lawsuits and contracted with local merchants for construction materials and food. As an indication of how unprepared Camp Upton's command was to accomplish courts-martial, Wilson had to write to the publisher John Wiley and Sons to obtain "a copy of the latest edition of Winthrop's treatise on *Military Law and Precedents*." However, he did have some spare time on the weekends. Even as the division prepared to sail to France, he continued to draft appellate briefs for attorneys who had taken over his civilian cases. His wife was also able to travel to New York and lease a house near Camp Upton so that they could reside together on the weekends. And while he immediately assumed his military duties, he continued to advise Lexington's attorneys on his former civilian trial cases throughout the division's training in the United States.[80]

On August 22, 1917, Samuel Pepper received an order to report to Camp MacArthur in Waco, Texas, to begin training with the newly formed Thirty-Second Division. It took him only four days to travel from Detroit to Waco, and once at the divisional headquarters, he reported to General William G. Haan. The division's first court-martial occurred on October 15, and it involved two National Guard soldiers who deserted from the military post and tried to return home to Idaho. Both of the guardsmen were captured, prosecuted, and sentenced to a dishonorable discharge and one year in confinement. Within a week, a letter arrived from Senator Borah asking that the soldiers be given leniency and returned to the ranks. Pepper recommended to Haan's temporary replacement, General Henry Allen, to grant the two guardsmen leniency by reducing the sentence to two months of hard labor and then return them to the ranks, and Allen ultimately agreed to do so. Between August 1917 and January 1918, the majority of the courts-martial Pepper oversaw arose from either desertion or alcohol-related offenses such as fighting or being drunk on post. He also oversaw a court-martial for a unique military offense, which continues to occur during the modern military conflicts in Iraq and Afghanistan. A few soldiers refused to be inoculated against smallpox, and their refusal constituted a disobedience of lawful orders. Pepper sympathized with the soldiers who refused their inoculations, because he too suffered through a horrendous fever and diarrhea after his vaccinations. Nonetheless, he informed General Haan that the refusals, if permitted to pass, would weaken discipline. Pepper's advice to Haan essentially mirrored the modern practice of military law.[81]

The most serious general court-martial Major Mendel Smith reviewed arose from Private Jeff W. Lankford's murder of a corporal on October 20, 1918. Lankford, in full view of a mess hall, twice stabbed a corporal named Robert E. Nelson in the back of the head. The night before the murder, Lankford informed his barracks mates that he was "going to fuck up with Corporal Nelson if it cost fifteen years" and that "Nelson had given him a dirty deal." Nelson had, in fact, placed Lankford on kitchen patrol duty and then revoked Lankford's off-base pass after discovering that Lankford had hoarded bread. When, on October 19, Nelson confronted Lankford with evidence of the bread theft, Lankford lunged at Nelson, but Nelson struck Lankford in the mouth, which caused Lankford to require "hospital stitches." Not only did Lankford seek revenge, but after stabbing Nelson he shouted to the soldiers in the mess hall to "take the son of a bitch outside and let him die." Several newspapers, including the *Washington Times* and *Harrisburg Telegraph*, reported on the murder and trial.[82]

At trial, Lankford's defense counsel attempted to argue that he had acted in self-defense and only used the knife after Nelson assaulted him. But even

Lankford's own witnesses testified that Nelson only responded to Lankford after the first stabbing. Although Smith concluded that Lankford's guilt was obvious, in reviewing the record of trial he noted several troubling irregularities. The first had to do with the substitution of court-martial members throughout the trial. The influenza pandemic caused seven of the thirteen officers to be hospitalized, and in conformity with the Articles of War, the substituted members were read the record of trial in open court. But none of the witnesses was recalled for further questioning, and the trial judge advocate failed to tell the members they had the right to question them. Another shortcoming that Smith noted had to do with Lankford's defense counsel, who conceded that a bloody knife found by military police officers belonged to Lankford without demanding a further analysis of the knife. Smith also found "numerous departures from the established rules of evidence manifest in the asking of many improper leading questions by trial counsel."[83]

To Smith, the most troubling aspect of the trial had to do with Major Louis Korn, the trial judge advocate. Unlike many trial judge advocates who were new to the army and were not necessarily lawyers, Korn was a commissioned judge advocate who had earned a law degree from Georgetown University and previously served as a cavalry officer. However, Smith believed that Korn and the court-martial president colluded to limit Lankford's cross-examination rights. "In our system of trial there is no safe-guard more effective in testing the integrity of human testimony than the right of cross-examination with its generally recognized common law incidents," Smith advised. "No person should be required generally, to forfeit his life, liberty, or property without an opportunity of applying this test to the hostile witness." In spite of the trial's shortcomings, however, Smith recommended that the findings and sentence be approved because of the weight of the evidence against Lankford. "The necessity for his own defense as presented by him, under all the surrounding circumstances, was so improbable as to make the plea almost ridiculous. It is plain that the accused nursed, during the night before the killing, a deadly revenge," Smith concluded. The army executed Lankford on December 18, 1918, after Baker approved of the findings and sentence.[84]

The experience of John Philip Clayton Boynton Hill provides another example of how the army was built and disciplined in the first year of the United States' entry into the war. Unsurprisingly, on July 29, 1917, when the Twenty-Ninth Division formed out of Maryland, Virginia, New Jersey, and West Virginia National Guard units, the War Department promoted Hill to the rank of lieutenant colonel and assigned him as the division's judge advocate. His attentions were redirected from studying the German Army to military discipline in the American Army. From 1917 until it departed for

France in June 1918, the Twenty-Ninth Division trained at both Camp Meade, Maryland, and Camp McClellan, Alabama. On December 1, 1917, rumors circulated through the army that the War Department would permit almost a quarter of the soldiers in training to be on furlough until the New Year. The rumor proved false; no more than 5 percent of the army was permitted leave. As the division trained over the Christmas holidays, fifteen hundred soldiers determined to take "French Leave," a term for AWOL. Between January 2 and February 1, 1918, the Twenty-Ninth Division conducted over two hundred special courts-martial, which resulted in demotions, loss of pay, and prison sentences averaging two weeks. But no dishonorable discharges were issued because of the limited jurisdiction of the special courts-martial. The high number of AWOL cases stemmed from the location of the division's training cantonments. Most of the soldiers came from Maryland, eastern Pennsylvania, Delaware, West Virginia, and New Jersey, and as a result, the travel of soldiers to their homes did not require a great amount of time or distance. However, because of the war's strain on the railroads, many of the soldiers were unable to return to their training before being caught. On the other hand, the division also adjudicated eighty general courts-martial before it shipped to France. Sixteen officers were dismissed after being found guilty of such offenses as being drunk on duty and failure to obey a superior officer.[85]

While singular examples of courts-martial enable some understanding of military law during the war, a broader analysis of the army's wartime discipline while it trained in the United States requires quantification in the form of the number of general courts-martial. That is, the general courts-martial of soldiers in training could both remove miscreants from the ranks as well as serve as a deterrent to all soldiers. Of course, innocent soldiers could be tried and convicted as well. Approximately four million soldiers went through training in the United States. Of these, two million were shipped to France to become part of the American Expeditionary Forces. Out of the four million who trained, slightly less than 11,400 were prosecuted in general courts-martial in the United States. There were over 125,000 special courts-martial conducted as well, but the majority of these trials resulted in reductions of rank, fines, and hard labor or imprisonment for periods of less than a month.

Early in the war, it was clearly evident that there was a disparity of punishments for similar offenses, even in courts-martial conducted within the same month in the same command. On December 17, 1917, a general court-martial held at Governors Island, New York, sentenced Private First Class John N. Mitchell to five years in confinement and a dishonorable discharge after finding him guilty of breaking into a house and assaulting a woman "with the intent to inflict great bodily harm to her." Two months later, a court-martial convicted Private John A. McLoud for assault with intent to commit rape and sentenced him to twenty years in confinement and a dishonorable discharge. Although the records of trial do not record the facts of either crime, both Mitchell's and McLoud's offenses occurred at the same New York City address.[86]

According to the General Courts-Martial Offense Ledger Sheets for trials in the United States, beginning in May 1917 and ending in June 1918, forty-one soldiers were court-martialed for impersonating an officer. While the most severe sentence adjudged was twenty years in confinement and a dishonorable discharge, over half of the convicted soldiers were sentenced to six months in confinement and no discharge at all. Two thousand one hundred sixty soldiers were court-martialed in a general court-martial for the purely military offenses of sleeping on post while assigned as a sentinel, being drunk while serving as a sentinel, abandoning a sentinel post, or provoking or insulting a sentinel in the performance of the sentinel's duties. More than 90 percent of these cases resulted in a conviction, and the overwhelming majority of those resulted in a sentence of less than three months' imprisonment. However, for an army about to deploy into the frontline trenches and artillery batteries in France, the fear of sentry posts being abandoned and trenches fled caused the army's commanders to vigorously prosecute such purely military offenses. Likewise, disrespect to a superior commissioned officer and disrespect to a superior noncommissioned officer were vigorously prosecuted, though the numbers of these offenses were in the hundreds rather than thousands.[87]

One thousand six hundred seventy-nine general courts-martial were adjudicated for the crime of larceny, and of these approximately one-fifth resulted in a finding of not guilty. The sentences ranged from a reprimand to fifteen years in confinement and a dishonorable discharge, but with an average of roughly six months in confinement and no discharge. One problem with comparing this category of sentences is that larceny can range from anything as simple as the theft of a watch to the theft of thousands of dollars. Larceny as an offense appears to have been the most numerous general court-martial offense as the army built up its strength. Second to larceny as a widespread offense was the crime of robbery, which resulted in over one hundred courts-martial but with similar statistical results. The difference between larceny and robbery under the Articles of War is that the latter offense was defined as a theft committed in a house or dwelling, and carried with it a greater possible punishment.[88]

One hundred forty-three soldiers were prosecuted in general courts-martial for the crime of murder in the United States. Of these, almost half the trials resulted in an acquittal, while one death sentence was adjudged, three soldiers were sentenced to life, and the rest to terms of years. Fifty-nine soldiers were court-martialed for manslaughter, with nineteen of these resulting in an acquittal. What may perhaps appear shocking is the leniency of some of the sentences. On January 4, 1918, a general court-martial conducted in the Eastern Department determined that Private John W. Nungesser was guilty of killing Private Hugh E. Hasson with a .45 caliber army pistol following an argument at a shooting range. But the general court-martial sentenced Nungessor to only one year in confinement. Nungessor's crime was deemed to be manslaughter, but the irresponsible nature of his actions, which resulted in the death of another soldier, might have been thought to merit a sentence closer to the ten-year maximum rather than simply one year in confinement.[89]

Eighty-five general courts-martial were conducted for the offense of mutiny in the United States, with nine soldiers given fifteen years as the harshest sentence being adjudged. On the other hand, approximately one-third of the trials resulted in an acquittal. However, soldiers found guilty of mutiny in the American Expeditionary Forces were sentenced far more harshly. Other offenses included loaning money at usurious rates of interest charged under the Eighty-Eighth Article, and refusing to submit to a surgical operation, as a violation of lawful orders. The sentences for these offenses ranged from a reprimand to two years in confinement.

Another aspect of quantifying the army's discipline during training is the Judge Advocate General's Office's directions to the stateside divisional and departmental commands. Prior to the war, it had customarily taken thirty days for the record of a general court-martial to reach the Judge Advocate General's Office, be reviewed, and be transmitted to the secretary of war for final determination. Beginning in the fall of 1917, Crowder informed the fielded judge advocates that in some instances, courts-martial that had been conducted in April had yet to reach Washington, DC. In June 1918, Major Mendel Smith, then assigned to Camp Wadsworth, South Carolina, informed Crowder that a lack of trained trial judge advocates, court members, and reporters caused delays in the earlier courts-martial, but as a result of the camp's commanding general issuing an order requiring all general court-martial records to be authenticated within forty-eight hours of the trial, no court-martial held after April 1918 had taken more than a month to be forwarded to Washington, DC. However, the rush to forward the records resulted in several omissions, which caused other delays.[90]

Also, on March 7, 1918, Crowder directed all of the stateside judge advocates to inform officers serving in a temporary duty prosecuting courts-martial that too many judge advocates had disregarded the rules favoring joint trials when more than one offender had been alleged to have committed an offense. One purpose underlying the preference for joint trials was to prevent a soldier accused of an offense from being ordered to testify against other soldiers, particularly with a promise of leniency. Crowder believed that such promises enabled perjured testimony to result in wrongful convictions. At the same time he admonished the fielded judge advocates to comply with this rule, he also lauded Captain Edward Greenbaum after Greenbaum advised that eighty soldiers charged with the offense of failure to obey orders should not be court-martialed at all. Medical personnel had classified the soldiers as "encumbered by a sluggish mentality," and therefore Greenbaum determined the soldiers were unfit for infantry duties altogether. Instead, the "dull and stupid" soldiers were assigned as stevedores. On the other hand, the stevedores were African American conscripts, and Greenbaum's description also evidenced the prevailing prejudices both within the War Department as well as in society.[91]

THE DISCIPLINE OF THE ARMY AND AFRICAN AMERICAN SOLDIERS

Three hundred fifty-seven thousand African American citizens served in the army during World War I, and the majority of these men were conscripted. The wartime experiences of African American soldiers, or for that matter, the nation's "colored citizenry"—as Crowder referred to African Americans—is deserving of more than mention in a few chapters, but this topic is not the primary focus of this book. Nonetheless, because the War Department, like the nation, treated African American soldiers differently than it treated Caucasian soldiers, it is essential to note these differences both in the conscripting and training of the army, in the American Expeditionary Forces, and in the War Department's approach to suspected subversive activity. Military law was designed to be colorblind in its application to courts-martial. The judge advocate general's *Digest of Opinions* had removed any mention of witness competency based on race or religion, and courts-martial were supposed to permit the testimony of African American witnesses, even when such witnesses testified against white soldiers. However, a colorblind law alone could not remove the prejudices of military officers and civilian leadership within the War Department.[92]

Despite the fact that African Americans had honorably fought in the Revolution, the War of 1812, the Civil War, several Indian conflicts, and the Spanish-American War and Philippine Insurrection, they continued to face a virulent prejudice in which whites doubted their discipline, bravery, and integrity. In 1906 a white bartender and a Hispanic police officer were killed in Brownsville, Texas. Local residents focused their suspicions on the soldiers of the Twenty-Fifth Infantry Regiment, which consisted of "colored soldiers." There was a marked tension between the soldiers and local residents arising from overt white prejudice and legalized segregation. The soldiers had, after all, been assigned to protect the local citizenry from incursions from Mexico and Native Americans, but they encountered hostility from the white and Hispanic population. Although a Texas Ranger attempted to implicate some of the soldiers for the murders, an army inspection determined, after interviewing the Twenty-Fifth's white officers, that there was no possibility the soldiers had taken part in the shooting. Nonetheless, President Theodore Roosevelt dismissed 167 African American soldiers from the army. None of the soldiers was court-martialed, but their retirements and pensions were lost as a result. Judge Advocate General George Davis supported Roosevelt's authority to dismiss the soldiers, and although Crowder voiced his objection on due process grounds, he too conceded that Roosevelt had the authority as commander in chief to discharge the soldiers. The soldiers attempted to bring suit against Roosevelt in a habeas action, but Roosevelt, represented by United States Attorney and future secretary of war Henry L. Stimson, prevailed. In Congress, Senator William Borah led a majority of legislators to support Roosevelt over those who supported the aggrieved soldiers.[93]

Just as President Wilson displayed an open bigotry against African American citizens, so too did prejudice against African American soldiers permeate the Judge Advocate General's Office. While it is difficult to find in Crowder's correspondences any overtly derogatory statements, it is not hard to find distasteful references to "colored soldiers" or "negroes," or derogatory terms, in some of the other judge advocates' correspondences. On January 2, 1918, Major Edwin McNeil, the Ninetieth Division's judge advocate, reported to Crowder that "colored soldiers were marrying to enable a government allowance of $15.00 per month for their new spouse simply to get more money." He asked Crowder to work to initiate a policy prohibiting the allowances for "colored marriages which occurred after induction into the Army." Crowder, however, refused to create a policy based on race. In another matter, Senator Tillman forwarded complaints from South Carolina constituents about the presence of African American soldiers training in that state. The senator also suggested that the War Department could order such soldiers in training to plant and harvest crops for the local farmers as a means of reducing food prices. Although Crowder normally responded to legislative inquiries, he chose to ignore Tillman on this matter, drawing Tillman's ire. Whatever Crowder may have felt about African American conscripts, he found Tillman's demagoguery repulsive.[94]

Major Guy Despard Goff, the son of a West Virginia senator, referred to colored soldiers as "darkies" and "rastus" and relayed to his father that they were "the least capable and most untrustworthy of all soldiers." William Mellard Connor, a South Carolina–born judge advocate who served in the Philippines during the war and was instrumental in later assisting Crowder and the War Department to resist Ansell's and congressional attempts at altering courts-martial, wrote to his father that "the one way of handling the negro is the Southern way, which some-day the rest of the country will learn." In this same letter, Connor related in an anecdotal story he believed to be humorous that "negro soldiers" could not be made to understand that desertion was an offense. Notwithstanding that thousands of "colored soldiers" had taken part in beating his home state into submission during the Civil War, he refused to acknowledge the contributions that such men made toward Germany's defeat. This attitude was shared by Lieutenant Colonel Hugh Ogden, the judge advocate for the "Rainbow Division," who wrote to his wife that "negro soldiers … haven't any of them guts and would run away just as soon as they were shelled." Ogden had no personal knowledge of this claim, but he believed the rumors of African American cowardice to be true and conveyed them as such to his family.[95]

One month after the nation's entry into the war, white violence against African Americans in East Saint Louis became widespread to the point that Governor Frank Lowden ordered the National Guard to police the city. American metal and packing industries hired African Americans, to the consternation of white labor unions whose leaders argued that the corporate owners had acted to undercut wages. Union leaders initiated a strike in mid-June 1917. In Illinois, there was no prohibition against African Americans voting, and the African American residents in East Saint Louis had become an important local political power. On July 2, after a newspaper reporter was shot at and two police officers were shot at and killed during the strike, thousands of white residents assaulted African Americans in the city. Over six thousand African American families were left homeless as whites committed arson in African American residential areas, and between 30 and 150 African Americans were killed. When Lowden removed the state guardsmen in late June, a federalized guard unit remained in place because the strike had occurred at an aluminum plant that Baker considered to be a vital war industry. Although community leaders criticized the National Guard for its inability to ensure the safety of the city's African Americans, Crowder supported the use of the National Guard to stop riots, whether caused by white or black agitation, but he remained reticent to advise using the federalized guard soldiers to participate alongside the guard in police-like activities such as quelling riots.[96]

On August 23, 1917, an African American soldier attempted to assist an African American woman during an arrest by Houston police officers. The police beat the soldier in view of a crowd and then arrested him. Later that day, an African American corporal went to the police station to retrieve the soldier, and he too was beaten and arrested. Houston was a segregated city, and several of the African American soldiers stationed near the city were long-serving veterans who had good reason to distrust the local authorities. But what followed was a breakdown in military discipline. That evening over one hundred armed soldiers from the Twenty-Fourth Infantry Regiment left their post and confronted both the police and white supporters of the police department. By the next morning four soldiers, four police officers, and twelve civilians had been killed. Two white soldiers who had been mistaken for policemen were also killed. Officers commanded the African American soldiers not to leave their posts, but the soldiers ignored their officers. General Ruckman ordered 169 soldiers confined in a roughly constructed military prison. He also directed most of the regiment's other soldiers to return to their New Mexico post. However, because San Antonio was the location for the confined soldiers' courts-martial, the distances between the sites of the offenses, the trials, and the regiment made it more difficult to secure witnesses.[97]

The army conducted three general courts-martial in which groups of soldiers were jointly prosecuted. The first court-martial resulted in thirteen soldiers being sentenced to death. The second court-martial resulted in another fifteen soldiers convicted, with five sentenced to death, and a third court-martial, in which forty soldiers were prosecuted, resulted in twenty-three verdicts of guilty and eleven death sentences. Combined, these three courts-martial were the largest mass military trial in American history, including the various war crimes trials following World War II. Colonel Hull served as the trial judge advocate, and he was assisted by Major Dudley V. Sutphin, a recently commissioned judge advocate. Born in Ohio in 1875, Sutphin attended Yale University for his undergraduate degree and, for his legal education, the University of Cincinnati's law school. By 1914 he had become a well-known litigator in Ohio. Taft recommended Sutphin to Crowder in 1917, and he was one of the first civilians to obtain a judge advocate commission after the declaration of war. Both Hull's and Sutphin's assignment to prosecute the trials came as a result of an appointment order from Ansell. Dunn, the judge advocate for the Southern Department, reported that the results of the trials were fair in all respects.[98]

Between the first and second court-martial, the War Department issued General Order 7, a regulation that required either Baker or Wilson to approve all sentences of death before any execution could be carried out. This regulation was primarily designed to prevent a "shot at dawn" approach to courts-martial that had been endemic to the British and French armies, and it was not issued only because of the Houston riot trials. Wilson would ultimately approve of six more death sentences from these trials. After several congressmen wrote to Baker asking for him to convince Wilson to commute the remaining death sentences, Wilson ordered all sentences of execution to be commuted to terms in prison. Problematic to the courts-martial were that only one lawyer was assigned to defend the accused soldiers. Not all of the soldiers accused of participating in the riot and shooting were equally culpable, and several soldiers were likely innocent of any wrongdoing. Thus, the soldiers did not all share in the same legal defenses. The conduct of the first trial angered Crowder because Dunn and Hull failed to notify him as well as Baker of the outcomes, and he believed that the grouping of the defendants into three trials was in error. On December 12, 1917, Ansell wrote to Crowder that both Ruckman and Dunn were ineffective and that given the short time between the announcement and sentence, Dunn could not possibly have conducted a thorough review. Some soldiers were, in fact, executed before Crowder, Baker, or Wilson knew of the outcome of the first trial, and as a result, neither Baker nor Wilson had the opportunity to overturn the first trial's verdicts or grant clemency had they decided to.[99]

Without question, the results of the so-called Houston Riot trials were an injustice, though even W. E. B. DuBois conceded that the soldiers' refusal to follow orders was a significant breach of discipline. Crowder concluded that because Baker had determined to create a whole division from African American soldiers to send to fight in France, these soldiers had to be confident that the administration of military justice was fairly conducted. Indeed, two divisions were ultimately created of African American soldiers, and although the majority of African American conscripts served as stevedores or in other non-combat tasks, the two divisions, numbering roughly fifty thousand soldiers, participated in the major engagements of the war's final summer and fall. To this end, Crowder urged the commission of the first African American judge advocate in the nation's history. On January 20, 1918, Adam E. Patterson was commissioned judge advocate. Patterson was born in 1876 in Walthall, Mississippi, but in his childhood his parents moved him to Kansas City. In 1917 he became the Ninety-Second Division's judge advocate. For over a century African American soldiers had been prosecuted in courts-martial without any representative court-martial panels or representation in the legal administration of military justice. Now, for the first time in American history, an African American officer oversaw military justice within a division. Patterson earned his undergraduate and law degrees at the University of Kansas and worked as a federal employee in Oklahoma. In 1913 President Wilson nominated him as a register of the Treasury Department, but withdrew his nomination after southern Democrat congressmen threatened to refuse to confirm his nomination. Oswald Garrison Villard championed Patterson for the register position as well as to Crowder for a judge advocate commission, and in doing so he called Wilson a coward for succumbing to Tillman and Vardaman. Patterson initially earned a commission with the rank of captain, but his performance as a trial judge advocate brought him to Crowder's attention and by the end of 1917 he was promoted to major.[100]

THE COURT, THE JUDGE ADVOCATE GENERAL, AND THE WAR EFFORT

When the Supreme Court upheld the constitutionality of selective service in what became known as the *Selective Draft Law Cases*, more appropriately titled *Arver v. United States*, the justices did so not only with the facts presented by the petitioners who contested the constitutionality of conscription, but also with an understanding of how the War Department's discipline was administered and who administered this discipline, and equally, if not more importantly, with insight into how the United States' entry into the world war had altered the nation's civil-military construct. In retrospect it is unsurprising that the Court affirmatively answered the question of whether the Constitution enabled the conscription of citizens into a federal army, but that the Court did so unanimously requires greater analysis of its reasons beyond the plain language of the decision. Crowder had cultivated a relationship with Brandeis through Frankfurter, and he had corresponded with Chief Justice Edward Douglass White. When Wilson became president, the Supreme Court consisted of White and Horace Harmon Lurton, both Civil War veterans of the Confederate army; Holmes, a Civil War veteran of the Union army; and William Rufus Day, Willis Van Devanter, Joseph McKenna, Mahlon Pitney, Joseph Lamar, and Charles Evans Hughes.[101]

By the end of Wilson's first term, Lurton and Lamar had died and Hughes had left the Court to contest the presidency in 1916. All three of these justices would have likely sided with the administration's war measures. Wilson's three judicial appointments, James McReynolds, Louis Brandeis, and John Hessin Clarke, supported parts of Wilson's progressive policies but for different reasons. McReynolds had initially served as Wilson's attorney general and prior to holding that position he had been a staunch antimonopolist. In other matters he turned out to become one of the Court's most conservative members. He also was the Court's most outspoken bigot in the twentieth century. Neither

Baker nor Crowder directly corresponded with McReynolds on selective service, courts-martial, or Executive Branch authority in wartime. But as Wilson began to accept the need to prepare the nation for a possible war, McReynolds privately told James O'Laughlin, the editor of the *Army-Navy Journal*, that he supported conscription in principle. He added that it was best left to the civil government, rather than the military, to administer a draft. O'Laughlin regularly corresponded with Crowder, and he passed along McReynolds's opinion to him. Whether Crowder used it to formulate the draft conscription legislation is unknown, but it cannot be missed that Crowder at least knew the opinion of one justice prior to formulating how conscription would occur. Crowder also likely knew of Justice Day's support for the War Department's conception of conscription. In April 1917, Day met with Crowder, Secretary of State Lansing, and Field Marshal Joseph Joffre, the French "hero of the Marne," and the four men discussed the need for a rapidly built American army. From Crowder's perspective, the most important product of this meeting was not the justice's endorsement of conscription, but rather, a "gentlemen's agreement" he entered into with Joffre. Joffre promised to lobby the French War Ministry to permit the United States to extend its full jurisdiction over American soldiers and limit the French courts from prosecuting Americans during the conflict. French officials had approved of the "gentlemen's agreement" by the time Pershing and his advance force organized in France. On March 22, 1918, the British government amended the Defense of the Realm Act to likewise recognize the United States' exclusive jurisdiction over American soldiers. There is no record that Justice Day participated in the actual discussion with Joffre, but he was present to see the "gentlemen's agreement" created.[102]

While it would be an overstatement to attribute to Brandeis the lion's share of credit among the justices for guiding the Court to its wartime decisions expanding Executive Branch authority, he was, perhaps, the Court's most important contributor to conscription as well as the War Department's ability to discipline its forces. As the Court's leading liberal, he was the most likely to dissent against governmental encroachments into individual liberties, but he did not do so until after the war. After the Senate confirmed Brandeis to the Court in 1916, Crowder sought him for advice on a variety of War Department matters. In 1916 Brandeis recommended Wambaugh and Wigmore to Crowder for reserve judge advocate commissions, and there is ample evidence that shortly before the declaration of war, both Wigmore and Frankfurter gave Brandeis a copy of Crowder's draft conscription bill. Moreover, on April 14, 1917, Wallace P. Donham, a future dean of the Harvard Business School, met with General Bliss and presented Bliss with a proposed law for compulsory military training that he had written for the Massachusetts Legislature. The intent of the state law was to require all males between the ages of eighteen and thirty to train with the National Guard for one summer. Brandeis had assisted Donham in writing the bill the prior year, and, through Frankfurter, he shared the bill's draft with Crowder. Although Crowder was not familiar with the Massachusetts state constitution, he and Brandeis concluded that as written, the draft would withstand constitutional scrutiny in the federal courts.[103]

Like Brandeis, Clarke regularly corresponded with President Wilson and Secretary of War Baker on military matters and foreign policy. When Wilson nominated Clarke to the Court, he had hoped that Clarke would couple with Brandeis and Holmes to form a liberal judicial core. "I shall look forward with the greatest confidence to your winning real distinction as a member of that tribunal, upon which the country is so dependent for liberal and enlightened interpretation of its laws," Wilson wrote Clarke after his Senate confirmation in July 1916. In August 1916, Clarke conveyed to Wilson that the nation could tolerate conscription, but for it to be accepted, the means for getting civilians into the military establishment had to be run by the civil government and not the army. In December 1916, Clarke informed Wilson that he supported the administration's preparedness plans as well as the president's peace efforts. Wilson responded that of all of the jurists, he wanted Clarke to know he appreciated his "generous judgment."[104]

On April 3, 1917, the day following Wilson's war declaration speech to Congress, Clarke informed Wilson not only that the president had proved he was the only leader to "match the trying days ahead," but that William Rufus Day, a Roosevelt appointee to the Court, exclaimed, "I really think there is not another man in America who could have done so well." Throughout the conflict Clarke spoke publicly for a war without conquest and "a peace without victory." He applauded Wilson's communications with the Vatican and hoped that the combination of the president and pontiff could end the conflict through negotiation before the United States became involved in it. And most importantly from Wilson's perspective, he was a firm believer in the League of Nations.[105]

When, in 1916, Wilson became infuriated with General Leonard Wood's public political statements on military readiness, despite a presidential order to refrain from such conduct, Clarke, rather than Crowder, came to Wood's defense. This would not be the only time Clarke would do so, even when Wilson felt Wood's lack of support for the presidential direction of conscription caused the general to side with Theodore Roosevelt and undermine public support for conscription. On August 5, 1917, Clarke advised Baker that despite Wood's arrogance, "the general, in the fundamentals of integrity has no superior." At the end of that month Clarke informed Baker that he agreed that selective service was necessary to successfully prosecute the war. Thus, Wilson's three appointees were firmly on the side of upholding conscription, and neither Holmes nor White, the two remaining Civil War veterans, gave any indication of opposition. In October 1914, White mentioned to Vice President Thomas Marshall that he not only believed the German government to be in the wrong, but also that eventually the United States would have no choice but to enter the conflict on the side of the Allies.[106]

Arver arose from a consolidation of three appeals. On June 8, 1917, Joseph F. Arver and Otto H. Wangerin were indicted for draft evasion, and one month later they were prosecuted and found guilty of refusing induction into the army in the United States District Court of Minnesota. Almost contemporaneously, Alfred E. Grahl, Louis Kramer, and Meyer Grabaud were also convicted in the United States District Court for the Southern District of New York for refusing to register for the draft. Grahl's and Grabaud's appeals were consolidated into a single appeal because both had been convicted together. None of the five appellants had been prosecuted by the War Department in a court-martial, even though this had been a possibility. The Court would not, at any time during the war, grant an appeal from a court-martial. Indeed, from World War I through the end of conscription during the Nixon administration, the Court deferred to Congress on the basis of determining when and where court-martial jurisdiction began, rather than determining when a citizen could be court-martialed.[107]

At the same time the Court heard the appeals of draft resisters, it also considered appeals from prominent civilians who had publicly encouraged men to refuse to register for conscription. Charles E. Ruthenberg, Alfred Wagenknecht, and Charles Baker were prosecuted for encouraging citizens to refuse to register for selective service. All three of these citizens belonged to the Socialist Party. More notably, in a separate decision, the Court also considered the appeals of Emma Goldman and Alexander Berkman, two Russian-born immigrants who hybridized anarchism with communism. Berkman had previously been convicted for attempting to murder a wealthy industrialist after the Homestead Strike of 1892, and Goldman had likewise served time in prison for incitement to riot the following year. All of these appellants were convicted under the Espionage Act of 1917. During World War I, the Justice Department prosecuted citizens under this act for simply advocating that conscription violated God's commandments as well as those who called for the toppling of the government. However, none of the appellants before the Supreme Court had committed acts of violence in resisting conscription.[108]

It did not take long for the justices to determine the constitutionality of selective service. The Court heard argument in December 1917 and issued its unanimous decision on January 7, 1918. It is, perhaps, a small irony that Chief Justice White, a veteran of the Confederate army who had fought for, among other principles, states' rights and a limited federal power, authored the decision. White understood that World War I was a different conflict than the so-called "War Between the States." The Court's decision itself is not complex or deeply academic, and a number of scholars, particularly during the Vietnam Conflict, criticized the Court. Nonetheless, it became the foundation for not only a wartime draft for the First World War, but also for World War II and for the peacetime draft during the Cold War. Missed by most, if not all, of the critics of the decision was that Brandeis advised White to author a sparse decision.[109]

The petitioners in *Arver* had argued that the Constitution's militia clause restricted the federal government from conscripting citizens into the army, and instead, left to the individual states the responsibility to do so. Such an enlistment scheme had, after all, been in existence in the War of 1812, and more importantly, during the Civil War. The justices dismissed this contention with the simple answer that the Constitution expressly provided to Congress the authority "to raise and support armies." The Court concluded this part of its decision by noting that if it were only up to the states to conscript, the Constitution would be nullified. As to the broader constitutionality of drafting individuals into the military, the Court recognized that only one state appellate court had ever decided a challenge to conscription, and this occurred in Pennsylvania in 1863. The justices also pointed to several Confederate state supreme court decisions that enabled conscription. However, those decisions were of limited precedence since they rested on state, rather than federal, authority and the Confederacy did not possess an operative supreme court as a court of final review. Often missed in the constitutional analysis of the Court's decision was that the justices emplaced Emory Upton's work as a reason for the federal government not to rely on state militia conscription. As to the second argument advanced by the appellants—that because Congress had exempted theological students, ordained ministers, and religious sects that advocated total aversion to war, the government created a law favoring particular religious beliefs, thereby violating the Constitution's Establishment Clause— the justices dispensed with this argument with a short discussion and a notable lack of case law. The oddest aspect of the decision was the Court's use of the fact that other Western nations with democratic aspects to their governments had conscription to find that the Selective Service Act was constitutionally sound. Legal conservatives have historically disfavored the use of foreign or international law in American courts, but the justices made an exception with the challenge to conscription. Both the inclusion of Upton's work as well as the justices' use of the conscription practices of other nations were partly the Judge Advocate General's Office's contribution to the decision. Crowder and three of his subordinates—Warren, Wambaugh, and Wigmore—advised Solicitor General Davis to argue that the conscription programs of other nations with representative governments evidenced the constitutionality of conscription.[110]

CONCLUSION: THE DISCIPLINE OF THE NATION

It troubled Crowder that the Court never determined the constitutionality of extending court-martial jurisdiction to citizens called into military service who refused to comply with their draft order. Although he believed that such persons were essentially deserters, there was a debate between judge advocates such as Chiperfield, Frankfurter, and Wigmore, as well as politicians and academics who supported Crowder, against a small number of judge advocates along with a minority of legislators such as the Speaker of the House of Representatives, James Clark, who urged that military jurisdiction began when a civilian first donned a uniform and swore an oath of allegiance. On the other hand, this was the only aspect of the Court's decision that gave Crowder cause for concern. He realized that the justices could have believed that the administration of military justice was arbitrary and haphazard, and to this end, he had ensured that several of the nation's leading scholars, as well as state court judges, former legislators, and prominent attorneys whose jurisprudence and political ideology ranged from conservative to progressive, were commissioned as judge advocates. The Court could have granted certiorari from at least one decision in which a court of appeals determined that citizens who failed to enter the army after being ordered to do so by an induction notice could be court-martialed for desertion.[111]

Shortly after the Court's decision to grant certiorari to Arver's and Wangerin's challenges against conscription, Crowder, on Frankfurter's advice, concluded that the creation of a civilian-led board to review the condition of persons who were denied conscientious objector status and court-martialed or housed in military prisons, was necessary to ensure that in the future, the federal judiciary would continue to defer to the War Department. On Crowder's recommendation, Baker appointed Harlan Fiske Stone and Julian Mack, a United States District Court judge, to the board. In August 1917, Mack crafted a draft bill for Baker to send to Congress that would enable the War Department to withhold pay from soldiers in France until their return to the United

States. The purpose underlying this bill was to prevent comparatively well-paid American soldiers from inundating the French economy with dollars and causing inflation, which in turn would demoralize the French population. Notwithstanding the fact that it might have been considered a dangerous idea for a sitting federal judge to draft a law at the behest of the War Department and thereby abandon the Constitution's separation of powers, it is interesting that Pershing sought out Frankfurter as an intermediary with Mack to get the law passed.[112]

In addition to the War Department controlling the sale of alcohol off base, regulating bridge construction, and condemning foodstuffs that had yet to be contracted for, there were doubtless hundreds of other instances in which the military establishment, with the involvement and sometimes oversight of the Judge Advocate General's Office, asserted control over society. Regardless of whether the military establishment had encroached into the lives of ordinary American citizens beyond what the drafters of the Constitution intended, by the summer of 1918 as the American Expeditionary Forces had positioned themselves to begin an enormous offensive operation against the German Army, there was little doubt in the federal government that the army had been constitutionally created and disciplined.

4

JUDGE ADVOCATES IN THE AEF

WHEN GENERAL JOHN J. PERSHING sailed for France in June 1917, he brought with him Lieutenant Colonel Walter Bethel and Major Hugh A. Bayne, and Pershing expected that these two officers would remain his judge advocates for the duration of the war. In August, Bethel sent Bayne to London to serve as a liaison to Britain's chief of the imperial general staff for one month, and on his return Bayne was responsible for assisting in the creation of a supply command that later became known as the Services of Supply. Bethel's duties ranged from courts-martial review to what would be termed today as interoperability with the French, British, and Belgian armed forces, including financial obligations to foreign governments and citizens. He also advised Pershing on the extent of First Amendment rights of servicemen and of American prisoners, the status of civilian volunteer organizations, and law of war issues such as the treatment of German prisoners of war and the status of German properties. Throughout the war, Bethel and his staff authored most of the major administrative and legal orders applicable to the American Expeditionary Forces. Although the "gentlemen's agreement" crafted by Crowder and Joffre, and approved by the French War Ministry, precluded any French assertion of jurisdiction over American soldiers, one of Bethel's first actions was to draft an agreement with Paul Painleve, France's minister of war, to authorize American military police to arrest French soldiers who were caught committing offenses in American military encampments, and for French police to have the authority to arrest American soldiers throughout France. On August 5, 1917, Pershing turned to Bethel to draft an order for secrecy similar to the order Crowder had previously authored for the General Staff. Colonel John Hines, Pershing's temporary adjutant general, had noticed that senior officers stationed at Pershing's headquarters in Chaumont were heard openly discussing American troop movements at a cafe. Two days later Pershing signed Bethel's draft order without any editing. But of all Bethel's myriad duties, his primary focus was the discipline of the soldiers assigned to the American Expeditionary Forces.[1]

In some instances Bethel dissuaded Pershing from implementing disciplinary policies involving both imprisoned soldiers and prisoners of war. For example, Pershing wanted to establish a military disciplinary prison in France where long-term offenders would serve their sentences, rather than have such prisoners sent to the United States. He believed that sending convicted soldiers to the United States encouraged disaffected soldiers to commit crimes. But Bethel countered that from an efficiency standpoint alone, a military prison required guards, doctors, and cooks, and because transport vessels returning to the United States were generally empty of any cargo, the shipment of prisoners to the United States was of little cost to the government. More importantly to Bethel was that the removal of prisoners serving long sentences at hard labor reduced the chance of a prison riot in the main theatre of war. Bethel reminded Pershing that both the British Expeditionary Forces and the French Army had suffered through mutinies and riots. Pershing ultimately agreed with Bethel, and American prisoners who were sentenced to more than a year in confinement were shipped to military prisons at Governors Island, Alcatraz, and Fort Leavenworth. On the other hand, Bethel's suggestion to Pershing that all German prisoners of war captured by American soldiers be turned over to France did not gain Pershing's approval. Another instance in which Pershing determined that Bethel's advice was in error had to do with the American Expeditionary Forces' response to venereal disease. In January 1918, Bethel informed Pershing that it was likely that the federal courts would determine the army's withholding of pay from soldiers who contracted venereal disease to be unlawful because, unlike the statute governing the withholding of pay from deserters, no statute existed to withhold the pay of soldiers who contracted venereal disease. Pershing nonetheless determined to maximize the punishment as a deterrent against promiscuity. During the war dozens of soldiers were prosecuted in summary courts-martial for contracting the disease. Indeed, as of December 6, 1917, Bethel reported to Pershing that seventy summary courts-martial had been conducted in the aviation detachments alone. Yet Pershing was not always the more conservative of the two. Bethel advised Pershing to issue an order banning all marriages between American soldiers and French women for the duration of the war. However, Pershing determined that it was not in the best interests of the army, relations with France, or the morale of soldiers to issue such an order.[2]

After six months in Europe, Bethel articulated his conception of how a Judge Advocate General's Department in France would contribute to the war effort in a memorandum to Bliss and Crowder. He informed both generals that while the primary duty of the judge advocate was to advise on all disciplinary matters, in reality, at the higher headquarters including not only the American Expeditionary Forces, but also at the Corps level and at the Services of Supply, "disciplinary work constitutes a relatively small portion of the whole." Although Bethel miscalculated on how labor-intensive and time-consuming disciplinary matters were to become, he was correct in noting that "on account of the many statutes and regulations made pursuant thereto, perplexing legal questions continually arise in all branches of military administration and the advice of the Judge Advocate General's Office is therefore, sought." But this was not all, and he further explained, "the relations of the American military to the French government, the municipalities and the French people give rise to many legal questions of a novel nature requiring their solution a study of the French law and of international law." He concluded by noting that it was difficult, if not impossible, to define the limits of what judge advocates might be called on to do, and then asked for "one dozen or more judge advocates to work in his headquarters office." Crowder agreed to transfer more judge advocates to France but responded that it would take several months to do so. From this point forward the Headquarters Judge Advocate's Office in France would alternatively be referred to as the American Expeditionary Forces, Judge Advocate General's Department or the Judge Advocate General's Department in France.[3]

On April 20, 1918, German forces attacked elements of the American Expeditionary Forces' Twenty-Sixth Division near the town of Seicheprey, and while the Americans initially retreated, by the end of the day all of the ground initially lost was retaken. The division was placed into a French sector for training purposes, and its leaders did not expect an attack to occur. On May 28, 1918, American soldiers went into a divisional-sized action against the German Army at the Battle of Cantigny. Regardless of criticisms Allied generals levied against American military leaders, this was the first time that an American division confronted a first-rate European adversary on European soil, and American soldiers took and held their objective, the French town for which the battle was later named. From June 1 through June 28 of that year, American soldiers and marines fought in the Battle of Belleau Wood, first taking part in stopping a German offensive and then counterattacking. Again, this was an Allied victory. On July 28, US soldiers participated in the Battle of Chateau Thierry, prevailing over their German opponents. At the same time, American soldiers fought alongside the Australians at the Lys River and with the French in Soissons. By August 1, 1918, American soldiers had contributed to stopping the last of the major German offensives.[4]

All of the pre-September battles were minor in size compared to the British and French battles at Verdun and the Somme in 1916, and the "Nivelle" Offensive and Battle of Third Ypres (or Passchendaele) in 1917. However, on September 12, the American Expeditionary Forces went into battle to destroy a German salient at St. Mihiel, in which the operation was primarily American in nature and began with a coordinated air and artillery campaign. In three days, American forces, numbering one-half million soldiers, backed by four French divisions, routed a German army in the midst of a withdrawal action. After the destruction of the St. Mihiel salient, Pershing ordered a substantial number of soldiers into a northwestern transit to take part in what he believed would be a decisive offensive to push the German Army into a retreat from France so that in 1919 the war would continue into Germany. From September 26 through November 11, over one million American soldiers fought through the Argonne Forest and along the Meuse and Marne Rivers in conditions that rivaled those of the 1916 Verdun battle. Over 26,000 American soldiers were killed and over 90,000 injured while advancing against well-constructed German defensive positions and through poison gas and artillery barrages, machine gun fire, and exhaustion. At no time was there a mutiny, a unit-wide refusal to fight, or a discernable degradation of discipline in the American Expeditionary Forces.[5]

ESTABLISHMENT OF AN OFFICE OF THE JUDGE ADVOCATE GENERAL FOR THE AEF

By June 26, 1917, 14,000 American soldiers had arrived in France and transited to various staff and training centers. Two weeks earlier, Pershing, along with Bethel and Bayne, had docked at Boulogne and proceeded to a temporary headquarters in Paris. Crowder and Pershing earlier agreed that an office of the judge advocate general had to be created specifically for the American Expeditionary Forces. Because the expected size of the American Expeditionary Forces was to be over one million soldiers, it would be impossible to oversee its discipline from the United States. Pershing had already conceived that the enormous American divisions, at war's end forty-two in number, would eventually be formed into six corps controlled by two or more armies. An American division typically went into battle with over twenty-four thousand soldiers, making it almost twice the size of British and French divisions. On December 1, 1917, Bethel sent a message to the corps and divisional staffs that the American Expeditionary Forces were in need of judge advocates to serve in a semipermanent staff capacity at the divisional and corps levels, as well as in the various schools and rear echelon commands then being planned. Because of the rapid buildup of the army, he rightly assumed that hundreds of civilian lawyers had volunteered or were conscripted for military service, but with no clear War Department intention of having them serve as judge advocates. To this end, he asked the divisional and corps commands to actively seek out new officers who "practiced law for at least five years with excellent success." Bethel's request was one of the earliest, if not the first, important benchmarks for the Judge Advocate General's Department in the American Expeditionary Forces.[6]

Secretary of War Baker established a second important benchmark on January 17, 1918, when he issued General Order 7. This order prohibited the immediate implementation of a death sentence. An execution could not occur until the Judge Advocate General's Office or one of its designated branches in the United States had conducted a full review of the record of trial, and only with Baker's final approval could an execution be carried out. Additionally the order prohibited the dismissal of an officer from the army until a similar review was conducted. Essentially, this order meant that no soldier sentenced to be executed could be hung or "shot to death" unless either Baker or one of his designees had the opportunity to read through the judge advocate general's review or, if Baker so chose, the record of trial. The purpose underlying General Order 7, as Crowder explained to the fielded judge advocates, was to ensure that errors in trial would not result in a soldier suffering harsh punishment or death, and that given the number of recurring errors, the order was essential. Baker commensurately also ordered the establishment of "a branch of the office of the Judge Advocate General, at Paris, France, or at some other point convenient to the headquarters of the American Expeditionary Forces in France." This part of the order simply made official what Crowder, Bethel, Pershing, and Bliss had already begun. Baker made it clear in the order, however, that the judge advocate assigned to lead this branch would be "controlled in the performance of his duties by the Judge Advocate General of the Army." Thus, the judge advocate placed in charge of administering courts-martial would not directly fall under Pershing's authority, but rather would be responsible to Crowder. One day after the issuance of this order, Baker appointed Bethel to assume temporary charge of the branch office.[7]

One month later, Pershing cabled Crowder that he wanted Bethel to remain as his judge advocate. Problematic to Pershing's cable was that the day prior, Crowder had nominated Lieutenant Colonel Kreger to become the American Expeditionary Forces' judge advocate. Indeed, Crowder informed the fielded judge advocates on March 8, 1918, that Kreger was to become the "Judge Advocate General for the American Expeditionary Forces," and he placed Kreger in charge of ensuring compliance with General Order 7. To Pershing, because "all matters pertaining to courts-martial have been most faithfully and conscientiously handled by General Bethel," there was no reason that any other officer should fill this post. Crowder acquiesced to Pershing with the understanding that Kreger would assume the next important assignment in France. Kreger became the First Army's judge advocate in early 1918, and because Pershing was both the American Expeditionary Forces commander and, until August 1918, the commander of the First Army, there were overlapping duties between Bethel and Kreger. On July 6, 1918, Lieutenant Colonel Blanton Winship replaced Kreger as the First Army's judge advocate, but the overlapping duties remained a feature of legal practice in the American Expeditionary Forces. Kreger, in turn, became Crowder's representative in France, which required Bethel to pass on to Kreger all general court-martial records for review. While Kreger's posting was designed to add to the efficiency of the Judge Advocate General's Office, it irritated Pershing that there were multiple reviews for courts-martial convictions, and Kreger pointed this out to his wife when he described his duties as "deep but not broad." But Bethel had some blame in Kreger's remaining in France. As of April 5, 1918, Bethel had not formally organized the Judge Advocate General's Department in France, leading Crowder to angrily chastise him that regardless of Pershing's disagreement with General Order 7, Baker had mandated the creation of a headquarters judge advocate branch not only to expedite courts-martial review for transmission to the Judge Advocate General's Office, but also to ensure that in the future, both the president and secretary of war would be able to consider the propriety of executions and dismissals with the benefit of that judge advocate's review in hand.[8]

It is certain that General Order 7 angered Pershing and his senior ranking staff officers and corps commanders. After all, Crowder had taken it upon himself to draft the order for Baker to issue without consulting Pershing. Harbord, while serving as Pershing's chief of staff, argued that because General Order 7 enabled a junior officer not subject to Pershing's authority to halt the American Expeditionary Forces' commander's decision to execute a sentence of death or dismissal, the order was a flawed usurpation of command authority. "The commander in chief has at present, no power to hurry this review in order to make punishment more summary and this junior officer— independent of the commander in chief—is in a position to say that the C in C's sentence shall not be carried into effect," Harbord complained to Bethel, concluding that both he and Bethel needed to lobby Baker to reverse his order.

(By "C in C," Harbord meant Pershing and not President Wilson.). Harbord later went so far as to accuse Crowder of being "undependable" and of having sent Bethel to France to ensure that General Order 7 would remain in place. Pershing never accepted Harbord's criticism against either Crowder or Bethel, but he asked Baker to consider retracting the order. Likewise, General Charles Pelot Summerall took issue with General Order 7, arguing that "cowards and repeat stragglers would escape the summary punishment required to maintain discipline." Crowder and Bethel disagreed with Pershing, Summerall, and Harbord on the effect of General Order 7 and urged the generals to consider that the order would shield the army's discipline from reform efforts both during and after the war.[9]

Baker overturned the death sentences in four early general courts-martial, which further caused Pershing to complain to Bethel and Crowder. In February 1918 Baker commuted the sentences of Privates John Cook and Forrest Sebastian, who were found guilty of sleeping at their posts. Both soldiers were restored to their units, and Cook was later killed in the Aisne, while Sebastian was wounded in the Meuse-Argonne Offensive. Baker also commuted the sentences of Privates Stanley Fishback and Olen Ledoyen for their refusal to obey the orders of their officers to reconnoiter enemy lines in a dangerous patrol. Bethel noted, in his review of the four cases, that each of the four soldiers had been inadequately defended, but as a technical matter, each was also guilty. He quoted an observation of Emory Upton who claimed that because early in the Civil War, Lincoln had commuted several sentences, the Union army later required severe discipline. Pershing was particularly galled at the commutation of the two latter offenders' sentences because he believed if it became known that Baker would freely grant commutations, then discipline would erode. Ansell later claimed that Crowder favored executing all four soldiers. However, in a private meeting with Baker, Crowder passed to him a memorandum in which he noted that while it was important to support Pershing, the execution of the soldiers was unwarranted by the facts of each case. Moreover, Crowder included the research of another judge advocate, which evidenced that soldiers similarly convicted received terms of imprisonment in months rather than a death sentence. In a letter to Wilson, Baker cited the youth of the soldiers and the lack of a political reason for their actions as a basis for commuting the sentences, adding that the death penalty was best suited for armies in which men had been compelled to fight to enrich a sovereign. The four men, Baker concluded, had been conscripted into the army, and neither he nor Crowder believed in "ceremonial executions" such as what was occurring in the British and French armies.[10]

Bethel repeatedly stressed throughout the war that severe punishment could only be inflicted following a court-martial and that summary punishment such as shooting a soldier fleeing from the front was antithetical to the United States' military laws. As he built up a structure of judge advocates to serve the various command levels, he also wanted to ensure that courts-martial were conducted in both a fair and efficient manner, at least as "fair and efficient" was defined at the time. On April 18, 1918, he instructed the judge advocates attached to the various commands that they should not routinely serve as prosecutors in general courts-martial since they would also be called upon to review the records of trial for procedural reliability. He noted that thousands of lawyers could be found in the American Expeditionary Forces who could serve with zeal as both prosecutors and counsel for an accused soldier on a temporary basis, and he then informed the divisional judge advocates that while he was confident that accused officers had been well defended at courts-martial, he doubted whether enlisted soldiers had received "due care in the selection of their counsel." To this end, he made it clear that divisional commanders should not deny the appointment of experienced counsel for accused enlisted soldiers, and when such denials occurred, he expected to be immediately informed of the reasons why.[11]

While Crowder wanted Bethel and Kreger to have a wide degree of independence, he remained in contact with both officers and would occasionally reach beyond them to excoriate judge advocates who he believed had failed to adequately accomplish their duties. On April 13, 1918, Crowder admonished Captain Edward S. Greenbaum for failing to explain why, out of the twenty-two general courts-martial the Thirty-Third Division prosecuted for desertion in January, there were only seven convictions. Greenbaum had only recently arrived in France, but his response that the prosecuting judge advocate had been removed from duties did not satisfy Crowder, who further threatened Greenbaum that his own failure to achieve a higher conviction rate on desertion trials would result in his removal. Ultimately Kreger came to Greenbaum's aid and mollified Crowder by explaining that Greenbaum had discovered significant errors in other trials, which freed eleven wrongfully convicted soldiers from imprisonment.[12]

In January 1918, Bethel secured a formal written agreement from the French government that no American soldiers would be prosecuted in French criminal courts. This made the gentlemen's agreement binding on both the American Expeditionary Forces and the French government. Three months later both the Belgian and British governments also agreed to the principle of sole jurisdiction being vested in the American military. However, no agreement was arrived at as to whether French, Belgian, or British courts could issue garnishment orders against the pay of American soldiers who damaged property. All three Allied governments stated a preference for American military commanders to determine when to honor garnishment orders. To this effect, the examination of damage claims became a commonplace duty, alongside courts-martial reviews, for the American Expeditionary Forces' judge advocates.[13]

EARLY COURTS-MARTIAL AND THEIR "ANATOMY" IN THE AMERICAN EXPEDITIONARY FORCES

One of the first questions in military law is not simply whether the military possesses jurisdiction over a citizen who happens to be in uniform, but which officer has the authority to convene a court-martial. Under the American Expeditionary Forces construct, general courts-martial could be convened by Pershing, the commander of the Services of Supply, and the commanders of numbered armies, corps, and divisions. With the exception of the enormous Services of Supply, all general courts-martial sentences had to be either approved or disapproved at the American Expeditionary Forces headquarters. Thus, any soldier convicted in a general court-martial could appeal for redress to the American Expeditionary Forces headquarters. This construct reflected the Eighth Article of War, but it did not account for the authority of the myriad separate commands found throughout France, Belgium, Italy, and Britain. It took until September 10, 1918, to confirm that the commanding officers of "separate brigades," such as the various coastal artillery brigades or railroad brigades, could not convene general courts-martial unless Pershing had earlier expressly authorized this authority. On November 15, 1918, Pershing, on Kreger's advice, returned sixty-four general courts-martial convictions and sentences that had been convened by four separate coastal artillery brigades. Because of the "evolutionary complexity" of the American Expeditionary Forces structure, Pershing had never authorized the four brigades to convene general courts-martial. When approached by Kreger as to whether Pershing could retroactively confer authority, Majors Arthur Hill, Patrick Cosgrave, and C. V. Porter cited Winthrop's *Military Law and Precedents* and advised that "retroactivity was a legal impossibility." Bethel ultimately agreed with the three judge advocates, and as a result Private Claude F. Curtis, who had been convicted of murder and sentenced to five years' imprisonment and a dishonorable discharge, and sixty-three other soldiers convicted of lesser sentences, were freed from their convictions and prison terms. While Major General Ernest J. Hinds, the American Expeditionary Forces chief of artillery, was offended at the result, Pershing appears to have accepted Kreger's reasoning that these courts were held without proper jurisdiction and those soldiers convicted in them had to be freed. Pershing also accepted Bethel's advice that double jeopardy did not prevent retrials for the "most serious offenses."[14]

Although most of the American Expeditionary Forces' courts-martial occurred from the summer of 1918 through the first four months of 1919, military trials were conducted from the time the first brigades arrived in France, and Pershing's conception of military discipline can be discerned in the army's initial trials in France. Between August 1, 1917, and the close of that year, the American Expeditionary Forces conducted sixteen general courts-martial in which all but one of the accused soldiers were found guilty of at least one of the specifications under which they had been charged. One court-martial ended in a death penalty while the others resulted in sentences ranging from a reprimand to imprisonment to a dismissal from the army. Major Bayne conducted the initial reviews of most of the courts-martial before Bethel advised Pershing on a proper disposition for the convicted soldiers.[15]

Private Frank Cadue's court-martial sentenced him to death after adjudging him guilty of raping and murdering a seven-year-old French girl. Cadue confessed to French military police and admitted to the court-martial that he had committed the rape and murder, but he claimed he was intoxicated and did not know that he had murdered the victim. Despite Bethel's concern over the rapidity with which British courts-martial sentences were carried out, it is noteworthy that on October 20, 1917, Cadue committed the offense, two days later the army held the court-martial, and two weeks later, on November 5, he was hung. Even before General Order 7, the two-week interlude between the sentence and Cadue's execution gave both Baker and Wilson the time to intervene and either overturn the court-martial or order clemency, but neither did so. While the *New York Times, Washington Post,* and other city newspapers such as the Carlsbad, New Mexico, *Evening Current* and Ogden, Utah, *Standard* reported on Cadue's court-martial and execution, he did not garner any notable public sympathy.[16]

Throughout the war, Pershing was particularly forceful on criminal conduct that victimized French citizens, and he set a tone for maximizing punishment for this class of offenders from the start. A month before Cadue's trial, the army prosecuted a Private Joseph McGlade for stealing 84 francs from a civilian. The court-martial found McGlade guilty and sentenced him to nine months in confinement and a dishonorable discharge. Pershing added a reprimand of sorts to the execution of the sentence, which read: "The sentence, though inadequate, is approved and will be duly executed. The Atlantic Branch, United States Disciplinary Barracks, Governors' Island,

New York, is designated as the place of confinement, to which prisoner will be sent." Unlike in the cases of hundreds of other convicted soldiers, the War Department never restored McGlade to duty.[17]

Nine of the first seventeen courts-martial were of officers whose offenses ranged from being drunk on duty to making false statements. To Pershing, Captain Leroy Overpeck was the most egregious of the offending officers. Overpeck brought a French woman into a barracks and had sexual intercourse with her in front of his lieutenants. That the woman was likely a prostitute and the sexual intercourse fully consensual was of no consequence to Pershing. The court-martial sentenced Overpeck to a dismissal but recommended clemency. "The recommendation of the members of the court-martial for clemency cannot be favorably considered because of the nature and gravity of the offense of which the accused has been found guilty," Pershing wrote on the order executing the sentence. Bethel had, in this instance, recommended reducing Overpeck's punishment to a reprimand, but Pershing countered that officers had to be held to the highest standard in order to command enlisted forces to fight.[18]

Of the enlisted soldiers court-martialed, the most significant trial, other than that of Cadue, arose from the killing of a French civilian by Private Leo Renn. Although Renn shot an adult civilian, the court-martial found him innocent of murder or of any lesser criminal degree of guilt. What appears to have occurred is that during the night of September 3, 1917, an intoxicated Frenchman failed to announce himself while Renn was on guard duty, and Renn mistook the man for a German. Bethel advised an agreeing Pershing that the acquittal was warranted and, moreover, French officials including General Henri Petain supported the acquittal. On the other hand, Pershing, against Bethel's advice, determined not to support clemency for a Private Norman Rhodes, who, on October 17, publicly criticized Captain George S. Patton, stating, "the damned captain is no good. I wish some of these sons-of-bitches would report me, I would tell the son of a bitch of a troop commander where to get off at." Rhodes, a career soldier, also proclaimed that he was Dutch and therefore only loyal to the Netherlands, a neutral country. Rhodes had twice previously been court-martialed but was permitted to remain on duty, which might further explain his dishonorable discharge and sentence of ten years in confinement. The young Patton, who himself was given to profanity, was a favorite of Pershing's, and Pershing had an intimate relationship with Patton's sister, which also might explain the general's refusal to consider clemency. Bethel supported the dishonorable discharge but advised that ten years was an excessive sentence.[19]

The other courts-martial of enlisted personnel who were found guilty included a term of six months' confinement for Private Frederick Peloquin for the theft of shoes from a French civilian. Pershing believed the sentence to be too lenient but approved it. In the case of Private Richard Prina, who was found guilty of willful disobedience of orders, Pershing commented that a sentence of six months' confinement was too lenient. In all but one of the enlisted trials, Pershing would likewise approve sentences of confinement and dishonorable discharges for offenses ranging from drunkenness on duty to disobedience of orders. The one court-martial that Pershing did not approve was that of a Private James Mosely, who deserted while absent without leave from the army, lost his pistol, and stole a watch from a French civilian. Bethel apprised Pershing that the evidence strongly indicated Mosely was not mentally responsible for the theft of the watch or the desertion, and Pershing agreed by overturning the court-martial findings.[20]

There are thousands of examples from the National Archives that could be used to illustrate a typical general court-martial in the American Expeditionary Forces. What made courts-martial unique to the American Expeditionary Forces was that for the first time in American history, conscripted soldiers were prosecuted overseas. There were a few other notable differences from stateside courts-martial. Oftentimes a court-martial involved French, British, or Belgian victims or witnesses, in which case French Military Mission officers served as a liaison between the American Expeditionary Forces and the various local governments and military commanders. Throughout the war Bethel appears to have maintained a high opinion of these French officers. Another unique aspect was that offenses that arose from absences, desertions, accusations of cowardice, or mutinous conduct were not only solely military in nature but also so in a foreign war zone. As an example, on August 8, 1918, Pershing expressed his concerns about self-inflicted wounds to Bethel and his subordinates, reminding them that during the Civil War self-inflicted wounds and other acts of malingering harmed the Union army at critical times. Bethel responded by instructing the fielded judge advocates to vigorously prosecute such offenses.[21]

On October 3, 1918, French gendarmes caught three soldiers in the act of stealing 600 francs and three bicycles from a store in Calais and placed them under arrest. Four days later the soldiers were court-martialed and sentenced to six months' confinement. The divisional commander commuted the sentences and assigned the men to a labor battalion for four months, where they forfeited two-thirds of their pay. However, the bicycles were either lost or destroyed, and the local commander sought advice from the divisional judge advocate as to whether the soldiers could be forced to forfeit all their pay to repay the store owner. The local commander's question percolated to Bethel who, in turn, advised that Pershing could order the soldiers' pay garnisheed to compensate the French store owner. One officer defended all three accused soldiers, but in this instance, the conviction was a foregone conclusion because the men had confessed in writing to their crime. An ad hoc judge advocate prosecuted the case, and Major Arthur Dehon Hill, a judge advocate assigned to the Services of Supply, read through the trial record and advised Harbord that the court-martial was fairly tried with no errors to the detriment of the accused soldiers. This entire process concluded by the end of October.[22]

On October 26, 1918, Private Thomas P. Oates of the Seventh Division absented himself from the front lines near St. Mihiel and did not join his peers in a reconnaissance patrol of the German lines as he had been ordered to do. Military police apprehended him on November 5, and he was brought to trial in a general court-martial on February 26, 1919. This was not Oates's first offense. On August 1, 1918, he failed to move to the front and was charged with an unauthorized absence but was acquitted by a special court-martial. At his general court-martial, he pleaded not guilty to desertion but guilty to a lesser offense of unauthorized absence. The court-martial found him guilty of the lesser offense and sentenced him to one year in confinement. Had the court-martial occurred prior to the Armistice and had he been found guilty of desertion, he likely would have been sentenced to a much greater term of confinement. Had he been in the British, Italian, Belgian, or French armies, he might have been executed. Major Joseph W. Bartlett, the first assistant judge advocate for the Seventh Division, advised Kreger that he believed the sentence was fair. Kreger agreed with the result and recommended Oates be returned to duty after his confinement.[23]

The general court-martial of Sergeant First Class Charles Jensen ended differently than Oates's trial. Also assigned to the Seventh Division, Jensen fled from his unit on October 26 while the unit was under fire in the Meuse-Argonne. The second of four charges against Jensen read that while "outside of Bois St. Claude he ran away from his company which was then engaged with the enemy, and did not return thereto until after the cessation of hostilities." Compounding Jensen's offense was the fact that his commanding officer twice ordered him to return to his unit, which was then engaged in the important task of demining its sector. Given the horrific nature of combat in World War I, there can be no doubt that Jensen, like many of his peers, was surrounded by carnage and feared for his life. But because of his rank, it was unsurprising that the court-martial sentenced him to fifteen years' confinement and a dishonorable discharge on January 1, 1919. On June 9 of the same year, Kreger, against the advice of Major Nathaniel, the division's judge advocate, successfully prevailed on Pershing to reduce Jensen's sentence to seven years in confinement. At the same time Jensen fled his unit, a Private Gus Schrader assigned to the Thirty-Sixth Division likewise fled while under fire in the Meuse-Argonne. A general court-martial found him guilty of desertion and sentenced him to four years of confinement and a dishonorable discharge. However, Major Victor Ruehl, the divisional judge advocate, convinced the divisional commander Major General Edmund Smith to find Schrader guilty of absence without authority and reduce the sentence to six months.[24]

Although efficiency was a mainstay goal of military justice, not all courts-martial were rapidly convened nor did all result in a conviction. On August 2, 1918, Camille Richy, a farmer living near the town of Etival, claimed that an American soldier went into his food and wine stores to purchase food for his unit but also stole 2,100 francs. Both Richy and his wife filed affidavits with a French police inspector. The inspector identified Private Samuel B. Rowe as the culprit in the theft. It took approximately five months for Rowe to be court-martialed because after the allegations were forwarded to the American Expeditionary Force's adjutant general, Rowe's unit went into action in the Meuse-Argonne. When, on October 26, 1918, it became known that Rowe had yet to be court-martialed, the adjutant general ordered Major General Hanson E. Ely, the Fifth Division's commander, to explain the delay. Ely, of course, had far more pressing issues than the court-martial of a single soldier accused of theft, but he nonetheless responded that he would ensure a trial would commence at the first available time.[25]

On March 5, 1919, Ely referred a charge of larceny to a general court-martial against Rowe, but two days later the court-martial acquitted Rowe. An officer with some legal training, in the sense that he had been a policeman prior to the war, defended Rowe, pointing out that the Richys were unable to specifically identify who had entered their store. Regardless of the fact that Rowe had admitted to the French inspector as well as an army investigator that he did, in fact, enter the store, the missing francs were never located, and there was no evidence that Rowe had purchased anything beyond his means. It is possible that Rowe was guilty, or that another soldier or person committed the theft, or, as the "defense counsel" emphasized, that the Richys had made the story up. In the end, the court-martial acquitted Rowe and the army reimbursed the Richys 2,100 francs, despite the fact that a French Military Mission officer pointed out that had a "Poilu"— as French soldiers were called—been acquitted, the French government would not have recompensed the Richys, and the American Expeditionary Forces were not obligated to do so.[26]

One aspect of American courts-martial that has not been commented on in the treatises and polemics on US military discipline is the quality and amount of oversight judge advocates and other personnel put into courts-martial review. As an example, on January 21, 1919, a general court-martial sentenced Private Gaudio Dominick to death and a dishonorable discharge after finding him guilty of abandoning his post during the St. Mihiel Offensive, "finding safety in the rear," and also of absenting himself from his unit during the Meuse-Argonne Offensive, from October 5, 1918, to January 15, 1919. The trial judge advocate produced evidence that Dominick had once before absented himself from his unit on September 12 and was returned by the military police on October 1, 1918. He was then accused of feigning sickness on October 5 and therefore did not accompany his rifle company into a trench-line. Five days later when his company was ordered into an attack, he disappeared and was not found until January 15. Dominick testified in his own defense that his failure to go into the line on September 12 occurred as a result of "not being able to keep up with the other soldiers due to pneumonia." He admitted that on October 10, he did not advance with his fellow soldiers because court-martial charges had been preferred against him and he feared that he would be wrongfully convicted. On Winship's advice, Liggett disapproved the offenses related to the first absence as well as the charge that accused Dominick of feigning illness, and then reduced the sentence to twenty years. One month later Pershing followed Bethel's advice to reduce Dominick's sentence to five years. Major Mendel Smith conducted a final review for Crowder on May 26, 1919, and recommended that Dominick be released from prison and returned to the ranks for the duration of his enlistment "in order to be considered for an honorable discharge."[27]

In October 1918, Major Samuel Wilson oversaw the general court-martial of a private who impersonated a Canadian brigadier general and was given luxurious accommodations and access to the Seventy-Seventh Division's officers' mess for a week. The private disappeared into the ranks but his true identity was discovered in a hospital one week after his impersonation. After being shot in the head in an assault against a German machine gun nest, the private was found with Canadian general officer ranks and a corresponding identity card in his pocket. Wilson urged the court-martial to find the soldier, who at times professed to be not only a general but also a priest, mentally incompetent and therefore not responsible for his earlier ruses. The court-martial, to Bethel's disgust, agreed with Wilson and acquitted the soldier. Bethel challenged Wilson as to whether the fact that the private had the wherewithal to follow orders to advance against German lines served as proof that he was sane at the time of the offense. Wilson responded that the soldier had lost part of his skull and could not assist in his defense at the time of trial, and as a result, it was impossible to conduct a fair trial.[28]

Although capital trials garnered more interest than routine trials for larceny, disobedience, or assault, soldiers convicted of less severe offenses likewise had their records reviewed at the various command levels. On December 1, 1918, a general court-martial convicted Private Charles Hayward of stealing an army truck and "visiting Paris without permission." The court-martial sentenced Hayward to a dishonorable discharge and five years in confinement. However, on the initial review Lieutenant Colonel Marion Howze, a judge advocate, who had been part of the 1916 expansion, discerned that Hayward had been shot in the stomach during the battle at Chateau Thierry, and it was common practice for the hospital to assign recovering soldiers driving duties. It was clear that Hayward violated the general order against touring in Paris without permission, and he certainly did not have permission to take the truck into Paris. But after Hayward's arrest in Paris, the truck was either illicitly sold, confiscated, or misplaced and there was no evidence that Hayward intended for this to occur. Howze recommended to Pershing that Hayward's sentence be reduced to six months and the larceny offense disapproved. Pershing, for reasons unknown, reduced Hayward's sentence to three months and ordered him returned to the army.[29]

On the other hand, Howze recommended Pershing sustain a twenty-five-year sentence to prison and a dishonorable discharge for Private Arthur Fuller, who had been convicted of desertion. Fuller deserted from his unit on July 5, 1918, at Meaux and was not found until January 11, 1919, in Paris, living under an assumed name with an Italian deserter and working as a cobbler. Fuller was apparently fluent in French, and the French military police accepted his story that he had been injured at Verdun in 1916. Howze also recommended upholding Private Samuel Markowitz's conviction and sentence of a dishonorable discharge and fifteen years for the larceny of two watches, sixty francs, and a bayonet. While serving on a burial detail, Markowitz stole items off of dead soldiers and split the proceeds with two other soldiers, who, perhaps because they were tried separately and assisted in Markowitz's prosecution, were sentenced to one year in confinement each. Both Howze and Major Charles Teare urged Pershing to sustain Markowitz's sentence because his conduct endangered discipline and was "an affront to propriety."[30]

JUDGE ADVOCATES OF THE AMERICAN EXPEDITIONARY FORCES

With the exception of hundreds of officers who served as ad hoc or temporary judge advocates, there were, by August 1918, 117 judge advocates serving in the American Expeditionary Forces. Yet Bethel urged that this number needed to double by October, and to do so required divisional commanders to permit transfers from the line. Almost all of the judge advocates in France had legal training prior to entering the army, and almost all were considerably older than their counterparts serving in the infantry and artillery. Their advanced age, which appears to have averaged forty-seven years, had to do with Bethel's and Crowder's beliefs that longevity in the legal profession was important to due process. Bethel also wanted judge advocates who had at least briefly served as line officers. Several of the judge advocates were prominent lawyers prior to the war. For instance, Dudley V. Sutphin had represented Ohio banks and railroad industries, leading former President Taft to recommend him to Crowder, and although Crowder was angry at the "Houston Riot" trials, he held Colonels Hull and Dunn accountable. Sutphin served as the Eighty-Third "Depot" Division's judge advocate. Another judge advocate, Arthur Dehon Hill, a Harvard Law graduate and former student of Oliver Wendell Holmes Jr., had worked for Theodore Roosevelt's 1904 presidential campaign, and later Roosevelt encouraged him to run for state office. Hill applied for a judge advocate commission with letters of support from Roosevelt, Taft, Holmes, and Frankfurter. Hill and Frankfurter established a friendship in 1908. During the war Hill was assigned to the Services of Supply, and then a forward base section, largely because Crowder doubted Hull's legal abilities, and on Frankfurter's advice he assigned Hill to serve as a "professor of law for Hull." After the war, Hill represented Sacco and Vanzetti in their postconviction appeals. Alongside Hill served Hugh Ogden, another Harvard Law graduate taught by Holmes. Likewise Patrick Cosgrave left his Nebraska judgeship to become a judge advocate, and Bernard Gorfinkle left a Boston law firm to do the same. Ogden, Cosgrave, and Gorfinkle had served in the state national guards but not on a regular or lengthy basis.[31]

On January 2, 1918, Major Hill boarded a vessel in New York and, with over four hundred other soldiers, he headed to France. During the transatlantic voyage, he shared a cabin with another judge advocate whom he informed his wife was a Spanish-American War veteran, describing the officer as a "conservative-minded man from Wisconsin." Given his description, Hill might have shared a cabin with Guy Despard Goff, the son of a West Virginia senator who had left the United States Attorney's Office in Wisconsin for a judge advocate commission. Two other officers that he berthed with were "like minded regular Army men." One of the discussions on the "political situation"—a term Hill repeatedly used in his letters—was that of Victor Berger, a former Wisconsin congressman whose *Milwaukee Leader* was alleged to be a subversive newspaper designed to undermine the war effort. Hill did not consider Berger a threat to the nation and urged his cabin-mates that Berger's right to publish the *Leader* was in the best interests of the Constitution. Other than for his views on Berger, Hill also expressed a distrust of General Leonard Wood, an opinion that aligned him more with Woodrow Wilson than with his cabin-mates. Throughout the war Hill commented disapprovingly on Wood's political activities, but he expressed his continued admiration for Roosevelt. He was also unique among his peers in the American Expeditionary Forces in that he had studied in France and corresponded with French legal scholars in the decade before the war.[32]

Shortly after Hill's arrival in France, the army assigned him to the Services of Supply, a rear area responsible for training soldiers and getting soldiers and materiel to the front, contracting with the French population, settling claims against the United States with French citizens, monitoring prisoners of war, and overseeing rear area courts-martial. For most of his assignment, Hill reported to Colonel Hull, who took a liking to Hill and came to rely on his expertise in tort and contract law. Hull also had fun at Hill's expense by drafting charges against him for such matters as "wrongfully taking abandoned property, namely a mademoiselle, name and value unknown." Another spoof charge had Hill acting in "a manner discreditable to the military service by deeds, means, and methods unknown, but of the existence of which no one can have any doubt."[33]

In comparison to service in the front lines, Hill's assignment was relatively safe and he acknowledged to his wife and son that he was lucky to have avoided the trenches. He developed an affinity for soldiers who had been wounded in battle, and in his recommendations to avoid courts-martial he regularly advised commanding officers to simply reprimand wounded soldiers who were caught in acts of petty thievery or minor absences without authority. On November 5, 1918, he advised Hull that a captain who had been shot in the foot during an advance could be forgiven for overstaying his convalescence leave in light of the fact this was the captain's second wound. On the other hand, in an instance where three soldiers were accused of raping a French girl, he recommended convening a general court-martial, and after securing a conviction that sentenced the three soldiers to long terms of imprisonment, he recommended that none of the three receive any commutation of sentence.[34]

The first two duties of any significance that Hill undertook on his arrival in France were to draft a general order for Harbord that prohibited American soldiers from consorting with prostitutes and other "women of questionable character." The order had a limited duration of one year, and on its expiration Hill redrafted it. The second duty of significance had to do with settling a claim of property destruction by American soldiers, or rather, their hoofed transports. Two sergeants responsible for guarding a brigade's artillery mules became intoxicated and fell asleep on post. Several dozen mules broke free of their paddocks and ventured into orchard fields, where they consumed fruit and destroyed vegetation. Given the food shortages on the Western Front and the high price of agricultural commodities, Hill believed that the issue was serious enough to recommend both disciplining the sergeants and settling claims in favor of French farmers who asserted damages against the United States. An attached French legal officer opposed Hill, claiming that the French military could assert domain against the farmers on the basis of a war necessity, but Hill opted to recommend following American rather than French law.[35]

On April 3, 1918, Hill's headquarters moved to the city of Tours, southwest of Paris, where he joined over twenty thousand American officers and soldiers serving in the various supply, medical, and logistics staffs. His headquarters became overwhelmed with casualties stemming from a German attack on the Lys River in what was captioned as Operation Georgette. Although he was stationed in Tours, he was responsible for venturing into the multitude of towns across France where American servicemen were stationed. Each French town had a "town major" who could be a French officer of any rank, and usually the town majors were either older officers or those who were wounded earlier in the war and could not be returned to the trenches. Hill found the majority of the town majors fair in their negotiations over payments for damages or goods and services. In one instance, a town major informed Hill that an entire village was untrustworthy and no claim could be considered valid.[36]

On his way to Tours, Hill ventured into Paris, which was subjected to an ongoing German bombardment by one of the giant German artillery pieces situated over seventy miles away. When Hill returned, he learned that Harbord relieved his first supervisor, a colonel, and placed Hill in temporary charge until Hull arrived from Britain. The relieved supervisor had made, in Hill's estimation, "a stupid mistake as a guardian of prisoners." Hill discovered that his first supervisor had permitted prisoners of war to leave their confinement for brief periods of time with nothing more than a promise to voluntarily return at nightfall. Most of the early claims Hill settled occurred not from the incompetence or misconduct of soldiers but simply because, as large units of soldiers traversed the French roads on their way to the front, gardens and wheat fields were trampled, livestock animals were taken or set free, and the drivers of motorized transports lost control of their vehicles on the poorly constructed roads. French legal advisors repeatedly encouraged Hill not to settle any of the claims because most of the damages were incident to the war, but Hill continually advised payments to make the aggrieved French citizens "whole."[37]

From the start of his posting in France, Hill attempted to refine his knowledge in French law, which, he informed his son, "is pretty hard work, because the people of one country never seem to think quite the same way that the people of another country do, and because law language is always a little different than other language." In order to master French law, Hill moved into a chateau with an injured French officer named Captain Legrande, who, in his civilian life, had been a prosecutor. "He was a very brave soldier and wears three decorations, two for honor and one for being wounded," Hill informed his son. "He went out with four other officers to reconnoiter and a German shell exploded among them and killed the other four and wounded him twenty four times." By August 1918, Hill had mastered French admiralty laws so well that when an American barge carrying army munitions and personnel collided with a dock, he was able to satisfy the local magistrates. By October 1918, Hill became so proficient in France's military and civil laws that Harbord assigned him to escort General Philippe Petain through the Services of Supply zone. Six months after the Armistice, Hill was also selected to escort General Ferdinand Foch through the Services of Supply. In 1919 Hill indicated to his son that Foch's fear of renewed hostilities with Germany was convincing enough to reaffirm the importance of discipline.[38]

One of the recurring themes in Hill's letters to his wife and son was that the courts-martial conducted under his oversight were generally fair. He oversaw a range of trials arising from larceny and rape charges to three courts-martial originating out of a barge collision during the offloading of ships. Apparently, once a sailor traversed into France, the army asserted jurisdiction under the Articles of War. "Sailors are notorious around the world for telling lies in law suits and to get at what happened is very difficult," he noted. Another court-martial, in his estimation, was necessary to maintain goodwill among the Allies. Two American soldiers assaulted Mohamed Iolch, an Egyptian teamster serving in the British Expeditionary Force. The assault occurred while Iolch transported barrels of wine along the Lys and Somme areas. The soldiers hit him with a rock, stole his shoes, and carried off the wine. Hill conceded that the soldiers might have been drunk at the time but held that a general court-martial was in the best interests of military discipline.[39]

Hill also developed a dislike of supply officers who he believed frequently enriched themselves at government expense or were involved in graft schemes with French merchants. "Today I am busy about an officer in charge of a Hospital and who bought provisions for his own table and that of his friends with the government money and used government automobiles to take ladies he knew to Paris," Hill noted to his son. The officer was court-martialed, found guilty, and sentenced to a reprimand. Neither Hill nor Harbord approved of the light sentence. Hill charged another officer with fraud after the officer purchased gasoline under an unknowing officer's name and then permitted the French to file a claim against the innocent officer following an automobile collision. Hill's court-martial docket became so busy that by 1918 he recruited injured officers and sergeants recovering at the hospitals from war wounds to assist in prosecutions and defend accused soldiers. His only complaint about the structure of courts-martial was not that the procedures were unfair, but rather, that the courts-martial were conducted more slowly than intended, to the benefit of accused soldiers. While waiting for one trial to commence, he was able to read an entire Balzac novel in French.[40]

To Hill, one of the more aggravating investigations arose from several quartermasters' officers who purchased supplies from an agent "who sold the supplies for about five times what they were worth, and seemed to have spent something like a million dollars of government money, when they ought to have spent no more than half that amount." Hill was initially unable to prove that the officers had enriched themselves or received kickbacks from the agent and concluded that "they were simply fools who allowed themselves to be cheated." He advised Harbord to forgo a court-martial and to send the officers to do other duties in "a disagreeable or dangerous place." The general followed Hill's advice, but one of the suspected officers decided he would rather face a court-martial then serve in the trenches and confessed that his peers were complicit in a fraud conspiracy. Ultimately four officers were court-martialed and dismissed from the service.[41]

The vast overexpenditure of dollars at six times above the actual value of the goods was a cause of concern to the American Expeditionary Forces. Hill was aware that during the Civil War, fraud and embezzlement undermined the Union's war efforts and many officers went unpunished for their self-enrichment. Some of the quartermaster officers were too smart in their graft for Hill to recommend prosecution for theft, and instead he urged the commanding officer to charge such officers with "breaches of orders." He also drafted a model reprimand which, when issued against an offending officer, created a permanent army file. The letter explained that officers serving in quartermaster and commissary duties had to understand that the United States placed considerable trust in their judgment and intelligence, but the recipient failed "to hold himself to such a standard ... creating grave doubt as to the fitness for any position of responsibility." Such a letter would make any promotion within the army difficult and would be open to any prospective employer after the conflict.[42]

Major Samuel Pepper's experience in the American Expeditionary Forces, like Hill's, provides an insight into how the army disciplined its soldiers and interacted with Allied officers and government officials. On January 3, 1918, in the midst of gas-mask training in Texas, Pepper received a cable informing him that the Thirty-Second Division was to transit by rail to New York and then sail to France. Some of Pepper's friends in New York City held a party at the Tennis and Racket Club the night before his departure, which lasted until the morning. Pepper, in his own words, was "pickled" when he boarded the RMS *Adriatic* to begin his journey to France. It took the *Adriatic* a month to sail from New York to Le Havre, and within a week after arriving, he traveled to Etaples, where Bethel informed him of a British Army mutiny. On February 26, Bethel introduced Pepper to Pershing at the Chaumont AEF Headquarters.[43]

In March Pepper journeyed to the British sector near the Somme—the scene of the horrific 1916 battle—to observe an ongoing German offensive against their lines. He recorded in his diary, "the Germans seem to be making a very furious drive, have taken 16,000 prisoners and have advanced as much as ten miles. Otherwise the British seem to be holding up well." However, his assessment was overly optimistic, as the German successes had surprised the Allied commands and caused the French to worry that the British Expeditionary Forces would be driven to the French and Belgian coast, leaving Paris an open city. Indeed, the German offensives could have resulted in the disintegration of the Allied forces before enough American forces were brought into the front lines. Pepper knew that Pershing had insisted that the American Army fight as a complete entity, but he sided with General Ferdinand Foch's and French Prime Minister Georges Clemenceau's desperate insistence to get American soldiers to the front. One of the aspects of the German spring offensives against the British and French that impressed Pepper on the need for discipline was his observation of the tenacity and discipline of the French Senegalese and Moroccan soldiers. At the end of March 1918, Pepper recorded that the "very intelligent, splendid looking fellows, bright and well-dressed Senegalese had to serve as an example for American soldiers."[44]

In early April, Pepper reported to General Liggett to assume his duties as the staff judge advocate to the First Corps. Once there he visited the judge advocates serving in the divisions and recorded that "Major Hugh Ogden, a judge advocate assigned to the Forty-Second 'Rainbow' Division, impressed him for his zeal" in working in the frontline trenches. "He seems to be more of a trial JA than anything else, going right out to the front lines to accommodate members of the court. He also goes out there to investigate his cases," Pepper recorded. "They have as many as seven courts running concurrently to cover the locations of the regiments. Maj O seems a very pleasant gentleman and very enthusiastic, comes from Boston." The next month, Liggett appointed Pepper as a liaison to French general Maurice Gamelin, in part because

Pepper was fluent in French from his Canadian upbringing, but also because Liggett discovered that Pepper was "a stellar negotiator." While working in Gamelin's office in May, Pepper reviewed the French Army's disciplinary procedures, and although he believed that exposing miscreants to additional danger had a beneficial effect on discipline, he informed Liggett that, in his view, the creation of "punishment companies was antithetical to the rights of service-members."[45]

On June 4 Pepper prosecuted his first court-martial in France, a murder case. The trial had to be held in abeyance as a result of a German artillery barrage that destroyed the makeshift courtroom and killed one of the court members. Moreover, as the surviving court members, the accused soldier, the guards, and Pepper emerged from a bunker, a German aircraft dropped a load of bombs near them, necessitating a return to the bunker. It was not until June 29 that the trial resumed, and the following day the accused was found guilty and sentenced to death. Pepper noted that the death sentence surprised the command. "It was a shock when we thought of the consequences," he penned in his diary before noting that another murder case was to occur shortly.[46]

While Pepper did not approve of French summary punishments or Pershing's view of summary discipline, and he was an adherent to the principle that no soldier could be punished without a trial, he was not averse to the death penalty or harsh sentences. In a lengthy diary entry he recorded that he believed in capital punishment for murderers as well as for other lesser offenses. He penned that the army had been too lenient on deserters and cowards who fled from their units at the front. "Our principal aim is to hold every man to service and to not permit any man to escape service by the mere commission of petty crimes in order to get a D.D.," Pepper wrote. "We may have to go farther, however, later on, and apply capital punishment in a few cases of disobedience of orders. I imagine the W.D. is opposed to extreme penalties being applied in any but the worst cases of murder, rape, spying, treason ... etc." On July 27, Pepper was reassigned to a division staff judge advocate position and would ultimately participate in the St. Mihiel and Meuse-Argonne Offensives. From that time until the Armistice Pepper did not record any impressions of courts-martial though he reviewed twenty five general courts-martial and sixty special courts-martial. Two of the general courts-martial arose out of allegations of mutinous conduct for spreading IWW literature on the wrongness of the war, and eight courts-martial arose from cowardice allegations. None of the trials resulted in a sentence of more than ten years. On the other hand, he did record that German artillery had injured his roommate, a chaplain, and killed the chaplain's enlisted assistant, and on two occasions he donned his gas mask as a result of a chlorine or mustard gas attack.[47]

Patrick James Cosgrave served alongside Ogden and Pepper as the Fifth Division's judge advocate. Cosgrave was born in 1871 in Wilkes-Barre, Pennsylvania, and moved with his parents to Lincoln, Nebraska, thirteen years later. In 1891 he graduated with an LLB from the University of Michigan, and one year later he earned an LLM from the same institution. He was elected president of his law class, and in 1891 the university chancellor selected him to escort Grover Cleveland through the campus. At Cleveland's invitation, Cosgrave traveled with the former and future president to Chicago. From 1902 to 1907 he served as a police court judge for the city of Lincoln, then as a county judge until 1912. That year, Nebraska governor Chester Aldrich appointed him district judge, a position in which he adjudicated the most serious of state felony trials. Despite an impressive resume, Cosgrave's judicial experience might not have been enough to have enabled him to receive a direct commission as a judge advocate in July 1917, but he had substantial military experience.[48]

In 1892 he enlisted as a sergeant in the Lincoln Light Infantry, a city militia organization that was created to defend against Indians as well as to augment the state militia against internal insurrection. In 1895 he was commissioned into the Nebraska state militia. As a captain commanding a company of the First Nebraska Volunteers, he fought in the Philippines against both the Spanish Army and Philippine insurgents from 1898 to 1899. Writing to a fellow captain, Cosgrave penned, "I have now been in three lively engagements and fully appreciate—those indescribable feelings one undergoes when receiving his baptism of fire." He witnessed Dewey's fleet fire into Spanish lines: "We have had the pleasure of witnessing the 'old man' (as the Marines call him), George Dewey and his fleet hurl missiles of destruction against the forts on the ever memorable 18th of August; the scene though grand and majestic was terrible in its execution." He also served as a regimental judge advocate and as a trial judge advocate over a soldier charged with murder. But in 1899 he was shot in the stomach and returned to Nebraska, where he entered into a law practice and became a member in the state Republican Party. As of 1902 he was no longer in the National Guard.[49]

On April 10, 1917, Cosgrave applied for a judge advocate commission, and by July he was in uniform once more. Like Pepper, he trained in Texas. On February 14, 1918, Crowder assigned Cosgrave as the Fifth Division's judge advocate. His military record and Distinguished Service Medal states that he took part in the Voges Mountains Sector Defensive from June 1 to July 17, 1918; at St. Mihiel from September 12 to 15; and in the

Meuse-Argonne Offensive from October 11 to November 11. Like Pepper, Cosgrave recorded his experiences in a diary that indicated shelling, gas attacks, and near-death experiences.[50]

On April 29, Cosgrave attended services in Winchester Cathedral, and one day later he landed at Le Havre, France. On May 26 he "had a brief personal meeting" with Pershing and noted that he believed Germany could not be defeated until the spring of 1919. Two days after meeting Pershing, he observed the British Expeditionary Forces holding against the German offensive in the Somme River area and recorded that the sky was red with the British counter-battery fire, and that the British soldiers were highly disciplined. Shortly afterward, his division was assigned to take part in the Voges Mountains defensive operations. In the course of one month, he reviewed six special courts-martial and twelve summary courts-martial. Of these he recommended approving four of the special courts-martial. On July 1 a German gas attack disrupted one of the trials and killed Cosgrave's horse. He wrote that the gas attack frightened him more than his experience of being shot in the abdomen.[51]

During the St. Mihiel Offensive, a German artillery shell destroyed a truck that he had left moments earlier, and two soldiers were killed. On September 25 Cosgrave was promoted to lieutenant colonel, and two days later Bethel called on him to see if he wanted to transfer to the headquarters at Chaumont, but he remained with the division on his own accord. He apparently believed that he had a duty to share in the dangers of war, and on several occasions he volunteered to retrieve wounded and dead soldiers in front of the trench-lines. On October 23 a German shell explosion killed a soldier who was assisting Cosgrave, and Cosgrave likely suffered collapsed lungs and damaged ribs. He had difficulty breathing until after the Armistice. Cosgrave's son was killed in the Argonne Forest in early October, but he was not informed until December, and when told, he asked not to be immediately relieved from his duties. From October 1 through November 11, 1918, Cosgrave prosecuted two courts-martial as a trial judge advocate and reviewed seven general courts-martial, eleven special courts-martial, and thirty-eight summary courts-martial. He recommended his divisional commander approve of the findings in half of these cases. From the Armistice until December 22, he reviewed another twenty-eight general courts-martial and recommended approval in fifteen but also recommended clemency in each of the eleven desertion convictions. At the end of that month, Winship visited Cosgrave and informed him that Bethel and the Fifth Division's commander, Major General Hanson Ely, wanted to recommend him for a permanent commission. But Cosgrave demurred, insisting he wanted to return to his judicial duties in Nebraska. This would not occur until May 28, 1919, because, as he recorded after dining with Charles Teare, there was a likelihood of renewed hostilities.[52]

On the same day Cosgrave was promoted to lieutenant colonel, so too was Charles V. Porter, the Seventy-Ninth Division's judge advocate. Born in 1883 in Louisiana, Porter was one of the younger officers commissioned as a judge advocate. He was a Yale-educated lawyer and had served as the Louisiana governor's private secretary. Along with Colonel James Mayes, both of Louisiana's senators pushed for Porter's judge advocate commission, and he satisfied Bethel with his legal work. Bethel and Hull alike were pleased with Porter's performance throughout his service in France. In August 1918 Porter was cited for bravery after rescuing injured soldiers trapped in a no-man's land during a German artillery attack. Porter reviewed over one hundred special courts-martial and advised overturning nearly one-third.[53]

Hugh Ogden arrived in France on November 17, 1917, and Winship successfully lobbied for him to become the judge advocate to the Forty-Second or "Rainbow" Division. On June 15, 1918, Ogden wrote to his wife that although he had experienced German shellfire for the six months that he was in France, the bombardment of the prior day was the most horrific, being "Fritz's last chance at military victory." One day later Ogden described his sorrow at the loss of American lives: "You have served with these men for months, you grow very fond of them, and it is horrible to see them butchered in this bloody, brutal, ghastly war. Out they pull the stretchers and every kind of battered humanity comes out, gas, blue-skin, shell-shock, trembling like a leaf all over, arms, legs, feet, abdomen."[54]

Ogden was a prominent Boston attorney and the descendant of early Seventeenth Century Puritan settlers, Revolutionary War officers, abolitionists, and Protestant religious leaders. Born in 1871 in Bath, Maine, he graduated from the University of Pennsylvania in 1890 and Harvard's law school in 1896. Shortly after being admitted to the bar, he formed Whipple, Sears, and Ogden and specialized in corporate law. In 1897 he also joined the state militia and served on coastal defense duty. In 1903 he was commissioned as a second lieutenant in the Massachusetts National Guard, and in addition to his militia and legal pursuits, he also served as a lay minister in the Episcopal Church. Another interesting aspect of Ogden's life is that he and Arthur Hill had been friends since childhood. On June 20, 1917, Senator John Weeks interceded with Crowder on Ogden's behalf to ensure that Ogden was sent to France as a divisional judge advocate.[55]

Ogden was called into active duty on May 2, 1917, and proceeded to train at Camp Mills, Long Island, with the Forty-Second Division at the end of summer. He later reported that the division conducted as many courts-martial in its six weeks of training in Long Island as it did during its eighteen-month service in France. To Ogden, the most serious general court-martial he oversaw stemmed from a soldier's desertion. The soldier spoke nominal French, and while wearing civilian clothes was apprehended by the French gendarmes near the Swiss border. A French divisional commander assumed that the soldier was a German spy and ordered him to be summarily shot. Only after being brought before a firing squad did the deserter admit to being an American soldier. A general court-martial convicted the soldier of desertion and sentenced him to death, a sentence that Ogden recommended to Major General Charles Menoher be upheld. However, Bethel advised Pershing to reduce the sentence to five years' imprisonment, and in this instance Pershing followed Bethel's advice. On November 22, 1917, Ogden informed Senator Weeks that if given time, the American Expeditionary Force would be "the best army the world ever saw."[56]

Ogden had, in Blanton Winship, a benefactor. For reasons that are absent from Ogden's and Winship's letters, Winship lobbied to have Ogden be commissioned as a judge advocate at the start of the war over the application of Senator Oscar Underwood's son. Ogden supported the prohibition against soldiers consuming alcohol in the United States, and although he doubted that it could be enforced in France, he concluded that alcohol "led to 75% of the Army's disciplinary problems." One of Ogden's unique wartime duties was to serve as a censor. On only one occasion did he discover that a soldier intentionally divulged prohibited information to a civilian in the United States, but the civilian was the soldier's wife and Ogden concluded that the soldier "provided the information to impress his girl." Ogden was assisted by his legal orderly, Sergeant Major B. Webb, who was not only a Harvard classmate but a relative of Cornelius Vanderbilt, and he credited Webb with "conducting a large volume of legal research."[57]

Major Samuel Wilson, the Seventy-Seventh Division's judge advocate, had, perhaps, the most interesting of the transatlantic crossings to France. Two days before he sailed to France he served as a trial judge advocate in the general court-martial of Private William A. Kerner, but the trial did not conclude before embarkation and it continued on board ship. Found guilty of refusing to obey an officer's order, Kerner was sentenced to "be shot to death with musketry." Kerner had been confined in a guardhouse when he refused to drill after his lieutenant ordered him to do so. Wilson had only argued for a dishonorable discharge, and the severity of the sentence shocked him. But Kerner had previously been convicted in a special court-martial of absence without leave and in a summary court-martial for petty larceny. The findings and sentence were announced on board ship as well. Wilson

urged Howze to recommend to the divisional commander not to approve the
sentence. Howze, however, advised the opposite, and Major General Franklin
Bell, the outgoing division commander (and Wilson's cousin) indicated he
would approve the sentence as adjudged. On June 1, 1918, Major General C.
B. Duncan, Bell's successor, approved the sentence, but the next day, Brigadier
General E. M. Johnson assumed command and reversed. On June 4 Howze
noted to the corps judge advocate and commander that although Johnson
had assumed command, he was not under orders at the time he reversed
Duncan's approval, and therefore only a higher ranking officer such as a corps
commander could reverse Duncan. Ultimately, Kerner's fate was held in
limbo until Baker disapproved the sentence, and Kerner was returned to the
United States after being dishonorably discharged. This episode did not lower
Wilson in Howze's estimation and when, on June 11, Howze was ordered to
become the division's operations officer, he urged that Wilson be promoted as
the division's judge advocate.[58]

Wilson was present to experience his division's first casualties. On June 5,
1918, a German artillery shell landed in an enlisted soldiers' mess and killed
one soldier. One day later, another German round crashed into a number of
soldiers drilling on the British "Stokes Mortar," but the round did not explode.
One of the soldiers picked up the "dud," while a number of other soldiers
surrounded him. A sergeant ordered the soldier to "drop the round," but
this time the artillery round exploded, killing fifteen soldiers. The sergeant,
however, survived. Wilson advised pursuing a special court-martial for the
sergeant for being derelict in his duties. For the duration of the war Wilson
had no permanently assigned assistant judge advocate and appears to have
operated his office on an ad hoc staffing basis by culling injured officers with
legal training to serve as temporary assistants. This was not the condition of
affairs that he desired, however. On November 6, 1918, he made his seventh
request for two assistant judge advocates to Winship, but he did not gain an
assistant until after the Armistice.[59]

Although for most of the war Major Hugh Bayne was assigned to the
Services of Supply or attached to a mission in Geneva to establish a prisoner
of war agreement with Germany, he became the Eightieth Division's judge
advocate on November 1, 1918. During his time with the division, which
lasted until December 18, 1918, he oversaw twelve general courts-martial
and seventy lesser trials. He was gassed during the Meuse-Argonne Offensive
and suffered minor injuries. He later recorded that he had taken a special
interest in one general court-martial involving an officer. "The testimony was
sickening to hear—the accused had gone over the top with his platoon, but
then he lay on the ground groveling in fear while the battle went on and

the shells burst around him," Bayne wrote. "Finally, stretcher bearers carried him to the rear while wounded men walked." Bayne acknowledged that it was likely that had this occurred in the British or French armies, the lieutenant would have been convicted and sentenced to be shot or imprisoned for life. However, a psychiatrist testified that the lieutenant's nervous system was such that "he was incapable of resisting the nervous terror which took possession of him." The court-martial acquitted the lieutenant and Bayne advised General Adelbert Cronkhite, the divisional commander, to accept the verdict, because the lieutenant had been rightfully adjudged as insane. However, in approving the verdict Bayne penned into the general court-martial order that the lieutenant was "an uncontrollable coward." Bayne did not relish stigmatizing the lieutenant for the rest of his life and recorded, "it made me sad to write it and damn the poor fellow, but we cannot afford to make it easy for cowards to pretend they were overcome by an irresistible impulse to avoid the danger of battle."[60]

From late 1917 to April 1919, Bernard Gorfinkle, who had failed in his efforts to obtain a judge advocate commission during his stateside training, served as the Twenty-Sixth Division's assistant judge advocate, and in June 1918 he obtained a judge advocate commission with a promotion to captain. Although he was persistent in his efforts, his commission ultimately came about as a result of happenstance. After arriving in France, in December 1917 his company of truck drivers boarded a train that took them to the divisional headquarters instead of the location of the regiment to which he was assigned, some thirty miles away. The divisional adjutant commandeered the enlisted truck drivers and assigned Gorfinkle as a scout. Gorfinkle took it upon himself to complain to Lieutenant Colonel Cassius Dowell, the division's judge advocate, who, in turn, assigned Gorfinkle as an acting judge advocate. Gorfinkle told his father that he found Dowell "difficult and hard to approach," but he praised Dowell's legal acumen. Although it was not until early August 1918 that Gorfinkle's judge advocate commission was approved, in the interim he prosecuted over forty courts-martial and crafted a model regulation for repaying French claims of less than 1,000 francs.[61]

In March 1918 Dowell nominated Gorfinkle to be commissioned as an assistant judge advocate, and Bethel endorsed Gorfinkle as well. However, in late March, Ansell informed Dowell that he opposed Gorfinkle because of questions about his loyalty. When Gorfinkle's letters of support were discovered, Crowder superseded Ansell and favorably acted on Dowell's request. But Gorfinkle almost did not get the opportunity to remain in the army at all, for three reasons. The first challenge to confront Gorfinkle stemmed from a nasal operation in which the surgeon prescribed him cocaine in March 1918. For a three-week period Gorfinkle followed the surgeon's direction and daily used cocaine. Surprisingly, he did not become addicted to the substance, but he had to be hospitalized a second time as a result of an infection and again was given cocaine.[62]

On April 24 Gorfinkle observed the fighting at Seicheprey and was injured by German shrapnel after getting caught in an artillery attack. A Boston friend named Harry Ditmars, while standing alongside Gorfinkle, was killed in the barrage. That same day, Bethel elevated Dowell from his divisional duties to serve as a judge advocate for the II Corps. Gorfinkle wrote to his parents that he was "S.O.L. if Dowell left France," and this occurred two weeks later. Gorfinkle again came under fire in August and September 1918, witnessed aerial combat, and was in attendance at air ace Major Raoul Lufbery's funeral. A German aircraft dropped a bomb near Gorfinkle after the funeral. And on November 1, 1918, he was slightly wounded once more in the Meuse-Argonne Offensive near Verdun.[63]

Equally as serious as his exposure to enemy fire, in May 1918 a colonel accused Gorfinkle of stealing medals and eyeglasses from German prisoners of war for his own enrichment. Although Gorfinkle accounted for the medals and eyeglasses, in asserting his innocence he called the colonel a "mamzer," which in Yiddish unkindly translated to a child born out of both incest and wedlock. Not surprisingly, Gorfinkle's public use of the term resulted in a charge of disrespect to a superior commissioned officer. A general court-martial was rapidly held, and it acquitted him rapidly as well. Gorfinkle was lucky to be represented by Dowell's eventual replacement, Major Harry Anderson, a Protestant who facetiously but convincingly argued that "mamzer" was a humorous term of endearment. Prior to the war, Anderson was the president of the Tennessee State Bar and a well-regarded corporation attorney. In 1924 President Calvin Coolidge appointed him to the United States District Court for Tennessee. In April 1918 Anderson apparently attempted to introduce Gorfinkle to the Jewish women of Memphis from a far distance. "He and I get along famously, he knows I am a Jew and says he will fix it up for me with some of his Jewish friends who have daughters back home," Gorfinkle informed his law partners.[64]

By January 1918 Gorfinkle prosecuted over one hundred special courts-martial, and he served as a summary court officer in roughly two hundred trials. He exuberantly explained to his law partners in Boston that he not only convinced a court-martial to convict a soldier accused of desertion and cowardice and would press for the death sentence, he had "licked" his opposing counsel, "a distinguished Boston attorney named Joseph O'Connell whose brother is in Congress." From August 1918 until the end of the war, one of Gorfinkle's duties was to determine whether men who claimed to have been injured as a result of weapons misfire had actually intentionally inflicted a wound to avoid further service. Gorfinkle found this duty distasteful, but after joining in a patrol "through territory that a few days ago was filled with Boche," and seeing "hundreds of mangled bodies along with smelling the odor," he understood why a few men attempted to avoid frontline service.[65]

Lieutenant Colonel John Philip Hill's experience of serving in France was similar to those of his peers in the other divisions. While serving as the Twenty-Ninth Division's judge advocate, he came under fire on several occasions. On August 1 the division took its place next to a French division outside of the Meuse-Argonne. In the two months of its line duties prior to the Meuse-Argonne Offensive, the division conducted five general courts-martial and over one hundred special courts-martial. The offenses ranged from murder and desertion for the general courts-martial to AWOL and failure to obey for the special courts-martial. Three of the general courts-martial were of officers. Alcohol appears to have accounted for over a third of the special courts-martial. In September 1918, Hill suffered injuries to his throat and eyes from chlorine gas after his mask failed him. He recovered after a week-long hospitalization and returned to his judge advocate duties. Following the Armistice, the division conducted another two hundred special courts-martial, but no general courts-martial.[66]

Major Hill took Bethel's missive regarding the quality of defense counsel to heart and after scouring the officer ranks for attorneys, he discovered that a Red Cross officer named Captain Harold Content was the most qualified of all the officers who had been attorneys prior to the war. Content had attempted to obtain a regular army commission, but the War Department determined him to be medically unfit for duty. Instead the Red Cross commissioned him as a captain, and while this rank did not give him any military authority over soldiers, it enabled him to share the risks of war. Content graduated from Columbia University's law school in 1908, and both Harlan Stone and John Bassett Moore praised his abilities. In 1913 he joined the US Attorney's Office in New York and prosecuted politicians accused of corruption. In 1917 he prosecuted Alexander Berkman and Emma Goldman as well as dozens of draft delinquents. He also became well known for prosecuting Margaret Sanger in 1916. Through a special agreement and with Bethel's approval, Content defended over seventy soldiers and officers in courts-martial and obtained acquittals for twenty-seven.[67]

On October 8, Bethel assigned Hill to the French XVII Corps, where he remained for the duration of the war. In a short time, he became the American liaison officer to French general Henry Gouraud, and on one unique occasion,

Gouraud assigned him as a trial judge advocate in a French court-martial for desertion and spreading subversive literature. The court-martial sentenced the French soldier to fifty years at hard labor, likely served at Devil's Island. After the Armistice, Hill returned to the Twenty-Ninth Division. In December, Bethel assigned him to lead an investigation into claims that American officers had summarily executed soldiers for military offenses such as fleeing from the front lines. He also began to reinvigorate his political ambitions and campaigned against Prohibition by writing letters from France to the Baltimore and Annapolis newspapers. In 1920 the Maryland Republican Party encouraged Hill to run for Congress in the largely Democrat bastion of Baltimore. *The Baltimore American*—at the time Maryland's largest circulating newspaper—backed Hill, and its editors professed: "In many divisions the judge advocate tried everybody in sight and had poor discipline. In the Twenty-Ninth, Col Hill held only five general courts-martial the whole time we were in France. He went up and down the line in the mud, exposed to the fire of the enemy, religiously doing his duties in settling cases."[68]

Two months after the Armistice, Bethel and Hull provided Crowder their assessment of the judge advocates that served in the American Expeditionary Forces. Without any prompting from Crowder, Hull divided the judge advocates under his supervision into two categories: "Jew" and "others." He informed Crowder that Lieutenant Colonel Julian A. S. Meyer was "a clever Jew, ambitious, capable, and energetic" and Gorfinkle "another jew was not as good as Meyer, but would work hard and get results." During the war, Meyer served at the American Expeditionary Forces headquarters and reviewed hundreds of courts-martial records. Hull degraded Victor Ruehl as "cheap camouflage and lazy," and called Lieutenant Colonel Paul Tucker "a weak sister" and Major Alfred M. Craven "garrulous, a damned fool." Tucker specialized in real estate law and while in Europe he drafted contracts with the French municipalities. Hull also criticized Bayne to Bethel, who replied that Bayne was "not up to the task from the beginning." On the other hand, Hull admired Dudley Sutphin and recommended that the War Department offer him a regular commission, but he reserved his highest praise for Arthur Hill.[69]

Bethel informed Crowder that Arthur Hill "rendered most valuable service" and was "a lawyer of high order." Bethel also relayed that Cosgrave, Pepper, Ogden, and Frederick Bauer were his top candidates for gaining a regular army commission, and as "second tier candidates" Whitsett and Porter likewise deserved promotion. Although the historic record is sparse on Bauer, he earned a law degree from Harvard University in 1900, was in private practice in Massachusetts prior to the nation's entry into the war, and served as a second lieutenant in the state national guard. Bethel gave Cosgrave his highest praise and asked Crowder to ensure that Cosgrave would be offered a regular commission with the rank of lieutenant colonel when he returned home. However, Cosgrave made it clear that he intended to return to Nebraska to his family, which had suffered from the death of his son, and to his judicial duties. Interestingly, Bethel also lauded Adam Patterson and conceded that of all the judge advocates, Patterson had the most difficult duty as "a colored officer of a colored division." In recommending to Crowder that Patterson be offered a permanent commission, he noted that Patterson "has prosecuted a number of important cases and the records convince me that he is about as good a trial judge advocate as could be found."[70]

In December 1918, Patterson advised Bethel that the conviction of Private George Hicks for the murder of another soldier was not warranted by the evidence. The deceased soldier had threatened Hicks with a rifle after Hicks and a group of other "colored soldiers" inadvertently awakened him in the early hours of November 15. Hicks attempted to grab the rifle, but as he did so, the weapon discharged into the deceased's face. Additionally, a nearby captain had ordered the deceased soldier to "drop his weapon" prior to the shooting. Both Bethel and, more importantly, Liggett accepted Patterson's review, and Hicks was freed from his life sentence. That the deceased soldier was white and Hicks an African American soldier makes this instance all the more remarkable.[71]

INTERACTION WITH THE ALLIES: COURTS-MARTIAL, CLAIMS, AND RELATIONS WITH THE CITIZENRY

From the first arrival of US forces in France, American judge advocates like Pepper and Hill interacted with their Allied counterparts and observed British, French, and Belgian disciplinary methods. Sometimes these observations caused judge advocates to consider solutions to problems they had yet to encounter. In July 1917, the judge advocate general of the British Army sought information on how the War Department intended to administer the estates of deceased soldiers if such estates were contested between a competing party in the United States and a French or Belgian party. Bethel advised Crowder that there was indeed a likelihood that American soldiers would father French and Belgian children and then be killed in combat. Many such soldiers would not have made allotments in their estates or war insurance to their French and Belgian children, but undoubtedly French and Belgian mothers would pursue claims of support to the War Department. Bethel also urged that the British model of only enforcing the actual statement contained in a will would not be in the interest of harmony with the Allies or fair to French and Belgian mothers. To Bethel, the best means to prevent discord with the Allies was to require soldiers to acknowledge their relations with foreign civilians on their legal documents, even to the point that such an acknowledgment could be found as proof of a violation of orders prohibiting fraternization with French and Belgian civilians. He could have advocated the British solution because the probate laws of several states did not recognize the rights of children born out of wedlock. Indeed, it was not until 1968 that the Supreme Court found discrimination against children born out of wedlock unconstitutional. Simply, Bethel and others believed that if a soldier failed to uphold a moral obligation to the French citizenry they would also fail to adhere to the discipline required to both fight a war and not alienate the local population. This failure, in turn, could cause difficulties in dealing with the defeated Germans.[72]

While there was an open question as to whether American soldiers would serve under French or British command, there was never serious consideration given to subjecting American soldiers to foreign disciplinary systems. Early in the war, Lord Roberts, the British chief of the Imperial General Staff, suggested to General Hugh Scott that Americans being trained by the British Army should be subject to British discipline, but the War Department's leadership universally opposed the idea, and there is no record that it was brought to Wilson's attention. Nonetheless, from Crowder on down through the ranks of judge advocates, significant study of British and French military law was undertaken, both to consider whether American courts-martial and disciplinary processes should be modified and to gain a better understanding of how American forces might integrate into an Allied-commanded operation. In early 1918, Bethel turned to Winship to examine British and French courts-martial and other Allied mechanisms for maintaining discipline and then report his findings to Pershing, Liggett, and himself. Winship largely echoed Bethel's sentiments that American soldiers, the government, and the public would not tolerate anything approximating a "shot at dawn" approach to discipline. On the other hand, Winship had to overcome Brigadier General Alvord, the American Expeditionary Forces' adjutant general, who argued to Pershing that "an appropriate as well as the most effective punishment for malingerers is hard labor in the most dangerous place where the labor of soldiers is necessary."[73]

Winship reported to Liggett that while French and British disciplinary systems had similarities to American courts-martial, there were enough significant differences that neither should be adopted, and he opined that under no circumstances should American soldiers be subject to any type of foreign discipline. He added that the Australian government had exercised its independence by refusing to permit British courts-martial to sentence Australian soldiers to death. Additionally, he noted that while British courts-martial were conducted in a manner that mirrored American courts-martial, British sentences, such as public whipping, "rail-riding," and "spread eagling," were more "severe and degrading" than permissible under American law.

As for French courts-martial, Winship advised that the French practice of sending persons who openly committed crimes to avoid frontline service into "punishment companies" had a significant effect on reducing crimes but likewise could not be instituted in American courts-martial. Assignment to a "punishment company" in the French Army was tantamount to a death sentence, because convicted soldiers were placed in daylight raiding and wire-cutting parties where they were openly exposed to enemy fire. If the prisoner refused to advance beyond the French forward trench-line, then French soldiers would shoot the prisoner. "The main feature of these companies is that men serving in them are subjected not only to hard labor but to labor of the most dangerous character in the front line trenches, and in No Man's Land," Winship reported to Liggett, before advising that there were two reasons for not following the French model. He argued that a sentence to a "punishment company" would be the same as "dignifying a thief, with an assignment that carries exceptional honor." The second reason Winship advanced was that the creation of such a sentence would likely undermine discipline instead of enhancing it, even though he believed there were "no real legal difficulties that would prevent its institution."[74]

Bethel took an opposite position from Winship's, however. To Bethel, assignment to a punishment company was misnamed, because hazardous duty such as serving in a listening post or on a raid was a legitimate duty, and he countered that "those who attempt to evade dangerous duty should be all the more compelled to perform it; if the straggling is due to cowardice, compelling the straggler to serve in the most dangerous places is the most effective means to stop it." Although Bethel insisted on trials before the imposition of punishment, he believed that exposure to hazardous conditions was not, in and of itself, a punishment and went on to add that such deterrence had been successful in the British and French armies.[75]

In late 1918, Liggett expressed his concern to Kreger that a number of general and special courts-martial were delayed after it was discovered that the accused soldier was a minor who had lied about his age and then informed the court-martial of this fact in an effort to avoid prosecution. Liggett had learned that in both the British and French armies, youth was not a bar to a court-martial and that the British had executed an under-age soldier. On the other hand, Crowder had made it clear that at least in the United States, a soldier who was too young to have enlisted in the first place was to be treated differently than a soldier over eighteen years of age. In March 1918, Crowder transmitted an opinion to the senior judge advocates in Europe as well as in the US geographic commands that the age of minority had to be a mitigating factor in courts-martial. Crowder's missive occurred as a result of the court-martial of a Private Thomas J. MacVey, held at Governors Island on November 7, 1917. MacVey was, in reality, fifteen years old and lied about his age to enlist immediately after Congress declared war on Germany. Once the lie was discovered in early November, he deserted and was apprehended two days later. A court-martial sentenced him to six months in confinement and a dishonorable discharge, but Crowder successfully prevailed on the commanding general of the Eastern Department to disapprove the verdict and send MacVey home to his parents.[76]

On the issue of youth in France, Kreger turned to the newly arrived Lieutenant Colonel George Wallace for guidance on this issue since Wallace had assisted Crowder in the MacVey case. Wallace, in turn, informed Kreger that while there was no specific legal bar against prosecuting a youthful soldier in France, especially since the lie about age constituted a fraudulent enlistment, he advised against court-martialing minors who lied about their age and enlisted in the army for all but the most serious crimes. Wallace urged that the British had set an example of what not to do in prosecuting minors, including meting out sentences of death. He accurately predicted that following the war, Parliament would take notice of public pressure to significantly curtail the British system of military justice. In the 1920s, a political movement in Britain led by Ernest Thurtle, a member of Parliament, succeeded in reforming British courts-martial. By 1930 British courts-martial could no longer sentence a soldier to death for cowardice or desertion without an appeal to the government. As for the French, Wallace accepted the fact that France, more than Britain, had been in a war for its very existence, and after the 1917 mutiny the punishment of youthful offenders was all the more reasonable. Nonetheless, he recognized that there could be significant constitutional challenges arising from long terms of imprisonment imposed by courts-martial on youthful offenders.[77]

Although Bethel and the other ranking judge advocates attached to the American Expeditionary Forces opposed the implementation of the harsher extrajudicial aspects of the Allied systems, Pershing and several of his corps and divisional commanders did not always agree with their advice. In what might be considered an act of bypassing his headquarters judge advocate, Pershing complained that there was "too little discipline meted out to repeat stragglers, deserters, and cowards" and informed select corps and divisional commanders that summary execution of soldiers fleeing from the front was a necessary and permissible part of the Meuse-Argonne Offensive. Not all of the generals agreed with Pershing on the necessity of draconian measures. For instance, Generals Henry T. Allen and Joseph T. Dickman agreed with Pershing that on the most extreme occasions subordinate officers serving at the front possessed the authority to summarily execute soldiers who fled from battle but thought it was both unwise and unnecessary to issue an order at that time. Following the war, Senator Thomas Watson, a Georgia Democrat, claimed that there were widespread summary executions and that over twenty-five "shot at dawn" type executions for military offenses had occurred. However, there was no evidence, other than Pershing's memorandum, that any summary executions had occurred.[78]

Analyzing Allied disciplinary systems was only one of several types of interactions that judge advocates had with their foreign counterparts. Wherever soldiers traverse in wartime and regardless of the high level of discipline of the army, there is inevitable damage to private property and loss to civilians. In 1917 Baker assigned the Judge Advocate General's Office the duty to investigate and adjudicate claims made by French, Belgian, and British citizens against soldiers. In this role, judge advocates from Bethel, Hull, and Kreger down through their staffs had a degree of interaction with Allied military governments and military officials that was alien to other soldiers. Bethel investigated claims ranging from an affray involving over twenty soldiers in the town of Delouze where the mayor alleged the soldiers had wrecked his house, to one in which soldiers inadvertently trampled a prized London garden belonging to an English aristocrat. In both cases the army paid restitution for damages. Likewise, Hull substantiated an allegation of a soldier's theft of a "carcass of mutton" from a farm, and the army reimbursed the farmwoman. Of the thousands of files in the National Archives, some of which are found in odd areas such as penitentiary correspondences and bakeries, the overwhelming majority of claims were substantiated and payments were made to civilians. But not in all claims were civilians recompensed. In one instance where a French railroad conductor claimed that American soldiers stole thirty wheels of cheese, Colonel James J. Mayes, a headquarters judge advocate, concluded that the claim was false and Hull, who accepted Mayes's findings, refused to pay the claim. French authorities pursued this claim until dropping it in 1920.[79]

In each investigation Bethel, Kreger, or Hull was responsible for informing local officials as to the outcome. Thus on May 15, 1918, Bethel confirmed to the chief of the French Military Mission a report that five American soldiers were "fishing by means of explosives on private property in violation of French law" and that the five soldiers would be court-martialed. Moreover, Bethel assured the French that the chateau owner would be compensated for the loss of his fish stock. Likewise, on March 20, 1919, Bethel informed the chief of the French Military Mission that two soldiers who "heisted" a wagon containing two hundred loaves of bread were promptly punished by a court-martial.[80]

Between 1918 and 1919, judge advocates investigated hundreds of cases of looting including 138 bicycle thefts and dozens of claims of American soldiers fathering French children, as well as a separate prejudicial category of claims made against "Negroes." This separate category had nothing to do with the prejudices of French citizenry, which many African American soldiers observed to be far less than the prejudice and segregation faced in the United States and within the army. Rather, the Judge Advocate General's Office in France had as a policy adopted the belief that African American soldiers were of a lesser quality than their white counterparts. As an example, when Bethel promised harsh punishment against a Negro soldier accused of assaulting a woman, the citizenry of the town of Nevers filed a petition with him asserting that the woman was "of questionable character." But Bethel pursued the charges because, as he noted, "the negro soldier, has weak self-discipline." In spite of Bethel's incorporation of prevailing prejudicial stereotypes, a court-martial accepted the testimony of French witnesses and acquitted the soldier.[81]

Bayne, like Bethel, also concluded that African American soldiers were more likely to assault white women. In one of the first courts-martial he reviewed, he advised Pershing that several "negro soldiers" who were accused of attempting to rape a French laundress in their barracks were guilty. Bayne claimed that the attempted assault had been "witnessed by scores of people." Yet only two witnesses came forward for the government. The alleged victim did not testify, and one of the witnesses, "a negro soldier," claimed that the guilty soldiers had jostled the laundress. Had the facts been the same for a white soldier, Bayne would likely have arrived at a different result in his advice, because he inferred the intent of the convicted soldiers without any evidence that they had said anything of a sexual nature and in contradiction to the testimony of the soldiers that they had merely attempted to take clean sheets from the laundress.[82]

One area in particular in which Bethel divided African American soldiers from "white men" was venereal disease. In January 1918 General Francis Kernan, the first commander of the Services of Supply, issued an order criticizing the officers who conducted summary courts-martial for adjudging "lenient sentences" to "black stevedores" who contracted venereal disease. In response, Bethel advocated leniency for these soldiers because, as he informed Pershing, "The mode of life of these soldiers was not of the average white recruit."[83]

In addition to the thousands of claims processed against the United States, on occasion the French government found itself investigating misconduct committed by its soldiers and civilians against American forces. One of the most serious of these investigations arose when an American soldier mistook a French police officer for being a spy and shot him. Several French soldiers then attacked the American soldier as well as another American soldier and beat them to death. By the time the French military investigated the offenses, American military witnesses were difficult to locate and the French turned to Bethel for assistance. Although the French government offered compensation, Bethel informed his Allied counterparts that there was no legal mechanism for the army to transfer any funds to the deceased soldiers' families from the French military.[84]

THE VARIED VOLUME OF JUDGE ADVOCATE DUTIES IN THE AMERICAN EXPEDITIONARY FORCES

On October 3, 1918, Major Charles Teare reported to Kreger that in the month of September, the Fourth Division prosecuted four officers and twelve enlisted soldiers in general courts-martial, and in these trials, one officer and two soldiers were acquitted. The offenses included desertion, drunk on duty, and in the case of one officer, abusive treatment of enlisted personnel. In addition, the Fourth Division prosecuted twenty-seven special courts-martial, of which twenty-six resulted in a conviction, as well as 339 summary courts-martial, of which all but twelve resulted in a conviction. Of the general courts-martial, three convicted officers were sentenced to dismissals and confinement, and several of the enlisted sentences exceeded a year in prison. The Fourth Division had 19,491 soldiers on its rolls at the time of Teare's report. It had also conducted operations against the German Army during the entire month.[85]

The same month that Teare issued his report, Major Ogden, the Forty-Second—or "Rainbow"—Division's judge advocate, reported that his division prosecuted one officer and two enlisted soldiers in general courts-martial, as well as twelve special courts-martial and fifty-two summary courts-martial. The officer was court-martialed for an unauthorized absence and assaulting a military police officer, and based on the record it appeared that the officer had been intoxicated at the time. The enlisted offenses ranged from larceny and disrespect to noncommissioned officers to six absences. Only one of the Forty-Second Division's trials resulted in a sentence to a dishonorable discharge, but several soldiers received imprisonment of over six months. It is possible that the numeric difference in courts-martial between the Fourth and Forty-Second divisions had to do with the fact that the Rainbow Division was created out of National Guard forces, and hence its soldiers already had a greater degree of military training. On June 27, 1918, Ogden informed his wife that in the prior twelve months, the division "tried 175 General courts-martial cases, about 200 special courts-martial cases, and about 6,500 different charges in summary courts-martial." Both divisions were involved in the Battle of St. Mihiel during the month of September 1918, and both would take part in the Meuse-Argonne Offensive.[86]

On November 1, 1918, Chiperfield reported to Bethel and Crowder that in October, the Thirty-Third Division prosecuted one general court-martial, twenty-seven general courts-martial, and 116 summary courts-martial. Chiperfield and his assistant, Lieutenant Colonel James H. Stansfield, had taken to heart Crowder's direction to send the majority of charges to the lowest court-martial. From the division's arrival in France in May 1918 through November 1, 1918, there were two general courts-martial, sixty-eight special courts-martial, and 517 summary courts-martial. On learning of these low numbers, Ansell asked Bethel to investigate how it was possible for independent brigades to have conducted triple the number of general courts-martial than a division comprising three brigades. It was not until April 1919 when Crowder appointed Nathan MacChesney to investigate the division that the reasons came to light. MacChesney interviewed Pershing as well as Major General George Bell, the division's commander. Bell answered that because much of the division was created from the Illinois National Guard, and its veterans had not only served in the Philippines, in Cuba, and on the Mexican border, but also with the British and Australians in their front lines in June 1918, its discipline was already strong. Moreover, the division "had been able to shed itself of undesirables long before it departed to France." While MacChesney pointed out that by war's end, eight thousand draftees served in the division as replacements, which somewhat undermined Bell's reasoning, he could not discover a single instance in which he disagreed with Chiperfield's advice.[87]

As in the case of the Thirty-Third Division, the majority of the Twenty-Ninth Division's courts-martial occurred prior to its shipment from Maryland to France in June 1918, and until the Armistice, its court-martial numbers were commensurate to those of the other divisions. In July 1918, the division conducted four general courts-martial, including a trial of an officer accused of desertion. Lieutenant Colonel John Hill informed Bethel and Kreger that the small numbers of courts-martial had to do with the composition of the division's soldiers. Many of the soldiers had served on the Mexican border with the National Guard, and prior to June 1917, courts-martial had rid the division of its miscreants during the division's long training in Maryland and Alabama. In January 1919, the division conducted sixteen general and over one hundred special courts-martial. Hill reported that drunkenness was responsible for the majority of the crimes. Ironically, following his election to Congress in 1920, he would become one of the nation's more outspoken anti-Prohibitionists.[88]

The Twenty-Eighth Division adjudicated four general courts-martial following the Battle of Chateau Thierry in July 1918. The division, while providing support to the French Army during a defensive struggle, experienced hand-to-hand fighting against German soldiers. All four of the soldiers were found guilty of deserting their posts, and each was sentenced to five years in confinement and a dishonorable discharge. There were nineteen special courts-martial for what was considered lesser conduct, such as stealing property from captured German prisoners of war. Between November 1, 1918, and the end of December of that year, the division prosecuted over sixty general courts-martial for cowardice, misbehavior, desertion, and other specific military offenses that occurred during the division's combat in the Meuse-Argonne Offensive. In over half of these cases Major Cleon Berntheizel, the division's judge advocate, recommended to Major General Charles Muir to disapprove of the findings or grant clemency. In most instances Muir accepted Berntheizel's advice and commuted the sentences so that soldiers could return to the front.[89]

A "depot division" such as the Fortieth Division was structured somewhat differently than divisions that served in the front lines. There were, in all, six divisions classified as "depot divisions," and for most of the period between April 1918 and the Armistice these six divisions were responsible for outfitting replacement units before sending them to a frontline division. Thus a depot division was considered both a reserve force near the front and a unit in constant training. A depot division also served as "an intermediate supply unit" situated between the Services of Supply and the front lines. From September 1917 until war's end, Major James A. Howell served as the Fortieth Division's judge advocate. He had graduated from Harvard's law school in 1897 and served as a state judge in Utah from 1905 until the nation's entry into the war. His staff included a sergeant major and Major Fred G. Folsom, Captain Julian G. Dickinson, and Lieutenant John E. Price as assistant judge advocates. Between its arrival in France in December 1917 and the Armistice, the division conducted 137 general courts-martial, 195 special courts-martial, and 1,773 special courts-martial of soldiers. The most serious of the general courts-martial included two convictions for murder and one for rape. Each of the three soldiers received hard labor for life, but their sentences were later commuted to twenty years. The division also prosecuted twenty civilian laborers in general courts-martial and twelve civilians in special courts-martial. According to Bethel, *Milligan* did not apply to American laborers working for the army in France. Bethel's advice was not unfounded. In 1952 the Supreme Court upheld the assertion of military jurisdiction over citizens who worked for the War Department or lived in military installations in foreign countries as constitutional, though by 1960, the Court had fully reversed itself. On December 1, 1918, Howell reported to Kreger that his office also provided "matrimonial advice of a confidential nature to hundreds of soldiers" and settled hundreds of claims with French government and military officials. The most telling aspect of Howell's report was that the bulk of the courts-martial occurred within the first three months of the division arriving in France, and as training for combat increased, the numbers of courts-martial drastically declined.[90]

In October 1917, the Ninety-Second Division was formed out of African American soldiers and officered by senior white officers and a mix of African American and white junior officers, the latter of whom were given only rudimentary training. Their commander, Major General Charles Ballou, like many senior ranking officers in the army, had a pronounced prejudice against African American soldiers, going so far as to issue a regulation governing disputes arising between "negro and white soldiers" which insisted that "the burden of proof rested on the former." Ballou, however, at least acknowledged that underperforming white officers were part of the division's weakness, and he feuded with General Robert Bullard over this point. The division had difficulties from the start. It was common for Pershing to place American divisions into the British and French front lines for training purposes, but Field Marshal Douglas Haig, the British Expeditionary Force commander, refused to accept the Ninety-Second Division. Pershing conceded that the division, and particularly its officers, lacked the requisite training to succeed—he claimed that because of their lower standard of education and temperament, African American officers required more time in training to rise to the same standards as white officers—but that the division could only receive the training in the front lines. White officers reported to the War Department and members of Congress that the division's soldiers committed numerous rapes and threatened mutiny. Hugh Ogden joined in the criticism by alleging that the division's soldiers had a habit of running away from combat and claimed that T.N.T. stood for "travel nigger travel" rather than the explosive. The one bright spot for the division, as Major Adam Patterson, the division's judge advocate, noted to W. E. B. DuBois, was that the French citizenry protected African American soldiers.[91]

In reality, from August 1, 1918, until October 1, 1919, the division conducted forty-seven general courts-martial and over one hundred special courts-martial. These numbers were only slightly higher than those reported by Major Teare for the Fourth Division over the same time frame. Nonetheless, Patterson had a more difficult task in administering discipline than his judge advocate peers for reasons that few officers such as Ogden would understand or acknowledge. The clear reality of the division's record of military discipline was more reflective of the army holding African Americans accountable for conduct that white soldiers would not be held to account for. Tellingly, of the nine general courts-martial for rape, only two resulted in a finding of guilty by largely white courts-martial panels. During the height of the Meuse-Argonne Offensive, the division conducted five general courts-martial of African American officers accused of cowardice, and all five were adjudged guilty. All of the officers were dismissed from the army and stigmatized with a mark of dishonorable service. Four of the officers were sentenced to be executed. None of the officers was executed after Patterson advised Ballou and Bethel that the guilty findings were unwarranted. Even the most effective senior white commanders in the American Expeditionary Forces could not seem to understand that the constant public criticism of African American soldiers diminished their morale and discipline, in all likelihood more than German propaganda, the general harshness of military discipline, or the experience of frontline service.[92]

The divisional examples of courts-martial workload can be extrapolated to the entire American Expeditionary Forces, which conducted over three thousand general and special courts-martial between the Armistice and December 1, 1918. How the judge advocates were able to read records of trial and advise their commanders during this time is not simply answerable by highlighting their legal acumen, work ethic, or talent. They had significant help not only from line officers who were lawyers before the war but also from enlisted personnel. Each division had at least four sergeants to assist in the adjudication of trials and claims. These sergeants, known as "legal orderlies," also doubled as court reporters. During the first months of the war Crowder suggested to Bethel that civilians could be employed by the War Department to serve as transcribers or reporters for courts-martial. Bethel, with Pershing's support, countered that enlisted court reporters would be more valuable in performing a full range of duties to include legal research. Although the term *paralegal* had yet to enter the nation's lexicon, over two hundred enlisted personnel performed duties, including legal research and the drafting of documents, that would properly fit under the "paralegal" rubric. Most of the orderlies were brought into the Judge Advocate General's Department as privates, but the headquarters correspondences reveal not only rapid promotion to sergeant for the orderlies but also that the American Expeditionary Forces judge advocates placed great reliance on the services of legal orderlies and court reporters. As an example, Colonel A. W. Brown, a judge advocate assigned to the First Army, urged Bethel to promote Private DeHirsch Bransky to the rank of battalion sergeant major as a result of his "exemplary services." Not only had Bransky conducted court-reporter duties in dozens of general courts-martial, he had also drafted a number of special orders for the command and researched French law. At the same time Brown lobbied on behalf of Bransky, Colonel Wiley Howell, the acting First Army judge advocate, likewise urged Bethel to ensure that Sergeant Howard J. Vogt, who had performed similar duties, be promoted to regimental sergeant major. Both Bransky and Vogt were law school students who were drafted in 1917. On April 16, 1919, Winship urged Bethel to ask Crowder for more enlisted personnel because of "their invaluable service in investigating claims and researching complex issues of fact and law." By 1919 legal orderlies were doubling as criminal investigators for American soldiers suspected of crimes, and also were investigating German misconduct.[93]

Judge advocates who deployed with the American Expeditionary Forces, like their commanders, could be sticklers for following military protocol and other regulations. For instance, Howell noted to Liggett that although he supervised Colonel A. W. Brown at First Army headquarters, the fact that in the regular army and without Howell's brevet promotion, Brown outranked Howell, precluded Howell from writing an efficiency report on Brown. One week before Howell wrote to Liggett, he had toured the Services of Supply along with his enlisted orderly and a military cook with the rank of private named John T. Abbott. Howell discovered that "Cook Abbott" knowingly received double rations and informed the headquarters company commander that the cook's pay had to be withheld so that the army did not become victim to "a scheme."[94]

The fielded judge advocates were able to exercise a good deal of independence regardless of the large numbers of regulations. Despite Winship's guidance to Pershing on not employing the harsher aspects of British and French discipline in the US Army, several brigade, divisional, and corps commanders believed that harsh visible punishment served as an effective deterrent. In June 1918, Liggett authorized punishment battalions in the rear areas so that persons punished by special courts-martial could serve their sentences laboring in the

midst of their peers. One of the duties assigned to court-martialed soldiers
placed in such battalions was to feed and exercise horses and mules and tend
to other animals. Animal cruelty became widespread to the point where
one divisional commander issued an order for sergeant majors in charge of
offenders to "subject soldiers instantly to the same procedure (kicking, beating
over the head, and similar forms of brutality)." Lieutenant Colonel James A.
Gallogly, the First Army Corps judge advocate, tried to advise Liggett that his
subordinate division commander's order was illegal, but Liggett was absent at
the time and the officer who issued the order, General William Siebert, was
unwilling to rescind it. Gallogly enlisted Winship's help and he journeyed to
Chaumont to confer with Liggett. Based on Winship's advice, Liggett rescinded
Siebert's order.[95]

On other matters, Gallogly proved willing to endorse draconian measures.
French roads were not conducive to the mass movements of soldiers and war
matériel. The celebrated "Voie Sacrée" or "Sacred Way" connecting Bar-le-Duc
to Verdun served as a single lifeline for the French Army holding the Verdun
area, and it became an important supply artery for the American Expeditionary
Forces. Traffic jams and accidents not only slowed the transport of soldiers to
the front at critical times, Pershing became convinced that such occurrences
could "bring the loss of battle." To effectively deter carelessness on the
roads, Gallogly advised Liggett to establish summary courts to immediately
prosecute careless drivers at major intersections. Such courts required only
a single officer sitting in judgment and could strip an enlisted soldier of
rank and pay or result in confinement for thirty days. To Gallogly, the need
for a visible public deterrent was sufficient reason to justify swift tribunals
without the time to develop a defense. Not all of the judge advocates endorsed
Gallogy's idea, however. Pepper noted in his diary that "the use of summary
courts-martial to take care of traffic violators is a faulty scheme and will not
produce the best desired results."[96]

While the judge advocate hierarchical structure was designed to promote
consistency in the application of law throughout the American Expeditionary
Forces, there were occurrences where judge advocates assigned at higher
echelon headquarters became livid at the performance of their peers in
subordinate commands. On September 18, 1918, Major R. C. Stewart, assigned
to the First Corps, chastised Captain S. G. Thornton for advising the First
Division commander that the theft of monies from a dead captain "failed
to state an offense." Thornton apparently believed that for larceny to occur,
a victim of theft had to be alive. On August 27, 1918, the army prosecuted
Private Martin Dillon in a general court-martial for "desertion and flight from
his unit while it was engaged with the enemy, on July 20, 1918." The desertion

and flight took place in an engagement near Soissons during the Second Battle of the Marne. Dillon took refuge in a field aid station, and a French surgeon caught him taking eighteen hundred francs from "a dead American captain." The court-martial sentenced Dillon to be dishonorably discharged and confined for twenty-five years, but on Thornton's advice, the commander did not approve the guilty verdict as to the theft and commuted the sentence to five years. A livid Stewart informed Winship that Thornton's "incompetence in basic criminal law militated against his further service" and recommended he be sent home.[97]

One common theme throughout the correspondences and official memoranda of judge advocates was the elimination of errors in records that, to the judge advocates, evidenced not only a slipshod approach to significant administrative legal issues but also a diminution of the procedural rights afforded to service-members. For instance, army officers obtained their commission through a delegation process that originated with the president. As a result, an officer could not be discharged or demoted without an administrative procedure approved by the secretary of war. Likewise, officers who were "brevetted" to a temporary higher rank as a result of the army's rapid expansion could only be demoted through a similar administrative procedure. Known as an elimination board, this procedure required a trial format similar to a court-martial. Following the Armistice, large numbers of officer elimination boards were conducted, including in the American Expeditionary Forces. But problems with these boards arose before the Armistice, even though fewer than eight hundred were conducted prior to then.

When Kreger discovered in August 1918 that over one-third of the elimination boards had failed to adhere to the rules governing basic administrative rights, he reminded the judge advocates throughout the American Expeditionary Forces that these failures were an affront not only to the American Expeditionary Forces but also Secretary Baker and President Wilson. The majority of the records of elimination boards, according to Kreger, had failed to note that witnesses were sworn and that the reasons for reduction to permanent rank or recommendations of removal from the army were often "too loosely and irregularly framed" to constitute a basis for removal. In the Civil War, an officer could be removed without cause, but by 1917 this wasn't the case, and Pershing supported Kreger regarding this. The army had become a creature of statute and its judge advocates became sticklers on this point.[98]

Some of the basis of the elimination of officers arose as a result of misconduct that could have been prosecuted in a court-martial, and some of it came after the discovery of an incompetency in leadership. Senior officers, including career officers, were not immune from such boards. On January 22, 1919,

Colonel Wallace was tasked with investigating an allegation of cowardice against a Lieutenant Frederick Huff. Huff had been drafted into the army as a dental surgeon, and on October 28 he became separated from his unit in the Meuse-Argonne. Rather than return to the rear, he assisted surgeons under fire in a makeshift hospital, but after he rejoined his unit, his colonel, William R. Pope, called him a coward and beat him to the ground with a walking cane. Pope also challenged Huff to a fight in front of his staff and then attempted to prefer charges of cowardice. In his investigation, Wallace advised Kreger and Pershing that Huff was wholly innocent and Pope "had failed the standards required of an officer in the American Expeditionary Forces." As a result of the investigation, the army forced Pope into retirement through the elimination board process, and Huff received an honorable discharge at the end of his service.[99]

Following the Armistice, processing naturalization orders was added to other judge advocate duties. During the war, the United States Naturalization Service had enabled the War Department to process and recommend approval of citizenship applications. The Naturalization Service only required an attestation form from the reviewing officer instead of the statements the reviewing officer took into consideration. In December 1918 alone, judge advocates processed over one thousand citizenship applications of soldiers who were born in foreign countries but served faithfully in the United States Army or in attached United States Marine Corps units. On December 16, 1918, Captain V. Webb, the junior-most judge advocate attached to the First Army, forwarded five hundred citizenship applications recommending approval that he had investigated since the Armistice. Such investigations included attaching two officers' affidavits that attested to an applicant's loyalty and "moral soundness." Webb's duties also included ensuring that an applicant's name be properly reflected in citizenship documentation. As a result, he corrected a name reversal that occurred at Ellis Island in 1911 from Diego Hugo Martorelli to Hugo Diego Martorelli. There are dozens of applications in the National Archives files where Webb corrected what appears to have been a common occurrence of misspellings at the various immigration centers such as Ellis Island. More tellingly than Webb's keen eye to make sure that names were properly reflected for soldiers who had earned their citizenship, was that he opined that rumors of Bolshevik sympathies were not enough to deny citizenship. To Webb, the law required an affirmative act such as stoking a mutiny or aiding Germany for a denial of citizenship, and in such instances, courts-martial were the only instrument of proof. Bethel and Kreger supported him on this point.[100]

CONCLUSION: THE ROLE OF THE JUDGE ADVOCATE GENERAL'S OFFICE IN
THE DEFEAT OF GERMANY

From 1917 through the Armistice, soldiers in the American Expeditionary
Forces shipped to France and trained throughout that nation, including
in the front lines. Many of the over two million soldiers in the American
Expeditionary Forces experienced the horror and human suffering of trench
warfare. They were also subjected to an austere alien legal system based
both on discipline and due process. From June until November 11, 1918, but
particularly in the last three months of the war, the American Expeditionary
Forces fought almost continuously against entrenched German forces. At
no time was there a mutiny or large-scale refusal to "go over the top." While
there were several reasons for this success, one of them had to do with the
composition and philosophy of the fielded judge advocates. Beginning with
Bethel and Kreger, the career judge advocates were attuned to the need to
balance discipline with notions of fairness based on the legal jurisprudence
of the time. Moreover, a number of attorneys who could be categorized as
legal progressives, but had minimal to no prior military experience, served
as judge advocates in the American Expeditionary Forces. They also not
only provided critical guidance to the commanders on courts-martial, they
cemented legal relationships with the Allies. At times, some, like Arthur
Hill, were placed on liaison duties with the ranking French and British
military and government officials. This too served as a critical duty so that
the American Expeditionary Forces could function as an American Army
in an American offensive, and had the war continued, the American army
would have supplied the preponderant numbers of soldiers in an invasion
of Germany.

When, in June 1919, Brigadier General Ansell tried to alter the army's
disciplinary construct and publicly argued that courts-martial conducted
during the war were devoid of due process, most of the judge advocates
who served in France took offense. The fielded judge advocates had, after all,
worked to ensure that discipline would not be the sole factor in trials, and
they approached military justice as part of an interlocking legal structure that
made the American Expeditionary Forces interoperable with the Allies in such
matters as contracting and the treatment of prisoners of war. Judge advocates
such as Ogden, Cosgrave, Pepper, both Arthur and John Hill, and Patterson
labored under austere conditions, and although they would return to their
largely progressive pursuits in 1919—such as defending Sacco and Vanzetti on
their appeals—they universally would side with Crowder over Ansell.

5

INTERNATIONAL LAW AND ADMINISTRATIVE
DUTIES IN WAR AND AFTER THE ARMISTICE

ON NOVEMBER 11, 1918, FRENCH general Ferdinand Foch, British admiral Roslyn Wemyss, and four representatives of the German government signed an armistice to terminate hostilities for a period of thirty-six days on the Western Front and in Italy. Although no American took part in the signing, the Allies expected American military involvement in the enforcement of the Armistice's provisions. Section V of the Armistice mandated the evacuation of German forces from the left bank of the Rhine, including an eighteen-mile extension into Germany proper. Between the eighteen-mile "bridgehead" into Germany and the permissible forward line of the German Army, the Armistice established a neutral zone of six and one quarter miles, extending from the Dutch border to the Swiss frontier. No German or Allied forces were permitted to enter the neutral zone. Essentially, the Allies occupied a region known as the Rhineland. Allied forces were entitled to requisition foodstuffs and other material in the Rhineland, and "the upkeep of the troops of occupation in the Rhineland (excluding Alsace and Lorraine)," was chargeable "to the German government." Other obligations were placed on the German Army, including notifying the Allies of the locations of minefields, poisoned wells, and buried ordnance stores, to minimize the loss of life. Although it was not listed in the Armistice's language, American forces were to be responsible for the governance of the German cities of Trier and Coblenz and the area surrounding both cities.[1]

One month before the war ended, Crowder met with John Bassett Moore, the influential Columbia University international law scholar and occasional State Department special counsel, and Crowder predicted to Moore that the

Meuse-Argonne Offensive, coupled with the British and French offensives, would result in the collapse of the German Army in France within thirty days. Crowder did not necessarily believe that the war with Germany would end. The purpose of Crowder's discussion with Moore, which occurred on a train traveling from Governors Island to Washington, DC, was not to predict the end of the war, but rather, to decide how to militarily govern Germany. Moore advised Crowder that the extension of military jurisdiction over the German population was necessary because Germany was in political upheaval, and the only means by which to have an impartial and apolitical German judiciary was through the military's oversight. Moore also advised that the military governance of the southern states during Reconstruction could serve as a model, but he cautioned that the army ought to refrain from censoring or suppressing newspapers and political activity to the extent possible.[2]

On November 17, 240,000 American soldiers of the newly constituted Third Army under Joseph T. Dickman's command crossed over the front lines, and within two weeks, this force entered into the Rhineland. The numbered army was renamed after the War Department established a new command to govern the area of Germany assigned to the United States titled the "American Forces in Germany." Within three months, the War Department separated responsibility for governing Germany from the American Expeditionary Forces in France. However, Pershing remained in overall command of all American ground and air forces in Europe. The first two commanders in Germany, Generals Dickman and Liggett, lasted in command for less than seven months. Dickman returned to France to organize a defensive line in case the war were renewed. Liggett remained in Germany for one month and then returned to command the First Army in France, because there were considerably more American soldiers in France, and Pershing wanted to retain Liggett in command of a fighting force should war begin anew. From July 1919 until the termination of the mission in Germany in 1923, General Henry Tureman Allen served as commander of the American Forces in Germany. For most of Allen's command tenure, Colonel Kyle Rucker served as the mission's judge advocate, and he, in turn, supervised four judge advocates.[3]

Rucker was commissioned into the cavalry after graduating from the United States Military Academy in 1899, and he served in the Philippines the following year. In 1913 he was attached to the Signal Corps, and in 1916, he was commissioned as a judge advocate as part of the Judge Advocate General's Office's expansion. Both Pershing and General Frederick Funston endorsed Rucker's application for a judge advocate commission. While stationed in Georgia in 1905, he had attended the Atlanta Law School in the evenings, earned highest honors, and continued in his cavalry duties during the day. He had served as an acting judge advocate on two separate occasions, including in Tampico, Mexico, in 1915. In 1917 he was promoted to major and assigned as the judge advocate to the Southeastern Department, responsible for administering courts-martial on the Texas-Mexico border near Brownsville and Laredo. In reporting to the War Department on his duties, he noted that the National Guard was "crippled by informality between the officer and enlisted ranks," and several guard officers were shocked that a soldier caught sleeping on post could serve considerable time in prison.[4]

The American Forces in Germany's chief of civil affairs later noted in his official report that despite the army's experience in establishing military governments in Mexico and California following the Mexican-American War, in the southern states during Reconstruction, and in the twentieth century in Puerto Rico, Cuba, the Philippines, China, and Tampico, the War Department had no training or doctrine for using the military as a governing force. However, the Judge Advocate General's Office, and in particular Winthrop, Lieber, and Davis, had written treatises on the legal mechanisms of military government, and their texts were standard reading in the Judge Advocate General's Office, the General Staff, and the United States Military Academy. Rucker repeatedly referenced Winthrop's treatise in his advice to Dickman and Allen. On December 13, 1918, Pershing issued General Order 1, instructing the occupied German population that the German courts and other public functions would continue as before, but under the supervision of army authorities and only insofar as the municipal courts did not interfere with the safety of American soldiers. In settling disputes between US soldiers and German citizens, American military tribunals were to have sole jurisdiction. Moreover, in all cases involving both US soldiers and civilians, or civilians alleged to have violated military regulations or the laws of war, military trials would have full jurisdiction over German citizens. The order as originally drafted by Rucker for Pershing originated in Winthrop's treatise.[5]

For the first time since Reconstruction, an American military government was established with full jurisdiction over an occupied population and with the intent of its existing for a long duration. Although at the time *Milligan* applied only to US citizens located in the United States, and specifically only where the civil courts functioned, there were historic sensitivities to the reach of military jurisdiction over civilians, and Rucker was unsure as to how Congress would react. Congress was, for the most part, willing to tolerate military trials over indigenous peoples. Native Americans in California following the Modoc Wars were prosecuted in a military trial despite the fact that the federal courts in California fully functioned. In the Philippines, military courts prosecuted civilians for committing common law offenses. For instance, on April 1, 1902, while serving as the Northern Division's judge advocate in Manila, Blanton Winship reported that in addition to twenty-eight general courts-martial of soldiers and scouts, his command prosecuted two civilians in military commissions for larceny. Rather than comparing military jurisdiction to what occurred in the Civil War, Rucker advised Dickman that it was best to publicly explain that the military courts in Germany were similar to what Funston had attempted to establish in Tampico, Mexico in 1915, and what General Wesley Merritt established over the Philippine population. But Rucker recognized that the Germans were not persons of a different race or considered to be "uncivilized," and he added that it was best not to advertise that the trials were exempt from *Milligan*, to avoid the appearance of a constitutional issue. He learned that Secretary of State Lansing had queried Attorney General Gregory and Secretary of War Baker as to whether the creation of military tribunals over Germans ran afoul of *Milligan*, and Lansing's question caused him to worry that other government officials might argue that the post–Civil War decision prevented military trials in Germany. Moreover, it was well known that Wilson did not approve of the military government over the southern states during Reconstruction. Although Crowder advised Baker, March, and Pershing that *Milligan* did not prevent the military trials of Germans, and he equated the German population to Philippine civilians, he too worried whether southern congressmen or Lansing would try to stop the trials. Crowder also reminded Rucker that for the trials to gain domestic support, the discipline of the army would have to be vigorously enforced.[6]

One day after General Order 1's issuance, Rucker advised Dickman to publish a further order detailing not only the duties of soldiers in occupied Germany but also a list of prohibited conduct. Rucker worried that soldiers would justify acts of looting and assaults on German civilians as part of their police duties over occupied Germany. His worries were well founded. In the thirty days following the first American soldiers arriving in Germany, his office was asked to draft courts-martial charges for forty-eight cases of looting alone. Rucker's model order for Dickman began, "the erroneous view frequently entertained by the enlisted personnel that their occupancy of enemy soil gives a privilege of unrestrained search and seizure of personal effects of private individuals and the appropriation of their own use of enemy property, will receive on the part of each organization commander immediate consideration and correction." This language remained intact in the actual published order.[7]

THE LAW OF WAR AND THE JUDGE ADVOCATE GENERAL'S OFFICE

Analysis of the army's governance of occupied Germany requires, in addition to an understanding of the legal relationships between the Allied forces, consideration of the Judge Advocate General's Office's approach to the law of war. Senior American military commanders in France and Germany following the Armistice had, in addition to the discipline of the army and the governance over part of the German population, the duty of enforcing the laws of war by investigating and prosecuting war crimes and investigating and enforcing reparations payments to the Allies. The containment of communism—or as it was commonly titled, "Bolshevism"—was also part of their duties. All of these duties were interlinked, and the zealous enforcement of one duty could affect the others. Put another way, the maintenance of the army's discipline, the enforcement of law and order on the German civilian population while achieving trusting relations with the United States, the containment of Bolshevism, the principle of both holding German officials accountable for war crimes and the new German government to the reparations terms of the Armistice and eventual peace treaty, required a judicious approach.[8]

Shortly after the declaration of war on Germany, an odd issue originating in a military arrest of a soldier arose in a federal court, which not only reaffirmed the War Department's authority to assert its full jurisdiction over US soldiers but also provided the department a basis for an almost unlimited power to classify foreign-born noncitizens as prisoners of war, interned aliens, or saboteurs. In July 1917, Private John Hackenberg, an Ohio National Guard soldier, refused to be mustered into the army. Hackenberg was born in Vienna and emigrated with his mother to the United States in 1912. In 1915 he enlisted in the Ohio National Guard at the age of sixteen, and when his unit federalized for service on the Mexican border, he willingly swore a federal oath attesting to a false age. However, in July 1917, he decided to implicate himself for fraudulently enlisting rather than be federalized and ship to France to fight German and possibly Austrian soldiers. His commander ordered his arrest and charged him with various violations of the Articles of War, but most notably fraudulent enlistment and refusing to obey a lawful order to report to a training cantonment. In response, Hackenberg's brother-in-law appealed for a writ of habeas corpus to the United States District Court for Ohio and argued that Hackenberg was not liable to the army's jurisdiction because he had been too young to enlist, and secondarily, that as an Austrian subject who had never become an American citizen, he was either an alien national or a prisoner of war and therefore could not be forced to train or ship to France to fight.[9]

Crowder assigned Nathan MacChesney and James Brown Scott to draft the government's response to Hackenberg's challenge, but he permitted Colonel Hubert J. Turney, the judge advocate of the Ohio National Guard, to argue the merits of the response with MacChesney present in court. In 1914 MacChesney and Turney had represented Ohio in a significant appeal to the Supreme Court involving the authority of the secretary of war to regulate National Guard commissions. Judge David C. Westenhaver, a Wilson appointee who later sentenced labor leader Eugene Debs to ten years in prison, sided with the War Department over its assertion of its jurisdiction to court-martial Hackenberg. It might also have been a matter of significance that Baker lobbied Wilson for Westenhaver's judicial nomination in February 1917. Westenhaver recognized that the army retained jurisdiction to prosecute soldiers who fraudulently enlisted on the basis of age, and he determined that Hackenberg's asserted allegiance to the Habsburg emperor did not terminate this jurisdiction. Implicit in Westenhaver's decision was that the federal judiciary could not review appeals arising from the War Department classifying foreign-born individuals who had not attained citizenship as enemy aliens or prisoners of war, any more than the judiciary could determine an appeal that challenged the fairness of a court-martial. Although the judge advocates involved in defending the War Department did not base their arguments on a unitary Executive Branch theory in a manner that several White House attorneys in President George W. Bush's administration would later assert—that is, that in wartime the president has virtually unlimited authority to ignore domestic laws and international covenants related for reasons of national security—the Judge Advocate General's Office's approach to Hackenberg's challenge might have unintentionally presaged the so-called "neoconservative" jurisprudence of the post–September 11, 2001, attacks.[10]

The war brought questions of nationality to the War Department not seen since the San Patricio Battalion incident during the Mexican-American War, when a small number of Irish immigrants who had enlisted in the army prior to the conflict found it morally impossible to fight against Catholic Mexico and deserted. Over fifty of these men were captured in Mexican Army uniforms while fighting against the United States and were executed after a quick trial. The World War I example of Henry Bode shows how nationality, citizenship, and loyalty intersected in a court-martial. Bode was born in Germany in 1870, emigrated to the United States in 1898, and enlisted in the Montana Volunteer Infantry. He enlisted in the army in 1911 after working as a miner in Butte, Montana, and participating in union attempts to organize labor. He deserted in 1912, and a court-martial sentenced him to six months in confinement. However, he returned to active duty and became a naturalized citizen.[11]

He deserted from the army in 1914 while stationed in Texas and crossed the border into Mexico before heading to Germany. Once in Germany, he enlisted in its army and initially served on the Eastern Front. However, he was injured, and while recuperating in Berlin in late 1915 he encountered Ms. Frank Gerard, the wife of the US ambassador to Germany. She reported to the War Department that Bode was a German soldier. In 1916 Bode, along with his unit, was transferred to the Western Front, and he fought against the British at the Battle of the Somme. After the United States' declaration of war against Germany, Bode obtained his release from the German Army and traveled to Mexico. In early 1918 he crossed back into Texas and willingly surrendered. General Marlboro Churchill, the acting chief of the Military Intelligence Branch, was concerned that Bode had claimed that he had been sent into the United States to act as a spy. Bode pleaded with Churchill that in exchange for avoiding a court-martial and possible death sentence for treason, he would inform on other Germans. The judge advocate in the Southern Department had, in fact, recommended charging Bode with treason and pursing an execution. But Crowder relayed to Churchill as well as to the commanding general of the department that Bode had not yet committed treason because at the time Bode joined the German Army, the United States had yet to enter the war. A day after Crowder departed for a conference in New York, Ansell advised Churchill that "should any evidence develop that the accused held correspondence with or gave intelligence to the enemy, either directly or indirectly, he should be charged with treason."[12]

Bode ran into trouble after Witzke identified him as a potential accomplice, but for reasons that are no longer evident in the case files, Crowder discounted Witzke's claims. After Crowder advised Churchill that Witzke was unreliable because he wanted to avoid his own execution, Churchill obtained evidence from the Swedish consul general that Bode had been caught in Sweden in January 1917 and claimed to be working for the Department of Justice, investigating a German spy. In December 1917, shortly before he turned himself in, he had contacted a German-born soldier named Max Jacobs and a Swedish-born soldier named Birger Carlson and tried to convince them to desert into Mexico. Ultimately Bode was court-martialed at Governors Island for both desertion and espionage and sentenced to ten years in prison, of which he served less than two. In 1920 Bode applied for reentry into the army, and as a result of the War Department's bureaucracy, he was released from confinement at Alcatraz and restored to duty. The cause of Bode's restoration originated with Dunn, who after the trial transmitted to the War Department only that Bode had been convicted and sentenced for desertion without providing the underlying conduct for the offenses. This provided Crowder with another reason to disparage Dunn, this time to Secretary of War John Weeks, who had succeeded Baker. In spite of the personalities involved in what Crowder called "the Bode affair," it is important to note that at no time did the Judge Advocate General's Office seek to replay what had occurred with the San Patricio Battalion. To the contrary, Crowder and, surprisingly, Wigmore advised that if the army were to court-martial Bode for treason, then the German government could prosecute any of the thousands of German-born nationals serving in the United States Army for treason against Germany as "a law of war matter in equity." On the other hand, had Crowder been alive in 1939 when the War Department issued Bode a war service bonus, he would have likely written an angry letter to President Roosevelt.[13]

Even before the United States' entry into the war, the General Staff examined the laws of war regarding prisoner of war treatment as well as other aspects of the law of war as this body of laws applied to the European war. On March 29, 1917, Chief of Staff Hugh Scott signed Special Regulation 26 governing the treatment of prisoners of war. Crowder, Bethel, and Major James Brown Scott authored the regulation the day prior for General Scott's signature, after learning that Secretary of the Navy Josephus Daniels agreed that all captured German servicemen would come under the War Department's custody and control. The order embodied the prevailing international law norms for protecting the rights and health of prisoners of war, but in addition, it mandated that prisoner of war letters from both French and stateside encampments were to be sent free of cost to the prisoners. Additionally, there were to be no restraints on religious practices or voluntary employment. On the morning of March 29, Major Scott gained Solicitor General Davis's agreement that the regulation was legally sound. For understandable reasons, General Scott issued Special Regulation 26 on April 17, over a week after the declaration of war.[14]

One of the immediate questions arising out of the war was to what extent German nationals living in the United States who held German military commissions or other obligations to the German military were liable to prisoner of war status. As of January 18 there were over 250,000 males of German birth living in the United States who were classified as "alien enemies." Under international law, persons in this category were subject to internment, but internment was not a mandatory feature of the United States' laws. Historically, internment was likely to occur when an "alien enemy" had a military obligation to an enemy state. In July 1917, Ansell advised General Bliss that a German Navy reserve officer was lawfully interned as a result of the declaration of war. The reserve officer worked at an American bank in New York at the time, and because he was not in uniform at the time of capture, Ansell concluded, there was no requirement to move him into a prisoner of war status. On the other hand, by early 1918 the army held over one hundred prisoners of war at Fort McPherson in Georgia, and a prior camp commander had ordered the prisoners to construct their own barracks. All of these prisoners were in the United States on April 5, 1917. Colonel James Mayes interpreted the 1907 Hague Convention to require the War Department to compensate the prisoners of war for their labor, at the same rate contractors would have been paid for similar work. As a result, the War Department paid the prisoners of war in US dollars.[15]

There was little revolutionary about the War Department issuing orders governing the treatment of prisoners of war. In 1863 Francis Lieber headed an army committee that authored a codified law of war to apply to both the Union and Confederacy. Once approved by Secretary of War Stanton, the codified laws, which became known as General Order 100, guided the army to formally conform to the laws and customs of war. General Order 100 was in use in the Spanish-American War, the Philippine Insurrection, and the China Relief Expedition, as well as the "Punitive Expedition" into Mexico in 1916. One of the tenets of General Order 100 was that its protections only applied to the forces that conformed to Western notions of the laws of war. In 1899 and 1907, the major European powers, the United States, China, and Japan signed on to a series of conventions at The Hague which adopted and expanded on General Order 100. The signatory governments agreed to comply with the two Hague prohibitions against waging aggressive warfare without notice to an opposing state, as well as to prohibit the use of poison gas and aerial bombardment. That General George Davis, Crowder's predecessor, accompanied the American ambassador Joseph Choate to the 1907 conference likely gave credence to the conventions insofar as the army's leadership was concerned. There is no evidence that Wilson, Garrison, Hugh Scott, Bliss, Pershing, Crowder, Ansell, or any of Pershing's subordinates, with the exception of James Harbord, complained about the two conventions' restrictions. On the other hand, by 1917 the warring powers had violated several of the restrictions, to include the use of poison gas and the waging of economic warfare through a naval blockade.[16]

Another influence on the laws of war becoming a concern to the judge advocate general had to do with Germany's approach to neutrality. It is true that the British freely conducted intelligence activities in the United States, but they did not commit acts of espionage on American soil. During the Civil War, Confederate agents conducted espionage from Canada into the northern states. Prior to the United States' entry into World War I, German agents planned to destroy Canadian industries from operations originating in the

United States. From the beginning of the century, a small number of German reserve officers had been detached as observers to the various Mexican Army commands, and these officers were able to transit through the United States. In August 1914, Captain Franz Von Papen, Germany's military attaché to the United States, originated a scheme to buy motor-boats mounted with cannon and machine guns to fire on Canadian villages along the Great Lakes as well as to destroy canal locks. He ordered Horst Von der Goltz, a German officer who used the alias Bridgeman Taylor, to enlist Irish nationals for the operation. However, Von der Goltz was unable to conduct the raids and traveled to Italy before being captured by the British military and interned. Although Von Papen's initial scheme was never carried out, other operations were.[17]

In 1915 Assistant Attorney General Charles Warren informed both General Scott and Crowder that a German-funded "Hindu plot" existed in the United States and its members worked in tandem with Irish nationalists to disrupt the British military's war efforts. Warren claimed that the "Society of the Advancement of India" was a front to dynamite British flagged vessels in New York and San Francisco. He advised Scott and Crowder that John Heinrich von Bernstorff, the German ambassador to the United States, funded suspected agents Raim Chandra, Jodh Singh, and Heramba Lal Gupta. There was very little that Crowder or the army could do with this information since the United States was not yet at war, and the laws were unclear on such activity. At best, German agents could be prosecuted for committing ordinary crimes in federal court. But Crowder nonetheless urged Garrison to pressure the Secretary of State Bryan to expel German government officials and extradite the three Indian agents to the British government. In early 1917, agents of the Department of the Navy arrested and imprisoned three persons purporting to be Swiss citizens. In reality one of these men was a German naval officer and the other two German agents, caught spying near the Brooklyn Navy Yard shortly after the declaration of war. Although the fate of the three Germans rested with the secretary of the navy and attorney general, Crowder was interested in the outcome of their trials.[18]

By 1916 the War Department was well aware of German espionage activities in the United States. That year a munitions depot on "Black Tom Island," New Jersey, exploded, killing seven people and causing millions of dollars in property damage. War Department officers believed that German agents were responsible for the explosion, in part because the munitions that were destroyed were headed to Britain. Once again, Crowder lobbied to have Secretary of State Bryan expel the German diplomatic corps from the United States and have the Bureau of Investigation arrest Lothar Witzke, a German naval officer. Crowder had evidence that Witzke planned the explosion, and it was well known that he and German diplomats attempted to stoke antiwar sentiments among Irish-Americans by spreading propaganda alleging that Roger Casement—an Irish patriot whom the British caught smuggling arms into Ireland—was wrongfully prosecuted and executed. The British government prosecuted Casement in a civil trial, but many of his peers who took up arms and fought for full Irish independence from Britain were not treated in the same manner.[19]

Crowder strongly believed that public perceptions of Casement's fate were important to the War Department and that President Wilson had the ability to support Britain's treatment of Casement. Crowder, however, misjudged Wilson's willingness to endorse a foreign country's treason laws. Although Casement was prosecuted in a civil trial, in 1915 Parliament suspended the right to a jury trial through the Defense of Realm Act. Following the 1916 Easter Rising, the British Army court-martialed 183 civilians, and these trials sentenced ninety prisoners to death. None of the prisoners were British soldiers at the time of the trials, and most had never been. In all, the British Army executed fifteen civilians. After a small number of members of Parliament expressed their doubts on the legality of the military trials, on May 15, 1916, Prime Minister Herbert Asquith ordered all executions to cease. However, the British judiciary upheld the government's authority to apply the law of war to Irish nationalists who took up arms against Britain, and Asquith's successor, David Lloyd George, was free to rescind Asquith's order.[20]

Casement's situation led to a perplexing division between the State, Justice, and War Departments. Secretary of State Lansing and Attorney General Gregory had determined to publicly downplay German espionage activities in the United States, and in regard to the British execution of Casement, Lansing advised Wilson that the Executive Branch should remain silent on the matter and neither endorse nor oppose a Senate resolution of condemnation. A broad cross section of senators, ranging from progressives James Phelan of California and Thomas Walsh of Montana to the reactionary James Vardaman of Mississippi, vocally condemned the British government. Crowder was fully aware of the political ramifications of Britain's military trials of Irish nationals, but he believed that under British law, the military trials were lawful. He urged Garrison to counter to Lansing and Gregory that Casement's trial and execution comported with British law. He also argued that Irish nationalists who had taken up arms against the British government in wartime were amenable to trial by court-martial. Garrison agreed with Crowder's assessment on British jurisdiction but informed him that "political considerations" blocked any statement of support from Wilson. Tumulty explained to Lansing and Garrison that Wilson sided with the State

Department and that because "the Casement matter played a prominent part in the New Jersey primaries and resulted in bringing many votes to [the Republican candidate], the President would issue no statement of support to Britain on the matter."[21]

Witzke fled to Mexico shortly after the "Black Tom" explosion, but in early 1918 he returned to the United States under the name Pablo Waberski. Because the nation was now at war, Crowder and Ansell advised Baker not to cede the responsibility for prosecuting Witzke to the Justice Department. Ansell went so far as to blame the Department of Justice for incompetently enabling Witzke's escape. While neither of the two judge advocates agreed with Assistant Attorney General Charles Warren's plan to prosecute citizens who committed espionage and encouraged draft resistance and mutiny in military trials, because Witzke was an enemy alien who happened to also be a commissioned officer, they argued that the law of war permitted his prosecution in a military trial. Ultimately the army prosecuted Witzke in a secret trial and sentenced him to death. He would not, however, be executed, as Wilson commuted his sentence to life in prison, and in 1921 President Warren G. Harding, to Crowder's consternation, freed him from prison altogether. In 1918 Gregory and Lansing advised Wilson that *Milligan* was "an unsettled matter" and urged him to commute Witzke's sentence. Crowder disagreed with Gregory's and Lansing's analysis as to the stretch of *Milligan*, but he did not lobby Wilson to execute Witzke.[22]

In 1915 the War Department interned German sailors from the *Kronprinz Wilhelm*, a passenger liner that the German Navy had converted into a surface raiding vessel. For two years, the German sailors were permitted a limited freedom of movement in the Norfolk area. In late April 1917, Adjutant General McCain informed Baker that the sailors remained "interned," which meant they could be confined to the vessel and its immediate surroundings. The sailors had been permitted to build a small village by their vessel, and perhaps because they had abided by their restriction, McCain believed it was in the nation's best interest not to change their status. Crowder, however, disagreed with McCain and concluded the sailors were now prisoners of war, which, as an oddity, gave them different rights and greater protections, such as the ability to be employed as found in the Hague Conventions. Moreover, Major Scott had already advised Lansing that the sailors had to be regarded as prisoners of war in army custody. Bliss informed Baker and General Scott that he agreed with Crowder and added that the commanders of prisoner of war camps had to be educated on the various international conventions regarding the rights of prisoners of war. Although General Peyton March supported McCain, ultimately Solicitor General Davis sided with Crowder and in addition to classifying the interned sailors as prisoners of war, on March 28, 1918, Davis and Crowder authored a set of regulations for the treatment of prisoners of war.[23]

As the United States' armed presence increased in France, the American Expeditionary Forces took control over larger numbers of prisoners of war. By September 1, 1918, the army controlled 10,986 enlisted German prisoners of war. There was a lack of consistency in the Allies' treatment of prisoners of war. German prisoners of war held by the French Army were subjected to French military laws and regulations, and those held by the British Expeditionary Forces were subjected to British military law. In September 1918, the French undersecretary of state for military justice, a civilian position with no analog in the War Department, sought to have the American Expeditionary Forces apply French military law to the governance of captured German soldiers held in American prisoner of war encampments. There was merit to the request in the sense that uniformity of treatment would make the behavior of prisoners during transfers between the Allies more predictable. On the other hand, the United States Army enjoyed a reputation for civility, deserved or not, in Germany. Winship assigned Captain J. A. Webb, one of the judge advocates at Chaumont, to formulate a response to the French minister, in which the American Expeditionary Forces agreed to apply French law in most, but not all, matters. One French rule that Winship, Bethel, and Kreger insisted the American Expeditionary Forces could not follow was the right of permanent seizure of private nonmilitary property. Dating to Winthrop's *Military Law and Precedents*, the War Department's position was that the private property of prisoners such as pictures, books, watches, and letters could be inspected but not seized unless such property was intended to be used for an escape.[24]

In early November 1917, the British Expeditionary Forces relinquished control over a prisoner of war camp factory in Le Havre to the American Expeditionary Forces. Captain Bernard Gorfinkle, who was to become the Twenty-Sixth Division's assistant judge advocate, briefly supervised the factory as he waited to transit to the front to join his ammunition train detail. To his mother, he wrote, "the German (skilled) prisoners make all sorts of delicate instruments. Each gets paid and gets better food than even the Tommies do at certain times." The employment of prisoners of war was permissible under international law, though it usually occurred on a voluntary basis.[25]

In December 1917, Bethel advised Pershing that there was no prohibition against using German prisoners of war to construct and repair roads necessary for getting soldiers and supplies to the front, as long as the prisoners of war were not placed in danger of being exposed to German artillery or poison gas. Harbord, who at the time was acting as Pershing's chief of staff, advocated placing German prisoners at the front to act as a shield from German artillery attacks. He had also urged that placing German prisoners of war on American flagged vessels heading to the United States would dissuade German U-boat attacks. To Harbord's ire, Bethel countered that the intentional exposure of prisoners of war to harm violated international law, and Pershing sided with Bethel on this point. Crowder also supported Bethel, and to overcome Peyton March's agreement with Harbord, Crowder also gained Lansing's support.[26]

From the time of the United States' entry into the war through the Armistice, the Judge Advocate General's Office made it clear that the treatment of captured German soldiers had to conform to the laws of war to the effect that such prisoners were to be fed, given medical care, permitted to communicate through a neutral intermediary to their families, and protected from abuses. In 1917 Crowder informed Pershing that the 1799 Treaty of Berlin remained binding on the United States, and in that treaty were the terms, "prisoners of war whom they take from the other shall be placed in wholesome situations." Pershing agreed with Crowder's assessment that the treaty remained binding unless the German Army violated it first. In May 1918, Bethel advised Pershing that mail to prisoners of war that transited through Switzerland by means of the International Committee of the Red Cross should not be withheld from prisoners as a sanction against Germany. On September 21, 1918, Pershing cabled Peyton March a memorandum regarding the American Expeditionary Forces' policies on holding Americans accountable for mistreating prisoners of war. Earlier in the week, Kreger questioned two German officers who claimed that while they were under interrogation, two American officers grabbed them by their throats and demanded answers as to the position of German artillery batteries. Following Kreger's investigation, Pershing formally admonished the two American officers, stripped them of their brevet ranks, and returned them to the United States.[27]

Generally, Crowder and other ranking officials were satisfied that the United States comported with the international law regime governing prisoners of war. In September 1918, John W. Davis, who by this time had left the Solicitor General's Office to head the American Mission on Prisoners of War, reported to Secretary of State Lansing that the treatment of German prisoners was exceptional and that their sole complaint had to do with the lack of "black bread." Davis noted to Colonel George Wallace that he had informed Lansing that he credited the treatment of prisoners of war to Crowder and Kreger. Of course, in spite of the adherence to international law, there were individual violators.[28]

On November 8, 1918, Gorfinkle preferred charges against two soldiers who stole watches from six captured German soldiers, and the following day,

the US soldiers were prosecuted in a general court-martial. Gorfinkle reported
to the Twenty-Sixth Division's commander that the two American soldiers
took the Germans into custody and confiscated their watches after exiting "no
man's land." He noted that while the captured Germans were young, appeared
happy to be captured, and did not want to complain about the loss of their
watches, he vigorously pursued the court-martial because he believed the theft
of the watches "more heinous as a barracks theft by one soldier against others." The general court-martial convicted the two soldiers and sentenced them
each to a month of hard labor.[29]

In April 1917, former president Taft advised Crowder that a prisoner of
war conference with Germany and Austria would be helpful in developing
postwar relations with Germany, and the German government would likely
accept an invitation to enter into negotiations as a means to protect German interests after the war. There were reports that the German treatment
of French and Belgian prisoners of war fell short of international standards
as well, and Taft suggested that the conference would help protect American prisoners of war. On September 23, 1918, a German delegation met with
Major General Francis Kernan, Solicitor General Davis, and John Garrett, the
US ambassador to the Netherlands, in Berne, Switzerland. Major Hugh Bayne
served as legal advisor to the delegation. Both delegations agreed on the need
to repatriate prisoners of war as soon as practicable after the conclusion of
hostilities, the requirement to protect personal property, and protection from
abuse and mistreatment. Both sides also, interestingly, agreed that guard dogs
had to be muzzled at all times and could not be used as a means to intimidate
prisoners of war. According to Bayne, the two major points of contention
between the delegations had to do with the isolation of prisoners and the
status of German government officials. Since only a few Americans had been
captured, the Germans scattered them into camps of French, British, Belgian,
Italian, and Russian soldiers. In several instances, American prisoners did
not speak any of the languages that surrounded them. The German position
was that this condition could not be ameliorated. The American delegation
insisted that the German kaiser and other royal family members such as the
crown prince had to be considered prisoners of war. The German delegation,
in opposite, argued that as heads of state, the kaiser and other members—
although serving in uniform—had to be immediately repatriated to a neutral
country. Ultimately a prisoner of war agreement was not signed until the
Armistice, and the American delegation conceded the status of the kaiser and
royal family members to the German position. Bayne and the delegation left
Berne to bring the agreement to the War Department on October 12, 1918,
for Baker's consideration.[30]

Prisoner of war treatment was only one of many of the law of war issues in which the Judge Advocate General's Office would advise the War Department. In August 1918, the German government protested the arming of American soldiers with shotguns, long a staple of American hunters. On September 26, 1918, Ansell issued a response to Baker, noting that while international law permitted the maximum killing of enemy soldiers, it did not permit the design of weapons for the purpose of inflicting injuries and thus prolonging suffering. Ansell likened shotgun pellets to shrapnel and concluded that the pellet sizes in each round were capable of killing several advancing opponents, and therefore the weapon did not violate international law. Baker's assistant, Benedict Crowell, agreed with Ansell's assessment, and shotgun weapons continued to be deployed in the trenches. On the other hand, given the widespread use of poison gas, it is possible that Ansell simply concluded that the German protest was meritless, considering Germany's wartime conduct.[31]

Another law of war matter included a prohibition against misusing the "Red Cross" emblem to protect war materiel. On May 14, 1918, Bayne drafted a memorandum for Harbord to issue to all divisional and brigade commanders making it clear that the misuse of the protective emblem was not only a violation of the law of war, and commensurately the Articles of War, it also invited the German military to cease recognizing the emblem's protection.[32]

When the "American Forces in Germany" command was created, its commanders and judge advocates intended that the laws of war would be applied in a uniquely American and somewhat benevolent manner. Concerns over the German population's political stability and the prevention of reigniting hostilities were part of the reason for this approach, but a benevolent policy also comported with Wilson's Fourteen Points. In essence, there was no desire to replicate the methods of pacifying the Philippine population in Germany. Yet the War Department also intended that whatever war debt Germany incurred would be enforced. On December 1, 1918, Bethel drafted an order to the "inhabitants of Trier, and the counties of Daun, Prum, Bitburg, Wittlich, and Bernkastel," which promised that the United States would not "wage war on law abiding and peaceful citizens" but warned that "every violation of the laws of war, every hostile act, and every attempt at violence as well as disobedience to the regulations of the military authorities will be severely punished." One week later, Pershing had the order distributed to the "Rhine-Prussian" population and its outlying areas.[33]

The governance of prisoners of war and civilians in occupied Germany was a duty contemporaneous with the investigation of war crimes. It was well known that during the German invasion of Belgium and France in 1914, German soldiers were ordered to execute Belgian and French citizens as a reprisal for the killings of German soldiers. The German Army destroyed the medieval University of Louvain, and on August 23, 1914, German soldiers summarily executed 674 Belgian civilians in the town of Dinant. Submarine warfare and the widespread use of poison gas also violated international law, but all of the belligerents, to include the United States, utilized such weapons. Crowder planned for the eventuality that some war crimes trials would occur and decided that Kreger would supervise the American contribution to prosecuting such cases.[34]

On September 21, 1918, General Noel de Castlenau, the French commanding general of the "Armies of the East," noted to Liggett that he had discussed German war crimes with Bethel and Kreger, both of whom agreed that German officers had to be held accountable for the murder of civilians, assaults committed against women, and the unnecessary destruction of historic and private properties. Both judge advocates also articulated to de Castlenau that accountability had to be achieved through a legal process. The French general claimed he was impressed with Bethel's exposition of how, during the Civil War, the Union prosecuted war crimes in military trials such as the trial of Henry Wirz, the commandant of the Andersonville prison.[35]

On September 29, 1918, Pershing assured de Castlenau that "every facility will be afforded to the representatives of the French Army charged with the duty of investigating damages and other acts committed by the enemy in violation of international law." On November 10, 1918, Liggett instructed the First Army's divisional commanders that in response to the French government's request to assist in the investigation of "violations of the law of nations committed by the enemy against property in French territory," divisional judge advocates would be tasked with gathering evidence of atrocities and other violations. In turn, he expected judge advocates to forward all reports promptly to the judge advocate for the First Army within twenty-four hours of noting an occurrence. One month earlier, Kreger had advised Liggett that the American Expeditionary Forces "should undertake to assist the allied governments in investigating war crimes."[36]

In July 1919, Sir Felix Maximilian Schoenbrunn Cassel, the British judge advocate general, invited Winship and Lieutenant Colonel William Cattron Rigby, a recently arrived judge advocate assigned to study Allied military justice systems, to briefly assist in a general court-martial that could be fairly characterized as a war crimes trial. Their temporary service on the court-martial occurred as a result of Rigby's interview of the British judge advocate general to obtain information in an effort to counter Ansell's attack on the fairness of American courts-martial. The court-martial, which was held in Guildhall, London, took place after the chief of the Imperial General Staff charged Assistant Surgeon William Fratel, "a Eurasion officer," and several other Ottoman soldiers captured after the Armistice with complicity in the maltreatment and murder of British prisoners of war taken after the British defeat at Kut el-Amara in 1916. Of the 13,000 British and Indian soldiers taken as prisoners at Kut, over half died in Turkish prisoner of war camps. Fratel was born in India and attached to an Indian Army brigade, but he may have accepted a commission in the Ottoman Army after the fall of Kut. If true, his conduct could have constituted treason, but the British did not court-martial him for this offense.[37]

The British alleged, in nineteen separate charges, that Fratel withheld medical treatment from hundreds of prisoners as well as starved, kicked, and whipped sick prisoners at a location known as the Bagtsche prisoner of war camp. Remarkably, the British trial judge advocates permitted Rigby to question Fratel and establish that the surgeon had the authority to command enlisted soldiers as well as other officers to perform functions around Bagtsche. Rigby presented to the court-martial an important part of the evidence against Fratel and others. Although the British were well aware of the doctrine of command responsibility, Rigby was able to argue that by possessing the authority to command, Fratel could be held criminally liable for the criminal acts of soldiers under his command. The court-martial found Fratel guilty of four of the charges and sentenced him to two years. Had the court-martial occurred while hostilities continued, Fratel would have likely been sentenced to death. Rigby apparently did not ask the War Department for permission to take part in the Allied court-martial, and he only remained for two days of the trial which stretched, albeit with several long adjournments, from July to November. However, his experience in the trial would later prove helpful in countering Ansell's allegations that American courts-martial were uniquely unfair among the Allies. The *Times of London* and several Dominion and Commonwealth newspapers such as the *Sydney Herald* reported on the court-martial. But no American newspaper seems to have done so, and Rigby's role in it has largely disappeared from American military and legal history.[38]

MAINTAINING A DISCIPLINED OCCUPATION FORCE

For the first six months following the Armistice, the majority of American soldiers in Germany were veterans of the 1918 summer and fall offensives. But by the summer of 1919, very few soldiers assigned in Germany had experienced combat. Most of the new troops had only recently finished basic training in the United States and had no advanced training in France, such as their predecessors had undergone. Concerned that his new forces were of a lower disciplinary quality and therefore unsuitable for occupation duties, Allen urged Bliss to accept the premise that while soldiers who committed offenses during wartime undermined the discipline of the army, in occupied Germany, the criminal acts of his soldiers would "embolden Bolshevist and Spartacist leaders" to openly recruit citizens against the Allies. "These men are going to represent the United States in a part of the country that thinks rather highly of us and it would be a crime to have our prestige given a black eye by a lot of rough necks," Bliss responded. Pershing added to this conversation by notifying Allen of his full support for thoroughly prosecuting misconduct among his forces.[39]

In January 1920, Allen informed Liggett that while his command had dwindled in number, his force's disciplinary problems had not lessened. "I have had more trouble in keeping down AWOLs, courts-martial and venereal disease than in a force many times larger," he complained. "The quality of the replacements was not nearly equal to the drafted men, nor have these men had such a great cause for which to train as did the others." Of course Allen had commanded a division in combat, which was different from commanding an occupying force.[40]

Allen's concern with maintaining good relations with the German population lasted throughout his tenure, and he believed it to be essential to respect the local domestic law enforcement and judicial systems in unoccupied Germany. To do this, he repeatedly turned to Rucker to serve as a liaison with German prosecutors and judges. In 1921 German police officers arrested two American officers assigned to the provost marshal and transported them to a prison in Mosbach, Baden. Allen instructed Rucker to have the two arrested officers repatriated and to assure the German authorities that if the officers had exceeded their authority or caused any disturbance, "the full measure of disciplinary action would be taken against them." Rucker succeeded in this mission and invited the German prosecutors to attend a court-martial.[41]

Allen would also repeatedly and vocally stress that the discipline of the American occupation forces was paramount to German stability and preserving a tenuous peace. In that light, a primary judge advocate duty in Coblenz from January 1, 1919, to the termination of the American Forces in Germany's mission was to safeguard German citizenry from soldiers committing offenses. This included Rucker drafting an order to prohibit "sexual intercourse with females under sixteen years of age" regardless of whether the female consented to the act. In what might be considered the first time that a federal law, in this case the "Mann Act," was assimilated into a military prohibition overseas, under a unique aspect of the Articles of War the order provided for a fifteen-year maximum sentence for any soldier convicted of this offense. Allen expected both his judge advocates and the local inspector general to investigate such offenses, along with all other offenses committed against the local population. Because many of the offenses that occurred in the occupied areas happened while the offending soldier was intoxicated, Rucker crafted another order against alcohol consumption. The catalyst for the order was the murder of a British officer by a Private Yobski, who "was raving drunk," as well as six courts-martial of officers accused of being drunk on duty, which were prosecuted on a single day.[42]

The historic record bears out that Rucker and his subordinates gave serious consideration to German allegations of American wrongdoing. Between 1918 and January 10, 1919, German police accused twenty-five American soldiers of committing homicide. Rucker's office determined that eleven soldiers had no justification for the killing of a German civilian and preferred murder charges. Of the eleven courts-martial, six soldiers were convicted, and each of these soldiers received greater sentences then two Germans who were convicted in a military court of the same offense. Seventeen rape allegations were brought to Rucker's attention, and it was only in instances where the victim could not identify her assailant that no charges were preferred. A total of eight courts-martial were conducted, resulting in five convictions, and each soldier received a term of over five years' imprisonment. By January 1920, a total of 118 courts-martial were held against Americans accused of crimes against German citizens. In September 1921, Winship reported to Kreger that during his inspection of the Judge Advocate's Office in Coblenz, he concluded that American soldiers were regularly court-martialed on the basis of civilian complaints, almost without question.[43]

A typical judge advocate investigation included interviewing German citizens who alleged that a soldier committed an offense such as larceny, rape, or assault, and then recommending to General Allen to convene a general or special court-martial. In one instance, Rucker assigned H. H. Morisette to investigate an assault on an American soldier by German citizens outside of Coblenz, followed by five American soldiers assaulting Germans. Morisette concluded that the soldiers' commander, a Major R. C. Barton, had not only encouraged the assault, he had also obstructed justice by intimidating the local populace. The soldier initially attacked by the Germans had grabbed a female and stolen her handbag. Complicating the investigation was that Barton, an infantry officer, appointed himself to serve as defense counsel for the five soldiers. As for the conduct of the five soldiers, Morisette informed Allen, "The seriousness of the situation is increased by the fact that this alleged assault was not an isolated case, but one of an increasing number of such incidents that were causing serious bodily injuries to unoffending civilians." In concluding his investigative report, Morisette recommended to Allen that Major Barton "be court-martialed for violating the customs of the service as these pertained to the laws of war, and the other soldiers court-martialed in a general court-martial as well." Rucker supported this course of action, and while Barton avoided a court-martial, his five soldiers were not so lucky.[44]

Every month the judge advocates were tasked with reporting to the Judge Advocate General's Office the number of civilians prosecuted in military trials as well as courts-martial of soldiers who committed offenses against the German population. In June 1922, Morisette reported that eighty-four American soldiers were court-martialed for committing crimes against German citizens during the prior six months. That same year Rucker noted that over four hundred courts-martial had been conducted for such offenses since the command had been created. However, after 1921 some of the sentences appear to have been light in comparison with courts-martial sentences in the American Expeditionary Forces. For instance, a private who shot a German teenage girl was sentenced to a year and a dishonorable discharge, but Allen commuted the dishonorable discharge. A general court-martial convicted a private of smashing a beer stein on a German's head and hospitalizing him, but only sentenced the private to a month in confinement. On October 7, 1921, a court-martial found Private Abelardo Diaz guilty of striking Frau Elizabeth Ott on the head with a wine bottle and tearing off her dress in a café in daytime, but only sentenced Diaz to forfeit two-thirds of his pay for three months. In June 1921, a court-martial determined that Private Adelard Gadbois was guilty of assaulting a fifteen-year-old female named Anna Wiehs Engers by punching her, tearing off her dress, and cutting her hair with the intent to rape her. His sentence was one year in jail, but with no dishonorable discharge. On December 1, 1920, a general court-martial sentenced Private Joseph Evans to six months' confinement after he shot an elderly German citizen named Adolf Vendel without provocation. Apparently the fact that Evans was intoxicated at the time mitigated the offense. Rucker and his judge advocates would repeatedly advise Allen that these lenient sentences would undermine both the mission of the American Forces in Germany, and the discipline of these forces to confront an enemy if the war began anew or in any fight against Bolshevism.[45]

Although there were few desertions from the American Expeditionary Forces, there were citizens who refused induction into the army and then evaded prosecution by fleeing overseas or into Canada. As noted earlier, unlike in World War II and after, such persons could be considered deserters and subject to military jurisdiction. In 1917 Grover Cleveland Bergdoll refused his induction into the army and successfully evaded arrest until 1919. After his arrest, the army court-martialed him, and he was found guilty and sentenced to five years in confinement at Governors Island. However, he managed to escape to Germany, leading the army to accuse Colonel John E. White, the officer in charge of the military prison, for dereliction of duty. Bergdoll was not an ordinary citizen. He was born in Philadelphia, and he became a well-known aviation pioneer. His father was a wealthy German immigrant who owned a large brewery. According to Bergdoll, in an affidavit he provided to a German prosecutor after his escape, he traveled to Chicago and then Saint Paul before walking into Canada and then sailing to Germany under an assumed name.[46]

On January 18, 1921, Sergeant Franz Zimmer, an American soldier, and Charles Naef, an American civilian detective attached to the provost marshal, traveled to Karlsruhe and attempted to seize Bergdoll and his chauffer, a Mr. Stecher. Zimmer and Naef possessed German passes indicating their final destination was Rostock, a city north of Karlsruhe, in an effort to conceal their true intentions. Along the way, they confirmed that Bergdoll was, in fact, in Karlsruhe. Using the same passes, the two men attempted to arrest Bergdoll near the city of Eberbach in Baden. However, not only was Bergdoll able to escape in his car, when Naef fired his gun at Bergdoll's tires, one of the bullets struck a German child. Not surprisingly, German police arrested Zimmer and Naef.[47]

Rucker initially failed in his efforts to convince the German government to repatriate the two agents, and the *New York Times* reported on the German refusal, leading to a public outcry for Zimmer and Naef to be freed. In response, Rucker advised Allen to cease handing over German citizens for trials in German courts and resume prosecutions in military tribunals until the German government returned Naef and Zimmer. For a defeated government desperate to establish good relations with the United States, the German officials had acted boldly. Allen ultimately issued an apology to the German government, and the German prosecutor still brought Zimmer and Naef to trial to obtain a conviction. Bergdoll and Stecher remained at large, only to return to the United States over a decade later. Rucker succeeded in the end in convincing the Baden government officials to release Zimmer and Naef after the two men were found guilty but before serving their sentence. Allen only passingly referred to this episode in his autobiography, and he did not mention Rucker at all. Yet in March 1921, he personally praised Rucker for his efforts in obtaining freedom for the two agents.[48]

JURISDICTION OVER GERMAN CITIZENS

On December 10, 1918, Pershing issued General Order 225, which established three types of military tribunals with jurisdiction over civilians. Somewhat mirroring courts-martial, the lowest type of court— the inferior provost court— possessed the jurisdiction to sentence a German defendant to three months in prison or a 1,000DM fine. In the next type of tribunal, the superior provost court possessed the jurisdiction to sentence a German defendant to six months in prison or a 5,000DM fine. The third type of tribunal, the military commission, was a trial akin to a general court-martial. This trial had unlimited sentencing jurisdiction with one exception. No German could be sentenced to death in an American military tribunal regardless of how heinous the crime was. Somewhat different from courts-martial conducted in the American Expeditionary Forces was that Colonel Rucker's office was the final appellate review instead of a higher command. That is, General Order 7 did not extend to trials of German citizens. There were, in addition, two other courts of special jurisdiction, juvenile courts and vagrancy courts, with the latter designed to curb prostitution. However, the Judge Advocate General's Office did not provide oversight or review for these proceedings. Pershing, Dickman, Liggett, Rucker and Allen desired to maximize jurisdiction over the local population, especially over former German soldiers. To accomplish this end, Dickman appointed Hugh Ogden to become the first chief provost court judge for Coblenz. During the last two months of the war, Dickman became thoroughly impressed with Ogden, and on Winship's advice Dickman asked Ogden to volunteer.[49]

Ogden only sat as a judge on a few cases, but he supervised all provost court officers as well as the German judiciary in the zone of occupation. In December 1918 he relayed to his wife that he was busy instructing the provost judges in Coblenz on how to run their courts, concluding, "this military law is great stuff, you make your own laws and then you enforce them." In actuality, Ogden's claim was not quite true because he followed the trial procedures outlined in Winthrop's *Military Law and Precedents*. Between January 1, 1919, and January 20, 1920, the American Forces in Germany conducted a total of 9,699 trials of German civilians. In these trials, 2,317 Germans were prosecuted for failing to obey posted orders such as the sale of alcohol to American soldiers, 357 Germans for assaulting American soldiers, 781 for theft of US military property, and 302 for unlawful possession of firearms classified as "deadly," such as machine guns and grenade throwers. Interestingly, ninety-one German women were convicted of "practicing prostitution while diseased." The majority of these trials, with the exception of violent crimes, were prosecuted in the provost courts. As a signal trial for the containment of Bolshevism, 314 Germans were prosecuted for "unauthorized assembly," an offense designed against promonarchist and Bolshevik and Spartacist movements, but in reality wholly directed against the two latter groups.[50]

Dickman's and Allen's desire to maximize American jurisdiction over Germans in their area of command stemmed from a German military police patrol killing of an American soldier in an area considered to be "a neutral zone" in early September 1919. American soldiers were prohibited from entering the "neutral zone," but the "neutral zone" area was poorly marked, and when a German patrol attempted to arrest two American soldiers, one of the soldiers drew a pistol at the Germans, who in turn killed the soldier. The German military police arrested the other soldier, tied him to a horse which dragged him across a muddy field, and then refused to repatriate him to Allen's command. At Allen's behest, Rucker enlisted the assistance of Ferdinand Foch's staff in retrieving the soldier, and Foch threatened to shoot a number of German prisoners. Allen recognized that none of this was conducive to the American Forces in Germany's mission, and he turned to Rucker to draft rules establishing military trials over German soldiers and police officers who committed offenses against American servicemen as a means of avoiding a future need for French intervention.[51]

However, Allen did not get his wish to prosecute the German soldiers responsible for killing the American. In late September he sent Rucker into a contentious meeting with French general Maurice Weygand, who admonished Rucker that since the killing had occurred in the neutral zone, an area where the Americans were prohibited from entering, the Inter-Allied Commission would not demand the surrender of the German soldiers. Interestingly, the retired marshal of France, Joseph Joffre, sided with the Americans, but neither Foch nor Weygand wanted a trial of Germans, and Joffre no longer possessed any command authority. Although Allen believed that Foch and Weygand were wrong, he realized that he could not proceed without their help.[52]

The failure to arrest and prosecute the German military police did not stop the army's extension of its jurisdiction over German citizens, in part because this process was already well under way. Indeed, the first military trial of German citizens occurred before the killing of the American soldier, while Dickman remained in command. On January 29, 1919, a military commission convicted two German citizens of smuggling seven hundred cases of cognac into Coblenz, using a fraudulent French-issued pass, and selling the spirits on the black market. The civilians, Joseph Scheid and Jakob Ring, were defended by two German attorneys and an American officer. The military commission determined Scheid and Ring were guilty and then sentenced both to be confined at hard labor for a year. In appealing for clemency to Dickman, Ring conceded that while he was guilty, prior to the war he was a hotelier in Coblenz and had lost all of his property. In essence, Ring claimed his smuggling was to support his family. Dickman selected Brigadier General

Wendell Cushing Neville as the presiding officer to the trial, along with two other generals, Harvey Bishop and Charles E. Kilbourne (a Medal of Honor recipient from the Spanish-American War), and two colonels, Marion Battle and Arthur Mackie. All of the officers were frontline veterans. On Kreger's advice, Dickman also appointed Major Nathaniel Barnwell, who had served as the Seventh Division's judge advocate during the war, as the trial judge advocate. Barnwell had earned a law degree from the University of Virginia in 1894 and a second law degree from the University of Grenoble in France two years later. Prior to the war he represented railroads and campaigned against Senator Tillman. Because the trial necessitated French governmental and military witnesses to attest to the false pass, it had an added complexity. Rucker was able to secure Weygand's agreement to bring French witnesses to the military commission.[53]

During his judge advocate review of the record of trial, Rucker noted that the seized cognac and the boat on which it was transported had to be handed over to the French as part of Germany's reparation requirements. After Rucker concluded that the trial had been fairly conducted, Colonel Guy D. Goff, a newly arrived judge advocate, undertook a second review, and Goff determined that "the record and sentence were sufficient and justified." This second review occurred as a result of Crowder's concern that the Ring-Scheid trial "be considered fair in all its aspects."[54]

In comparison to the more well-known military trials of civilians such as those of Mary Surratt and her companions and the intended war crimes trial of high-ranking German officials to include Kaiser Wilhelm, the trial of Ring and Scheid appears to be of little magnitude. Yet the trial was significant because it was the first of its kind. Indeed, Rucker advised Allen that the trial would form the basis for assessing whether more important cases could be fairly adjudicated. To Rucker and Goff, the trial of Ring and Scheid not only proved to the local German population that the military would ensure a fair application of the law, but it would also show to potential doubters in the United States that the army would treat Germans fairly in military trials. After World War II, a small number of prominent Americans, to include Senator Joseph McCarthy, alleged that the army had prosecuted German soldiers responsible for the 1944 "Malmedy Massacre" without due process of law. Between 1919 and 1923, there were no such high-level claims.[55]

In March 1919 the army prosecuted a German citizen named Karl Bode who stabbed a Private McEarnery to death. During the trial it was uncovered that McEarnery was intoxicated and attacked both Bode and Bode's sister. The judge advocate assigned to investigate and prosecute the matter informed Rucker that while at most, Bode was guilty of unpremeditated manslaughter, the army should charge him with the maximum offense of murder. At first Rucker was willing to entertain the judge advocate's reasons for pressing forward, but after observing witness testimony on the first day of trial, Rucker advised both Dickman and Allen that no crime had occurred and Bode was justified in his acts on the basis of self-defense. Rucker was particularly galled that one of McEarnery's peers, a private Patrick J. Brown, had lied under oath that neither he nor McEarnery was intoxicated, and also that Brown testified that Bode had attacked McEarnery without provocation. Allen ordered Bode freed and withdrew the charges against him, and then charged Brown with committing perjury. Not all trials ended in this manner. On June 14, 1919, a military commission convicted another German citizen for murdering an American soldier and sentenced him to twenty years in confinement. The murder resulted from a mutual fight, but in comparison to courts-martial held in the occupied areas of Germany, the sentence was severe.[56]

Some of the investigations were more complex than Bode's case. In one instance, a German family consisting of a wife, a husband, and a son was alleged to have assaulted a civilian named M. Sevestre attached to the French Military Mission in Germany, but Captain James E. Morisette, a judge advocate assigned to Rucker, determined that the assault occurred after the French civilian threw a hot coffee urn at the family's patriarch, a former German colonel. The investigation became more troublesome after Morisette discovered that American military police confiscated the French civilian's pistol and refused to return it. Rucker advised Allen that while German disrespect toward members of the Inter-Allied Rhineland High Commission was intolerable, in this instance there should be no prosecution against the retired German colonel or his family, and the firearm was returned to the French civilian. Rucker also reported that he "was of the opinion that M. Sevestre is at fault." His advice proved difficult for Allen to implement. While the French high command had not been willing to hold German police accountable for killing and abusing American soldiers, Weygand insisted that the former German colonel be prosecuted regardless of the French civilian's actions. "To do less," according to Weygand, "was an assault on the honor of France." But while Weygand represented the passions of the French military, he could not direct an American military commission to a verdict. In the end, the former colonel and his family were prosecuted in a military commission, and unsurprisingly, the commission acquitted them after Rucker argued for it to do so.[57]

On February 1, 1919, Goff inspected the Rhine District of Germany and investigated the military commission trials over the citizenry. Writing to his father who was, at the time, serving in the Senate, he recounted that the establishment of criminal courts and civil provost courts, as well as making the local population subject to "the corrective and punitive control of American law," was essential to maintain order. Goff reported to his father that the German population did "not take kindly" to the American forces even though they preferred the Americans over the French and British. He recognized that the imposition of an American legal system through a military administration was, to the German population, too alien to be trusted. Likewise, he observed that American soldiers who had fought against the Germans at St. Mihiel and in the Meuse-Argonne were intolerant of the German citizens.[58]

Nonetheless, of the recorded 142 military commission trials of Germans, over one-third resulted in an acquittal, and for the most part, the sentences of those found guilty were comparable to those in courts-martial in the American Expeditionary Forces. In one trial of a German accused of attempted murder against a major, the trial judge advocate, Lieutenant Colonel Roy Holderness, argued that the evidence showed that the German male likely had acted in self-defense and should be found not guilty. Holderness had been court-martialed in Deming, New Mexico, in early 1918 after being accused of conduct unbecoming an officer and gentleman for bringing an "immoral woman into his tent for immoral purposes," but he too was acquitted. Every month the judge advocates were tasked with sending information about the numbers of trials and results to Allen and then on to the War Department. In April 1920, there were thirty- two trials of Germans who were alleged to have assaulted American soldiers. Twenty-one of these trials resulted in acquittal on the grounds of self-defense. It would be difficult to know if similar results would have been achieved in the German civil courts, or if the trials had occurred under French, Belgian, or British authority. But it does appear that the judge advocates assigned to the trials often did seek to dismiss charges once it became known that an American soldier was culpable in the affray.[59]

Although it was clear that the containment of Bolshevism was a paramount mission, Rucker and Goff advised Allen to refuse to support the German government in its political and treason trials. In January 1919, the German Criminal Court in Dusseldorf issued an arrest warrant for a Herr Metzler for treason. While serving in a German Army headquarters, Metzler had provided the French Army with intelligence during the war, and Rucker not only concluded that he was entitled to French protection but also that because the United States technically remained at war with Germany since Congress had not approved of the peace treaty, it would violate the law of war to assist Germany in a treason trial. Rucker also advised Allen to refuse to support the German trials of Rhenish separatists so that the United States would not become involved in an indigenous dispute. In addition to the prohibition against aiding German political prosecutions, Baker instructed Allen that in the event French and German forces clashed, the United States could not offer German forces asylum.[60]

The impressions of the judge advocates assigned to Germany, or those who simply passed through for an inspection, provide another context for the performance and necessity of the United States' role in its occupation mission. On June 8, 1919, Lieutenant Colonel Cosgrave wrote to his wife and daughter that he, along with several officers from the Fifth Division's staff, had inspected the areas of Germany occupied by the British, French, Belgians, and Americans. The staff was late in arriving at Coblenz because, as Cosgrave cheekily noted, the ranking officer had taken the entire entourage on detours to the Waterloo battlefield in Belgium and the great Cathedral in Cologne. Cosgrave did not share Allen's sentiments that the American soldiers assigned to the occupation forces lacked the discipline of their predecessors in the American Expeditionary Forces. But he urged his wife and daughter to be patient for his return, warning that Bolsheviks were encouraging the normally law-abiding German population to riot against the Allies as well as against the German police, and this could result in a renewed conflict. He concluded by assuring his wife that he did not volunteer to remain on duty in Germany. On the other hand, he warned that he, along with Lieutenant Colonel Charles Teare, believed that a resumption of fighting was inevitable.[61]

Although most of the judge advocates assigned to the American Forces in Germany had served as judge advocates at the divisional and corps levels during the war, there were four judge advocates who transferred from the Judge Advocate General's Office to the First Army Headquarters and then to Coblenz after the Armistice. Guy D. Goff was the most prominent of this group. Throughout the war, judge advocates serving in Washington, DC, and in other stateside postings lobbied Crowder for transfers to Europe, but most did not succeed. In late 1918, Crowder approved of Goff's transfer to France and then Germany to serve as a deputy judge advocate to Rucker as well as to liaison with Secretary of State Lansing and other American dignitaries involved in the Versailles peace negotiations.

A West Virginia contemporary of George Wallace, Goff later became a US senator. The son of Senator Nathan D. Goff, a Civil War veteran of the Union army and one-time secretary of the navy under President Rutherford Hayes, the younger Goff was a Republican who shared Wallace's conservatism, particularly toward organized labor. Like Wallace, Goff had a pronounced fear of socialism and the IWW. He graduated from Harvard's law school in 1891 and then moved to Milwaukee, Wisconsin, where he established a law practice. In 1895 he was elected prosecutor for Milwaukee, and in 1904 he unsuccessfully ran for mayor. In 1911 Taft appointed him United States attorney for Wisconsin. This appointment proved contentious because Senator Robert La Follette had lobbied Taft for another attorney to fill the post, and the senator, convinced he had been slighted, opposed Goff's nomination. However, Irvine Luther Lenroot, a Wisconsin congressman, supported Goff. After April 1918, when Lenroot was elected senator, Goff advised him not to join with Ansell and Chamberlain in their efforts to reform courts-martial.[62]

Shortly after becoming United States attorney, Goff spoke to a business meeting where he warned of the perils of labor agitation and called socialism an "evil." He argued that the IWW constituted a dangerous threat to the United States because instead of trying to gain converts, the union intended to put urban voters in fear so that their votes would be suppressed. In 1910 three International Association of Bridge and Structural Iron Union workers from Wisconsin traveled to Los Angeles and bombed the *Los Angeles Times*, killing twenty-one employees and injuring over one hundred. Goff claimed that the local union was affiliated with the IWW and therefore could be outlawed. In reality, the three men involved in the bombing, J. J. McNamara, J. B. McNamara, and Ortie McManigal, did not intend to kill anyone. The *Times* editor, Harrison Day Otis, a Civil War and Spanish-American War veteran, was an antiprogressive conservative who used the newspaper to keep Los Angeles a union-free city. The bombers simply intended to destroy the means to print and distribute the newspaper. Goff ordered the arrests and pursued indictments of fifty men in Milwaukee who belonged to the same union as the three bombers. Although he was unable to obtain evidence that the Milwaukee-based union was complicit in the bombing, he claimed that the bombing was proof that the IWW and "communist elements sought the overthrow of the government."[63]

Despite Goff's political differences with Wilson, in February 1917, Wilson appointed him as a special assistant to Attorney General Gregory. Goff helped craft legal arguments supporting Wilson's positions on German violations of US neutrality as well as the Executive Branch's exceptional wartime authorities to regulate commerce. The next day, Goff was commissioned into the Wisconsin National Guard with the rank of major. One day after Wilson asked Congress to declare war on Germany, Goff applied for a reserve commission in the Judge Advocate General's Office, and on May 1, 1917, the army commissioned him as a colonel. While in Washington, DC, he conveyed to Gregory and Crowder that former Congressman Victor Berger was a danger to the war efforts in the upper Midwest. Goff's political views reflected the military establishment's fear that if the army did not contain Bolshevism or anarchism in Germany, then both political movements would grow in numbers throughout

Europe and into the United States. Immediately worrisome to Goff was the prospect of both movements gaining an influential presence in the army's ranks, as had occurred in the German Army and Navy.[64]

Goff's letters to his father were important not only because of their potential to influence Congress, but also because these letters presented the complex duties of senior officers and judge advocates in Europe. Maintaining law and order both in the United States Army and in the German population, containing Bolshevism, and holding German officers and governmental officials accountable for war crimes, and doing all this in concert with the Allied powers, required tremendous skill and diplomacy. On April 19, 1919, Goff informed his father that the United States provost marshal in Trier was the brother of a man he had prosecuted for syndicalism in Milwaukee in 1912. The provost marshal apparently did not share the radical views of his brother. He thanked Goff for the prosecution of his brother and then added that there were radicals in the army consorting with Spartacists. Goff also informed his father that he agreed with the provost's assessment of the German population: "they are two faced; they give you the right hand of welcome, leaving the left hand free to stick a knife in you if they thought they could get away with it."[65]

It angered Goff that Germany was not truly defeated and, as a result, its officials were able to negotiate over conditions at Versailles. In May 1919, he told Crowder that he observed German dignitaries "taunting Italian officials that they had backed the wrong horse." By that time the Italian premier, Vittorio Orlando, and Wilson had argued over Italy's intended expansion of territory in the Balkans, and Goff concluded that Wilson unintentionally emboldened the German government to assume it possessed the ability to confront the Allies. To Goff, the most troubling part of the Versailles negotiations was that a number of American and British officers and government officials, including Secretary of State Lansing, had determined that German government officials could not be held accountable for war crimes. Goff encouraged the creation of a judge advocate delegation including not only Crowder, but also Frankfurter, James Brown Scott, and Wigmore to convince Lansing to reverse course.[66]

Lansing's view of war crimes trials matched his earlier position on not prosecuting German saboteurs in 1916 as well as avoiding any statement on the British prosecution and execution of Roger Casement or the military trials of Irish nationalists. On November 14, 1918, Elihu Root warned Lansing that Bolshevism was the greatest danger to achieving peace in Europe, but he also urged that war crimes trials were necessary. Root tried to advocate that the battle to contain Bolshevism from spreading began in Germany, and the War Department was responsible for the containment. If German war criminals were to go free, Root reasoned, the failure to enforce international law would embolden the Bolsheviks for several reasons, and in particular, that the rule of law was malleable. Root also noted to Lansing that Crowder believed that removing war criminals from Germany not only would be morally required, it would further strengthen the Allies. Lansing agreed with Root that the containment of Bolshevism was an essential policy but countered that the prosecution of Germans labeled as war criminals by the Allies "would drive the German population into the Bolshevik camp."[67]

Lansing, in turn, argued to Goff that an 1812 Supreme Court decision, *United States v. Hudson and Goodwin*, prevented the prosecution of war crimes because the contemplated war crimes offenses had not been specifically enumerated into an international criminal code. Goff gave Lansing a Judge Advocate General's written opinion—the War Department's equivalent of an Attorney General Opinion—that *Hudson and Goodwin* was never believed to apply to military law, and that the law of war enabled the punishment of government officers who "failed to prevent or suppress violations of the laws of war." To this end, Goff added that Chief Justice John Marshall had, in 1815, written into American law the principle that international law "consisted of both formal rules and unwritten rules which reflected the great principles of reason and justice." To Goff, the law of war, when applied to Germany, which "since 1914 violated every rule of international law, conventional and otherwise and disregarded every principle of humanity, and caused the world to revert to barbarity," made it inconceivable that Lansing would urge immunity based on a narrow technicality. If, Goff warned, Germany's government and military officers, to include Kaiser Wilhelm, were to escape liability, "international law would lose rational jurisdiction and power capable of responding to reason and reacting to the requirements of exact justice." Goff foresaw that international law could serve as a bulwark against future dictators from launching new wars, and he also saw the enforcement of international law as a basis to hold the alliance of France, Britain, Belgium, and the United States together. Although he was a conservative Republican, he encouraged the United States to become part of a strong "League of Nations" as a means to prevent a future war and to contain Bolshevism.[68]

Goff became so irritated with Lansing over the State Department's tepid response to prosecuting major war criminals that he wrote to John W. Davis— who had left the prisoner of war mission to become the US ambassador to Great Britain— that Lansing's opposition was premised on the irrational fear that war crimes trials would embolden Bolshevism. To Goff, Lansing's excuses were problematic for three reasons. First, the fact that the kaiser had "run away like a white livered craven coward" would not engender to him any personal sympathy in Germany. Secondly, Goff presciently argued, the failure to prosecute war criminals simply "emboldened militarism and prussianism." In the 1930s, Adolf Hitler was to be acutely aware that the post–World War I trials failed to materialize to a meaningful degree. Goff added that a third reason to prosecute war criminals in Allied tribunals was that the failure to do so would result in a breakdown of international peace efforts.[69]

Hugh Ogden and James Brown Scott likewise found Lansing's opinion on war crimes perplexing, and both sided with Crowder in arguing that not only did the law of war permit the prosecution of German war criminals, the law required the prosecution of those German officers who were responsible for murdering Belgian and French citizens. Ogden informed his wife that he supported holding Germans accountable for war crimes because "the Germany of Goethe is gone and this new one only understands the rule of force." Scott agreed with Goff that the failure to hold German officials accountable would embolden future governments to defy international law. He enlisted Wigmore to add to a forthcoming speech to the New York Bar Association, statements on the importance of establishing international trials to hold German officials accountable for the murder of Belgian citizens in Dinant in 1914. Scott also supported the United States joining the League of Nations, and he went so far as to lobby Elihu Root to publicly support Wilson to the Senate. Root agreed with Wilson in concept, but in 1920 he penned to an agreeing Scott that it was Wilson's incompetency that caused the failure of the United States to enter into the League rather than the success of the senators who resisted. However, by 1922 Scott advocated permitting Wilhelm to remain in exile, and he supported the concept of permitting Germany to prosecute military officers who had committed offenses in the absence of Allied trials. Because of Germany's instability, he worried that prosecuting Wilhelm or former officers would create martyrs, and he particularly opposed forcing the Netherlands to abdicate its sovereignty when historically deposed monarchs and tyrants had been given safe haven in France and Britain.[70]

Not all of the judge advocates who transited into France and Germany following the Armistice agreed with Crowder, Rucker, Scott, and Goff on holding German officials accountable for war crimes, joining the League of Nations, or the need to remain in Germany until stability was achieved and the security of France and Belgium assured. In late 1919, J. Reuben Clark traveled to Coblenz and Trier while still on active duty, but while doing so he provided his observations to Senator Philander Knox, one of Woodrow Wilson's more ardent opponents. Clark differed from Crowder on the need to have the United States Army remain in Germany, and for the United States to join the League of Nations. Writing to Knox, Clark noted his opposition to using soldiers to enforce reparations or to joining the League of Nations. Indeed, Clark opposed any promise that bound the United States to the Allies if Germany resumed the conflict. "It is true that we now have, according to the press, only some sixteen thousand men on the Rhine, but of course Viviani wants these merely to be the shadow of the great force he would expect us to throw across the water in case of real trouble," Clark advised. "I think there is nothing to do but immediately to return the troops to this country. That I believe is what we promised in our party platform and let us not at this early date begin to go back on that." [71]

On April 7, 1921, four years after the declaration of war against Germany and with Warren G. Harding in the White House, Knox introduced a resolution into Congress declaring an end to war with Germany. Knox would have certainly sought a statutory end to the war without Clark's prodding. The two men were simply aligned in their early isolationist beliefs. However, the fact that Goff and Crowder, two Republicans in their political sentiments, were aligned with internationalist Democrats against a nascent isolationist movement that was also primarily Republican in its origins, was, in addition to a dispute over military justice, another example of an ideological split in the Judge Advocate General's Office, albeit one of a more reflective nature that never truly divided the office into warring camps. [72]

JUDGE ADVOCATE DUTIES IN FRANCE AND BELGIUM, 1919–1921

The army's occupation mission in Germany, as well as its application of international law to military operations, can be further contextualized by examining the oversight of the enforcement of discipline and other judge advocate duties in France regarding the redeploying of divisions of the American Expeditionary Forces. In the two months following the Armistice, the number of courts-martial in the American Expeditionary Forces increased, and from January 1, 1919, through July 1, 1919, courts-martial in France occurred on a level equivalent to that during the last six months of the war. For example, between the Armistice and July 1, 1919, the Services of Supply held over thirty thousand summary courts-martial and 508 general courts-martial. On August 1, 1919, Lieutenant Colonel Gallogly reported to Winship that during the prior two months, the Services of Supply reviewed fifty-two general courts-martial records, including the records of six officer trials that had been forwarded from the First Division after that division departed from France. In July 1919, the Services of Supply held seven officer trials from the First Division. The First Division's trial numbers were almost identical during the period from June 1 to December 31, 1918. Courts-martial in the six months after the Armistice were only one of the duties taxing judge advocates. In October 1918, General van Horn Moseley, the chief of the American Expeditionary Forces' fourth section, a unit responsible for ensuring the delivery of supplies from the Services of Supply to the front, recorded in his diary, "the problem of settling accounts with the French after this war is going to be an annoying one." Moseley understated how burdensome the issue of French claims would become, but he added that a staff of judge advocates was already gainfully employed in sorting through the French demands. After November 11, tens of thousands of damage claims from French merchants and property owners began to pour into the Services of Supply, which established a Rents, Requisitions, and Claims department under Gorfinkle's supervision.[73]

The United States Merchant Marine inquired to the War Department over how to handle deserters found on ships debarking from France. Clearly the soldiers who had fought in the war wanted to go home, but the orderly process of shipping soldiers home was disrupted by a number of factors, and desertions could undermine mission readiness. In response to the inquiry, Blanton Winship advised that since army deserters remained subject to court-martial jurisdiction, all such persons found on merchant ships under sail should be returned to the army in the United States. He noted that as "the county was still in a state of war," court-martial jurisdiction remained in effect over such persons, but such cases would be treated more leniently in the United States than in France.[74]

The sentences of general courts-martial in France could, at times, continue to be severe when a victim was French or when the offense was violent. In spite of the preference for trials to be conducted with single accused soldiers, the use of joint trials also continued. On October 19, 1919, three privates— John Kellie, William LeBuff, and Ernest N. Knight—were prosecuted for breaking into a stockade with the intent of murdering another private. The victim in this case, Private First Class Sam Evans, had pleaded guilty to having sexual intercourse with an underage French girl along with his three assailants, and the three soldiers wanted him silenced to keep him from testifying in their court-martial. Kellie, LeBuff, and Knight pleaded not guilty to assault, but the general court-martial found them guilty and sentenced them to five years in confinement and a dishonorable discharge. Then the army prosecuted the three for their offense of what has become known as statutory rape and sentenced them to another twenty-five years. Blanton Winship advised the Third Army commander against granting clemency. At the same time, a general court-martial sentenced Private Carl Blair to five years' confinement for stealing 900 francs from a hotel safe. On the day Blair was prosecuted, so too was Sergeant First Class Holbert McClane for pointing a firearm at the head of a private who refused to do his duty, and then, once in pretrial confinement for this offense, for assaulting a prison guard by shoving the guard into the contents of a latrine. The general court-martial sentenced McClane to five years in confinement and a dishonorable discharge. However, in this instance, Winship advised that the charge involving the prison guard and the latrine was not sustainable by the evidence.[75]

Following the Armistice, Crowder advised Bethel that because the workload of the Judge Advocate General's Office in France was likely to vastly increase, he should solicit volunteers from the line officers who wished to remain in France. Bethel, in turn, noted to Winship, who in December became the Services of Supply judge advocate, that he "believed the heaviest disciplinary work in the next few months will devolve upon the various sections of the S. O. S. and the work is fast becoming heavier than the office can handle it." In August 1919, Winship asked Harbord to consider ordering the retention of judge advocates assigned to the Services of Supply if there were not enough volunteers. Winship noted that because the American Expeditionary Forces headquarters had closed, the Services of Supply, with its headquarters at Tours, was tasked with the review of thousands of general courts-martial that had been held immediately after the war. In addition to this duty, the withdrawal of forces from France "led to the arrest of many offenders and increased the trial court work," and there were "several serious cases of fraud against the government." Because the judge advocates assigned throughout the war to the Services of Supply had become familiar with French law, Winship pleaded that their loss would prove detrimental to the hundreds of claims and contract negotiations with the French government. Between the Armistice and September 1919, the Services of Supply processed over fifty-five thousand claims. Harbord agreed to retain several judge advocates, but he reinforced Crowder's direction to seek volunteers from the corps and division judge advocates as well as line officers to take their place.[76]

Some judge advocates, such as Lieutenant Colonel Albert Smith of the Thirty-Seventh Infantry Division, informed Winship that his law firm partners in Los Angeles had dissolved their firm in his absence during the previous two years and he needed to return home to rebuild a law practice. Likewise, Winship learned that four of the judge advocates assigned to the Ninety-First Division, except for the detailed judge advocate, Lieutenant Colonel Charles McCorkle, intended to return home at the first possible opportunity. For reasons similar to Smith's, most of the judge advocates intended to return from Europe as soon as they could. Other judge advocates, such as Major Cleon Berntheizel, who by all accounts had performed his duties to the satisfaction of General Charles Muir, the Twenty-Eighth Division's commander, failed to achieve promotion, in his case because of a latent hostility from General Moseley. Failing promotion, Berntheizel desired to return home to resurrect his political career.[77]

After Bethel left France in July 1919, there was still a shortage of judge advocates to fulfill the duties of reviewing general and special courts-martial, claims payments to Allied governments and citizens, War Risk Insurance issues, and investigations into war crimes. The shortage was not caused by a lack of volunteers, but rather by the continual application of stringent standards for judge advocate duties. For instance, on January 26, 1919, Captain Herman Decius, an infantry officer assigned to the Ninety-First Division, volunteered to remain in Paris for a year as a judge advocate. Decius graduated from the University of Southern California School of Law in 1911, served as a trial judge advocate in a general court-martial, and fought at St. Mihiel. McCorkle endorsed Decius's application. Yet Bethel believed Decius was too inexperienced in military law to become a judge advocate. Decius, like two dozen of his peers, was sent home. On the other hand, Bethel did not have a similar opinion of Malcolm S. Lauchheimer, who became Pepper's assistant at a forward base camp. Prior to the war Lauchheimer was a professor of labor relations at Johns Hopkins University, and during the war he served in the American Expeditionary Forces Adjutant General's Office. He did not become an attorney until 1916, but his decade-long tenure as a professor of labor relations placed him in good stead with Bethel.[78]

The two primary duties of the judge advocates assigned in France after June 1919 remained courts-martial and settling the vast numbers of foreign claims. By this time the Services of Supply headquarters had been reduced from its peak number of thirty-four judge advocates to five commissioned judge advocates, four infantry officers who had been lawyers prior to the war and were awaiting orders to return to the United States, and eleven legal orderlies. In addition to Winship, the legal staff included Major Charles Albert, a Washington state lawyer who championed universal suffrage prior to the war. Albert was born in Pennsylvania in 1878 and was educated at George Washington University and the University of Minnesota. Before moving to Spokane in 1910, he represented the Great Northern Railway and was a member of the state Democratic Party. Major Charles H. Moorman, a Kentucky judge educated at Ohio State University and a contemporary of Samuel Wilson, served alongside Albert. Moorman left his legal practice in Lexington, Kentucky, and served in the Red Cross in France prior to April 1917. After the war, President Coolidge appointed him to the United States Court of Appeals for the Sixth Circuit. Major Leon Fraser was the third officer assigned to Winship. He began the war as a private, was promoted to sergeant major, and after the Armistice commissioned as a major. Fraser was adopted and raised near Albany, New York, and graduated from Columbia University in 1899, but then remained for another eleven years earning a law degree as well as a doctorate in political science. Following his admission to the bar he represented General Electric while teaching political science and law at Barnard College and journalism at Columbia. In 1912 he was employed as the *New York World*'s editor. Following the war, he would assist Charles Dawes, become a director of General Electric's international division, and have the foresight to warn that Adolph Hitler was "a dangerous religious fanatic" after meeting him in 1931. Ironically, in May 1917, Columbia did not renew his teaching contract because of alleged "pacifist tendencies" and questions about his loyalty. Major Hugh Bayne asserted to Bethel in early 1918 that Fraser was neither a pacifist nor disloyal but rather would be a superb officer.[79]

On August 1, 1919, Winship reorganized the Services of Supply's Judge Advocate General's Office with four judge advocates and sixteen sergeants at Tours, thirty-one judge advocates and an equal number of sergeants assigned to nine base sections throughout France, and eighteen judge advocates and seven sergeants in Paris. Another seventeen judge advocates were assigned to embarkation centers and depots. The judge advocates in charge of the embarkation centers had served in France throughout much of the war. Samuel Pepper was the judge advocate for the Le Havre embarkation center, Arthur Dehon Hill was in charge of Base Section Number 8, and Wiley Howell led the large Paris office. Assisting them were a large percentage of new judge advocates. For instance, Major Stacy B. Lloyd, a University of Pennsylvania Law School graduate, was commissioned as a judge advocate in July 1918 and was sent to France in February 1919. Born in 1876, Lloyd had been the Pennsylvania director of food administration after the declaration of war. His legal experience prior to 1917 included a general counsel position at the Pennsylvania Railroad Corporation.[80]

All of the nine base sections were staffed with judge advocates who had either considerable line or judge advocate experience during the war. For instance, Major George Dabney and Lieutenant A. G. Hebling were assigned as judge advocates to "Base Section Number 1," a post near Verdun. Hebling was admitted to the Pennsylvania Bar in 1914 after graduating from the University of Pittsburgh's law school. In his first civilian trial, he obtained an acquittal for a client accused of "moonshining and murder." He enlisted in June 1917 as a private, was quickly promoted to sergeant major, and only in January 1919 commissioned major as a judge advocate. He did, however, lead enlisted infantrymen into combat during the Meuse-Argonne Offensive and earned the Bronze Star. Dabney graduated from Harvard's law school in 1902 and went to work for the Massachusetts governor shortly after. He began the war as an engineering officer and arrived in France in November 1917. Dabney also assisted the French in a mining operation under a German trench section in early 1918. In January 1919, he was assigned as a judge advocate and placed in charge of a section responsible for settling civil disputes with French municipal governments. For the first six months of 1919, the two judge advocates settled nineteen claims with French municipalities totaling six million dollars.[81]

In May 1919, the judge advocates assigned to "Base Section 2" attempted to prosecute Spanish laborers in military trials. The laborers were accused of routine crimes such as larceny, robbery, and fraud. The three judge advocates, Lieutenant Colonel Jasper Yates Brinton, Major Elias Field, and Lieutenant Irving Kurz, advised the section commander that *Milligan* did not protect the Spanish from military jurisdiction, and the French agreement with the American Expeditionary Forces enabled American jurisdiction. Winship, however, disagreed with the use of American military courts to prosecute the Spanish laborers without first consulting with the Spanish government. The Spanish government protested the subjugation of their citizens to American military trials and, as a compromise, the French civil courts asserted jurisdiction. The difference between the Spanish and Germans was that Spain had been a neutral during the war. Prior to the war, Brinton, a University of Pennsylvania law graduate and scholar of Greek and Latin, not only taught law at his alma mater, he headed a political organization dedicated to outlawing child labor. He was also a close friend of Major Hugh Bayne. During the war, Brinton had served as the judge advocate for the Port of Bordeaux. Field, a Harvard Law graduate and contemporary of Arthur Hill, arrived in France in November 1918. Before being commissioned into the army he practiced law in Boston, and at times he represented the city in the state supreme court. After the war, he joined Hill in representing Sacco and Vanzetti on their appeals. Kurz likewise had graduated from Harvard, but in 1914, making him one of the younger judge advocates.[82]

Although the numbers of courts-martial records caused a backlog at the judge advocate headquarters, additional matters consumed much of its efforts and resources. Foremost of the issues to require judge advocate oversight was a significant prisoner abuse scandal. In August 1918, the Services of Supply took control of a prison farm outside of Paris designated as "Prison Farm no. 2" as well as a military stockade in nearby Chelles, a suburb of Paris. Both Prison Farm no. 2 and the stockade were designed to confine soldiers who were caught in Paris while absent without leave, deserters, and other stragglers. Although Pershing had earlier issued an order prohibiting excursions to Paris, hundreds of soldiers were caught in France's capital city. In October 1918 Major General Frederick Strong, the Fortieth Division's commander as well as the commander of the district of Paris, instructed Colonel Edgar Grinstead, the prison commandant, "to be ruthless in securing the discipline of stragglers." Prison Farm no. 2 and the Chelles stockade each contained over a thousand prisoners, many of whom had not yet been convicted by a court-martial, and of this number several would never be court-martialed. Between October and December 1918, dozens of prisoners were abused by military guards, and one prisoner committed suicide. Additionally, enlisted prison guards assaulted commissioned officers brought into the prison.[83]

Beginning in September 1918, the Judge Advocate General's Office in France became aware of prisoner mistreatment in the American Expeditionary Forces' military prisons. Specifically, on September 1, Major James L. Kincaid, the Twenty-Seventh Division's judge advocate, notified Bethel that several of the division's soldiers had been detained at prisons and assaulted by the guards. Kincaid's initial letter went unanswered, but in December he penned a detailed summary of prison abuse to his division commander, Major General John F. O'Ryan, which led Kreger to advise Pershing to order an investigation into the prisons. Pershing, in turn, appointed Winship to oversee the investigation. Winship assigned Major Arthur G. Black, a Kansas City attorney and graduate of Washington University's law school, and Major John J. Kuhn, a Brooklyn attorney who graduated from Cornell in 1896 and served as the Eightieth Division's judge advocate, to investigate the prison abuses and recommend charges against all personnel to include Colonel Grinstead and General Strong. Following an investigation, Colonel Winship forwarded to Harbord charges against eleven soldiers, including the worst of the offenders, a lieutenant named Fred Smith, who was nicknamed "Hard-Boiled Smith." The prison scandal investigation consumed a large amount of the judge advocates' time and resources.[84]

Winship also removed the judge advocate in Paris and replaced him with Colonel Wiley Howell. Winship's reasons for the removal were that the original judge advocate had failed to inquire into prison conditions during his tenure in Paris, and Winship concluded that the judge advocate was not competent to be in charge of personnel. Crowder agreed with Winship's action. In all, four judge advocates were removed from France as a result of Winship's conclusion that they had failed to properly advise the responsible commanders on their duties to treat imprisoned soldiers—many of whom had not yet been court-martialed—humanely.[85]

Harbord convened seven courts-martial. A general court-martial convicted Smith of beating prisoners and sentenced him to a dismissal and three years in prison. Three other lieutenants, along with Sergeants Clarence E. Ball, Fred Wolfmaier, and Savo Ragnovich, were convicted of abusing prisoners. With the exception of Smith, none of the convicted soldiers received a sentence of greater than one year in confinement, though all were either dismissed or dishonorably discharged from the army. Pershing commented that all of the sentences were inadequate, but rather than order a resentencing, he approved of each. However, Harbord reduced "Hard-Boiled" Smith's sentence to eighteen months in confinement, and two of the other officers were restored to duty, despite Lieutenant Colonel Mendel Smith's advice to approve of the convictions and sentences as adjudged. More galling to the judge advocates was that neither General Strong nor Colonel Grinstead was prosecuted. With a surprising lack of political foresight, neither the Judge Advocate General's Office nor the American Expeditionary Forces' command seems to have planned for a congressional hearing into the matter.[86]

While the judge advocates at the headquarters offices worked to review courts-martial, examine claims, and investigate allegations of war crimes as well as prisoner abuses, the divisional judge advocates' workload remained both large and varied. Shortly after the Armistice, and prior to an influx of courts-martial records, the Seventy-Seventh Division's commander, Major General Robert Alexander, assigned Lieutenant Colonel Samuel Wilson to write an article for *Stars and Stripes*, detailing the division's origins as well as the history underlying its nickname, "the Statue of Liberty Division." Wilson was also ordered to create a private reunion association for the division's veterans, and although similar associations had sprung up across the American Expeditionary Forces, he drafted the bylaws and tax status application for the association. Perhaps most importantly, Wilson drafted division-wide orders ranging from prohibiting soldiers from consorting with prostitutes and requiring the consumption of "boiled water" to reduce the risk of typhoid, to mandatory weekly delousing as well as using rubble from villages to repair roads. Wilson, on behalf of the division, contracted with local quarries to obtain "road metal" for this latter purpose.[87]

Wilson also advocated for political matters of national importance. In the four months following the Armistice, he corresponded with former associates in Kentucky, urging them to support the League of Nations while at the same time championing the cause of making Prohibition a permanent national law. He also drafted position papers to sustain war crimes trials against not only German officials but also former Ottoman government officials for the massacre of tens of thousands of Armenians. Wilson went so far as to suggest that if the Allies would not conduct criminal trials against the deposed Ottoman government, then the common courts of Kentucky might extend jurisdiction.

"The world has been astounded by the authenticated reports from Armenia and Syria of the unbelievable acts of atrocity and savage brutality committed against these inoffensive and indefensible people by the Turkish forces," he concluded. In addition to his insistence on prosecuting war criminals, Wilson came out forcefully against a measure to ban the teaching of German in Kentucky schools and called the proposal "anti-American."[88]

On December 8, 1918, General Alexander ordered a program of drill and discipline so that the division would be prepared to engage in combat if Germany renewed fighting. He ordered the quarantine of whole companies where soldiers had a high rate of sickness or significant indiscipline. Between December 15 and February 15, the division conducted over two hundred summary courts-martial, thirty-nine special courts-martial, and seventeen general courts-martial. The large number of summary courts-martial arose from charges of soldiers failing to salute officers and wearing civilian clothes. On December 15, Alexander issued a bulletin reminding all soldiers that saluting officers was required since soldiers were not permitted to either be out of uniform except while participating in athletic events or acting in "stage shows." On February 15, a *New York Times* reporter informed several soldiers of a rumor that the division would transit to Le Havre at the end of the month and sail to New York on March 5. This rumor resulted in a large number of soldiers becoming publicly drunk and further flaunting regulations. Alexander had Wilson draft a memorandum to dispel the rumor and inform the division's soldiers that they were not likely to sail for New York before the end of April. Another sixty-two lesser courts-martial were conducted between February 15 and March 1.[89]

Although Wilson's workload increased after January 1, 1919, the most significant of the Seventy-Seventh's trials originated prior to the Armistice. In December 1918, the division conducted two general courts-martial arising from the "Lost Battalion" episode. Lieutenant Maurice S. Revnes was accused of "misbehavior before the enemy" for sending a note to Lieutenant Colonel Charles Whittlesey which asked him to surrender the battalion's survivors to the Germans if no relief arrived by the middle of the day. Revnes had been shot through the foot and witnessed a number of deaths, and he treated gangrene in other soldiers. The court-martial initially acquitted Revnes. However, Wilson, after reviewing the record of trial advised Alexander not to approve the acquittal, but rather, to send the record of trial back for reconsideration. Wilson discovered that while the trial judge advocate had alluded to Revnes's note to Whittlesey, he had never produced the note for evidence. To Wilson, the failure to produce evidence justified disapproving the acquittal, which, under the unique aspects of the Articles of War, enabled such an action. Whittlesey had already returned to New York at the time of the trial and thus was unavailable to testify. On reconsideration and with the addition of a telegraphic affidavit from Whittlesey, the court-martial found Revnes guilty and sentenced him to a dismissal. On a second review, following the conviction and sentence, Wilson then advised Alexander not to approve the sentence of a dismissal in light of mitigating circumstances, including the possibility that Revnes's own gangrene infections might have caused delusions and the fact that Revnes had been a courageous officer prior to his letter to Whittlesey. Ultimately Revnes was honorably discharged from the army.[90]

A second general court-martial occurred despite Wilson's advice to Alexander not to proceed to trial. On September 28, 1918, Colonel Samuel Vidmer, a regimental commander, ordered Major Lewis Sanders, an artillery officer, to move two cannon under his command to an advanced forward position. Sanders objected to moving the two cannon from their position because they were situated in a place that minimized the possibility of having American shells explode on advancing American infantrymen. After Vidmer ordered Sanders to move the cannon a second time, the cannon were moved but were unable to fire due to heavy foliage. On his own initiative Sanders moved the two cannon back to their initial positions and provided artillery support to the infantry by destroying several German machine gun nests. On October 1, 1918, Wilson took statements from a dozen participants and concluded that while Sanders had disobeyed Vidmer's orders and therefore "it could be proved that he was guilty of a willful disobedience of orders, the artillery had accomplished the mission which the divisional command assigned to it." Had Sanders maintained the cannon in the location Vidmer insisted, Wilson reasoned, hundreds of American infantrymen would have been killed by American cannon fire. "In justice to Major Sanders, and in all candor, I must say that I think he was actuated by unimpeachable motives and was absolutely sincere in his belief in futility of changing the position of his guns," he advised. Despite Wilson's reticence for a court-martial, General Alexander ordered Sanders to be tried in a general court-martial. On December 1, 1918, the court-martial resulted in an acquittal, and this time the verdict was approved. But Sanders was not informed of the acquittal until January 3, 1919.[91]

In early March 1919, the Seventy-Seventh Division did, in fact, transit to Le Mans rather than Le Havre, but Wilson was confronted by a number of issues regarding holding soldiers accountable for larceny against French citizens as well as for public drunkenness that resulted in the destruction of private property. On March 8 the division rapidly convened seventeen special courts-martial and one general court-martial to set an example that soldiers found guilty of offenses would not sail home with the division. All of the soldiers were found guilty and sentenced to periods in prison ranging from one month to six months. On March 11 Wilson informed Alexander that there was an immediate reduction in the number of criminal acts. However, the deterrent Alexander and Wilson desired was short-lived. One week later, Winship informed Wilson that Kreger initiated a policy in which soldiers imprisoned for less than six months would be permitted to return to the United States with their respective divisions and would then serve out their remaining sentence under guard until discharged. Kreger worried that the military prisons would overflow with soldiers convicted of minor offenses and then result in riots. He had another worry as well, stemming from the prisoner abuse investigation. In June 1919, the *New York Times* reported that dozens of American soldiers who had been arrested near Paris were assaulted by American military police in army prisons. However, Kreger, along with the other judge advocates in Chaumont, Paris, and Tours, knew that newspaper reporters were aware of the abuse as early as March 4.[92]

In his last days in France, Wilson gave Bethel his copy of Winthrop's *Military Law and Precedents*. Bethel had earlier informed Wilson that "there were many important offices in the A. E. F. in need of this treatise," and since "it had not been possible to purchase the treatise on the market," Bethel "promised he would be grateful for the favor." Ironically, by this time Ansell had testified to Congress that the War Department's reliance on Winthrop's treatise caused hundreds of injustices. On April 14, the division transited to Brest over a four-day period. Its twenty-four thousand soldiers boarded vessels to New York. When the division returned to New York and following its victory parade, an enormous "victory dinner" was held for its officers and noncommissioned officers. At the "victory dinner," Wilson was seated next to a number of influential men in the War Department and American politics, including Alfred Smith, Reverend Francis Duffy, Newton Baker, and Assistant Secretary of the Navy Franklin D. Roosevelt. On May 21, 1919, Wilson returned home to Lexington and resumed his legal practice.[93]

RUSSIA AND ARMENIA

Although the majority of judge advocates in Europe after the Armistice were located in France, and secondarily in Germany, four judge advocates took part in two foreign missions that had a significant impact not only on the shaping of the nation's foreign policies throughout the twentieth century, but also on the redesigning of international borders and the relationship between the Soviet Union—and then its partial successor, the Russian Federation—and the United States since 1919. One other judge advocate was attached to a War Department mission that examined the Ottoman Empire's treatment of Armenians during the war and advised President Wilson on the viability of an independent Armenian state.

In July 1918, Wilson ordered American soldiers into Russia, ostensibly to enable Czechoslovakian soldiers and other pro-Allied forces to escape through Vladivostok as well as to prevent German soldiers from being redirected to the Western Front. American soldiers took part in two Allied expeditions into Murmansk and Archangel, in reality as a means to distract German forces in Russia from transiting to the Western Front as well as to contain Bolshevism. The fall of the Kerensky government enabled hundreds of thousands of German and Austrian soldiers to shift from the eastern theatre of war to fight in France, Greece, Turkey, and Italy. Wilson was initially reluctant to commit American soldiers to a Russian expedition, and Congress never expressly sanctioned using conscripted soldiers for a Russian expedition. Moreover Speaker of the House James Clark lobbied Wilson against sending any American soldiers into Russia. On the other hand, Wilson gambled that the expeditions into Russia would withstand judicial scrutiny because of the Constitution's war powers grant to the Executive Branch as well as fears of the spread of Bolshevism. Lansing later hinted that Supreme Court Justice Stephen Day had quietly approved of Wilson's reasoning, and given that Day was a McKinley appointee, and the likelihood that Brandeis, Clarke, Holmes, and McReynolds would support Wilson, a majority of justices were unlikely to entertain challenges to Wilson on the matter. One week after the Armistice, Frankfurter reported to Baker that Brandeis had distrusted Kerensky but believed the Bolsheviks were a greater menace.[94]

In June 1918 Crowder informed Baker that he worried over whether Wilson had the constitutional authority to send American soldiers to Russia without a clear statement that the purpose for doing so was to prevent German soldiers from transiting to the Western Front. Baker, for his part, concluded that sending American soldiers into Russia was a mistake that would detract from offensive efforts on the Western Front. While Crowder doubted the authority of Wilson to act without the sanction of Congress, he sought Pershing's support for his efforts to be appointed to command the expedition to Vladivostok along Russia's Pacific coast. Crowder was not unqualified to do so, since he had familiarity with the Japanese forces sent into Vladivostok, as well as the region from his posting as an observer during the Russo-Japanese War in 1904.[95]

Crowder's worries over the legality of sending American forces into Russia were misplaced in the sense that neither Congress nor the federal judiciary

determined that Wilson had exceeded his constitutional authority. In February 1919, Wambaugh informed Baker that the president's stationing of
soldiers in Archangel and Vladivostok was in full accordance with the Constitution and that the federal courts would not grant any judicial challenges. In
1922 the Supreme Court indirectly addressed the use of military forces against
Bolshevism in a decision originating in a court-martial held in Vladivostok.
In 1920 the army court-martialed Private Roy Marshall in Vladivostok for
robbery and sentenced him to five years' imprisonment. While awaiting transfer from Alcatraz to the McNeil Island military prison, Marshall appealed to
the federal courts. He claimed that his confession was obtained under duress,
the specification under which he was charged was faulty, and the stationing of
forces in Russia without an express declaration of war or congressional authorization rendered the court-martial without jurisdiction. In other words, he
urged that because President Wilson sent soldiers to a conflict in Russia without congressional sanction, no court-martial possessed jurisdiction. This may
have been the first instance of a service-member attempting an appeal of a
court-martial on the basis of having been ordered into a war or military operation that Congress had never expressly sanctioned. The Supreme Court, in
Collins v. McDonald, relying on a half century of precedent, found that criminal charges did not have to be drafted with precision, and it determined that
a claim of an unlawfully coerced confession was not a proper habeas matter.
Most importantly, the Court held that the question of court-martial jurisdiction over soldiers serving in what came to be commonly referred to in the
Vietnam era as "an illegal war"—though not in the language of 1920—was
"trivial." Even Brandeis did not believe that the Court should enter into the
question of whether Wilson exceeded his authority.[96]

    Collins is an important contextual backdrop to the American forces' situ-
ation in both Murmansk and Vladivostok. At the same time Generals Dickman, Liggett, and Allen tried to enforce a tough disciplinary regimen on the
soldiers under their commands in France and Germany, a similar difficulty
occurred in Russia. In Vladivostok, American soldiers took part in a coalition
operation that included British, French, and Japanese forces. Commanded by
Major General William Graves, the expedition conducted over four hundred
general and special courts-martial. The indiscipline of this force of slightly
less than eight thousand soldiers was reminiscent of the China Relief Expedition twenty years earlier. The courts-martial records evidence a low morale
that manifested in refusals to obey orders to guard American posts, rampant
alcohol consumption, and over thirty desertions. The latter offense is puz-
zling since a deserted soldier had little opportunity to leave the area. Overseeing military justice and other aspects of military law in Vladivostok was

Lieutenant Colonel Albert J. Galen. Prior to the war, Galen had served a term as Montana's state attorney general, and earned his LLB from Notre Dame and his LLD from the University of Michigan. A commensurate deployment of American soldiers to Murmansk occurred with Lieutenant Edward S. Thurston as its judge advocate. Commanded by Colonel George Evans Stewart, 5,000 American soldiers joined 6,000 British soldiers and sailors and 1,700 French soldiers.[97]

The Vladivostok expedition got off to a remarkably poor start as three of the first five general courts-martial arose out of the conduct of officers. One court-martial found an officer guilty of consorting with prostitutes in Osaka and entering into a prohibited area. A second court-martial convicted an officer of being drunk and disorderly and then "assaulting a friendly Cossack." The third court-martial determined that a lieutenant was not only drunk in public, but when questioned by a British colonel as to his identity, provided the name of an innocent officer. Although officer misconduct is always detrimental, the most serious of the early courts-martial arose from the murder of one soldier by another soldier. On October 10, 1919, a general court-martial found Private William Penman guilty of "murdering Private James Long with premeditation" and sentenced him to be imprisoned for life. The same day that Penman was convicted and sentenced, a general court-martial found Private Hugh T. Murtaugh, a cook, guilty of being drunk on duty and defecating in a vat of soup that was about to be served in the officers' mess.[98]

Courts-martial were only one indicator of the difficulties that confronted the American expedition. Poor relations with the British commander, an unwelcoming local population, and the constant threat of confrontation with Bolshevik forces were constant detractions from discipline. One of the aspects of the Vladivostok expedition was the large number of Japanese soldiers. By September 1919, there were 60,000 Japanese soldiers in Siberia, and they came into open confrontation with Bolshevik forces in spite of assurances to the Allies that there would be a minimum contact with the warring Russian factions. Graves tried to convey to the soldiers under his command an understanding that because Russia was in the midst of a brutal civil war, any victimization of the local populace by a soldier would only advance the Bolshevik cause. On September 11, 1918, a general court-martial determined that Corporal M. L. Bryant was guilty of assaulting citizens in Vladivostok and thrice stealing from the local population, as well as being drunk and disorderly, and the court sentenced him to a dishonorable discharge and a year in prison. Graves also published a reprimand he drafted for Bryant to the entirety of the American force reminding the force that "individual soldiers who, by their single misconduct, attempt to undo the work of all or obstruct the accomplishments of our success, will be met with severe punishment."[99]

Despite Graves's concern for discipline, he was unable to control the outcomes of courts-martial. On December 19, 1919, a general court-martial found Lieutenant Edward Gallegos guilty of being drunk on duty and assaulting an enlisted soldier but acquitted him of conduct unbecoming an officer and gentleman. Moreover, the court-martial only sentenced him to forfeit five dollars of his pay per month for six months. Galen advised Graves not to approve the sentence because it was too lenient. Graves concurred, and after admonishing the court for the acquittal, penned, "to approve the findings and the sentence of the court would be tantamount to participating in this travesty of military justice." Ultimately Gallegos was returned to duty.[100]

In terms of courts-martial, the situation in Murmansk under the command of Colonel Stewart was similar to the conditions in Vladivostok. Stewart and his British counterparts were visibly hostile to each other, and the British commander, Major General Frederick Poole, ordered Stewart's forces to a frontal area where confrontations with Bolshevik forces became a common occurrence. One of the differences between the two expeditions was that while Major General Graves had the authority to convene and approve general courts-martial, Colonel Stewart did not, and it fell to Pershing to convene and approve such trials. One soldier attempted to desert while the force transited through Britain by wearing a Canadian uniform and boarding a vessel traveling to Halifax. The soldier was convicted of desertion and sentenced to two years in prison and a dishonorable discharge. Another soldier was convicted of murder and sentenced to life. On February 28, 1919, Thurston reported to Kreger that with the exception of a single officer sentenced to a dismissal, disciplinary matters were "routine." However, by June 1919, eighteen general courts-martial and over one hundred lesser courts-martial had been adjudicated in Murmansk. Over the course of one year, there were 284 general courts-martial and over 600 special courts-martial. For a five thousand—strong soldiers force, these were higher per capita numbers than experienced in the American Expeditionary Forces' divisions.[101]

Thurston turned to Captain Charles E. Lewis to serve as trial judge advocate for almost all of the expedition's general courts-martial. Born in 1889, Captain Lewis was a Michigan attorney prior to the war. He graduated from the University of Michigan's law school in 1913 alongside Frank Murphy. Although he applied for a judge advocate commission and had the backing of Charles Beecher Warren, he was unsuccessful in his attempts to join the Judge Advocate General's Office. Commissioned as a lieutenant and assigned to an "intelligence platoon," he trained at Camp Custer in Michigan and, in

July 1918, departed with a battalion for Britain and then Murmansk rather than France. He also kept a diary of the 339th Regiment's duties for his regimental commander. The soldiers protested an order to turn in their American Springfield rifles in exchange for Russian rifles. One battalion left with over six hundred soldiers, but ten of them died of Spanish Influenza shortly after arriving in Murmansk. Once in Archangel, Lewis supervised the employment of "Bolsheviki prisoners," equating them to prisoners of war in terms of their rights. In late September 1918, Lewis oversaw the construction of a rifle range using "Bolshevikis." In October he recorded that Bolsheviks on fatigue duty had hidden Mills grenades and rifles under the camp hospital for retrieval during a planned uprising. Between Lewis's arrival and January 1, 1918, there was no mutiny of American soldiers, but over one hundred soldiers fell ill to influenza and forty died.[102]

Lewis later recalled that there were several acts of indiscipline, though he attributed these to a loss of morale occurring as a result of mistreatment by British officers in overall command of the expedition as well as interactions with the Russians. "The general relations between the Americans on the one hand and the French and Canadian elements on the other were, in general, cordial, while our relations with the English were strained," he informed the Army War College in 1932. By the time American soldiers left Murmansk, the expedition had conducted forty-two general courts-martial which resulted both in sentences of a year or more and dishonorable discharges.[103]

There were aspects to both expeditions that made it a far different operation than the occupation of Germany. Initially, in Vladivostok, Galen had attempted to convince the Allied forces to treat captured Bolshevik soldiers as prisoners of war because the Japanese government considered the expedition part of an ongoing war. However, in November 1918, Crowder made it clear that detained Russians, regardless of their political affiliation, could not be treated as prisoners of war or forcibly employed in the expedition's defenses. However, he noted that prisoners could be employed to assist in their own subsistence in such work as farming. Because the Bolsheviks were considered a dire threat, captured Bolshevik soldiers could expect little from the Japanese Army.[104]

The Russian expedition, according to Wilsonian scholar Thomas Knock, is often forgotten by American leaders. President Ronald Reagan once made the claim that despite the United States' differences with the Soviet Union, the United States had never invaded Russian territory. Not only was Reagan mistaken, the two Allied expeditions to Russia left a legacy of Russian distrust of the West. Not since the expedition into China in 1900 was an American force encumbered by rampant disciplinary problems. After November 11,

1918, both Major General Graves and Colonel Stewart asked Baker to approve a quick removal of forces from Russia, and Crowder advised an agreeing Baker that as a matter of constitutional law, the expeditions were once more on shaky ground. However, after consulting with Lansing, Wilson instructed Baker that American forces would remain in Russia until after the Paris Peace Conference concluded. On January 13, 1919, Senator Hiram Johnson introduced a resolution to the Senate demanding the speedy withdrawal of American forces from Russia. Only the tie-breaking vote of Vice President Marshall prevented the resolution's passage. When the last of the US forces finally left Russia in July 1919, the lives of over two hundred soldiers had been lost. Crowder also had come to the conclusion that while the American Army was capable of confronting any foreign power on a conventional battlefield, it was not prepared to fight against the mass ideology of communism in Russia.[105]

Crowder was convinced that the battle lines against communism were in Germany and Western Europe, not in Russia. He believed that communism could be defeated without resort to war if the United States took a prominent international role in assisting the nationalist aspirations of ethnic minorities as well as holding the perpetrators of war crimes accountable. To this end, he took a particular interest in the various enclaves of the former Ottoman Empire, particularly the fate of the Armenian population. When, in early 1919, Lansing proposed that the War Department send a mission to the former Ottoman Empire to assess whether the United States could protect that region's ethnic minorities, Crowder sought Baker's permission to have a judge advocate detailed to serve on the mission. He initially proposed that Colonel Wambaugh travel with the mission but then decided that he would permit Winship to select a judge advocate in Europe to take part.[106]

During the war, the Ottoman government either ordered the massacre or permitted the deaths of over one and a half million of its Armenian inhabitants. Armenian leaders sought the creation of a nation within the former Turkish Empire based on conceptions of an ancient homeland stretching from the Caspian Sea to the Black Sea. President Wilson believed that Ottoman officials were responsible for the deaths of hundreds of thousands of Armenians, and he supported the creation of an Armenian state. Crowder lobbied for war crimes trials against Ottoman officials. On June 25, 1919, Henry Morgenthau, the former ambassador to the Ottoman Empire, with Lansing's approval, asked General Harbord to serve as the head of an investigative mission to report on conditions in Armenia. During the war Morgenthau protested the mass killings of the Ottoman Empire's minority Armenian population to the Ottoman government as well as to Lansing and Wilson. Morgenthau also recommended to Harbord that he bring with him Lieutenant Jasper Brinton as the mission's judge advocate. Winship approved of permitting Brinton to leave France and join Harbord in Turkey. Brinton not only collected evidence of atrocities committed against the Armenian minority population, he also assisted Harbord in interviewing Mustapha Kemal, who was shortly to become the leader of the new Turkey. Harbord ultimately advised Wilson that an Armenian nation was untenable as long as "Constantinople" remained under Turkish control, and because that city was historically a Turkish capital, it was unlikely that a foreign power could hold on to it.[107]

Although Harbord was lukewarm to creating an American protectorate, he permitted his staff not only to exercise independent judgment throughout their mission, but also to report their conclusions to the State Department and Baker. Brinton advocated the opposite of Harbord, urging the War Department to send several thousand soldiers to bolster the fledgling Armenian government and protect the citizenry from both Ataturk's forces and Bolshevik aggression. He did, however, convince Harbord to recommend that the United States push the Allies to establish war crimes trials over former Ottoman officials responsible for the massacres. After consulting with Brinton, Bainbridge Colby, who had succeeded Lansing as secretary of state, advocated that the United States support a "greater Republic of Armenia." Harbord's mission into Asia Minor lasted thirty days. He issued his report to the State Department on October 16, 1919, but it was not made public until 1920, and the Senate ultimately rejected its conclusions.[108]

In 1919 Brinton wrote to Senators James Wadsworth and Henry Cabot Lodge, asking them to support Allied war crimes trials of Ottoman officials. Both senators had criticized the Ottoman government and spoken in support of the Armenians. By this time Wadsworth had replaced George Chamberlain as the chairman of the Senate Military Affairs Committee. Lodge was one of the few senators to support stationing a small number of American soldiers in Armenia. In his letter, Brinton noted that the British Army had court-martialed four Ottoman military officers for their treatment of prisoners of war and that the trials were fair. But by the time of Brinton's letter, most of the Republican senators not only opposed joining the League of Nations, they were also determined to rapidly end the United States' military presence in Europe.[109]

Brinton's role in the mission has never been historically detailed, and he did not leave his impressions or correspondences to a repository. After the war, President Warren Harding appointed him as a judge to the Egyptian Mixed Courts. Although General George van Horn Moseley, who accompanied Harbord as a deputy, had earlier derided Major Cleon Berntheizel, he effusively praised Brinton, calling him "a wonderful man in every way." Brinton, like Samuel Wilson, was appalled with the Turkish treatment of Armenians during the war, and for a decade he urged that conducting military trials over the former "Young Turk government" officials were far more of a necessity than prosecuting the former Hohenzollern Kaiser. While he agreed with Harbord and Moseley that it was important for the United States to support Mustapha Kemal as a bulwark against the spread of Bolshevism, he did not conclude, after meeting with Kemal, that prosecuting former government officials responsible to the deposed sultan or part of the former "Young Turk" government would contribute to the spread of Bolshevism in Asia Minor. Brinton not only earned the praise of his commanders, he also impressed his fellow officers after getting the State Department to approve his written legal opinion enabling the mission's participants to bring large quantities of Greek and Turkish wines and hard spirits into the United States for personal use as "lawful foreign gifts."[110]

CONCLUSION: THE SHAPING OF THE PRACTICE OF AMERICAN INTERNATIONAL LAW

In January 1919, James Brown Scott returned to his State Department duties to assist Lansing in establishing a peace agreement between the Allies and Germany. Crowder viewed Scott as a personal emissary between the War Department and Lansing, and Scott represented the War Department's interest in various peace negotiations. At the same time Scott departed for Europe, Gorfinkle was temporarily assigned to aid Bernard Baruch in determining reparations and debts owed to the United States by Germany as well as to examine Allied claims. Other judge advocates served as advisors to State Department officials on the question of German disarmament as well as the status of various League of Nations mandates. Judge advocates thus had a role in each of these areas of international importance. However, the primary roles of the judge advocates in Europe continued to be not only the maintenance of discipline and the examination of foreign claims but also the protection of American sovereignty over the nation's soldiers.

President Wilson and War Department officials might have assumed that, with their emphatic rejection of the British Military Mission's request to assert British jurisdiction over American soldiers training in British encampments in 1917 and the "gentleman's agreement" with the French government, no further suggestions to extend foreign jurisdiction would be made. Yet in 1921, the Belgian government sought to extend jurisdiction over the few remaining American soldiers on its soil. On December 22, 1921, Captain C. C. Todd informed Generals Liggett and Allen that to surrender the jurisdiction of American forces, even to an ally such as Belgium, would violate a fundamental principle of international law that permitted each of the victors to maintain full jurisdiction over their soldiery regardless of the nationality of any victim. Todd noted to the generals that the Supreme Court in *Coleman v. Tennessee*, a post–Civil War decision, used international law to prevent Tennessee, a state which had seceded, from prosecuting a former Union soldier for a murder that occurred while the soldier was on active duty. In all likelihood, the American rejection of Belgium's request was not surprising to either side. One important aspect of the rejection, however, was the continued application of a combination of both domestic and international law to the War Department's approach to overseas operations as well as the influence of international law in the decision processes of its legal officers.[111]

6

―――

POLITICAL OVERSIGHT OF MILITARY DISCIPLINE

ON JANUARY 7, 1916, PRESIDENT Wilson's confidant Senator John Sharp Williams of Mississippi wrote to Joseph Tumulty that a court-martial of an officer named Edward L. Keyes was "a relic of old time abuse." Williams, who had earlier articulated his fear of standing armies, specifically distrusted courts-martial. Keyes's court-martial had actually occurred in 1877, and he had unsuccessfully sued to obtain back pay in both the Court of Claims and the Supreme Court by arguing that his court-martial failed due process. In 1877 Colonel Wesley Merritt not only charged Keyes with committing an offense, he also testified against Keyes and then served as a member of the court-martial that found Keyes guilty. Like Captain Oberlin Carter, Keyes could not obtain redress in the federal courts. Williams recognized that the War Department had since created rules to prevent the recurrence of the kind of ruling Keyes faced, but when he urged Tumulty to have Wilson pardon and restore Keyes, he also argued that the fairness of military trials remained suspect. Williams's advocacy for Keyes was not the only time he would try to gain favor for a court-martialed soldier. On June 14, 1917, Williams approached Wilson on the court-martial of a Private Harry E. Newham, who had gone absent without leave from the Mexican border and returned home to Mississippi. Newham's sister had earlier pleaded to Williams that she and her mother were soon to become destitute. Williams conceded that Newham's court-martial was fairer than Keyes's trial had been and that the sentence of a nine-month imprisonment and a dishonorable discharge was reasonable. But he asked Wilson to grant Newham's sister's request to disapprove the dishonorable discharge and permit Newham to return home. Throughout the war, Williams and his legislative peers frequently lobbied Wilson to overturn courts-martial and grant convicted soldiers clemency in the form of commuting sentences.[1]

Since the nation's founding, courts-martial have occasionally launched political careers for the officers involved in the prosecutions of accused soldiers or for those officers sitting in judgment. In the War of 1812, Martin Van Buren, a barely known New York legislator who had no direct connection to the army, was tasked to serve as a judge advocate in the trial of General William Hull. During a campaign near Detroit, Hull surrendered his forces to the British without engaging in battle. The court-martial sentenced Hull to be shot to death but recommended clemency. It also catapulted Van Buren into national prominence. General Andrew Jackson learned of Van Buren through newspaper reporting of the court-martial, and had Van Buren never achieved notice for his work on the court-martial, it is unlikely he would have become Jackson's second vice president. As a result, he probably would not have become president in 1836. Courts-martial of officers during the Civil War, the Indian campaigns, the Spanish-American War, and the Philippine Insurrection garnered legislative and newspaper interest. During the Civil War, General James Garfield served on a controversial court-martial of another general named Fitz-John Porter and a year later was elected to Congress, and in 1880, to the presidency. Congressman John Bingham not only provided oversight to the Fitz-John Porter court-martial, he also served as a trial judge advocate in the military trial of Mary Surratt and others implicated in the conspiracy to assassinate President Lincoln. Bingham went on to return to Congress and author the Fourteenth Amendment. Once the war in Europe began in 1914, Congress took an increasingly heightened interest in courts-martial, and this interest accelerated after 1917. By the Armistice, the United States possessed an army four times larger than the Union army during the Civil War. While a number of young men came from prominent families with political connections, conscription, more than any other aspect of the army's demographics, would heighten the legislative interest in courts-martial.[2]

Prior to 1916, Wilson received legislative requests to overturn a court-martial or reduce a sentence on an average of roughly once per month. Between 1912 and the declaration of war, a common request was not necessarily based on the premise that a court-martial was unfairly conducted, but rather, that the needs of a constituent wife, mother, or child necessitated a change in prison site or an early release from prison. One of the unique features of congressional inquiries into courts-martial was that Tumulty, Wilson's personal secretary, reviewed most of the congressional queries before sending these on to Crowder, Garrison, and eventually, Baker. Tumulty also usually drafted a brief summary to Wilson on the assertions contained in each inquiry. After April 5, 1917, as a result of the marked increase in legislative queries, a part of the Judge Advocate General's Office's daily duties was to recommend to the president, secretary of war, or Tumulty a proper action on a request for clemency.

On occasion Wilson expressed a personal interest over a legislative query into a court-martial and would personally write to Crowder asking for a thorough review. "The enclosed has appealed very much to my interest and sympathy and I would be very much obliged if you would have the case carefully looked into for my information," Wilson penned to Crowder when such an instance occurred. The historic record evidences that Wilson understood he could not ignore congressional inquests into military justice, and he expected thorough answers from the Judge Advocate General's Office. At times, the president permitted a court-martial inquiry to take temporary precedence over other wartime matters.[3]

In June 1917, Baker sent Frankfurter to examine labor relations in the western mining industries. Before Frankfurter left to do so, Baker asked him, at Wilson's behest, to investigate the court-martial and year-long imprisonment of a Private John M. Kelsey at Fort Leavenworth. Congressman William Ayers of Kansas earlier requested that Baker review the conduct of the officers involved in the court-martial, but Baker did not quickly respond to Ayers, and the congressman appealed directly to Wilson. Baker advised Frankfurter that when Kelsey enlisted in 1912, he did not inform the army recruiters that as a child he had been diagnosed with epilepsy. For four years Kelsey was able to keep his condition from being discovered, but once he was assigned to Fort Leavenworth, his sergeants and officers concluded that he malingered and on one occasion mocked a sergeant. Baker believed that a one-year term of confinement and a dishonorable discharge were, in all likelihood, not required in this instance, and he insisted Frankfurter conduct a thorough investigation. It took Frankfurter one day to conclude an injustice had occurred, and the future Supreme Court justice advised Baker that Kelsey should be freed from prison and returned to the care of his mother. The distinguishing aspect of Frankfurter's investigation is not that it occurred, but rather, that it caused a delay for Henry Morgenthau, who traveled with Frankfurter to meet with mining corporation owners and labor union leaders in Arizona.[4]

It would be difficult, if not impossible, to consign to a chapter or for that matter a one-volume book all of the correspondence between Congress and the Judge Advocate General's Office, with an appropriate accompanying analysis. The importance of singular examples of congressional interactions is that in many instances, these highlight how prominent the military establishment became in the Legislative Branch. The Constitution assigns Congress the duty of establishing laws governing the military establishment, and to a large extent, Congress relied—and still does—on the military establishment for advice. During World War I, Congress took an active rather than passive role in matters of courts-martial and military discipline. Often, the Judge Advocate General's Office responded favorably to congressional inquiries, but Crowder and his subordinate officers could also aggressively oppose congressmen, to a point where the military gained an authority that it had not known since the Civil War.

LEGISLATIVE OVERSIGHT OF COURTS-MARTIAL: 1914–1920

On March 3, 1914, Congressman William Gordon, an Ohio Democrat, introduced a draft bill to the House Military Affairs Committee that would curtail the extension of courts-martial jurisdiction over soldiers who fraudulently enlisted. Gordon reasoned that because a soldier who fraudulently enlisted should not have been in the army in the first place, it violated *Milligan* to court-martial this type of soldier. He argued that soldiers who fraudulently enlisted ought to be prosecuted in federal court for committing frauds against the United States. Although he did not leave his correspondences to a repository, his speech on the matter clearly showed that he believed that courts-martial were deficient in due process, particularly because trials conducted under the Articles of War did not provide the right to a jury. Gordon pointed out that since 1904, the army had court-martialed a total of 2,872 soldiers for the offense of fraudulent enlistment, and he wanted Congress to retroactively grant to these soldiers the right to a retrial in federal court. Congressman Frank Lester Greene, a Vermont Republican, consulted with both Garrison and Crowder and then led the other committee members to oppose Gordon. Gordon's draft bill failed to leave the committee for a full congressional vote. It is not difficult to understand the views of both sides. Gordon represented the traditional view of distrusting a standing army, and Greene accepted Garrison's and Crowder's arguments that the army required full jurisdictional reach over all persons in uniform to enable a disciplined force for the nation.[5]

Because the federal judiciary relegated its jurisdiction over courts-martial to the sole question of whether the military possessed jurisdiction over the accused person, it is unsurprising that Congress would be flooded with complaints that courts-martial were conducted in violation of due process or were inherently unfair for other reasons. The Judge Advocate General's

Office's approach to congressional inquiries provides not only an insight into how the War Department's legal leaders viewed the military's responsibilities to the Legislative Branch, but also how the possibility of the nation entering into the war altered the military's relationship to that branch, even before 1917. One court-martial of note that occurred prior to the 1914 Austrian ultimatum to Serbia led to a congressional inquiry, and Crowder's response evidenced that he believed the United States' involvement in a large-scale war was a possibility.

In late 1913, several enlisted soldiers and two officers alleged that their commander, Major Benjamin Koehler, fondled their testicles and made lewd remarks toward them. An army investigation concluded that Koehler also had unusual relationships with enlisted soldiers that today would be referred to as "fraternization." In February 1914 a court-martial convicted Koehler of most of the charges against him and sentenced him to a dismissal from the army. Considering that the nature of the alleged offenses was both rooted in the prohibition against officers having relationships with enlisted soldiers based on equality, and the homosexual aspect of Koehler's alleged conduct, one might conclude that given the "Victorian Era morality," the court-martial would have imprisoned him. This did not occur, and several political leaders supported Koehler. No less than William Jennings Bryan came to Koehler's defense, and Senator Thomas Walsh and Congressman Charles Sloan, both from Montana, joined Bryan in seeking clemency for Koehler. Crowder, who was a stickler for adherence to military rules, conceded that Koehler was a decorated officer and had fought in Cuba against the Spanish and in the Philippine Insurrection, but then noted that a grant of clemency for Koehler would undermine the trust that soldiers placed in their superior officers and result in a loss of effectiveness should a war come. Wilson and Garrison agreed with Crowder's assessment, and Koehler was not returned to the army.[6]

Congressmen occasionally aligned with the Judge Advocate General's Office to effectuate a change in the law. Senator Wesley L. Jones of Washington, a progressive Republican, approached Crowder about restoring Private Matt A. Dortscheid to duty after his court-martial for desertion, sleeping on post, and escaping from prison in 1912. Although Jones did not believe that the court-martial was unfair or the sentence of a dishonorable discharge and eighteen months in prison excessive, he urged that the loss of citizenship resulting from the court-martial failed due process. To an extent, Crowder agreed with him, although he did not cite the Eighth Amendment's prohibition against cruel and unusual punishment. Rather, Crowder believed that the stripping of citizenship in peacetime was unwarranted, even when a soldier distributed subversive literature such as Dortscheid was alleged to have done prior to his desertion. Jones had wanted Crowder to assist in drafting a bill to end the coupling of a loss of citizenship to desertion, and Crowder was amenable to testifying as to the lack of necessity for the loss of citizenship in peacetime. However, as long as the law remained intact, Crowder would only advise that the loss of citizenship be considered as a matter in granting clemency such as reducing a sentence of confinement or disapproving a dishonorable discharge. It was not until 1958 in *Trop v. Dulles* that the Supreme Court finally determined that the loss of citizenship as an ancillary punishment to courts-martial violated the Bill of Rights' prohibition against cruel and unusual punishment. Although the appeal in that particular decision arose from a World War II court-martial, the Court issued a broad ruling encompassing all criminal trials, military or civilian.[7]

In 1914 Senator George Chamberlain attempted to intercede in a court-martial of a United States Military Academy cadet named Albert B. Mason. As in the case of several cadets throughout the history of the academy, Mason was caught cheating on an examination. He was charged with conduct unbecoming an officer and gentleman, found guilty, and sentenced to a dismissal. Although his father was a large landowner and grocer in Oregon, Mason was from Illinois, and notwithstanding Mason's Illinois residency, Chamberlain selected him for appointment to the academy. In his letter to Wilson, Chamberlain criticized courts-martial in a manner similar to Senator Williams and then accused the academy of treating Mason worse than "the most friendless and debased character, who, even in a criminal trial could not be convicted entirely on circumstantial evidence, as had been the case with Mason."[8]

Crowder took offense at Chamberlain's characterization of military justice, but he conceded to Garrison and Wilson that the witnesses against Mason were fellow cadets and therefore stood to benefit in their class standing by his removal. However, Crowder countered that the officers sitting in judgment of Mason "were exceptionally well qualified" and had considered this very fact. In response to Chamberlain, and on Crowder's advice, Wilson penned to the senator, "I would not interfere without doing perhaps irreparable damage to the honor system at West Point.[9]

Wilson's refusal to entertain Chamberlain's demand for clemency contributed to a long-term difficult relationship between the senator and the president, and it may have marked the beginning of Chamberlain's efforts to alter the system of military justice. Other than Chamberlain, none of the participants appears to have realized that a long-term dispute would occur as a result of Mason's dismissal from the academy, and Crowder, Garrison, and Wilson must have simply thought of it as another routine congressional inquest into a court-martial. Indeed, the three men likely forgot the episode by April 1917, because Chamberlain had assisted Crowder in bringing the selective service bill into law.[10]

Chamberlain was not the only congressman to argue with Crowder. In 1914 Crowder entered into a long-term disagreement with Congressman Henry Bruckner of New York over the appeal of a Private Clyde Hyde, who was sentenced to a year in prison and a dishonorable discharge after being found guilty of drunkenness on duty and larceny. Bruckner called the larceny charges baseless and urged Wilson to overturn the conviction. Neither Crowder's assistant, Lieutenant Colonel Herbert A. White, nor Crowder supported Hyde's reenlistment. To both officers, it did not matter that Hyde's mother and wife had written Bruckner that they needed Hyde to find quick employment to keep them out of poverty. Bruckner took exception to Crowder's characterization that Hyde could not be redeemed for further service, but Wilson and Garrison sided with Crowder. In January 1918, Crowder argued with Bruckner over the court-martial of a Private Stephen Mueller, who had enlisted under the name Steve Lavay, and claimed to have been born in New Jersey with no prior military service. A general court-martial found Mueller guilty of making a false statement. Mueller was, in fact, born in Salzburg, Austria, and had served in the National Guard in 1914. It may have been the case that Mueller was suspected of being an enemy agent, but given the sentence of fifteen days in confinement and a return to the ranks, the court-martial certainly did not conclude any malfeasance other than the concealment. Bruckner urged Crowder to recommend disapproving the verdict altogether, given the weak sentence, but Crowder responded that the "sentence was grossly inadequate to the offense." In this instance Bruckner was unable to obtain clemency for Mueller from the War Department, and in 1919 Bruckner joined with Chamberlain in decrying the lack of fairness of courts-martial.[11]

In 1917 Lieutenant Colonel Walter Bethel corresponded with Senator Williams regarding the court-martial of Lieutenant A. J. Dunn, who had been sentenced to a dismissal for residing with prostitutes in San Antonio in late 1915. The court-martial itself had recommended clemency to the War Department, but Garrison had approved the sentence without comment in December 1915. Williams supported Prohibition and had been endorsed by the anti-saloon league. He was not sympathetic to Dunn, but he wanted to make sure that Baker, who replaced Garrison, had at least considered Dunn's application for clemency. He found Bethel to be a willing supporter, and in turn, Bethel lobbied Baker to reconsider the approval of the original sentence. Baker ultimately restored Dunn to the army and sent him to France.[12]

Three months later, Ansell responded to Congressman Daniel Garrett's inquiry into the court-martial of a private Tom Bonner of the Third Texas Infantry regiment, a National Guard unit called into federal service on the Mexican border. Garrett earlier urged Baker that Bonner had a stellar reputation in civilian life and ought to be restored to active duty. A court-martial had convicted Bonner of stealing laundry and sentenced him to a dishonorable discharge and six months in confinement. Bonner's offense may not have been serious, but he had already twice been court-martialed and convicted for absence without leave and disobedience of orders. And one of the absences occurred during the Punitive Expedition into Mexico. Ansell responded to Baker that because Bonner had been convicted of "moral turpitude," he should not be reenlisted in the army. Baker agreed with Ansell, and Bonner received no clemency. As a result, when the Third Texas Regiment sailed for France, Bonner was not part of it.[13]

Contemporaneous with Ansell's response on Bonner, he also responded to Congressman Aaron Kreider over the trial of Private Longenecker, who had gone absent without leave and was sentenced to eighteen months' confinement and a dishonorable discharge. Longenecker had deserted from his post in Texas in December 1914 and then turned himself in on February 22, 1917, in Harrisburg, Pennsylvania. Kreider noted to President Wilson that a physician had concluded that Longenecker was "not physically adapted to perform the duties of a soldier" and urged Wilson to order his release from prison. Ansell, however, advised Baker to reenlist Longenecker and give him a chance to prove himself in France. Longenecker was brought back into the army and sent to France, where he performed his duties sufficiently well to earn an honorable discharge.[14]

At the same time Ansell responded to Kreider, Crowder responded to an inquiry from Congressman Asher Hinds, a Maine Republican. Hinds attempted to intercede on behalf of a Private Herbert Ballard, who had been convicted in a court-martial for both stealing cavalry horses and desertion. The court-martial sentenced Ballard to five years, and General Leonard Wood recommended to Baker that Ballard receive no clemency. Crowder first advised Baker and then Wilson that while Ballard's offenses in peacetime might deserve some clemency, the fact that there was a shortage of horses on the Western Front merited the five years' imprisonment to serve as a deterrent. To Crowder, Ballard's conduct had the potential to erode the war effort, and ultimately Wilson agreed with him.[15]

In January 1917 Senator Willard Saulsbury urged Wilson to disapprove a guilty verdict for Private Charles H. Moore, Delaware National Guard soldier. In late 1916 Moore determined that he no longer wanted to serve on the Mexican border and absented himself from his duties. He was arrested in San Antonio, four days after his flight from Deming, New Mexico, and the court-martial sentenced him to forfeit two-thirds of his pay per month for four months and to be confined at hard labor for six months. General H. P. McCain, the army's adjutant general, informed Saulsbury that General Funston was willing to remit Moore's sentence and permit him to rejoin his regiment but not to overturn the conviction. A Vermont National Guard colonel who knew Moore's family noted to both Funston and McCain that Moore had "acquired the cocaine habit and while under the influence of the drug, he left his wife and enlisted." Moreover, Moore was an attorney in his civilian life and had represented the Young Man's Christian Organization. One of the association's officers advocated permitting Moore to return to his now destitute family. Whatever the mitigating circumstances of Moore's case, after McCain consulted with Crowder, he replied to Saulsbury that Moore's fate rested with Funston, and neither he nor Crowder would advise Baker or Wilson to intervene.[16]

In 1918 Congressman Carter Glass became dissatisfied with Ansell over the court-martial and imprisonment of a Private Paul Clement. Born in 1901, Clement enlisted in the Virginia state guard for service on the Mexican border in 1916 after lying about his age. He was discharged in February 1917 but resumed his military service after being conscripted in 1918. While drunk in Roanoke, he fought with a civilian and after besting the civilian, Clement stole his watch. A general court-martial sentenced Clement to two years in confinement and a dishonorable discharge. Ansell responded to Glass that he believed Clement's trial was "fairly conducted and the sentence justified." In July 1918 Glass appealed on Clement's behalf once more and pointed out to Colonel Easby-Smith, who was left temporarily in charge of the Judge Advocate General's Office, that Clement desired to return to the army to fight in France and had two brothers already on the Western Front. Glass warned one of Clement's supporters, a minister, that he had "never found the military authorities much inclined to show any leniency in such cases" because "they do not concede that intoxication affords any extenuating excuse." However, in this instance Easby-Smith recommended to Baker to restore Clement to duty, and Clement was able to rejoin the army to serve in Coblenz. Ironically, Ansell later accused Easy-Smith of inflexibly defending a harsh courts-martial system.[17]

In 1919 Senator David Walsh, a Massachusetts Democrat loyal to Wilson, appealed on behalf of a Private William Moran who, along with three other soldiers, was convicted of assaulting German civilians. A general court-martial sentenced him to a dishonorable discharge and two years' confinement. Walsh urged Tumulty to inform Wilson that Moran "came from an excellent family and had earned a splendid record in the Army." At the same time, Congressman James Gallivan, another Democrat from Massachusetts, lobbied Tumulty on the basis that Moran came from "an excellent family." There were two features of this appeal that distinguished it from the majority of the others. Moran was a native of Oklahoma whose father was the president of the Texas Pipeline Corporation, and according to Gavillan, "a director of several banks in that locality." Gavillan enclosed letters of support from an Oklahoma congressman and the state governor, but more tellingly, these men noted their support for the League of Nations. On Wilson's direction, Tumulty turned to Kreger, who by this time had transferred from France to the Judge Advocate General's Office, to investigate Moran's appeal. Initially Kreger informed Tumulty that Moran had used a deadly weapon in an assault against a German civilian, and this action not only undermined discipline, it also placed other soldiers in danger by eroding German goodwill toward American troops.

Following Kreger's recommendation to deny clemency, Congressmen Everett Howard, Scott Ferris, and James McClintic, all Oklahoma Democrats, appealed to Tumulty. "We feel that further benefit cannot be accrued to the military organization or to any one concerned by his further punishment," the three congressmen argued before reminding Tumulty of Moran's father's support of Wilson. After Tumulty's further inquiry, Kreger noted he would recommend a transfer to a disciplinary battalion so that Moran "could prove worthy to be a soldier and be returned to the ranks." However, Moran's coactors in the same criminal activity would not receive favorable consideration.[18]

In April 1919, Congressman Lever was able to convince Crowder to recommend reversing the conviction of Lieutenant John C. Baskin, a forty-six-year-old officer who had been court-martialed and sentenced to a dismissal for negligently releasing a prisoner from a stockade. Before Crowder became involved, Colonel Dunn responded to Lever that "the verdict was justified and sentence was appropriate to the offense." The prisoner had asked Baskin for permission to use the post office, and after being temporarily released to do so, fled to his home. Lever wrote directly to Crowder, who forwarded Lever's letter to Baker with his support. By the end of April 1919, Baskin was brought back into the army and given an honorable discharge. By this time, Crowder had become so disenchanted with Dunn that he based his recommendation to support Baskin on Dunn's incompetency.[19]

Idaho senator William E. Borah received hundreds of letters pointing out what the writers believed to be injustices in courts-martial. Elected to the Senate in January 1907 as a Republican, Borah quickly exercised an independence from his party and rose to become one of the nation's more influential legislators. He reluctantly voted to declare war on Germany and would ultimately oppose joining the League of Nations. He was also incensed that Congress had permitted the military establishment to exercise courts-martial jurisdiction over conscripted citizens who had refused to submit to induction and therefore had not yet willingly subjected themselves to military discipline. (In World War II, the Supreme Court determined that Congress had not expressly permitted courts-martial jurisdiction over civilians, and as a result, those citizens who resisted induction into the military by refusing to take an oath or receive initial pay could only be prosecuted in federal court.) By late 1917, it had become well known that Borah expressed doubts on the fairness of wartime courts-martial. Hundreds of court-martialed service-members and their families, including those who had no connection to Idaho, lobbied him for help.[20]

Interestingly, Borah earlier sided with President Theodore Roosevelt over the dismissal of 167 African American soldiers in 1907 following the so-called "Brownsville Raid." Roosevelt and Stimson considered Borah their most vocal military affairs advocate in the Senate. Roosevelt reflected to Stimson in 1908 that Borah was "leading the fight on our side in this Brownsville Affair" after Borah noted to Stimson that "the legality of the President's acts are not in doubt." Even assuming that Borah permitted racism to enter into his decision to endorse Executive Branch supremacy in military affairs as he battled with Senator John Spooner over the justness of the dismissal of the African American soldiers, Borah certainly understood that his position on legislative noninterference in military discipline would apply equally to aggrieved soldiers regardless of their race. But he abandoned his earlier stance on congressional noninterference during the war, and Crowder claimed to Stimson that the senator's challenges to the War Department were hypocritical. On the other hand, Crowder recognized that Borah enjoyed a more prominent status than most of the nation's other legislators.[21]

Several of the court-martialed soldiers or their families who petitioned Borah suffered through a strange harshness in military discipline. For instance, Ralph E. Mitchell, a court-martialed soldier, claimed to Borah that while he was walking on a road near Chateau Thierry in France, an army truck driver had "offered him a lift." When Mitchell found out that the driver was traveling to Paris, he decided to go along with him. He admitted that he had no authorization to depart his encampment near the front but had only intended to go for a short time. "Although I did not remove the uniform of a U. S. soldier or conceal the fact that I was a member of the A. E. F., I was charged with desertion in the face of the enemy, convicted, and sentenced to be dishonorably discharged from the service, to forfeit all pay and allowances, and to serve for the term of my natural life at hard labor at the U. S. Disciplinary Barracks at Fort Leavenworth, Kansas," he informed Borah. Another soldier named Arnold McBride wrote to Borah that he was sentenced to five years for stealing one set of civilian clothing. McBride admitted to the theft but explained, he was "just eighteen years old and at the date of the sentence I was seventeen years and two days." To verify his claim, McBride sent his birth certificate to Borah. Borah was able to help both soldiers be restored to duty.[22]

In another instance, the Abraham Lincoln Post of Detroit asked Borah to pressure the War Department to grant Private John Fitzgerald a release from prison. The army court-martialed Fitzgerald for desertion after he absented himself from the front lines for three days beginning on October 9, 1918. Fitzgerald's unit had been in action against the Germans in the Meuse-Argonne at the time of his desertion, and the court-martial sentenced him to ten years in confinement. But as Borah pointed out to Crowder, Fitzgerald was also cited for prior bravery and could not be concluded to be a "constitutional coward." Crowder took it upon himself to review Fitzgerald's record of trial and recommended to Baker to restore Fitzgerald to duty so that he could complete his term of enlistment and receive an honorable discharge. In the other appeals, Borah was not as successful.[23]

One mother whose son was absent without permission for ten days, found guilty of desertion, and sentenced to five years in confinement, wrote Borah, "your effort to reform military injustice is a most commendable and urgent one as there are hundreds and thousands of our Army boys who are suffering from unjust courts-martial trials and sentences, besides the near relatives of those same boys are greatly incapacitated and aged, grieving over such shameful proceedings." The woman informed Borah that her son had served for two-and-a-half years with the army in Manila and became addicted to alcohol. When preparing to ship to France, he took an unauthorized leave in the United States and stayed at a Young Men's Christian Association house in uniform. Because the secretary of war had denied clemency, the soldier's mother believed that Borah could lobby President Wilson. Borah tried to intervene but did not succeed in gaining a pardon.[24]

The papers of Senator Robert La Follette evidence a dichotomous view, as with Borah, that the War Department was harsh in discipline but not unyielding in individual soldier's cases. Because La Follette had voted against both the declaration of war against the Central powers and conscription, it might have been expected that the Judge Advocate General's Office would be unreceptive to his queries in individual cases. However, Crowder respected La Follette for his work on the War Risk Insurance Act and instructed the Judge

Advocate General's Office to investigate soldiers' grievances that the senator brought to the War Department's attention.

In October 1919 La Follette wrote to Baker and Crowder that a prisoner held at Fort Leavenworth named Private Arnold Jensen was underage. Jensen enlisted in 1917 at the age of fifteen but claimed to be twenty-two years old. He fought in the First Division at St. Mihiel and in the Meuse-Argonne. On November 1, 1918, his gas mask failed and he was hospitalized for over a month. Instead of returning to his unit, Jensen decided to explore Paris. A general court-martial not only found him guilty of desertion, it sentenced him to four years in prison and a dishonorable discharge. La Follette conceded to Baker and Crowder that Jensen was responsible for his absence, but given his youth and battle experience, the four-year sentence was extreme. Crowder successfully prevailed on Baker to remit Jensen's sentence and return him to the army so that he could receive an honorable discharge.[25]

On January 10, 1920, Private Alexander Cadotte wrote to La Follette for his help to avoid being imprisoned. Cadotte had enlisted in "the machine gun company, second Wisconsin National Guard, in 1916." He served at the front for a total of eight months in the Thirty-Second Division and was gassed and shot through the shoulder in the Meuse-Argonne in late October 1918. Sent to an army hospital at Camp MacArthur, Texas, Cadotte became "disgusted with his treatment and left the Army with his uniform still on." Writing that "the doctors would not even fix my teeth which was ruined by the German poison gas," Cadotte claimed that he could not lie on his back without his lungs filling with liquid. Yet he was court-martialed in absentia for desertion, and he went into hiding at the Knights of Columbus Hall in Milwaukee. La Follette appealed Cadotte's case to Crowder and on Crowder's advice, Baker did not approve the findings of the court-martial.[26]

Ten days after Cadotte's appeal was resolved, Private Juan Gonzalez sought La Follette's help. Gonzalez informed La Follette that he had been court-martialed in Bordeaux, France, with another soldier, after being accused of robbing items from French houses. While the general court-martial found both soldiers guilty and sentenced them to three years at Fort Leavenworth, the other soldier was set free as a result of a clemency board recommendation. Gonzalez's justifiable complaint was that the same officer who charged him also defended him in the court-martial and "made only a half-hearted defense." La Follette inquired to Crowder about the propriety of having an officer serve as both an accuser and a defense counsel, and Crowder assured La Follette that, if this was true, Private Gonzalez's court-martial was devoid of jurisdiction. Ultimately Baker overturned Gonzalez's conviction.[27]

Congressmen did not stop with the Judge Advocate General's Office in their attempts to gain clemency or the reversal of a court-martial. In November 1920, Senator Walsh sought clemency for a Private Robert Browning but directed his request to the Adjutant General's Office instead of Crowder. Browning deserted from his duty near Metz, France, for over a three-month period and was caught trying to return to the United States while his regiment was transiting to serve in the American Forces in Germany near Cologne. In trying to have his discharge upgraded to honorable and have him released from his two-year prison sentence, Browning's family hired a Montana attorney named A. W. O'Rourke. The adjutant general forwarded Walsh's request to Crowder, but instead of waiting for Crowder's inquiry, the adjutant general responded to Walsh that Browning's "case does not look very hopeful." Interestingly A. W. O'Rourke spent a good deal of his correspondence to Walsh and the adjutant general discussing the potential success of James Cox's presidential campaign against Warren Harding in Montana. They were convinced that if Cox prevailed over Harding, Browning would obtain a pardon.[28]

In February 1918, Senator Hoke Smith, a Georgia Democrat, approached General George Goethals, the acting quartermaster general of the army, to lobby Ansell to prevent the court-martial of a Lieutenant Ernest Watson. Goethals admitted to Smith that he believed Watson's conduct would not have been serious in civilian life. Watson had sneaked away from his training camp for the evening and when he returned, he gave the military police a false name. But, Goethals explained to Smith, Watson's conduct was serious to the army, though he promised to "take up the matter with Crowder." In the end, Watson was permitted to resign his commission rather than face a court-martial.[29]

In November 1918, Nebraska Governor Keith Neville became frustrated with the Judge Advocate General's Office after it determined that Private Louis Gibson's general court-martial conviction and two-year imprisonment for sleeping on post were justified. In August 1918, Gibson had fallen asleep during his sentry duties, and a German patrol managed to conduct a raid without being detected. Four US soldiers were wounded and two taken prisoner during the raid. Had Gibson been in the British or French Army, he might have been sentenced to decades in prison or shot. But Gibson had also been in combat with little sleep for the previous six days. Ansell reviewed the record of trial and concluded that it was likely the court-martial took his condition into consideration as a matter of mitigation. Neville enlisted Senators Gilbert Hitchcock and George Norris to lobby Baker and Wilson to commute Gibson's sentence. Neither Ansell nor Baker determined it was necessary to investigate the specific facts of Gibson's trial. In response, the three Nebraska politicians allied with over a dozen newspapers throughout the state to gather citizens' petitions seeking a presidential pardon for Gibson. After receiving over ten thousand petitions, Baker relented and commuted Gibson's sentence to six months. In June 1919, Wilson pardoned Gibson and ordered that he be given an honorable discharge. Neither Crowder nor Ansell supported this course of action, but it showed that popular support for a single soldier could be dispositive on the question of whether that soldier would be shown clemency.[30]

Aggrieved soldiers appealed not only to their own legislators but also legislators who may have had nothing more than a circumstantial connection to the soldier. On December 22, 1920, the army court-martialed Corporal John T. McLean for taking a fourteen-day absence without leave and for embezzling government monies of approximately $350. McLean had served in the front lines during the Meuse-Argonne Offensive as an infantryman and had also been stationed in Trier until September 1920. He was originally from Birmingham, Alabama, but when he landed in New York, the army transferred him to Fort Sheridan, Chicago. Perhaps feeling resentment for being prevented from seeing his family or from being assigned as a quartermaster sergeant without a commensurate promotion in rank, he decided to steal the monies from an army commissary and visit his family. The court-martial sentenced McLean to a dishonorable discharge and eighteen months in confinement, but the commanding general did not approve the discharge and approved only six months' confinement and a reduction to the lowest enlisted grade of private.[31]

McLean appealed to Tennessee senator Kenneth McKellar, a native of Alabama who was born in McLean's hometown, and Congressman James Byrnes, a South Carolinian who once visited McLean's training camp in 1916. Both legislators took up McLean's cause and appealed to Crowder to intervene. Crowder was, at the time, in Cuba, and Colonel Hull ordered Major Mark Guerin to investigate whether the court-martial had been properly conducted. Guerin reported to Hull that McLean's conviction for the theft had been based entirely on circumstantial evidence. That is, the day after McLean absented himself, the monies were found to be missing. The convening authority took this into consideration when reducing McLean's sentence, but he did not dismiss the conviction for the theft. Guerin advised Hull to respond to the legislators that "in this state of the record, this office cannot say that the conviction or sentence is illegal." He added that the convening authority enabled McLean to return to the army and "work out his own salvation." Hull attached Guerin's advice to his own response to the two legislators and added, "McLean's admitted course of conduct shows that he is not without need of discipline and if he has all of these good qualities which it is hoped he has, his confinement will serve to bring them out and to make a man of him." McLean returned to the army and ultimately received an honorable discharge in 1925.[32]

In 1922 Congressman Henry Wurzbach of Texas approached General John L. Hines to support clemency for a Private Arlington Hardwicke, who had been sentenced to ten years in confinement in late 1919. Hines had initially only approved of a five-year sentence even though the court-martial sentenced Hardwicke to ten years. In 1920 Wurzbach was unsuccessful in convincing Crowder that an injustice had been done to Hardwicke, and two years later the congressman petitioned both Hines and Hull. Hardwicke had, in fact, been prosecuted for an unauthorized absence from his infantry regiment in the front lines in early November 1918 but was not imprisoned. He deserted and attempted to return to the United States in disguise in order to avoid service in Germany. Hull determined there was no reason to commute Hardwicke's sentence. In this instance, Hines, who himself had been court-martialed in 1902, was more lenient than Hull, and he noted that he would have Hardwicke released from prison six months early.[33]

In a few instances, a legislator and the Judge Advocate General's Office allied to prevent a court-martial from occurring. In November 1917, a Virginia farmer convinced General Henry Carter Stuart to court-martial fourteen soldiers who trampled over his farm and destroyed produce during a battle exercise near Fort Lee. Stuart forwarded the farmer's demands and the charges against the soldiers to Congressman Carter Glass, but Glass disagreed with the army court-martialing the soldiers, and he brought the matter to Crowder's attention. Crowder assigned Lieutenant Colonel Arthur Brown to travel to Fort Lee and convince General Stuart to retract the charges as well as advise the farmer to claim damage against the War Department. Brown succeeded in stopping the courts-martial with the argument that the "unintended depredations to the melon patch were reimbursable by the War Department, and not caused by mischief, but the court-martial would constitute a greater mischief."[34]

A small number of legislators expressed a concern for the treatment of African American soldiers, and on occasion, the issue confronting the War Department was not whether a court-martial had been fairly conducted, but rather, whether the War Department should publicize the conviction and sentence. On August 18, 1918, the army court-martialed Lieutenant Ulus C. Miller, a white officer, for assaulting four African American privates

at Fort Wadsworth, South Carolina. The court-martial sentenced Miller to a
dishonorable discharge, and President Wilson affirmed the conviction and
sentence. Senator Tillman demanded the War Department restore Miller to
duty. In contrast, the National Association for the Advancement of Colored
People along with Senator William Calder and Congressman Adolph Sabath
lobbied Crowder to have the War Department publish the results of trial. The
secretary of the NAACP urged that publicity "would be helpful in that there is
so much discrimination against colored men, and that such publication would
have a distinctly beneficial effect on colored people."[35]

THE JUDGE ADVOCATE GENERAL'S OFFICE, CONGRESS, AND NEUROLOGY

Prior to the war, insanity was accepted as a defense to criminal conduct
in courts-martial, and in some instances, soldiers who became delusional
were allowed to retire or were hospitalized in federal and state hospitals. In
1859 Congressman Daniel Sickles, who was later to achieve notoriety as a
Union general, was acquitted of murder on the basis of temporary insanity.
At the time of his trial in a New York civil court, Sickles had no connection
to the army, but within three years of his trial, he commanded a corps in
the Army of the Potomac as a major general. Perhaps because his defense
counsel was future secretary of war Edward Stanton, the War Department
later recognized insanity as a bona fide medical condition. In 1884 the War
Department permitted General Ranald MacKenzie, a Civil War veteran and
famed Indian fighter, to retire from the army after he became delusional.
Until World War I, the legal test for determining insanity was based on
proving that the accused soldier suffered from "an irresistible impulse" to
commit an offense and that the accused soldier could not comprehend the
wrongness of his acts. Although insanity was an accepted defense against
criminal liability, soldiers who claimed insanity were usually unsuccessful in
avoiding a conviction and imprisonment.

Crowder, Ansell, and the judge advocates assigned to the Judge Advocate
General's Office were attuned to advances in psychiatry, and with the addition
of judge advocates who came into the army after serving as state judges,
federal prosecutors, or professors of law, the Judge Advocate General's Office
accepted that the rigors of modern warfare would cause a fraction of the
soldiers sent into battle to become unable to function. They also collectively
realized that congressional oversight over military discipline might be at
its most vigorous in the army's treatment of persons suffering from "shell-
shock" or other warfare-caused neurosis. In 1917 Crowder informed Baker

that from a military law standpoint, there were no impediments to placing psychiatrists throughout the American Expeditionary Forces in positions commensurate with the status of surgeons. He also added that the courts-martial of soldiers determined to be unfit for duty without the protection of a psychiatric diagnosis would undermine Congress's confidence in the fairness of courts-martial.[36]

In 1914 Congressman Andrew R. Brodbeck asked Secretary of War Garrison to move a Private Lisle Crabtree from the Government Hospital for the Insane in Washington, DC, to a Pennsylvania state hospital so that his mother could attend to him. Crabtree's offenses were serious. A court-martial convicted him of murder and assault and sentenced him to life in prison after he shot two officers at Fort Leavenworth and killed his commanding officer "without provocation." Crowder responded to Garrison that a medical investigation determined Crabtree was sane at the time of the offenses, but in prison he had become dangerously delusional and would commit a violent offense if he gained his liberty. Moreover, after reviewing Pennsylvania's state laws, Crowder concluded that the state hospital was expressly prohibited from accepting Crabtree as a patient because of his offenses and diagnosed dangerousness. Not satisfied with Crowder's response, Broadbeck sought Congressman A. Mitchell Palmer to lobby the War Department, but Palmer was unable to convince either Garrison or Crowder to recommend Crabtree's release. Palmer later became attorney general and worked alongside Crowder during the "Red Scare." However, the two men did not work cohesively. Crowder later expressed to Baker his disagreement with Palmer's willingness to deport persons suspected of anarchism without a full trial.[37]

Crowder did not limit the defense of insanity to what had commonly been referred to as "shell shock." For instance, on January 22, 1918, he asked Baker to disapprove the finding of guilty for a Private Albert Singer, who had been convicted of sleeping on post and sentenced to be imprisoned for one year and dishonorably discharged. The judge advocate review uncovered that although Singer had served on the Mexican border and his military record was sound, he also had been diagnosed by a medical doctor of being "mentally unfit." This evidence never made it to the court-martial because Singer pleaded guilty. However, evidence of Singer's mental condition was known to the trial judge advocate prior to the trial, and this troubled Crowder. Baker ultimately disapproved the verdict and sentence, and Singer was discharged from further service with an honorable discharge.[38]

The term *shell-shock* is not a defined malady, and by 1916 British psychiatrists determined that it did not occur only as a result of fear. Rather, exhaustion due to a lack of sleep, exposure to the constant probability of death, and proximity to explosions were all contributors to a variety of mental and physical deteriorations. By 1917, as a result of both medical advances and a change in political attitudes toward the mentally ill, War Department officers were not inclined to automatically consider shell-shock a sign of cowardice. By the end of the war, the American Psychiatric Association concluded that "shell-shock" was a legitimate psychological state. Nonetheless, there were hundreds of courts-martial for offenses ranging from disobedience of orders to desertion and cowardice that may have been rooted in a soldier's mental deterioration as a result of concussions, poison gas, and the constant exposure to death. In part, these trials occurred because officers commanding regiments, brigades, and higher echelons were likely to believe that many soldiers malingered and faked having "shell-shock," rather than dismissing the existence of "shell-shock" as a fiction.[39]

On June 19, 1919, Colonel J. S. Easby-Smith, the acting deputy judge advocate general, advised Tumulty that Lieutenant Harry E. Glock should be released from imprisonment at Fort Leavenworth. Glock's court-martial arose from a case of shell-shock, and it had the interest of congressmen including Champ Clark, the Speaker of the House of Representatives, who sought clemency for Glock. In opposing Clark, Pershing proclaimed the ten-year sentence too lenient and opposed any clemency. During the trial Glock admitted that he had abandoned his platoon and deserted the front lines prior to "going over the top" out of fear. Easby-Smith noted that Glock "was under severe shell-fire and was more than once knocked down by the force of nearby explosions of shells before he ran away" but also added that there was no evidence in the record of trial that Glock was "suffering a mental aberration." As a matter of circumstantial evidence, Easby-Smith conceded that it was likely Glock had "shell-shock" but he would not recommend a retrial based on Pershing's stated opinion that ten years was too light a sentence and the record of trial indicated no errors in its procedure. By modern standards, it is probable that a mental competency hearing would be ordered with the possibility of a retrial. On the other hand, had Glock been in the British or French army, it is possible he could have been rapidly executed. After reading Easby-Smith's review, Crowder supported commuting Glock's sentence to one year and releasing him home.[40]

After the war, as the medical community became more open to the reality of "shell-shock," legislative inquiries into courts-martial on the basis of mental health increased in number. Both New Jersey senators, David Baird and Joseph S. Frelinghusen, along with the state governor and Enoch Thompson (the political boss of Atlantic City), appealed to Wilson to commute the sentence of a Lieutenant Blatchford Sherman, who had been convicted of desertion in the face of the enemy but later diagnosed with a neurological condition. In this instance, the term *shell-shock* was used by the civilian doctors who advised New Jersey's governor. Blatchford enlisted in the army in early 1917, was commissioned in France, and then saw action in Alsace. During the Meuse-Argonne Offensive he refused to lead his men forward under fire and was later found incoherent in a rear area. By the time Sherman was court-martialed, he "was bleeding profusely through his gums and nose." Even Sherman's immediate commander appealed to the War Department that his sentence, "in light of the New Jersey State Hospital's conclusion that he labored under a mental condition and was therefore not responsible for his crimes, was too severe." Crowder responded that he had thoroughly examined the record of trial as well as numerous letters appealing for clemency and he supported freeing Blatchford from confinement. But he did not believe restoration to rank was appropriate because there were no legal errors in the trial.[41]

Crowder provided a similar analysis in 1920 in response to the appeal of Captain Harry S. Rowley. Rowley had fled from the front lines during the Meuse-Argonne Offensive but was not court-martialed until April 1919. Initially, some of the record of Rowley's court-martial was missing from the appeal file, and Crowder recommended overturning the verdict altogether. However, after the missing portion was located, Crowder reversed course and recommended to Wilson that Rowley be freed from confinement though not restored to duty. Crowder recognized that La Follette had urged the War Department to restore Rowley to duty and then issue an honorable discharge, but he countered that in the absence of a legal error in the record of trial, remission of the lengthy sentence to imprisonment was the more appropriate course.[42]

On one occasion La Follette teamed with both Senator Chamberlain and General Charles Summerall to have a general court-martial reversed on the basis of "shell-shock." Private Earl Sanders, a native of Antigo, Wisconsin, enlisted in the National Guard at the age of seventeen in 1916 and shipped to France in November 1917. He lied about his age when he enlisted and claimed to be twenty-one years old, but he desired to see service on the Mexican border at the time. By the Armistice, Sanders was not only a veteran of the battles of Soissons, St. Mihiel, and the Meuse-Argonne, he had also been shot and gassed in the final days of the war and sent to a hospital. Following the Armistice, his regiment went into Germany, but he left the hospital and toured France. For reasons that Sanders did not explain to La Follette, he joined a group of freed Russian prisoners of war who had no desire to return to Russia, and he began to drink and fight with them. While he encamped with the Russians near Verdun in July 1919, American military police discovered that he was in hiding, and he refused to return to his unit. During an attempt to arrest him, he drew a revolver on two American officers and threatened to shoot them, all the while shouting to his Russian companions to come to his aid. After a physical melee resulting in several injuries, the military police, assisted by French gendarmes, arrested Sanders, and on September 1, 1919, a general court-martial sentenced him to five years in prison and a dishonorable discharge.[43]

Sanders had been cited for bravery during the war—his company commander had recommended him for a promotion to sergeant—and in his defense, he neither fictionalized the extent of his wounds nor claimed as a defense that he began to hallucinate after breathing mustard gas. Most of Sanders's peers were either killed or wounded during the final months of the war as well. Perhaps out of personal pride, Sanders denied suffering shell-shock or any other mental infirmity in his court-martial. In late 1919 the clemency board recommended denying Sanders's application for a reduction in his sentence. But while he was imprisoned at Fort Leavenworth, army doctors diagnosed him with shell-shock, and he wrote to La Follette, Chamberlain, and Summerall. All three urged Baker to overturn the court-martial, but Baker refused to do so. In May 1921, Kreger convinced Secretary of War John Weeks to reverse the court-martial verdict and permit Sanders to return home on the basis that he was not responsible for his conduct.[44]

In 1919 Senator Hitchcock sought General Peyton March's help in effecting the discharge of a Private Robert Sorenson from the army. Sorenson was hospitalized for shell-shock but was also awaiting a special court-martial for disrespect to commissioned officers. He had served in an artillery unit and participated in the Meuse-Argonne Offensive. He was wounded in the head by German shrapnel in the closing days of the war, and it was likely that the wounds caused him to expectorate when he spoke as well as constantly intersperse his words with profanities. At least one officer was offended at being spit on and cursed at, and Sorenson was charged with disrespect to a commissioned officer. Following a judge advocate inquiry, the army discharged Sorenson with an honorable discharge rather than conducting a court-martial, and he returned home.[45]

"Shell-shock" and other related neurological conditions had other implications for courts-martial that were unlikely to have been foreseen prior to the war. On January 18, 1918, the army convened a general court-martial to try Lieutenant Walter S. Church, who had been assigned to the First Division. He had also served as an enlisted soldier for eight years before being commissioned into the Idaho National Guard. Church had been accused of cashing checks from one of the cooks assigned to his battalion and then keeping the monies for his own use, which was known as the crime of "conversion." The army charged him with larceny as well as a failure to pay a debt to the cook and conduct unbecoming an officer and gentleman. The court-martial convicted Church of one of the specifications, acquitted him of the rest, and sentenced him to be dismissed from the army. Pershing approved of the findings and sentence on March 19. In June Borah attempted to help Church overturn his court-martial.[46]

Shortly before Pershing approved the court-martial in late February 1918, the army returned Church to the United States, where it warehoused him in a sanitarium at Ellis Island, New York. Problematic to both the court-martial and the army's transfer of Church was that Church had been gassed and suffered from "delusions" prior to the offenses for which he had been court-martialed. The American Red Cross confirmed this fact to Borah as well. By the time he had shipped off to France, he had eighteen years of military service, including participating in the army's pursuit of Pancho Villa as well as fighting guerillas in the Philippines. J. H. Gibson, the Idaho state Republican Party chair, relayed his concerns over the court-martial to Borah, including the fact that army officials had informed Church's wife that Church's health was in generally "good condition." Gibson later noted that "so far as Church is concerned, he may be entirely unworthy of our efforts but he has a wife and child to be looked after and it may be possible that a great injustice was done him by the Military authorities." Moreover, Church's wife traveled to Ellis Island and found that her husband was "totally deranged."[47]

Equally, if not more, problematic to the court-martial was that Church, who had no legal training, represented himself. Borah enlisted Idaho's other senator, John F. Nugent, a Democrat, to find a means to vindicate Church. The army's inspector general informed Nugent that although Church lacked any education after the age of sixteen, he "made an intelligent extenuating statement to the court, questioned witnesses for the prosecution, and showed an ability to remember dates and conversations." Once Church was at Ellis Island, federal psychiatrists diagnosed him as suffering dementia. On March 8, 1918, the army transferred Church to a military hospital at Fort McHenry, where he escaped and fled to Idaho. By April, Church was confined in an Oregon sanitarium.[48] "Lieutenant Church bore an excellent reputation in his home community before he entered the Service," Borah informed Baker, before complaining that the War Department had failed to answer previous inquiries. Baker assured Borah that he would take a personal interest in Church's court-martial, and because of Borah's intervention, Baker ordered the Judge Advocate General's Office to review Church's court-martial record for a second time.[49]

The Judge Advocate General's Office recommended reversing the court-martial conviction for the most obvious of legal reasons. Lieutenant Colonel E. G. Davis, the judge advocate assigned to investigate the case further, found that officers serving with Church, including the convening authority, had known that Church was suffering from some form of "insanity." Indeed, one army psychiatrist concluded that Church's insanity predated his military commission. Thus, having represented himself, Church could not "be expected to raise the issue of his own insanity." Moreover, military regulations authored by Crowder between 1912 and 1916 required that the convening authority appoint a counsel to raise the defense of insanity, and the judge advocate general's *Digest of Opinions* required the defense be raised when some evidence of insanity was apparent, even if the soldier on trial opposed doing so. None of this had occurred, but Baker refused to budge on granting a new trial. Baker conceded to Borah that Church had suffered from dementia but held he was nonetheless "legally responsible for his acts" and added that since he had been discharged, the government was not responsible for his treatment. Thus, despite the fact that two senators lobbied the War Department to rescind the court-martial conviction and sentence and the Judge Advocate General's Office advised that there were significant errors, Baker believed that the court-martial comported with the law.[50]

There were hundreds of soldiers court-martialed, found guilty, and sentenced to dishonorable discharges and terms in confinement in the American Expeditionary Forces that would not likely be court-martialed in the nation's modern wars, because many of these men today would be diagnosed with a neurological disorder. In British courts-martial, even the appeals of junior officers and sergeant majors for soldiers who were accused of cowardice, but likely suffering neurosis, were not enough to overcome death sentences. In the American Expeditionary Forces, each division had an assigned psychiatrist. At war's end, there were 4,309 soldiers sent to the United States who were diagnosed as unfit for further service. In all of these instances, Crowder and his subordinates acknowledged the existence of shell-shock, and unlike some of their Allied counterparts, they did not confuse the neurological condition with cowardice. However, they tempered their understanding of "shell-shock" with the expectation that officers had to be more immune from it than the enlisted soldiers, or the discipline of the soldiers would be at stake. Congress played a role in the acceptance of "shell-shock" as a mitigating factor in military discipline, but without the Judge Advocate General's Office, a military acceptance of the legitimacy of this condition would not have occurred to the extent that it did. In essence, the Legislative Branch's oversight coupled with the Judge

Advocate General's Office's efforts helped prevent a wholesale disregard of neurological impairments caused by the war.[51]

CONGRESS AND THE COURTS-MARTIAL OF CITIZENS

On May 17, 1918, Crowder issued an order to the country which he captioned as a "work or fight" order. Earlier in the month he had been informed that hundreds of citizens who were exempted from the draft by virtue of their employment in farming, mining, and manufacturing, or because of their status as the sole source of parental authority over minor children, had "idled" in their work. Worse, to Crowder, was that in early 1918 labor union employees in various manufacturing industries who had been exempted, threatened to strike. He advised Baker to have strikers immediately conscripted into the army. It also galled Crowder—and in all likelihood senior War Department officials as well as many soldiers—that those men who were exempted from conscription were not forced to work seven-day weeks, took vacations, and engaged in other activities that did little to support the war. He concluded, as he later testified to the House Military Affairs Committee, that hundreds of men had married women who had children and independent sources of income, for the purpose of obtaining an exemption. As a result of Crowder's order, hundreds, if not thousands, of men found to be working less than full-time could be swept into the army. The "work or fight order" was also widely reported across the country, and labor unions opposed it. On March 31, Crowder explained to a receptive Brandeis that the order was a necessity to alleviate the shortage of manpower in uniform, and that with an increase of women in the industrial workforce the order would not affect the nation's manufacturing capacity.[52]

On November 16, 1917, Senator Hiram Johnson conveyed his anger at Crowder over the "work or fight order" to Senator Philander Knox. "Practically, now, he is adopting an entirely new scheme after he accustomed the country to a different one, and he is reverting to his original views regarding dependents, and will put in his first class of those to be called at once, men with wives and children who have relatives able to support the dependents in case the bread winner were drafted," Johnson complained. "The difficulty with him is that he has neither conception nor understanding of the family relation and that his enthusiasm to raise a very large army obscures every social and human consideration." Johnson's anger with Crowder had begun with Crowder's refusal to exempt his son. The Selective Service Act did not specifically exempt fathers from being drafted. The law did, however, permit the War Department to exempt fathers whose children would become "public charges" if the father were forced into military service. In August 1917, Crowder fashioned a regulation that enabled draft boards to issue exemptions to prevent burdens on state orphanages. Senator Johnson had wanted his twenty-nine-year-old son, who was a husband and father of two children, to gain an exemption. Johnson believed that an exemption was justified because another of his sons was already in the army. After the exemption was denied, Johnson appealed to Crowder to intervene, arguing that a strict adherence to the law would create "a discontented, dispirited, and embittered Army." However, after pointing out to Johnson the fairness of the exemption regulation, Crowder refused to intervene. Johnson next complained to President Wilson, but Wilson simply directed Baker to look into the matter, and Baker agreed with Crowder's assessment. Not satisfied with Baker's agreement with Crowder, Johnson responded by calling Crowder's reasons for his refusal to intervene "outrageous" and accused him of "Prussianism." In the end, Wilson intervened and Johnson's son was exempted, but from this point forward, Johnson claimed that if Congress failed to oversee conscription, it would be used as a means to selectively draft dissenters and then court-martial them as a means of overcoming the First Amendment.[53]

Several senators and congressmen asserted that their states were disproportionately represented in the army. Senator Thomas Walsh of Montana claimed that the rural and mountain states of North Dakota, South Dakota, Montana, and Idaho provided more men per capita to the army than the industrial states in the Northeast. He challenged that this meant that a higher proportion of citizens from those states were subject not only to the German "death machine" but also to the military's jurisdiction. Crowder provided his data on the raw numbers of draftees to Walsh and countered that New York's governor had likewise complained that his state had been drained of its citizenry more than farm states because of the Selective Service Act's farming exemptions. Neither Walsh nor New York's governor had opposed conscription or the war. Congressmen who opposed selective service could become vitriolic in their attacks against Crowder, Baker, and Wilson. In August 1917, former congressman Thomas Watson of Georgia, an ardent populist who campaigned against both the declaration of war and conscription, publicly compared Crowder to Freiherr Moritz von Bissing, a German general responsible for numerous war crimes in Belgium in 1914. Watson argued that any court-martial of a conscientious objector applicant violated the Constitution. Crowder understood that even some legislators who voted in favor of selective service would challenge the courts-martial and imprisonment of their constituents who refused to comply with induction orders or other orders pertaining to enlistment, and for this reason he had tried to carefully craft limited exceptions into the Selective Service Act so as not to have the War Department accused of favoritism.[54]

Crowder also understood that citizens drafted into the army might, on receipt of their draft order, try to enlist in the navy or marine corps in the hopes of avoiding shipment to France, and he enforced the Selective Service Act to prevent wholesale occurrences of this. Though it was true that marines fought in France, it was equally likely that a volunteer into the marine corps might be sent anywhere in the world and in particular, Cuba, the Caribbean Islands, the Philippines, or Central America. Crowder's vigorous enforcement in prohibiting citizens from joining the navy could be problematic because congressmen serving on the two naval committees were in a position to influence the recruitment of volunteers into either the marines or the navy and might resent Crowder. After consulting with Secretary of the Navy Daniels, he tried to lessen congressional anger by having the act permit two exceptions to citizens volunteering for naval service. The first exception applied to doctors, and the second exception was for persons offered naval or marine corps commissions. In August 1917, Senator Miles Poindexter of Washington asked for Crowder's assistance in permitting a constituent to reenlist in the navy rather than have to honor his induction notice into the army. The constituent had been honorably discharged from the navy in 1916 and was "a trained machinist who wanted to serve the country in war." While Crowder was sympathetic to the constituent's request, he informed Poindexter that the sailor would have had to reenlist in the navy prior to receipt of the induction notice in order to be exempted from the army. In spite of Crowder's response, Poindexter supported conscription, and in a speech to his Spokane constituents, he argued that the nation had to place great trust in the provost marshal.[55]

Despite the exception permitting citizens to accept navy and marine corps commissions, there were instances where a citizen was arrested for failing to comply with an army induction order when the citizen already had accepted a commission in another service branch. In one instance, the Kalispell, Montana, mayor's son had registered for the draft but was offered a naval commission. When he failed to appear for an army medical examination, it was because he was already undergoing naval training. Nonetheless, War Department agents arrested him and threatened him with prosecution. Senator Walsh asked Crowder to intervene with the local provost marshal and ensure the future naval officer would not be prosecuted or court-martialed for draft evasion. A simple telegram from Crowder enabled the War Department to avoid wasting resources in prosecuting the young man for having done "nothing more than zealously followed his patriotic dictates."[56]

Just as the prosecution of soldiers in courts-martial was to have congressional and other political interest, so too were the courts-martial of citizens who refused induction and were subjected to military trials or were treated roughly by the military. Between the declaration of war and the Armistice, the army convened 371 courts-martial over citizens claiming conscientious objection who refused to either work to support the war effort or be inducted into the army. There were hundreds of other citizens prosecuted in the United States District Courts. The majority of the men prosecuted in courts-martial were charged with disobedience of lawful orders, though roughly 10 percent were court-martialed for desertion. One of the men convicted was sentenced to death, but the convening authority reduced the sentence to twenty-five years.[57]

By November 11, 1918, there were 450 citizens imprisoned at Fort Leavenworth and Alcatraz who were denied conscientious objector exemption from military service but who also refused to follow orders. This was a small number in comparison to the number of citizens who failed or refused to comply with the Selective Service Act. Of the twenty-four million citizens who were required to register, three million did not do so. When, on April 10, 1917, Baker transmitted a proposed conscription bill to Congress, he only recommended that persons belonging to "pacifist religious sects" be permitted to be assigned to noncombatant duties in the medical and chaplain fields. After providing the draft to Congress, Baker and Crowder consulted with Jane Addams, one of the nation's more prominent social reformers and a member of the antiwar American Union Against Militarism. Roger Baldwin, the future head of the American Civil Liberties Union, and Oswald Garrison Villard also lobbied Baker and Crowder for a broader conscientious objector exemption. In response, Baker chose to defer the issue of exemptions to Congress. Addams then met with congressmen prior to the vote on selective service, and two Colorado legislators, Congressman Edward Keating and Senator Charles Thomas, lobbied to expand conscientious objection exemption to citizens who sincerely believed that military service was contrary to their conscience. These arguments failed and the Selective Service Act was basically passed as Crowder and his subordinates had originally drafted it. In the first six months following the declaration of war, it became evident to Charles Beecher Warren that several local boards in Wisconsin, Minnesota, and Ohio had liberally granted exemptions. Warren reported to Crowder that these boards considered the individual beliefs of applicants rather than a faith's doctrinal teachings. In response, Crowder asserted to the various boards and several congressmen that conscription had to be administered as Congress intended, and neither the Provost Marshal's Office nor the local and state boards had the authority to exempt persons based on a nonsectarian or individualized objection. As a result, soldiers who went into the army but later sought noncombatant positions could be court-martialed for disobedience of orders if they refused to carry a weapon. Wigmore became Crowder's most outspoken advocate on this point. Both Crowder and Wigmore were not opposed to pacifist organizations, but they believed that such organizations were likely to increase in number and then be used by militant socialists and Bolsheviks to strengthen antiwar sentiments.[58]

However, Frankfurter drafted a memorandum supporting an expanded exemption policy in September 1917. Although not contained in this memorandum, Frankfurter conveyed to Crowder that the harsher aspects of French and British courts-martial could be avoided by enabling a liberalized means to claim conscientious objection. Like Crowder, Bethel, and Kreger, Frankfurter believed that public confidence in courts-martial was essential to maintaining the war effort, and the American public and Congress would not approve of the British or French practices. Frankfurter eventually swayed Crowder, and more importantly Wilson, to enable an expanded exemption. On March 20, 1918, Wilson issued Executive Order 2823. The order expanded conscientious objector status to persons claiming that their faith opposed killing, rather than relying on the religious leaders of a faith to make the assertion. In a sense, this permitted an individual to argue that while a broad doctrinal position of their faith might have enabled military service, the literal reading of the tenets of the faith prohibited killing in war. Additionally, the order established a board to review courts-martial convictions and sentences arising from conscientious objector cases. The board consisted of a judge advocate, Judge Julian Mack, and Dean Harlan Fiske Stone. Frankfurter recommended both civilians to Baker.[59]

President Taft appointed Julian Mack to the federal judiciary in 1910. Raised in Cincinnati, he was educated at the University of Berlin, University of Leipzig, and Harvard's law school. He taught law alongside Wigmore at Northwestern University Law School from 1901 to 1910. Although he aligned with the Republican Party before his nomination, he was friendly with Brandeis, and when Frankfurter suggested Mack to Baker, Brandeis endorsed the appointment. So too did Crowder and Wigmore. Although Mack had no prior military experience, he served on the National War Labor Board and was respected for protecting the rights of children after establishing a special court that segregated children accused of crimes from hardened adult criminals.[60]

This board made it possible for imprisoned citizens to seek noncombatant service if it determined that the imprisoned soldier's conscientious objection to killing was sincere. Congress never specifically created the board, and Ansell surprisingly opposed it to the army's Chief of Staff Peyton March. By this time Crowder had accepted the necessity of the board and opined that its creation was within Wilson's "war power" authority under the Constitution. While the two men had a difference of opinion on the treatment and rights of conscientious objector claimants, neither Crowder nor Ansell would later testify that this contributed to the friction between the two. But it is notable that Mack and Stone obliquely challenged the legal sufficiency of several courts-martial, and Crowder did not oppose this. Ansell objected to this aspect of the board as well as the board's existence. In his opposition to the board, Ansell gained an ally in the House of Representatives, the newly elected Republican Walter Hughes Newton of Minnesota. Ansell and Hughes were in the minority, as the majority of congressmen supported the implementation of the board, even though it had not been created by statute. But there were instances where Crowder disagreed with the actions of congressmen who tried to affect the administration of conscription.[61]

Shortly after the Selective Service Act became law, Crowder opposed the selection of one state's selective service officials. In May 1917, Congressman Claude Kitchin, the chairman of the Ways and Means Committee and majority leader, lobbied North Carolina's governor to appoint three state officers to determine the appeals of persons denied conscientious objector status. Because Kitchin had voted against both the war and conscription, accused northern industrialists and bankers of profiteering, and claimed that the British blockade of Germany violated international law, Crowder feared Kitchin's nominees would grant wholesale exemptions and ultimately was able to convince the state governor to nominate three different citizens. To Kitchin's credit, he did not fight Crowder over the War Department's intrusion into state appointments.[62]

One of the unexpected aspects of conscientious objection was the possibility that a citizen might be inducted into the army but then assert conscientious objection to further military service. In 1971 the Supreme Court recognized that conscientious objection could "crystalize" after induction into the military, and the justices, led by William O. Douglas, determined that the federal courts had jurisdiction to decide whether the military establishment had disregarded the laws and regulations covering such instances. However, neither Congress in World War I nor the judiciary required the military establishment to enable conscientious objection exemption after induction. In December 1917, Congressman Carter Glass sought Crowder's guidance on whether a soldier already in the army could claim conscientious objection on the eve of being sent to France. Crowder replied that the soldier could apply for conscientious objection back to his original board, but the War Department would not enable the soldier to remain in the United States while the board considered the appeal. He also advised Glass that the soldier could appeal to his commanding officer for a discharge. Importantly, Crowder noted that conscientious objection could not serve as a defense in a court-martial against a charge of disobedience of orders. Glass agreed with Crowder's assessment and noted to his constituent, "to depart from this inexorable regulation in one case to please one public man would open wide the flood-gates." On two other occasions, Glass repeated his support for Crowder's position, and in one of these instances he responded to an aggrieved mother that the court-martial of her son Private Robert J. Dooley for disobedience of orders was required under the law.[63]

In 1918 Senator Poindexter asked Crowder to inquire into the imprisonment of a Private Cecil Cooper, who had deserted and been sentenced to two years in prison. Once at Fort Leavenworth, Cooper sought to be restored to active duty and renounced his previous assertion of conscientious objection. A captain stationed at the prison also supported Cooper being returned to duty and wrote an affidavit that Cooper had been a model prisoner. Cooper's father, a Seattle banker, asked Poindexter to add that his son's sentence was too severe. Crowder responded to Poindexter that Baker had already approved Cooper's return to the army, and he could expect to be shipped to his division in France.[64]

On April 25, 1918, Congressman Tillman informed Major Charles Beecher Warren that if a white inductee facing a court-martial for refusing to serve in uniform was not retroactively given an exemption, not only would the soldier's deaf mother suffer the lack of support, "the negroes on the place, would commit crimes." Tillman implied to Warren that he would publicly blame Crowder for causing a racial insurrection unless the court-martial was prevented. Warren replied to Tillman that there were proper channels for the soldier to apply for an exemption, and the War Department was not responsible for the law enforcement of South Carolina. Warren could have added that given Tillman's history of inciting riots against African Americans, he too might be held responsible for any "riots." Most troubling to Crowder was that Tillman had attempted to assert as a basis for conscientious objection, a religious opposition to serving in the army with African American soldiers. To this end, Warren, with Crowder's approval, informed Tillman that there was "no justified religious reason to grant conscientious objection based on a refusal to serve with colored soldiers."[65]

In 1919 the Saint Paul *Enterprise* reported that a conscientious objector named John A. Hardesen had been tortured at the Alcatraz Military Prison.

Hardesen was a Montana native, and the newspaper's editors encouraged its readers to write to Senator Walsh so that he could demand an investigation. In April 1918, the army court-martialed Hardesen, and he was sentenced to twenty-five years in confinement. Walsh, in turn, demanded an explanation from Baker as to why Hardesen had been placed into solitary confinement in a cell with little light and placed on bread and water for fourteen days on two recent occasions. Baker responded that Hardesen discovered his conscientious objection only after being shipped to France and refused to follow orders to transit to the front with the rest of his division. From June 1918 to April 1919, Hardesen was housed at Fort Leavenworth, but then transferred to Alcatraz, where he refused to perform the labor assigned to him. As a result, he was court-martialed once more for disobedience of orders and placed in solitary confinement with a limited diet. The prison rules only authorized a bread-and-water diet for fourteen days, but because he had been sentenced to a month in solitary confinement, he was given a two-week respite from the diet and then placed on it once more. Baker ended his response with the admonition that if a prisoner such as Hardesen were to be let off of punishment, then other prisoners would follow suit and the prison population would lose all discipline. Prior to sending his response, Baker gained Crowder's support for it.[66]

In 1920 Senator George Norris of Nebraska demanded an inquiry into the condition of a prisoner named Robert Simmons who had been convicted of refusing induction into the army and then also placed into solitary confinement at the Alcatraz prison. Norris claimed to Baker that the penitentiary authorities had ignored a prison medical diagnosis prohibiting Simmons from working in outdoor prison labor and then tortured him. To investigate this matter Baker turned to Crowder, who determined that Simmons had, in fact, wrongly been placed in solitary confinement, and he ordered Simmons returned to his regular cell.[67]

Crowder could not have foreseen all of the jurisdictional implications created by selective service, and on occasion, he was unable to solve challenges in the War Department's favor. In early 1919, he became involved in a three-way jurisdictional claim over the prosecution of a citizen named Guy L. Gregory. In 1917 Gregory failed to register for the draft. After being informed that his failure could be prosecuted in November 1917, he registered but claimed to be thirty-three years of age, when he was, in fact, twenty-four years old. Shortly afterward he murdered a woman named Marion Harle who had discovered his lie. For unknown reasons, the authorities were unable to arrest Gregory for a year, and in late 1918, Crowder advised Baker that the War Department should assert jurisdiction over him for his intentional avoidance of the draft. Both the prosecuting attorney for Phillips County, Montana, and the United States Attorney for Montana also wanted to prosecute Gregory for murder and then combine the murder charge with the crime of draft evasion. Ultimately Senator Walsh intervened and the United States Attorney prosecuted Gregory in federal court, where he was convicted of murder and draft evasion and sentenced to life imprisonment.[68]

Vice President Thomas Marshall viewed himself as a legislator as much as vice president, if for no other reason than that Wilson had not included him in much of the cabinet's decisional processes affecting the war. Marshall would have ordinarily been a strong advocate against mass conscription. After graduating from law school, he partnered with Lambdin Milligan and later claimed that Milligan had influenced him to oppose prosecuting citizens for publicly opposing the war. When John Sharp Williams sought to have Robert La Follette removed from the Senate in late 1917, Marshall voiced support for La Follette. Although Marshall opposed conscription, he did support the nation's entry into the war on the side of the Allies, and he had good relations with Crowder. Marshall queried Crowder as to whether a less draconian response than courts-martial could be used to deal with citizens who were denied exemption and refused to follow orders. In 1918 Crowder informed Marshall that the courts-martial of conscientious objectors who refused to perform work were merited because the refusals constituted disobedience of orders, and a summary punishment would afford accused persons no due process. Marshall accepted Crowder's reasoning but asked Crowder to encourage Baker to reduce the sentences of citizens in military prisons who had been denied conscientious objector status. That the vice president asked Crowder to influence Baker is a remarkable example of the judge advocate general's increasing power.[69]

On June 2, 1920, a concerned citizen wrote to Senator Claude Swanson of Virginia asking whether persons deemed as "slackers" remained subject to the military's jurisdiction. Swanson forwarded the letter to Crowder, who responded that wartime deserters could still be court-martialed because Congress had not repealed the selective service laws. It was true, Crowder pointed out, that President Wilson suspended conscription in conformity with his authority as commander in chief, but until Congress acted, "draft deserters and delinquents still [were] amenable to trial and punishment." Crowder added that it was in the best interest of a person who was subject to the military's jurisdiction to "immediately surrender" because it was possible for a "slacker" to avoid a court-martial by enlisting in the army.[70]

In October 1921, Senator Thomas Watson wrote to Crowder with a kinder tone than he had used at the beginning of the war, addressing him as "my dear general." Watson attempted to gain the release of a Private Fredrick Whitehead,

who had refused induction and deserted in 1918. The War Department
captured Whitehead and court-martialed him in 1920, and he was sentenced
to four years in confinement. Crowder recommended to Secretary of War
Weeks to free Whitehead but not overturn the guilty findings. In the end,
Whitehead served a quarter of his sentence before being freed.[71]

CONGRESS AND THE "INDEFENSIBLE CASES"

In every American war, there are trials in which the guilt of an accused
service-member is so plain that one might expect Congress or the public not
to embrace the convicted soldier as a victim of injustice. Yet historically, some
of the public and their elected officials have rallied to the accused service-
member despite the plain evidence of guilt and the heinousness of the crime.
For instance, during the Vietnam Conflict, a part of the public claimed
Lieutenant William Laws Calley was wrongfully prosecuted, and several
congressmen including Mendel Rivers and F. Edward Hebert, as well as James
Carter, the governor of Georgia and future president, advocated on Calley's
behalf. While there were no trials arising from offenses such as Calley's in
World War I, there were a few trials in which, despite the evidence of a soldier's
guilt, legislators and prominent citizens rallied to the soldier.[72]

In 1914 Captain Joseph H. Griffiths, a quartermaster officer, deserted his
post near Portland, Oregon, and fled under an alias to San Francisco. The War
Department discovered that Griffiths had transferred army funds into his own
bank account, and after being questioned, he convinced a woman to disguise
herself as his wife and convinced her to travel with him to the Orient. Griffiths
was already married to another woman. A San Francisco policeman and army
officers arrested Griffiths on a docked ship, and a court-martial sentenced him
to ten years in confinement and a dismissal. Griffiths had attempted to argue
that he was "duped by swindlers" and that his confession was taken under
duress. The court-martial was also widely reported across the western states,
and given the embarrassment to the army, it might have appeared unlikely that
the War Department would afford him any leniency. However, after Crowder
reviewed the record of trial and recommended clemency, President Wilson
approved only a three-year sentence and a dismissal. For unknown reasons,
Senator Wesley Jones of Washington tried to convince Crowder to support
restoring Griffiths's commission in 1917. Griffiths may have been a talented
quartermaster but his bigamous conduct offended Crowder.[73]

Southern legislators such as Congressman Claude Kitchin and Senators
Benjamin Tillman and James Vardaman opposed not only the conscription of

African American soldiers but any attempt at achieving their equal treatment in the War Department. Throughout their political careers, the three legislators worked to disenfranchise African Americans from the nation's political and economic life. Senator Thomas Watson of Georgia likewise worked to achieve the same ends. On July 25, 1921, Kreger responded to a demand from Watson to release Private George W. Jackson. In August 1918 Jackson either abandoned his post or became separated from his unit for two days. He murdered Corporal Smart, a military policeman, during Smart's attempt to arrest him. Witnesses testified that Jackson had not only shot Smart, who was unarmed, but also fired four rounds into his body after Smart fell to the ground, and he exclaimed that Smart was "a nigger ... worse than the Germans." A court-martial convicted Jackson of premeditated murder and sentenced him to death, but in December 1918, Wilson commuted the sentence to life in prison. A clemency board further recommended to Baker that the sentence be reduced to twenty years. In spite of the overwhelming evidence against Jackson, Watson claimed the court-martial verdict to be "a sham." Watson argued that because Smart was an African American soldier and Jackson was white, the murder was an understandable act of self-defense. Kreger responded to Watson that it was unlikely that any further clemency would be afforded to Jackson or that Secretary of War John Weeks, who replaced Baker, would overturn the conviction. Jackson was not the only soldier that Watson tried to defend on the basis of race.[74]

In 1920 Watson argued to Crowder that the conviction for murder and sentence to twenty years of a Private Richard Lewis was unjust because the murder victim, a colored soldier named Private Harry Lewis, had offended the white Richard Lewis, and African American soldiers were permitted to testify against Private Lewis in San Antonio. Watson either believed that the United States District Court in Texas had sole jurisdiction or that its jurisdiction was preferred because, under the Texas evidentiary laws, colored persons were not deemed to be competent to testify against whites. In this instance, Hull, on Crowder's behalf, responded that the War Department had the authority to retain full jurisdiction since the murder occurred on post.[75]

A different type of example of legislative oversight in an "indefensible trial" arose out of the court-martial conviction of Captain Edward M. Harding. On April 8, 1919, the army court-martialed Harding at Camp Alfred Vail, New Jersey, for commandeering a government-owned Cadillac automobile at Governors Island for his personal use. Harding's commanding officer had previously discovered he used the vehicle, which was intended to convey foreign dignitaries and high-ranking officers through the city, for "an evening out with his fiancée and his friends." Moreover, the gasoline used during

Harding's frolics belonged to the army. In an effort to convince Harding of the wrongness of his conduct, the general commanding Governors Island ordered Harding not to leave the post. Harding did not follow the order and continued to use the Cadillac for his personal amusement, including visits to houses of prostitution and "speakeasies." The court-martial sentenced Harding to be dismissed from the army, and while he served no time in jail, the dismissal had significant personal effects.[76]

Harding not only had political aspirations of his own, he also had a family connection to James B. Regan, the finance committee chair of New York's state Democratic Party and proprietor of the swank Knickerbocker Hotel. Regan, in turn, had a connection to Tumulty and wrote to the president's secretary in the hopes of the president not approving the findings and sentence of Harding's court-martial. Three New York congressmen rallied to Harding's defense as well. Kreger, acting in place of Crowder who was in Paris at the time of the appeal, conveyed to Tumulty that Harding's court-martial had an unusual aspect to it. Normally after a court-martial sentenced an accused soldier, the officers empaneled on the court-martial would immediately decide whether to recommend clemency. In Harding's case, the empaneled officers voted to wait on their recommendation to see whether Wilson would approve the sentence in the first place. Kreger advised that although the Articles of War did not expressly permit a court-martial to be reconvened after a presidential determination, it would be fair to restore Harding to the army and permit him to be honorably discharged since, "in being ordered to remain within the limits of Camp Alfred Vail, New Jersey, he had also suffered through a de facto imprisonment." Ultimately Wilson did restore Harding to the army. Whether Tumulty or Wilson were influenced by fellow prominent Democrats cannot be known, but the brief judge advocate review of Harding's court-martial and his ultimate restoration were a microcosm of the interplay between political interests and the fate of court-martialed service-members in World War I, even where an officer wasted military resources and flaunted a visible disregard of regulations and law.[77]

Although Crowder appreciated Congressman Francis Lever's support of the War Department throughout the war, he and Kreger were perplexed over one of the congressman's inquiries. In May 1919, the army court-martialed a Private William J. Laver for the offense of bigamy, and after he was found guilty, it sentenced him to a dishonorable discharge and two years in confinement. Prior to entering the army, Laver was married to a woman in Texas, and then after finishing training, he married a woman in South Carolina without first obtaining a divorce. In August 1918, Laver married a third woman in Melbourne, England, "after an acquaintance of five or six weeks." Laver testified in his own defense that he did not know he was married the second and third times, because he "had become a dope fiend." Compounding Laver's difficulties was that when his unit had left Britain for the front lines in France, he remained in Britain without permission, and it was during this time that he was married. Kreger noted that while it was possible that the addiction to "dope" might serve as a defense to Laver's third marriage, it could not be a defense to the unauthorized absence or for the second marriage. Although the record of trial was determined to be sufficient, Kreger advised Lever that the postwar clemency board might remit Laver's remaining confinement and send him home. There were two interesting aspects to Laver's appeal that neither Crowder nor Kreger adduced until after Kreger's response was mailed to Lever. Private Laver's name was misspelled and the correct spelling was "Lever," and Private Lever had not informed his second cousin, Congressman Lever, of the full extent of his misconduct, in particular, the second marriage and the absence from duty.[78]

A more poignant example of an "indefensible case" arose from the trial of Captain George Chamberlain, a United States Marine Corps aviator who was prosecuted in a navy court-martial, but one in which the Judge Advocate General's Office became involved. During the war, marines serving in the American Expeditionary Forces were commanded by John Archer Lejune and were disciplined in their own courts-martial but with army oversight. On occasion, army officers served as judge advocates in marine courts-martial. Kreger aided the prosecution of Chamberlain's court-martial, in part because the trial directly impacted the army due to the number of army officers called as witnesses.[79]

Prior to the United States' entry into the war, hundreds of American citizens crossed into Canada and joined the British and Canadian expeditionary forces. Likewise, hundreds of citizens enlisted or were commissioned into the French military, the most famous of these being the Lafayette Escadrille. Less known than the Americans who flew for the French Air Service were several dozen American servicemen who flew for the nascent British Royal Flying Corps. One of the officers who flew with the British, albeit on an "unofficial visit" and not as part of the Royal Flying Corps, was Captain Edmund G. Chamberlain. A native of San Antonio who attended Princeton University, Chamberlain was credited with shooting down five German aircraft on July 28, 1918, as well as landing behind enemy lines, capturing a German soldier, and carrying an injured French colonial soldier to safety. However, the only source of information for the reports of his "heroism" came from Chamberlain himself, and he also claimed to have taken part in over fifteen bombing raids against the Germans. Based on his self-reporting, a British staff officer submitted Chamberlain for a Victoria Cross, Britain's highest medal, and the British War Ministry transferred Chamberlain's record to the American Expeditionary Forces for a nomination for the Medal of Honor. Chamberlain did, on one occasion, fly with the Royal Air Force, and he was shot down over Allied territory. Beyond that fact, his claims of air combat and other heroism became impossible to prove.[80]

Chamberlain's exploits were well documented in the American press. The *New York Times* lauded him as an example of American manliness, and the Chicago, Philadelphia, and Boston newspapers followed suit. But Colonel Harold Fowler, an American recently attached to a British aviation headquarters staff commanded by Brigadier General John Maitland Salmond, doubted Chamberlain's integrity. Ultimately Fowler was able to expose the fact that all of the British officers who submitted affidavits attesting to Chamberlain's bravery were dead. During the war, Fowler was assigned to the United States Army Air Service, and he planned night bombing raids against German positions and developed joint air and ground operations. Based on his wartime experiences, he was convinced Chamberlain had concocted a fraud. In late 1918, Fowler reported Chamberlain's ongoing fraud to Secretary of the Navy Josephus Daniels. In spite of Fowler's accusations, Chamberlain continued to publicly advertise his valor, and Admiral William Sims appointed him to Colonel Edward House's staff in Paris at the time the Versailles treaty negotiations were under way. However, Fowler's father and House were long-time friends, and once House was convinced he had been lied to, he pushed for a court-martial.[81]

When confronted by House, Chamberlain was unable to produce the location of the British officers, the German prisoner of war, or any of the French participants who allegedly took part in the events. Given the ferocity and high casualty counts of the Western Front, Chamberlain's inability to find witnesses might not, in and of itself, have been harmful to his case. But when it was coupled with the fact that all of the documents addressing his exploits appeared to have been authored by the same person, an understandable suspicion arose, even among the British staff. There was, in contrast, a great deal of evidence that while Chamberlain was on leave in Paris during the time of his self-attested bravery, he consumed a quantity of alcohol with several British officers and accompanied them to their duty stations. And notably, Chamberlain never shot down a German aircraft while flying in an American sortie.

In May 1919, the navy court-martialed Chamberlain in London for falsifying records of his aerial accomplishments, but it was not entirely a naval court-martial. Kreger and Winship assisted with the prosecution.

Chamberlain was specifically charged under the Naval Articles (as opposed to the Articles of War) with "scandalous conduct detrimental to good order and discipline" and "falsehoods." He testified in his own defense and claimed that while he was on leave in Paris on July 26, 1918, a British officer named "Henderson" approached him and claimed to have met him prior to the war in New York. Henderson then invited him to a British aerodrome near the Marne River and introduced him to other British pilots. Chamberlain further testified that these men invited him to fly on a mission, but because he had no familiarity with the Sopwith Camel, he fell out of formation and returned to the base alone. He stated that two days later, on July 28, the British again invited him to fly on a bombing mission, and he accepted. On this mission he claimed to have shot down several aircraft while protecting a French bomber formation. Chamberlain's version of his personal exploits becomes a bit comical after this point. He testified that the citations correctly described what he had accomplished, but under oath, he disavowed all knowledge of who authored the citations. He also testified that he landed his stricken aircraft behind enemy lines and removed the compass from the plane, but then lost the compass. While trying to traverse back to the British and French forces, he swore that he eluded three German infantrymen and discovered a wounded "French colonial" as well as a German whom he captured as a prisoner of war. After seizing the German's rifle, he claimed that he ordered the German prisoner to carry the wounded French colonial until they entered Allied territory and then found a medical aid station. After he had the German prisoner over to a French officer, another French officer brought Chamberlain back to the British aerodrome, where he, or some other officer, wrote a formal statement of the exploit. Some British servicemen apparently believed his statement and forwarded it to the Paris edition of the *Chicago Tribune*, whose writers forwarded the news story across the United States.[82]

In opposite of Chamberlain's testimony, the trial judge advocate provided an affidavit from General Salmond, which stated that several of the officers Chamberlain claimed to fly with were either not locatable, dead, or on other assignments during the time of Chamberlain's "heroism." Equally importantly, no officer in the Royal Flying Corps knew of an officer named Henderson fitting Chamberlain's description, and few remembered Chamberlain at all. Salmond added that the Royal Flying Corps had itself conducted a full investigation and concluded that the "whole affair was a concoction of lies and forgeries." Another American naval officer testified that two of the individuals Chamberlain claimed to fly with were in service in Italy, and both had died. Additionally, British officers serving in the squadron that Chamberlain claimed to fly with disavowed any knowledge of his flight. All Chamberlain

could offer in response was that these officers would have been disobeying
orders if the British Expeditionary Forces' command had discovered that a
non–Royal Flying Corps aviator had been permitted to pilot a new Sopwith
Camel. Moreover, no French officer or enlisted personnel could be found to
testify in Chamberlain's defense.[83]

After conferring with Crowder as well as the judge advocate general of the
navy, on December 8, 1919, Secretary of the Navy Daniels announced the result
of Chamberlain's court-martial, and in early February 1920, President Wilson
approved the court-martial's guilty findings and sentence to a dismissal.
Because Kreger had assisted in the prosecution, Crowder wanted to ensure that
Chamberlain's conviction and sentence remained intact. He also believed that
as a result of Chamberlain's father's influence, the court-martial could be used
to reopen congressional debates into the fairness of courts-martial. Crowder's
fear of this proved to be prescient. In early 1920, Ansell began to lobby Texas
legislators on behalf of Chamberlain as a means to reopen a congressional
inquiry into the fairness of courts-martial. On June 10, 1921, Senator Morris
Sheppard, who earlier agreed with Crowder and Garrison that the claims of
Captain George A. Armes—the wayward frontier officer—were meritless,
introduced a bill to the full Senate to reinstate Chamberlain as a captain in
the marine corps and argued that the trial was unfair. Both Sheppard and
Chamberlain's father were Wilsonian Democrats, and the elder Chamberlain
had financially backed Sheppard's senatorial bid. Even President-elect Warren
G. Harding considered granting Chamberlain an audience, but Crowder and
future attorney general Harry Daugherty dissuaded him from doing so. While
Ansell's assistance to Chamberlain upset Crowder, he was particularly worried
after learning that former attorney general Thomas Watts Gregory had joined
in Chamberlain's cause.[84]

Gregory, for his part, supplied Sheppard with information about the
authority of Congress to reinstate a court-martialed officer, analogizing
Chamberlain's court-martial to Fitz-John Porter's case during the Civil War.
Court-martialed in late 1862 after the Second Battle of Manassas, Porter
was found guilty of disobedience of orders and dismissed from the army.
The trial was controversial for several reasons, and under congressional
pressure, President Chester Arthur restored Porter to the army two decades
after Appomattox. Gregory also decried the "Ku Klux Klan" methods of the
trial to Gordon Auchincloss, an influential attorney who had helped shepherd
the Selective Service Act through Congress and then prosecuted citizens
who refused induction in federal courts. After Gregory impugned Fowler's
motives, Auchincloss responded that he had spoken to Colonel House, and the
two men had concluded that "of all the men in our acquaintance that were in

the war, Fowler had without question the most brilliant record." Auchincloss added that both he and House had a "high personal regard" for Fowler, and Crowder supported Fowler as well.[85]

Not mollified by Auchincloss's response, Gregory responded by conceding that Fowler's integrity might be without question, but in an effort to appease the British military, Fowler had pushed too hard for a court-martial, and this benefited the British. "I have known some American officers of the Admiral Sims type who became very much enamored of the British, frequently to the extent of forming and expressing views indicating that they considered the British officers and soldiers superior to those of the United States." Gregory claimed, however, that he was unlikely to gain many congressional adherents to this line of attack, even among the isolationists, because the British had not benefited from the court-martial. For unknown reasons, Chamberlain's complaints to Congress went into a two-year dormancy, but in 1924 Gregory successfully lobbied Senator Walsh to convene a Senate investigation. Senator Sheppard served on the investigative committee and not only kept Chamberlain apprised of its progress, but when the secretary of the navy could not locate British witnesses, he tried to convince Walsh to force an end to the proceedings.[86]

At some point, the committee concluded that Chamberlain's guilt largely rested on the question of handwriting. Treasury Department experts concluded that the Victoria Cross medal applications were, in fact, in Chamberlain's handwriting. With Sheppard's assistance, the elder Chamberlain and Gregory convinced Albert O. Osborne, who later became the Federal Bureau of Investigation's leading forensic document examiner and a pioneer in the field of handwriting, ink, and paper analysis, to assist in Chamberlain's defense. Osborne urged the committee to conclude that the government's forensic case was "weak, unscientific, and inconclusive," in large measure because the government had failed to make allowances for the difference in writing styles and letter drafting between the British and Americans. But he agreed that the documents attesting to Chamberlain's exploits were written by the same person.[87]

After the committee adjourned but before it issued its findings, Gregory raised a significant evidentiary issue that had not been brought to the attention of the committee. A French farmer in Saint Gemmes found a British aircraft compass near the location where Chamberlain claimed he landed to rescue the British officer. Gregory then lobbied Walsh to reopen the investigative hearings until the British military could confirm the origin of the compass. However, by this time, Walsh's patience was at an end and he adjourned the committee permanently. Walsh, like Crowder, Kreger, House, and most of the participants, concluded that Chamberlain had incompetently crashed an aircraft in no-man's land and then concocted a heroic exploit to explain the loss of the aircraft.[88]

In 1924 Ansell advised Chamberlain to sue the Department of the Navy in Court of Claims. When he did so in 1928, that court concluded that the statute of limitations prevented it from taking jurisdiction over the claim. The Supreme Court upheld the claims court the following year. Ansell had wanted to use Chamberlain's court-martial as proof that courts-martial could not be trusted to fairly decide a serviceman's fate, but Chamberlain was unlikely to be held a public martyr. On the other hand, he was not left destitute. Although he left the marine corps in disgrace, he later became a prominent figure in the banking industry.[89]

WAR RISK INSURANCE, ADMINISTRATIVE MATTERS, AND THE PRISONER ABUSE SCANDAL

Although the Judge Advocate General's Office had contentious relationships with several legislators throughout the war, of all the parts of the government, it was with the Treasury Department that Crowder and his subordinates most frequently argued. On several significant matters, the Judge Advocate General's Office found itself allied with Congress against Secretary of the Treasury William Gibbs McAdoo, the president's son-in-law. On December 18, 1918, Crowder directed the War Department law librarian, Major T. R. Hawley, to catalog instances where he believed McAdoo and his subordinates had disregarded statutes to the detriment of the War Department. In 1918 the Treasury Department refused to pay Veterinary Corps officers at their brevet rank after Crowder had informed McAdoo that Congress had enabled brevet promotions for the Veterinary Corps. The Treasury Department also refused to pay officers a rate of four cents per mile for their travel if they traveled by aircraft, even though the regulations governing travel rate pay did not distinguish this as a nonpayable mode of travel. In August 1917, nineteen senior officers were denied travel pay after they departed from the Philippines and traveled directly to Europe, because they did not first return to the United States, as their orders indicated. The nineteen officers apparently believed that the needs of military efficiency coupled with the permission of the adjutant general outweighed the needs of bureaucracy. Worse still, the officers had initially been paid, but the Treasury Department initiated a repossession order, and this infuriated Crowder.[90]

The most numerous of the disagreements between the Judge Advocate General's Office and McAdoo, however, had to do with War Risk Insurance Act payments. "The frequent occurrence of such conflicts cause continual uncertainty in the War Department as to the effect of laws and even of its own orders," Hawley concluded before suggesting that Crowder lobby that "specific and detailed legislation be enacted, placing the War Department as the judge of the limits of its own jurisdiction, over the Treasury Department." Crowder believed that because of McAdoo's unique relationship to Wilson, there was little he or Baker could do to oust him. Baker, likewise, was upset with McAdoo over what he perceived as the Treasury Department's refusal to timely comply with the governing statute to the detriment of the army's morale. In a letter to McAdoo, Baker complained of "exasperating delays by the Treasury Department" and noted that several congressmen were angry with the treatment of constituent families. However, within a month of Armistice, Carter Glass, one of Crowder's congressional allies, replaced McAdoo.[91]

A Virginia Democrat, Glass was elected to the House of Representatives in 1902 and served continuously as a congressman through December 16, 1918, when Wilson appointed him secretary of the treasury. By this time, the Judge Advocate General's Office had consistently battled with the Treasury Department over the prompt payment of War Risk Insurance to beneficiaries. Several treasury agents had insisted that beneficiaries were required to prove their financial dependency on a deceased soldier or sailor, even though the War Risk Insurance Act did not require dependency as a prerequisite for receipt of insurance payments. One month after the Armistice, Crowder met with Glass to end the Treasury Department's noncompliance with the act. Two weeks later Glass sent a memorandum to all treasury agents informing them that the only proof required for receipt of insurance payments was a copy of the signed policy, which was already in the possession of both the War and Treasury Departments. He also pushed for the appointment of Henry D. Lindsley as the Treasury Department's War Risk Insurance director. Linsdley had served under Pershing as a liaison to the Treasury Department during the war, and Crowder welcomed his appointment to oversee payments to beneficiaries.[92]

Crowder's meeting with Glass had its roots in a joint effort with Senator La Follette to convince McAdoo to more closely oversee the Treasury Department's War Risk Insurance responsibilities. Although La Follette was against the nation entering the war and opposed Selective Service, in May 1917 he sought to protect servicemen and their families by introducing a bill to expand the War Risk Insurance Act to all servicemen brought on active duty and to make the act retroactive to April 6. La Follette also drafted the act to continue until two years after the cessation of hostilities. After La Follette's draft bill became law, it enabled injured servicemen or their survivors to receive $5,000 in various payment forms from the government. Crowder enthusiastically supported La Follette's efforts to protect servicemen as well as to keep private insurance companies out of the War Department's operations. Both men did not trust the commercial insurance industry to treat servicemen fairly, and they agreed that the government had to guarantee financial protection to the millions of men and families affected by military service. In several instances, the Judge Advocate General's Office aligned with La Follette to inform the Treasury Department that it had wrongfully withheld insurance payments from rightful beneficiaries. In May 1918 Crowder endorsed a letter from La Follette to McAdoo, excoriating the Treasury Department for requiring beneficiaries to provide their insurance certificate before collecting any payments. "The certificate is merely evidence that the contract exists and you do not need to prove that you are the beneficiary named by the soldier or sailor, because this is already in the War Department's and the Treasury Department's possession," La Follette concluded.[93]

Senator M. Hoke Smith, a Georgia Democrat, and Congressman Asbury Francis Lever also aligned with the Judge Advocate General's Office in criticizing McAdoo's performance. In October 1919, Smith informed Crowder that a widow, whose husband was killed in the Spanish-American War, had also outlived her son, who had been killed in France in late 1917. Even though she was the named beneficiary on the insurance form, the Treasury Department denied her claim because she was not listed as a dependent. As a lawyer, Smith knew that the Treasury Department had failed to comply with the law but needed Crowder's assistance because, as he complained to Crowder, McAdoo was unresponsive. In January 1918, Lever asked the Judge Advocate General's Office for assistance in ensuring that War Risk Insurance payments were provided to named beneficiaries and that the parents and children of deceased soldiers did not have to prove to the Treasury Department that they were also the dependents of the deceased or injured soldier. Lever, with Crowder's help, drafted a memorandum to Glass and complained that "despite the plain language of the statute, McAdoo had ignored that dependency—that is persons who relied on the soldier's salary for their existence—was not a requirement under the law to be classified as a beneficiary." A beneficiary, they insisted, was merely a person designated by a soldier, and therefore entitled to receive insurance payments after death or a significant injury. Glass promised Lever and Crowder that he agreed with their position and ordered treasury agents to comply. As a result, thousands of citizens received insurance payments at a quicker distribution rate, and thousands who would not have received their lawful insurance payments at all were ultimately paid under Glass's stewardship. However, through 1920, there remained a backlog of claims because of what Crowder and Glass believed to be the Treasury Department's bureaucracy under McAdoo.[94]

Even though in December 1918 Glass and Crowder had come to an agreement on accelerating the process to enable named beneficiaries to receive insurance payments, a large number of citizens were still caught in a gridlock a year after the Armistice, resulting in other legislators aligning with the Judge Advocate General's Office. The experience of Congressman Wallace H. White, a Maine Republican, is a case in point. From January 1, 1919, through the end of April of that year, he and the Judge Advocate General's Office worked on thirty-seven "war widow's claims." In each of these cases, the Treasury Department yielded to Crowder and paid the beneficiaries. However, in one of the cases, a lawyer representing a deceased soldier's wife asked White to "get a good sized hatpin and insert it in the most delicate part of the anatomy of someone so that she can get results before death relieves her of her misery." Lieutenant Colonel Cassius Dowell, who had returned from France, responded on behalf of Crowder that he agreed with the lawyer's proposed course of action.[95]

If one congressman received thirty-seven complaints regarding insurance claims in a four-month period, then it is not difficult to extrapolate that thousands of complaints arising from uncontested insurance claims flooded Congress and the Judge Advocate General's Office. These complaints, however, were easy to solve because of the type of proof required. A more difficult issue arose when a person not named as a beneficiary claimed the insurance payments. For instance, Private Edmund J. Arsenault was conscripted into the army in August 1917 and killed in France in August 1918. Arsenault listed payments of twenty dollars per month to his mother and five dollars per month to his sister. Shortly before being shipped to France, Arsenault married and, perhaps unbeknownst to him, fathered a child. Not surprisingly his wife claimed a right to the insurance payments. But Arsenault never listed his wife on the War Risk Insurance policy and, after reading Dowell's legal analysis, White concluded that the wife's support was contingent on the charity of the beneficiaries. Crowder reluctantly agreed with White.[96]

A more difficult problem arose for Crowder and White in the appeal of the mother of Vaughn Ramsdell, who enlisted in the army under the false name of Vernon Roberts at the age of fifteen. Ramsdell listed "my mother Charlotte Roberts" as his beneficiary. The only accurate part of his enlistment papers was the emergency notification form that listed Ms. Ethel Palmer of Bangor, Maine, as his sister. Sadly, Ramsdell was killed in the closing days of the war, and he had never placed his widowed mother's name on an insurance statement, in all likelihood fearing that he would be discharged. He had, however, mailed his mother money during his service in France, and he was her sole source of support. Complicating this issue was the fact that "there were two Vaughn Ramsdells in the Army." It took Dowell eight months to convince the Treasury Department that the term "my mother" could suffice alone, and it was not unlawful to disregard the false name of Charlotte Roberts.[97]

Crowder, on occasion, acted without regard to Congress over the disbursement of payments. In January 1918, Baker, at Crowder's urging, issued an order that would deny War Risk Insurance payments to soldiers who died while in a desertion status. However, he did not try to stop the payments to beneficiaries when a soldier died in an army prison. Congress had not expressly approved of War Risk Insurance payments arising from the death or injury of imprisoned soldiers, even though soldiers imprisoned as a result of a court-martial were not eligible to receive pay. Prior to his shipment to France, Major Samuel Wilson pointed out to Congressman Alben Barkley, a future vice president, that the War Risk Insurance Act could be coupled with the statutory prohibition against pay to imprisoned soldiers to deny beneficiaries. Barkley, in turn, advised Crowder that in the absence of Congress acting to clarify payments in such instances, the judge advocate general was free to make his own determination. But Crowder adopted the position that imprisoned soldiers were still protected by the act.[98]

Perhaps the judge advocate general's oddest experience with Congress over the War Risk Insurance Act had to do with Senator Poindexter. After the fall of the Tsarist government, the War Department contracted with the Russian Railway Corps, a part of the Russian Army loyal to Kerensky, to transport armaments to pro-Allied forces in Russia. In October 1918, after receiving letters complaining that the officers were underpaid, Poindexter introduced a bill to the Senate that would extend the act's coverage to the Railway Corps' officers. Some of the officers were American citizens who volunteered to travel to Russia, but these officers were not subject to the Articles of War. Both Secretary of State Lansing and Crowder opposed the extension because it would make the United States liable to foreign individuals as well as Americans who were not subject to the Articles of War. By this time, Poindexter had fixated on Bolshevism, to include accusing Brandeis of being a Bolshevist, and he wanted to use the act to increase morale in the Russian officer corps. Although Crowder conveyed to Poindexter that the extension "would result in the misallocation of funds and be an unprecedented obligation," the senator continued to push for it.

In response to Poindexter's intransigence, Lansing and Wigmore convinced Chamberlain, as well as Republican stalwarts John Weeks, James Wadsworth, and Henry Cabot Lodge, to quash Poindexter's bill.[99]

War Risk Insurance was only one matter outside of military justice that brought the Judge Advocate General's Office into frequent contact with Congress. Once the war began, large numbers of citizens sought officer commissions, including persons who had previously been commissioned or served in an auxiliary military force. Between 1901 and the entry of the United States into the war, the War Department maintained a quasi-army known as the Philippine Scouts. This force was officered by Americans who left the army to remain in the Philippines, although several of the Scouts' officers had served as sergeants in the regular army, and the promise of better pay and status were the reason for the transfer. After the declaration of war, many of these officers attempted to be commissioned into the army. In early May 1917, Colonel Dunn advised Congressman Charles Manly Stedman that a transfer from the Philippine Scouts to the army without a physical and written examination was illegal in all cases. Stedman, a North Carolina Democrat and Civil War veteran, sought Crowder's intervention. Crowder not only negated Dunn's advice, he advised Baker that the War Department could transfer scouts' officers who previously held a commission in the regular army back into the regular army, and the former noncommissioned army officers could be given preference for commissions. Baker concurred with Crowder.[100]

On occasion, the Judge Advocate General's Office served as an ambassador between the State Department and Congress, particularly where alien residents had served in the army. In April 1916, Fritz—or Frederick—Reichers, a Missouri resident, traveled to Germany to see his sister after his nephew had been killed fighting in the German Army at Verdun. After the United States' entry into the war, Reichers attempted to return to Missouri through the Netherlands, but he was denied entry. He also discovered that his wife, who had remained behind in Missouri, had ceased receiving his veterans' pension. Reichers was an eighty-year-old man who emigrated to the United States as a child, enlisted in the Union army, and fought at both Vicksburg and during General Sherman's "March to the Sea." While in Germany, he discovered that the Justice Department considered him "an enemy subject" and caused his military pension to cease, even though there was no evidence of his being disloyal to the United States. Speaker of the House of Representatives James "Champ" Clark worked to have Reichers returned to the United States and his pension restored but was initially unable to do so. Colonel James Mayes provided evidence of Reichers's loyalty to the Justice and State Departments, and on July 9, 1917, he was permitted to return to Missouri.[101]

Crowder had urged Congressman Julius Kahn and Senator Henry Cabot Lodge not to amend the Selective Service Act of 1917 to permit the furloughing of agricultural labor. Congress nonetheless amended the act in 1918 to permit commanding officers to temporarily release soldiers who had completed training to return to farm work until their shipment to France or assignment to a stateside installation. But the Judge Advocate General's Office and Provost Marshal's Office interceded on behalf of furlough applicants. On April 24, 1918, Congressman Henry De La Warr Flood of Virginia asked Crowder for his assistance in obtaining furloughs for several hundred applicants at Camp Lee in Virginia. Major General Adelbert Cronkhite, the Eightieth Division's commanding general, had earlier informed Flood that he lacked the authority to grant furloughs. Given that the division was populated with over nine thousand Virginians, it is understandable that Flood took an interest in the agricultural conditions of his state. Crowder quickly responded to Flood and informed Cronkhite that he had the lawful authority to grant month-long furloughs before the Eightieth Division shipped to France. However, he also cautioned Flood that the soldiers would be considered AWOL if they failed to return.[102]

For several decades, but particularly during Wilson's presidency, the Executive Branch had tried to prevent the military establishment from campaigning for political causes. In August 1919, Congressman Cordell Hull asked if Sergeant Alvin C. York, a military hero who earned a Medal of Honor, could stand beside him as he campaigned in support of the United States joining the League of Nations. Crowder supported Wilson on joining the League and believed that collective security was essential to prevent both a resurgent Germany and a global Bolshevik revolution. Nonetheless, he informed Hull that York could not appear in uniform at a political event because to do so would violate the prohibition against political activities. Crowder recognized that York could persuade people in Tennessee and Kentucky to support Wilson, and his visible presence in national rallies would present Republican opponents of the League such as Senator Henry Cabot Lodge with difficulties in arguing that an international agreement was un-American. But York's presence would run afoul of the requirement for an apolitical military.[103]

With the exception of Senator Chamberlain's efforts to drastically change courts-martial procedure, one of the most significant legislative interactions with the Judge Advocate General's Office to occur after the Armistice arose as a result of the prison scandal in France. On June 19, 1919, a House Military Affairs subcommittee opened an investigation into the treatment of American soldiers confined in army prisons in France. The subcommittee was, in reality, part of a larger House of Representatives investigation into the War Department's expenditures from 1917 to 1919, and it determined that the War Department had not safeguarded the nation's finances in a number of significant areas such as food distribution. By the time the subcommittee was formed, the Republicans had established a majority in the House of Representatives. This fact did not distress Crowder. He believed that Winship and Bethel would be able to present the War Department's actions in court-martialing the guilty prison guards as proof that the prison scandal had not been "whitewashed." However, Crowder was disturbed that the Republican majority hired Ansell, who by this time was a civilian, as the subcommittee's legal counsel and Ansell would then be in a position to question Kreger, Winship, or any other person called to testify.[104]

Headed by Congressman Royal Cleaves Johnson, a South Dakota Republican who served as an infantry officer during the Meuse-Argonne Offensive, the subcommittee traveled to France in April 1919 to investigate not only the prisoner abuse claims but also American payments to the French government. After Johnson voted against declaring war on Germany in 1917, he enlisted in the army and was commissioned shortly afterward. He was incensed not only over what he considered too small a number of courts-martial, but also grants of clemency to the commissioned offenders of the scandal. Congressmen Oscar Bland, an Indiana Republican, and Henry Flood joined Johnson. Flood later criticized Johnson for exaggerating the prison conditions after Johnson claimed the Paris prisons were worse than the notorious Andersonville Prison during the Civil War. But Johnson had the credibility of being a recently discharged officer who served on the Western Front, and he had earned both the Distinguished Service Cross and the French Croix de Guerre. In February 1919, Johnson accused Pershing of refusing to send general courts-martial records to the Judge Advocate General's Office for review and revision. He also excoriated the oversight of courts-martial in the Southern Department. Although Johnson was not necessarily allied with Chamberlain at the time of his accusations, he later supported the senator's investigation into courts-martial. But Johnson caused two impediments to the prison scandal investigation. The first was that he hired Ansell after Ansell had publicly attacked the fairness of courts-martial and accused Baker and Crowder of being dishonest. Flood and Bland criticized Ansell's hiring because the former acting judge advocate general had alienated the army's leadership, to include calling several senior generals "jokes." For one other reason, Johnson was unlikely to gain any support from the Executive Branch. He had accused Wilson of permitting his cabinet members to secure safe duties for their sons far away from the front lines.[105]

Johnson ordered both General Peyton March and Colonel Winship to testify to the committee. One of the aspects of Congress's investigation of prisoner abuse that neither March nor Winship could satisfactorily answer was why only junior lieutenants and noncommissioned officers were brought to trial. Congressman Bland poignantly queried whether the army had scapegoated the lower ranks and given senior officers immunity from prosecution. Additionally, Ansell questioned March as to the ability of enlisted soldiers to complain about the conduct of superior officers not only in military prisons but also as to the fairness of the courts-martial.[106]

On July 29, "Hard-Boiled" Smith tried to defend himself to Johnson's committee by arguing his chain of command approved of his actions. He noted that he had enlisted in the Arizona National Guard in 1913, served on the Mexican border in 1915, and then was commissioned as a lieutenant in early 1916. He complained that the army never prepared him to command military policemen in charge of a prison and claimed that Colonel Grinstead regularly visited the prison farm and that the farm operated under his orders, including "the most ruthless kind of discipline." Most troubling, Smith informed the committee that even if Prison Farm no. 2 was an appalling facility, it was "a pleasure resort compared to other prisons in France."[107]

On September 8, 1919, Winship testified that while he believed Grinstead should have been court-martialed, he advised Harbord that the available evidence was not sufficient to sustain serious charges against him. While Winship agreed with Johnson that Grinstead, and for that matter two general officers above him, had a duty to investigate prisons and hospitals, it would be difficult to prove that the senior officers had failed to do so as a dereliction. While Winship's reasoning did not fully mollify Flood, the subcommittee had its attentions diverted by other matters, including campaigning both for and against the nation joining the League of Nations. Moreover, Flood accused Johnson and Bland of wasting the subcommittee's resources for political gain and pointed out that of the over four thousand pages the subcommittee generated, less than one thousand were actually dedicated to expenditures. Johnson, for his part, had already moved on toward recommending major overhauls in the army's disciplinary processes and did not respond to Flood. Bland, on the other hand, defended the investigation into the prison conditions as a necessary function "of enforcing accountability to the Congress."[108]

CONCLUSION: THE CONGRESSIONAL ALLIANCE

It is unlikely that Crowder and his subordinates intended to enter into an alliance with members of Congress against Secretary of the Treasury McAdoo, but he believed it necessary to ensure that the beneficiaries of deceased servicemen were promptly paid as a matter of maintaining morale and discipline in the ranks. In matters of military justice or administrative issues, the Judge Advocate General's Office often agreed with congressmen over specified issues or cases, but Crowder seldom considered these agreements to be permanent. Most importantly, Crowder and his subordinates enjoyed good relations with many legislators, even those such as La Follette who voted against the nation's entry into the war. On the whole, there was very little legislative call for an alteration in the practice and procedure of courts-martial during the war. And Congress's trust in Crowder did not diminish despite the significant alteration of civil and military relations that had occurred.

Following the war, Senator Chamberlain and Congressman Johnson would press for dramatic changes in courts-martial procedure, including expanding the judge advocate general's authority to a level above that of commanding generals who convened courts-martial and second only to that of the secretary of war. Crowder opposed this expansion and for differing reasons, the majority of legislators would side with him. One reason, already noted, had to do with the fear of a renewed war coupled with the belief that the nation's military law construct had been instrumental in shaping a disciplined army to defeat the strongest land power in the world at the time. But added to this reason was the fact that throughout the war, the Judge Advocate General's Office was responsive to Congress, and even when individual congressmen could not obtain relief for their clients, the disagreement usually ended with little residual effect in the relationship between the office and Congress.

7

COURTS-MARTIAL, CONCERNS OVER

SUBVERSION, AND CONSCIENTIOUS OBJECTION

IN 1913 THE ARMY COURT-MARTIALED Private Waldo Coffman and four other soldiers for making seditious statements. After being found guilty, Coffman was sentenced to two years in confinement and a dishonorable discharge. While stationed at Fort Stevens in Oregon, he preached support for the IWW to his fellow soldiers, and he advocated for a soldiers' labor union. He also published an editorial in *Appeal to Reason*, a socialist-oriented newspaper, describing his desire to "stir up trouble in the ranks." During Coffman's trial, the body of a key prosecution witness was found floating in Grays Harbor, Washington. The witness was likely murdered to stifle testimony against Coffman and the four other soldiers. Three other soldiers that the trial judge advocate expected to testify against Coffman deserted. Perhaps believing that Coffman's offenses were not too serious a threat to the army's discipline, Secretary of War Garrison, on Crowder's advice, reduced Coffman's sentence to one year but kept intact the dishonorable discharge. Crowder advised Garrison that because Coffman was in confinement at the time the witness was killed, he could not be held responsible for the murder, and that IWW leader William Dudley Haywood's followers were likely responsible without any prodding from Coffman. Haywood had been instrumental in founding the IWW, and in 1905 future senator William Borah and other Idaho officials prosecuted him for murdering a former state governor. However, noted defense attorney Clarence Darrow was able to prove that the government's main witnesses against Haywood committed perjury, and his trial resulted in an acquittal.[1]

Newspapermen reported Coffman's court-martial across the northwestern states. Unions passed resolutions supporting him and claimed that Garrison's act of freeing him prevented a challenge in federal court under a writ of habeas. In 1913 Kansas senator William Thompson argued to Garrison that Coffman was innocent of attempting to spread mutiny or subversion in the ranks. Senator Miles Poindexter of Washington, who was later to become an outspoken anti-Bolshevik, joined Thompson in urging the War Department to reverse the court-martial. Thompson claimed to have known Coffman's parents for several years and openly vouched for Coffman in the Senate. Because Kansas state law, like its federal counterpart, stripped Coffman of the right to vote, Thompson further lobbied the War Department to exonerate him. Although Garrison was unwilling to remove the dishonorable discharge or overturn the conviction, he further reduced Coffman's imprisonment to time served and recommended that Thompson work with Crowder to restore Coffman's citizenship. On December 12, 1913, Crowder advised Thompson that the best means to restore Coffman's citizenship was through a legislative act for Coffman's relief, and while he did not support restoring Coffman to duty, he drafted the bill for Thompson to introduce in the Senate. By this time, one of the other soldiers was acquitted and the three remaining soldiers were sentenced to six months in confinement. None of the three other convicted soldiers was dishonorably discharged, and as a result they were permitted to remain in the army. On August 7, 1914, Senator George Chamberlain, the chairman of the Senate Military Affairs Committee, convinced Congress to enact Crowder's draft bill for Coffman's relief, elevating him to an honorable discharge.[2]

In 1916 John Reed, a contributing author to *The Masses*, a socialist magazine, described Coffman's court-martial as "an exercise in tyranny." He went on to label all army courts-martial as "the most shocking example of injustice and tyranny in America." Despite Reed's characterization of the army's peacetime courts-martial, in comparison to the wartime courts-martial of soldiers convicted of subversion, espionage, or mutiny, Coffman's sentence was lenient, and the fact that one of his peers was acquitted evidenced that "guilt by association" was absent from at least one prewar court-martial. In contrast, in July 1919 a general court-martial found a soldier guilty of sedition and sentenced him to be shot to death, but Wilson disapproved the sentence and instructed Baker to reassess the sentence to a term of imprisonment. Baker, in turn, reduced the sentence to five years in prison. The soldier, along with 138 of his peers during the war, was found guilty of making disloyal statements to his fellow soldiers with the intent to incite mutiny. After April 5, 1917, the

army dealt harshly with soldiers accused of sedition, and the sentences of soldiers convicted of this offense ranged from ninety-nine years in confinement
to one year.[3]

Even soldiers acquitted of subversion-type offenses were not necessarily
safe from later imprisonment or harsh discipline. In the trial of Americo V.
Alexander, an enlisted soldier who received conscientious objector status
and was assigned to noncombatant hospital duty, the court-martial heard
evidence that prior to the war Alexander had been an "active participant" in
New Jersey's Socialist Party. Assigned to an army hospital near Philadelphia,
Alexander apparently impressed his commander, who recommended him for
a commission. Alexander declined the promotion, responding that he welcomed serving in the trenches as a stretcher bearer but opposed the killing of
anyone or the supervision of others who were charged with the duty of killing.
While at an opera, another patron overheard a conversation between Alexander and his wife and inquired as to how he became a conscientious objector.
The patron was, in fact, an army agent and informed the Camp Dix commander that Alexander had sown dissension and was a subversive. Charged
under the Ninety-Sixth Article of War for encouraging and counseling others
to avoid duty as well as soliciting others to undermine military discipline,
Alexander was court-martialed. However, he was found not guilty and set free.

Alexander's experience of being accused of disloyalty did not end with his
acquittal. After his initial arrest, a captain alleged that he had acted disrespect-
fully toward commissioned officers and refused to clean the military police
stables after being ordered to do so. Such "fatigue duty" may or may not have
been legitimate. Considering his hospital orderly position, the duty may also
well have been punitive. Found guilty of three specifications of disrespect to
officers, in a second court-martial Alexander was sentenced to twenty years'
imprisonment. Alexander sought Senator Borah's help, and Borah agreed that
at the least, the sentence was disproportionate to the offenses. As part of his
appeal to Borah, Alexander provided a section of a transcript in which the
aggrieved officer and trial judge advocate alluded to his socialist ties. Borah,
in turn, urged Crowder to advise Baker to lessen Alexander's sentence. Ultimately Baker reduced the sentence to one year in prison.[4]

Just as Borah's criticisms of the fairness of courts-martial contradicted his
earlier support of Theodore Roosevelt over the president's act of discharg-
ing African American soldiers, his support of Alexander was contrary to his
earlier positions on socialism. When he ran for office, Borah's opposition to
socialism was well known because he had campaigned against it as a foreign
influence. Borah's biographer John Vinson explained that by 1917, the senator
developed a desire to protect the freedom of speech rights of socialists and

labor unions. During the war, many legislators were not as inclined to advocate for soldiers accused of disloyalty as was Borah. However, Hiram Johnson, Robert La Follette, and several congressmen were willing to do so.[5]

Professor Roy Talbert, in his *Negative Intelligence: The Army and the American Left, 1917–1941*, persuasively argues that because it was essential to achieve stability in the manufacturing, mining, and timber industries, particularly in the coal and copper fields, there was a heightened fear in the War Department of organizations such as the IWW, which had led strikes in these industries prior to the war. Taking Professor Talbert's thesis one further step, the fact that judge advocates such as George Wallace, Cleon Berntheizel, and Samuel Pepper had, as national guard judge advocates, taken part in the suppression of strikes prior to 1916 made it more likely that a soldier's suspected affiliation with the IWW or other so-called radical labor organizations caused heightened scrutiny into the soldier's activities while in training and on duty in Europe. It then became more likely that a soldier would face a court-martial or other difficulties for criticizing the war.[6]

Yet notwithstanding Professor Talbert's thesis as well as anecdotal examples such as Private Alexander's experience, or for that matter the disciplinary experiences of hundreds of other soldiers, the army did not always vigorously prosecute or punish soldiers suspected of disloyalty or subversion. While serving as a trial judge advocate in France, Captain E. Barrett Prettyman recorded his impressions in his diary after a commanding officer reversed a court-martial against a procommunist soldier who had been convicted of mutiny: "Sunday—Sept 8, 1918: Oh yes, Capt Mullen told me that the Malekovich case, my first case, the Bolshevik was set aside because the commanding general did not think that it was evident beyond a reasonable doubt, but there was no criticism of my conduct of the case, and even bolshies deserve fair process." Private Malekovich had been caught with a pamphlet authored by Emma Goldman and Alexander Berkman and was charged with inciting a mutiny. A general court-martial convicted him and sentenced him to a dishonorable discharge and five years in confinement. However, on the advice of the divisional judge advocate, the commanding general determined that Malekovich had not attempted to undermine discipline.[7]

THE EXPERIENCE OF WAR AND THE TRIPLE FEAR: THE IWW, BOLSHEVISM, AND GERMANY

On August 1, 1916, Congressman Edwin Y. Webb, the chairman of the House Judiciary Committee and a North Carolina Democrat elected in 1902, asked Secretary of War Baker whether the nation's laws were sufficient for the War Department "to protect against the publication of certain information which may be inconsistent with the defense of the country or the preservation of peace therein." Baker responded to Webb that the judge advocate general and the General Staff had crafted proposed legislation "to guard against elements undermining the national defense." He also added that Crowder had advised him that "the constitutional prohibition against laws abridging freedom of speech and of the press is not violated by a statute making punishable the publication of information which the safety of the nation requires should not be disclosed." While Crowder's reasoning was not necessarily original, because the government severely limited freedom of the press six decades earlier during the Civil War, his advice to Baker showed that, along with the General Staff, he believed that the War Department needed to possess the authority to restrict newspaper access to military installations and have the Justice Department vigorously prosecute persons who published secretive information on the movement and training of forces.[8]

Two months prior to the declaration of war on Germany, Frankfurter discussed with Baker a possible judicial response to the War Department's censorship of mail and newspapers. Both men agreed that the War Department should have no role in censoring nonmilitary mail but should instead advise the postmaster general and attorney general of the need for an official censorship office within either department. However, Frankfurter also informed Baker that Justice Brandeis had indicated he would support a War Department censorship program. At almost the same time, Crowder instructed Frankfurter and Wambaugh to author a detailed analysis of the United Kingdom's Defense of the Realm Act to see whether he should lobby Congress to adopt similar measures to combat and prosecute espionage. On April 3, 1917, Baker asked Frankfurter to meet with Samuel Gompers, the president of the American Federation of Labor, so that if war occurred, strikes and labor stoppages could be avoided. There is nothing surprising in Frankfurter's conduct. He had been aligned with Brandeis for over a decade and selected the justice's clerks. In retrospect, Frankfurter's mission between Brandeis (the Court's leading liberal) and the War Department, prior to the declaration of war, evidences how greatly Baker and other senior War Department officers feared the prospect of espionage and subversion before the declaration of war and how much they wanted to be confident that the judiciary would not curtail their efforts.[9]

One day before President Wilson asked Congress to declare war, Major General Thomas Barry, the commanding general of the Central Division, met with Guy D. Goff in Milwaukee. Goff was, at the time, serving as a special prosecutor for Attorney General Gregory, but he was also investigating

German espionage activities in the United States. Goff advised Barry that Captain Franz Von Papen had placed at least seven agents in Milwaukee to recruit German immigrants to destroy critical steel and shipping industries in case of war with Germany. Goff had also discovered that there were over a dozen German naval reservists and retired officers in Wisconsin who likewise posed a danger to the nation's security.[10]

On June 15, 1917, President Wilson signed the Espionage Act into law. The law was designed to punish persons who interfered with conscription, military training, or the deployment of forces overseas. The use of a federal law to prohibit a citizen from aiding a foreign government was fairly new to the United States. In 1911 President Taft signed into law a "Defense Secrets Act," which enabled prosecutions of persons accused of divulging military secrets to foreign governments. However, prior to 1917 there were no prosecutions under the 1911 act, and the conduct prohibited by that act had to do with providing military information to foreign entities rather than a broader prohibition against speech that the attorney general determined aided an enemy nation. In 1907 the Supreme Court in *Patterson v. Colorado* decided that neither the First nor Fourteenth Amendments t prohibited a state from prosecuting a newspaper editor who criticized the state supreme court. The law in question in *Patterson* was a state law, and generally, the First Amendment was believed to prohibit only the federal government from restraining speech. Crowder, however, believed that *Patterson* could serve as a basis to prosecute antiwar speech, just as it could be enforced to prevent public criticism of a state supreme court. He assigned Major J. Reuben Clark to assist Attorney General Gregory in developing a framework to prosecute persons who encouraged citizens to resist complying with induction orders and draft registration requirements. From that point forward the War Department's influence spread to multiple prosecutions of civilians in federal court.[11]

In prior conflicts, particularly during the Civil War, free speech protections eroded, and celebrated prosecutions such as the military trial of a former congressman named Clement Vallandigham evidenced that the federal judiciary could be tolerant of the Executive Branch prosecuting citizens in military trials who advocated against the nation's war efforts. By 1919 the federal government had arrested over two thousand citizens for suspected violations of the Espionage Act, but the Justice Department was primarily responsible for these arrests, even though the War Department provided intelligence on citizens and residents to the attorney general. The Espionage Act was controversial, and progressive congressmen such as Borah, La Follette, Johnson in the Senate, and Clark and Kitchin in the House of Representatives opposed it. A poignant example of how Baker and Crowder regarded congressional opposition to the Espionage Act lay in their responses to Senator Charles Thomas and Representative Edward Keating. Both Colorado legislators tied their opposition to the Espionage Act to their earlier fight against conscription. In early 1917 Thomas and Keating failed to convince Congress that citizens had to be afforded the right of conscientious objection based on individual belief rather than having to prove adherence to a religious denomination such as the Quakers or the "Bible Student Movement," the forerunner of the Jehovah's Witnesses. They also unsuccessfully advocated that political objection to the war had to be considered a viable exemption from conscripted military service. Crowder argued to Republican conservative stalwarts Senator Francis E. Warren of Wyoming and Henry Cabot Lodge of Massachusetts that if Thomas and Keating succeeded in expanding the basis for conscientious objection, the government would be significantly limited in using the Espionage Act to prosecute citizens. Baker raised a similar argument to Democrats John Sharp Williams and Lee Slater Overman. In the end, the Espionage Act became law, the federal government vigorously enforced it, and often judge advocates assisted federal law enforcement to do so. On occasion, judge advocates also assisted state prosecutions under the various state antisyndicalism laws. Whether by intent or unintended consequence, the Espionage Act brought the army closer to serving as a domestic police force than at any time since Reconstruction.[12]

On the other hand, there were instances where judge advocates intervened to prevent prosecutions as well as other injustices under the Espionage Act. For instance, on January 4, 1919, Captain John B. Campbell, an acting judge advocate, informed George Albert Carpenter, a district court judge for the Northern District of Illinois, that the Military Intelligence Branch had investigated Privates Danow Orlovsky and Eduardo Paredes and in his duties as a judge advocate, he concluded that neither soldier had committed any offenses chargeable under the Articles of War and therefore should be naturalized. The American Protective League, a private organization that intruded into the lives of citizens, had alleged that both men consorted with pro-Bolshevists. In reality the two soldiers had attended a meeting to raise money to advise Russian immigrants who were erroneously inducted so that these immigrants could appeal their mandatory military service. Another judge advocate, Captain Edwin P. Grosvenor, informed Brigadier General M. Churchill, the army's acting chief of intelligence, "that no violation of any of the provisions of the Selective Service Act is made out. An offer to help Russian citizens erroneously inducted is not unlawful, particularly when the papers show that there was not any attempt to evade the draft, but merely an effort to advise ignorant aliens of the rights accorded to them by the law.[13]

Since the Civil War, the Judge Advocate General's Office had developed a legal doctrine for instances when the president or secretary of war ordered the army to be used as a police force after a declaration of martial law during an insurrection or in response to other emergencies such as the San Francisco earthquake. Usually, judge advocates advised the secretary of war and the commanding officers of geographic divisions that while the army could be used to protect citizens and property, it could not be used to enforce the labor laws governing union organization. For instance, in 1899 General Lieber advised Secretary of War Alger that "the Army must have nothing to do with enforcing rules for the government of miners unions. That is a matter for local authorities to deal with." In 1919 Crowder opposed the use of uniformed soldiers and sailors to break strikes in Seattle and Boston, even though he feared that IWW members had tried to infiltrate the army to cause a mutiny during the strike. Four days after the declaration of war, Senator Thomas Walsh of Montana asked Baker to delay the federalization of national guardsmen so that they could be used to suppress an IWW strike in the Montana lumber fields. Walsh believed that the IWW would try to undermine the nation's war efforts, and Crowder informed Baker that the belated appearance of the guardsman would not affect the army's training timetable. Moreover, Crowder advised that it was preferable not to have the guardsman conduct suppression duties after they were federalized. When Arizona senator Henry Ashurst claimed in August 1917 that the IWW's initials stood for "Imperial Wilhelm's Warriors," Crowder and Ansell agreed with Ashurst that the union's leadership had indirectly aligned with Germany to prevent the country from prosecuting the war, just as the German government had used Vladimir Lenin to remove Russia from the war.[14]

Although the period 1917 to 1920 may well have been the height of the suppression of civil liberties in the United States, there was never a declaration of nationwide martial law. President Wilson, cabinet members, and senior War Department leaders were convinced that there was a foreign threat to the nation, not only as a result of German espionage and spying but also from the IWW, communist, anarchist, and socialist organizations, which they believed received support from Germany or acted independently. On April 14, 1917, President Wilson created the Committee on Public Information to relay to the public the justification for entering the war as well as to counter antiwar publications. He selected newspaper editor George Creel to head this committee. Much of the committee's efforts were spent on countering and censoring IWW, socialist, and communist organizations. In the summer of 1917, Creel warned the country that an unnatural alliance between Imperial Germany and Bolshevism plotted against the United States. He wanted to increase prosecutions under the Espionage Act and conveyed to Wilson that "disloyal newspapers" would sow dissension in the ranks. Crowder mostly agreed with Creel's assessment, though he did not approve of several of the draconian measures taken against suspected persons during the war.[15]

There were three interrelated reasons for Baker and other senior War Department officers' fears of espionage and subversion. Crowder—and for that matter the judge advocates attached to his staff—shared in these fears. The first of these had to do with the conduct of the IWW's leaders as well as prominent anarchists. At first glance it might appear that because the IWW had no alignment with Germany, there was little reason to investigate IWW subversion in the ranks as part of a German war operation. But the IWW along with "radical" organizations had campaigned against the United States entering the war, and in 1914 a number of similar organizations in France and Britain urged against going to war. There were similarities in the antiwar rhetoric among the war's transatlantic opponents. Without the context of the five decades prior to the United States' entry into the war, it is impossible to analyze how the War Department conducted its internal security policies, or for that matter, how the Executive Branch utilized its nationwide law enforcement functions. Within a decade of the end of the Civil War, violent strikes became commonplace throughout the industrial states. In 1886 during the "Haymarket Strike," a bomb killed seven policemen, and several anarchists were prosecuted for the act. Contemporaneously a strike occurred in Wisconsin, and on the orders of the state governor, the militia fired into the strikers, killing seven. In the 1890s labor demonstrations resulted in violent riots in Cleveland, Pittsburgh, and Chicago. The IWW was not yet in existence, but in 1905 anarchists and a small number of labor union leaders formed that organization.[16]

In the decade before World War I, the IWW concentrated its efforts in both the western states and the industrial East. In 1911 the *Los Angeles Times* was bombed, and in 1913 the IWW initiated a large strike in the textile industries in Paterson, New Jersey. In 1915 a strike occurred at the Bayonne, New Jersey, refineries and seven strikers were killed. On July 22, 1916, a bomb exploded during a preparedness day parade in San Francisco, killing ten citizens. A trial devoid of due process convicted Thomas Mooney, a socialist who had been an IWW member, and his associate Warren K. Billings. On November 24, 1917, a bomb exploded in a Milwaukee Police building killing nine policemen, and although it appeared that a church was the original target, the police deaths were reported as being caused by anarchists. In 1920 a bomb exploded on Wall Street killing thirty people and injuring several hundred others, and while the IWW was not directly implicated in the bombing, its members remained suspected of the act. Crowder and Baker believed that the 1916 Preparedness Day bombing was proof that the IWW intended to foster mutiny in the army and wage a war within a war. In 1918 Frankfurter, who would later advise that Mooney and Billings were likely innocent, informed journalist Walter Lippman that the bombing itself caused the War Department to be convinced that there was "an enemy from within" that sought to use the war to topple the government by causing a mutiny in the ranks and a revolution at home. In October 1917, Crowder not only advised Baker that it would be worthwhile to lobby Congress to expand the federal criminal definition of treason to include radical strike organizers at armaments plants and in other industries supplying the military, he also wrote a pamphlet advocating the change for distribution to the draft boards.[17]

A second reason for fearing subversion from the IWW and other radical organizations had to do with the French and, to a lesser degree, the Italian and British experiences during the three years prior to the American entry into the war. After the Italian government allied with Britain, France, and Belgium against the Central powers in May 1915, one of their battleships, the *Benedetto Brin*, mysteriously blew up in its Brindisi harbor. Over four hundred sailors were killed. On August 2, 1916, another battleship, the *Leonardo da Vinci*, suffered a similar fate in the port of Taranto, and this time over two hundred sailors drowned. Although the Italian internal police later determined that Austrian agents plotted both acts, they were convinced that anarchists carried them out at the prodding of Austria. Crowder believed that German agents could convince anarchists or the IWW to carry out similar acts in the United States, or that the IWW, Bolsheviks, or anarchists would try to do so on their own.[18]

In April 1917, General Robert Nivelle, the commanding general of the French Army, committed his forces to a disastrous offensive in the Chemin des Dames, and within a month the French Army's discipline collapsed. In August 1917, Frankfurter informed Baker that the French people had learned that a number of French generals vociferously opposed Nivelle, and this fact became powerful propaganda to subversive groups. One month earlier, the United States Army's chief of engineers informed Bliss and the staff bureau heads that he witnessed French soldiers joining a strike in Paris, and the French government responded by bringing in a brigade of colonial soldiers "who could be relied on to shoot if the order was given." For a nation fighting desperately for its existence, a labor strike in any of France's industries was a concern. Yet if labor strikes in France were troubling, the French Army's condition after the "Nivelle Offensive" was of greater worry to the Allies. By May 1917, the French Army was unable to conduct any major offensive, and this inability was not simply because the French were short on equipment or soldiers. The French Army was plagued by a widespread mutiny.[19]

Prior to the outbreak of war in 1914, the French minister of the interior, Louis Malvy, with the assistance of the French War Ministry, established a list of persons to be arrested if a war with Germany occurred. The list, titled "Carnet B," contained two legislators and a number of radical socialists as well as others who were thought to harbor German allegiances. Malvy rather than the army was placed in charge of ordering the arrests, but he determined that it was not in the national interest to order any arrests after the German invasion. Miguel Almereyda, a young syndicalist who had been arrested and imprisoned for inciting French soldiers to mutiny in 1905 and again in 1908, and imprisoned for possessing explosives in 1901, was prominent on "Carnet B." Instead of arresting Almereyda, Malvy attempted to convince him to provide information on other subversives and support France's war efforts. Malvy was naïve in his assessment of Almereyda. In 1913 Almeryeda founded *Bonnet Rouge*, a socialist newspaper, and as the war continued the newspaper espoused pacifism and argued that while armaments manufacturers, investors, bankers, and merchants became wealthy, the working poor of France were being slaughtered in the trenches. For the first two years of the war, Malvy had the French treasury subsidize *Bonnet Rouge* as well as other socialist-oriented newspapers in an attempt to moderate their radicalism. Malvy's approach to the French press was problematic because the German government also secretly funded Almereyda's newspaper and other antiwar publications.[20]

Two months after the United States declared war on Germany, whole regiments in the French Army mutinied and refused to attack German positions. Almost half of the divisions in the French Army experienced refusals to "go over the top" as well as the formation of "soldiers' unions" that demanded senior officers promise to undertake no further offensives. Unlike in the Russian Revolution, there was never a wholesale attempt to overthrow the government, but the French mutinies occurred in tandem with labor strikes, and there was evidence that Bolshevik propaganda was used to appeal to the French working-class soldiers, particularly with the distribution of newspapers such as *Bonnet Rouge*. The French government ultimately arrested and prosecuted Almeryeda and several other writers.

Although Almereyda's *Bonnet Rouge* was not the only German-funded operation in France, the French government's response to it influenced the War Department's investigation and prosecution of American soldiers suspected of espionage and subversion because one of the newspaper's backers had operated in the United States. Another French citizen named Paul Bolo, operating as a German agent, channeled German money through Switzerland into *Bonnet Rouge* to ensure a wide distribution throughout the French Army. Bolo also established relationships with Joseph Caillaux, a former French premier, and several other French legislators. While there has been a debate as to what degree the horrific conditions of trench warfare, the high death and injury numbers that accompanied each offensive, distrust of the French Army's disciplinary system, or the infusion of defeatist and leftist propaganda into the ranks of soldiers caused the mutinies, senior French generals and the country's new premier, Georges Clemenceau, believed that propaganda was an underlying cause. Their fears of Germany's use of communist and pacifist organizations were not irrational.[21]

Caillaux was a prominent prewar radical socialist, and while he did not argue for measures similar to those advocated by the IWW or the Bolsheviks, he remained antiwar and he desired to return to the premiership. Prior to the war he espoused pro-German policies and was hostile to France's alliance with Britain. In early 1914 his wife murdered a critical newspaper editor and her trial, which resulted in an acquittal, was well reported throughout the United States. As Caillaux worked toward his return to France's highest office in 1916, he received support from Almereyda and Bolo. Indeed, the three men met on several occasions at Caillaux's home.[22]

War Department officials suspected Bolo's activities in the United States two years before the nation's entry into the war. In February 1914, Bolo traveled to Cuba and Florida and unsuccessfully attempted to dupe the J. P. Morgan Corporation into establishing a bank under his directorship. Morgan officials informed Secretary of the Treasury Robert Gibbs McAdoo that Bolo was a fraud who had spent his wife's income and tried to swindle wealthy Americans. Crowder concluded that while in Cuba, Bolo had intended to meet with anti-American and socialist leaders to foment strikes in the sugar fields to drive the price of sugar skyward. Both Britain and France imported Cuban sugar, and neither country's economy could tolerate an inflationary spiral in the price of imports. Because of Crowder's special relationship with the Cuban government, he was attuned to their internal police activities as well as the island's labor stability, and the Cuban police forced Bolo to leave the island. Shortly after departing Cuba, Bolo met with Abbas Himli Pasha, the deposed Egyptian khedive in Switzerland. The khedive was interested in removing British and French control over the Suez Canal, and he plotted to return to Egypt as its ruler after Bolo succeeded in causing an uprising to remove his British-supported uncle. The khedive provided Bolo with official credentials and monies to spread "pacifist and defeatist propaganda against Great Britain and France." Bolo returned to the United States to begin this work, and it was during this time that he attempted to develop a connection with the

Judge Advocate General's Department. In early 1916 a wounded French officer convalescing in San Francisco with his extended family introduced Bolo
to Major Hugh Bayne at a rally for Belgian and French orphans. After Bolo
was arrested, French officials discovered Bayne's name in an address book.
However, prior to the declaration of war, Bayne had informed military intelligence of his brief encounter with Bolo, and he told Crowder that Bolo was
interested in labor conditions in the United States. But because he observed
that Bolo "spent much of his time trying to impress women with lectures on
the subject of love," he wrongly underestimated the possibility that Bolo was
more dangerous than simply being "a fraud who presented little danger to the
national security."[23]

In early 1916 a conservative French senator named Charles Humbert
informed J. P. Morgan that Bolo had attempted to transfer over one million
francs into the senator's American account at J. P. Morgan in order to take over
a prowar newspaper. Humbert did not realize that Bolo intended to blackmail
him into publishing articles critical of the French government. Once more,
J. P. Morgan officers informed the Treasury Department of Bolo's activities.
In February of that year, Bolo traveled to New York and met with Ambassador Bernstorff and Adolph Pavenstadt, a wealthy German expatriate who, in
reality, helped fund clandestine German operations in the United States and
Mexico. Bolo also met with William Randolph Hearst, apparently under the
impression that the newspaper magnate was pro-German and could be relied
on to publish anti-British editorials as well as pro-German articles. Hearst,
however, notified the attorney general about Bolo's attempts to purchase his
paper. By the time Bolo left the United States, the War Department knew of
his meetings.[24]

War Department officials believed that Caillaux also had traveled to the
United States and Mexico in 1915 to create a political lobby to pressure France
to make peace with Germany. Had either Bolo or Caillaux reentered the
United States after the declaration of war, Crowder, with Baker's approval,
intended to have them tried as spies in a court-martial similar to Witzke's
trial. He assigned Colonel James Mayes to convey all intelligence files on
Bolo to the French government in May 1917. On February 3, 1917, the War
Department interned Pavenstadt, and on April 11, 1917, Crowder determined
to charge him with spying in a court-martial. However, Baker demurred and
Paventsadt remained interned until the end of the war. To Crowder's consternation, in early 1919 Pavenstadt was freed to return to Germany. In early 1918
Caillaux was accused of treason, prosecuted, and found guilty in the French
civil courts. Sentenced to three years in prison and expulsion from France for
five years, Caillaux was the highest ranking French politician to be convicted.

Malvy was also accused of treason, as were several lesser government officials. However, a criminal trial acquitted Malvy of wrongdoing, and several lesser persons were likewise acquitted. On the other hand, the French Army executed Bolo, and Almeryda died under mysterious circumstances in prison.[25]

American newspapers reported on the arrests of Caillaux, Malvy, Bolo, and Almeryda, although not on the trench mutinies. By April 1917, senior officers in the American Expeditionary Forces were well attuned to the problems caused by subversive propaganda in the French Army. For instance, General Hunter Liggett closely studied the trench mutiny of 1917 and accepted French intelligence reports that German agents had encouraged the spread of propaganda and subversion. He read *Bonnet Rouge*, believed that the execution of Bolo was justified, and wanted to ensure that the War Department would vigorously prosecute soldiers who spread antiwar literature. Pershing, March, and other line officers had similar fears. In addition to relying on intelligence officers, they turned to the Judge Advocate General's Office to ensure that there would be no American version of Almeryda or Bolo. In June 1917 Frankfurter reported to both Crowder and Secretary of Labor William Wilson that the trench mutinies "were caused by Caillaux's recrudescence" as well as Bolshevik propaganda and that French socialists would likely launch a nationwide strike if Caillaux were convicted.[26]

A third reason for suspecting an "enemy from within" had to do with the United States' changing population. In the Civil War, members of Lincoln's cabinet, notably Secretary of War Edwin Stanton and Brigadier General Joseph Holt, the judge advocate general of the army, believed that the existence of the Union was threatened by proslavery forces within the Union. Anticonscription riots and pro-Confederate groups, as well as Confederate raids and espionage campaigns into the Union, provided credence to their worries. Moreover, Confederate secretary of war Judah Benjamin oversaw Canadian-based espionage operations such as the arson of hotels and destruction of rail bridges in New York and Chicago. Notwithstanding strong Irish immigrant opposition to conscription during the Civil War, most "enemies from within" tended to be American by birth. The demographic changes in the United States between 1865 and 1917, however, made it more likely that if there were an "enemy from within," that enemy would be foreign-born or the offspring of immigrants. Moreover, American elites often considered socialism and anarchism to be foreign causes exported to the United States.[27]

In 1860 the United States' population was 31 million, but in 1910, it numbered almost 100 million. Of this number, 2.5 million Americans had been born in Germany, and over 5 million had at least one German parent. There were over five hundred German language newspapers as well. More numerous than the German-American population were the descendants of Irish immigrants as well as persons born in Ireland, many of whom migrated to the United States to leave British oppression. The US Army had a tradition of enlisting large numbers of immigrants from both the German states and Ireland. War Department leaders believed that subversives would be able to recruit conscripted soldiers to commit espionage and spread seditious information. Not surprisingly, the Judge Advocate General's Office took a prominent role in investigating and prosecuting subversion among German and Irish soldiers and also sought to prevent a widespread campaign to ferret out subversion from within the army.[28]

Two further events occurred in 1915 that caused the War Department to conclude that there was "an enemy from within." In early 1915, the Secret Service uncovered a bomb plot and arrested an individual named Robert Fay who later admitted to being a German officer. Fay was also suspected of attempting to bomb American munitions factories. His arrest occurred after fifteen foreign ships exploded while departing the United States for Great Britain and France. Fay had also attempted to recruit IWW members to place bombs along New Jersey's shipping docks. Secondly, Franz von Rintelen, a German Navy intelligence officer, arrived in the United States in 1915 and set up the Bridgeport Projectile Corporation, which turned out to be a fictional business entity. He planned to purchase large amounts of gunpowder at higher than normal prices to create an inflationary spiral so that British, Belgian, and French purchasers would more quickly exhaust their nations' treasuries when they purchased American-manufactured munitions. In addition to destroying much of the gunpowder he purchased, Von Rintelen directed espionage operations to plant bombs on ships bound for Britain, lobbied Mexican government officials to declare war on the United States, and also tried to stoke labor strikes among longshoremen and munitions workers. When, in 1916, Mexican guerilla fighters led by Pancho Villa raided Columbus, New Mexico, killing several American citizens, the War Department suspected German involvement. After the war, and while sitting in a prison, Von Rintelen admitted to many of the activities he was accused of committing, although there was no connection between Villa and him. He also gave the attorney general evidence that enabled the prosecution of Americans who accepted German money, encouraged strikes, and plotted sabotage. More importantly, Fay's arrest and interrogation, as well as von Rintelen's, convinced Baker, Crowder, and other senior officials that not only had the German government directed the espionage operations, it had recruited radicals to accomplish the bombings.[29]

Professor Niall Ferguson, in his acclaimed *The Pity of War: Explaining World War I*, notes that the victorious armies not only prevailed by killing their enemy but also by getting them to desert, mutiny, or surrender. Though he dedicated a chapter to explaining the means by which governments attempted to maintain cohesive forces, he did not detail the Central powers' efforts to undermine discipline in the Allied armies. He also did not analyze the internal social and economic forces in Britain, France, and the United States that could have resulted in a widespread mutiny. He appears to be among the majority of military, political, and economic historians who do not analyze such social forces in great detail—or, for that matter, the Allies' responses to what they perceived as a real danger to military discipline.[30]

THE JUDGE ADVOCATE GENERAL'S OFFICE AND DOMESTIC SUBVERSION

Fears of the IWW permeated the army, and the Judge Advocate General's Office was no exception. But Crowder and his subordinates recognized that there were constitutional limitations on what the War Department could do. In September 1917, two military intelligence officers tried to find a means to have George M. Bourquin, a United States District Court judge in Montana, removed from draft evader cases because he had issued light sentences, including a single day in prison for citizens convicted of failing to comply with induction orders. The officers believed that the judge and the US attorney, Burton Wheeler, had enabled anarchists and IWW leaders to convince people that draft evasion resulted in little personal harm. Crowder went to Baker to oppose their efforts, realizing that the War Department's involvement in a judge's removal would draw congressional ire, if not outrage the federal judiciary. At the same time, Attorney General Gregory chastised the two officers for laying the groundwork for a constitutional crisis. This episode provides a contextual limit to what Crowder believed was a prohibition against the army's domestic use. However, the Judge Advocate General's Office advised on the legality of many surveillance operations and arrests.[31]

In April 1917, Frankfurter drafted a memorandum to the Council of National Defense suggesting how the War Department should respond to the IWW's planned strikes in the western mining industries. The Army War College's intelligence division had informed the chief of staff that the IWW would try to thwart the army's enlistment and procurement efforts through labor strikes, and Baker assigned Frankfurter to suggest a War Department response. Prior to submitting his suggestions to the council, Frankfurter obtained Brandeis's concurrence on the need for the War Department to monitor the IWW. Frankfurter also kept Crowder informed on his interactions with Brandeis, and as a result of the justice's quiet support. Based on his

understanding of Brandeis's views, Crowder concluded that the War Department's actions involving the collection of domestic intelligence on the IWW
and other "radical" organizations would withstand judicial scrutiny. He also
concluded that Congress would support the army's domestic surveillance of
citizens. In January 1919, Senator Atlee Pomerene, the chairman of the Senate
Privileges and Elections Committee, informed Baker and Crowder that the
army needed to redouble its monitoring of the IWW and Bolshevism to prevent soldiers from being recruited into a national mutiny. This aspect of the
judge advocate general's conduct in World War I, as well as that of the War
Department, provides a critical context to any analysis of the War Department's leaders' view of the existence of malleable constitutional constraints on
national security programs.[32]

Even before the nation's entry into the war, judge advocates served alongside intelligence officers and federal law enforcement agents while investigating claims of subversion. There was a widespread belief that the German
government endorsed Pancho Villa's raid into New Mexico in 1916. In February 1917 Crowder instructed Colonel George Dunn to ascertain whether
there was any evidence that Margaretha Gertruida Zelle, a German spy more
commonly known as "Mata Hari," had agents in northern Mexico or in the
southern United States, and whether she and Witzke had any relationship. It is
unclear why Crowder thought such a connection might be a possibility, but he
later claimed that a French civil officer had approached a judge advocate on
his staff with some evidence of a connection. On December 14, 1917, Crowder
received information from Colonel Ralph Van Deman, the acting chief of the
Military Intelligence Branch, that two Mexican government officials, Senator
Francisco Mancilla and Deputy Sylvester Aguilar, received payments from the
German government to help agents cross the border into Texas, report on
army movements, and spread anti-American propaganda throughout Mexico.
Crowder suspected that Witzke directed these cross-border spying acts.[33]

In March 1917, Major John Philip Hill, Maryland's judge advocate, spoke
to an audience in Baltimore and accused Germany of having an extensive
spy and espionage network in both Mexico and the United States. He also
criticized the Justice Department for failing to arrest known German spies
and warned that the German government had consorted with radical labor
leaders, socialists, and Bolsheviks. Hill claimed, based on his experiences in
Germany and as a United States attorney, along with his time on the Mexican
border, that Germany's main goal was to keep American soldiers from traveling to Europe if war came, by stoking labor strife in the United States and
goading the Mexican government into declaring war on the United States.
By this time, Hill's accusations against Germany were believable because not

only had Wilson publicized the "Zimmerman Telegram," the author of that communication had admitted to its authenticity. Hill also informed his audience that Americans had no choice but to suspect German immigrants and their children.[34]

From the start of the war, suspicions of the loyalty of German immigrants and their descendants permeated American society. Several states banned the teaching of German in schools, German-American–owned stores were destroyed, and Postmaster General Albert Burleson barred German language newspapers from the mails. In 1917 there were ninety-two army officers who were born in Germany, and while most were readily welcomed to remain on duty, initially Colonel Carl Reichmann was not. Born in Germany in 1859 and educated at Tubingen University, Reichmann served for a brief time in the German Army and emigrated to the United States in 1880. He enlisted the following year and was commissioned lieutenant in 1884. In addition to taking part in Indian campaigns, he served as a military observer during the Boer War and in the Russo-Japanese War. His turn-of-the century reports on the efficiency of foreign militaries assisted the War Department in preparing for the possibility of a modern total war. But while he was assigned as an observer in South Africa, a British officer accused Reichmann of leading British soldiers into an ambush. Although a British Army investigation debunked the accusation and concluded that the officer making the claim had incompetently maneuvered his forces, the fact that the German government had vocalized support for the Boers caused the War Department to conduct its own investigation. This investigation likewise resulted in Reichmann being cleared. Two years later in 1906, Reichmann confided to Henry Claus, a retired officer of German extraction, that he was denied a position on the general staff because of his German heritage. Claus made Reichmann's letter public, and it caused a minor furor in the War Department. However, Reichmann's career progressed, and in July 1917, Baker, on General Scott's advice, recommended to Wilson that Reichmann be promoted to the rank of brigadier general.[35]

Within a month, Senator Miles Poindexter of Washington accused Reichmann of being a German spy and claimed that Reichmann was unfit to command Americans. Baker did not consider Poindexter's evidence against Reichmann to be compelling and initially ignored it. So too did Attorney General Gregory, although Crowder warned both men that Poindexter was likely to try to derail Reichmann's career. Poindexter's attack on Reichmann occurred after a Canadian woman named Ms. James Anderson informed him that in February 1917, she overheard Reichmann comment in a conversation with the wife of a colonel that all of the warring factions had violated international law and that the British naval blockade of Germany was little different from the German Navy's use of submarines. Given the senator's earlier support for Waldo Coffman, it might have been considered odd that he would use this information to accuse Reichmann of disloyalty. The accusation was odder still in light of Poindexter's other political activities prior to the war.[36]

Until 1917 Poindexter was one of the Republican Party's more outspoken progressives. As late as 1916, he advocated for the IWW's right to demonstrate against unsafe labor conditions. Poindexter was born in Virginia in 1868 and earned a law degree at Washington and Lee's law school at the age of twenty. Shortly after graduating he headed to Walla Walla, a small town in eastern Washington, where he campaigned for William Jennings Bryan. He moved to Spokane in 1904 but switched to the Republican Party, albeit as a progressive in the model of La Follette. In 1908 he was elected to the House of Representatives and joined with a group of young Republicans to divest the Speaker of the House's power over committee appointments and the scheduling of bills. Two years later he was elected to the Senate and found himself in close alignment with La Follette. As a freshman senator, he publicly argued that the IWW had the right to strike in Lawrence, Massachusetts, and he accused mill owners of exploiting workers. He also supported Wilson's efforts at banking reform and was one of only three Republicans to vote to confirm Brandeis. In 1916 Republican Party leaders accused Poindexter of siding with the IWW and socialists and convinced a traditional conservative candidate to challenge him in the state primary. Nonetheless, Poindexter was popular with the state's longshoremen, paper mill workers, miners, and lumbermen, and he won both the primary and the election. By Wilson's second term Poindexter was a more reliable supporter of the president than he was of conservatives such as Henry Cabot Lodge or James Wadsworth. The war either changed his political beliefs, or he became an opportunist.[37]

Like Theodore Roosevelt, Poindexter criticized Wilson's adherence to nonintervention, and he called for a large federal army. He also championed France and Britain and accused Germany of violating international law. In February 1917, he tried to prevent La Follette from filibustering Wilson's proposed "armed ship bill," and in May of that year he accused the IWW of being a dangerous enemy to the country. He voted to remove La Follette from the Senate as a result of La Follette's vote against declaring war, and he accused Senator George Norris of being in league with Germany. When Hiram Johnson spoke against the Espionage Act, Poindexter accused him of disloyalty. In early 1918 Poindexter claimed that the nation's labor unions were infested with Bolsheviks who intended to prolong the war so that the population would overthrow the government. However, by March 1918 Poindexter had overplayed his accusations by March 1918. In addition to attacking Reichmann, he accused Attorney General Gregory and other members of Wilson's administration of being disloyal. Toward the end of the war, he accused Brandeis of being a Bolshevist. Although Crowder had not taken offense at Poindexter's early support of Waldo Coffman, he was disgusted with the senator's attack on Reichmann, in part because Crowder had, for many years, been friends with the colonel. Interestingly Crowder had known Reichmann since 1892 when he represented Reichmann before the Court of Claims over a pay dispute with the army.[38]

The army's general officers also largely sided with Reichmann. Neither Bliss nor Hugh Scott questioned Reichmann's loyalty to the United States. On learning of the allegations against Reichmann, Leonard Wood commented that "no officer would fight harder against Germany in the trenches than old Carl." Pershing advised Crowder that he believed Reichmann was one of the army's more "forward-looking" officers after Wilson forwarded the promotion to the Senate. The husband of the wife that Reichmann had spoken to alleged that Ms. Anderson, a divorcee who remarried a minor British official, was "nothing more than an angry woman after Reichmann spurned her."[39]

In response to Poindexter's allegations against Reichmann, Senator Chamberlain formed a special investigative committee. Senators Duncan Fletcher, a Florida Democrat, and John Weeks, a Massachusetts Republican, joined Poindexter but did not agree with the soundness of Poindexter's allegations against Reichmann. During questioning, Reichmann admitted he had stated that both the German government and Allied governments had violated international law, but countered that his comments echoed the prewar sentiments of several congressmen, including Senators Saulsbury, Phelan, Tillman, La Follette, Norris, and Borah, and Representative Kitchin. Weeks also questioned Anderson's motives in alleging Reichmann's disloyalty. Several War Department officers including Crowder provided affidavits attesting to Reichmann's loyalty as well. Both Weeks and Fletcher concluded that Poindexter's allegations against Reichmann were meritless, and he was permitted to remain in the army. However, he was not promoted to the rank of general or sent to France. With the exception of his criticism against Chamberlain, Crowder usually did not voice derogatory opinions against legislators. He did, however, chastise Poindexter for trying to seek personal gain in committee assignments by attacking Reichmann.[40]

Ironically, after the hearings, Reichmann was assigned as an intelligence officer and investigated allegations of disloyalty among the civilian population around Chicago. One of the citizens he reported as being pro-Bolshevik was journalist and future iconic author Carl Sandburg. Reichmann also tried to recruit African American community leaders to form loyalty leagues and to ascertain whether the Bolsheviks or IWW influenced African American organizations. Reichmann provided evidence of subversion in federal trials conducted before Judge Kenesaw Landis, and he worked alongside Colonel Mayes in his investigation of Espionage Act violations.[41]

While Reichmann, with War Department backing, was determined to be found innocent of disloyalty and returned to duty, Captain Victor C. von Unruh was accused of subversion and then deserted from the army. Born in 1868 in Germany and educated as a doctor in Trier, von Unruh emigrated to the United States in 1908 and was commissioned as a reserve officer in the New York National Guard. Von Unruh specialized in viruses and he studied how influenza spread. Ordered to Georgia in 1917, he was accused of disloyalty because he had hidden an aspect of his life before he emigrated to the United States. When he entered the United States in 1908, von Unruh claimed to have no military experience, when in fact he had served as a reserve officer in a Prussian cavalry regiment. One of his fellow officers in Georgia reported that Von Unruh had taken an interest in a local internment camp housing Germans and had stolen or unlawfully commandeered an army horse. On May 5, 1918, von Unruh left his posting and as of the Armistice had not been brought back into army custody. By 1919 the War Department had still not located Von Unruh, but there was evidence that he had crossed the border into Mexico with another officer of German extraction named Carl Heynen. In early May 1919, Mayes drafted an extradition request to the Mexican government for both Von Unruh and Heynen, but the Mexican government either had no interest or no ability to retrieve either of the deserted officers.[42]

Shortly after the Committee on Public Information was created, Baker informed Secretary of the Navy Josephus Daniels that he and Crowder had advised several senators that while a pending censorship bill was important to the war effort, the bill's proposed penalties were too drastic. In particular, the bill, authored by Chamberlain, made it possible for the army to court-martial civilians accused of spying, and both Baker and Crowder opposed it. On July 10, 1917, Baker gave Daniels a legal memorandum drafted by Blanton Winship detailing the authority of both secretaries to censor mails and news publications on military installations. Winship also advised Baker that the Judge Advocate General's Office concluded that while Daniels possessed the wartime authority to monitor all undersea cable communications, the War Department could likewise monitor the same cables once out of the water, as well as monitor and quarantine telegraph and telephone access from citizens and organizations suspected of aiding Germany or subversive organizations.[43]

Crowder's caution against having the War Department encroach into the population's civil liberties came to light following an instance when one of

Creel's subordinates publicly claimed that most conscientious objectors were pro-German, and Crowder complained to Baker that this statement had no merit. In another instance, the Justice Department arrested over one hundred Swedish immigrants for failing to comply with their induction notices. The Swedes pleaded guilty in federal court before Judge Kenesaw Landis based on their belief that their failure to comply, in and of itself, was a crime under the Espionage Act. In reality, several of the arrested Swedes did not comply with their induction notice because they did not understand that they were required to report for induction on a specific day. Creel wanted to display this mass arrest as evidence that the IWW had attempted to thwart conscription in Chicago. In February 1918, he informed Wilson that the Swedes were part of a Bolshevist plot, and that the War Department desired to exercise jurisdiction. But this was not true. Ansell had advised in favor of taking jurisdiction, and Crowder opposed this course of action. He complained to Baker that presenting the arrests and trials as a matter of subversion would ultimately undermine confidence in the War Department, and court-martialing the Swedes would result in anticonscription demonstrations. Ansell's advice was not, at the time, contrary to the Selective Service Act, but Crowder believed it was unwise to follow his advice because it would enable legislators such as Hiram Johnson to further allege that courts-martial were a means to suppress the First Amendment. In the end, Crowder prevailed and those Swedes who desired to serve in the army were released to attend basic training.[44]

On November 11, 1918, the army numbered 3,685,458 soldiers, of whom two-thirds were conscripted. Twenty-four million citizens and residents registered for Selective Service. Of the sixty-five thousand who sought noncombatant service, the army placed fifty-seven thousand into noncombatant duties, including as stretcher bearers who shared the most intense frontline dangers with the infantry. Over 300,000 civilians refused to report for duty after being ordered to do so. Five hundred four civilians who were brought into War Department custody and refused to drill were court-martialed, with seventeen sentenced to death. None of these persons was actually executed and most were freed by 1925. However, their treatment in captivity was often brutal. Crowder did not blame Creel for the treatment of conscientious objectors held in military prisons, but he objected to judge advocates adopting Creel's positions in their advice on charging prisoners with crimes such as mutiny or disloyalty without evidence.[45]

In spite of his concerns over Creel's zealousness, Crowder worried over the prospect of widespread German subversion through the nation's newspapers. In the two months prior to the United States' entry into the war, Breckinridge Long, the third assistant secretary of state, apprised Crowder on the numbers of newspaper articles that the State Department suspected to be German-funded or German-influenced. Following the entry into war, Long continued to provide Crowder with articles criticizing the administration of selective service and military training. Crowder responded by forwarding the articles to Attorney General Gregory with the comment that although he had no evidence as to German funding of the newspapers in question, he requested the Justice Department to investigate the newspaper editors and owners. He cautioned that just as Bolo and Almereyda had used *Bonnet Rouge* to undermine the French Army, a similar subversive operation in the United States could occur.[46]

While Crowder was not opposed to the War Department working alongside the Justice Department to stifle espionage and subversion in the United States, particularly where there was specific evidence linking individuals to criminal acts, he rarely approved of involving the War Department in state antisyndicalism efforts. For instance, in August 1917, Oklahoma's governor R. L. Williams asked Baker to have the army help enforce an arms embargo on private shipments of firearms into Oklahoma, if not all of the plains states. Williams claimed that "persons opposed to the selective draft such as these belonging to the socialists, IWW and WCU organizations are buying arms." Major R. K. Spiller, Ansell's friend, promised the governor that the War Department would assist in policing the state. Crowder, for his part, determined that an arms embargo as a war measure was intrusive into property rights as well as state's rights. Certainly the governor could enact an internal embargo, but Crowder advised that the governor's proposal would extend the War Department's authority too far.[47]

The Oklahoma governor's request to the War Department did not arise in a political vacuum. In what might be considered the United States' oddest internal rebellion—and one doomed to fail—in August 1917, a small number of Oklahoma tenant farmers belonging to an organization called the "Working Class Union" aligned with a smaller number of Native Muscogee Creek Indians to oppose conscription. The IWW did not foment this particular uprising, known as the "Green Corn Rebellion"; it caught their leaders by surprise. Some of the tenant farmers shot at a county sheriff and his deputy and then attempted to destroy telegraph line and railroad tracks. They planned to march across the country and gain supporters before laying siege to Washington, DC. Within a short period, the rebellion disintegrated and several hundred of its members were arrested. A pitched battle with state law enforcement officers and a posse also resulted in three deaths. Although the rebellion was easily suppressed, it served as a reminder that some of the nation's more vocal opponents of the war also intended to replace the nation's form of government.[48]

Governor Williams was not the only state executive to seek War Department help against suspected internal subversion. In early 1920, Thomas Riggs, Alaska's territorial governor, sought an increase in the number of soldiers because an escaped army prisoner, Private B. R. Sawyer, had been observed distributing Bolshevik and IWW literature in Ketchikan. While in the army, Sawyer was charged with attempting to incite a mutiny after being caught espousing the IWW's merits, but he deserted before his court-martial began. He was captured, charged with desertion, and sentenced to five years in confinement. However, he escaped from custody prior to being sent to Alcatraz. Kreger advised Baker that Riggs should have local police arrest Sawyer and then turn him over to military custody. He also derided Riggs as an "alarmist."[49]

On September 29, 1919, Baker directed the army's departmental commanders to favorably respond to requests from state governors for the use of soldiers not only to guard industrial plants and shipyards during strikes, but also to take part in arrests. Crowder protested to Baker that the order was illegal under the Posse Comitatus Act and contrary to the Constitution's intent to have the army be subservient to the federal civil government. Crowder's opposition to Baker's direction came at a critical point where both he and Baker were fighting in Congress to maintain the 1916 Articles of War against Ansell's reform efforts. But Crowder believed that if Baker's directive were to stand, then state politics would become militarized to the detriment of civil liberties, and popular trust in the military would erode.[50]

Judge advocates, in following Crowder's position over limited military jurisdiction, usually cited *Milligan* when advising generals against ordering the arrest of civilians. However, noncitizens were a different matter. On September 1, 1917, army officers apprehended two men working under aliases in an industrial plant in Toledo, Ohio, and detained them without trial for over a month. Colonel Hubert J. Turney, the Ohio National Guard's judge advocate, who was to become the Thirty-Seventh Division's judge advocate, advised Major General Charles Treat that the arrest was lawful. However, since Treat had graduated with distinction from the Columbia University Law School in 1885, he likely concluded the legality of the arrests on his own. In late October, the two men obtained legal representation and sought a writ of habeas corpus. Breckinridge Long intervened on behalf of the two men, who turned out to be Serbian citizens rather than German agents. Colonel Frank L. Dodds, the department's judge advocate, advised the War Department to release the two men into the custody of the Justice Department.[51]

Historians who analyze the United States during the war often focus on the nation's anti-German sentiment, but there were instances of persons of other nationalities falling victim to irrational accusations. For instance, Solomon

Bujdud and Amin Chanin were born in the Ottoman Empire, and for reasons which are absent from the historic record, both men emigrated to Eagle
Pass, a remote Texas town on the Mexican border where they opened a small
hotel in 1908. On June 1, 1918, army officers arrested both men for suspicion of spying for Germany, particularly "after being found associating with a
suspicious German Jew." After ninety-eight days of military confinement and
without a formal charge being levied against them, both men were able to find
an attorney to petition Judge Duval West, who had issued harsh sentences to
civilians throughout the war for selling alcohol to soldiers, for a writ of habeas
corpus. On October 14, Attorney General Gregory asked Ansell whether the
War Department intended to maintain jurisdiction and prosecute the men as
had been done with Witzke. Ansell responded that the Southern Department
was likely to prosecute both men in military trials for providing information
on army movements to Mexican agents, who would then pass on the information to Germany. However, two weeks later, Crowder intervened and informed
Gregory that no evidence existed linking the two men to any foreign government, and Budjud and Chanin were released.[52]

While the government concentrated its prosecutions on persons accused
of spreading IWW literature or advocating socialist, anarchist, or Bolshevik causes, there was a broad War Department prohibition against political
activity in the ranks. As in the case of several issues to arise during the war,
the Judge Advocate General's Office reached to the Civil War experience for
guidance. In 1864 General Ulysses Grant issued an order prohibiting political
speeches in the Union armies regardless of who was speaking. In November
1917, General J. Franklin Bell sought Baker's permission to allow candidates
for local office to briefly speak to the soldiery in training at Camp Lee, Virginia. Ansell and Crowder advised against doing so, pointing out that Grant's
standing order in 1864 was designed to maintain discipline in a fair-handed
manner and therefore ought to be replicated. Ansell and Crowder also noted
that nothing in Grant's order prohibited the circulation of newspapers or off-
base meetings, but if the War Department were to allow a Republican or Democrat to campaign, then it would have to permit a Socialist Party candidate to
likewise campaign. The Supreme Court in 1972 in *Flower v. United States*, and
in 1976 in *Greer v. Spock*, would, without actually stating it in their decisions,
adopt Grant's, Crowder's, and Ansell's reasoning. That is, the Department of
Defense could prohibit political activities on base as a means for maintaining
an apolitical military.[53]

Throughout the war, the Judge Advocate General's Office was tasked with
developing policies to respond to antiwar literature distributed outside military posts. In July 1918, Colonel Mayes informed the chief of the Military

Intelligence Branch that President Wilson had the authority to "stop the sale and distribution of such publications as are calculated to obstruct and interfere with the successful operation of the military force of the government." Mayes advised Baker that "although the Constitution itself was silent on the authority of Executive Branch to grant military officers the power to seize political literature, Emerich de Vattel, the prominent eighteenth century international law jurist expressed that a nation has the right to harness its military power to ward off imminent danger." Mayes justified his use of Vattel by pointing out that the Supreme Court in *Coleman v. Tennessee* relied on Vattel's treatise. In retrospect, Mayes's use of Vattel, like the Court's in *Coleman*, is questionable. *Coleman* arose from Tennessee's prosecution of a former Union soldier for a murder that a court-martial had previously acquitted the soldier of. The Court, rather than apply a double jeopardy analysis, likened Tennessee—a part of the Confederacy when the murder occurred—to a foreign state and then concluded that a foreign state (such as Tennessee) had no jurisdiction over a transiting army. Vattel, concededly, was one of the more influential scholars to shape international law, but as a Swiss scholar, he wrote for an audience of monarchies rather than governments constrained by a bill of rights. In another instance, Mayes advised that the prohibition against soldiers possessing, or civilians distributing, a Seventh Day Adventist Tract titled *The World in Perplexity* was justified because it espoused arguments similar to socialist claims of the war benefiting bankers and financiers at the expense of the poor.[54]

Prominent scholars of the Progressive era have noted that of all Wilson's cabinet officers, Postmaster General Albert Burleson was the most reactionary, and he was determined to eradicate communism, anarchism, and socialism. In 1915 he issued postal regulations prohibiting the mailing of non-neutral material. To Burleson, this meant that any newspaper espousing a socialist affiliation was suspect and therefore could be prohibited from the mails. Following the declaration of war against Germany, he extended postal regulations to prevent the mailing of antiwar material, and he lobbied Attorney General Gregory to prosecute antiwar leaders who he believed interfered with conscription. One of Burleson's targets was former Wisconsin congressman and Socialist Party of America leader Victor L. Berger. In addition to Berger's political activities, he also owned and edited the *Milwaukee Leader*, which publicized its opposition to the nation's involvement in the war. Unlike the IWW, anarchists, or Bolsheviks, Berger never advocated the violent overthrow of the government. He believed that socialism could be achieved through mass unionization, strikes, and ultimately the electoral process. Ironically, in early 1917 Berger argued to Edward House, Baker, Gregory, and Crowder that the IWW constituted a real threat against the nation's war efforts because of its contacts with Russia's revolutionary leaders. Berger pointed out that his newspaper had merely stated its opposition to the Selective Service Act because it undemocratically compelled men into service instead of relying on volunteers, and he reminded them that he and the Socialist Party opposed violence. The IWW, he reasoned, had pursued "direct action" such as strikes and bombings. When Berger was indicted in February 1918 for advocating resistance to the draft under the Espionage Act, Crowder opposed the government's prosecution of him. However, Ansell felt the indictment and conviction were justified, and he advised Baker that the War Department could assist in the Justice Department's prosecution of Berger. Ultimately, Baker permitted the Military Intelligence Bureau to collect intelligence on the former congressman.[55]

The War Department's assistance in prosecuting Berger was problematic for several reasons even though he was no longer in Congress. From 1911 to 1914, Berger chaired a congressional subcommittee responsible for overseeing federal construction and maintenance in the capital city and he regularly corresponded with Crowder and Colonel William Judson, the assistant bureau chief of engineers responsible for the District of Columbia's sanitation and bridges. In May 1917, Bliss assigned Judson to serve as the chief of staff and military attaché to the United States' military assistance group to Russia. Judson's primary purpose was ostensibly to remain neutral in Russian internal affairs and to secure transit for American arms to be shipped to the Rumanian forces still engaged against Germany. A combined Rumanian and Russian offensive, known as "the Kerensky Offensive," was planned for June 1917, but the two armies were underequipped for the operation. Judson also sought to discover whether any prominent American had aided or aligned with the Bolsheviks.[56]

During the time Judson spent in Russia, he discerned that the Bolsheviks were likely to take Russia out of the war, and he also concluded that Lenin had employed a strategy to spread communism by destabilizing the armed forces of the warring powers through propaganda and subversion. Judson conveyed to the War Department that the Bolsheviks not only were informing German soldiers that the allied powers intended to dissolve Germany but also that communists were emplaced in the Allied forces in the hopes of spreading mutinies. In spite of his warnings about Bolshevik designs, Judson was convinced that American socialists such as Berger not only were not part of Lenin's plans, they were as likely as any other political leaders to be eliminated by the Bolsheviks.[57]

Judson shared his observations with Crowder, who in turn informed Baker that he opposed the government's prosecution of Berger if for no other reason than that it would fuel Bolshevik subversion in the army. But he also noted to Baker that Berger was not a threat to selective service because he had never advocated violence, and if imprisoned, Berger's political supporters would move into more radical organizations. In spite of Judson's well-reasoned defense of Berger and Crowder's reticence to involve the War Department in the prosecution of the former congressman, the Department of Justice, with War Department assistance, prosecuted Berger for obstructing the war effort. On February 20, 1919, Berger was convicted in federal court, and Judge Landis sentenced him to twenty years in prison. When the House of Representatives moved in 1919 to refuse to permit Berger to claim his seat in Congress after he was elected, Crowder informed Senator Henry Cabot Lodge that Berger had not damaged the nation's war efforts. In 1921 the Supreme Court determined that Judge Landis had undermined the trial through his plainly evident bias.[58]

A similar prosecution occurred against labor organizer Eugene Debs. In 1918 Debs was convicted in United States District Court and sentenced to ten years for violating the Espionage Act. Following the 1894 Pullman strike, Debs and Berger aligned to promote unionization of the railroad workforce. Debs had taken part in the founding of the IWW, but by 1912 he led the socialists within the union to depart from the IWW and spoke out against its violence. Debs, like La Follette, Kitchin, and Berger, opposed the war and conscription but also had never advocated violence. However, unlike Berger, Debs publicly encouraged resistance to conscription. While President Wilson was relatively quiet on his opinions about Berger, he called Debs "a traitor." Crowder supported Debs's arrest and conviction, but he also later urged that Wilson commute Debs's sentence. Not so Ansell, who considered Debs a traitor and opposed any commutation of Debs's imprisonment. In reality, neither Berger's nor Debs's fates occupied much of Crowder's or Ansell's time, but their difference of opinion in these matters evidences that at times, Crowder could be more protective of civil liberties than Ansell. As Wilson left office, Baker and Crowder supported Debs's release but Wilson denied clemency. In May 1921 Crowder noted to Secretary of War John Weeks that he never believed Debs threatened the nation's war efforts. In December of that year President Harding commuted Debs's sentence.[59]

While the Berger and Debs trials were prominent in the national newspapers, little was reported on African Americans, who were not immune from suspicions of disloyalty any more than whites. In several instances, congressmen and state officials insisted the War Department investigate claims amounting to threats of an African American insurrection reminiscent of Nat Turner's 1831 revolt in Virginia. Because the IWW had actively recruited religious and racial minorities, Military Intelligence Bureau officers investigated

African American officer applicants for pro-German or IWW sympathies, but there was no evidence of disloyalty ever uncovered. The NAACP in 1916 had advocated for African Americans to support socialist candidates, and in 1918, the Justice Department arrested A. Philip Randolph and Chandler Owen, two socialist-oriented African American newspaper editors, for advocating resistance to conscription. None of this proved disloyalty. Prior to the war, there was little interaction between communists, anarchists, and African American intellectual leaders, and in reality there was no reason to suspect any universal disloyalty. Indeed, W. E. B. DuBois, perhaps the most prominent of African American leaders, advocated for African Americans to support the war effort and went so far as to demand that African Americans be included in the draft. Nonetheless, suspicions of disloyalty occurred throughout the war.[60]

In May 1919 Colonel George Dunn advised that the army search all "negro soldiers" before they embarked from France to return to the United States. Dunn was convinced that African American soldiers were in the process of smuggling handguns and rifles out of the army to use in a planned nationwide armed uprising. He apparently believed an anonymous intelligence report to this effect, but his advice infuriated Crowder because not only was there no evidence that African American soldiers were disloyal, Dunn had failed to inform Crowder of the memorandum prior to its being shared with Peyton March. The chief of staff, on reading Dunn's memorandum, accepted the possibility of an African American uprising. While it is true that there were race riots in 1919 in Omaha, Chicago, and three dozen other cities, white citizens were responsible for the riots. March, moreover, should have realized that it was not the first occasion on which Dunn accused African Americans of disloyalty. Following the "Houston Riot" trials, he urged General Ruckman to quickly approve the verdicts and death sentences in order to stem a planned "negro uprising, fomented by IWW and negro subversives." Crowder and Mayes concluded that given that DuBois and other leading African Americans criticized the soldiers' conduct, Dunn's advice to Ruckman in 1917 was baseless as well.[61]

Crowder believed that the German military had made a nominal attempt to influence African Americans to refuse to comply with induction orders, but in terms of a higher African American desertion rate, he was convinced that African American desertions were rooted in their poverty and migratory civilian work patterns. Other judge advocates dismissed as "far-fetched" the intelligence reports suspecting African American subversion. For instance, on April 28, 1918, the Southeastern Department's intelligence officer claimed that he had evidence of German agents using fortune tellers and gypsies to inform African American civilians—and particularly women—that unless

Germany prevailed in the war, slavery would become law once more. Perhaps, because this "evidence" arose in South Carolina and Senator Tillman had been an unapologetic outspoken bigot, this type of rumor might have caused worry in the state's African American population that white-led riots would occur. Although the German military had created a semi-effective espionage network, it was not that broad, well funded, or detailed as to employ "hundreds of gypsies and fortune tellers." Mayes referred to this report as "nonsense" and advised against drafting an order prohibiting fortune tellers in towns near military installations. In 1917 Colonel Dodds advised General Bell that reports of German or IWW attempts to "foment a movement among colored doctors, to refuse to assist to War Department, and instead join the German Army" were "foolish" and should "be ignored." Likewise, in September 1917, Frankfurter penned to Van Deman that the Military Intelligence Bureau was wasting its time investigating "Negro subversion," and that persons who reported it likely were either trying to undermine the war effort by minimizing African American contributions or having the War Department employ draconian measures against African American soldiers.[62]

In addition to protecting soldiers from enemy or pacifist propaganda and rooting out disloyalty from the army, one of the Bureau of Intelligence's functions, with judge advocate assistance, was the protection of soldiers from attempts to induce sickness and disease in the ranks. In an era with a small number of food inspectors, it might be understandable that instances of food contamination would be suspected as enemy or IWW activity. In early May 1918, ground glass and sand nodules were discovered to have been mixed into chocolate candy and peanuts from the Planters Nut and Chocolate Corporation. Because Planters had a large Italian immigrant workforce, there were suspicions about anarchists working in the factories. Indeed, the corporation's security office informed the War Department that the company had unknowingly hired anarchists to work in its Virginia factories. In an unusual twist, Mayes and Van Deman jointly commanded the Food and Drug Administration's investigation into the corporation's industrial plants. After the FDA concluded that the presence of ground glass was an inadvertent lapse in safety, the corporation was permitted to resume its contracting with the War Department.[63]

Before the American Expeditionary Forces were organized to transit to the United States and soldiers waited to be demobilized, Frankfurter worried that Bolshevik organizers would be able to clandestinely recruit idle soldiers. On November 18, 1918, he warned Wilson, Baker, and Crowder that it was critical to transition soldiers quickly into industrial jobs and return farmworkers to their homes to prevent Bolshevik recruitment. In early January 1919,

British soldiers mutinied in Southampton and refused to be transported to France. The soldiers had been informed they were soon to be discharged but instead were ordered to be part of the postwar occupation forces in Germany. Frankfurter fretted that the longer soldiers were kept in uniform, the more likely they would believe Bolshevik-spun rumors that they too would be sent to Germany as part of an occupation force. Frankfurter's worries were prescient not only for the immediate aftermath of the war in Europe, but also because in 1945, the Communist Party of the United States attempted to ignite strikes in the armed forces stationed overseas following the Japanese surrender. Ultimately Bolshevik attempts to cause soldier riots in early 1919 and the Communist Party's attempts to do the same in late 1945 failed, but there was evidence implicating both organizations.[64]

SEDITION IN THE RECRUITMENT AND TRAINING OF THE
NATION'S SOLDIERY

On August 3, 1917, General H. P. McCain, the army's adjutant general, issued a confidential directive to senior army officers that "the names of all German nationals and those of her allies" had to be reported to his office as well as to the chief of military intelligence and the Judge Advocate General's Office. One month later, McCain cautioned that foreign organizations had clandestinely appeared at embarkation ports and interactions between "soldiers of German alienage and such organizations had to be recorded in the event that prosecutions for mutiny or disloyalty were conducted." By the summer of 1918, this concern was overcome by a fear of "communist, bolshevist and anarchist influences into the Army."[65]

With the exception of the San Patricio Battalion episode of the Mexican-American War, the army had rarely encountered instances where a soldier deserted to an opposing foreign state. In those rare instances, there could be a harsh response. For instance, in 1916 the army court-martialed Captain Robert H. Hall, who had deserted into Mexico and was later captured commanding a unit of José Venustiano Carranza's forces. Hall had been assigned to an Indiana National Guard unit, and he forged the names of soldiers under his command on various financial instruments in Austin, Texas. When he realized that military investigators had discovered his misconduct, he fled into Mexico, sold his military equipment, and offered his services to Carranza. A British journalist, who found it interesting that a US national had been commissioned as a colonel in the Mexican Army, obtained an interview with him. The journalist discovered that Hall was married to a woman in Indiana—but he also had married a fifteen-year-old Mexican national in Texas prior to his desertion—and conveyed this information to a number of newspapers. The newspaper reporting apparently solved the mystery of Captain Hall's disappearance. Unsurprisingly, when Hall was captured, the War Department charged him with bigamy, desertion, larceny, misappropriation of funds, and providing confidential topographic maps to Carranza. This last charge was tantamount to treason. Crowder assigned Ansell to serve as a judge advocate in the trial, and under Ansell's direction, the assistant judge advocate argued for Hall to be sentenced to life. The court-martial sentenced Hall to a dismissal and twenty years in confinement, but he ended up serving four years in total before his release.[66]

During the Civil War, the army court-martialed soldiers for seditious activity, and so during World War I, it was unsurprising that this would occur again. Crowder never sought to incorporate the 1917 Espionage Act into the Articles of War because there were already prohibitions against the conduct that the Espionage Act covered, as well as constraints on soldiers' speech. While courts-martial could mete out severe sentences for espionage, sedition, treason, and mutiny, the Articles of War were not unique in the possibility of severe sentences for such offenses. In the British Army, sedition and mutiny could result in a death sentence, though most offenders were sentenced to lengthy terms in prison. Civilians in the United Kingdom who had taken up arms against the British war efforts could be court-martialed and sentenced to death. The French Army was a different matter. Notwithstanding the infamous Dreyfus court-martial in the late nineteenth century, as a result of "Carnet B" and the trench mutiny, the French Army's leadership had good reason to fear espionage and subversion. By 1917 Premier Georges Clemenceau, himself a prewar socialist, had become convinced that radical socialists and communists had provoked disobedience and mutiny in the trenches with the aim of making France sue for peace and forcing the French population to turn to Bolshevism and revolt. As a result, the French Army harshly suppressed newspapers and prosecuted soldiers suspected of mutiny, and dozens of death sentences were adjudged during the conflict. Moreover, some French soldiers accused of directly aiding Germany could expect summary punishment, or if court-martialed, a death sentence or a sentence to a penal colony, which amounted to a de facto death sentence.[67]

How fears of subversion, espionage, or disloyalty translated into the army's wartime courts-martial can be discerned not only by reviewing the Judge Advocate General's Office memoranda as well as the Military Intelligence Group files, but also by culling through courts-martial records, notwithstanding the fact that many soldiers court-martialed for offenses such as disobedience of orders or disrespect might have first been suspected of loyalty to Germany or subversive organizations. It is difficult to definitively ascertain how such offenses would have been treated in the army had the war continued through 1919, but the War Department's conduct in 1918 does give some indication. From July 1918 to the end of the war, five soldiers were prosecuted in general courts-martial for giving aid to the enemy. Of these, none was acquitted and all were sentenced to terms ranging from five to twenty years of imprisonment. One hundred sixty-six soldiers were prosecuted for inciting mutiny or joining a mutiny. Of these, none was sentenced to death, but several soldiers were sentenced to terms of twenty years or less. Thirty-eight soldiers accused of mutiny were acquitted. Forty-six soldiers were prosecuted in a general court-martial for using contemptuous words against President Wilson, Secretary Baker, or other ranking government officials, and of these, almost all were convicted and sentenced to terms ranging between one year and ten years.[68]

Not all soldiers accused of disloyalty were prosecuted in courts-martial. For instance, on July 19, 1917, military intelligence officers informed the Southern Department that a Herman Rothenbucher—occasionally spelled as Rotenbucker—had been dishonorably discharged from the army in 1914 after being convicted of disobedience of orders and disrespect to a noncommissioned officer. However, the bureaucratic machinery of military intelligence took over a year to uncover that he was in the army once more. Rothenbucher enlisted in the army under the name Edward Rotenbucker, and after basic training, the army assigned him to Kelly Field as an aircraft mechanic. On July 16, 1918, the army arrested him for fraudulently enlisting, but he claimed his purpose in enlisting was to serve honorably and rebuild his reputation in the United States. After Rothenbucher refused to answer questions regarding any communications he made with Germany, the judge advocate assigned to Kelly Field in San Antonio recommended court-martialing him for refusing to obey orders as well as fraudulently enlisting. In early September, the army transferred Rothenbucher to Camp Wheeler, Georgia, and in November, he was processed for a discharge without a court-martial. Although Rothenbucher's conduct was suspicious, military intelligence officers as well as the judge advocate at Camp Wheeler were only able to determine that his claimed purpose for rejoining the army was meritorious, though he had, in fact, fraudulently enlisted. By December 1918, Rothenbucher was a civilian once more, but in 1920 the Office of the Director of General Intelligence concluded that Rothenbucher had attempted to provide intelligence on aviation operations in Texas to German agents.[69]

Between February 1, 1918, and the end of March of that year, judge advocates in the Western Department investigated eighteen soldiers accused of being pro-German. One of the allegations was absurdly pornographic and ran afoul of Victorian morality, but the soldier's conduct did not connote any disloyalty. A sergeant named Gustav May in San Francisco had asked his soldiers for the locations of German women engaged in the laundry trade so that he could "'f*&' them as he intended to do the same to the Kaiser, instead of the Asian laundresses that he had been fornicating." Apparently, the sergeant's stated carnal desire for German laundresses was taken as a preference for Germany over the United States, and he was court-martialed. He was ultimately acquitted. On the other hand, both Privates Frederich Lechner and Otto Ludwig refused to leave the western states for France after stating their loyalty to Germany. Both men were US citizens, and both were court-martialed and convicted of disobedience of orders. Each received one year in prison and a dishonorable discharge.[70]

Between January 2 and June 23, 1918, Major General John Ruckman, the Southern Department's commander, approved twenty-nine general courts-martial convictions for disloyalty and four convictions for contemptuous statements against the president. Bookending these dates were the general courts-martial of Musician Third Class Alfred Stanhove and Private Michael Prush. Shortly after commencing training in August 1917, Stanhove proclaimed that "the Kaiser is the greatest leader and best friend the world had ever had," and "the English stole all the possessions they have, and the Americans stole the United States from the Indians and stole the Philippines from the Spanish." On October 17, 1917, a general court-martial sentenced Stanhove to five years in prison and a dishonorable discharge, and on January 2, 1918, Ruckman, following Dunn's advice, found no reason to mitigate the sentence. On February 15, 1918, a general court-martial found Private Prush guilty of disloyalty after he stated that not only would he refuse to kill any Austrian soldiers, he would "kill any American who fired on the Austrians." Prush had emigrated to the United States from Vienna as a four-year-old, but his older brother served in the Austrian Army, fighting against Italy. To Dunn and Rucker, none of this was mitigating, and Prush's sentence of ten years in prison and a dishonorable discharge was approved. Ruckman's decisions against clemency were unsurprising given his oversight of the "Houston Riot" trials.[71]

On July 1, 1918, Major General Willard Ames Holbrook assumed command of the Southern Department, but there was little change from Ruckman's tenure in the severity of courts-martial for persons accused of disloyalty. On July 17, 1918, a general court-martial found Sergeant Albert Unger guilty of disrespect to President Wilson and sentenced him to ten years in prison and a dishonorable discharge. Unger, a naturalized citizen who had been born in Germany and served in the Punitive Expedition and in Tampico, informed several privates that Wilson and the other Allied leaders were "lying sons of bitches" and Kaiser Wilhelm II was "an honorable man." Neither Dunn nor Holbrook saw a reason to disapprove the findings or sentence. Yet in spite of Dunn's, Ruckman's, and Holbrook's unbending attitude toward subversion, they could not direct courts-martial to find soldiers guilty in all trials.[72]

In July 1918, Lieutenant Edward Jerome Vogeler was charged with mutiny and sedition for allegedly stating to a number of conscripts that he had hoped "Germany would win the war and rule the world." Another allegation was that Vogeler conflated reporters of casualties on the Western Front to trainees in order to undermine discipline and their willingness to fight. Held at Fort Sam Houston, the court-martial ultimately acquitted Vogeler of all eleven offenses. One week later, a court-martial conducted at the same post convicted Private Delbert Dolph and sentenced him to twenty years in confinement and a dishonorable discharge for proclaiming to a number of draftees that "just as McKinley had been shot, Wilson deserves to be killed the same way too." Vogeler and Dolph were both born in Germany and therefore suspect, but the panel concluded that Dolph meant to undermine discipline and morale, while Vogeler was simply a tough instructor who used intimidation to instill discipline.[73]

The commanders of other geographic divisions had an approach similar to that of the Southern Department in prosecuting sedition and subversion. On November 27, 1917, a general court-martial conducted at Governors Island determined that Captain David A. Henkes was guilty of disloyalty under the Ninety-Fifth and Ninety-Sixth Articles of War. Born in Iowa in 1879, Henkes enlisted in the Wisconsin National Guard in 1898 and fought in Cuba and then in the Philippines. After transferring into the regular army in 1901, he was commissioned as a lieutenant in the cavalry and then served on the Mexican border. Assigned to the Sixteenth Cavalry Regiment, he was one of the first officers to go to France, but he refused to advance into the front lines, claiming that because his parents emigrated from Germany, he could not take up arms against his relatives and "mother country." Henkes thrice unsuccessfully tried to resign his commission, urging that his loyalty would be questioned and therefore he would be an ineffective officer. However, military intelligence discovered that in January 1917, he had also corresponded with Ambassador von Bernstorff. Henkes's discussions with von Bernstorff were not evidence of actual espionage, but rather, they showed his desire to move to Germany and serve in the German Army. Ansell believed that Henkes's sentence of twenty-five years in confinement and dismissal from the army was fair, and he recommended to a willing Baker to approve it in full.[74]

While Henkes's punishment was among the most severe sentences assessed by courts-martial held in the United States against soldiers accused of aiding the enemy, he was by no means the only one to be severely sentenced. One month prior to Henkes's court-martial, a general court-martial held at Governors Island convicted Private James M. Plotnik of spying on behalf of Germany and sentenced him to seven years in confinement and a dishonorable discharge. Plotnik used the alias James Montgomery when he enlisted, and he provided German agents with maps of the army's aviation field at Essington, Pennsylvania. Oddly, Crowder urged, over Ansell's protest as well as that of Colonel Frank L. Dodds, the Eastern Department's judge advocate, to have General Bell commute Plotnik's sentence to four years. What made Plotnik's offense less egregious to Crowder was that unlike Henkes, Plotnik had not accepted a commission from the president with the promise to fight all of the nation's foreign and domestic enemies. Yet as Ansell countered, Plotnik had actually been caught providing sensitive military information to the enemy and could have been sentenced to death.[75]

In May 1918, Dodds drafted charges against Lieutenant John McAllister, a medical officer who was accused of making "seditious comments" against Wilson and the Allies. Dodds also saw to it that a Lieutenant Bertrand Balkema was court-martialed for telling sergeants and other enlisted personnel that the federal income tax was unconstitutional, Germany was a more democratic nation than the United States, and "dishonesty prevails in Government circles, and the hullabaloo about raising American flags is all rot on the part of the American people." The court-martial sentenced Balkema to be dismissed and confined for ten years. In this instance, despite Dodd's and Ansell's objections, Crowder advised Baker that the evidence presented at the court-martial was factually insufficient to sustain the conviction and sentence, and Baker ordered Balkema restored to the army. McAllister was not as lucky. Sentenced to a dismissal and with no clemency granted, he committed suicide.[76]

On October 19, 1917, Major General Thomas H. Barry, the Central Department's commanding general, approved of Private Clarence Cotter's court-martial conviction and sentence of six months in confinement. Cotter had informed his fellow soldiers that he intended to desert and would not go to France to fight Germany, concluding, "there is very little to the U. S. Flag anyway." On March 15, 1918, a general court-martial found Private Joseph Tomanocy guilty of uttering treasonous statements and sentenced him to twenty years in prison and a dishonorable discharge. Tomanocy was alleged to have stated in his barracks that he "was going to rip his uniform off and return to Germany to fight." But following a review by Lieutenant Colonel Charles Beecher Warren, General Barry disapproved the findings and sentence and ordered Tomanocy restored to duty. An odder verdict and sentence came to Warren four days after he reviewed Tomanocy's case. On June 20, 1918, the army court-martialed Private Marcus Breitfeller for mutinous and disloyal statements after he publicly refused to wear a uniform or carry a rifle. Breitfeller unsuccessfully asserted as a defense that he was a foreign national—indeed, an enemy alien of Austrian birth—and therefore not required to serve in the United States Army. Although he did not assert conscientious objection or resist his induction, Warren advised Barry that Breitfeller's statements, "I won't fight for the United States, why should I drill?" and "I am not in favor of the United States. I am an Austrian," could not be upheld as mutinous or disloyal as a jurisdictional matter, and the War Department would have to discharge him. As a result, Breitfeller would not have to serve the five years in prison that the court-martial sentenced him to. Recalling Hackenberg's appeal to the federal courts, Warren noted that while Hackenberg had voluntarily enlisted, Breitfeller was a conscript.[77]

On August 11, 1918, Major General William Carter assumed command over the Central Department, and on the same day a general court-martial at Fort Riley, Kansas, acquitted Private Guy Weitman of making disloyal and contemptuous statements against President Wilson and attempting to organize a mutiny among his fellow soldiers. Weitman admitted to repeating rumors that Secretary of the Treasury William Gibbs McAdoo had accepted seven million dollars from bankers to lobby Wilson to enter the war and that an entire division in Texas had mutinied against the war. Warren reviewed the record of trial and concluded that the evidence could have justified a conviction, particularly since Weitman had claimed to be a member of the IWW. Since none of the government's witnesses testified that Weitman had any influence on them, Warren recommended to General Carter to uphold the acquittal. However, neither Carter nor Warren was "soft" on disloyalty cases. On April 15, 1919, a general court-martial convicted Private Frank P. Prassel of mutiny and contemptuous language against the president and sentenced him to fifteen years in prison. Under a pseudonym, Prassel published a letter in a newspaper alleging that Wilson, at the behest of "money interests," had intentionally placed American ships in sight of German submarines to enable the declaration of war to succeed in Congress. Prassel also condemned the British government "for being worse than the German government for its treatment of Ireland." Although Warren recommended to Carter that he make a reduction in Prassel's sentence to five years (and Carter did so), he concluded that the findings were merited and the sentence justified.[78]

Some of the investigations and prosecutions into alleged subversion were later discovered to be nothing more than a product of the delusions of the investigators. On December 18, 1918, Lieutenant Colonel Mendel Smith terminated an investigation after determining that a Major Noel Gaines, who had been ordered into psychiatric observation in Saint Elizabeth's Hospital, was deluded. Smith also advised the acting secretary of war that Gaines's prior investigations were tainted by his psychosis. While serving in the Southern Department, Gaines accused two captains and a lieutenant of disloyalty, and in the lieutenant's case, Gaines accused him of putting ground glass into the mess hall food as well as into horse feed. Gaines also caused a general court-martial conviction of a Private Wrantizky for disloyalty and disobedience of orders. Smith discovered that Wrantizky, an Estonian immigrant, had done nothing more than form a Lutheran bible study group for other Baltic immigrants. Gaines, however, claimed that the Estonian language was a secretive German-Bolshevik cipher. The army arrested and hospitalized Gaines after he accused General Henry T. Allen of secretly conspiring with the IWW to overthrow the government. In working to free Wrantizky and clear all doubt of loyalty from the accused officers, Smith wrote to Ansell, "the evidence submitted in these alleged investigations present a voluminous mixture of some pertinent evidence, much hearsay and irrelevant matters, rumors, and an undue emphasis of purely inconsequential detail."[79]

Even in cases not as egregious as Gaines's false accusations that resulted in courts-martial for four service-members, Smith also recommended disapproving Private Edward Monson's conviction for uttering disloyal statements. On August 26, 1918, Monson, while drunk, announced that "he lived in one hell of a country" and boasted that since he did not have to go to France and fight, "he was having a good time in the Army." Unfortunately Monson also informed a general that he would consider going AWOL if sent to France. Smith advised both the commanding general of the Western Department and the War Department that none of this evidence warranted a conviction for disloyalty or a sentence to two years in confinement and a dishonorable discharge. Apparently the geographic commander agreed, and he transferred Monson to the Presidio in San Francisco.[80]

On occasion, the use of judge advocates in the investigation of persons accused of subversion or disloyalty yielded unforeseen consequences for courts-martial. On March 27, 1918, the judge advocate for the Western Department advised the departmental commander to disapprove a court-martial conviction of a soldier for disloyalty after discovering that Lieutenant Chester A. Bayles, the trial judge advocate, had an unsavory past. In 1913 the New York Court of Appeals disbarred Bayles. A state investigation uncovered that he procured men to provide alcohol and cocaine to a client's wife and then have sex with her prior to a divorce proceeding. Bayles was able to secure a favorable divorce settlement after proving the client's wife was a drug user and committed adultery. He unsuccessfully appealed his disbarment, and the state appellate court published the disbarment in its reporter. Given the rapidity with which officers were commissioned, it is unsurprising that the War Department was unaware of Bayles's disbarment when it commissioned him. On Crowder's advice, Baker dismissed Bayles from the army shortly after the discovery.[81]

Advising on death sentences arising from charges of disloyalty, mutiny, espionage, or sedition became a critical responsibility for several judge advocates. In November 1918, Wilson ordered three soldiers previously sentenced to death to be returned to duty after Charles Beecher Warren advised him to do so. Privates Nicholas Locassie, Benjamin Breger, and Herman Kaplan were convicted of refusing to obey lawful orders and seditious conduct. Although a trial concluded that the three soldiers committed mutiny because they possessed antiwar literature, there was no evidence they intended to undermine military training or wartime discipline. Rather, each of the three soldiers had personal reasons for opposing military service based on their personal faith.[82]

In July 1918 the army prosecuted Privates Edwin E. Schonofsky and Alfons Dalloen in a joint general court-martial in the Western Department. Both men had committed larceny and deserted, but both were also accused of being German spies prior to the theft and desertion. One month later, Baker turned to Crowder to advise him as to whether Shonofsky's death sentence and Dolloen's sentence to fifty years in confinement and a dishonorable discharge were warranted. One day after the Armistice, Senator Hiram Johnson urged Baker to review the guilty verdicts, arguing that the presentation of false evidence that Schonofsky was a spy undermined the trial's fairness. Crowder agreed with Johnson and advised Baker that while Schonofsky had been overhead saying that "the German Army is the best in the world," there was no evidence that he was a spy, and the accusation of disloyalty likely influenced him to desert out of fear for his life. Dalloen had not been accused of spying, but he was Schonofsky's close friend and he feared "guilt by association." Rather than rely on his own review, Crowder turned to Wigmore for an additional opinion. Wigmore, in turn, concluded that the larceny and desertion were a common transaction and therefore the joint trial was warranted, but the trial judge advocate was in error for claiming that Schonofsky was a spy. Wigmore then recommended Baker consider that while Schonofsky's sentence should be commuted, there was no reason to commute Dalloen's sentence. Crowder went further and advised Baker to overturn the verdict against Schonofsky altogether, while reducing Dalloen's sentence to a dishonorable discharge and five years in prison. Crowder intimated, without specifically articulating it, that Schonofsky was under duress as a result of a false allegation. Ultimately, Baker approved both convictions and reduced the sentences to twenty years apiece. In 1919 Ansell would allude to the two courts-martial as further evidence of unfair trials.[83]

INVESTIGATING AND PROSECUTING SEDITION IN THE AMERICAN EXPEDITIONARY FORCES

Courts-martial for disloyalty, sedition, subversion, mutiny, or espionage within the American Expeditionary Forces had a greater potential to result in drastic sentences than courts-martial conducted in the United States. Throughout the conflict, the warring armies and governments had created sophisticated propaganda operations to undermine confidence in the opposing forces. In December 1917 a rumor spread through the American Expeditionary Forces that the United States had to purchase trenches as part of a real-estate contract with the French government. The rumor, while unfounded, had the potential to stoke resentment toward the French population. General Bethel and General D. E. Nolan, the American Expeditionary Forces' intelligence chief, were convinced that the rumor was more than the usual griping from soldiers. Trench rumors were nothing new to the Allies, and occasionally both sides used agents to spread rumors to foment surrender, degrade morale, or incite a mutiny. By August 1918, Bethel believed that the trench rumor originated with French communists rather than pro-German soldiers in the American Expeditionary Forces. General Johnson Hagood, an officer assigned to the Services of Supply, likewise notified General Harbord that he and Colonel Hull believed that Bolsheviks were attempting to cause disaffection in the army. However, Nolan insisted that two pro-German privates assigned to the Rainbow Division's headquarters staff encouraged the rumor. By the end of the war, most of the American Expeditionary Forces' soldiers had heard the rumor, and many soldiers believed it to be true, going so far as to insist on a congressional inquiry into it. There were no courts-martial or arrests resulting from the rumor prior to the departure of American soldiers from Europe in 1922. However, in 1938 Major General Allen Gullion, the army's judge advocate general, reported to the director of intelligence that the two privates Nolan earlier named were in fact the source of the rumor, and he forwarded their names to the Federal Bureau of Investigation. Nothing more appears to have been done in regard to the two soldiers.[84]

During the time American forces served in France and Germany, judge advocates investigated over six hundred soldiers who were suspected of ties to pro-German organizations, the IWW, other socialist groups, or Bolshevik organizations. Most of the investigations yielded no evidence of subversion. Even in the investigations that caused military intelligence officers and judge advocates to believe that a soldier engaged in subversive activities, only a fraction of the soldiers were court-martialed for mutiny or disloyalty. Whether a soldier was brought to trial depended on whether the investigation established that the soldier had actually engaged in some activity that could erode discipline. However, just as with Private Americo Alexander's experience, it was not always the case that subversion or mutiny became the offenses charged against soldiers.

On December 19, 1918, the American Expeditionary Forces' chief of intelligence requested that the Twenty-Ninth Division's commander assign an officer to investigate a Private John Cybulski for spreading propaganda designed to demoralize his fellow frontline soldiers. Cybulski was not accused of being pro-German, but rather, he was a reported IWW member and publicly spoke against the conflict as "a bankers and manufacturers war." Nolan informed Bethel, "it has been ascertained that the IWW has planned to plant its members in the service in order to create disturbances, and it is possible that he is one of their agents for this purpose." Whatever the limited impact of Cybulski's activities, he was a likely candidate to be arrested and court-martialed if he had distributed IWW literature to his fellow soldiers or made public statements to the effect that none of them "should go over the top" or fire a weapon. Cybulski was court-martialed, found guilty, and sentenced to five years in prison and a dishonorable discharge.[85]

In another instance, a lieutenant attached to a depot division was convinced that a Private Howard L. Ditterle was either a member of the IWW or a German agent posing as an IWW member, after hearing that Ditterle had called the war "a capitalists' war" and defended Germany's invasion of France and Belgium. But other than a letter Ditterle wrote to his wife denying German responsibility for the war, there was no evidence he encouraged mutiny. Bethel did not permit a court-martial to go forward based on this limited evidence. Likewise, a San Antonio civilian swore in an affidavit that a Sergeant Alfred Swearingen was a German agent and had possessed IWW literature while he trained in Texas. A judge advocate investigation conducted by Lieutenant Colonel Chiperfield concluded that the civilian was "a jilted woman." Swearingen had served in the West Virginia National Guard during the coalfield strike, and Albert B. White, a former West Virginia governor, noted to Chiperfield that Swearingen "is a young man of splendid qualities and has 'the right stuff' in him." Similarly, the Parkersburg mayor came to Swearingen's defense. As a result, Chiperfield ensured Swearingen transited to the front. Another case Chiperfield investigated arose after a Sergeant Charles Ostendorf had openly expressed his willingness to fight Bulgarians, Turks, and Austrians, but since his father had been a veteran of the Prussian Army during the War of 1870, he did not want to kill Germans. Chiperfield concluded that the sergeant's statements were nothing more than a reluctance to kill family members, and that he was a loyal American and could be assigned elsewhere.[86]

Even in investigations where judge advocates or military intelligence officers determined that a soldier had distributed subversive literature or publicly defended the IWW, Bolshevism, or Germany, there remained a question of intent. Private Herman Becker was investigated for making pro-German statements and claiming that France was as guilty as Germany for the war. Major R. C. Stewart, the First Division's judge advocate, concluded that a court-martial was not warranted because of Becker's personal circumstances. Becker was born in Chicago to immigrant German parents, and he had unsuccessfully attempted to be classified as a conscientious objector. He nonetheless complied with his induction order and was enlisted in the army. Military intelligence agents intercepted Becker's letters to his sister, which were found to contain derogatory statements about President Wilson and the army. But Stewart concluded that "the investigation brought out the fact that he is a young man of extremely limited intellect, and would be incapable of having any success in an attempt to demoralize his fellow soldiers."[87]

In one of the more confusing investigations, a Private Gabriel Cabrera claimed that he was a Mexican citizen, and despite being born in the United States he did not consider himself an American citizen and therefore was not amenable to conscripted military service. Although he attempted to challenge his conscription orders, he was inducted into the army under the threat of arrest. Once in France, Cabrera was discovered to have mailed his mother a letter asking her to have the Mexican Consul in San Francisco reclaim him, and he concluded his letter stating that he was "staining the flag of Mexico by wearing an American uniform." Military intelligence officers intercepted the letter and asked Major J. Van Ness Phillip, a judge advocate attached to the American Expeditionary Forces headquarters, whether Cabrera could be court-martialed "for the inflammatory letter." After investigating the matter, Phillip advised Nolan that although Cabrera was a US citizen by birth, he was also entitled to claim Mexican citizenship because his parents were citizens of that country. To Phillip, the prudent course of action was to send Cabrera back to the United States and have the attorney general convey him to Mexico. Cabrera was returned to the United States and deported to Mexico.[88]

On the other hand, Bethel drafted charges against a Sergeant Charles Schroeder, who was accused of intentionally withholding clothes and blankets from soldiers in June 1918 for the purpose of causing a loss of morale. While in training at Camp Wadsworth, South Carolina, Schroeder publicly spoke in favor of Germany and claimed that the United States was "fighting a banker's and merchant's war." Prior to the war Schroeder was employed as a code transmitter by the W. R. Grace Corporation, a company specializing in shipping, chemicals, and vaults. After Schroeder left the company, its security officers suspected that he gave the IWW corporate codes, and they provided evidence to the War Department. If Schroeder was guilty of anything, he was likely a pro-German agent who wanted to use the IWW to undermine morale. He partially confessed to communicating with IWW members but claimed he did not know that the people he gave corporate codes to belonged to the organization. Schroeder was court-martialed for mutiny, found guilty, and sentenced to five years in confinement and a dishonorable discharge.[89]

Not all cases were as clear as Schroeder's. Private Clarence Wold made the IWW his war insurance beneficiary in the event he was killed. Nolan lobbied the Judge Advocate's Office to have the Fourth Division court-martial Wold for "any slight violation of the Articles of War." Wold's failure to follow orders to report to his platoon commander resulted in a special court-martial sentence of confinement for two months. The court-martial charge indicates that Wold was simply late in following his orders, but it is clear that the underlying reason for the court-martial was the fact that he had been encouraging fellow soldiers to adhere to the IWW's principles and "refuse to go over the top." Surprisingly he was not court-martialed for his encouragement of mutiny. Likewise, a Private Frank Balling had asked his father to send the IWW's antiwar literature so that he could distribute it to his fellow artillerists. Unfortunately for Balling, the army intercepted his letters, and Nolan lobbied Bethel to ensure Balling would be court-martialed. Ultimately Balling was brought to trial. However, he was not charged with mutiny or subversion, but rather, the court-martial found him guilty of an unauthorized absence, disrespect to a noncommissioned officer, and disobedience of orders. He was sentenced to six months in confinement. Balling's example may have been replayed dozens of times throughout the army during the war, making it difficult to give a full analysis as to how many soldiers were suspected of subversion or mutiny but prosecuted for common military offenses.[90]

On October 31, 1918, Major Samuel Wilson served as a trial judge advocate in the general court-martial of Private First Class Julian Jarecky. Assigned as an artilleryman, Jarecky entered a field hospital after being caught in a bombardment and announced that he would no longer serve in the army. He called the war "nothing more than the basest hypocrisy" and "refused to take part in the slaughter." He then went on to claim that he "instinctively favored the German effort, so much so, that [he was] positive that no amount of persuasion and argument could make [him] change his mind." A second specification alleged that while he acknowledged that he could be called a traitor, "it was the president, secretary of war, and the generals who were traitors to the American people, and that merchants and bankers profited from the war." Wilson discerned, while cross-examining a doctor, that Jarecky suffered from a concussion and shell-shock and that there was no real evidence of disloyalty. Following his closing argument, the court-martial found Jarecky "not guilty because of temporary insanity at the time the wrongful acts were committed."[91]

Because the United States' population had rapidly expanded as a result of Central, Southern, and Eastern European immigration, it was unsurprising that some soldiers found it difficult to fight against their country of origin. Sometimes, however, reluctant soldiers did not express their misgivings until already in France. In January 1918, the First Division prosecuted Private Theodore Falatovich after he informed his fellow soldiers that he could not fire upon Austrian or German soldiers because he had brothers serving in both enemy armies. A general court-martial convicted Falatovich for making disloyal statements and disobeying orders and sentenced him to a year's imprisonment and a dishonorable discharge. None of the judge advocates in the review process recommended clemency, and Falatovich's sentence was carried out. Two weeks before Falatovich's court-martial, the commander of the Forty-Second Division charged Private Stanley Poturlaski with the same offenses, and a court-martial sentenced him to a year in prison and a dishonorable discharge. Again, he did not receive any clemency. On March 2, 1918, a general court-martial held by the Ninety-First Division determined that Private Reuben McConnell was guilty of mutiny, disloyal statements, and sedition, and then sentenced him to twenty years and a dishonorable discharge. McConnell had not only called Prime Minister Lloyd George "a criminal" and urged his fellow soldiers of Irish lineage to refuse to fight Germans, he also swore that he would "kill more English officers than any Germans as the Germans had never enslaved anyone."[92]

McConnell's court-martial evidences one difficulty in assessing how the War Department defined loyalty. Great Britain was one of the United States' two most important allies, and by consensus it remains the United States' most important ally to this day. Yet a sizeable number of Americans were sympathetic to Irish demands for unconditional independence from Britain and were appalled at the British government's treatment of Ireland over the previous centuries. Once in uniform and in France, American soldiers were expected to curtail expressions of support for Ireland and criticisms of the British government. On January 2, 1918, a general court-martial convicted Private Macon R. Slaughter of making disloyal statements and sentenced him to a dishonorable discharge and six months in prison. While serving in the Forty-Second Division he informed his fellow soldiers that the British government was "no better than the Germans" and "Ireland deserved its independence." On review, military intelligence officers found additional evidence that Slaughter had corresponded with Irish nationalists, and while the United States had taken a neutral position on Irish independence, the judge advocate review concluded that Slaughter's statements were designed to undermine Allied unity.[93]

Accusations of disloyalty could lead a soldier to desert the ranks out of fear. Such was the case of Private Charles Pfleger, who arrived in France in April 1917 only to find himself under suspicion of being pro-German. After being questioned by military intelligence personnel and threatened with a court-martial, Pfleger fled his unit and as of February 26, 1919, he had not been located in France. Sadly for Pfleger, the judge advocate review of his files concluded that "while he was wrongly maligned by a fellow soldier prior to embarkation for France, he should be court-martialed as a deserter." The army was unable to capture Pflegler, in part because while his name was Germanic, his parents emigrated from Alsace and he was raised speaking French. As of 1919 he had been spotted in Nancy, France, but the army was unable to bring him into custody.[94]

After the Armistice, worries over Bolshevik and IWW influence in the American Expeditionary Forces was replaced with a fear that such organizations would make inroads with the American soldiers remaining in Germany. General Henry T. Allen, who assumed command in occupied Germany, feared that Bolshevism would consume Germany and then cause mutinies among the occupied forces. In December 1918, he wrote to both Peyton March and Senator J. C. W. Beckham of Kentucky that it would be a sound policy to intervene in Russia because Germany's future was intertwined with Russia's. Two months later he reiterated his fears to Pershing, and though he noted that the discipline of the soldiers under his command was "superb," he believed that Bolsheviks had attempted to spread propaganda to American soldiers.[95]

In October 1919, Allen urged General Bliss to lobby Baker to station more soldiers in Germany to stem the spread of communism in the Rhineland as well as permit him to order the arrest of Spartacist leaders. Bliss pushed back on Allen, arguing that the Allies could not afford to occupy Germany and it would have to be a strengthened German government that contained communism. "I doubt whether the United States would go into Germany to put down a Spartacist insurrection any more than it seems willing to go into Russia to put down a Bolsheivk insurrection." Not satisfied with Bliss's answer, Allen wrote to Pershing that he agreed with General Michel, the Belgian commander in Germany, that the "growing Spartacist movement in Germany, coupled with the expansion of Russian Bolshevism into the east will eventuate in an effort to drive out the occupying forces." In the same letter Allen noted that he had growing difficulties maintaining discipline over his forces, particularly those who had been drafted in 1918 and came to Europe after the Armistice. He feared that some of the soldiers had become enamored by Bolshevist propaganda, and he promised to vigorously court-martial persons suspected of fomenting mutiny. While Allen's worries over the reliability of soldiers under his command were exaggerated, his fears were sincere.[96]

Lieutenant Colonel Guy D. Goff's letters from Germany to his father, Senator Nathan Goff, as well as his letters to other judge advocates on the possibility of a Bolshevik takeover of Germany, reflected common fears of subversion in the army. Although in hindsight Goff believed that Bolshevism had expanded far more than it actually had, his fears of its expansion, like Allen's, were sincere. In April 1919, Goff told his father that he agreed with Lord Northcliffe's *Daily Mail* editorials, which accused David Lloyd George of having "Bolsheviki tendencies." One month later, when Northcliffe accused American labor leaders Samuel Gompers and John L. Lewis of "fomenting a class war, from which only the Bolsheviks would benefit," Goff again agreed with Northcliffe's assessment. In June 1919 Goff claimed that Hungarian communist Bela Kun ordered communists to infiltrate into the American forces in Germany. After interviewing a Hungarian expatriate, Goff ascertained that Bolsheviks targeted ethnic Slavic and Hungarian soldiers serving in the United States Army with propaganda designed to encourage desertions as well as defections to the Bolshevik forces in their home countries.[97]

OVERMAN COMMITTEE

On August 10, 1917, Wilson signed into law "An Act to Provide Further for the National Security and Defense by Encouraging the Production, Conserving the Supply, and Controlling the Distribution of Food Products and Fuel." Crafted by Congressman Asbury Francis Lever, the law had little to do with subversion, and it was intended to prevent inflation in the costs of foodstuffs as well as to focus farming and manufacturing on the nation's war needs. The law greatly expanded the president's power to regulate commerce, and for this reason, several legislators objected to it. The law also, by no design of Lever, enabled Congress to open an investigation into suspected subversive activity in the nation. Several prominent brewers such as the Anheuser-Busch and Pabst families had Germanic origins, and the nation's brewers and distillers had, in the decade prior to the war, spent large sums of money on political campaigns. Adolph Busch also purchased hundreds of thousands of dollars in German bonds prior to the war, and he did not divest his family of these bonds after the nation entered the war.[98]

On September 27, 1918, the Senate Judiciary Committee, using the Lever Act as a basis, formed a subcommittee to investigate subversive activities in the United States. Headed by Senator Lee Slater Overman, a North Carolina Democrat, the investigative body was formally titled the "Subcommittee on Brewing and Liquor Interests, and German Propaganda and Bolshevik Propaganda." Along with Lever, Carter Glass, and John Sharp Williams, Overman was one of Wilson's stauncher supporters in Congress. Based on allegations made by A. Mitchell Palmer, the subcommittee first investigated the United States Brewers Association and specified distillers for ties to Germany. In February 1919, the Judiciary Committee extended the subcommittee to investigate Bolshevik efforts to undermine the government and military. Senators Knute Nelson, a Minnesota Republican, Thomas Sterling, a South Dakota Republican, William King, a Utah Democrat, and Josiah Wolcott, a Delaware Democrat, also served on the subcommittee. All of these senators had not only voted to declare war on Germany, they had also voted in favor of the Espionage Act. Because the committee investigated German and Bolshevik efforts to undermine conscription and foster mutinies in the army and navy, Baker convinced Crowder to assist Overman. Crowder initially tried to resist Baker by arguing that aiding a legislative committee to investigate sedition in the United States would unduly politicize the army. But on Baker's insistence, he appointed Major Edwin Lowry Humes to the subcommittee as its counsel.[99]

Major Humes was an unsurprising choice to serve on the subcommittee. Perhaps the only surprising aspect of his service was that Ansell had lobbied Baker and Nelson to have Humes appointed. A United States attorney and staunch Prohibitionist, Humes had prosecuted liquor manufacturers before the war. Several of the prosecutions he conducted had to do with political corruption. In 1914 he served in the Pennsylvania state legislature alongside Cleon Berntheizel. Humes had also worked on A. Mitchell Palmer's unsuccessful Pennsylvania senate campaign in 1914 and had become convinced that German brewers were behind Palmer's defeat in the Democratic primary. Shortly after the declaration of war on Germany, Humes announced that the United States Attorney's Office would prosecute any civilian wearing a military uniform, and he secured indictments against two civilians for doing so. He also publicly accused the IWW of aligning with Germany and enabling Bolshevism to enter the United States. In July 1917, he was commissioned as a judge advocate, partly as a result of Palmer's support and the state governor's recommending him to Baker. By this time, Palmer was appointed as the nation's alien property custodian, in charge of the disposition of German-owned properties and bank accounts. Neither Crowder nor Ansell opposed Humes's commission, and he had the type of prewar experience Crowder sought. Humes had graduated from the University of Pennsylvania's law school, and he served in the National Guard for a decade, including briefly on the Mexican border.[100]

Although Humes was employed as the subcommittee's counsel and directly responsible to Overman, he was most closely aligned in his hatred of Bolshevism, socialism, and the IWW with Knute Nelson. A Norwegian immigrant who fought for the Union in the Civil War, Nelson was wounded and taken prisoner at the Battle of Fort Hudson. He not only approved General Benjamin Butler's heavy-handed administration of New Orleans as well as the harshest aspects of Reconstruction, he also supported the United States' expansion into the Pacific and vocally sided with Great Britain during the Boer War. Throughout World War I, Nelson accused people opposed to the nation's involvement in the war, regardless of whether their opposition was religious or political, of trying to undermine the United States much as the Copperheads had attempted to enable the Confederacy to become an independent nation.[101]

One of the many schemes that Humes claimed to uncover to Nelson was the formation of the Hungarian-American Loyalty League. The league was established by Alexander Konta, a Hungarian Jewish immigrant. Born in Budapest in 1862, Konta established a newspaper called the *Magyar Figaro*, but the Habsburg authorities arrested him for publishing obscene stories. He fled from jail to France and then entered the United States in 1891 as a purchasing agent for a French newspaper corporation. Between 1914 and the United States' declaration of war, Konta met with German government officials, including Von Papen and Bernstorff. In June 1917 Konta formed a loyalty league to establish the government's trust in the Hungarian communities. Konta had invested his own monies, as well as the monies taken from applications to the loyalty league, into two German-owned breweries. Humes concluded that Konta had duped patriotic Magyar immigrants into providing him their money so that he could, in turn, filter their monies through the breweries and fund IWW-led strikes. Nelson lauded Humes for his work.[102]

On July 28, 1919, the subcommittee's investigation reported on its findings to the Senate. Their report concluded that German-American brewing

interests had, during the war, contributed monies to disloyal causes and purchased interests in newspapers to oppose Prohibition and defend Germany.
The subcommittee linked German cultural organizations, which predated the
war by decades, to von Bernstorff or other German government officials. It
also accused the German government of trying to influence leading academics and scholars, as well as publishing news articles favorable to Germany. "The
commercial field in many industries was dominated by Germans or those of
German extraction and sympathy," the subcommittee noted before it listed
banking, exports, chemicals, and textiles as having overarching Germanic
influences. It was able to pinpoint that German officials had attempted to purchase military supplies and even establish a German-owned munitions firm
in the United States. None of these facts should have been surprising. Nor
should the fact that the German government sanctioned espionage operations
in the United States have come as a surprise, given that US industries had
shipped tremendous amounts of war matériel to the Allies prior to April 1917
and American banks had loaned millions of dollars in gold bullion to both
Britain and France.[103]

The subcommittee went further, however, and claimed that Germany was
able to manipulate at least one congressman and a large labor-based peace
organization into pushing for a vote against war. It tied Irish nationalist leaders to Germany as well. Perhaps the most controversial aspect of the subcommittee's investigation had to do with its claim that a Bolshevik revolution was
essentially under way. The subcommittee partly arrived at this conclusion as
a result of communist doctrine. Beginning with Karl Marx, communist leaders had argued that communism would either be a worldwide movement or
would be doomed to failure. The subcommittee acknowledged that while
few Americans were true Bolsheviks, of the many people who were attracted
to Bolshevism—derided as "parlor Bolsheviks"—few actually understood
the conditions inside of Russia. "The Bolsheviki have inaugurated a reign of
terror unparalleled in the history of modern civilization," the subcommittee
warned. Although the Armistice was signed by the time the subcommittee
published its findings, their report warned that Germany had set in motion a
Bolshevik propaganda program to weaken American banking institutions and
undermine agriculture. The subcommittee also claimed that Bolshevism had
intruded into public and university education, and that if it were not stopped,
the country could experience greater numbers of bombings and strikes.[104]

Humes accused American scholars who had studied in Germany of har-
boring Bolshevist sympathies. While not well remembered today, prominent
professors such as David Starr Jordan, Charles Beard, and George Brinton
McClellan Jr., the son of the Civil War general and unsuccessful presidential

candidate, were claimed to have Bolshevist sympathies. Humes also accused Jane Addams of being in league with the Bolsheviks. Even two of Brandeis's students were accused of disloyalty to the United States. When Amos Pinchot— a former ally of Theodore Roosevelt and one the nation's leading war opponents—accused Humes, in a letter to Overman, of seeking to topple the nation's freedoms, Overman and Nelson accused Pinchot of disloyalty after he publicly repeated Congressman George Huddleston's claim that Crowder was "a military satrap." Ironically, Crowder had concluded that Humes had gone too far in his accusations, and he permitted other judge advocates to testify on behalf of persons whom the subcommittee had implicated as disloyal. For instance, in February 1919, Colonel Wambaugh testified to the committee that in his opinion, Professor Albert Bushnell Hart, a well-regarded historian, was a loyal citizen after anonymous people informed the committee that Hart was pro-German and Humes claimed the accusations to be merited.[105]

CONCLUSION: THE RECEDING OF ABRIDGEMENTS OF RIGHTS

On December 21, 1918, Crowder attended a joint War and Navy Department meeting to discuss labor strikes in Seattle and the use of soldiers and sailors not only to safeguard war industries but also to suppress Bolshevik and IWW demonstrations. One month earlier, Crowder advised Van Deman and Baker to transfer all investigative files on civilians to the Department of Justice "because the *Posse Comitatus Act* and *Milligan* appear to require that the Army no longer police the nation's civilian population." However, during the meeting, Crowder agreed with Van Deman that "the IWW, Bolsheviki, radical socialists, and on some issues the AF of L have joined, and formed a dangerous combination to American institutions." Crowder advocated continuing to court-martial soldiers for sedition in instances where soldiers were discovered to be openly espousing IWW or Bolshevik policies. He also noted that Bolsheviks had attempted to convert soldiers serving in the coastal defenses in Louisiana and in the Northeast. In spite of his agreement on the dangers of Bolshevism and the IWW, by the middle of 1919 the number of courts-martial for sedition precipitously dropped as did the sentences for soldiers caught trying to undermine discipline through Bolshevik propaganda.[106]

Just as Congress began to retreat from investigating communism in late 1919, the army returned to its prewar approach to fears of internal subversion. In reality, this process began in 1919. In January of that year, a recently discharged officer who had served as a temporary judge advocate on General

George van Horn Moseley's staff informed the general that "since the Armistice, numbers of discharged soldiers roamed through New York City, and near Governors Island they intentionally refused to salute officers." The officer then claimed that this led soldiers awaiting discharge to do the same and then concluded that Bolsheviki were behind the indiscipline, and because "democracy is only capable of a veneer of discipline except on the front line where the men have come to learn that discipline is really life insurance," Bolshevism might take root in the army. Moseley certainly believed this to be the case, and throughout the two succeeding decades he tried to prevent foreigners and Jews from enlisting in the army. Moseley shared his impressions with Winship, who in turn advised Crowder that Moseley was "misguided."[107]

On June 11, 1920, Crowder asked Wigmore to assess whether the conviction and sentence of Private Wallace Patch at Langley Field was legally sound. By this time Wigmore was no longer in the army. Patch had been court-martialed and sentenced to two years in confinement for larceny at the beginning of 1919. In March 1920 Patch "led a mutiny of several prisoners to refuse to work and then taunted the guard officers with communist sayings." A general court-martial convicted him of mutiny and sentenced him to six months' confinement. Wigmore reviewed the record of trial and concluded that it was legally sound but then recommended to Crowder to have the War Department disapprove the sentence. Wigmore reached a similar conclusion under almost identical facts in the case of Private Maurice Adams, except that Adams had been imprisoned at Camp Holabird, Maryland.[108]

In 1922 Paul Crouch, the son of a North Carolina preacher and Civil War veteran, joined the army with the express purpose of committing subversive acts at the behest of the newly formed Communist Party of the United States. The army court-martialed Crouch in Hawaii for attempting to foster a mutiny, creating a secret organization within the army, and communicating with Soviet intelligent agents. A court-martial found him guilty and sentenced him to three years in prison. Crowder and Hull advised Secretary of War John Weeks that the sentence was appropriate to the offense, but Crouch would cause no harm if released early. The two judge advocates forwarded this advice, knowing that American communist leaders and their Soviet supporters wanted to use the army to train American communists so that Americans would not have to travel to the Soviet Union for military training. Additionally, the Soviet agents wanted to hide procommunist soldiers in the army so that when the expected revolution did come, or if the United States went to war against the Soviet Union, these soldiers would stoke indiscipline in the ranks. Considering what Crouch had intended to accomplish, his time in prison was rather short. After his release, he tried to form a clandestine operation to place communists in naval yards for a similar purpose. However, by 1945 he shed his communist affiliation and became one of the nation's more vocal anticommunists. During the Cold War he assisted congressional investigations and organized entrapment schemes for J. Edgar Hoover. Crowder and his subordinates were not prescient to the point that they predicted Crouch would assist the government against subversion. They merely viewed him similarly to the way they viewed Waldo Coffman in 1913—as a noxious soldier deserving a dishonorable discharge.[109]

8

COURTS-MARTIAL AND DISCIPLINE
CONTROVERSY: 1918–1920

BETWEEN THE ARMISTICE AND THE New Year, several of the nation's newspapers and dozens of prominent politicians vocally lauded Crowder. William Howard Taft asked Baker to promote Crowder to a fourth star, bypassing the rank of lieutenant general and with a date of rank placing him only behind Pershing and Bliss in seniority. Senator Henry Cabot Lodge wanted Wilson to appoint Crowder to the American delegation in Versailles. On December 11, 1918, Crowder spoke to an audience at Georgetown University and advocated for a permanent selective service so that if the nation had to confront a resurgent Germany or a future Bolshevik enemy, the army would be manned by trained soldiers from all parts of society and American industry could plan for a depletion of its male workforce. The *El Paso Times, Salt Lake Herald, Washington Star, Brooklyn Daily Eagle, New York Times, New York World, New York Sun, Saint Louis Globe Democrat, Chicago Tribune, San Francisco Chronicle, Louisville Courier Journal, Detroit Journal, Albany Knickerbocker Press,* and *Philadelphia Ledger* endorsed Crowder's idea. The *Salt Lake Herald* called universal conscription "the antidote for Bolshevism," and the *Philadelphia Ledger's* editors proclaimed Crowder to be "one of the ablest men in Washington who has performed difficult services brilliantly." Crowder and several of his subordinates collected the nation's newspapers as a means for assessing the population's willingness to continue conscription but also as evidence of the nation's confidence in the Judge Advocate General's Office.[1]

Crowder envisioned a conscription program in which male citizens underwent a three-month basic military training regimen followed by three months of active service. Conscripted citizens would be expected to drill as federal reservists for thirty days per year, with six years of total obligation.

While Crowder must have been pleased with the support of the newspapers, he refused to take credit for the success of bringing four million men into a trained army. Instead, he publicly complimented Congressman Julius Kahn and Senator George Chamberlain as well as his staff of judge advocates and the hundreds of citizens who administered the draft boards. Crowder did not expect that the postwar accolades for the Judge Advocate General's Office would soon come to a sweeping halt. At the end of December 1918, Chamberlain publicly accused Baker and Crowder of permitting thousands of soldiers to be prosecuted in unfair courts-martial. Congressman Royal Johnson of South Dakota, a decorated veteran recently returned from the Western Front, joined Chamberlain in condemning the administration of military justice. Ansell was, in fact, the catalyst for Chamberlain's and Johnson's actions, though Crowder did not realize this until the end of February 1919.[2]

Ansell was clearly dissatisfied with Crowder's governance of the Judge Advocate General's Office throughout the war. Baker's decisions had resulted in a diminution of Ansell's status within the War Department, and Ansell blamed Crowder. In the early part of the summer of 1918, Crowder and Ansell advocated to Baker to create a board to examine general courts-martial records for both legal sufficiency and to advise the War Department on the propriety of reducing individual sentences. While Baker followed their advice, Ansell protested the board's construction for two reasons. First, the board was not a true appellate court and it simply advised Baker, though it did so in a detailed format akin to a court of appeals decision. As a result, the board did not create binding precedents and it became colloquially known as a "clemency board," denoting that it was not an adjudicatory body. Second, with Baker's approval, Crowder assigned Ansell, Wigmore, and Major A. Stevens Heckscher to serve on the board. Ansell did not oppose Heckscher's appointment. Heckscher had attended Harvard at the same time as Frankfurter, represented railroads in Pennsylvania, and was also a director of the Central National Bank of Philadelphia. But when, at the end of February 1919, Ansell was reduced to his prewar rank, Wigmore became his superior officer on the board. The two men had clashed since the war began. By the end of 1918, Ansell knew that Wigmore would be in a position of authority over him.[3]

A second source of Ansell's anger had to do with his expectation to become judge advocate general. He expected Crowder to retire in early 1919 and support his ascension to head the office. But by December 1918, Ansell learned that Crowder not only intended to serve a third term as judge advocate general, he also favored Kreger and Bethel because he considered their service in France more important than Ansell's wartime duties. For Crowder to succeed to a third term, President Wilson would have to forward his nomination to

the Senate Military Affairs Committee before February 1, 1919. Regardless
of whether Crowder were renominated, statutorily regular army officers who
had been brevetted during the war had to return to their prewar rank, which
for Ansell meant a demotion to lieutenant colonel. Whoever was selected to
become assistant judge advocate general would serve as a brigadier general
and likely be the next officer to become judge advocate general. Thus only one
brevetted officer would be able to keep his rank. The other officers reduced
in rank faced another troubling fact. Judge advocates brought in as reservists
prior to the declaration of war would retain their wartime rank until the term
of their service expired. Once Ansell reverted to his prewar lieutenant colonel
rank, Wigmore, Wambaugh, Easby-Smith, and several other reservists would
outrank him, and he did not enjoy good relations with these officers. Instead
of remaining on active duty for another three years so that he could retire or
compete for colonel, Ansell informed Crowder that he "would likely resign
his commission and begin the private practice of law." Although Crowder did
not want Ansell to leave the army prior to his retirement eligibility, he asked
Lindley Garrison and Henry Stimson "to hire Ansell or find him a position in
a prominent law firm." On July 1, 1919, Ansell resigned from the army.[4]

In one sense, Ansell's frustrations dated to his inability to become the acting judge advocate general. He believed that he could not perform his duties
unless he was fully vested with the authority inherent in the judge advocate
general position. But throughout the war Crowder remained responsible for
the assignment of judge advocates as well as the approval of published legal
opinions. In November 1917, when Baker instructed Crowder to perform the
duties of judge advocate general contemporaneously with his assignment as
provost marshal of the United States, it angered Ansell that Crowder had not
objected to supervising both War Department agencies. On the other hand,
even though Crowder disagreed with Ansell's response to the "Texas Mutiny
trials," he did not disparage Ansell to either Baker or the general staff, and it
was solely Baker who made the decision not to permit Ansell to be appointed
as acting judge advocate general.[5]

Crowder remained adamant that the 1916 Articles of War, when coupled
with wartime safeguards such as General Order 7, not only ensured due
process to soldiers but maintained the basic structure of the 1916 Articles
necessary for the army's reliability. He insisted, moreover, that Germany had
only been temporarily defeated by a disciplined American soldiery. He did
not believe that harsh sentences were required or that soldiers charged with
committing offenses were automatically guilty, and he stressed that as the
burden of proof remained on the government, there was nothing inherently
unfair about maintaining a command-directed system of military justice. In

response to the argument that a court of appeals was necessary, he cautioned that any formal appeals process, to include a binding appeals court, undermined the president's constitutional authority as commander in chief as well as those powers the president delegated to a secretary of war. Crowder's argument over presidential authority comported with President Wilson's belief in Executive Branch primacy. A court of appeals would also, Crowder believed, undermine one of the principal features of courts-martial, namely the speed of adjudication from trial to the final disposition of the case.[6]

In January 1919 Baker presented Ansell with the Distinguished Service Medal. Undoubtedly Ansell deserved this highest recognition for his wartime staff work. Within two months, the War Department reduced him to his peacetime grade. In between those two events Ansell criticized courts-martial to a hastily formed Senate Military Affairs subcommittee, so that his demotion—regardless of the fact that hundreds of other officers were similarly reduced to their peacetime grade—appeared to Ansell and his allies Senator Chamberlain and Congressman Johnson as a punishment for his advocacy of having Congress reconstruct courts-martial to mirror federal criminal trials and to divest commanders of their authority to convene and control courts-martial. In March 1919, Baker informed newspaper reporters and Congress that Ansell's demotion was part of a normal course of business and that Ansell was not the only officer so treated. Ansell responded by accusing Baker of dishonesty. By the end of that month, Baker ordered Ansell to cease from publicly disparaging Crowder. However, by this time a small number of other judge advocates, politicians, and newspaper editors characterized Crowder as a martinet. Between August and November, a second Senate subcommittee conducted hearings into military justice. During this period Ansell openly accused Crowder of lacking integrity and Crowder responded in kind. Supporters of both officers, to include prominent men such as Taft, Henry Stimson, and Elihu Root, joined in a public fight over not only the fairness of courts-martial but also the army's role in society. After all, the fact that the army had added approximately 30,000 convicted felons and created over 300,000 federal records of convictions in lesser trials, evidenced the military's influence in the nation, in particular in regard to the employability and social standing of those soldiers convicted. Public dissatisfaction with courts-martial, Crowder's supporters feared, could lead to widespread criticisms against the War Department's other actions, particularly conscription and the army's domestic activities during the war.[7]

More important than the accusations of malfeasance by Crowder, Ansell, Baker, and their surrogates was the fact that the two subcommittee investigations occurred at a time when the participants believed not only that universal military training and an enlarged reserve force would soon come into being, but also that there was a realistic possibility of a renewed war as well as a Bolshevik attempt to cause an army-wide mutiny. For instance, on December 23, 1918, General Bethel wrote to Crowder that he desired to remain in France, because to go home at that point would be "an abandonment of important work when we are only in the midst of it." More to the point, Bethel, like Crowder, believed that Bolsheviks and their allies planned to topple the French, Italian, and German governments, and only the presence of a strong American military force in Europe could prevent this. Bethel and Crowder embodied what appears to have been the prevailing War Department belief in the dangers of Bolshevism, and this belief was rooted in the wartime experiences of the Allied forces. In 1919 Major Samuel Pepper wrote in his diary that "discipline is the *sine qua non* of a military organization." He reasoned that if the army ceased to be disciplined, then it would fall apart much as the French Army had during the mutinies of 1917— and then Bolshevism would seep into it.[8]

Several of the army's commanding generals likewise feared a new war. In late 1919 General Henry T. Allen apprised Baker of his worries over the American forces in Germany being caught in a Civil War between promonarchist and Bolshevik forces. Allen stressed the need to maintain absolute discipline over his soldiers to prevent them from causing an anti-American demonstration or sparking a revolt against the Allies. On December 20, 1919, Major Lewis Colfelt, a judge advocate stationed at Camp Zachary Taylor, wrote to General Charles Pelot Summerall that Bolsheviks and anarchists were trying to influence soldiers awaiting discharge. He encouraged Summerall to push Congress to increase the pay of soldiers and to expand the Department of Justice's ability to use the Espionage Act to prosecute civilians who distributed "Bolshevik propaganda" near military installations, and he added that it was important to reemphasize to the Legislative Branch the importance of harshly disciplining soldiers who introduced communist ideas into the ranks.[9]

Perhaps one of the best examples of the linkage between the fears of Bolshevism and opposition to Ansell's push for reform came from one of Ansell's own friends. On May 21, 1919, William Judson, who had returned to Washington, DC, and was reduced to the rank of colonel in the Corps of Engineers as part of the postwar reduction in the size of the army, informed General Peyton March and Baker of his opposition to Ansell's proposed reforms, particularly in reducing the role of commanders from the military disciplinary process. Judson acknowledged that like March, he had no personal affinity for Crowder and was one of Ansell's friends, but he believed Ansell's reforms would undermine military discipline. Drawing from his experiences in observing the Russian Army under Kerensky and then the Bolshevik government under Lenin, Judson concluded that the United States Army would be crippled by a diminution in discipline if Ansell prevailed. "The first thing that happened following the revolution that ejected the Czar was a 'reform' in the Military Code, practically eliminating the authority of commanding generals over courts-martial and their activities," Judson began, and he concluded, "they did not know that this greatest asset of an army—discipline—cannot be certainly preserved unless the administration of military justice, which is one of the principal means of preserving discipline, is in the hands, and known to be in the hands, of the line officers set over the men of any command."[10]

ANSELL AND CROWDER: A PRIVATE DISAGREEMENT

From July 1918 through the end of the year, over one hundred civilian lawyers were commissioned as judge advocates and assigned to the Judge Advocate General's Office. Their numbers included Richard Billups, an Oklahoma legislator who attended the 1912 Democrat Convention and cast his state's vote for Wilson; Homer Hall, a United States Attorney and Illinois Republican who campaigned for Taft in 1912; Aubrey Strode, a Virginia legislator who drafted a state statute mandating sterilizations for the "feeble minded," which the Supreme Court later infamously upheld in *Buck v. Bell*; and Francis E. McGovern, a former governor of Wisconsin and La Follette ally. Academics were also represented in this group. On August 1, 1918, the War Department commissioned Noel T. Dowling judge advocate with the rank of major. Dowling was a professor of law at Columbia University. He not only headed the War Risk Insurance Division, he also chaired a fourth clemency board. Major George C. Beach joined Dowling on this board. Beach was an adjunct professor at the University of Missouri Law School. But when he left Missouri for a judge advocate commission, he also left his position as a justice on the Missouri Supreme Court. Captain Hugh Fegan, a Georgetown law professor and future dean, served as a third officer on this board. Between 1908 and 1911, Fegan served as the Department of Agriculture's solicitor. Edmund Morgan, who was later to be instrumental in the design and passage of the Uniform Code of Military Justice in 1950, also had an occasional role on the boards. He was commissioned in September 1918 with the rank of major and left the army in May 1919. A graduate of Harvard's law school, prior to entering the Judge Advocate General's Office he was a professor at the University of Minnesota, and after the war he taught law at Yale University. These eight officers, like their ninety-seven counterparts assigned to the Judge Advocate

General's Office, represented an almost complete cross section of the nation's legal thinking.[11]

On November 12, 1918, Crowder issued a memorandum informing judge advocates serving in Washington, DC, that while he was sympathetic to their desire to return to their homes and civilian legal work, he would not endorse any application to separate from the army. "The demands upon the Department are likely to increase, rather than decrease, for some time to come," he began. "To serve as long as the department needs you during this war is your official obligation and your personal duty; and neither the war, legally speaking, nor the work of the war, practically speaking, is yet over." In reality, the Judge Advocate General's Office was about to be flooded with thousands of general courts-martial records as well as claims against the War Department from foreign entities and domestic corporations, and a tremendous increase in statutorily mandated War Risk Insurance examinations. Crowder ended his memorandum by explaining that he had confidence in the patriotism and commitment to duty of all of the personnel assigned to the Judge Advocate General's Office. Ansell responded to this memorandum with a challenge to Crowder to explain why, if the Judge Advocate General's Office required over one hundred judge advocates with temporary commissions, the termination of his brevet promotion was warranted. Crowder reasonably appears to have ignored Ansell on this matter. After all, Crowder had no statutory authority to prevent Ansell's reduction in rank.[12]

Ansell had, the week prior to Crowder's memorandum, attempted to impose a legal and policy change on the clemency boards without Crowder's approval. Six days before Crowder issued his memorandum, Ansell issued a memorandum regarding the clemency board's review of courts-martial. He acknowledged that the federal courts of appeal and the majority of state appellate courts utilized the "scintilla rule, in applying the facts of a criminal trial when determining whether the sufficiency of the evidence was such to sustain the conviction." That is, the federal and state appellate courts would not, as a general rule, overturn convictions unless no evidence had been brought to the attention of the jurors that could establish that a person on trial was guilty. Normally under the "scintilla rule," only challenges based on law, such as a defendant being denied the right to question witnesses or a judge permitting a jury to consider inadmissible evidence, could be used as a basis for overturning a conviction. The "scintilla rule" was the prevailing American practice in appeals. However, Ansell directed the judge advocates reviewing general courts-martial records to apply an "English legal standard, requiring reversal when there is not a reasonable sufficiency of evidence or when substantial injustice has on the whole case been done to the accused." Ansell conceded that the more permissive "English legal standard" was likely to result in greater numbers of recommendations for reversal, particularly because several judge advocates had served as trial and appellate judges prior to the war and would understand the liberal character of the "English standard." The next day, Crowder, on Wigmore's advice, reversed Ansell's order and directed the judge advocates to adopt the more traditional and stringent "scintilla rule." However, Crowder also stressed that this rule applied to the determination of guilt, and he expected the boards would recommend that most of the sentences would be mitigated.[13]

In the last two weeks of November 1918, Ansell would resend a number of his wartime memoranda to Baker and Crowder criticizing courts-martial practice, and he once more advocated for a court of military appeals staffed by judge advocates who would have the authority to overturn convictions and reverse sentences. Crowder does not appear to have been angered by Ansell's renewed efforts, and while the two men had several private conversations, Crowder continued to advocate for Ansell to obtain a position in a law firm or in government. Ansell gave no indication that he had met with Senator Chamberlain or other legislators in an effort to effectuate a change to courts-martial, and he remained as chairman of the clemency boards until his reduction in rank. Yet Crowder also had an inkling that he would have to respond to Ansell's arguments in a forum outside of the War Department.

On December 4, Crowder created two working groups, partly to examine and respond to Ansell's claims of the unfairness of courts-martial. One group, formed under the title "Judge Advocates' Military Society," was headed by Colonel Robert Kemper Bailey, who had served in the army as an infantry officer until his retirement in 1911. After a brief career as a probate judge in Virginia, Baker recalled him from retirement to active duty. Having been born in 1848, Bailey was the oldest judge advocate to serve in uniform during World War I. Although he graduated from the University of Virginia's law school before being commissioned, he spent only six months as a judge advocate. He served in campaigns against the Sioux, Cheyenne, and Apache, and he was also General Nelson A. Miles's aide during the Apache campaign. Majors Jacob Ruppenthal and James Sidney Sanner joined Bailey on this working group. Like Bailey, Sanner was also a state judge prior to the war. Born in Maryland in 1872, he emigrated to the Montana Territory in 1884, and at the age of fifteen he graduated from high school. Rather than attend college, Sanner studied law under the tutelage of a local judge and was admitted to practice law in 1892. In addition to heading the Miles City School Board, he was elected as the city's judge in 1907. In 1912 he became a justice on the state's supreme court. On October 9, 1918, Sanner resigned from the state supreme court and secured a judge advocate commission.[14]

By the time the German Army invaded Belgium in 1914, Jacob Ruppen-
thal was a well-regarded Kansas trial judge. Born in Philadelphia to German
immigrant parents in 1869, he moved with his family to Kansas in 1876.
He was educated at Saline State Normal College and then the University of
Kansas and was admitted to the bar in 1896. One year later he was elected
Russell County's district attorney. In 1906 he was elected a county judge.
He was active in the Republican Party and campaigned for Taft in 1908 and
again in 1912. He was married in 1895. When his wife died in 1914 and he
accepted his commission, he was the single father of three young daughters.
In 1917 Crowder, at Taft's urging, wrote to Ruppenthal to see if he would
accept a commission. Ruppenthal delayed his commission until August
1918, when he believed his oldest daughter could help raise his younger
two. When he left for the army, a local district attorney attempted to have
him removed from the bench as a result of his accepting a federal commission. Under the state constitution, Ruppenthal's removal might have been
required. However, the state supreme court refused to entertain the merits
of the district attorney's filing.[15]

Wambaugh headed a second committee, the "Judge Advocates Memorial
Volume." Majors John Reed Scott and William M. McKinney joined him.
Educated at Gettysburg College, Scott was admitted to the bar in 1889 after
studying under a Pennsylvania judge. In the decade prior to the war he represented railroads and steel corporations, and he also served as a part-time
magistrate. In 1898 he was commissioned as a lieutenant in the Pennsylvania
National Guard. On June 29, 1918, he was commissioned as a judge advocate with the rank of major and served through the end of 1920, leaving the
army as a lieutenant colonel. Bernard Baruch recommended Scott to Crowder,
with an important caveat. Scott had drafted legal protections for Baruch's vast
investments in the steel industry, and Baruch wanted to avoid any impropri-
ety in War Department contracting. Born in Illinois and educated at Union
College, McKinney was a prominent New York lawyer who served as a state
legislator and occasional professor. He authored several treatises on the state
laws of New York, Massachusetts, and California, and he also undertook
efforts to further the acceptance of psychiatry in criminal trials. During the
war he drafted orders for Baker to place psychiatrists into the American Expeditionary Force's divisions and enable commanders to forgo courts-martial if
a soldier was diagnosed as not responsible for his conduct. After his wartime
service, he moved to Los Angeles and became the American Bar Association's
Pacific Coast chairman.[16]

On January 4, 1919, Crowder utilized the work of the two "working groups"
to defend the Judge Advocate General's Office to Baker. He pointed out that

in September 1917, he had drafted an order for Baker to issue to all generals commanding geographic departments as well as the American Expeditionary Forces' corps and divisional commanders. The order instructed them to reduce the large numbers of dishonorable discharges and permit convicted soldiers to return to their duties whenever possible. It was true that throughout the war Crowder argued that dishonorable discharges and long terms of confinement were necessary for soldiers who committed rape or murder, assaulted foreign civilians or noncommissioned officers and officers, sowed dissension, attempted mutinies, committed egregious larcenies, or abused prisoners of war. However, he stressed that minor offenses, such as unauthorized absences, failures to obey regulations, certain disrespects to higher officials, and "small-time" larcenies were not a reason to stigmatize citizens with a dishonorable discharge for the duration of their lives. Baker endorsed Crowder's memorandum in late 1917 and issued a broad policy statement to its effect. Thus, from Crowder's perspective, the Judge Advocate General's Office had been proactive in preventing injustices.[17]

On January 11, 1919, Ansell conveyed a long letter to Baker noting that the clemency boards had reviewed over one hundred general courts-martial from Camp Dix, but because Crowder had refused to permit the "English standard," many of the convictions, though legally sound, resulted in unjust sentences that remained intact after the clemency review process. Ansell once more argued that given the thousands of trial records, Baker could not possibly thoughtfully consider the gravity of all of the sentences, and only an appellate court would alleviate much of the secretary's workload. Some of the sentences were indeed harsh, even by army standards. For instance, a private was sentenced to thirty years' imprisonment for refusing to drill with a rifle, and the sentence was only reduced by the convening authority to ten years. The board recommended a reduction to one year, keeping the dishonorable discharge, but Ansell dissented and recommended overturning the dishonorable discharge. Ansell must have assumed that Baker had not read through the record because he adopted the board's advice with no further inquiry. A soldier convicted of a one-month absence without leave was sentenced to forty years, and the clemency board recommended a reduction to five years. Again, Baker rapidly approved the board's recommendation, even though Ansell dissented from the other two judge advocates and urged that the secretary only approve a six-month term in prison. A private who smoked a cigarette during an open ranks inspection and on being ordered to hand his cigarettes over to an officer stated that he "did not give a God damn for anybody" was sentenced to forty years. Although the convening authority reduced the sentence to ten years, and the clemency board further recommended a reduction to one year,

Ansell urged this was still an unjust sentence, and only a court of appeals could reduce it without troubling Baker.[18]

Ten days after reading Ansell's letter, Baker ordered the expansion of clemency review boards and in response, Crowder created a second and third board. One month later he created a fourth board. Baker also added in his order that the boards not only had a duty to recommend the reduction of sentences for minor offenses, they also had a duty to recommend disapproval of dishonorable discharges, even in "serious cases." Although Crowder was pleased by the work of the boards, and Baker assured Crowder that he was confident in the boards, Crowder worried about whether he would be permitted to serve a third term. Perhaps Crowder was unaware that Baker had sided with him on almost every issue, but in late January, Frankfurter informed Henry Stimson, "Baker is vigorously behind Crowder and I am sure that he can be counted on to carry through the fight." Still, Frankfurter doubted that Baker alone could prevail over a growing number of critics of military justice in Congress, and he asked Stimson to enlist Elihu Root's support to convince the American Bar Association to endorse the Judge Advocate General's Office's wartime performance. One week after Frankfurter's first communique to Stimson, he conveyed to Stimson that Ansell was guided by personal ambition to the detriment of the army.[19]

Frankfurter's suspicions of Ansell were understandable. On January 25, 1919, Ansell decried the unfairness of courts-martial at a luncheon of Chicago Real Estate Board members. Later that day, he gave a similar speech to the Chicago Bar Association. The *Chicago Daily News* reported Ansell's comments, but Crowder did not learn of them for several days. Ironically, Crowder appears to have encouraged Ansell as well as other officers to lecture to audiences about how the Judge Advocate General's Office contributed to the Allies' victory, and in late January, Crowder asked Ansell to speak to a large gathering in Washington, DC. By the end of the month, however, he ordered Ansell to cease making public appearances for the purpose of criticizing courts-martial. This did not prevent Ansell's opinions from becoming known to the public. Even if Ansell were silenced, he had an ally in Edmund Morgan, who had returned to his civilian professorship at the University of Minnesota, and Morgan was not restrained in his support. Four other judge advocates also sided with Ansell.[20]

There were events not directly related to the criticisms of military justice that Crowder believed his critics concocted to discredit him. On January 19, 1919, the *Sacramento Bee* printed a news story that claimed General March had offered Crowder important overseas postings to include command of a division, but Crowder objected to these assignments. (That same day, the *New*

York World headlined stories on courts-martial abuses.) The *Bee* was in error because Crowder had forcefully petitioned Baker, March, and Pershing for command of a division as well as command over the Port Arthur expedition, but Baker refused to let Crowder leave Washington, DC. Justice Brandeis forwarded the story to Crowder, who in turn disavowed it, adding that he wondered whether the story was created to put him in a poor national light as intentionally avoiding danger. Almost contemporaneously, an anonymous officer accused Crowder of consorting with Asian prostitutes in a letter to Baker that was also sent to the Richmond, Virginia *Times Dispatch*. That newspaper's editors did not print the letter and forwarded it to Crowder. There was no evidence that Ansell encouraged the officer to accuse Crowder of consorting with prostitutes, but in 1919, General Van Deman informed Crowder that George C. Beach, a former judge advocate, was the source of the allegation, and Beach was one of Ansell's few vocal supporters.[21]

There was one particular aspect to Ansell's conduct that infuriated Crowder prior to February 1919. In early January, Ansell informed Alabama congressman John Lawson Burnett that Crowder had supported the death sentences of Privates John Cook, Forrest Sebastian, Stanley Fishback, and Olen Ledoyen, which Baker ultimately overturned under General Order 7. Burnett had voted against declaring war on Germany, conscription, and the Espionage Act, and he was generally opposed to courts-martial. Ansell claimed to Burnett that he "went over Crowder's head" to ensure that the four soldiers were not sentenced to death. Ansell did, in fact, tell another congressman during the war that the army would execute the four soldiers unless he or someone else could convince Wilson to intervene, but that congressman did not meet with Baker. Although Crowder had initially found no errors in the four courts-martial, he also privately met with Baker to express his misgivings on permitting the four executions to proceed, and he informed Ansell of this fact. Ansell failed to tell Burnett that Crowder not only opposed the executions, he ultimately supported restoring the four soldiers to duty, and this would become a contested issue in the two subcommittee investigations.[22]

POLITICAL AND PUBLIC DISAGREEMENT: CHAMBERLAIN, JOHNSON, AND ANSELL

On December 30, 1918, in a speech to several of his constituents, Chamberlain turned his public criticisms of the War Department's wartime performance specifically to courts-martial. In a speech to Congress four days later, he claimed that the legal academy had begun to cast doubts on the fairness of courts-martial and urged that a court of appeals be established. Four days later, the American Bar Association announced that it would undertake an independent study of courts-martial to determine whether it was appropriate to recommend changes in court-martial procedure. Ultimately, however, the bar association found no general due process shortcomings in courts-martial, though the investigating attorneys recognized that individual cases had resulted in unfair verdicts and sentences. Chamberlain would not know of the bar association's findings until months later, and he determined that it was unwise to wait for the association to conclude its report to take action in the Senate. On January 9, 1919, he announced that he had formed a subcommittee and drafted a bill that would empower the judge advocate general to reverse findings and reduce sentences as well as order new trials.[23]

By the beginning of February, Crowder was worried that he would not be reappointed to a third term as a result of congressional opposition. If, by February 14, the Senate failed to confirm his appointment, he would be forced to retire. For Crowder to succeed to a third term, President Wilson had to transmit the nomination from Europe, and this only came before the Senate on February 12. Crowder did not, at first, suspect that Ansell sought to undermine his reappointment, but he informed Frankfurter and Stimson that he believed Chamberlain and Royal Johnson wanted to use newspaper criticisms of courts-martial to ensure that Ansell would be promoted into the post. Crowder had a sound reason to be concerned with Chamberlain, who until March would continue to chair the Military Affairs Committee.[24]

From the distance of almost a century, it is difficult to pinpoint what motivated Chamberlain to criticize military justice. Just as Senator Borah received hundreds of letters complaining of courts-martial, by the end of the war, Chamberlain received hundreds of letters supporting him for pointing out the War Department's shortages in uniforms, medical supplies, and weaponry, as well as its inefficiency in basic training, and this may have caused him to suspect all of the staff bureaus. Chamberlain was not antimilitary by any means. On July 31, 1919, in the midst of the court-martial controversy, he backed a bill drafted by Kahn mandating universal military training. Like Crowder, Chamberlain believed that war with Germany could be renewed, and he also was concerned at the spread of Bolshevism. However, he insisted that if greater numbers of citizens were brought into the army, his courts-martial reform bill would have to become a reality. Yet there were sound reasons for Crowder to suspect Chamberlain's sincerity beyond the fact that during the war Chamberlain lauded Crowder and insisted on expanding military jurisdiction over civilians accused of espionage, whereas now he had accused Crowder of overseeing unfair trials. In January 1918, against the pleas of Baker and Secretary of the Navy Daniels, Chamberlain drafted a bill to create a new cabinet position titled "secretary of munitions," modeled after the British minister of munitions. This cabinet post would take over all procurement and contracting duties from the War and Navy Departments. Chamberlain also supported Senator Weeks's efforts to create a Joint Committee on the Conduct of the War. During the Civil War a congressional committee with this name investigated a spectrum of matters from contracting fraud, to the treatment of African American soldiers, to allegations of disloyalty. The committee accused several military officers of being sympathetic to the Confederacy.[25]

In a speech before the Senate on January 16, 1918, Chamberlain excoriated Baker and Peyton March over the conduct of the war. Chamberlain was particularly angered with the medical treatment of tuberculosis cases, which resulted in the deaths of dozens of soldiers. As he later noted to an Oregon confidant, he and Wilson had twice met to discuss his concerns, and Wilson had become irritated with him. This was an accurate assessment, and Wilson privately observed that Chamberlain had been more in league with Republican critics than with the administration. Chamberlain also noted to his confidant that beginning in April, he had received dozens of constituent letters criticizing military discipline.[26]

Crowder's personal opinion of Chamberlain first surfaced after the January 16 speech. After Chamberlain criticized Baker in the Senate, Carter Glass defended Baker and Wilson against Chamberlain's allegations in the House of Representatives and accused Chamberlain of seeking personal gain. Crowder thanked Glass for his defense of the administration even though Chamberlain had not criticized conscription or courts-martial. Crowder was not alone in thanking Glass. Secretary of State Robert Lansing called Glass's speech a "masterful defense," and Wilson's advisor Edward House told Glass that Chamberlain was "a willful idiot." Crowder did not use this type of strident language against Chamberlain, but he was aware of Lansing's and House's comments and expressed his agreement.[27]

On January 13, 1919, Chamberlain introduced his draft bill listed as S. 5320 and titled "A Bill to Promote the Administration of Military Justice." In reality, it was Ansell who drafted this bill, but this was not discovered until March. One month later, Congressman Johnson followed suit in the House of Representatives, but unlike Chamberlain, Johnson did not chair the House Military Affairs Committee. In the absence of Stanley Dent, an Alabama Democrat, Kahn, a California Republican, controlled the scheduling of Johnson's investigation. Moreover, although Kahn determined to wait until the Republicans controlled both chambers of Congress before acting on any military justice reforms, he continued to side with Crowder. One of the analytical factors absent from Professor Lurie's study on the origin of the Court of Military Appeals was that Chamberlain needed the Senate to act quickly. That is, the Democrats held a majority in the Sixty-Fifth Congress, but Congress could not vote on the bill unless the Senate Military Affairs Committee speedily held hearings. Until March 4, Chamberlain would serve as chairman of this committee and control the calling of witnesses. After that date, the Sixty-Sixth Congress would come into session, and with the Democratic Party in the minority, James Wadsworth, a conservative New York Republican wedded to preventing the United States from entering into an international league, would become the committee chairman. It is true that Chamberlain had allied with Republicans during the war in criticizing the War Department, but he sensed that, as a result of Taft's influence, most Republicans would side with Crowder. Chamberlain's efforts for a quick hearing and vote would fail for several reasons, and although debates over the League of Nations, women's suffrage, and Prohibition were part of the subcommittee's inability to investigate quickly, he also caused a delay by attempting to appoint senators to the investigation who he believed would agree with him.[28]

Chamberlain's draft bill contained several features of due process that today have become a part of courts-martial after the enactment of the Uniform Code of Military Justice in 1950 but were absent from courts-martial through the end of World War II. The draft bill called for a judge advocate to perform the duties of a trial judge in terms of ruling on objections and instructing officers serving on the court-martial. As a judicial officer, this judge advocate would not perform any prosecutorial functions. However, unlike a civilian judge, the judge advocate would not be vested with the authority to dismiss a charge on the basis of a lack of jurisdiction. The draft bill contained a provision for permitting an enlisted soldier to serve on a court-martial in judgment of an accused enlisted soldier. Other features advanced by Chamberlain became law in 1920, such as a prohibition against a convening authority reopening a court-martial after an acquittal. The bill also barred a convening authority from referring charges against an accused soldier to a general court-martial unless a divisional or departmental staff judge advocate determined that the available evidence merited a trial. However, the most controversial aspect of Chamberlain's draft bill, other than Ansell's advocacy for it, was their attempts to expand the term *revise* to include the authority of the judge advocate general to disapprove a finding of guilty and to mitigate sentences.[29]

Chamberlain initially approached Kenneth McKellar to serve on the investigation, but the Tennessee Democrat informed him that he was satisfied with the overall administration of courts-martial, even taking into account deplorable aberrations in individual cases. In late January 1919,

McKellar asked Crowder for his assessment as to whether courts-martial had been conducted "fully and fairly." Crowder turned to Wigmore to respond to McKellar, and Wigmore, in turn, informed the senator that soldiers convicted in a court-martial not only had the benefit of a judge advocate review "scrutinizing the legality of its action" but also "the clemency review boards as an additional safeguard with no equal in civilian appeals." Wigmore described the clemency boards to McKellar as "a large corps of officers (all but two or three of them being civilian lawyers of extensive practice including some former judges—appointed as reserve officers) who had carefully scrutinized every record, sending many back with recommendations for disapproval on legal grounds." McKellar accepted Wigmore's response as reasonable and questioned the need for any radical change. Chamberlain also sought Duncan Fletcher, a progressive Florida Democrat, but he too informed Chamberlain that he was unlikely to join him. Fletcher had spoken with Baker and concluded that there was no need for a new Articles of War or any other statutory change, other than making the clemency boards a permanent part of the advisory process. Chamberlain also attempted to convince senators not serving on the committee as well as to reach across party lines, and he invited M. Hoke Smith and Robert La Follette to join him. Smith, a Georgia Democrat, had joined his political rival for his Senate seat, Thomas Watson, in criticizing the War Department for mistreating soldiers, but he also wanted to campaign to support the League of Nations. He also was one of the only senators to express an interest in taking up Crowder's draft bill to empower the president to overturn courts-martial in early 1918. Smith may have had another reason for resisting Chamberlain. In late November 1919 Smith informed his chief of staff that it was critical to support Wilson and not provide political fodder for Theodore Roosevelt. Chamberlain's invitation to La Follette is a mystery, given La Follette's vote against the nation entering the war and an ongoing expulsion threat against him. Had La Follette joined the committee and associated with Chamberlain, his presence would have likely harmed Chamberlain's efforts. Chamberlain's invitation to La Follette is odd for another reason. In June 1918, Chamberlain had aligned with Senator Atlee Pomerene to expel La Follette from the Senate.[30]

Instead of a subcommittee composed of three senators, Chamberlain opened the hearing to the Military Affairs Committee for any interested participants. As a result, the investigating subcommittee, in addition to Chamberlain and McKellar, was composed of Republicans James Wadsworth, John Weeks of Massachusetts, Francis E. Warren of Wyoming, Joseph Sherman Frelinghuysen of New Jersey, Philander Knox of Pennsylvania, Harry S. New of Indiana, Howard Sutherland of West Virginia, and Hiram Johnson of California, and Democrats Charles Spalding Thomas of Colorado, John Beckham of Kentucky, and Henry Lee Myers of Montana. Party affiliation was not necessarily an indicator as to whether a senator would side with Crowder and Baker over Chamberlain and Ansell. For instance, although Johnson had been Theodore Roosevelt's running mate in 1912, he was an outspoken critic of standing armies and voted against the Espionage Act. And it was also well known that Johnson disliked Crowder after his married son was conscripted and Crowder refused to intervene. On the other hand, Myers championed the Espionage Act and had joined with Taft in lauding Crowder. Weeks had criticized Baker during the war and pushed for the creation of a congressional committee to examine the War Department's efficiency in training and supplying recruits, but he also allied with Crowder. Thomas not only voted against the Selective Service Act, he had objected to the extension of court-martial jurisdiction over citizens who were denied conscientious objection exemption. He had also called courts-martial "un-American" and would again use this term during the investigation. In January 1918, Wadsworth made it clear to General John McAuley Palmer that he opposed Chamberlain and Ansell.[31]

On February 13, 1919, the subcommittee hearings began with Chamberlain asserting that he had received hundreds of letters from aggrieved parents whose sons were court-martialed and sentenced to lengthy periods in prison, and then introduced Ansell. Early in Ansell's testimony, which lasted through four sessions over two days, Frelinghuysen pointed out that no judge advocate prior to Ansell had advocated for an expanded revisory authority. Weeks hinted to Ansell that at best, one could only surmise that during the Civil War, Judge Advocate General Joseph Holt had assumed an expanded authority. Ansell seemed to recognize that the historic record did not support his claim that in the Civil War, Holt was authorized to overturn courts-martial, and he conceded that he assumed it to be true. Most of Ansell's testimony over the first day consisted of providing memoranda such as Wambaugh's advocacy in 1917 to create an appellate court as well as his own memoranda to Baker to expand Section 1199 to define *revisory* as the authority to reverse or overturn. Ansell also assured the subcommittee that he harbored no ill feelings toward Crowder, and that his career had not suffered as a result of his advocacy for change. Up to this point, Ansell's testimony was unlikely to offend Crowder because there was little inconsistency between what had actually occurred in the Judge Advocate General's Office in 1917 and 1918, and Ansell's testimony. And when Knox equated Ansell's disagreement with Crowder over the meaning of "revisory authority" to a disagreement between collegial Supreme Court justices, Ansell agreed.[32]

In the afternoon of his first day of testimony, Ansell noted that in February of the prior year, he had undertaken a study of the British and French courts-martial systems. He then made a claim that astonished Kreger, Bethel, Winship, and likely dozens of other judge advocates who had served in France and Britain. Ansell insisted that enlisted soldiers in the Allies' courts-martial had greater rights than in American courts-martial. He also claimed that it was likely that Italian soldiers enjoyed fairer trials than their American counterparts. It was true that Ansell had traveled to France and Britain in 1918, but he did not venture to the front lines or witness any of the Allies' military trials. Nor did he understand the large numbers of rapid trials, summary executions, and other summary punishments endemic to the Allies' armies. He does not appear to have been aware of the French mutinies after the disastrous "Nivelle Offensive," even though other judge advocates who had been relegated to Washington, DC, throughout the war understood what the French Army underwent. When he juxtaposed the "enlightened" military justice of the Allies to American courts-martial by characterizing opponents of his view, including Crowder, as failing to understand the requirements of "the new Army of America" and instead embracing the "counsel of a reactionary past, whose guidance will prove harmful, if not fatal," it undoubtedly caused many of the judge advocates to conclude that Ansell was disingenuous. Whether or not Ansell designed his comments to insult Crowder or other senior judge advocates, they also perceived his testimony as a personal attack.[33]

Ansell began his second day of testimony on February 15 by providing a final synopsis of his study of Allied courts-martial. He either did not know, or chose to ignore, that significant political efforts in Britain and France were under way to reform courts-martial, and the governments of both countries had sealed thousands of courts-martial records under various national secrets acts. Because of the absence of knowledge in Congress as to what had actually occurred in the Allies' wartime disciplinary systems, Ansell was able to shift his testimony to advocate for Chamberlain's draft bill without resistance from the senators. At this point, Wadsworth, perhaps presaging the ultimate defeat of Chamberlain's draft bill, questioned Ansell as to whether the bill undermined the authority of commanders to maintain and enforce discipline. Ansell did not directly answer Wadsworth's question. Instead he testified that no civilian practice of law permitted nonlawyers to control courts. But when Chamberlain tried to support Ansell, Sutherland cautioned that although directors of large corporations such as railroads relied on their lawyers for advice, ultimately corporate decisions rested with the directors.[34]

In the midst of this discussion, Knox and McKellar pushed for a provision that would prohibit a commanding officer from convening a general court-martial without a judge advocate first advising that the available evidence warranted a court-martial. This provision, which became law in 1920, was already in Chamberlain's draft bill, and Ansell might have thought that since Knox, a conservative, and McKellar, a progressive, had aligned, he would be able to convince them on the need to enhance the "revisory authority" as well as to create a court of appeals. However, Knox, along with Weeks, Sutherland, and Wadsworth, was opposed to a court of appeals or a judge advocate review that was empowered to reduce sentences and remove dishonorable discharges. They ultimately aligned with Crowder over the meaning of *revise*. Still, as Ansell concluded his testimony, he must have felt some confidence that Chamberlain might prevail. This was not to be.[35]

Four days after Ansell testified, the subcommittee called the three judge advocates who had directed the Judge Advocate General's Office's military justice division during the war. The first of these officers, Lieutenant Colonel Alfred E. Clark, favored the contemporary practice of military justice. Like the majority of judge advocates assigned to the Judge Advocate General's Office, Clark had little relation to the War Department prior to April 5, 1917. He was born in Ontario, Canada, in 1873, but his father moved him to Minnesota five years later. He attended the Northwestern Christian College, where he earned a degree in history, and then studied law at the University of Minnesota. Following a short tenure as a prosecutor in Mankato, he moved to Portland, Oregon. In 1911 the Oregon legislature appointed him to redraft the state's criminal code, and the following year, he chaired a state committee to revise the state judicial code. His sole army experience was as a commissioned officer in the Minnesota militia for three years. In May 1917, not only Governor James Withycombe endorsed Clark for a judge advocate commission, but Chamberlain also advocated for Clark. Clark went so far as to testify that he supported a divisional commander's authority to reopen a court-martial, even in cases where the judgment resulted in an acquittal. More importantly, he informed the subcommittee that while he was initially impressed with Ansell's advocacy to expand the definition of *revise*, on further examination, he opposed Ansell taking unilateral action in the "Texas Mutiny cases." Clark, however, showed a degree of independence from Crowder by testifying in favor of establishing a military court of appeals to have an authority commensurate with civilian courts of appeal.[36]

Lieutenant Colonel Edgar Davis followed Clark. Commissioned from the United States Military Academy one year after Ansell, Davis retired from the army in 1910 after service in the Philippines and a term as a law professor at the academy. From 1910 until 1917, Davis practiced law in Boise, Idaho, and in 1917 the War Department recalled him to active duty. He testified that he advised Ansell not to reverse the convictions or set aside the sentences of the "Texas Mutiny cases," but rather, to advise Baker to reenlist the soldiers so that they could serve their enlistments and then be discharged with honorable discharges. Both Davis and Clark asserted that they had advised Ansell that *Ex Parte Mason* negated the argument that a judge advocate general had the power to set aside a finding or sentence. After all, in the events leading to that decision, a federal judge had determined that the judge advocate general could not bind the president or the War Department to overturn the court-martial conviction of a soldier who had attempted to murder Charles Guiteau, the man who assassinated President James Garfield. Davis also went further than Clark in urging the subcommittee to agree that Crowder's view of the limited authority of the judge advocate general was correct and Ansell was in the wrong. Davis reminded the senators that some of the army's early disciplinary difficulties arose as a result of the IWW but that the army had been able to contain the threat from subversion by using the existing disciplinary system. Thus, Davis implied that Chamberlain's bill would weaken the army's reliability by making it more difficult to investigate and court-martial Bolsheviks, IWW members, or other subversives.[37]

Colonel Beverly Read was the fourth officer to testify, and at the time of the subcommittee's investigation he headed the military justice division. Read was far more conservative than Clark or Davis. He vigorously opposed Chamberlain's draft bill, argued to keep the 1916 Articles of War as the law governing the army's discipline, and added that the fifty judge advocates assigned to the military justice division were largely in agreement that Chamberlain's draft bill would undermine military readiness. Read also informed the subcommittee that while there were over ten thousand soldiers serving long sentences in the three military prisons, most of these soldiers were likely to have their sentences significantly shortened by the clemency boards. Moreover, he added that hundreds of these soldiers would be returned to the army to complete their enlistments through the secretary of war's unilateral action.[38]

In the late afternoon of February 26, Crowder appeared before the subcommittee. Within minutes of his beginning to testify, Warren pointed out that Crowder opposed giving his own office greater authority, which was a rarity. This is a contextually important matter for understanding how Crowder both shaped his testimony and responded to Ansell after the subcommittee concluded its investigation. In essence, he viewed the importance of defeating Chamberlain's bill as a matter of constitutional magnitude rather than an academic debate or a question of mere convenience to the War Department, and because of this, he tried to prevent his office from accumulating power. He did not bring a prepared statement to read into the record but instead preferred

to answer questions on the topic of Chamberlain's draft bill as well as Section
1199. In doing so, he argued that the draft bill was "an attempt to engraft upon
the American practice certain essentials of the English practice, but carries
the English practice and its applications much further than the English themselves have carried it." Implicit in Crowder's statement was that Ansell had
sloppily studied British military law prior to assisting Chamberlain to draft
his pending bill. Crowder pointed out that in the nine years prior to World
War I, the British Army, which numbered 250,000 soldiers, prosecuted twelve
general courts-martial within the United Kingdom and 180 such trials in
the dominions and Empire. During the same period, the United States Army
had tried over 41,000 general courts-martial. He opined that the reason for
the disparity in numbers of general courts-martial between the two nations
was that the British equivalent to the special court-martial carried with it a
two-year imprisonment possibility and in the overseas territories, unlike in
American special courts-martial, the British Army's lesser courts possessed
the jurisdiction to dishonorably discharge soldiers. Thus, even if the British
general courts-martial enabled a greater degree of judge advocate control over
the proceedings, this control was absent from the majority of British lesser
courts-martial, of which tens of thousands were conducted during the war.[39]

What Crowder failed to mention about British courts-martial is as important as his testimony about them. The British Expeditionary Forces court-martialed thousands of soldiers in field courts-martial in which British soldiers
had no right of appeals, including when a soldier was sentenced to death. A
field court-martial required three officers instead of the general court-martial
requirement of five, and unlike a general court-martial, a field court-martial did not mandate a defense counsel for the accused soldier. And field
courts-martial did not require transcribed records of trial.

Crowder also cautioned that newspaper reporting on the "unfairness"
of American courts-martial often ignored the end-result of the trials. He
pointed to a general court-martial that had acquitted a recruit of disobedience of orders, but General J. Franklin Bell had directed the court-martial to
reconsider the question of the lawfulness of the order. The court-martial then
convicted the recruit and sentenced him to five years in prison and a dishonorable discharge. None of the newspapers reported, however, that Bell disapproved the dishonorable discharge and only approved of a sentence of one
month in prison. The recruit returned to the army to complete training and
was ultimately honorably discharged at war's end. To Crowder, an important
aspect of general courts-martial was the fact that soldiers, with the exception
of the gravest offenders, had an opportunity to be readmitted into the army.
By the time subcommittee had met, Crowder pointed out that 1,200 soldiers

imprisoned at Fort Leavenworth had already been restored to duty and after serving their enlistments were honorably discharged.[40]

In spite of Crowder's conservatism, he agreed with several aspects of Chamberlain's bill. For instance, he testified that an accused soldier should have the right to select a commissioned officer as a defense counsel if that officer were reasonably available. He also testified that while he did not believe that any injustices had occurred as a result of divisional commanders ordering courts-martial to reconsider evidence after voting for a finding of not guilty, he supported a statutory termination of this authority. Crowder's reasoning for supporting an end to the authority to order reconsideration of acquittals was not grounded in the Constitution's prohibition against double jeopardy, but rather, was based on his belief that the practice of doing so "shocks the American people."[41]

The most important part of Crowder's testimony occurred in the last half hour of it. Chamberlain challenged him that the term *revise* in actuality meant the judge advocate general had the power to overturn a conviction, and he claimed that Crowder represented "the militarist view." Wadsworth came to Crowder's defense on this point and countered that empowering the judge advocate general was no less militarist than maintaining the existing system. Crowder, for his part, assured the subcommittee that within two months, the clemency review boards would examine the majority of the general courts-martial records, and most of the imprisoned soldiers would be released by the end of the year. Crowder concluded his testimony by opposing an appellate court and instead recommending that Congress enact a provision clearly defining the president as the appellate authority over courts-martial, with the caveat that the president could delegate this authority to the secretary of war.[42]

Crowder's testimony was brief and succinct in comparison to Ansell's, and after he departed the subcommittee, the participating senators focused their attentions on other matters, particularly, the possibility that the United States might join the League of Nations. This did not mean that the debate over courts-martial had ended, or that Congress had accepted Crowder's position, or for that matter that there was a general disinterest in military law. Congressmen continued to communicate with the Judge Advocate General's Office on War Risk Insurance, courts-martial, and the status of seized alien property. Crowder likely knew that Ansell and Chamberlain would not let the issue remain out of the forefront of either Congress or the citizenry. Shortly after the close of the investigation, Crowder opined to Baker that of Chamberlain's proposed alterations to the Articles of War, "some of them are silly, some ridiculous, and some vicious." He also added that Generals Pershing, Liggett,

Bullard, and Haan had written him not only opposing Chamberlain's reforms but also condemning Ansell's conduct. From this point forward, the army's senior-most commanding officers, including Pershing, who was by this time a nationally revered figure, were in lockstep against Ansell and Chamberlain.[43]

INTERREGNUM: FOREIGN STUDIES AND INTERNAL INVESTIGATIONS

Between the end of Chamberlain's subcommittee investigation and August 1919, several events occurred that led to an irreversible break between Ansell and his supporters, and on the other side, Crowder, Baker, and their allies. By the end of March, it became impossible for the two groups to work in a cooperative manner on any issue related to military justice. For instance, in early April Baker directed Ansell to write a list of proposed reforms. On February 10, Baker disagreed with Ansell over a board's recommendation for disapproving the general court-martial conviction of a lieutenant named Lewis Hanks. On reading Baker's missive, Ansell complained to Crowder that Baker "had created a bit of asperity," a seldom used word defined as abrasiveness and sarcasm. Crowder shared Ansell's concerns with Baker, and the secretary responded that he expected Ansell and the other board members to "give [him] their honest conscientious views." In early March, Crowder and other judge advocates drafted a series of regulations for Baker to issue, including a prohibition on commanders from ordering courts-martial to reconsider an acquittal. Ansell disparaged these regulations as lacking the binding force of law.[44]

On March 10, the War Department published ninety thousand copies of a pamphlet entitled *Military Justice during the War*. At the beginning of the month, Baker had asked Crowder to vindicate the army as a result of "harsh criticisms" against courts-martial. Ansell determined that the pamphlet was designed as an insult to him. The pamphlet contained a basic overview of courts-martial procedure and explained various cases that had been criticized in Congress and newspaper articles. It also pointed out that in early 1918, Crowder had tried to advise Congress to make it statutorily clear that the president had the authority to reverse convictions after obtaining the judge advocate general's advice, but the Senate and House military affairs committees did not act on his advice. While the pamphlet contained no direct criticism of Ansell, it was designed to rebut Chamberlain's assertions on the unfairness of courts-martial, and it also presented the episode of the four privates from Crowder's perspective. Ansell would later assert that Crowder had formed "a propaganda bureau" in publishing this pamphlet.[45]

Three days before the publication of *Military Justice during the War*, Baker directed Major General John Chamberlain, the inspector general of the army, to "investigate controversies in the Office of the Judge Advocate General." Two months later, General Chamberlain reported to Baker that Crowder had been helpful in the investigation but Ansell had refused to submit to any inquiry and alleged that the investigation was in retaliation for his congressional testimony. Ansell also wrote a memo to the inspector general that accused Crowder of using the Judge Advocate General's Office to distribute patronage jobs. Along with Ansell, Senator Chamberlain accused Wigmore of "illegal franking," that is, using the government mails for personal purposes, and the *New York Times* reported on this accusation. Wigmore did use government stamps to send editorials to newspapers and bar associations in support of Crowder, but Attorney General A. Mitchell Palmer concluded that Wigmore had not committed any offense.[46]

Baker directed two other investigations. A small group of judge advocates were sent to Europe to conduct a detailed study of not only Allied courts-martial but also the German, Spanish, and Soviet modes of ensuring discipline. This study group was not only created to provide to Congress a detailed report on foreign courts-martial; Crowder and Baker also intended the group to discern and publicize the due process shortfalls in foreign systems. Ansell also rightly believed that the study was intended to undermine his earlier testimony on the fairness of foreign courts-martial. But his unfounded claims on the superiority of French and British courts-martial were also the cause of this study in the first place.

After Ansell's testimony, Crowder concluded that it was essential for the Judge Advocate General's Office to undertake a comprehensive study of the Allies' courts-martial. In late February, Kreger complained to Baker and Crowder that Ansell had, in his testimony to the subcommittee, "cherry-picked" aspects of British and French courts-martial procedures that were favorable to Chamberlain's draft bill. In a separate letter to Crowder, Kreger accused Ansell of intentionally ignoring the vast use of summary punishments in the British, French, Belgian, Italian, and Portuguese armies, as well as the nonexistence of appeals from courts-martial arising at the front. That is, even though there were rights of appeal in the laws governing French, British, and Belgian courts-martial, they did not apply in wartime zones of conflict. Contemporaneous with Kreger's accusation against Ansell, Wambaugh pointed out to Baker and Crowder that newspapers supporting Ansell likewise printed "inaccurate statements of British and French court-martial practice" because the British and French governments had effectively utilized their respective secrecy laws to "shroud injustices." Wambaugh further noted that the British

had not only refused to make wartime courts-martial records public, even
courts-martial conducted during the Boer War remained sealed to the public.
The only available British courts-martial information for Ansell to use pertained to peacetime trials. For reasons that are no longer evident in the historic records, Crowder determined that it was best not to select a long-serving
judge advocate to study the Allies' military systems and suggested to Baker
that he appoint Lieutenant Colonel William Rigby, one of the newly assigned
judge advocates. Baker, in turn, assigned Rigby to head a study of European
military justice and disciplinary systems but directed Colonel Blanton Winship to supervise Rigby.[47]

Born in 1871, Rigby was commissioned as a judge advocate in May 1918
and assigned to the Judge Advocate General's Office. His father, a Civil War
veteran of the Battle of Vicksburg, was a prominent attorney and later the
national park administrator for the Vicksburg battlefield. Rigby graduated
from Cornell College in Iowa in 1892 and then Northwestern University's law
school one year later. After graduation he entered private practice in Chicago
and developed a close relationship with Wigmore. Rigby was commissioned
into the Illinois Volunteers during the Spanish-American War and took part
in the Puerto Rican campaign. Like several of his judge advocate peers, he
not only had experience in criminal law, he also engaged in an international
law practice. In 1908 the Imperial Russian Government retained him in an
effort to have one of its citizens extradited for murder, robbery, and arson. The
subject of the extradition, Christian Rudowitz, was a revolutionary, and prominent Americans such as Jane Addams, Upton Sinclair, and several politicians
protested the extradition. Moreover, Clarence Darrow defended Rudowitz,
and the case drew intense newspaper interest. Rudowitz denied the allegations, but as a fallback position, he conceded that he belonged to the same
organization that committed the murder, arson, and robbery. He also claimed
these acts were political activity, and international law barred his extradition
on this basis. Rigby convinced a federal magistrate to order Rudowitz's extradition. But, in an interesting twist, Wigmore joined with Darrow in an appeal
to the State Department, and Secretary of State Elihu Root ultimately declined
to send Rudowitz back to Russia to face a certain execution.[48]

Rigby brought Major Calvin W. Wells to Europe as his deputy, along with
four junior officers and several noncommissioned officers who served as clerks
and translators. Prior to the war, Wells had graduated from the University of
Mississippi's law school and served as a judge advocate in the Mississippi
National Guard. He was also a state trial judge. Following World War II, Wells
opposed President Truman's position on civil rights and became a "Dixie-
crat." Sergeant Major LeRoy Vanderburgh was the ranking noncommissioned

officer to serve with Rigby. He had graduated from New York University's law school in 1909 and following the war became a New Jersey trial judge. During the course of the investigation, Rigby attempted to have Vanderburgh commissioned as a captain but did not succeed in doing so.[49]

By the end of June, Rigby not only was able to present statistics from the British and French Army's numbers of courts-martial and draconian punishments that would be alien to US courts-martial, he also obtained interviews with the Allies' leading military law and civil jurists and was able to gain British and French military opinions of military justice reforms. With the help of Ambassador John Davis, Rigby conducted a "lengthy interview with Winston Churchill," Britain's secretary of state for war.[50]

In interviewing Major General Borlase Childs, Britain's deputy judge advocate general, Rigby discovered that British military law did not require a stenographer for wartime general courts-martial, and this limited appeals to legal challenges. Childs agreed to be recorded by a stenographer in an interview, and what Rigby produced could have been a boon to Crowder, but for reasons noted below, some of the information was unusable. When Rigby asked Childs to comment on Chamberlain's proposal to permit noncommissioned officers to serve on courts-martial, Childs responded that it would likely undermine the fairness of the proceedings and cause an elevated severity in sentences. Other parts of the interview showed that the British Army tolerated harsh discipline and widespread departures from rights common to British civilian criminal trials. Childs criticized Australia's refusal to impose the death penalty for desertion and called the effect of their refusal on military discipline "deplorable," indicating that he believed that executions for desertion and cowardice were a necessary deterrent. He also admitted that it had been a practice in the British Army to permit officers to shoot a soldier for misconduct "in the line of battle without any court-martial" and added that such events were "the unwritten law of the soldier." Interestingly, Childs, who had served at the front for the first twenty months of the war, was well aware that the French Army permitted summary executions, including executions of junior officers, and opined that several instances of this had occurred in 1917. He did not, however, believe that the summary executions of miscreants violated French law or due process. Ultimately, Childs's statements on the expeditiousness of "field general courts-martial" were likely to defeat Ansell's argument that British courts-martial were more progressive than American. "A summary of the evidence for a field court-martial is not necessary," Childs asserted. "It depends on the surrounding circumstances. There was one man shot during the retreat from Mons. He was tried and shot in a half hour. The Germans were walking over his grave in an hour."[51]

The problem with Childs's testimony, as well as similar comments from Churchill and other British military and government officials, was that Crowder had to maintain the British desire for secrecy. Rigby faced a similar hurdle with the French Army. He was able to convey to Crowder that there had been large numbers of summary executions of French soldiers during the war, which Americans would find intolerable. Rigby also mentioned to Crowder an instance of a single trial and speedy execution of four corporals found guilty of a regiment's "cowardice." In what could be considered collective punishment for a regiment failing to achieve an objective, a French general who convened a court-martial apparently believed that the question of whether the individual corporals were guilty was irrelevant to the question of how to hold the regiment's soldiers accountable. The officers whom the general appointed to the court-martial had no doubt on this matter. One of the corporals had been an exemplary soldier. According to the French prosecutor, although the corporal bravely acquitted himself in the battle, he failed to force other men to follow his example. Equally important, the four corporals were executed within twelve hours of their sentence being adjudged. Rigby informed Crowder that French courts-martial had sentenced over 1,600 soldiers to death for "misbehavior before the enemy," and of these, over 1,000 were executed. This number did not include summary executions for the same offense. Additionally, French courts-martial sentenced over 5,000 soldiers to life in prison after finding the soldiers guilty of cowardice, and as of the time of Rigby's study, very few of the soldiers had had their sentence reduced. But neither the French minister of war nor the French general staff were willing to give detailed discussions on these events. However, a French prosecutor named Major Pressard passed on this information to Rigby. General Hallmin, the French judge advocate general, informed Rigby, "Many of our courts-martial were severe and are now being attacked in the Chamber of Deputies."[52]

On May 12, 1919, Hallmin permitted Rigby to participate in a court-martial in which a soldier was alleged to have deserted during the war after committing a political offense. From this experience, Rigby was able to highlight a glaring difference between the continental legal systems and the Anglo-American adversarial system. In the French, Italian, and Belgian armies, an accused soldier's refusal to testify was considered evidence of guilt, and soldiers accused of offenses could be ordered to implicate themselves. In American and British military law, a soldier could not be ordered to admit guilt, and a soldier's decision not to testify in his own defense could not be considered evidence of guilt. Indeed, it was not until the late nineteenth century that the state and federal courts began to permit a defendant to testify in his or her own defense. Although French military law required the government to provide an *avocat*—a defense counsel—because of a shortage of attorneys, during the war soldiers who before the war were law students and police officers were assigned as *avocats*. In response to Ansell's assertion of the right to appeal in the French Army, Rigby advised Crowder, "a convicted French soldier only has 24 hours to appeal," and there was no requirement for the appeal to be considered. In other words, just as in the "Houston Riot cases," an attempt to appeal was not a bar to an execution. By the end of Rigby's study, there was little in the French court-martial practice that could have been characterized as more progressive than American courts-martial.

Rigby's study had become so extensive that judge advocates traveled to Switzerland, Spain, and Sweden, nations that had remained neutral during the conflict, to examine their court-martial systems. And Kreger crossed into "White" Russia to try to learn of the new Soviet Army's courts-martial from captured Bolshevik officers. He concluded that one of the reasons for the Soviet failure to achieve a rapid and decisive victory was their abandonment of the old Czarist codes and failure to institute a new disciplinary code. In interviewing a Colonel Radish, a former Russian officer serving on the Latvian Army's general staff, Kreger learned that the early Soviet Army had instructions on discipline but not a formal code. In 1919 Lenin's government issued a formal code of prohibited acts, but the primary offense was "the commission of a crime against communism." Officers in the new Soviet Army were not accorded the absolute authority to order soldiers to perform tasks. Interestingly, Kreger also observed the nascent Polish Army and was impressed by the existence of a formal code of discipline. In 1919 he correctly predicted that the Polish Army would be able to defeat a Soviet invasion. Within two years of his prediction, Poland's military did, in fact, defeat the Soviet Army. In 1974, when the Supreme Court decided *Parker v. Levy*, an appeal that significantly bolstered the military's jurisdiction and recognized the military establishment's authority to impose restrictions on speech beyond what the Constitution would tolerate for civilians, Justice Harry Blackmun, in writing a concurrence, cited the Soviet Union's military's lack of discipline following World War I as a reason that Bolshevism did not successfully spread through Europe in the half decade after the Russian Revolution as well as a reason for Poland's victory.[53]

A second investigation, which began in May 1919, produced what became known as the "Kernan Report," titled after its chief investigator, General Francis Kernan. A panel composed of Kernan; General John F. O'Ryan, a divisional commander and National Guard general; and Lieutenant Colonel Hugh Ogden, this internal War Department investigation interviewed over two hundred officers and former officers. Kernan began the war by commanding a unit that was the predecessor to the Services of Supply, but in June 1918, he accompanied former Solicitor General John Davis to Switzerland to negotiate with the German and Austrian governments on the conditions and eventual release of prisoners of war. During the investigation, Kernan, O'Ryan, and Ogden discovered that the majority of officers wanted to maintain the system of courts-martial. A minority of officers urged a radical overhaul of the military justice system, while an equally sized middle group sought minor changes. The report also severely criticized Chamberlain's draft bill, and it did so by analyzing each of Chamberlain's modifications to the Articles of War. One of the aspects of this report that is missed by the few historians who analyze the court-martial controversy is that the War Department accepted comments critical of courts-martial procedure from not only regular officers but also National Guard officers and former officers who had returned to civilian life. A few historians note that Kernan was a martinet and then characterize the investigation as a "whitewash." Given the fact that over half of the officers who participated in the study were already out of the army or awaiting discharge and therefore relatively unhindered in expressing their views, Kernan's impact on the board's conclusions is questionable.[54]

Not all of the judge advocates providing their opinions to Kernan were in lockstep with Crowder. Colonel Samuel Wilson urged Kernan to consider advocating a new requirement that would make a trial judge advocate's advice binding to a court-martial panel on issues of law and then permit either the accused soldier or the president of the panel to appeal to the divisional judge advocate, who would advise the divisional commander to determine the appeal. He also advocated extending the jurisdiction of special courts-martial so that junior officers could be prosecuted in this type of trial for minor infractions. Like Crowder, Wilson opposed having a binding appellate court or expanding the "revisory" authority. Wilson also informed Kernan that Ansell had little understanding of how the rights of soldiers in courts-martial had been safeguarded in France during the war and after the Armistice.[55]

On June 28, 1919, Blanton Winship addressed a letter to Kernan detailing his views on needed changes to courts-martial. Winship agreed with Chamberlain that general courts-martial should possess a military judge with the equivalent authority of a civilian trial judge, to include the power to compel witnesses to testify. He also opined that a permanent board of review should exist to advise the secretary of war that a court-martial record either comported with the law or should be set aside on the basis of legal error. But like Crowder, he adamantly opposed both Ansell's view of the term "revisory," as well as a court of appeals, not only for the constitutional reason Crowder advocated but also as a matter of efficiency. "Late in May, 1919, the Judge Advocate General's Office at Chaumont was engaged in reviewing trials for acts of cowardice that took place the preceding October," he noted. "In times of war it is clearly of the utmost importance that penalties be promptly inflicted and that they should be really effective as deterrents." One other area Winship advocated for, which took until 1950 to become effective, was the requirement that unanimity was required for the death penalty.[56]

On May 23, 1919, Lieutenant Colonel J. H. Hayes, the Third Corps judge advocate, provided his assessment of Ansell's proposed reforms to General Hines to forward to Kernan. Hayes conceded that early in the conflict, enlisted soldiers faced unusually severe punishment. He asserted that "the rapidity of which four million citizens were brought into the Army" also meant that new officers were quick to resort to courts-martial. However, he claimed that as the war progressed, "courts-martial became fair, and could not be improved upon." The one area that Hayes suggested should change was that a court-martial should have a military judge, independent of the judge advocate prosecuting the case. On the other hand, Hayes noted that while Ansell's proposed reforms might cause a slowdown in the time it took for a court-martial to be accomplished, the reforms could be beneficial to the army in peacetime.[57]

The Kernan and Rigby reports provided an effective counter to Ansell's and Chamberlain's assertions in the sense that there were few organizations that rallied to Chamberlain. Chamberlain responded to the Kernan Report not only by criticizing it but also by introducing a new bill to the Military Affairs Committee that granted amnesty to all soldiers convicted in general courts-martial. He also sought to create, for the first time, a civilian court of appeals to review all future courts-martial, instead of his earlier plan for a court of appeals composed of officers. Crowder informed Baker that he could not conceive that Congress would pass such a bill and that it evidenced that both Chamberlain and Ansell had "been driven to an extreme position." He did not need Chamberlain's draft bill to come to this conclusion.[58]

THE CONTROVERSY TAKES PUBLIC FORM

Beginning in March, the controversy in which Chamberlain, Johnson, and Ansell opposed Crowder and Baker not only became well publicized, the various participants and their allies attacked each other's motives and integrity. On March 6, the *New York Times* informed its readers that Chamberlain accused Crowder of lying to him. That same day the *Times* reported that Johnson accused Baker of demoting Ansell out of spite. Four days later, the *Times* reported that Crowder asserted that during the war, Ansell had "tried to seize his powers." Ansell quickly countered that Crowder had lied and knew of both the memorandum seeking to expand the revisory authority of the Judge Advocate General's Office and his draft order for Baker to increase the authority of the acting judge advocate general to the full authorities of the judge advocate general. In between the printed accusations, Wigmore spoke to the New York Bar Association and blamed critics of courts-martial of making "grossly false inferences" from a small number of aberrant trials to push for alterations to the Articles of War.[59]

Shortly after the *Times* published its articles, the *Washington Post* published an article that claimed Crowder had tried to punish Ansell and had persuaded Baker "to flood the country with publicity." Although the *Post* had a wide readership, the *Christian Science Monitor* reprinted the *Post's* article to its nationwide audience. At the beginning of April, Ansell issued a stunning accusation against both Crowder and Baker. He claimed that Crowder had not only conceded the defects of courts-martial in a personal conversation but also stated that he had no choice but to argue to uphold the Articles of War to protect his own reputation as well as the reputations of past judge advocates. Ansell also claimed Baker had not acted in "good faith" in his explanations to Congress. The *Associated Press*, *New York Times*, and *Washington Post* headlined Ansell's accusations against Crowder and Baker. Crowder did not read these articles until April 18 while he was in Cuba, and he penned to Baker that he had never made a recommendation to punish Ansell and had never conceded to Ansell that courts-martial were defective in due process. Crowder complained to Baker that Ansell's conduct had made it "very difficult to remain silent with this defamation going on."[60]

On March 11, Ansell drafted a long letter to Baker detailing his view of the shortcomings in courts-martial, but he also blamed the secretary for permitting Crowder to publicly attack him. This was, to Baker, an odd allegation since Ansell, in his testimony to Congress, clearly alleged that he and Crowder, along with other judge advocates, had knowingly enabled a system of unfair trials. More troubling to Baker was that Ansell, for the first time, accused Crowder of privately admitting to widespread defects but covering these up out of a need for self-protection. Baker ignored Ansell's letter for almost two weeks, but he was concerned enough to inform Crowder about the contents of it. And for the first time, Ansell called for a court of appeals staffed by civilians rather than military officers. Baker also informed President Wilson on the status of the court-martial controversy, something in which the secretary had previously not involved the president. On March 27, Baker returned Ansell's letter, calling it "useless" and "improper for publication." At the end of the month, Ansell not only spoke to the North Carolina Bar Association about the unfairness of courts-martial, he was able to have his letter, along with Baker's terse response, published in several newspapers. On April 2, Ansell gave Crowder a more introspective and shorter letter listing thirteen suggested improvements to courts-martial. This shorter letter also appeared in several of the nation's newspapers. Baker must have been exasperated with the controversy for several reasons, including the fact that it followed him after he left the United States on April 4 for a two-week-long inspection of military forces in France and Germany. Indeed, as Baker boarded a vessel to depart the United States, a congressman implored him to investigate whether Ansell's view of courts-martial had merit.[61]

In April Chamberlain not only attacked Crowder's reputation on the Senate floor while Crowder was in Cuba, he accused Crowder of cowardice for going to Cuba to avoid the controversy. In reality, Crowder had objected to going to Cuba, but Cuban president Aurelio Menocal insisted on Crowder's presence in the rewriting of Cuba's election laws. Cuba's strategic importance to the United States made it unlikely that Baker, Lansing, or Wilson would have approved of Crowder remaining in the United States. In an act that could have only angered Ansell, Crowder convinced Baker to formally appoint Kreger as acting judge advocate general in his absence. This assignment puzzled Kreger, because he was junior to Hull and Bethel, and when he tried to ask Crowder why he was ordered to the position, Crowder explained that he wanted to protect Kreger from being demoted to his prewar rank. But this was only part of the reason, and Kreger discovered that Crowder no longer had confidence in Bethel to stand up to Chamberlain. Kreger commented to his brother that while Baker expressed that his selection to serve as an acting judge advocate general was "a high compliment," he was likely to be lambasted in Congress and in the nation's press. "It is quite likely that I will be discussed and cussed in the newspapers before my temporary direction of the office of the Judge Advocate General of the Army ends; but I am going to do my best to be just and do right under the law and then accept the verdict that is finally handed down," he promised.[62]

On April 6, 1919, Henry Stimson published a defense of the army's disciplinary system in the *New York Times* and called Crowder a "sincere and effective reformer of the administration of military justice, who had transformed military justice into a progressive system which reformed offenders without the stigma of felony." Stimson accused Chamberlain of picking limited anecdotal examples to cast doubt on the fairness of courts-martial and reinforced that it was Crowder, rather than Ansell, who impressed on Pershing the necessity of avoiding general courts-martial for all but the most severe offenses. Not only did Baker thank Stimson for his public support of Crowder, so too did Colonel William Judson, John O'Laughlin, the *Army-Navy Journal's* editor, and Thomas Walter Swan, the dean of Yale University's law school and a future judge on the Court of Appeals for the Second Circuit. Former attorney general and president of the New York Bar Association, George Wickersham, also volunteered to join in the defense of Crowder.[63]

Two days after the editorial, Crowder thanked Stimson, adding that if courts-martial had been unfair during World War I, then such trials were "scandalously bad in the days when Mr. Root, Mr. Taft, and Mr. Stimson helped to administer military justice." Crowder's anger toward Ansell and Chamberlain surfaced in the letter as well. As to Ansell's claim that Crowder felt bound to protect his own reputation, he countered that Ansell had "attacked every Judge Advocate General from Lieber down." He acknowledged that Ansell had "very great ability" but argued that he was "deficient in character and sanity." But Crowder too lost some measure of reality when he doubted that he would have the chance "to tell the story in a convincing way to any mind that is fair," which he would have to do because he thought that Bolshevism had already pervaded Congress.[64]

Other journals and newspapers printed editorials on their front pages. On April 13, 1919, the *New York Times* printed an editorial, authored by three former judge advocates, that scathingly criticized Crowder and courts-martial. George C. Beach was the lead author and one of the others was Roy Keehn, who left the army to become William Hearst's personal counsel. Wigmore responded to their editorial by pointing out that none of them had served in Europe or in the military justice division. The lead article in the *Collier's National Weekly* magazine contained a lengthy defense of Crowder and the fairness of military law. The author, Arthur Train, had served as a judge advocate in Washington, DC, during the war and he vigorously criticized Chamberlain for picking a small number "of misleading individual cases" to sensationalize alleged injustices in courts-martial. In contrast, *The National Weekly*, in a front-page editorial written by J. B. W. Gardiner, sided with Ansell and called courts-martial "archaic" and "not fairly tried."[65]

As the public became increasingly aware of the court-martial controversy, the leaders of influential organizations took an interest in it. In late March, the president of the American Bar Association appointed a civilian panel to investigate courts-martial. The panel consisted of William P. Bynum, a former North Carolina trial judge and assistant attorney general under President McKinley; Samuel S. Gregory, a former president of the American Bar Association; Martin Conboy, a prominent member of the New York Bar Association and advisor to Franklin Roosevelt; Andrew Jackson Bruce, a North Dakota judge; and John Hinkley, a former adjutant general of the Maryland National Guard who served in the Spanish-American War as an infantry officer and became president of the Maryland Bar Association. Hinkley was the only appointee with a military background, and Gregory frequently corresponded with Supreme Court justice James McReynolds, though he also, alongside Clarence Darrow, defended labor leader Eugene Debs in a contempt proceeding. The majority of the committee members recognized that there were due process shortfalls in individual courts-martial but concluded that these errors were not systemic and that structurally, the 1916 Articles of War, when followed, enabled fair trials. Although the American Bar Association was influential in Congress, one of the critical features of the investigation was that newspapers reported its findings. Ansell would later complain that the Judge Advocate General's Office influenced the committee by denying soldiers the ability to travel to testify, but the bar association denied his allegation.[66]

In addition to the American Bar Association, the leaders of several national organizations took an interest in the court-martial debate in the Senate. For instance, Thomas Sidle, the president of the Union National Bank and a contemporary of Andrew Mellon, argued to Baker that Ansell and Chamberlain "were on the wrong foot" but would be likely to stand on "that wrong foot for the next thirty years." Sidle was not merely expressing a personal opinion. Rather, he spoke on behalf of one of the nation's largest banking associations. Likewise, in March, John R. Shillady, the secretary of the National Association for the Advancement of Colored People, inquired of Baker as to whether his organization should take a stand in the court-martial debate. On Crowder's advice, Baker responded through an intermediary that the War Department "plans to throw around every protection so that soldiers may receive a fair trial and the rights to which they are entitled and protected." Baker also pointed out that the clemency review boards were freeing dozens of men, including African American soldiers. Baker's response likely influenced Shillady not to have the association enter into the court-martial debate. Of course, there may have been another reason for the NAACP's absence from the debate. With the War Department reducing the size of the army, Shillady feared that African American units would disappear. In late 1919 the NAACP forwarded to Senator Warren a proposed amendment to require the maintenance of one "colored infantry division" that included an African American judge advocate. It would have been difficult to oppose Baker and Crowder and lobby for the proposed amendment at the same time.[67]

On June 28, 1919, the Maryland State Bar Association hosted a debate in Annapolis pitting Wigmore against Morgan. The state bar published this debate in its annual proceedings, and the *New York Times* highlighted it. The state bar president introduced Wigmore as "representing Crowder's side of the question" and Morgan as "Ansell's understudy." Wigmore began his speech with the observation that in military law, justice had to be secondary in importance to "victory." This was an unfortunate predicate to the rest of Wigmore's speech, in which he tried to compare the rights of ordinary citizens accused of crimes to those of soldiers prosecuted in courts-martial, with an emphasis that courts-martial were at least as fair as criminal trials. The rights of soldiers, he informed the audience, included a verbatim transcript, an "appellate review," clemency reviews for all soldiers serving under a sentence of a dishonorable discharge or terms of imprisonment, and psychiatric evaluations. Wigmore was correct in noting that the majority of American citizens prosecuted in state and federal criminal courts in 1919 did not have similar rights, but Morgan latched on to the statement that justice had to be implicitly secondary to discipline.[68]

Morgan, for his part, began by commenting that the first time he publicly criticized military justice was in a brief comment to the Commercial Club of Washington, shortly after the inspector general of the army investigated him. He argued to the state bar association that military law was archaic and un-American and that it failed to provide procedural safeguards, including the right not to be prosecuted on "unfounded charges." Morgan was correct in this latter observation because no law prevented a divisional commander from convening a general court-martial even in the absence of competent evidence. He was also scholarly in his comparison of American courts-martial to ancient Roman courts, and he cited Hans Delbruk, a leading German military historian. Morgan also pointed out that in addition to the lack of a law preventing specious charges against an accused soldier, the Articles of War contained no right to a fair and impartial jury, and it permitted a commanding officer to order a court-martial that voted for an acquittal to be reopened to reconsider its vote. And, he derided the efforts of senior War Department officials to use the specter of "Bolshevism" as a reason not to weaken military discipline.[69]

The Wigmore-Morgan debate was not unique in the sense that judge advocates and officers engaged in several debates on military justice and publicly spoke on the subject. General Hugh Lennox Scott, the former chief of staff, argued to New Jersey's congressional delegation as well as the state legislature and Princeton University's student body that Ansell's criticisms of courts-martial were unfounded. On June 5, Columbia University conferred an honorary doctorate on Crowder, and during his acceptance speech he assured the audience that criticisms of courts-martial were unmerited. That Harlan Stone, the dean of Columbia's law school and a future attorney general and Supreme Court justice, nominated Crowder for this honor may have portended Stone's later judicial deference to the military establishment. On June 26, Ansell spoke to the Pennsylvania Bar Association and claimed that over half of the general courts-martial convened in the American Expeditionary Forces were unmerited.[70]

Given the federal judiciary's limited habeas review of courts-martial, it may have been the case that neither Ansell nor Crowder gave much thought to how the judiciary viewed the debates over military justice. In fact, several judges sided with Baker and Crowder, and none, including federal judges such as Gabriel Bourquin and Charles Amidon, who dismissed prosecutions under the Espionage Act and Selective Service Act, appears to have publicly sided with Ansell. On June 2, 1919, Judge David C. Westenhaver, who had issued one of the first decisions upholding conscription, wrote to Baker that courts-martial were structurally fair. Of course, Westenhaver's opinions were likely to be viewed as biased since he had been Baker's former law partner. Also, during the war Westenhaver's son had commanded a machine gun company in the Twenty-Ninth Division and served as a trial judge advocate in four general courts-martial under Lieutenant John Philip Hill's guidance. The opinions of the Supreme Court justices are far more important than the views of a district court judge. Between May and July 1919, Brandeis and Clarke informed War Department officials that Chamberlain's criticisms of the structure of courts-martial were foolish.[71]

REPUBLICAN-LED SENATE SUBCOMMITTEE

Unlike Chamberlain's subcommittee, the second subcommittee limited its investigation to three senators. Francis Emroy Warren served as the investigation's chairman, and Chamberlain, as the ranking minority member, was able to assign himself. Warren, Wadsworth, Lodge, and Knox decided to add Irvine Luther Lenroot as the third member. Lenroot was born in 1869 in Wisconsin and worked in logging camps while attending public school. He became a court stenographer and studied law under the tutelage of the judges to whom he provided records of trials. When Lenroot entered Wisconsin politics in 1900, he aligned with La Follette. Elected to Congress in 1908, he joined insurgent Republicans to undermine the power of Joseph Cannon, the Republican Speaker of the House of Representatives. However, in 1917 he was the only state Republican to vote to declare war on Germany, and he voted in favor of conscription and the Espionage Act. In October 1918 Lenroot ran for an open Senate seat against Victor Berger in a special election after Senator Paul Husting was killed in a hunting accident. By this time Lenroot and La Follette were political opponents, and Lenroot campaigned on the dangers of Bolshevism.[72]

Lenroot did not leave a volume of correspondence relating to his first two years in the Senate. When he campaigned for reelection in 1920, he stated that he opposed peacetime conscription because it led to a Germanic type of militarism that was a danger to freedom, and he claimed that Baker failed to hold divisional commanders accountable who permitted untrained men to go into battle against the German Army. He also retrospectively explained his opposition to Chamberlain and Ansell based on the possibility that a renewed war against Germany or a new war against Bolshevism could begin at any time, and he believed it important to keep Bolsheviks from infiltrating the army. "You may say that there is no danger of Bolshevism taking root in this country," Lenroot urged. "There is not when the people know what it is, but there are thousands of men in the United States, and some women, too, who are secretly preaching that Russian Sovietism is much better than our own system of Government." He added that a disciplined army was essential to deter Bolshevism.[73]

The subcommittee's first witness was not Ansell but rather a retired major named J. E. Runcie. Runcie had graduated from the United States Military Academy in 1879, served in the Spanish-American War, and retired from the army in 1903. After his retirement he was admitted to the New York Bar and practiced law for twenty years. Following a second retirement, he became the academy's librarian. He urged the subcommittee to consider that the continued vesting of commanders with authority over courts-martial created unpredictability in the law and that a military court of appeals would provide predictability through precedent. Runcie also advocated for a larger Judge Advocate General's Department that would supervise all counsel so that commanding officers could not control the futures of either trial or defense counsel. However, Runcie departed from Ansell and Chamberlain on the possibility of having enlisted personnel serve on courts-martial.[74]

Ansell testified over several days beginning on August 25. Toward the end of his testimony he articulated a truism of American military policy by stating that the army had seldom been prepared for the conflicts that the government directed it to engage in. Had he urged this point at the beginning of his testimony and avoided impugning Baker, Crowder, and several others, he might have been more successful in coupling the need for reform to maintaining a large standing army. Instead, by the time he brought this point to the subcommittee's attention, he had gone so far as to belittle senior army officers. There were other troubling aspects to Ansell's conduct in the subcommittee.[75]

He emphatically asserted that he was never empowered to establish policies and therefore never tried to do so. Yet this is precisely what he had attempted to do in reversing the courts-martial conviction arising out of the Texas Mutiny cases. On the second day of his testimony, Ansell disparaged the Kernan Report and, in doing so, insulted the army's senior officers. He alleged, without naming any specific major general, that "the surest means to attain a division or geographic command" was "unthinking conformance to a system which in and of itself tended to arrest mental and professional judgment." There can be little doubt that this angered Baker and several generals, particularly when he concluded with this statement: "I think I may be permitted to claim with entire accuracy, it can be said that many of the major generals are jokes to everyone else in the world, except ourselves and themselves." Ansell also testified that "landscape gardening" was a significant duty of officers in command of posts and that the 1903 General Staff Act had created a professional cadre of what could be called "red tape artists." Ansell could have at least conceded that prior to the entry into the war, the army was constructed much like Britain's prewar army in that it was small and designed for colonial policing. As a result of the United States Army's small prewar size, dozens of majors became generals in the army in rapid time, and although the first eighteen months of the war were a "learning experience" for these officers, had the war continued, a disciplined force of over two million strong was capable of fighting into Germany.

Ansell's disparagement of the Kernan Report and senior officers was problematic for at least two other reasons. He ignored the fact that beginning with General William Sherman's tenure as the commanding general of the army, the army had created various schools to professionalize the officer corps. Moreover, several officers had attained academic and legal distinction in the period between the Civil War and 1919. What was lacking in most of the army's senior leadership in World War I, to include its divisional commanders and higher command echelons, was experience in commanding large bodies of soldiers in war. Although it may have been fashionable to portray officers as doltish or hampered by limited intellectual curiosity, and while some of the army's senior officers could fit into that characterization, others such as Tasker Bliss were intellectually gifted officers.[76]

To be sure, Ansell was infuriated that the Kernan Report called his advocacy for altering courts-martial "uninformed." However, he mistakenly accused those officers who conducted the investigation as being motivated to advance their careers. Odgen had served as the investigation's legal advisor with the understanding that he would return to his civilian practice immediately after the report's publication. He had no career aspiration in the War Department, and he merely intended to return to a lucrative civilian practice. Indeed, by the end of 1919 Ogden was back in Boston representing banks and railroads, and eventually he was appointed to serve as a special investigator in a major industrial accident known as "the Great Molasses Flood."[77]

Another aspect of Ansell's testimony that infuriated Crowder had to do with their differing versions on the fates of John Cook, Forrest Sebastian, Stanley Fishback, and Olen Ledoyen, the four privates sentenced to death in France. Ansell continued to claim that Crowder insisted the death sentences had to remain as adjudged in order to support Pershing's authority, and that it was only after Ansell's intervention with a congressman that Baker commuted the death sentences and restored the four soldiers to rank. But the documentary record did not sustain Ansell's version. After all, Crowder merely found that the evidence adduced during the trial was sufficient to sustain the convictions and sentences. But he also advised Baker that it was important to extend clemency to the four soldiers. No congressman came forward to defend Ansell on this point, and Baker sided with Crowder.[78]

Over the course of his testimony, Ansell pointed out that many of the injustices arising from courts-martial had to do with the War Department's reliance on Winthrop's *Military Law and Precedents*. He conceded that Winthrop was enormously influential in shaping military law but was responsible for the belief that a court-martial was immune from judicial appeal. He stressed that in 1907, the Supreme Court, by implication, had renounced Winthrop in *Grafton v. United States*. This decision applied the Constitution's prohibition against double jeopardy to instances where a military trial acquitted a soldier and a federal prosecutor attempted to convict that soldier for the same offense. As Professor Lurie aptly noted in his study on the origin and functions of the Court of Military Appeals, Ansell exaggerated *Grafton's* importance in the application of the Bill of Rights to the military.[79]

Perhaps the most unfortunate aspects of Ansell's testimony was that he not only reiterated his claims that soldiers in the Allied armies enjoyed greater safeguards than American soldiers, he also attacked Crowder, Kreger, Wigmore, and a number of other officers for failing to employ these greater rights to American courts-martial. In this vein, he accused the Judge Advocate General's Office of being responsible for permitting the "oppression of men and officers who serve in it, and of the Army at large" and called Crowder "an imperious master." In response to Wigmore's caution on subversion undermining the army, Ansell countered with the obvious point that "liberalism in the law" did not cause Bolshevism to spread but that it grew as a result of "old reactionary systems." But he likely weakened this argument not only in his stunning criticism of his peers, but also when he called Easby-Smith an incompetent attorney.[80]

Ansell made it clear that he felt deeply insulted that the Judge Advocate General's Office conducted a study of European courts-martial. He resorted to belittling Rigby's qualifications as "having manifested no particular quality for the place unless it be his staunch adherence to the Judge Advocate General." Perhaps it is understandable that Ansell believed Rigby's selection was unsound, but he ignored that Rigby's selection had partly to do with the fact that Charles Evans Hughes, Harlan Stone, Elihu Root, and Wigmore endorsed him to Crowder, and since Rigby had not taken part in either side of the debate, Crowder believed that he was a sound selection.[81]

After Ansell concluded his testimony, Chamberlain convinced Warren to permit a W. B. Thomas to testify. Ansell had introduced Thomas to Chamberlain in late August as a worthy person to highlight the unfairness of courts-martial in the American Expeditionary Forces. Thomas was a Spanish-American War veteran, and he had served as a lieutenant in the Philippines. Between the two wars he attended the University of Minnesota and was admitted to the bar. In 1917 he enlisted in the army as an engineer, but on arriving in France he began to defend soldiers in courts-martial. Like Ansell, Thomas criticized courts-martial and although he had first-hand knowledge of several trials, the fact that he was never a commissioned judge advocate—and indeed an enlisted soldier—probably resulted in his testimony having little impact on the investigation's outcome.

On September 3, General O'Ryan criticized Ansell to the subcommittee by implying that he had been too distant from the conflict to understand the necessities of maintaining the 1916 Articles. O'Ryan conceded that the American Army had a small percentage of undependable soldiers but then argued that if commanders had to wait for judge advocates to act on "absence without leave cases while a battle commenced, the court-martial of such soldiers would occur too slowly to have a positive effect on discipline." Yet he also stretched credulity in testifying that the enlisted soldiers in his division were satisfied with the administration of courts-martial. O'Ryan could not have known the opinions of the twenty thousand soldiers who had served under his command. But he also candidly articulated the traditional belief in the need for divisional commanders to possess the fullest authority possible, including the authority to reopen trials and disregard the advice of divisional judge advocates so that soldiers could be relied on to defend a trench-line or attack an enemy stronghold, regardless of the conditions or costs involved in the order. Two weeks later, General Summerall articulated the importance of maintaining the Articles of War and cautioned the senators to be "very conservative in making radical departure from a system which has been vindicated in many varieties of circumstances."[82]

On September 24, Rigby appeared before the subcommittee for the first of several appearances, and although he knew that Ansell had disparaged him, he never criticized Ansell by name. At the start of Rigby's testimony, before listening to him, Warren and Chamberlain bickered over the nature of Chamberlain's draft bill and whether it would wholly replace the Articles of War. Rigby pointed out that British judge advocates served in an advisory capacity and did not have the authority to alter a finding or revise a sentence. This rebutted one of Ansell's claims. More importantly, he informed the investigation that the British Army made use of their field courts-martial as a substitute for general courts-martial, and hundreds of soldiers were sentenced to death and long terms in confinement without the benefit of an appellate review, a trial transcript, or the larger composition of a general court-martial. Likewise he informed the investigation that French courts-martial conducted during the war could sentence an accused soldier to death even when the courts-martial were summary in nature.

The remainder of the witnesses largely sided with Crowder. Generals Kernan, John Chamberlain, and Frank Parker testified, as did Bethel, Hull, and Kreger. Parker's testimony might have caused Crowder concern when he lamented that general courts-martial were too burdensome during the war, and the British practice of permitting field courts-martial to adjudge sentences of death for desertion and cowardice could be of benefit to the US Army. Parker had trained in the French Army prior to the war and observed their courts-martial following the 1917 mutiny. While he withheld testifying about the mutiny, he noted that French soldiers had few of the rights that American soldiers were entitled to. Although Bethel, Hull, and Kreger conceded, as would Crowder, that certain reforms such as the right to counsel were necessary, they implied that Ansell had misrepresented many of the wartime incidents he relied on to support his testimony. Bethel and Hull went slightly farther than Kreger in not opposing the creation of a limited appellate court staffed by officers, but both judge advocates insisted that a court of appeals had to be confined to appeals based on legal error rather than a lack of factual sufficiency as Ansell earlier espoused. Only Morgan, who followed Crowder and Baker, sided with Ansell.

Crowder did not appear before the subcommittee until October 24, almost two months after Ansell had testified. However, Chamberlain, having accused Crowder of wrongdoing, absented himself from the committee. Crowder almost immediately caught Warren and Lenroot off guard when he asked to swear an oath and be subjected to cross-examination. No other witness had testified under an oath, and on his own insistence, Crowder was now subject to the laws governing perjury.[83]

Crowder's defense of the Articles of War was consistent with his testimony in February. He conceded that there were "far too many excessive sentences" adjudged during the war, but then argued that in comparison to the large numbers of courts-martial, these sentences were anecdotal to the issues before the subcommittee. In other words, he was willing to accept a principle that one hundred injustices were one hundred injustices too many, but in comparison to the whole criminal justice system in which tens of thousands of trials occurred, the one hundred injustices were not a cause for reform. He also presented evidence that Ansell wrongly took credit for prior reforms, including the establishment of military disciplinary barracks that were designed to rehabilitate soldiers in place of prisons. At the end of his first day's testimony, Crowder tried to rebut Ansell's accusation that he and other "reactionary" lawyers had claimed that the Bill of Rights did not apply to courts-martial, and he presented a review of where the Bill of Rights had been incorporated into the Articles of War, including the prohibition against double jeopardy, the right to confront witnesses, and the right to obtain exculpatory evidence from the government.[84]

From the second day of his testimony on, Crowder countered many of Ansell's other assertions. He turned Warren's and Lenroot's attention to Ansell's claims that French, Belgian, British, and Italian soldiers were afforded greater protections of rights than American soldiers. Noting that the Allied governments had used their secrecy laws to shield information on their war-time courts-martial, Crowder was able to prove that there were no absolute rights of appeal in wartime courts-martial in any of the Allied militaries. He also rebutted Ansell's version of the "Texas Mutiny cases" as well as the fate of the four enlisted soldiers sentenced to death in the American Expeditionary Force that Baker later commuted. When Lenroot informed Crowder that the Senate was "given to understand that for the sake of efficiency and discipline, [he] was willing to rather give less weight to the rights of the accused," Crowder countered that he urged Baker to spare the lives of soldiers, including the four privates. Baker would later back Crowder on this point as well. One of Crowder's last statements to the committee was to accuse Chamberlain of presenting a bill "built on the distrust of every existing military authority," and then he provided to the senators an appendix refuting Ansell and Chamberlain's assertions on an item-by-item basis. Although Crowder may rightly be characterized as reactionary in defense of the military justice system, he was able to counter Chamberlain and Ansell.

It was not until the beginning of November that Baker testified to the subcommittee, and Chamberlain asked the secretary the majority of the questions. Baker remained steadfast in opposing an appellate court, citing the delays that a formal course of appeals would cause. He used the trial and execution of Sergeant Frank Cadue as an example. Baker reasoned that if, after Cadue were sentenced to be executed, a year or more passed before an appeal could occur, then the French citizenry would distrust the army's commitment to protecting civilians. Baker acknowledged that this example might appear harsh, but he added that he was not only opposed in principle to the death penalty, he and the judge advocates were able to fully read through the record of trial within a week. Of course, Cadue had confessed to committing rape and murder. Regarding the four privates sentenced to death, Baker not only sided with Crowder's version of the events leading to the grant of clemency, he also refuted Ansell's claim that Baker would not have acted but for Ansell's opposition to the execution. "General Ansell's statement that it was necessary to bestir himself to prevent execution of these sentences has no basis whatever in fact," Baker claimed. When Chamberlain challenged Baker that Ansell's demotion occurred as a result of his testimony, Baker responded that Ansell had "slandered his superiors," but the loss of brevet rank was already a forgone conclusion before his retirement.[85]

In his book on the origins of the United States Court of Military Appeals, Professor Lurie makes two comments on Senator Warren worthy of further exposition. The first is that Warren was familiar with military matters, "if only because his son in law was John J. Pershing." The second comment is that Warren and the rest of the subcommittee "seemed to be in no hurry to act on reforming military justice," mainly as a result of the pending vote on the League of Nations. Professor Lurie's first comment can be expanded by starting with the observation that Warren's knowledge of military affairs was, in fact, very extensive. From 1903 on, Warren served as a member of the Senate Military Affairs Committee and as a chairman of the Senate Appropriations Committee. Moreover, for many years, Warren had pushed to have greater numbers of soldiers stationed in Wyoming and Montana. Early in his political career, when he was a territorial governor, he asked President Grover Cleveland to order an army regiment to western Wyoming after the "Rock Springs Massacre of 1885," in which white lynch mobs murdered Chinese laborers. In his request, Warren recognized that the use of the army as a police force was unpopular, but he insisted it was necessary to safeguard the property of mine owners and railroads as well as to protect the Chinese laborers. It is also important to recognize another aspect to Warren's familiarity with the army. In 1919 Warren, along with John Hollis Bankhead, an Alabama Democrat, Nathan Goff, a West Virginia Republican, and Knute Nelson, a Minnesota Republican, was the last of the Civil War veterans left in the Senate. All four senators participated in that war's major battles around New Orleans and Port Hudson, though Bankhead fought for the Confederacy and Nelson, Goff, and Warren for the Union; and Bankhead, Nelson, and Warren voted to declare war on Germany. Goff would have voted to declare war as well but was ill and could not attend the Senate. But Warren was awarded the Medal of Honor for charging a Confederate position after most of his peers were injured or dead.[86]

Professor Lurie's second comment requires a further analysis of Warren's political orientation. Warren was the embodiment of a westerner who rose from little wealth to money and power. He moved to the rough Wyoming Territory in 1868 to take up ranching, was appointed territorial governor, and then was elected state governor. He was also elected as the state's first senator. By 1890 he was the richest man in the territory, not only from his thousands of cattle, but also because he had invested in electrical power generation for the city of Cheyenne, and he owned a share of the state's largest mercantile distribution company. He served a three-year term in the Senate from 1890 to 1893, and then took a two-year hiatus from government service. In 1895 he returned to Washington, DC, as a senator once more, but this time he remained in the Senate until his death in 1929. Warren was often antiprogressive, opposed the Seventeenth Amendment, and was wedded to Gilded Age values such as opposing unions and espousing "freedom of contract." Land reformers accused him of strong-arming small-time ranchers and sheep grazers off of open ranges so that he and other "cattle barons" could have sole use of the grasslands to maintain their virtual monopoly over beef production. Warren not only supported McKinley's foreign policies, which led to the war with Spain, he also was instrumental in securing federal funding for Theodore Roosevelt's efforts to create a volunteer regiment in that war, ultimately known as the "Rough Riders." He also believed that the government had an obligation to protect industry against the IWW and Bolshevik radicals. From 1916 through 1920, many of Warren's political efforts were spent battling progressive reforms and Wilson's internationalism.[87]

Of all the aspects of Warren's oversight of the subcommittee, perhaps the most important is that he did not want to serve on it. He complained to a retired general officer that the hearings would become a divisive political issue alongside the League of Nations, and he did not want to politicize the army while a renewed war remained a possibility. He called the subcommittee's investigation "the most troublesome duty." When Wadsworth asked him to be the subcommittee chairman, he responded that he was reluctant to do so because, among other reasons, he was not a lawyer, and the investigation was "a distraction that should be dealt with after the 1920 election." Wadsworth must not have believed that Warren had expressed his opposition strongly enough. Moreover, Senator Lodge, the chairman of the Senate Foreign Relations Committee and a stalwart conservative Republican, and Senator John W. Weeks lobbied Wadsworth to assign Warren as committee chairman.[88]

Warren was not a sop to the Executive Branch. He disliked Baker and Wilson. In 1917 he complained to a constituent that Wilson had failed to work in a bipartisan spirit on war issues. His dislike of the president mirrored that of his conservative peers who believed that Wilson's domestic progressive programs were unconstitutional and that in foreign relations, the president failed to understand that the League of Nations undermined national sovereignty. But he had a personal anger for Baker. In the midst of the hearings he informed Baker that army personnel overseeing the sale of war surplus had defrauded his son and dozens of other constituents over the purchase of bacon and other cured meats, and he held Baker responsible for not holding civilian officials accountable. Warren had also requested an immediate increase in the numbers of soldiers stationed at Fort McKenzie and Fort Russell to contain an IWW- and Bolshevik-led labor strike in the Wyoming and Utah coalfields. In this request he accused Baker and Wilson of being dilatory in failing to stop the spread of bolshevism in the United States.[89]

On the other hand, Crowder had a personal relationship with Warren, dating to his assignment to the Department of the Platte in 1892. In August 1918, Warren notified Pershing that Peyton March had tried to influence Baker to reduce both Crowder's authority as well as Pershing's overall command authority, and this was an affront to the War Department. Crowder was comfortable enough with the senator to refer to March as "a greedy man." Yet Crowder's relations with Warren did not always enable the results Warren sought from the Judge Advocate General's Office. Warren had recommended four candidates for a judge advocate commission to Crowder, but none was selected. In January 1919, Warren expressed his frustration with the Judge Advocate General's Office in not recommending clemency for a Major Scofield, who had been convicted in a court-martial for bringing alcohol into his quarters at Camp Funston and sharing a drink with sergeants and privates to celebrate the German capitulation. The court-martial sentenced Scofield to a dismissal, and General Leonard Wood approved the sentence. Warren conceded that Scofield's conduct momentarily degraded military discipline but argued to Crowder that the celebration was understandable. Most tellingly, in October 1918 Crowder, in a manner similar to how he treated Hiram Johnson, advised Warren that he could not intercede with a local draft board on behalf of the senator's son.[90]

Although Crowder had a relationship with Warren, there is no surviving correspondence between Crowder, Warren, and Pershing to indicate Warren's predisposition to tarnish Ansell or destroy Chamberlain's bill based on lobbying from either Crowder or Pershing. Perhaps, however, Warren had determined to do so without any prodding because of his conservatism and military experience. Warren's correspondences, now housed at the American Heritage Center in Laramie, Wyoming, are voluminous in comparison to Chamberlain's and Lenroot's collections. Yet among Warren's papers there is a noticeable absence of correspondence with other legislators or the War Department on the subcommittee investigation.

Warren was a busy senator, not only because of the pending vote on the peace treaty and commensurate League of Nations, but also because he was occupied trying to forestall a tariff war over wool imports with Great Britain and Australia. Although he had earlier opposed sheep herding on open ranges, by 1919 he realized that the wool industry was important to the western states. Throughout the summer and fall, Warren repeatedly felt compelled to assure the Wyoming Wool Growers Association and that organization's counterparts in Colorado and Nevada that he would prevail on the State Department to threaten the British government with tariffs on British imports if the British government placed a tariff on American wool in any of the British dominions or colonial holdings. "I am fully conversant with the sinister and dangerous tendencies of such importations by the British Government," he advised a constituent before informing him that Congressman Edwin Webb of Alabama was also an ally in the fight to keep wool markets open and free of protections. In contrast to the limited number of correspondences regarding courts-martial, there are hundreds of letters concerning wool and tariffs.[91]

Warren had other pressing congressional business besides sheep, the League of Nations, and courts-martial. Prohibition, women's suffrage, and the 1920 presidential election also occupied his time. Moreover, as the chairman of the Appropriations Committee, he had to devote his attention to a pending government deficiency bill that would enable the funding of the government after it had exhausted its appropriations. This was a time-consuming endeavor that required the testimony of almost every cabinet chief, and it taxed Warren's patience. For instance, although he vigorously opposed Bolshevism and the IWW, he was incensed with Attorney General Palmer's demands for greater expenditures to contain subversive organizations and spent two days demanding the results of investigations. He was also inundated with letters asking him to encourage Pershing to run for the presidency in 1920. At the end of October 1919, Wadsworth sought Warren's intervention with Pershing. Problematic to the influential Republicans seeking Pershing's nomination was that the general had no political ambitions, but Warren spent time responding to inquiries on the subject. Thus, unlike Chamberlain, Warren never claimed that the subcommittee investigation was his most pressing responsibility. Nonetheless, as an adherent to the principle of a strong federal army, he was interested in the investigation's outcome and hoped to conclude the hearings by the end of November 1919.[92]

While Warren barely knew Ansell, by the end of the summer he had developed a strong dislike of him. On October 7, 1919, Warren informed the army's inspector general that he would have a chance to testify in order to "refute some erroneous statements made by ex-Lieutenant Colonel S. T. Ansell," but the subcommittee had to be postponed "owing to pressing business in other committees." Two days later Warren advised Baker that while he had to devote the majority of his attention to the deficiency bill, he also wanted to have Ansell's testimony as well as the testimony of Major General O'Ryan printed and forwarded to Baker and Crowder. However, because Ansell had been permitted to revise his remarks and had "been very slow about getting the revised notes back," this was not possible. Warren implied that the reason for Ansell's slowness was to try to reshape his allegations against other judge advocates as well as retreat from his statements on the Allies' courts-martial. When Morgan likewise failed to adhere to a schedule, Warren suspected a less than honorable reason for it.[93]

There were aspects to Warren's supervision of the subcommittee that Ansell, Chamberlain, and Morgan could undoubtedly find fault with. The senator placed limitations on former soldiers who wanted to testify without a subcommittee invitation. For instance, on October 25, John J. Gallant asked Warren for permission to testify. After learning that Ansell had encouraged Gallant to come forward, Warren informed him that the subcommittee would only listen to him if he came to Washington, DC, before November 3, and at his own expense. Gallant had been a major with a distinguished prewar career, including a colonelcy in the Philippine Constabulary. But he had been accused of failing to comply with an order to counterattack German forces at Seicheprey. In July 1918 he was court-martialed for disobedience of orders, found guilty, and sentenced to a dismissal. He spent the next two years unsuccessfully trying to be exonerated. In essence, Warren gave Gallant only four days to travel from Boston to the capital at his own expense, and unsurprisingly Gallant was unable to do so.[94]

However, if Warren could be accused of limiting the number of witnesses favorable to Ansell and Chamberlain, he could also be accused of not permitting senior officers to testify against Ansell. In October 1919 Brigadier General Johnson Hagood, a frequent correspondent of Warren's, advised Warren to call Generals W. D. Connor and James McAndrew to testify, but Warren opted not to do so. Hagood, who had commanded a department within the Services of Supply, informed Kreger that he served on a court-martial of a doctor in 1901, and Ansell had been "a vitriolic prosecutor" in that trial.

Hagood was eager to testify that Ansell was motivated to become judge advocate general. On November 16, Warren explained to General Hines that there were "a number of high officers in the city, several of whom had experience in the field," who wanted to testify in favor of Crowder, but Ansell prevented them from doing so. Warren acknowledged that Hines considered Ansell "the basest hypocrite," but he did not want the subcommittee to have to determine "whether Crowder or Ansell was the better officer." Hines's desire to testify against Ansell is uniquely interesting, because Ansell had fought for his acquittal in a court-martial almost two decades earlier. Warren also stopped General Henry T. Allen from testifying against Ansell, which, given Allen's fears of a renewed war, surprised Crowder. Allen had cautioned Baker that as a result of "inadequate food and supplies," the German population could embrace Bolshevism and revolt, but "it could also welcome back the monarchy and become a militarized state." To Allen, conditions in Germany made it essential to maintain a disciplined force with the "old rules." Like Hines, Allen informed Warren that he wanted to testify that Ansell was "a poor officer."[95]

Warren's treatment of Morgan is also worthy of note. Morgan wanted the subcommittee to attach his Maryland Bar Association speech as well as Wigmore's to the final published report to show the public that Crowder was under Wigmore's influence and that Wigmore prized efficiency and discipline over due process. On November 14 Warren informed Morgan that the subcommittee would not place the speeches into the subcommittee's record. Warren had a sound reason for denying Morgan on this matter. Wigmore claimed to have spoken for the War Department, but in reality, Wigmore merely echoed some of Crowder's beliefs. Nonetheless Morgan attached his own speech to his testimony. After Morgan testified, Crowder wrote to William Bullitt, one of Wilson's assistants at the Paris Peace Conference, that "Morgan must have some mental aptitude but he is primarily a school man with no common sense ... he is the smallest man from the standpoint of character that I have ever come into contact with."[96]

On one occasion Warren corresponded with Crowder during the hearings. On October 17, he promised Crowder that he would have "an open discussion" with him prior to his testimony. Warren also let Crowder know that Bethel had suggested to the subcommittee to have Hull and Morrow testify, but again, because of the pending deficiency bill, he could not reconvene the investigation for at least a week. This gave Crowder time to consider whether Hull and Morrow were necessary for the committee. Although Crowder did not hold Hull in any esteem, he advised Warren that both Hull and Morrow could testify as to conditions in the Judge Advocate General's Office as well as courts-martial in France.[97]

Warren's only surviving correspondence to Lenroot and Chamberlain during the hearings was to resolve a scheduling conflict over Baker's testimony. During the course of the hearings, Warren wrote to Pershing about a number of matters such as the wisdom of maintaining an American force in Russia and General Wood's likely aspiration to become the Republican nominee. However, there is no evidence Warren wanted to include Pershing in the subcommittee, and there is an absence of any communication about Pershing's opinions on Crowder, Ansell, or the pending bill.[98]

RESPONSES TO THE REPUBLICAN-LED SUBCOMMITTEE

As the hearings were under way, Taft determined that he could no longer permit Ansell and Chamberlain to publicly disparage Crowder without coming to Crowder's defense. Taft's time was consumed with trying to lobby Republicans to support joining the League of Nations and convincing the party leaders that while he was not a presidential candidate, neither should several politicians be considered, and he earnestly wanted the nation to reverse Prohibition. He was a very busy former chief executive. But in mid-September he published two articles supporting Crowder. On September 15, the *Philadelphia Ledger* carried the first of his criticisms of Chamberlain's bill. Taft argued that Chamberlain's bill would reduce the discipline of the army at the cost of upending an already fair system of justice. That same day, Taft published a defense of the army's wartime administration of courts-martial and praised Crowder in the *New York Times*. Taft went further than defending Crowder. He accused Ansell of surreptitiously undermining Crowder for his own gain.[99]

Taft carried tremendous influence within the Republican Party, if not the legal academy and the nation. In addition to his political activities, at the time he wrote the editorials he was also a law professor at Yale University. Ansell responded by accusing Taft of writing the editorials at Crowder's behest. But this was not true, and Crowder was surprised by Taft's defense. Three months before Taft authored his letter, Julius Kahn asked Taft to defend Crowder, but nothing came of Kahn's request because Taft assumed that Chamberlain's draft bill would become moot once the Republican majority controlled the Senate committees. On September 19, Morgan wrote to Taft that Crowder had misled Congress and Ansell was a victim of retaliation. He added, "I cannot believe that you would approve this present system if you were to make a complete and thorough investigation of it." Taft responded to Morgan that not only had Crowder not known about his editorials, Ansell was "a publicity agent" and "a man of demagogic tendency." As proof of Ansell's poor character, Taft asserted, one only need look at his treatment of the American Bar Association president once that individual concluded that the War Department had generally protected the rights of the majority of soldiers. Morgan had recently joined the Yale law faculty, and both men wanted to work amicably alongside each other, but Morgan felt compelled to defend Ansell and responded to Taft that Ansell was, in his estimation, "a man of unimpeachable integrity." Morgan also added that Crowder neither had "the high abilities" Taft attributed to him nor was he responsible for the success of conscription. There is no record as to whether Taft responded.[100]

Taft received several letters supporting his defense of Crowder. Major General H. F. Hodges, the former commanding officer of the Seventy-Sixth Division, complained that Ansell tried to "capitalize on a feeling over courts-martial for his own benefit." He added, "What hurts the most is that the reputation which Crowder had built up and which his splendid work deserved, should be marred by an attack coming from within his own house by one he trusted and befriended." Hodges's disgust for Ansell clearly was the majority view within the War Department.[101]

Taft and Stimson were hardly the only politicians to come to Crowder's defense, and even the major newspapers tilted in Crowder's favor. In the midst of the hearings, Senator Knox introduced a bill to the military affairs committee to elevate Crowder to the rank of lieutenant general. Shortly after, Senators Wadsworth, Poindexter, and Weeks endorsed Knox's bill. Charles Evans Hughes, a former justice who ran for the presidency in 1916 against Wilson, informed the *New York Times* readers that he wanted Crowder to be promoted to lieutenant general. Predictably, having previously championed Crowder for a promotion, Chamberlain reversed himself and opposed Hughes's campaign to have Crowder promoted.[102]

Congressman Henry De La Warr Flood had little regard for either Royal Johnson or Ansell, who he claimed "gained much notoriety by his violent defamation of the Secretary of War." Flood protested Johnson's decision to hire Ansell as a legal counsel for a subcommittee investigation into military prison conditions, because doing so "rewarded him with a salary exceeding several times his compensation as an Army officer." Moreover, Flood believed he was able to prove that Johnson had agreed to Ansell's hiring and salary for the position prior to Ansell's resignation taking effect. If true, Ansell had violated a law in accepting the employment as a special counsel, but because the Republicans were in the majority and responsible for Ansell's hiring, Ansell was permitted to "thumb his nose" at the administration. Flood continued to criticize Ansell after the House subcommittee investigation ended. "The whole investigation was tinctured with the prejudices of this high-priced counsel, who, carried his quarrels with the Secretary of War and other officials of the War Department into nearly every day of the Committee," Flood complained. "Instead of confining his investigation to the field of jurisdiction of the sub-committee—war expenditures abroad—as it was clearly his counsel to do, this ex-officer applied himself almost exclusively to the purposes of attempting to discredit the War Department and the persons with which he had quarreled."[103]

On September 12, 1919, the *Honolulu Advertiser* published an editorial from a retired sergeant who accused Ansell of hypocrisy and claimed that "Sam Ansell" was, while assigned to the Eleventh US Infantry before the war, quick to court-martial soldiers. "Ansell was the most domineering and insulting officer to the men under him," the sergeant claimed. "He was an inbred martinet of the most extreme type." The *Advertiser* concluded by suggesting that Ansell was likely "employed at a large salary by the *Chicago Tribune*—an anti-Wilson newspaper—for propaganda purposes. On receiving the article, Flood had the text copied for dozens of representatives in both parties to read.[104]

CROWDER AND THE ARMY'S JUDGE ADVOCATES

On November 24, 1920, Crowder complained to General Dickman that he was left to meet "the fury of the controversy on his own," and with his "back against the wall as best he could to face the storm of accusation against the Army voiced by our critics in Congress, by the War Mothers of America, and by the American Legion." Crowder accused Pershing and Baker of engaging in "a conspiracy of silence, after the Judge Advocate General's Office was accused of blood thirst." Crowder's claim to Dickman was a gross exaggeration, in likelihood brought about from his exhaustion. After all, Pershing's duties in Europe had increased to supervising expeditions into Russia, the occupation of the Rhineland, and the army's withdrawal from France. Other generals asked Warren to testify against Ansell as well. And a wide range of progressives and conservatives had backed Crowder against Ansell, Chamberlain, and Royal Johnson. Brandeis and Taft—two powerful jurists who often disagreed with each other—backed Crowder. So too did Henry Stimson, Elihu Root, James Wadsworth, Carter Glass, Julius Kahn, and other lesser known legislators such as Frank Lester Greene and Henry Flood. Senator Knute Nelson questioned whether Ansell was guided by "Bolshevik sympathies" during his committee's investigation into Bolshevik influences in the United States. Moreover, Baker and Wilson were reasonably more concerned with the Treaty of Versailles and the withdrawal of forces from France and could not take an active day-to-day interest in the court-martial reform fights.[105]

Crowder should have also realized that in addition to his staff of judge advocates in Washington, DC, the majority of judge advocates returning from Europe believed that Ansell was in the wrong. Several judge advocates went so far as to accuse Ansell of seeking personal gain rather than trying to bring fairness into the system. Arthur Dehon Hill, who would go on to represent Sacco and Vanzetti on their appeals and champion free speech rights, not only opined to Frankfurter that Ansell was untrustworthy and had made fictionalized arguments to Congress, he also informed Justice Holmes and both of Massachusetts' senators of his negative opinion of Ansell, as well as the possibility that the army might be called on to fight for Polish independence against Bolshevist forces. For an attorney who would consistently fight for due process and champion civil rights both before and after the war, Hill's worries about the dangers of Bolshevism were notable in that he believed the military's existing disciplinary system was still necessary. Samuel Wilson likewise informed both of Kentucky's senators that Chamberlain's bill would prove to be a disaster to the national defense and that Ansell had little knowledge of the conditions of modern war.[106]

Guy Despard Goff returned from Europe in late 1919, angry that while judge advocates in the American Expeditionary Forces had served in dangerous conditions and faithfully performed their duties, Ansell had the temerity to criticize their performance. Goff informed his dying father that Ansell was not only in error, he sought advancement at the expense of those, like Kreger and Bethel, who had served in the war. Goff was elected to his father's seat in 1924 and four years later informed President Coolidge and Dwight Davis—Weeks's successor as secretary of war—that Herbert White should be nominated as judge advocate general after Hull's imminent retirement if Kreger could not be adjudged medically fit. Goff added that the War Department should have no conversation with Ansell over the line of succession or about any other matter.[107]

As the Twenty-Ninth Division reorganized for its return to the United States, Colonel John Philip Hill examined dozens of records of trial and recommended reductions in sentences as well as reversing the conviction of a soldier sentenced to twenty years for murder. He also corresponded with Maryland's Republican Party about running for Congress in 1920. On his return from Europe, Hill informed Crowder that Ansell had "operated out of ignorance or lied when he testified that French courts-martial had been fairer than American trials in all their respects." Hill had, after all, observed a dozen courts-martial in the French Fourth Army and even participated as an assistant judge advocate in a French desertion case. He was impressed with the resolve of the French soldiers during the war but added that when a French soldier accused of a crime refused to testify, the soldier would almost always be found guilty since the French military laws permitted an assertion against self-incrimination to be evidence of guilt. He also attacked fellow Republican Royal Johnson as "a fraud."[108]

On the afternoon of July 21, 1919, Patrick Cosgrave met with Crowder to discuss the conduct of courts-martial in the Fifth Division during the war. Although Crowder wanted Cosgrave to remain on duty, he explained to Crowder that he intended to return to his state judicial duties and his family. Cosgrave's wife had become ill and he had already lost a son in France. He recorded in his diary that he might have angered Crowder for arriving at the interview late, and he admitted that he had spent the morning touring the Bureau of Printing and Engraving and became engrossed in the stamping and printing of money. On the other hand, he told Crowder that Ansell's criticisms of courts-martial were meritless. He also assured Crowder that he would meet with Nebraska's congressmen and urge them to ignore Ansell. In only one instance throughout Cosgrave's diaries and letters is there a vulgarity, and while there is no evidence he ever personally met Ansell, Cosgrave called him "an ass."[109]

Two months after Cosgrave promised Crowder he would join in the public fight against Ansell and Chamberlain, Hugh Ogden spoke to the Boston Bar Association, and while doing so he was joined by Arthur Dehon Hill. Ogden provided a long defense of the military justice system, criticized Ansell and Chamberlain, and concluded with the observation that of the few wartime judge advocates who had joined with Ansell, none had worked in the administration of military justice, and none had served at the front lines. Ogden also labeled Ansell an "ass," and he obtained Senator Weeks's promise to support Crowder.[110]

Even judge advocates who had little to do with the war aligned with Crowder. William Mellard Connor provides an example of an officer who disagreed with Ansell. Connor was a commissioned judge advocate, but he did not serve in either the United States or Europe during the war. He was born in Charleston, South Carolina, in 1878 and attended Wofford College, graduating in 1897. He also pursued a special course of legal study at the University of Virginia in 1899 but was not a candidate for a law degree. In 1900 he moved to Spartanburg, joined a law practice, and was commissioned into the South Carolina National Guard. In 1902 he became a part-time municipal judge for Spartanburg but found this financially unfulfilling. In retirement he recalled to Secretary of State James Byrnes, whom he had known since 1901, that at that time "he practiced starvation under a law shingle" but the War Department had enriched his life. The following year, with Byrnes's father's help, Connor obtained a position as a law instructor in the Philippine Service and was appointed as a prosecutor for the Moro Province. In January 1914 he became the city attorney for Manila. From July 1914 to July 1917, he served as a trial judge in the Court of First Instance in Manila in the Eighteenth Judicial District, where he adjudicated both civil and criminal cases. In June 1917, Senator Claude Swanson, a Virginia Democrat, recommended Connor to Baker for an appointment as a justice on the Philippine Supreme Court. Both Leonard Wood and Pershing endorsed his appointment. When Connor was informed of Swanson's recommendation, he told Pershing that he would rather be appointed as a judge advocate and assist in the war effort. On July 2, 1917, Pershing informed the adjutant general of the army that he wanted Connor to join his staff. However, Connor became the judge advocate for the Philippines during much of the war. When the war ended, Crowder transferred Connor to his staff in Washington, DC, and assigned him to a clemency board headed by Colonel Easby-Smith. Lieutenant Colonel Myron Kramer, who rose to judge advocate general of the army in World War II, also served on this board.[111]

In April 1919 Ansell approached Connor for his views on courts-martial conducted during the war, and Connor drafted a brief to Ansell that he believed would be helpful to modernizing general courts-martial. However, Connor did not support the creation of a court of appeals or "an expansive revisory machinery." To Connor, "the worst defect inherent in courts-martial was the absence of trained legal personnel at all stages." He advised Ansell, "my suggested remedy is a general court-martial constituted of a judge who shall be a trained military lawyer, holding a commission in the Judge Advocate General's Department, empowered to hear and determine the cause; of a prosecutor which shall be likewise a trained military lawyer; so commissioned and a counsel for the defendant, likewise commissioned." Connor also urged that the trial and defense counsel rotate in their assignments so that future senior officers in the leading staff positions would be attuned to fundamentals of court-martial practice. "If these reforms were implemented," Connor posited, "the mischief of delay" would be avoided and "the sentence of every such general court-martial would be final and not subject to appeal." Rather than discussing Connor's recommendations, Ansell derided his suggestions as "cosmetic," leading Connor to inform Crowder that he viewed Ansell as "a detestable humbug." Connor also forwarded his brief to Ansell to the Kernan Board.[112]

CONCLUSION: CROWDER PREVAILS

On November 19, 1919, Senator Warren informed Baker that the galley proofs of all of the testimonies had been completed, with the exception of

Crowder's, and he expected a printed report to be issued by the first of December. The day before Christmas, Warren assured Crowder that Chamberlain's bill would not be forwarded to the Senate, and instead, his draft Articles of War, which were basically Crowder's design, would be voted on. The draft articles did contain some reforms, but these were far short of what Chamberlain and Ansell wanted. Ultimately the new Articles of War passed both the House and Senate and was forwarded to Wilson on May 31, 1920. On June 6, 1920, Warren "took pleasure" in informing Baker and Crowder that the Articles of War had become "the law of the Army." By this time Chamberlain was in a fight to retain his Senate seat, Ansell was a civilian, and the newspaper reporting of the event came to an end. This ended the court-martial controversy from World War I. However, there were two features to the controversy that require further, albeit brief, comment, because they contextualize the nervousness that both Baker and Crowder felt until the draft articles became law.[113]

Baker and Crowder were not in lockstep in all military justice issues during the court-martial controversy. This was particularly true in matters that had the potential to create political complications. For instance, in late 1918 the army court-martialed Colonel Virginius E. Clark for adultery, bigamy, conduct unbecoming an officer, and War Risk Insurance fraud. Clark's case was odd. His first wife died in 1912, and he remarried a woman whose divorce to her first husband had not yet been approved by the California courts. Clark, however, grew dissatisfied with this marriage and married a third woman after being advised by a civilian lawyer that his marriage to the divorcee had never legally occurred since California's marriage laws did not permit a marriage to a divorcee without the divorce first being lawfully recognized. The court-martial sentenced Clark to a dismissal for committing adultery and bigamy, but it acquitted him of fraud and conduct unbecoming an officer and gentleman. Crowder advised Baker that as a result of a state law, the most that Clark could have been convicted of was conduct unbecoming an officer for cohabitating with the erstwhile divorcee, but the court-martial acquitted him of this offense. Baker disagreed with Crowder and urged Wilson to approve the conviction but disapprove the dismissal because of Clark's wartime contributions and his status as a leading aeronautical designer. Baker basically opined that Clark was too valuable to the army to lose through a dismissal. However, he conceded to Wilson that if he were to sustain the conviction, the act of doing so would provide fodder to Ansell and Chamberlain. Ultimately Wilson disapproved of the conviction and Clark returned to the army.[114]

On April 15, 1920, Crowder advised Baker against Wilson's directing a general amnesty for all prisoners held in military prisons and disciplinary barracks. Crowder pointed out to Baker that he was unable to find a general amnesty declaration following "the Civil War or any of our prior wars" and that an amnesty would deprive Baker of his power to make "judicial or quasi-judicial findings in each case." Because Congress had yet to act on the new draft Articles of War, Crowder feared that Chamberlain's allies would claim that a general amnesty grant was tantamount to an admission that courts-martial conducted during the war were universally unfair. Moreover, only the Canadian government had granted a general amnesty following the Armistice. Crowder added, though, that the clemency review process had neared completion and that it was probable that all but the worst offenders such as murderers and rapists could be freed by the end of the summer.[115]

In spite of Crowder's resistance to most changes, the 1920 Articles of War did take into account several criticisms on the shortcomings of courts-martial. The new articles ended the authority of a commander to order a court-martial to reconsider its decision to acquit, and sentences announced by the court-martial were considered binding and final. As a result, not even a president could order a court-martial to reconsider its sentence, as had happened in the trial of General Swaim as described in chapter II. A permanent judge advocate board of review was created to advise the secretary of war as to whether a general court-martial comported with due process. In the event that the board and the judge advocate general disagreed, the secretary of war was required to state the reason for adopting the side he took. The board's decisions were not binding in the sense of a court of appeal, but the board's findings created a record from which Congress might examine the need for further action. One of the landmark changes in the 1920 Articles was a modification of Article 70. Prior to 1920, this article merely required that an arrested soldier be charged within eight days, which, after all, was the first basis of Captain Armes's appeal as described in chapter 2. Article 70 of the 1920 Articles of War listed among the duties of a staff judge advocate the duty to recommend on the disposition of charges after the pretrial investigation. By 1922 a judge advocate's advice was considered to be binding on commanders, and for the first time in history, a judge advocate could prevent a commanding officer from proceeding with a general court-martial if the judge advocate were to find that the evidence did not merit a trial. Another change had to do with the imposition of the death penalty. Prior to 1920, a two-thirds vote was required for the death penalty. The 1920 Articles of War required a unanimous vote. On the other hand, it would not be until 1968 that a military judge was created with an authority commensurate to a trial judge adjudicating a federal criminal trial.[116]

CONCLUSION: RETURN TO NORMALCY
AND A FORGOTTEN HISTORY

THE 1919 COURT-MARTIAL CONTROVERSY IS now largely forgotten. It seldom appears in history books on the United States in World War I, and only a few legal commentators give the controversy a passing mention in law reviews. Perhaps because the Uniform Code of Military Justice, which became law in 1950, embraced many of the reforms advocated by Ansell and Chamberlain, there is little interest in the controversy. In 1946 the House of Representatives Military Affairs Committee convened a subcommittee investigation into courts-martial. This began the process of creating a system of courts-martial to more closely mirror federal criminal trials. The subcommittee chairman asserted that during World War II, the absence of fairness in courts-martial was not only caused by the army's professional officers' valuation of discipline over due process, but also the fact that civilian attorneys brought into the military desired to prove their mettle by obtaining convictions and harsh sentences. This was almost a mirror of Ansell's accusations two and a half decades earlier. The 1946 subcommittee virtually lionized Ansell and derided the Kernan Report, but its members acknowledged that there were few people who remembered the 1919 controversy.[1]

Ironically, the 1919 debates over courts-martial effectively displaced a potentially bigger controversy that involved the Judge Advocate General's Office. Regardless of whether a judge advocate sided with Ansell and Morgan, or Crowder and Wigmore, the War Department's legal officers had taken part in a vast alteration of civil and military relations. The War Department asserted an authority that encroached into the personal lives of the nation's citizenry as well as into legal areas that had previously been the province of state legislatures and city and county governments. Baker and his subordinates established rules controlling prostitution and alcohol sales in areas outside of military installations, and breaches of these rules were prosecutable in federal court. These same men influenced the government's control of the freedoms of speech and assembly. Thus, if the court-martial controversy is now largely forgotten, so too is the War Department's legal reasoning for the means and methods of conscripting and disciplining a modern American army. Major General Crowder and the Judge Advocate General's Office were central to the War Department's actions. But beginning in March 1921 with President Warren G. Harding's presidency, the War Department's authority was rapidly curbed, and the often draconian enforcement of conscription and federal espionage laws curtailed. In 1930 the Judge Advocate General's Office numbered thirty judge advocates, roughly 7 percent of the staffing it had had at the time of the Armistice. Whatever else may be said about Harding's presidency, he kept his promise of a "return to normalcy." Yet with the coming centennial anniversary of the United States' entry into World War I, there may be a heightened interest in the court-martial controversy, along with the vast alteration in civil-military relations that occurred between 1917 and 1920.[2]

THE JUDGE ADVOCATE GENERAL'S OFFICE'S JUDICIAL RECORD

Beyond the nation's abrupt rejection of Wilson's ideology and the voters' desire for a "return of normalcy," there were other reasons the court-martial controversy faded into obscurity. The federal judiciary upheld almost every War Department action that was challenged in the courts, including Congress's delegation of power to Baker to issue regulations on civilian activities that occurred outside the army's installations. However, before analyzing the path of appeals through the courts, it must be recognized that it would be difficult to know whether Ansell's and Chamberlain's proposed reforms would have yielded results different from the process in place at the time. Certainly, the creation of a court of appeal and the divestment of court-martial authority from commanders would mirror courts-martial to civilian criminal trials. But the boards of review and the normal judge advocate review process also worked to undo injustices. And it is unlikely that reversals of convictions and sentences would have occurred at a faster rate than the boards issued them because appeals require lawyers to write briefs, lawyers to draft opposition briefs, and judges to analyze and apply the law and weigh the evidence from the trial against the appeals. This is a time-consuming process that today is all but considered to be a necessary aspect of due process, but this was not so in 1919.

On April 3, 1919, a general court-martial convicted First Lieutenant Ewell Ledford of larceny and sentenced him to a dismissal and eighteen months' imprisonment. Ledford was a former enlisted soldier with eighteen years of service. During the war, he had been responsible for collecting and maintaining civilian clothing and other personal property from soldiers transiting from training to the front. Much of this property "went missing," and Ledford's commander accused him of theft. After reviewing the record of trial, a board recommended disapproving the findings and sentence. Colonel H. A. White, while acting as judge advocate general, agreed and forwarded the recommendations to Baker who, in turn, agreed and forwarded these to President Wilson. On June 2, 1919, Wilson disapproved the guilty verdict and sentence that would have otherwise consigned Ledford to imprisonment and a lifetime of public disgrace. It is unlikely that a court of appeals could have acted as quickly.[3]

A similar occurrence played out in the case of Private Lambright who, on January 9, 1919, was convicted of larceny and "neglect of government property" and sentenced to a dishonorable discharge and imprisonment for two years. The board recommended disapproving the findings of larceny as well as the dishonorable discharge and reassessing the sentence to two months in confinement. Kreger, Baker, and Wilson agreed, and on April 29, Lambright was returned to the army to complete his enlistment and receive an honorable discharge. On March 10, 1919, a general court-martial convicted Private Lawrence Lee, "a colored soldier," of attempted murder. Lee had, in fact, shot a military police officer. But as discerned by a board of review headed by Colonel George Keedy, a University of Pennsylvania law professor, the government had failed to produce any evidence of Lee's intent, and at most, the record discerned only that after being yelled at by the military police, Lee discharged his rifle. Because there was nothing in the record to indicate that the discharge had been purposeful, the board concluded that at most Lee was guilty of neglect. Kreger, for his part, added that since neglect was not a lesser included offense of murder, Lee's conviction and sentence had to be disapproved. Baker and Wilson also agreed, and on April 4, Lee was returned to the ranks to serve out his term of enlistment.[4]

In 1921, in *Kahn v. Anderson*, the Supreme Court, with no dissenting justices, determined that under the strict habeas test, the judiciary could not review an appeal from a court-martial conviction where the general court-martial had fewer officers assigned to it than permissible under the Articles of War. The Articles of War mandated a panel of thirteen officers in a trial for murder unless exigent circumstances existed, but the record of trial contained no statement reflecting any exigent circumstances that explained why Kahn's court-martial only had five officers serving on it. Moreover, without explanation in the record, at least two of the officers serving on the court-martial were recalled from retirement specifically for the purpose of serving on court-martial duty. Throughout the war, Crowder had excoriated judge advocates for failing to ensure that the reasons for smaller panels were noted on records of trial. In *Kahn*, the Court not only decided that the claimed deficiency was not a jurisdictional matter, the justices also implicitly determined that the requirement of panel size was discretionary in spite of the plain language of the Articles of War. At the same time the Court decided *Kahn*, it also decided *Givens v. Zerbst*. This decision arose from a court-martial of an officer who killed an enlisted soldier. The officer challenged that the commanding officer who convened the court-martial did not possess the statutory authority to do so and that the Articles of War mandated that as the war had ended, the civilian authorities had to assert jurisdiction. The Court's holding was similar to *Kahn*, and it further reinforced the traditional notion of limited federal court jurisdiction.[5]

The lesser federal courts upheld the strict habeas test in several appeals as well. In *United States v. Drum*, the Court of Appeals for the Second Circuit in 1939 validated the Selective Service Act's extension of military jurisdiction to the time when a citizen received an induction notice. *Drum* arose from Grover Cleveland Bergdoll's appeal from his second court-martial. This decision was hardly a surprise. In 1923, in *Feld v. Bullard*, the same court issued a similar decision. That court upheld the extension of military jurisdiction over civilians who received an induction order but failed or refused to be conscripted into the army. Judge advocates argued both appeals on behalf of the government, and Crowder was finally assured that the courts-martial of citizens who refused to serve in the military was judicially sanctioned as a constitutional matter. In 1921 the Court of Appeals for the Eighth Circuit in *McRae v. Henkes* upheld a court-martial conviction against a claim that the general who convened the court-martial was not authorized to recall retired officers to serve in judgment. In *Kahn*, the Supreme Court found that the presence of retired officers on a court-martial did not divest the court-martial of jurisdiction. In *Henkes*, the appellate court determined that military officers appointed to command were presumed to possess the authority they exercised and therefore the federal courts would not grant habeas. That is, the federal courts could not review whether officers serving on a court-martial were lawfully assigned to the court-martial.[6]

In 1940 the Court of Appeals for the Fifth Circuit in *Sanford v. Robbins* held that traditional double jeopardy prohibitions did not apply to courts-martial, even though the Articles of War expressly protected soldiers from multiple trials on this basis. In 1918 sixteen African American soldiers were accused of rape and court-martialed. Two defense counsels represented all sixteen soldiers, and the court-martial tried all sixteen at the same time, even though the soldiers advanced different defenses. All sixteen men were convicted and sentenced to life in confinement. In 1919 President Woodrow Wilson declared the court-martial invalid and ordered the soldiers retried. In 1939 one of the convicted soldiers appealed on the basis of double jeopardy. However, the court of appeals determined that it would not grant review over the claim of double jeopardy since, according to the 1916 Articles of War, Wilson had the authority to order a court-martial to be reopened.[7]

Perhaps the most interesting decision was *Schita v. King*. In 1917 a general court-martial convicted Schita, a "colored soldier" at Governors Island, New York, of murder and sentenced him to life in prison. In 1943 the Court of Appeals for the Eighth Circuit, in issuing the first of two decisions, provided a descriptive characterization of Schita as "born a Zulu, became successively a member of the Native Constabulary of South Africa, the Canadian Army and finally the United States Army." In reality, Schita was a British Army veteran of the 1898 Sudan campaign against Islamist tribal forces, the Boer War in South Africa, and the battles of Mons and Loos on the Western Front in 1914 and 1915. How Schita came to the United States Army remains a mystery, but he was likely a disturbed veteran, suffering from battle fatigue. His medical records from a prison doctor stated that in 1915 he was neurologically impaired as a result of poison gas.[8]

Although over two decades had passed since his trial, Schita appealed by alleging that the army denied him the right to a defense counsel of his own choosing and that his belatedly appointed civilian counsel was unprepared to defend him. He also claimed that the court-martial did not permit him to call witnesses on his own behalf and it considered evidence without his presence, and that the judge advocate bullied defense witnesses. Equally troubling, he argued that he was convicted of felonious assault, "an offense he was never charged with" (though he was investigated for it) and the murder of a second enlisted man. By the time Schita appealed, he was confined in a federal hospital for "defective delinquents."

In a decision that almost mirrored *Runkle*, the Court of Appeals for the Eighth Circuit determined that a court-martial record could be so fundamentally defective that its jurisdiction was void. The army's record keeping in this instance was appallingly poor, and the War Department simply could not rebut Schita's claims. The appellate court conceded that Schita's allegations "taxed credulity," but in the absence of a complete trial record, it would not protect the court-martial from collateral attack. Rather than free Schita, however, the appellate court remanded the case to a district court to permit the army a chance to produce a record of trial. In 1944, army officials located the entire court-martial transcript as well as the judge advocate review, the clemency board review, and Baker's order to have Schita confined. On a second round of appeals, the appellate court denied Schita relief. The court discovered that Schita had, in fact, been represented by Martin Littleton, a former district attorney and congressman from New York who briefly served as a judge advocate. On June 5, 1944, one day before Allied forces landed in Normandy, the Supreme Court denied Schita certiorari. Frank Murphy voted to consider Schita's appeal, but a grant of certiorari requires four justices, and Murphy was only able to convince one other justice that Schita "deserved his day in court."[9]

THE JUDGE ADVOCATE GENERAL'S OFFICE'S PERSONNEL

Another reason both the controversy and the Judge Advocate General's Office's role in the realignment of civil and military relations faded into obscurity has to do with the judge advocates and civilians who assisted the War Department to enforce conscription. They were a cross section of the nation's academic, political, corporate, and judicial elites. For example, in 1924 Coolidge appointed Harlan Fiske Stone as attorney general. Stone purged the Department of Justice of corrupt personnel from Attorney General Harry Daugherty's tenure, and he restored respectability to that department. One year later Coolidge appointed him to the Supreme Court, and in 1941 Franklin Roosevelt appointed him chief justice. Stone advanced a civil rights jurisprudence, including rights to impartial judges and juries, finding state antisyndicalism laws to be unconstitutional and upholding the constitutionality of child welfare regulations as well as federal laws that created the right to organize labor unions. He also advocated for constitutional protections of minorities. Given that Stone never renounced courts-martial or the treatment of conscientious objectors, it would be unsurprising if much of the nation's citizenry concluded that the 1919 court-martial controversy was political in nature rather than a matter of due process. Of course Stone also voted to uphold the internment of citizens in World War II based on racial and national origin considerations to the detriment of due process, and he accepted the military's argument that national security made the internment a necessity.[10]

Enoch Crowder did not live to see the Uniform Code of Military Justice (UCMJ) become law, and he would have likely been opposed to it. The UCMJ gave judge advocates far more influence and control over courts-martial and other aspects of military discipline than Crowder believed the discipline of the army could tolerate. He retired from the army on February 14, 1923, but the next day he was sworn in as ambassador to Cuba. Secretary of State Charles Evans Hughes insisted on Crowder's ambassadorial appointment, and the nomination met no resistance in the Senate. The ambassadorship did not satisfy Crowder, and he complained to William Connor that Harding had "foisted Cuba" on him. In reality, the controversy exhausted Crowder, and in separate letters to Connor and Frankfurter, he observed: "When you get as old as I am and as far along on life's journey and your professional career, promotions, additional honors, or distinctions will mean very little to you. What a man wants is freedom from annoyances of a petty nature." Crowder returned to the United States two years later and attempted to engage in the private practice of law, but in reality went into semiretirement. He noted to Frankfurter that he had difficulty attracting the type of clients that he hoped to represent other than the Cuban government and that island's sugar interests. Crowder was a bright attorney but he spent a long professional life in government and was not able to create a lucrative law practice.[11]

Although Crowder has been portrayed as a stalwart conservative, he was responsive to claims of injustice. In 1921 he recommended to Harding that five soldiers who had been convicted of killing a British officer in an affray in Germany be pardoned. None of the testifying witnesses at the court-martial identified the soldiers as being involved in the fight. Harding pardoned the five soldiers on the same day he commuted Eugene Debs's sentence of ten years' imprisonment to time served. In 1923 Crowder allied with Senator Wesley Jones of Washington to restore full citizenship to a sailor who had been court-martialed by the navy in 1912. Charles Desmond Lambert had run away from home and enlisted on board the USS *Maryland* at fifteen years of age and under an assumed name. His father, a Civil War veteran and doctor employed by the Soldier's Home in Washington, DC, attempted to have the navy discharge him. Before the navy considered the request, Lambert deserted and disappeared under another assumed name. After he was caught, a navy court-martial found him guilty of desertion and sentenced him to six months in confinement and a dishonorable discharge. However, he escaped from confinement and then lived under a third assumed name until 1917. That year he enlisted in the army under his real name and fought in the Meuse-Argonne. He was promoted to sergeant in August 1918, decorated for bravery the next month, and then honorably discharged. In 1922 he and his reunited father discovered that he had lost his citizenship and that his honorable service in the army did not negate the navy court-martial. Crowder had no authority to overturn the naval court-martial, but from his retirement he wrote to Coolidge in 1924 that the loss of citizenship was unjust under most circumstances and certainly so in Lambert's case. In 1924

Coolidge restored Lambert's citizenship. Lambert was not Crowder's client; the former judge advocate simply wanted to decouple the loss of citizenship from the desertion.[12]

As Crowder neared retirement, he sought Pershing's assistance in lobbying for a successor. Crowder's dislike of Hull had not abated, and he characterized Hull to Pershing as a "poor lawyer, but gifted politically." Crowder went on to compare Hull to the disgraced former judge advocate general David A. Swaim, who had lied to Secretary of War Robert Todd Lincoln and was court-martialed during Chester Arthur's presidency. Crowder preferred Kreger, whom he called "unquestionably the best lawyer in the department ... the type of lawyer General Lieber was." If Coolidge did not pick Kreger, Crowder hoped that Pershing could lobby for Bethel, although he lamented that Bethel did not take a more forceful stand against Ansell. Crowder also recalled to Pershing that years earlier when Bethel taught at the United States Military Academy, he failed to revise Winthrop's *Military Law and Precedents* in spite of being directed to do so, and this still weighed against Bethel surpassing Kreger. However, Crowder noted that he "personally liked Bethel" and thought "the Department will be safe and thoroughly efficient in his hands if its charge is committed to him.[13]

In spite of Crowder's preference for Kreger, Bethel became judge advocate general in 1923. Because of a medical infirmity, Bethel retired a year later and Hull replaced him. Hull served a full four-year term as judge advocate general. In 1928 Hull reported to the chief of staff that the French war ministry had determined that efforts to push for reform in French courts-martial during the postwar period were led by communists. Hull made a surprising claim in stating that French communists conflated the numbers of French soldiers shot to death without trial and unfairly criticized their army's courts-martial. He went on to inform the chief of staff that the critics who joined with Ansell and Chamberlain could have been similarly motivated. Crowder had never gone quite that far in linking Bolsheviks to Ansell's allies.[14]

In 1925 Coolidge appointed Kreger to serve as a legal advisor for the Tacna-Arica Arbitration in an attempt to settle a land dispute between Peru and Chile. Pershing would write of Kreger's service in Chile: "In handling the difficult questions that arose during that period Kreger displayed marked legal ability, he is one of the best legal minds in the country." In early 1927, Kreger witnessed what he believed to be a Bolshevik attempt to create a mutiny in the Chilean Army, which resulted in General Carlos Ibanez's takeover of the civil government. Ibanez was an anticommunist minister of war. Although Kreger concluded that the Chilean military's takeover of the civil government and the deportation of persons suspected of communism failed to comport with democratic ideals and doomed the Tacna-Arica negotiations, he commented to Pershing that communists and IWW leaders in late 1918 had plotted mutinies in the United States Army. In 1928 Kreger became judge advocate general. During his tenure, he was confronted by the impact of the Great Depression on the army. He lived to see the Cold War and advised the army in both World War II and the Korean conflict. His final years would be spent in Iowa serving on the board of directors for Iowa State College, where he was instrumental in obtaining federal funding to expand the college into a large university.[15]

Blanton Winship followed Kreger and served a four-year term ending in 1933. In July 1932, Winship warned Douglas MacArthur that the army was not prepared to court-martial the hundreds of soldiers who would be influenced to mutiny by the "Bolshevik-led" Bonus March, a large demonstration of destitute Great War veterans. No soldier was court-martialed for refusing to obey MacArthur's orders or encouraging other soldiers to do so during the suppression of the Bonus March, evidencing that the dangers of subversion in the army were minimal. Winship went to Puerto Rico after his retirement and became governor general but was accused of suppressing individual rights. In 1942 Roosevelt recalled him to active duty, and he served as a member in the military commissions trials of accused Nazi saboteurs. Several other judge advocates who served under Crowder in World War I also served in World War II, to include William Rigby, Cassius Dowell, and Edwin McNeil. In 1938 Winship appointed Rigby as Puerto Rico's solicitor general. In 1942 Rigby expressed to Winship that had Ansell succeeded, the army "would not be able to fight the Wehrmacht." McNeil went on to become the judge advocate for the European Theatre of Operations in 1942, serving under Generals Dwight Eisenhower and Omar Bradley.[16]

In 1920, John Henry Wigmore returned to Northwestern University as dean of its law school. He remained an ally to Crowder for the rest of Crowder's life. Wigmore was also a reactionary. After Frankfurter and Arthur Hill worked on the appeals of Sacco and Vanzetti, Wigmore accused them of "coddling anarchists." On April 19, 1919, no less an influential figure than Justice Oliver Wendell Holmes complained to Frankfurter about Wigmore. "He certainly got the military sting good and hard—he is a damn sight more a soldier than I ever was and I shouldn't be surprised to hear him tell me that I didn't understand the emergencies of war," Holmes began. "I have been surprised at some of Wigmore's pronouncements before but I remember noting how tremendously military his bearing was, in uniform." As a scholar, Wigmore shaped the modern American trial in several aspects to include the judicial treatment of confessions taken under duress, but most particularly in developing the modern rules of evidence.[17]

The lives of several other judge advocates are worthy of note both for reasons of their continued influence in shaping the nation's military, and as a matter of social and political history. John Philip Hill was elected to Congress as a Republican in 1920. He waged a personal war against the Volstead Act in a unique manner. An avowed "wet," he went so far as to produce his own wine in large volume and then be arrested so that he could fight the indictment in court. He represented himself in court and in an example of blatant jury nullification, he obtained an acquittal. Hill also maintained an interest in military affairs. In 1921 he tried to link citizenship with military service, enlarge the army, and prevent Royal Johnson from opening a new congressional investigation into courts-martial. He succeeded only in the last effort, but this immensely pleased Crowder.[18]

James Brown Scott died in 1943 at the age of seventy-seven years. After the war he once more became an officer in the American Society of Internal Law, an organization he helped create. He worked to codify international law into the nation's statutes, corresponded with several secretaries of state, and supported Crowder's ambassadorial appointment. Nathan MacChesney returned to Illinois and taught law. In 1928 he served as Herbert Hoover's campaign coordinator. However, while serving as the general counsel to the nation's largest real estate organization, he advocated for communities to be permitted to draft restrictive covenants against African Americans. Coolidge appointed J. Reuben Clark as undersecretary of state in 1924, and Hoover appointed him ambassador to Mexico. He became prominent in The Church of Jesus Christ of Latter Day Saints and campaigned against communism. Eugene Wambaugh returned to Harvard and taught until his retirement in 1925.[19]

In 1928 Illinois voters returned Burnet Chiperfield to Congress, where he served two more terms before his death. However, in 1932 with mass unemployment and the rising popularity of Franklin Roosevelt, Chiperfield lost his seat to a Democrat opponent. He was one of the few congressmen who called for a larger standing army after the stock market collapse in 1929. Guy D. Goff left the army in 1920 and became an assistant to Attorney General Harry Daughtery. In 1924 West Virginia voters elected him to the Senate. He chose not to run for reelection in 1930 and died in 1933. Goff campaigned against socialism, and like Chiperfield, he advocated a larger standing army.

Samuel Pepper returned to Michigan and served as the state's judge advocate through the 1930s. He advised Governor Frank Murphy on maintaining the neutrality of the National Guard during a crippling strike at General Motors in 1936. Arthur Dehon Hill returned to Boston and taught at Harvard's law school. He also represented corporations and persons accused of syndicalism with equal vigor. He continued to correspond with Frankfurter in the 1920s and lamented that Wigmore had become reactionary to the point of criticizing attorneys who defended persons accused of syndicalism or other crimes of a subversive nature. In 1925 Coolidge nominated Charles Beecher Warren to succeed Harlan Stone as attorney general. However, Warren's opponents accused him of being aligned with the "sugar trusts," and the Senate did not confirm his nomination. Warren returned to his legal practice and academia.[20]

Patrick Cosgrave returned to Nebraska in 1919 and resumed his judgeship. Like Cosgrave, several other judge advocates, including Mendel Smith, Robert Kemper Bailey, Sidney Sanner, and Jacob Ruppenthal, returned to their state trial and appellate judgeships across the country. None of them seems to have publicly expressed that courts-martial failed due process, and their diaries and existing correspondences suggest that they never stopped siding with Crowder. In World War II Cosgrave was recommissioned and appointed to a state draft board. So too were other judge advocates, to include Bernard Gorfinkle. Of course, Felix Frankfurter was the most prominent of the judge advocates to ascend to the bench. Before he became a justice, he served on a committee chartered by Herbert Hoover to reform law enforcement and criminal trials. He also became an informal advisor to Franklin Roosevelt, and in 1940 Roosevelt appointed him to the Court. Even though, in 1920, Wigmore had accused Frankfurter of coddling anarchists and Frankfurter had become a leading advocate of individual rights, once on the Court he was conservative. On the eve of World War II, he led the Court to determine that a state could mandate that its students salute the US flag, and after the nation was in the war, he voted to uphold the internment of citizens based on their race. This decision placed the government's assertion of the needs of national security over the civil rights of citizens. In contrast, Frank Murphy was appalled and dissented. Yet Frankfurter also was a civil rights justice throughout the 1950s, and he did not blindly defer to the military establishment. He dissented from a decision that upheld the death sentences of two African American enlisted Air Force servicemen and vehemently argued that their courts-martial failed due process. Perhaps Crowder would have been surprised to learn that Frankfurter joined with Justices Hugo Black and William O. Douglas, both of whom had served in the army in the United States during World War I, in concluding that the habeas test should no longer be strict and the judiciary should overturn the court-martial. He also did not "rubber stamp" the government's anticommunist programs. Frankfurter was a

complex scholar, officer, and associate justice. Indeed, at the end of his judicial
tenure, he appeared ready to force the Department of Defense to ensure the
due process rights of servicemen accused of homosexuality. It can be fairly
argued, however, that to the extent a judicial officer can influence military
policy, he, more than any other twentieth-century justice, influenced national
defense. Beginning in 1940, Roosevelt followed Frankfurter's advice to appoint
Henry Stimson as secretary of war, Robert Patterson as Stimson's assistant,
and Frank Knox as secretary of the navy. Frankfurter was also responsible for
the appointments of other influential officers, including John J. McCloy and
Kenneth Royall. McCloy would oversee the military governance of Germany
in 1946. In 1942 Royall left his North Carolina legislative seat to become a
judge advocate. After the war President Truman appointed him secretary of
the army. On the eve of the Japanese attack on the Pearl Harbor naval base,
Frankfurter also advised Roosevelt on crafting a modern selective service law.[21]

When Adam Paterson returned to the United States, he and his fellow
soldiers who had served in the Ninety-Second and Ninety-Third Divisions
not only faced a heightened racism, they also witnessed their wartime efforts
minimized by white community leaders. For instance, Atlanta's chief of police
announced that the Ninety-Second Division had over three hundred courts-
martial convictions for rape and "that white officers were unable to control
the lust of black troops." In response to the police chief's accusation, Bethel
wrote a memorandum to Patterson detailing the actual number of courts-
martial the division conducted and noted that these numbers were similar
to those in several divisions. But the nation was not ready to commit itself to
the obvious fact that the color of one's skin has nothing to do with military
prowess, intelligence, or dedication. Patterson twice advised the NAACP that
the Articles of War were structurally fair. Sadly, he was disbarred in 1931 after
being accused of being paid by the City of Chicago for doing no work.[22]

Samuel T. Ansell lost the ability to reform courts-martial through a
combination of unfortunate happenstance and his own hubris. Shortly after
Bethel retired, Royal Johnson hoped that Ansell might be recalled from
retirement and appointed judge advocate general. Secretary of War John
Weeks informed Coolidge that under no circumstances should Ansell be
considered for a reappointment to the army. On the other hand, Weeks also
advised Coolidge that although Crowder had been a superb administrator, it
would be a mistake in the future to permit a judge advocate general to serve
for more than one term. Weeks concluded that too many capable officers had
not achieved promotion as a result of Crowder's longevity in the office.[23]

In 1920 Ansell campaigned for Chamberlain's reelection to the Senate
and went so far as to suggest that the senator should be considered as a

CONCLUSION

presidential candidate. However, Chamberlain was voted out of office. Ansell formed a successful legal practice in Washington, DC, but he also served as a counsel to several congressional committees. In 1933 Ansell advised a Senate subcommittee investigating election frauds, and during the questioning of witnesses he exchanged blows with Senator Huey Long. After Long falsely reported the incident, Ansell filed a libel suit against him. Long was unsuccessful in trying to convince the Supreme Court that he was immune from libel. In a unanimous decision authored by Brandeis, the Court determined that congressmen were not immune from libel suits for conduct that occurred outside of the legislature. From time to time Ansell represented clients on appeals to the Supreme Court. However, he enjoyed only a limited success before the nation's highest tribunal.[24]

Ansell would first argue in the Supreme Court in a challenge to regulations authored by Crowder and issued by Baker. In 1919 as the army downsized, Crowder crafted regulations for an administrative board to determine whether selected officers would remain on active duty, transfer to the National Guard, or be retired or released from the army. Crowder found it personally distasteful to be part of a process that forcibly retired hundreds of officers with reduced benefits, and in some cases no retirement payments at all as a result of rapid reductions in the army's size. However, he also believed that Baker had initiated the fairest system possible for shedding the army of underperforming officers. Just as Crowder had worked closely with the solicitor general on crafting the conscription laws, he likewise worked closely with the solicitor general in defending the government against the appeals of aggrieved officers.[25]

In 1895 John French enlisted in the army as a private and three years later, after a competitive examination, the War Department commissioned him as a lieutenant. French served in Cuba, the Philippine Insurrection, and the American Expeditionary Forces. On May 15, 1917, he was promoted to major, and in May 1918, the War Department brevetted him to the rank of colonel. In December 1920, an administrative selection board recommended that French be retired at the grade of major. After receiving this order, French retained Ansell as his attorney and unsuccessfully appealed through the federal courts, leading to the Supreme Court granting certiorari. Normally, Crowder would have appointed a junior officer to perform research duties and work alongside the solicitor general, but in this instance, he assigned himself and brought in Frankfurter and Goff to assist. The War Department prevailed in the Court of Appeals for the District of Columbia, and most gratifying to Crowder, a unanimous Supreme Court sided with the War

Department. The Supreme Court's decision was unsurprising in the sense that it mirrored *Reeves v. Ainsworth*, a 1911 decision that Crowder had taken part in. John J. Fitzgerald, a former congressman, wrote to Crowder, "There is a God in Israel and counsel for the opponent is a rascal and worthy of personal abuse."[26]

In 1920 Grover Cleveland Bergdoll retained Ansell for his court-martial defense. It was from Ansell's office where Bergdoll effectuated his escape into Canada and then to Germany. The Senate conducted an inquiry into the escape, and Ansell had to defend himself against charges that he was an unethical attorney. One of Ansell's last acts before leaving the army was to advise a prison commandant that Bergdoll's story of having buried $150,000 could be true, and that Bergdoll could be trusted for temporary release to retrieve this money. Bergdoll's conniving haunted Ansell for the remainder of his life, although unbeknownst to him, Crowder quietly came to his aid. In 1921 Attorney General Harry Daugherty advised Harding that the government could seize all of the Bergdoll family properties under the "Trading with the Enemy Act" and also declare Bergdoll's financial obligations void. This would have meant that any debt Bergdoll owed to Ansell was nullified. Crowder, however, argued that Bergdoll's desertion did not permit the government to seize Bergdoll's property or nullify his debts, and Harding agreed with him. In 1939, Harry Weinberger, who had represented Emma Goldman and a number of other IWW members during World War I, became Bergdoll's attorney after Bergdoll finally returned to the United States. Weinberger corresponded with Ansell and told him that Crowder's attacks on him in 1919 were "uncalled for and unjustified." Ansell responded to Weinberger by doubting the patriotism of the judge advocates who sided with Crowder.[27]

In 1939 Forest Arthur Harness, a Republican from Indiana, introduced a bill to Congress that stripped citizenship from deserters who resided in foreign countries. Harness had served as an ad hoc judge advocate in 1919, and as of 1939 he was a captain in the Indiana National Guard. The draft bill arose as a response to Bergdoll's voluntary return to the United States to face trial. Weinberger forwarded a number of letters opposing the bill to representatives and senators, including Robert La Follette Jr., Hiram Johnson, Emmanuel Celler, and Morris Sheppard. With Ansell's support he pointed out that while Harness's bill was a violation against an ex post facto punishment, even Crowder had opposed tying the loss of citizenship to desertion. In a strange twist, the Bergdoll case brought Crowder, who had since died, and Ansell into agreement on a significant due process matter. Harness's proposed bill was never considered by the Senate, and it too died.[28]

A QUIETLY INFLUENTIAL LEGACY

The Judge Advocate General's Office created a blueprint for the military's growth of power in World War II and afterward during the Cold War. In several respects, after 1941 the military establishment advanced an influence far more expansive than Crowder would have intended, but one that he and his subordinates inadvertently contributed to making possible. The nation's involvement in World War II, and the ensuing Cold War in which a conscription program became a facet of the nation's life from 1947 until Nixon's presidency, resulted in a military establishment with unprecedented power. For instance, during World War II, several civilians in the employ of the War Department were prosecuted in courts-martial. The judge advocate general of the army argued to the federal courts that *Milligan* did not prevent the military trials of civilians. After World War II, with Congress's acquiescence, the army set up military courts to prosecute civilians on military installations in Europe and Asia. Crowder had, three decades earlier, urged that such courts ran afoul of *Milligan*. In 1957 the Supreme Court determined that such courts were inherently unconstitutional and American citizens had the right to be prosecuted in civilian courts. Justice Hugo Black, a World War I veteran, authored the decision and was joined by Frankfurter, along with Earl Warren, William O. Douglas, and William Brennan. All of these justices were veterans, and with the exception of Brennan, all were veterans of World War I. However, between 1941 and 1957 the War Department prosecuted over four hundred citizens in military trials.[29]

Following the Second World War, Congress discovered that roughly one out of every eight soldiers had been court-martialed, and while most of these men were court-martialed in summary and special courts-martial, over 600,000 courts-martial were conducted per year. Moreover, at war's end 45,000 service-members remained confined in military prisons. These facts, along with the testimony of hundreds of lawyers, led to the enactment of the UCMJ. Unlike during the 1919 court-martial controversy, after World War II many judge advocates pushed for reform. Edmund Morgan would be instrumental in its creation, and Ansell would still be alive in 1950 when the new code became law. Perhaps if Crowder had compromised on the creation of a military court of appeals staffed by officers, the Uniform Code of Military Justice would have been nothing more than an evolutionary step rather than a revolutionary change in military justice. However, courts-martial were only one part of the Judge Advocate General's Office's legacy.[30]

In early 1917 Crowder advised Baker that the War Department possessed the authority, as a matter of a national emergency, to order bridges over a river to be elevated. In the Civil War, the army would have likely built a new bridge or elevated an existing bridge by using soldiers. In peacetime, the construction and maintenance of bridges over a river was a state or local matter. So too was grain production, the conditions of railroads and roads, and a community's health and sanitation standards. In World War I, the War Department exerted the authority to order state and municipal governments to adhere to Baker's decisions. The Judge Advocate General's Office was instrumental in this alteration of not only federal and state relations, but civil and military relations as well. This alteration would occur again in World War II and have a lasting effect through the Cold War. Of course, Crowder and his subordinates believed in the constitutionality of their actions, and they were reluctant for the military establishment to be as influential as it became. Nonetheless, the legacy of the Judge Advocate General's Office in the legal and political history of the nation is quietly profound.

Bibliography

PRIMARY SOURCES

NATIONAL ARCHIVES AND RECORDS ADMINISTRATION

RG 120 Records of the American Expeditionary Forces
RG 153.2.1 Records of the Judge Advocate General
RG 153.6 Records Relating to the French and Creary Retirement Cases
RG 163 Provost Marshal General's Records
RG 165 Records of the War Department and Special Staffs—Judge Advocate Records
RG 165 Office of the Director of Intelligence (G-2) General Records
RG 393 Records of the Continental Commands
        China Relief Expedition
        Department of the Platte
        Eastern Department
        Northern Department
        Philippine Department
        Southern Department
        Western Department

AMERICAN JEWISH ARCHIVES, BOSTON

    Bernard Gorfinkle [BG-AJA]

ATHAENEUM LIBRARY, PORTSMOUTH, NEW HAMPSHIRE

    Arthur Dehon Hill [ADH-AL]

CLEMSON UNIVERSITY, STROM THURMOND INSTITUTE

    Asbury Francis Lever [AFL-Clem]
    Benjamin Ryan Tillman [BRT-Clem]

DARTMOUTH COLLEGE—RAUNER SPECIAL COLLECTIONS LIBRARY

    John Wingate Weeks [JWW-RSC]

DETROIT PUBLIC LIBRARY

    Charles Beecher Warren [CBW-DPL]

EAST CAROLINA UNIVERSITY

Wade Phillips [WP-ECU]

GEORGETOWN UNIVERSITY

James Brown Scott [JBS-GU]

HARVARD UNIVERSITY LAW SCHOOL

Learned Hand [LH-Harv]
Oliver Wendell Holmes Jr. [OWH-UPH]

HERBERT HOOVER LIBRARY—STANFORD UNIVERSITY

Paul Crouch [PC-Stan]

LIBRARY OF CONGRESS

Newton D. Baker [NDB]
Louis D. Brandeis [LDB]
William Jennings Bryan [WJB]
Bainbridge Colby [BC]
Tom T. Connally [TCC]
Calvin Coolidge [CC]
Josephus Daniels [JD]
Stephen R. Day [SRD]
William O. Douglas [WOD]
Henry De La Warr Flood [HDF]
Felix Frankfurter [FF]
George Goethals [GG]
Frank Lester Greene [FLG]
Thomas Watts Gregory [TWG]
Herman Hagedorn [HH]
James G. Harbord [JGH]
John Philip Hill [JPH]
John L. Hines [JLH]
Gordon Hitchcock [GH]
Oliver Wendell Holmes Jr. [OWH-UPA]
Cordell Hull [CH]
Philander Knox [PK]
Robert La Follette [La Follette Family Papers—LFFP]
Robert Lansing [RL]
Irvine Luther Lenroot [ILL]
Breckinridge Long [BL]
Peyton C. March [PCM]
William McKinley [WMK]
John Bassett Moore [JBM]
George van Horn Moseley [GVM]
George W. Norris [GWN]
John C. O'Laughlin [JCO]
John McCauley Palmer [JMP]

John J. Pershing [JJP]
Elijah B. Prettyman [EBP]
William Rigby [WR]
Theodore Roosevelt [TR]
Elihu Root [ER]
Everett Sanders [ES]
Hugh Lennox Scott [HLS]
Charles Pelot Summerall [CPS]
William Howard Taft [WHT]
Joseph Tumulty [JT]
Willis Van Devanter [WVD]
James W. Wadsworth [JWW]
Thomas J. Walsh [TJW]
Wallace H. White [WHW]
John Sharp Williams [JSW]
James Harrison Wilson [JHW]
Woodrow Wilson [WWP]
Leonard Wood [LW]

MARYLAND HISTORICAL SOCIETY

Leon Adler [LA-MDHS]

MINNESOTA HISTORICAL SOCIETY

Knute Nelson [KN-MHS]

MISSOURI HISTORICAL SOCIETY

James "Beauchamp" Clark [JBC-MHS]
General Enoch Crowder [EHC]

NEBRASKA HISTORICAL SOCIETY

William Cosgrove [WC-NHS]

NEWBERRY LIBRARY—CHICAGO

William V. Judson [WVJ-NL]

NORTHWESTERN UNIVERSITY SPECIAL COLLECTIONS

John Henry Wigmore [JHW-NW]

OREGON HISTORICAL SOCIETY

George Earle Chamberlain [GEC-OHS]

PRINCETON UNIVERSITY—SEELEY G. MUDD LIBRARY

Bernard Baruch [BB-SGM]
Lindley Garrison [LG-SGM]

Edward Greenbaum [EG-SGM]
Henry Stimson [HS]

SOUTH CAROLINA HISTORICAL SOCIETY

Johnson Hagood [JH-SCHS]

SOUTHERN ILLINOIS UNIVERSITY

Hugh Ogden [HO-SIU]

UNITED STATES ARMY, JUDGE ADVOCATE GENERAL'S SCHOOL

Edwin C. McNeil [ECM-USA]

UNIVERSITY OF GEORGIA—RICHARD B. RUSSELL LIBRARY

M. Hoke Smith [MHS-UGA]

UNIVERSITY OF KENTUCKY

Samuel Wilson [SW-UK]

UNIVERSITY OF MICHIGAN

Charles Lewis [CL-UM]
Samuel Pepper [SP-UM]
Frank Murphy [FM-UM]

UNIVERSITY OF NORTH CAROLINA AT CHAPEL HILL, WILSON SPECIAL COLLECTIONS

Hugh A. Bayne [HAB-UNC]
Claude Kitchin [CK-UNC]
David A. Lockmiller [DAL-UNC]
Lee Slater Overman [LSO-UNC]
Charles Manly Stedman [CMS-UNC]
Thomas Watson [TW-UNC]
Edwin Yates Webb [EYW-UNC]

UNIVERSITY OF SOUTH CAROLINA

Mendel Smith [MS-USC]

UNIVERSITY OF TEXAS, BRISCOE CENTER

General Edward Kreger [EK-UT]
Morris Sheppard [MS-UT]

UNIVERSITY OF VIRGINIA SPECIAL COLLECTIONS

Claude Augustus Browning [CAB-UVA]
William Mellard Connor [WMC-UVA]

Carter Glass [CG-UVA]

UNIVERSITY OF WASHINGTON SPECIAL COLLECTIONS

Wesley Livsley Jones [WLJ-UW]
Miles Poindexter [MP-UW]

WEST VIRGINIA UNIVERSITY

Guy D. Goff [GDG-WVU]
Howard Sutherland [HS-WVU]
George Wallace [GW-WVU]

YALE UNIVERSITY

John W. Davis [JWD]
Edward Mandell House [EMH]
Harry A. Weinberger [HAW]

GOVERNMENT DOCUMENTS

Annual Report of the Director of the Bureau of War Risk Insurance for the Fiscal Year, 1920. Washington, DC: GPO, 1920.

Creel, George. *The German Bolshevik Conspiracy Issued by The Committee on Public Information.* Washington, DC: GPO, 1918.

Crowder, Enoch Herbert. *Second Report of the Provost Marshal of the United States to the Secretary of War on the Operation of the Selective Service System to December 20, 1918.* Washington, DC: GPO, 1919.

Dunham, Lurton Ingersoll. *A History of the War Department of the United States.* Washington, DC: GPO, 1880.

Dunn, William McKee. *A Sketch of the Duties of the Judge Advocate General's Department.* Washington, DC: GPO, 1874.

Establishment of Military Justice: Hearings Before a Subcommittee of the Committee on Military Affairs United States Senate, Sixty-Sixth Congress on S. 64 "ABill to Establish Military Justice. Washington, DC: GPO, 1919.

Hearings Before the Committee on the Philippines of the United States Senate. April 10, 1902. Washington, DC: GPO, 1902.

Hunt, Colonel I. L. *Report of the Officer in Charge of Civil Affairs, Third Army: American Military Government of Occupied Germany, 1918-1920.* Washington, DC: GPO, 1921.

Kitchin, Claude. *The Nation's Preparedness.* Washington, DC: GPO, 1916.

Subcommittee on Brewing and Liquor Interests, and German Propaganda and Bolshevik Propaganda. Washington, DC: GPO, 1919

PERSONAL REMINISCENCES AND DIARIES

Daniels, Josephus. *The Cabinet Diaries of Josephus Daniels.* Edited by David Cronon. Lincoln: University of Nebraska Press, 1963.

Greenwood, John T., ed. *My Life Before the World War, 1860-1917: A Memoir.* Reprint, New Haven, CT: Yale University Press, 2013.

Harbord, James G. *The American Army in France: 1917-1919.* Boston: Little, Brown, 1929.

Howard, Oliver Otis. *Autobiography of Oliver Otis Howard, Major General USA.* New York: Books for Libraries Press, 1971.

Marshall, Thomas R. *Recollections of Thomas Marshall: Vice President and Hoosier Philosopher.* Indianapolis: Bobbs-Merrill, 1925.

Scott, Hugh Lennox. *Some Memoirs of a Soldier.* New York: D. Appleton-Century, 1928.

Tumulty, Joseph P. *Wilson as I know Him.* Garden City, NY: Doubleday, 1921.

BOOKS AND ARTICLES

Adams, Graham. *Age of Industrial Violence, 1910–15: The Activities and Findings of the United States Commission on Industrial Relations.* New York: Columbia University Press, 1983.

Allen, Howard. *Poindexter of Washington: A Study in Progressive Politics.* Carbondale: Southern Illinois University Press, 1981.

Altschuler, Glenn, and Stuart Blumin. *The G.I. Bill: A New Deal for Veterans.* New York: Oxford University Press, 2009.

Ambrose, Stephen. *Upton and the Army.* Baton Rouge: Louisiana State University Press, 1964.

Arnett, Matthew W. *Claude Kitchen and the Wilson War Policies.* New York: Russell and Russell, 1937.

Astor, Gerald. *The Right to Fight: A History of African Americans in the Military.* New York: Da Capo, 1998.

Babington, Anthony. *Shell-Shock: A History of the Changing Attitudes to War Neurosis.* London: Pen and Sword, 1997.

Ballantine, Henry Winthrop. "Unconstitutional Claims of Military Authority." *American Journal of Criminal Law and Criminology* 5 (March 1915): 718–743.

Barbeau, Arthur E., and Florette Henri. *The Unknown Soldiers: African American Troops in World War I.* Philadelphia: Temple University Press, 1974.

Barton, Walter E. *The History and Influence of the American Psychiatric Association.* New York: APA, 1987.

Bassiouni, Cherif. *Introduction to International Criminal Law.* 2nd ed. Leiden: Brill, 2001.

Bates, James Leonard. *Senator Thomas J. Walsh of Montana: Law and Public Affairs from TR to FDR.* Champaign: University of Illinois Press, 1999.

Beaver, Daniel. *Newton D. Baker and the American War Effort, 1917–1919.* Lincoln: University of Nebraska Press, 1966.

Berg, A. Scott. *Wilson.* New York: G. P. Putnam's Sons, 2013.

Bevilacqua, Allan C. "The Strange Case of Edmund Chamberlain." *Leatherneck* 92 (May 2009).

Birkhimer, William. *Military Government and Martial Law.* Washington, DC: J. J. Chapman, 1892.

Black, Jeremy. *The Age of Total War, 1860–1945.* Lanham, MD: Rowman and Littlefield, 2006.

Borch, Frederic. "The Greatest Judge Advocate in History? The Extraordinary Life of Enoch H. Crowder, 1859–1932." *Army Lawyer* (May 2012).

Buekner, John D. *The History of Wisconsin. Vol 4: The Progressive Era, 1893–1914.* Madison: State Historical Society of Wisconsin, 1998.

Capozzola, Christopher. *Uncle Same Wants You: World War I and the Making of the Modern American Citizen.* New York: Oxford University Press, 2008.

Carter, William Harding. *The American Army.* Indianapolis: Bobbs-Merrill, 1915.

Cassar, George H. *Lloyd George at War: 1916–1918.* London: Anthem Press, 2011.

Cecil, Hugh, and Peter Liddle. *Facing Armageddon: The First World War Experience.* London: Pena and Sword, 1996.

Chambers, John Whiteclay. *To Raise an Army: The Draft Comes to Modern America.* New York: Free Press, 1987.

———. *The Tyranny of Change.* New Brunswick, NJ: Rutgers University Press, 1992.

Chew, William C. *National Stereotypes in Perspective: Americans in France, Frenchmen in America.* Amsterdam: Rodopi BV, 2001.

Chickering, Robert. "Total War: The Use and Abuse of a Concept." In *Anticipating Total War: The American and German Experiences, 1871-1914*, edited by Manfred Boemke et al. London: Cambridge University Press, 1999.

Christian, Garna L. *Black Soldiers in Jim Crow Texas, 1899-1917*. College Station: Texas A & M Press, 1995.

Clark, George B. *The American Expeditionary Force in World War I: A Statistical History*. Jefferson, NC: McFarland Press, 2013.

Clark, Thomas Ralph. *Defending Rights: Law, Labor, and Politics in California, 1890-1920*. Detroit: Wayne State University Press, 2002.

Coffman, Edward M. *The Hilt of the Sword: The Career of Peyton C. March*. Madison: University of Wisconsin Press, 1966.

———. *The Regulars: The American Army, 1898-1941*. Boston: Harvard University Press, 2004.

———. *The War to End All Wars: The American Military Experience in World War I*. Lexington: University Press of Kentucky, 1998.

Collins, Ann V. *All Hell Broke Loose: American Race Riots from the Progressive Era through World War II*. Santa Barbara, CA: ABC-CLIO, 2012.

Connelly, Donald B. *John M. Schofield and the Politics of Generalship*. Chapel Hill: University of North Carolina Press, 2006.

Cooper, Jerry. *The Rise of the National Guard: The Evolution of the American Militia, 1865-1920*. Lincoln: University of Nebraska Press, 1997.

Cooper, John Milton. *Pivotal Decades: The United States, 1900-1920*. New York: W.W. Norton, 1990.

Coppee, Henry. *Field Manual of Courts-Martial: to which are added the modes of procedure in courts of inquiry, military commissions, retiring boards, boards of survey, inspection reports and examining boards. With an appendix containing the Articles of War, supplementary acts of Congress and such portions of the revised regulations as bear upon the subject*. Philadelphia: J. B. Lippincott, 1863.

Craig, Douglas B. *Progressives at War: William G. McAdoo and Newton D. Baker, 1863-1941*. Baltimore: Johns Hopkins University Press, 2013.

Cramer, Clarence H. *Newton D. Baker: A Biography*. New York: World Publishing, 1961.

Cullum, George. *Biographical Register of Officers and Graduates of the United States Military Academy*. Saginaw MI: Seaman and Peters, 1920.

Davis, George B. *A Treatise on the Military Law of the United States Together with the Practice and Procedure of Courts-Martial and Other Military Tribunals*. New York: John Wiley and Sons, 1902.

de la Gorce, Paul Marie. *The French Army; a Military-Political History*. Translated by Kenneth Douglas. New York: G. Braziller, 1963.

Dembo, Jonathan. *A Life of Duty: The Autobiography of George Wilcox McIver, 1858-1947*. Charleston SC: The History Press, 2006.

Drake, Richard. *The Education of an Anti-Imperialist: Robert La Follette and U.S. Expansion*. Madison: University of Wisconsin Press, 2013.

Dubofsky, Melvin. *We Shall Be All: A History of the I.W.W.* 2nd ed. Champaign: University of Illinois Press, 1988.

Elkins, Stanley, and Eric McKittrick. *The Age of Federalism: The Early American Republic, 1788-1800*. New York: Oxford University Press, 1993.

Ellis, Mark L. *Race, War and Surveillance: African Americans and the United States Government During World War I*. Bloomington: Indiana University Press, 2001.

Erickson, John. *The Soviet High Command: A Military-Political History, 1918-1941*. London: St. Martin's Press, 1962.

Ewing, Keith D., and C. A. Gearty. *The Struggle for Civil Liberties, Political Freedom, and the Rule of Law in Britain*. London: Oxford University Press, 2000.

Farwell, Bryan. *Over There: The United States in the Great War*. New York: W.W. Norton, 1999.

Ferguson, Niall. *The Pity of War: Explaining World War I*. New York: Basic Books, 1998.

Ferrell, Robert H. *Five Days in October: The Lost Battalion of World War I*. Columbia: University of Missouri Press, 2005.

Fine, Sidney A. *Frank Murphy in World War One*. Ann Arbor: Michigan Historical Collections, 1969.

———. *Sit Down: The General Motors Strike of 1936-1937*. Ann Arbor: University of Michigan Press, 1969.

Fisher, Louis. *Nazi Saboteurs on Trial: A Military Tribunal and American Law*. Lawrence: University Press of Kansas, 2005.

Fleming, Thomas. *The Illusion of Victory: America in World War I*. New York: Basic Books, 2003.

Foner, Philip Sheldon. *Militarism and Organized Labor, 1900-1914*. Minneapolis: MEP Publications, 1987.

Fox, Frank W. *J. Reuben Clark: The Public Years*. Provo, UT: Brigham Young University Press, 1980.

Freeberg, Ernest. *Democracy's Prisoner: Eugene V. Debs, the Great War and the Right to Dissent*. Boston: Harvard University Press, 2008.

Frost, Richard H. *The Mooney Case: The San Francisco Preparedness Day Parade Bombing of 1916 and Its Aftermath—One of the Most Sensational Radical Labor Prosecutions in American History*. Stanford, CA: Stanford University Press, 1968.

Gaff, Alan D. *Blood in the Argonne: The Lost Battalion of World War I*. Norman: University of Oklahoma Press, 2008.

Galston, Miriam. "Activism and Restraint: The Evolution of Harlan Fiske Stone's Judicial Philosophy." *Tulane Law Review* 70 (1995).

Garthoff, Raymond. *Soviet Military Policy: A Historical Analysis*. London: Faber and Faber, 1966.

Gieske, Millard L., and Steven Keillor. *Norwegian Yankee: Knute Nelson and the Failure of American Politics, 1860-1923*. Northfield, MN: The Norwegian-American Historical Association, 1995.

Giffin, Frederick C. "The Rudowitz Extradition Case." *Journal of the Illinois State Historical Society* 72 (1982).

Gilbert, James L. *World War I and the Origins of Military Intelligence*. Lanham, MD: Scarecrow Press, 2012.

Gilbert, Martin. *The First World War: A Complete History*. New York: Henry Holt, 1994.

Gilchrist, Robert. *The Duties of a Judge Advocate, in a trial before a general court-martial, compiled from various works on military law*. Columbia, SC: Evans and Cogswell, 1864.

Gillette, Mary C. *The Army Medical Department, 1917-1940*. Washington, DC: Center for Military History, 1987.

Goemans, H. E. *War and Punishment: The Causes of War Termination and the First World War*. Princeton, NJ: Princeton University Press, 2000.

Goldberg, Gordon J. *Meyer London: A Biography of the Socialist New York Congressman, 1871-1926*. Jefferson, NC: McFarland Press, 2013

Goodall, Alexander. *Loyalty and Liberty: American Counter-subversion from World War I to the McCarthy Era*. Champaign: University of Illinois Press, 2013.

Gray, Wood. *The Hidden Civil War: The Story of the Copperheads*. New York: Viking, 1942.

Hagar, Gerald F. "Judge Advocate General's Department in the American Expeditionary Forces." *California Law Review* 8, no. 5 (1920).

Hagedorn, Ann. *Savage Peace: Hope and Fear in America, 1919*. New York: Simon and Schuster, 2007.

Hair, William Ivy. *The Kingfish and His Realm: The Life and Times of Huey P. Long*. Baton Rouge: Louisiana State University Press, 1991.

Hart, Basil H. Liddell. *The Real War: 1914-1918*. Boston: Little, Brown, 1930.

Healy, Thomas. *The Great Dissent: How Oliver Wendell Holmes Changed His Mind: And Changed the History of Free Speech*. New York: Henry Holt, 2013.

Herries, Meirion, and Susie Harries. *The Last Days of Innocence: America at War, 1917-1918*. New York: Vintage, 1997.

Holmes, William F. *The White Chief: James Kimble Vardaman*. Baton Rouge: Louisiana State University Press, 1970.

Horne, John, and Alan Kramer. *The German Atrocities of 1914: A History of Denial*. New Haven, CT: Yale University Press, 2001.

Hughes, R. M. *The Duties of Judge Advocates Compiled from Her Majesty's and the Honorable East India Company's Military Regulations and from the Works of Various Writers on Military Law*. London, 1845.

Inazu, John D. *Liberty's Refuge: The Forgotten Freedom of Assembly*. New Haven, CT: Yale University Press, 2012.

Iocobelli, Teresa. *Death or Deliverance: Canadian Courts-Martial in the Great War*. Vancouver: University of British Columbia Press, 2013.

Jankowski, Paul. *Verdun: The Longest Battle of the Great War*. London: Oxford University Press, 2014.

Janowitz, Morris. *The Last Half Century: Societal Change and Politics in America*. Chicago: University of Chicago Press, 1978.

Jensen, Joan. *Army Surveillance in America: 1775-1980*. New Haven CT: Yale University Press, 1991.

———. *The Price of Vigilance*. Chicago: Rand McNally, 1969.

Jones, Edgar, and Wesley Simon. *Military Psychiatry from 1900 to the Gulf War*. Sussex, UK: Psychiatry Press, 2005.

Jordan, David M. *Happiness Is Not My Companion: The Life of General G. K. Warren*. Bloomington: Indiana University Press, 2001.

Jordan, William L. *Black Newspapers and America's War for Democracy, 1914-1920*. Chapel Hill: University of North Carolina Press, 2001.

Kastenberg, Joshua E. *The Blackstone of Military Law*. Lanham, MD: Rowman and Littlefield, 2009.

———. *Law in War Law as War: Brigadier General Joseph Holt and the Judge Advocate General Department in the Civil War and Reconstruction*. Durham, NC: Carolina Academic Press, 2011.

———. "A Sesquicentennial Historic Analysis of *Dynes v. Hoover* and the Supreme Court's Bow to Military Necessity." *University of Memphis Law* Review 39 (2009).

Kaunonen, Gary. *Community in Conflict : A Working-Class History of the 1913-14 Michigan Copper Strike and the Italian Hall Tragedy*. East Lansing: Michigan State University Press, 2013.

Keegan, John. *A History of Warfare*. New York: Alfred A. Knopf, 1993.

Keene, Jennifer. *Doughboys: The Great War and the Remaking of America*. Baltimore: Johns Hopkins University Press, 2001.

Keiger, John V. F. *France and the Origin of the First World War*. New York: St. Martin's Press, 1983.

Keith, Jeanette. *Rich Man's War, Poor Man's Fight: Power in the Rural South during the First World War*. Chapel Hill: University of North Carolina Press, 2004.

Kennedy, David. *Over Here: The First World War and American Society*. New York: Oxford University Press, 2004.

Kessler, Jeremy K. "The Administrative Origins of Modern Civil Liberties Law." *Columbia Law Review* (June 2010).

Kirgis, Frederic. *The American Society of International Law's Century: 1906-2006*. New York: Brill, 2006.

Knock, Thomas J. *To End All Wars: Woodrow Wilson and the Quest for a New World Order*. Princeton, NJ: Princeton University Press, 1992.

Kohn, Richard A. "Using the Military at Home: Yesterday, Today, and Tomorrow." In *American Defense Policy*, edited by Paul J. Bolt, Damon V. Coletta, and Collins G. Shackelford. Baltimore: Johns Hopkins University Press, 2005

Laughlin, Rosemary. *The Ludlow Massacre of 1913-14*. Greensboro, NC: Morgan Reynolds, 2006.

Leonard, Elizabeth D. *Lincoln's Forgotten Ally: Judge Advocate General Joseph Holt of Kentucky*. Chapel Hill: University of North Carolina Press, 2011.

Lewy, Gunther. *America in Vietnam*. New York: Oxford University Press, 1978.

Linn, Brian McAllister. *The Philippine War, 1899-1902*. Lawrence: University Press of Kansas, 2000.

Livermore, Seward W. *Politics Is Adjourned: Woodrow Wilson and the War Congress, 1916-1918*. Boston: Wesleyan University Press, 1966.

Lloyd, Mark. *The Art of Military Deception*. London: Pen and Sword, 2003.

Lockmiller, David. *Enoch H. Crowder: Soldier, Lawyer, and Statesman.* Columbia: University of Missouri Press, 1955.

Loverman, Brian. *No Higher Law: Foreign Policy and the Western Hemisphere Since 1776.* Chapel Hill: University of North Carolina Press, 2010.

Lower, Richard Coke. *A Bloc of One: The Political Career of Hiram Johnson.* San Francisco: Stanford University Press, 1993.

Luebke, Frederick. *Bonds of Loyalty: German Americans in World War I.* DeKalb: Northern Illinois University Press, 1974.

Lukas, J. Anthony. *Big Trouble: A Murder in a Small Western Town Sets off a Struggle for the Soul of America.* New York: Simon and Schuster, 1997.

Lumpkins, Charles L. *American Pogrom: The East Saint Louis Race Riot and Black Politics.* Athens: Ohio University Press, 2008.

Lurie, Jonathan. *Arming Military Justice: The Origins of the United States Court of Military Appeals, 1775-1990.* Princeton, NJ: Princeton University Press, 1992.

"Major General George B. Davis: Judge Advocate General, 1901-1911." *Military Law Review* 31 (January 1966).

Marble, Sanders. *Scraping the Barrel: The Military Use of Substandard Manpower.* New York: Fordham University Press, 2001.

Martin, Benjamin. *The Hypocrisy of Justice in the Belle Epoque.* Baton Rouge: Louisiana State University Press, 1984.

McArthur, John. *Principles and Practice of Naval and Military Courts-Martial.* 4th ed. Vol 1. London: A. Strahan, 1813.

McFeely, William F. *Yankee Stepfather: General O. O. Howard and the Freedmen.* New York: W.W. Norton, 1994.

McNeill, William H. *The Pursuit of Power: Technology, Armed Force and Society since 1000 AD.* Chicago: University of Chicago Press, 1982.

Miller, Paul B. *From Revolutionaries to Citizens: Anti-Militarism in France, 1870-1914.* Durham, NC: Duke University Press, 2002.

Mjagki, Nina. *Loyalty in Time of Trial: The African-American Experience During World War I.* Lanham, MD: Rowman and Littlefield, 2011.

Murlin, Edgar. *The New York Red Book: An Illustrated Legislative Manual.* Albany: J. B. Lyon, 1902.

Neely, Mark E. *The Fate of Liberty: Abraham Lincoln and Civil Liberties.* New York: Oxford University Press, 1991.

Nelson, Keith L. *Victors Divided: America and the Allies in Germany, 1918-1923.* Los Angeles: University of California Press, 1975.

Newman, Roger K. *The Yale Biographical Dictionary of American Law.* New Haven: Yale University Press, 2009.

Okrent, Daniel. *Last Call: The Rise and Fall of Prohibition.* New York: Scribner, 2010.

Onofrio, Jan. *Missouri Biographical Dictionary.* 3rd ed. Vol 1. St. Clair, MI: Somerset, 2001.

Oram, Gerard. "The Administration of Discipline by the English Is Very Rigid: British Military Law and the Death Penalty, 1868-1918." *Crime, History and Societies* 5 (2001).

O'Reilly, Kenneth. *Nixon's Piano: Presidents and Racial Politics from Washington to Clinton.* New York: Free Press, 1995.

Patterson H. C., and Gilbert Fite. *Opponents of the War, 1917-1918.* Madison: University of Wisconsin Press, 1957.

Pearlman, Michael. *To Make Democracy Safe for America: Patricians and Preparedness in the Progressive Era.* Champaign: University of Illinois Press, 1984.

Pratt, Walter F. *The Supreme Court Under Edward Douglass White, 1910-1921.* Columbia: University of South Carolina Press, 1999.

Puleo, Stephen. *Dark Tide: The Great Boston Molasses Flood of 1919.* Boston: Beacon Press, 2004.

Renstrom, Peter G. *The Taft Court: Justices, Rulings, and Legacy.* Santa Barbara, CA: ABC-CLIO, 2003.

Richard, Carl J. *When the United States Invaded Russia: Woodrow Wilson's Siberian Disaster*. Lanham, MD: Rowman and Littlefield, 2013.

Ropp, Theodore. *War in the Modern World*. New York: Collier, 1962.

Schmitz, David F. *Henry L. Stimson: The First Wise Man*. Wilmington DE: Scholarly Resources, 2001.

Schrantz, George. *Guarding the Border: The Military Memories of Ward Schrantz, 1912-1917*. College Station: Texas A & M University Press, 2012.

Sellars, Nigel. *Oil, Wheat, and Wobblies: The Industrial Workers of the World in Oklahoma, 1905-1930*. Norman: University of Oklahoma Press, 1998.

Shenk, Gerald. *Work or Fight: Race, Gender, and the Draft in World War One*. New York: Palgrave-MacMillan, 2005.

Sherman, Edward F. "The Civilianization of Military Law." *Maine Law Review* 22 (1970).

Sherwood, John. *Georges Mandel and the Third Republic*. Palo Alto, CA: Stanford University Press, 1970.

Shinohara, Hatuse. *US International Lawyers in the Interwar Years: A Forgotten Crusade*. New York: Cambridge University Press, 2012.

Shoemaker, Rebecca M. *The White Court: Justices, Rulings, and Legacy*. Santa Barbara, CA: ABC-CLIO, 2004.

Smith, Louis. *American Democracy and Military Power: A Study of the Civil Control of Military Power in the United States*. Chicago: University of Chicago Press, 1951.

Sondhaus, Lawrence. *World War One: The Global Revolution*. London: Cambridge University Press, 2011.

Stokesbury, James. *A Short History of World War I*. New York: William Morrow, 1981.

Striner, Richard. *Woodrow Wilson and WWI: A Burden too Great to Bear*. Lanham, MD: Rowman and Littlefield, 2014.

Stuart, Reginald C. *Civil Military Relations During the War of 1812*. Santa Barbara, CA: Greenwood Press, 2009.

Sweeney, Jerry. *A Handbook of American Military History: From the Revolutionary War to the Present*. Lincoln: University of Nebraska Press, 1996.

Taafe, Stephen R. *Commanding the Army of the Potomac*. Lawrence: University Press of Kansas, 2006.

Talbert, Roy Jr. *Negative Intelligence: The Army and the American Left, 1917-1941*. Columbus: University of Mississippi Press, 1991.

Taylor, Telford. *Nuremberg and Vietnam: An American Tragedy*. Chicago: Quadrangle, 1976.

Temkin, Meshik. *The Sacco-Vanzetti Affair: America on Trial*. New Haven, CT: Yale University Press, 2009.

Terraine, John. *The Great War*. London: Wordsworth, 1965.

Thurtle, Ernest. *Shootings at Dawn: The Army Death Penalty at Work*. London: Victoria House Printing, 1924.

Trask, David F. *The AEF and Coalition Warmaking, 1917-1918*. Lawrence: University Press of Kansas, 1993.

Tuchman, Barbara. *The Proud Tower: A Portrait of the World Before the War, 1890-1918*. London: H. Hamilton, 1966.

———. *The Zimmerman Telegram*. London: Constable Press, 1959.

Unger, Nancy C. *Fighting Bob La Follette: The Righteous Reformer*. Chapel Hill: University of North Carolina Press, 2000.

Urofsky, Melvin L. *Louis D. Brandeis: A Life*. New York: Random House, 2009.

Vinson, John Chalmers. *William E. Borah and the Outlawry of War*. Athens: University of Georgia Press, 1957.

Walworth, Arthur. *Woodrow Wilson*. 3rd ed. New York: W.W. Norton, 1978.

Watson, Alexander. *Enduring the Great War: Combat, Morale and Collapse in the German and British Armies, 1914-1918*. London: Cambridge University Press, 2008.

Watt, Richard. *Dare Call It Treason: The True Story of the French Army Mutinies of 1917*. New York: Simon & Schuster, 1963.

Weaver, John Browning. *The Brownsville Raid.* New York: W.W. Norton, 1970.

Weber, Jennifer. *Copperheads: The Rise and Fall of Lincoln's Opponents in the North.* New York: Oxford University Press, 2006.

Wigmore, John Henry. *A Source Book on Military Law and Wartime Legislation.* Minneapolis: West Publishing, 1919.

Willett, Robert. *Russian Sideshow: America's Undeclared War, 1918-1920.* Washington, DC: Potomac Books, 2003.

Williams, Chad. *Torchbearers of Democracy: African American Soldiers in the World War I Era.* Chapel Hill: University of North Carolina Press, 2010.

Winthrop, William. *Military Law and Precedents.* Washington, DC: GPO, 1920.

Witt, John Fabian. *Lincoln's Code: The Laws of War in American History.* New York: Simon and Schuster, 2012.

Woodward, C. Vann. *Tom Watson: Agrarian Rebel.* New York: Oxford University Press, 1955.

Woodward, David. *The American Army in the First World War.* New York: Cambridge University Press, 2014.

Wooster, Robert. *The Military and United States Indian Policy, 1865-1903.* Lincoln: University of Nebraska Press, 1988.

Yanella, Philip. *The Other Carl Sandburg.* Jackson: University of Mississippi Press, 1996.

Yellin, Eric. *Racism in the Nation's Service: Government Workers and the Color Line.* Chapel Hill: University of North Carolina Press, 2013.

Zeiger, Susan. *Entangling Alliances: Foreign War Brides and American Soldiers in the Twentieth Century.* New York: New York University Press, 2010.

Notes

PREFACE

1. Taft to Ms. Carey Thomas, May 6, 1928 [WHT/301].

INTRODUCTION

1. On the numbers of men registered in the World War I draft, as well as the numbers of trials, see *Establishment of Military Justice: Hearings Before a Subcommittee of the Committee on Military Affairs United States Senate, Sixty-Sixth Congress on S. 64 "a Bill to Establish Military Justice* (Washington, DC: GPO, 1919), 687 [hereafter Hearings II]. See also Edward M. Coffman, *The War to End All Wars: The American Military Experience in World War I* (Lexington: University Press of Kentucky, 1998), 29; and John Whiteclay Chambers II, *The Tyranny of Change* (New Brunswick, NJ: Rutgers University Press, 1992), 240. For other evidence of the numbers of general courts-martial, see Newton D. Baker, Report to Congress for Fiscal Year 1921 [NDB/157]. On the Judge Advocate General's opinion regarding dishonorable discharges, see Adjutant General to all Commanding Generals, September 22, 1917 [RG 165 E310, Records of the War Department and Special Staffs—Judge Advocate B225].

2. On the fear of standing armies, see Stanley Elkins and Eric McKittrick, *The Age of Federalism: The Early American Republic, 1788-1800* (New York: Oxford University Press, 1993), 716. On the prewar army, see Robert M. Utley, *Frontier Regulars: 1866-1891*(New York: MacMillan, 1973), 11–44; John Whiteclay Chambers II, *To Raise an Army: The Draft Comes to Modern America* (New York: Free Press, 1987), 73; and Edward M. Coffman, *The Regulars: The American Army, 1898-1941* (Boston: Harvard University Press, 2004), 142–201.

3. *McClaughry v. Deming*, 186 U.S. 49 (1902). On the federalization of state militia forces, see Jerry Cooper, *The Rise of the National Guard: The Evolution of the American Militia* (Lincoln: University of Nebraska Press, 1997), 154–163.

4. On the Judge Advocate General's Department, see William McKee Dunn, *A Sketch of the Duties of the Judge Advocate General's Department* (Washington, DC: GPO, 1874), 1–7; Lurton Ingersoll Dunham, *A History of the War Department of the United States* (Washington, DC: GPO, 1880), 149–160; and Joshua E. Kastenberg, *The Blackstone of Military Law* (Lanham, MD: Rowman and Littlefield, 2009).

5. Gorfinkle to his mother, May 5, 1918 [BG-AJA/1]; Address by Lieutenant Colonel Hugh W. Ogden, printed in *Boston City Club Bulletin*, October 1, 1919, 41–58, 53.

6. Dunham, *A History of the War Department of the United States*, 155–160; Dunn, *A Sketch of the Duties of the Judge Advocate General's Department*, 1–7; *Ex Parte Mason*, 105 U.S. 696 (1881). However, the facts of Mason are found in *Ex Parte Mason*, 256 F 2 (DC 1882); and *McClaughry v. Deming*, 186 U.S. 49 (1902).

7. Joshua Kastenberg, *Law in War, War as Law: Brigadier General Joseph Holt and the Judge Advocate General Department in the Civil War and Reconstruction* (Durham, NC: Carolina Academic Press, 2011), 69; Stimson to Garrison, March 31, 1913 [LGP/9].

8. David Woodward, *The American Army in the First World War* (New York & London: Cambridge University Press, 2014), 114. There is an error in Professor Woodward's book. He notes, on page 58, that the judge advocate general suspended all sentences of a dishonorable discharge for the duration of the war. The judge advocate general did not possess the authority to suspend any sentence, and the secretary of war approved hundreds of dishonorable discharges during the conflict.

9. *McKinley v. United States*, 249 U.S. 397 (1919).

CHAPTER 1

1. See, e.g., Elizabeth D. Leonard, *Lincoln's Forgotten Ally: Judge Advocate General Joseph Holt of Kentucky* (Chapel Hill: University of North Carolina Press, 2011); Baker to Crowder, November 17, 1917; Crowder to Baker, November 18, 1917 [ECH/R3]

2. David Lockmiller, *Enoch H. Crowder: Soldier, Lawyer, and Statesman* (Columbia: University of Missouri Press, 1955); Frederic Borch, "The Greatest Judge Advocate in History? The Extraordinary life of Enoch H. Crowder 1859–1932," *Army Lawyer* (May 2012): 1–7; Meirion and Susie Hinds, *The Last Days of Innocence: America at War, 1917–1918* (New York: Vintage, 1997), 93; Edward M. Coffman, *The Regulars: The American Army, 1898–1941*, 121; Edward M. Coffman, *The Hilt of the Sword: The Career of Peyton C. March* (Madison: University of Wisconsin Press?, 1966), 27; Jonathan Dembo, *A Life of Duty: The Autobiography of George Wilcox McIver, 1858–1947* (Charleston, SC: The History Press, 2006), 188; Jonathan Lurie, *Arming Military Justice: The Origins of the United States Court of Military Appeals, 1775–1990* (Princeton, NJ: Princeton University Press, 1992).

3. On Schofield, see Donald B. Connelly, *John M. Schofield and the Politics of Generalship* (Chapel Hill: University of North Carolina Press, 2006), 257. On Howard, see Oliver Otis Howard, *Autobiography of Oliver Otis Howard, Major General USA* (New York: Books for Libraries Press, 1971); and William F. McFeely, *Yankee Stepfather: General O. O. Howard and the Freedmen* (New York: W.W. Norton, 1994). There is no mention of Crowder in these books. On Crowder's response to Roosevelt, see Senator John C. Spooner to Henry Stimson, May 20, 1908 [HS/R-16]. On Crowder's consideration of hiring a female attorney for the War Department, see Arthur Dehon Hill to Frankfurter, October 8, 1918 [FF-Harv/R-40].

4. Frederic Borch, "The Greatest Judge Advocate in History," 3; Jan Onofrio, *Missouri Biographical Dictionary*, 3rd ed. (St. Clair, MI: Somerset, 2001), 1:180–183.

5. Frederic Borch, "The Greatest Judge Advocate in History," 3.

6. Crowder to Adjutant General, April 15, 1896 [RG 393, Pt I, E 3338].

7. Crowder to Lieber, May 13, 1896 [RG 393 Pt I, E 3338]; Lieber to Crowder, September 2, 1894; Cockrell to Elkins, February 2, 1892; Proctor to Elkins, February 2, 1892; Ruger to Elkins, February 1, 1892; Caldwell to Elkins, April 21, 1894; Milton Moore to Elkins, February 3, 1892; Otis to Elkins, October 3, 1893; Bates to Elkins, May 4, 1894; Schwan to Lamont, July 16, 1894; and List of Endorsements, September 14, 1894 [all in EHC/R1].

8. Otis to Secretary of War Root, May 5, 1900 [EHC/34]; Elwell S. Otis, Report of the Philippine Commission to the President, January 31, 1900 (Washington, DC: GPO, 1901).

9. Brian McAllister Linn, *The Philippine War, 1899–1902* (Lawrence: University Press of Kansas, 2000), 51.

10. MacArthur to Root, October 21, 1901 [EHC/R1]; Crowder to Moore, July 19, 1910 [JBM/16]. In this letter Crowder recalls how Moore helped "heal" him through a debilitating sickness. Neither of Crowder's biographers, nor the historians who describe him, appear to have uncovered his relationship with Moore. Yet Moore influenced the War Department's practice of international law, and particularly the law of war, partly through this relationship.

11. Taft to Crowder, September 18, 1901 [WHT/31]; Taft to Crowder, February 24, 1902 [WHT/32]; Crowder to Taft, March 21, 1902 [WHT/32]; George W. Davis to Crowder, June 4, 1902 [WHT/33]; Taft to Elihu Root, June 9, 1908 [ERP/166]. In this letter, Taft informed Root of Crowder's

assistance. On Taft's mission to the Vatican, see David H. Burton, *Taft, Holmes, and the 1920s Court: An Appraisal* (New York: Farleigh Dickinson Press, 1998), 71.

12. Crowder to Root, n.d. 1903 [ER/33]. Crowder's memorandum is attached to a letter from Root to Senator John C. Spooner, dated March 3, 1903. For information on the Battle of Caloocan, see Brian McAllister Linn, *The Philippine War*, 56–57. However, Linn does not mention the issue involving the execution of prisoners of war, or several other instances where the law of war may have been violated by American soldiers. On the murder of prisoners, see *Hearings Before the Committee on the Philippines of the United States Senate*, April 10, 1902 (Washington, DC: GPO, 1902), 1427–1489.

13. In reality, Davis replaced General John Clous, who replaced General Thomas Barr as judge advocate general. However, Clous and Barr, who had also served in the Civil War, each served as judge advocate general for one day. Their tenure as judge advocate general was akin to an honorarium for having served in the army and the department faithfully since the middle of the Civil War. On George B. Davis, see "Major General George B. Davis: Judge Advocate General, 1901–1911," 31 *Military Law Review* (1966): i–iv.

14. Crowder to O'Laughlin, February 28, 1919 [JCO/16]. In this letter Crowder acknowledges Root's support for him, but disavows a desire either to enter politics or remain an officer on lifetime active duty. On Root's army, see Thomas S. Langston, *Uneasy Balance: Civil Military Relations in Peacetime America Since 1783* (Baltimore: Johns Hopkins University Press, 2003), 43–47; and especially Ronald J. Barr, *The Progressive Army: US Army Command and Administration, 1870–1914* (New York: St. Martin's Press, 1998).

15. On Crowder's view of desertion, see Adjutant General to Stimson, November 27, 1911 [HS/R-27], and Henry Stimson, "A Defense of Crowder's Administration of His Office," *New York Times*, April 9, 1919. On Wilson's view of Crowder see, Joseph P. Tumulty, *Wilson as I know Him* (Garden City, NY: Doubleday, 1921). Tumulty claimed that Crowder's republicanism was well known to Wilson, but Wilson determined he was trustworthy.

16. James O'Laughlin to Crowder, February 24, 1919 [JCO/16] O'Laughlin supported Crowder when Peyton March had publicly minimized Crowder's contribution to the war effort by calling Crowder a far more competent officer than March. Crowder to Moore, January 25, 1919 [JBM/16].

17. See, e.g., Mary C. Gillette, *The Army Medical Department, 1917–1940* (Washington, DC: Center for Military History, 1987), 137.

18. Brandeis to Jacob deHaas, March 17, 1918 [LDB/32]; Goethals to Brandeis, March 2, 1918; House to Brandeis, March 2, 1918; Brandeis to House, March 3, 1918 [EMH/18].

19. Crowder to Pershing, April 5, 1915 [JJP/56]; "Revision on the Articles of War," *Hearing Before the House Committee on Military Affairs*, Sixty-Second Congress, 2d Sess. on H.R. 23628, "Being a Project for the Revision of the New Articles of War," 21–31.

20. *Ex Parte Milligan*, 71 U.S. 2 (1866). On the number of Civil War military trials of civilians, see Mark E. Neely, *The Fate of Liberty: Abraham Lincoln and Civil Liberties* (New York: Oxford University Press, 1991), 168.

21. Garrison to Wilson, March 24, 1914 [LGP-SML/1]; Chief of the Ordnance Department to Garrison, September 17, 1914 [LGP-SML/1]; Crowder to O'Laughlin, February 28, 1919 [JCO/16]; O'Laughlin to Crowder, March 3, 1919 [JCO/16]. In this letter, Crowder describes his view of politics and conversation with Taft, and O'Laughlin responds that "Taft, notoriously, is not a politician." Crowder to Burleson, October 7, 1918 [RG 163 General File/12]. On the suffrage issue, see Crowder to Stimson, March 3, 1913 [HLS/R-32].

22. On Crowder's questioning of Wallace's assertion that West Virginia could prosecute its citizens in a state court-martial, see Wallace to Bethel, March 21, 1913. On Crowder's advice on enforcing the Dick Bill, see Ansell to Wallace, June 5, 1916 [GWP-WVL].

23. Crowder to Bliss, August 15, 1917 [THB/217].

24. Baker to Bliss, August 18, 1917 [THB/218]; Pershing to Crowder, June 28, 1918 [JJP/56].

25. Pershing to Crowder, March 30, 1915 [JJP/56]; Crowder to Pershing, January 19, 1918 [JJP/56].

26. Pershing to Crowder, June 8, 1911 [JJP/56]. On the attempts at staff reforms, see e.g. Donald B. Connelly, *John M. Schofield and the Politics of Generalship*, 301–304; Crowder to O'Laughlin, February 28, 1918 [JCO/16]. On the concern at the American Expeditionary Forces headquarters, see Harbord to Pershing, December 8, 1918 [JGH/11]. On Crowder's advice to Baker, see Scott to Frederick Palmer, quoted in Palmer, *Newton D. Baker: America at War* (New York: Dodd & Mead, 1931), 1:65; and Hugh L. Scott, *Some Memoirs of a Soldier* (New York: D. Appleton-Century, 1928), 546–547.

27. John Sharp Williams (JSW) to Wilson, Oct 26, 1915; Wilson to JSW [JSW/1]; Willard Saulsbury to James F. Price, September 23, 1915 [WS-U-Del/47 f-23]; Clinton Rossiter, *The Supreme Court and the Commander in Chief* (New York: Cornell University Press, 1951), 102; Thomas R. Marshall, *Recollections of Thomas Marshall: Vice President and Hoosier Philosopher* (Indianapolis: Bobs-Merrill, 1925), 75.

28. Jeanette Keith, *Rich Man's War, Poor Man's Fight: Power in the Rural South during the First World War* (Chapel Hill: University of North Carolina Press, 2004), 13–33; Gordon J. Goldberg, *Meyer London: A Biography of the Socialist New York Congressman, 1871–1926* (Jefferson, NC: McFarland Press, 2013), 157; Norris to A. T. Seashore, President Luther College, December 27, 1919 [GWN/46].

29. Ansell to Baker, October 8, 1918 [WWP/R189]; Acting Secretary of War Carrell to Wilson [WWP/R189]; on prisoners of war, see Taft to Ansell, August 15, 1918 [WHT/211]; Crowder to Wood, July 20, 1918 [LW/107]; Roosevelt to Wood, July 18, 1917; Roosevelt to Crowder, July 19, 1917 [TR/R393]; Crowder to TR, March 21, 1918 [TR/R269].

30. James L. Gilbert, *World War I and the Origins of Military Intelligence* (Lanham, MD: Scarecrow Press, 2012), 38–44; Roy Talbert Jr., *Negative Intelligence: The Army and the American Left, 1917–1941* (Columbus: University of Mississippi Press, 1991), 11–14.

31. On the fears of communist intrusion into the army, see *The German Bolshevik Conspiracy Issued by The Committee on Public Information*, George Creel, Chairman (1918). On the rise of anarchism and radical socialism in labor organizations, see Barbara Tuchman, *The Proud Tower: A Portrait of the World Before the War, 1890–1918* (London: H. Hamilton, 1966), especially ch. 2; and Richard A Kohn, "Using the Military at Home: Yesterday, Today, and Tomorrow," in Paul J. Bolt, Damon V. Coletta, and Collins G. Shackelford, *American Defense Policy* (Baltimore: Johns Hopkins University Press, 2005), 448–449. On the preparedness day parade bombing, see generally Richard H. Frost, *The Mooney Case: The San Francisco Preparedness Day Parade Bombing of 1916 and Its Aftermath—One of the Most Sensational Radical Labor Prosecutions in American History* (Stanford, CA: Stanford University Press, 1968).

32. Baker to Wilson, March 28, 1917; Wilson to Baker, March 28, 1917 [NDB/3].

33. W. C. Gorgas to Williams, May 11, 1917 [JSW/26]; Webb to Dr. J. M. T. Finney, May 15, 1917 [EYW-UNC/17]. On Webb's opposition to the war, see Webb to Mr. Charles Gibson, March 2, 1917; Webb to Mr. T. F. Stamay, March 5, 1917; Webb to Hon. T. L. Kirkpatrick, Mayor of Charlotte, March 5, 1917; Webb to H. B. Hemmeter, March 31, 1917; Webb to J. H. Fish, March 31, 1917 [EYW-UNC/15]; and Webb to J. L. Gilroy et al., April 10, 1917 [EYW-UNC/16].

34. Knox to Wilson, April 5, 1917; Knox, United States Senate Memorandum, n.d.; Commissioner, Alleghany County to Knox, April 7, 1917; Dwight Morgan, Allegheny River Improvement Association to Knox, April 28, 1917; Wilson to Knox, May 21, 1917; Baker to Wilson, May 18, 1917 [PK/29]; Baker to Knox, February 13, 1918 [PK/30].

35. H. C. Patterson and Gilbert Fite, *Opponents of the War, 1917–1918* (Madison: University of Wisconsin Press, 1957), 14.

36. Charles Warren to Overman, April 8, 1918 [CWP/1]. Warren addressed an identical letter to Senator Frank Kellogg, which is attached to the Overman letter.

37. Ansell to Baker, October 8, 1918 [WWP/R189]; Acting Secretary of War Carrell to Wilson [WWP/R189]; on prisoners of war, see Taft to Ansell, August 15, 1918 [WHT/R211].

38. Stephen J. Field to Nelson A. Miles, October 18, 1889; Field's advice to Miles was conveyed to the Judge Advocate General's Department. See Miles to Judge Advocate General, n.d. [NAM/1];

Nelson A. Miles to Daniel Lamont, July 14, 1894 [NAM/2]. On Miles, see Robert A. Wooster, *Nelson A. Miles and the Twilight of the Frontier Army* (Lincoln: University of Nebraska Press, 1992), 201–250.

39. On the Army of the Potomac, see Stephen R. Taafe, *Commanding the Army of the Potomac* (Lawrence: University Press of Kansas, 2006), 2–4. On the harnessing of society and economy as well as the casualty count of World War I, see John Keegan, *A History of Warfare* (New York: Alfred A. Knopf, 1993), 359–366; William H. McNeill, *The Pursuit of Power: Technology, Armed Force and Society Since 1000 AD* (Chicago: University of Chicago Press, 1982), 307– 345; Morris Janowitz, *The Last Half Century: Societal Change and Politics in America* (Chicago: University of Chicago Press, 1978), 194; James Stokesbury, *A Short History of World War I* (New York: William Morrow, 1981), 308–312; and especially Theodore Ropp, *War in the Modern World* (New York: Collier, 1962), 257–274.

40. Arthur Walworth, *Woodrow Wilson*, 3rd ed. (New York: W.W. Norton, 1978), 274. On Garrison's and Baker's lack of knowledge of the military, and Baker's pacifism, see also Douglas B. Craig, *Progressives at War: William G. McAdoo and Newton D. Baker, 1863-1941* (Baltimore: Johns Hopkins University Press, 2013), 65–67. See also Clarence H. Cramer, *Newton D. Baker: A Biography* (New York: World Publishing, 1961), 78–79. Cramer concluded that Garrison was sincere and able, but was also impatient, individualist, and tactless. Crowder left no impression of Garrison in this light.

41. On Tumulty, see Arthur Walworth, *Woodrow Wilson*, 276.

42. Tumulty to War Department, September 24, 1913; Winship to Tumulty, September 28, 1913 [WW/R297 C819]; Winship to Garrison and Tumulty, September 28, 1913; Tumulty to Garrison, September 29, 1913 [WW/R297 C819].

43. Newspaper Enterprise Association to General George Andrews, Adjutant General, October 13, 1913; Samuel Weakley to Tumulty, January 17, 1914; Tumulty to Wilson, January 28, 1914 [WW/R297 C817].

44. Crowder to Tumulty, January 24, 1919; Garrison to Tumulty, January 29, 1914 [WW/R297 C817].

45. Garrison, Memorandum for the JAG, June 30, 1915 [LG/6].

46. On the structure of the army, see Edward M. Coffman, *The War to End All Wars*, 48.

47. In 1974, in the Supreme Court case *Secretary of the Navy v. Avrech*, Justice William O. Douglas, who was conscripted into the army, wrote in his dissent: "in World War I we were free to lambast General 'Black Jack' Pershing who was distant, remote, and mythical. We also groused about the bankers' war, the munitions makers' war in which we had volunteered. What we said would have offended our military superiors." In Douglas's initial draft he also claimed that "lurid tales" about the generals' "blood lust" were commonplace, but this comment did not make it into the published dissent. Douglas, draft dissent, July 3, 1974 [WOD 1652]. For Douglas's military experience, see Military Discharge Certificate, William O. Douglas, dated December 20, 1918 [WOD/1771].

48. On Wilson's decision to send American forces to Russia, see Thomas J. Knock, *To End All Wars: Woodrow Wilson and the Quest for a New World Order* (Princeton, NJ: Princeton University Press, 1992), 155–158; Carl J. Richard, *When the United States Invaded Russia: Woodrow Wilson's Siberian Disaster* (Lanham, MD: Rowman and Littlefield, 2013), 38–41; and Douglas B. Craig, *Progressives at War*, 215.

49. Headquarters Eastern Department, General Court-Martial Orders no. 578, dated October 8, 1918; Headquarters Eastern Department, General Court-Martial Orders no. 581, October 12, 1918 [RG 393 Pt I, E 1593].

50. Judge Advocate, AEF to All Division and Section Judge Advocates, July 9, 1918 [RG 120 E594].

51. H. H. Morrow to Crowder, July 17, 1918 [NARA RG 120 E594]; Crowder, memorandum, July 17, 1918 [NARA RG 120 E594].

52. General Court-Martial Order 16, March 4, 1919, Trial of Corporal Julius Urbon [RG 120 E595, GCMO Orders 6th–77th Divisions/B1].

53. General Court-Martial Order 10, February 26, 1919, Trial of Private Homer Stevens [RG 120 E595, GCMO Orders 6th–77th Divisions/B1]; General Court-Martial Order 21, April 11, 1919, Trial of Bugler Urbon Meier [RG120 E595, GCMO Orders 6th–77th Divisions/B1].

CHAPTER 2

1. Pershing to Bliss, June 7, 1917 [THB/213].
2. On the Zimmerman Telegram, see generally Barbara Tuchman, *The Zimmerman Telegram* (London: Constable Press, 1959). On the concept of "total war," see e.g. Roger Chickering, "Total War: The Use and Abuse of a Concept," in Manfred Boemke et al., eds., *Anticipating Total War: The American and German Experiences, 1871–1914* (London: Cambridge University Press, 1999), 14–15. On one interpretation of the US contribution in the "total war" of World War I, see Jeremy Black, *The Age of Total War, 1860–1945* (Lanham, MD: Rowman and Littlefield, 2006), 81–83. Professor Black concentrates on the US industrial contributions to the Allied victory and posits that the nation's military contributions would have been overwhelming had the war continued into 1919. He does not, however, analyze how the US military prepared to take part, or actually took part, in the broader aspects of the war both as a disciplined force and in the degradation of German morale.
3. Ansell to Frelinghuysen, October 21, 1918 [NARA RG 153 E 390/ B1-f1]; Flood to H. D. Flood, July 30, 1917 [HDF/82]. Henry Flood eventually obtained a commission in the Quartermaster Corps, see J. Flood to Henry Flood, July 26, 1917 [HDF/82].
4. Bliss to Crowder, June 3, 1917 [THB/213]. On the efforts to curb the staffs' independence from the commanding general, see e.g. Donald Connelly, *John M. Schofield and the Politics of Generalship* (Chapel Hill: University of North Carolina Press, 2006), 232–233; and Allan R. Millett and Peter Maslowski, *For the Common Defense: A Military History of the United States* (New York: Free Press, 1994). On Davis's reputation, see Hugh Ogden to his wife Lisbeth, February 2, 1919 [HO-SIU/III]. Blanton Winship had informed Ogden that Davis would often be taken to task by the bureau chiefs because he was considered to be a poor lawyer.
5. See e.g. Pershing to Summerall, October 24, 1918. "When men run away in front of the enemy, officers should take summary action to stop it, even to the point of shooting men down who are caught in such disgraceful conduct" [CPS/2]. General Court Martial of Private Frank J. Gaffney, October 9, 1917, GCMO 901, Chicago IL [NA RG 393 E565, Central Division Records B/11]. In Gaffney's case, however, Baker commuted the sentence and permitted Gaffney to return to the ranks. He was also awarded the Medal of Honor for heroic action in the Belleau Wood battle in 1918.
6. Trial of Henwood GCMO 902, Chicago IL, October 20, 1915 [NRG 393 E565, Central Division Records B/10], Trial of Clark GCMO 834 Chicago IL, September 28, 1915 [RG 393 E565, Central Division Records B/10]; Adjutant General to All Commanding Generals, September 22, 1917 [RG 165 E310, Records of the War Department and Special Staffs—Judge Advocate Records B225].
7. John Leonard Hines, statement of defense, February 1, 1902, in JLH, court-martial record [JLH/38]; Warren to Hines, November 26, 1919 [FEW-AMC/V88-B17].
8. On the French mutinies, see Martin Gilbert, *The First World War: A Complete History* (New York: Henry Holt, 1994), 324–342; Richard M. Watt, *Dare Call It Treason* (New York: Simon & Schuster, 1963); and Paul Marie de la Gorce, *The French Army; A Military-Political History*, Kenneth Douglas, trans. (New York: G. Braziller, 1963); H. E. Goemans, *War and Punishment: The Causes of War Termination and the First World War* (Princeton, NJ: Princeton University Press, 2000), 156.
9. Pershing urged Baker to expand his authority to approve death sentences and argued to Baker that Field Marshal Douglas Haig and his subordinates, as well as their French counterparts, had far more authority over courts-martial than American generals. See Baker to Wilson, May 11, 1918 [NDB/6]. For the opinions of other officers, see James G. Harbord, *The American Army in France: 1917–1919* (Boston: Little, Brown, 1929), 113; David Stevenson, *Cataclysm: The First World War as Political Tragedy*, 174. For an excellent review of British discipline, see Gerard Oram, "The Administration of Discipline by the English is

Very Rigid: British Military Law and the Death Penalty, 1868–1918," *Crime, History and Societies* 5 (2001): 93–112; Colonel Rigby testimony, in Hearings II, 431.

10. James G. Harbord, *The American Army in France*, 113; Crowder to Baker, March 26, 1919 [EHC/R5]. The opinion of the army's senior officers on General Order 7 is further detailed in Chapter IV.

11. Hunter Liggett, *The American Expeditionary Force: Ten Years Ago in France* (Cranberry, NJ: Scholars Bookshelf, reprint, 2005), 329. Liggett further complained that "it took a grave offense to send a man to a military prison in the rear." This book was originally published in 1929; James G. Harbord, *The American Army in France*, 113.

12. Baker to Wilson, May 11, 1918 [NDB/6]; Hunter Liggett, *The American Expeditionary Force*, 212. On General Order 56, see Bethel to Stiness, May 29, 1918 [RG120 E802 B263—Forty-First Division Correspondence]. Bethel noted that "there are extremely few cases of enlisted men, except for capital cases, which may not be properly tried by special courts-martial under our present conditions." On "civilianizing military justice," see Edward F. Sherman, "The Civilianization of Military Law, *Maine Law Review* 22 (1970): 1–103.

13. On the maritime division, see H. A. White to Crowder, April 28, 1920 [RG 153 PC 29 E 13, Papers of Major W. J. Bacon/1]. During the war, Colonel H. A. White and Major Arlen G. Swiger oversaw the Maritime Division. In 1919, Captain William J. Bacon became the judge advocate responsible for convening boards to ascertain if the War Department was liable to vessel owners for damages caused by War Department negligence. On the War Risk Insurance, see *Annual Report of the Director of the Bureau of War Risk Insurance for the Fiscal Year, 1920* (Washington, DC: GPO, 1920), 5–6, 79; also, Glenn Altschuler and Stuart Blumin, *The G.I. Bill: A New Deal for Veterans* (New York: Oxford University Press, 2009), 23–25. See also E. M. Randall to Knute Nelson, August 20, 1917 [KN-MHS/26]. In this correspondence, Randall, the president of the Minnesota Mutual Life Insurance Company, complained to Senator Nelson that his company could not compete with the federal government over the sale of life insurance policies to soldiers.

14. Davis to Root, October 14, 1899 [ER/1899]; Crowder to Bryan, December 18, 1913 [WWP/R52]; Bryan to Wilson, December 19, 1913 [WWP/R52]; Major General C. P. Summerall, Chief of Staff United States Army to Secretary of War, February 3, 1927 [found in WCP-UVA/2]. Summerall had asked Colonel William Mellard Connor, a judge advocate, to proofread a draft to the secretary of war detailing the assignment of personnel and their role in the War Department.

15. Scott to Bethel, January 15, 1917 [HLS/27]; Crowder to Judson, April 2, 1919 [WVJ-NL/1]. As another example, in 1901 the House of Representatives' considered a bill that would prevent the sale of "intoxicating liquors" on military installations. In this instance Crowder advised using the language "ardent spirits," because otherwise, the sale of beer and "light wines" from the post stores could be banned as well. Lieber to Crowder, April 2, 1900; Lieber to Root, March 17, 1900 [ER/7].

16. Wallace to Ansell, December 15, 1917 [GWP-WVU/1]; Crowder to Judge Advocates, March 16, 1918 [SW-UK/CM-1918]; Carter to Glass to Mr. Daniel Ganus, July 23, 1918 [CG-UVA/100]. In this letter, Senator Glass explains that Congress did not approve of the extension, but Crowder "might be willing to advise or help the wife of a soldier."

17. See Kastenberg, *The Blackstone of Military Law*, ch. 9; George Breckenridge Davis, *A Treatise on the Military Law of the United States Together with the Practice and Procedure of Courts-Martial and Other Military Tribunals* (New York: John Wiley and Sons, 1902), 197, 326.

18. Crowder to Greene, July 26, 1918; Greene to Crowder, July 5, 1916; Greene to Crowder, July 4, 1916 [FLG/31]. See also generally Jonathan Laurie, *Arming Military Justice*, 1:52–54.

19. In an action known as the right of discovery, the Supreme Court in 1963 mandated that state and federal prosecutors were required to provide evidence in the state government's or federal government's possession to a defendant. In instances where the prosecution fails to provide exculpatory evidence or surprises the defense, courts of appeal may determine that a Sixth Amendment right has been violated. See *Brady v. Maryland*, 373 U.S. 83 (1963). In 1865 the *Digest of Opinions of the Judge Advocate General* instructed the War Department that the failure to provide exculpatory evidence to an accused soldier was a basis of not approving a court-martial conviction. On the right to counsel, see *Gideon v. Wainright*, 372 U.S. 335 (1963).

20. See e.g. Winthrop, *Military Law and Precedents*, 332–337; Article 24, 1916 Articles of War prohibited compulsory self-incrimination or the asking of degrading questions. See also General Court Martial of Homer Merwin, July 27, 1917, GCMO 574, Chicago IL, [RG 393 E565, Central Division Records B/11].

21. John McArthur, *Principles and Practice of Naval and Military Courts-Martial*, 4th ed. (London: A. Strahan, 1813), 1:291; R. M. Hughes, *The Duties of Judge Advocates Compiled from Her Majesty's and the Honorable East India Company's Military Regulations and from the Works of Various Writers on Military Law* (London, 1845), 118. On the Supreme Court, see *United States v. Berger*, 295 U.S. 78 (1935).

22. Baker to Westenhaver, January 22, 1918; Westenhaver to Baker, January 29, 1918 [NDB/6]. Also see Henry Coppee, *Field Manual of Courts-Martial: to which are added the modes of procedure in courts of inquiry, military commissions, retiring boards, boards of survey, inspection reports and examining boards. With an appendix containing the Articles of War, supplementary acts of Congress and such portions of the revised regulations as bear upon the subject* (Philadelphia: J. B. Lippincott, 1863), 41. Coppee was an influential officer prior to the Civil War who never served as a judge advocate, but his text was in wide use in the later nineteenth century. In advocating that junior officers volunteer for recorder duties, Coppee added, "Regimental courts are good schools in which young officers may, while acting as recorders, learn the duties of judge advocates." This construct was also adopted into the Confederate armies during the Civil War; see Robert C. Gilchrist, *The duties of a judge advocate, in a trial before a general court-martial, compiled from various works on military law* (Columbia, SC: Evans and Cogswell, 1864), 37–39. On the lack of a requirement of unanimity in criminal trials, see *Apodaca v. Oregon*, 406 U.S. 404 (1972) and *Johnson v. Louisiana*, 406 U.S. 356 (1972). Article 43, 1916 Articles of War.

23. *United States v. Hudson and Goodwin*, 11 U.S. 32 (1812); War Department Memorandum, August n.d., 1918; Ansell to Herbert Quick, Farm Loan Board, August 7, 1918 [WWP/R374 C4470] (Winthrop's view on conduct unbecoming). In 1974 the Supreme Court, in *Parker v. Levy*, determined that the offense of "conduct unbecoming an officer and gentleman" did not violate due process. *Parker v. Levy*, 417 U.S. 733 (1974). On Chamberlain and the 1916 Articles of War, see Senate Report 130, Revision of the Articles of War, 64th Con 1st Sess (Washington, DC: GPO, 1916), 90–91.

24. *Dynes v. Hoover*, 20 How. 65 (1857). On *Dynes v. Hoover*, see Joshua E. Kastenberg, "A Sesquicentennial Historic Analysis of *Dynes v. Hoover* and the Supreme Court's Bow to Military Necessity," U. Mem. L. Rev 39 (2009): 595. On criticisms of the lack of a court of appeals, see James Barnett Fry, *Military Miscellanies* (New York: Bretano's Press, 1889).

25. *Kahn v. Anderson*, 255 U.S. 1 (1921).

26. See e.g. *Warren Court of Inquiry* (Washington, DC: GPO, 1881). Sheridan reported to Grant that Warren did not "exert himself to get his corps up as rapidly as he might have done." Warren spent the next two decades attempting to prove that Sheridan had intentionally maligned him to affect his status in the army. See David M. Jordan, *Happiness is not my Companion: The Life of Gouvenor G. K. Warren* (Bloomington: Indiana University Press, 2001), 262–317.

27. Kreger to Department of Justice, March 31, 1919 [RG 120 E 1772 014.2/3]. This is a copy of a letter from Kreger to Mr. Claude C. Brogden, a former sergeant in the American Expeditionary Forces, in which Kreger explains that the Judge Advocate General's Office did not review special courts-martial, and therefore no records of Brogden's court-martial existed at the Judge Advocate General's, other than a record that he had been court-martialed in a lawfully constituted trial and that his sentence to forfeit one-third of his par per month, for nine months, had been a lawful sentence.

28. Winship to Judge Advocate, Department of the North Philippines, March 11, 1902 [RG 395 E 2246].

29. William Winthrop, *Military Law and Precedents* (Washington, DC: GPO, 1920), 49–55. Authored originally in 1895 by Winthrop, *Military Law and Precedents* is an expansion of his earlier *Military Law*.

30. William E. Birkhimer, *Military Government and Martial Law* (Washington, DC: J. J. Chapman, 1892); George B. Davis, *Military Laws of the United States* (Washington, DC: GPO, 1901).

31. See e.g. Colonel William Hagen, "The Rush Cases and the Class of 1887," *Army Lawyer* (May 1987): 18–20; Major William Frachter, "Colonel William Winthrop: A Biographical Sketch," *The Judge Advocate Journal* 1, no. 3 (December 1944): 12–14.

32. William Chetwood DeHart, *Observations on Military Law and the Constitution and Practice of Courts-Martial, With a Summary of the Law of Evidence as Applicable to Military Trials* (New York: D. Appleton, 1863); John O'Brien, *A Treatise on American Military Laws and the Practice of Courts-Martial With Suggestions for their Improvement* (Philadelphia: Lee and Blanchard, 1848); Alexander Macomb, *The Practice of Courts-Martial* (New York: Harper and Brothers, 1841).

33. In addition, see e.g. *Dynes v. Hoover, In re Grimely*, 137 U.S. 147 (1890). On the rights of militia members, see *McClaughry v. Deming*, 186 U.S. 49 (1902).

34. *Runkle v. United States*, 122 U.S. 543 (1887); *Grafton v. United States*, 206 U.S. 333 (1907).

35. *United States v. Page*, 137 U.S. 673 (1891).

36. See Papers of Ulysses Grant, August 5, 1875 (Carbondale: Southern Illinois University Press, 2003), 26:518.

37. Lieber to R. A. Alger, May 31, 1899 [WMK/7].

38. See e.g. *In re Carter* (CCNY, 1898); *In re Carter*, 97 F. 496 (CA 1, 1899); *Rose v. Roberts*, 948 (CA 2, 1900); and *Carter v. Roberts*, 177 U.S. 496 (1900); *Carter v. McClaughry*, 183 U.S. 365 (1902).

39. *Carter v. Woodring*, 67 App. D.C. 393 (CA DC, 1937), and *Carter v. Woodring*, 302 U.S. 752 (1937).

40. *New York Times*, August 21, 1902; *New York Times*, June 9, 1899; Charles Ewing, *In the matter of the review of the court-martial record in the case of Brevet Major Geo. A. Armes, Captain 10th U.S. Cavalry* (Washington, DC: R. O. Polkinhorn, 1877); and George Augustus Armes, *Ups and Downs of an Army Officer* (Washington, DC, 1900).

41. *Closson v. United States ex rel Armes*, 7 App. D.C. 460 (CA DC 1896); "Armes' Case an Issue: Discipline of the Army is Involved in this Affair," *New York Times*, December 14, 1895.

42. See e.g. "Will not be Arrested Again: Major Armes will be Paroled to Answer the Charges Against Him," *New York Times*, January 13, 1896.

43. "Charges Against Capt Armes," *New York Times*, October 4, 1895; "Armes' $250,000 Sequestered: Refuses to Pay his Wife Alimony and Stays in Canada," *New York Times*, July 25, 1896.

44. *New York Times*, May 14, 1914; LG to Armes, September 29, 1914 [LG/1]; LG to Senator Morris Sheppard, December 18, 1914 [LG/1]; Sheppard to Crowder, Dec n.d. [MS-UT/2G194].

45. Crowder to MacArthur, November 1, 1909 [RG 395 E 926]. On the China Relief Expedition, see Max Boot, *The Savage Wars of Peace: Small Wars and the Rise of American Power* (New York: Basic Books, 2002), 89–97. Boot did not cite court-martial records or judge advocate correspondences, but he analyzed the coalition relationships as well as the plundering and indiscipline of the multinational forces. He too arrives at the conclusion that the relief expedition presaged aspects of World War I.

46. Hutcheson to MacArthur, November 19, 1900 [RG 395 E926]; Hutcheson to Commander, China Relief Expedition, Colonel Liscum, December 27, 1902 [RG 395 E296].

47. White to Crowder, January 24, 1901.

48. Hutcheson to Davis, April 27, 1901 [RG 395 E296]; Hutcheson to Davis, May 19, 1901 [RG 395 E 926].

49. Hutcheson to Crowder, May 20, 1901 [RG 395 E926].

50. Trial record and correspondence found in [RG 393 E929].

51. Crowder to Franklin Bell, June 30, 1913 [EHC/R2].

52. Gilbert N. Haugen to Root, November 27, 1903; Benjamin P. Birdsall to Root, November 27, 1903; John A. T. Hull to Root, November 27, 1903; E. C. Burleigh to Root, November 27, 1903; James Wilson to Root, December 1, 1903; L. M. Shaw to Root, December 1, 1903 [ER/177 pt. 1, pp. 197–205].

53. Crowder to Edwards, January 30, 1919 [EHC/120]. Crowder, in this letter, underscored his displeasure with Dunn's advice on the executions of African American soldiers in Houston. Privately Crowder informed Edwards that the executions should have been remitted to prison

sentences. However, the final straw for Crowder was that Dunn had insulted Breckenridge Long at the State Department.

54. On Congressman John A Hull's influence with Root regarding the junior Hull, see John A. Hull to Root, February 7, 1901 [ERP/174-1, pp. 441]; and Hull to Theodore Roosevelt, March 4, 1908 [EHC/R1]; see also Crowder to Moore, February 23, 1911 [JBM/16]. On Shafter's support to Hull, see Root to Shafter, February 6, 1901 [ERP/174-1, p. 436]. On Crowder's aspersions on Hull, see Crowder to Pershing, December 28, 1926 [JJP/41].

55. Harbord to Pershing, December 8, 1918 [JGH/11]; Harbord to Pershing, October 19, 1918 [JH/178-8].

56. *The Yale Alumni Weekly*, September 24, 1920, vol. 30, no. 1478.

57. George W. Cullum, *Biographical Register of Officers and Graduates of the United States Military Academy*, Supplement VI-A (Saginaw, MI: Seaman and Peters, 1920), 268.

58. General Orders and Circulars, Adjutant General's Department (Washington, DC: GPO, 1903), 10.

59. Pershing to John Weeks, Secretary of War, January 17, 1923 [JJP/24]; Cullum, Biographical Register of Officers, vol. 6, Pt. 1, 515.

60. Crowder to Pershing, January 18, 1923 [JJP/24]; also Pershing to War Department, February 12, 1923 [JJP/25]; Joshua Kastenberg, *The Blackstone of Military Law*, 313.

61. "Their Father's Sons," *The Topeka Advocate and News*, June 8, 1898, p. 3; *Journal of the Executive Proceedings of the United States Senate*, vol. 31, Pt. 1; Hearings I, 213.

62. Root to Roosevelt, November 19, 1903 [ERP/177 pt. 1, 167]; Wood to Winship, June 12, 1917, in which he references his earlier support [LW/100].

63. Winship to Judge Advocate, March 28, 1902; Winship to Wood, June 8, 1917; Wood to Winship, June 12, 1917 [LW/100]; Hugh Ogden to Lisbeth (his wife), undated, but September [HO-SIU/I].

64. Pershing to Adjutant General, June 28, 1928 [JJP/113]; on Kreger's background, see *Keota Eagle*, April 10, 1891; *Tama Herald*, May 7, 1891 [EAK-DBC/1]; Bullard to Kreger, May 5, 1901 [EAK-DBC/1]; Bullard to Pershing, April 5, 1901 [EAK-DBC/1]; Kreger to Crowder, February 4, 1908 [EAK-DBC/1]; "Gen Kreger, J.A.G. of the Army, *Army-Navy Register*, November 2, 1928].

65. Jonathan Lurie, *Arming Military Justice*,1:51.

66. Crowder to Bell, June 20, 1913 [EHC/R2]; Crowder to Warren, February 28, 1917 [EHC/R2]; Crowder to Pershing, August 19, 1910 [JJP/56]; Pershing to Crowder, August 19, 1910 [JJP/56]; Crowder to Pershing, November 7, 1910 [JJP/56].

67. Jerry K. Sweeney, ed., *A Handbook of American Military History: From the Revolutionary War to the Present* (Lincoln: University of Nebraska Press, 1996), 158.

68. *United States v. Franklin*, 174 F. 163 (CCDY, 1909); *United States v. Franklin*, 216 U.S. 559 (1910); Ansell to Hand, January 16, 1910 [LH-Harv/12]; Hand to Ansell, Janaury 17, 1910 [LH-Harv/12].

69. Bliss to Scott, August 20, 1917 [THB/218].

70. Ansell to Williams, August 16, 1917 [JSW/30].

71. Wood to Adjutant General, December 5, 1918; Spiller to Wood, December 2, 1918; Spiller to Wood, September 14, 1918; Baker to Sinclair, August 15, 1918; Tumulty to Sinclair, July 30, 1918; Baker to Wilson, July 22, 1918 [LW/107].

72. Ansell to Baker, October 23, 1917; Bliss to Baker, October 24, 1917; Ansell to Baker, October 30, 1917 [NDB/1].

73. Crowder to Pershing, September 11, 1916 [JJP/56].

74. Hugh Scott to James Harbord, February 17, 1917 [JGH/8]. Scott notified Harbord about the list of officers to serve in the inauguration parade. Crowder to Pershing, September 11, 1916 [JJP/56]; McNeil, Fitness report for 1915; Crowder, Fitness Report for 1916. In 1915, Henry Morrow wrote that McNeil had shown fitness for duty in the Judge Advocate General's Department. On Bayne, see *Yale Alumni Weekly*, July 6, 1917, p. 1103.

75. George Washington Cullom, *Biographical Register of Graduates of the United States Military Academy* (Saginaw, MI: Seeman & Peters, 1920), 6-B:1281; "Supreme Court Likely to Rule on Spies Today: Biddle Attacks Bulwark of Civil Liberties," *Chicago Tribune*, July 31, 1942, p. 7.

76. Bethel, Fitness Report for McNeil, 1915; Crowder, Fitness Report for McNeil, 1916. Stone to Crowder, 1916; Stone to Board of Minnesota Bar Examiners, May 13, 1940. Although Stone's correspondences are no longer found in Crowder's papers, his original letter to Crowder is attached to McNeil's bar application for 1940. See Morrow to State Bar Examiners, May 1, 1940.

77. Crowder to Pershing, September 11, 1916 [JJP/4]. For more on Brown, see John J. Pershing, *My Life Before the World War: 1860–1917, A Memoir*, 341.

78. Crowder to Bliss, August 5, 1917 [THB/217]; Crwoder to Pershing, August 18, 1917 [JJP/56]; Crowder to Pershing, June 8, 1916 [JJP/56]. Crowder attached Johnson's record to his letter of introduction.

79. Johnson to Crowder, May 17, 1916 [DLP-UNC]. Professor Lockmiller's papers are housed at several repositories, including a collection of correspondences with Hugh Johnson at the University of North Carolina. Crowder to Pershing, June 8, 1916 [JJP/56].

80. Baruch to Johnson, November 24, 1919 [BB-SGM/236]; Baruch to Crowder, November 24, 1919 [BB-SGM/236]; Johnson to Baruch, November 28, 1919 [BB-SGM/236]. Looking back on their relationship, Johnson commented that the army was incapable of managing a wartime economy, and Baruch's knowledge of the nation's industries was essential to supplying the army.

81. Crowder to War Department, undated [WW/R 77]; Crowder to Frankfurter, February 18, 1917 [FF-Harv/30].

82. Fred L. Borch, "Civilian Lawyers Join the Department: The Story of the First Civilian Attorneys Given Direct Commissions in the Corps," *Army Lawyer* (May 2003), 2–6.

83. Frankfurter to Stimson, July 1, 1911 [FF-Harv/63]; Frankfurter to Stimson, March 21, 1913 [FF-Harv/63]; Crowder to Frankfurter, March 18, 1916 [FF-Harv/30]; Frankfurter to Baker, October 14, 1916 [FF-Harv/13]; Crowder to Frankfurter, August 14, 1916 [FF-Harv/30]; Frankfurter to Crowder, October 16, 1916 [FF-Harv/30]; Frankfurter to Crowder, February 8, 1917 [FF-Harv/30]; Samuel Ansell to General John M. Palmer, September 14, 1939 [John McCauley Palmer Papers/3]. On the British recommendation, see Eugene Wambaugh to Crowder, March 12, 1919 [RG 153, PC 29, E 28, B-15]. Wambaugh asked Crowder to recall this fact to Baker to gain the secretary of war's support to order a full examination of allied military justice systems. Frankfurter seems to have foreseen an argument that took root during the presidency of William J. Clinton, in which several service members challenged the legality of serving under United Nations command. See e.g. *United States v. New*, 55 M.J. 95 (CAAF, 2001).

84. Wilson to Baruch, August 6, 1918 [BB-SGM/44].

85. On Frankfurter's role in introducing Brandeis to Crowder, see Frankfurter to Stimson, April 29, 1916 [FF-Harv/63]; and Crowder to Frankfurter, February 23, 1916 [FF-Harv/30]. Also see Frankfurter to Wilson, June 12, 1917 [WWP/R88]; Taft to Root, n.d., 1921 [EHP/164]. See generally Daniel R. Beaver, *Newton D. Baker and the American War Effort, 1917–1919* (Lincoln: University of Nebraska Press, 1966), 52. On the Frankfurter-Brandeis relationship as well as a brief biography of Frankfurter, see Melvin I. Urofsky, *Louis D. Brandeis: A Life* (New York: Pantheon, 209), 336–337. On Frankfurter's role in serving as an "intermediary" between Justice Holmes and Crowder, see Holmes to Frankfurter, March 5, 1917 [OWH-UPA/21]; and Holmes to Harold Laski, December 18, 1917 [OWH-UPA/26].

86. Bethel to Wigmore, September 20, 1916 [JHW-NW/172]; Wigmore to Wilson, March 10, 1913 [WWP/R200]. Wigmore was a progressive who believed federal wage standards were a sound idea but cautioned that Congress and more importantly the Court was unlikely to permit a sweeping nationwide standard. During the war, Wigmore advised Wilson on industrial working conditions and suffrage. On Brandeis, see Wigmore to Brandeis, Decemebr 1, 1914 [JHW-NW/38]; Brandeis to Wigmore, July 29, 1890 [JHW-NW/38]. On Holmes, see Holmes to Frankfurter, April 25, 1919 [OWH-UPA/26].

87. Wigmore to Crowder, May 19, 1915 [JHW-NW/173]; Crowder to Wigmore, October 19, 1916 [JHW-NW/17-20]; Bethel to Wigmore, October 29, 1914 [JHW-NW/172]; William R. Roalfe, *John Henry Wigmore: Scholar and Reformer* (Evanston, IL: Northwestern University Press, 1977), 120.

88. Crowder to Wigmore, October 19, 1916 [JHW-NW/17-20]; Wigmore to Crowder, November 20, 1916 [JHW-NW/173]; Wigmore to Winship, November 23, 1916 [JHW-NW/172]; Winship to Wigmore, December 11, 1916 [JHW-NW/172]; Wigmore to Hull, May 5, 1915 [JHW-NW/172]; Wigmore to Lockmiller, February 19, 1940 [JHW-NW/17-20].

89. Scott to McKinley, February 13, 1899 [JBS-GUSC/71 f 6]; Root to Scott, December 30, 1905 [JBS-GUSC/7 f4]. Scott outlines his resume to Root in this letter. See also Scott to General Frank Hines, November 12, 1928 [JBS-GUSC/ 71 f 6]. Likewise Scott outlines his military service in his application for a veteran's pension. In re James Brown Scott, application for admission to the New York Bar, April 11, 1905 [JBS-GUSC/71 f 6].

90. Carnegie Endowment for International Peace, *The Reports of the Hague Conferences of 1899 and 1907* (London: Oxford University Press, 1917), 206; Lansing to Olney, August 14, 1914; Elihu Root to J. Scott, April 10, 1913 [JBS-GUSC/7 f4]; James Scott Brown to Lansing, July 31, 1914 [RL/2]; Richard Olney to Scott, August 10, 1914 [RL/2]; Lansing to Scott, August 12, 1914 [JBS-GUSB/5 f 9]; Lansing to Bryan, August 11, 1914; Lansing to Scott, August 15, 1914 [RL/2]; Scott to Lansing, August 17, 1914 [RL/2]; Crowder to J. Scott, June 19, 1915 [JBS-GUSP/2 f 14]; Crowder to Stimson, March 21, 1917 [HLS/R-48]; Crowder to J. Scott, February 9, 1918 [JBS-GUSP/2 f 14].

91. *Stearns v. Wood*, 236 U.S. 75 (1915); Wigmore to War Department, October 11, 1916 [JHW-NW/173].

92. J. Reuben Clark to Knox, January 11, 1916 [PK/21]; J. Reuben Clark to Knox, March 7, 1917 [PK/22]. On Clark, see generally Frank W. Fox and D. Michael Quinn, *J. Reuben Clark: The Public Years* (Provo, UT: Brigham Young University Press, 1980), 273.

93. On Whitsett, see George L. Schrantz, *Guarding the Border: The Military Memories of Ward Schrantz, 1912–1917* (College Station: Texas A & M University Press, 2012), 161. On Ruehl, see Indiana University, *Alumni Quarterly* 4 (April 1918): 323.

94. On Warren, see Baker to Wilson, May 17, 1917 [NDB/3]; James Brown Scott to Warren, April 2, 1917 [JBS-GUSC/8 fl 9]. On Warren drafting Crowder's note to the state governors, see Office of the Provost Marshal General to State Governors, and attached papers, March 18, 1918 [CBW-DPL/6].

95. On Bayne, see Memoirs in Bayne Family papers [HAB-UNC/R2]. Bayne's memoirs were originally housed at Yale and the University of North Carolina; Wilson Library has obtained a microfilm copy to place alongside the Bayne-Gale family papers. See also Bayne to Hand, October 17, 1911 [LH-Harv/14]; and Hand to Bayne, July 2, 1914 [LH-Harv/14].

96. On Chiperfield, see Congressman James H. Lewis to Tumulty, August 4, 1919 [JPT/12].

97. Judge Advocate General's Returns for 33d Division, May 1918 [RG PC 29 E 53 319.1/Box8]; MacChesney to White, April 26, 1919 [RG PC 29 E 53 319.1/Box8]; Bethel to Hines, April 26, 1919 [JLH/3].

98. Wambaugh to Ansell, December 11, 1917; Baker to Crowder, December 28, 1917 [in Hearings II, 91].

99. Baker, Memorandum for Major General Crowder, December 28, 1917 [NDB/1]. See also e.g. Report of the Inspector General to Secretary of War—Investigation of Controversies Pertaining to the Office of the Judge Advocate General, May 8, 1919, in [hearings 725–733]. Although Ansell would later claim the inspector general was directed to discredit him, it is noteworthy that the inspector general blamed the acting chief of staff rather than Ansell for failing to inform Baker of the unpublished order appointing Ansell as acting judge advocate general.

100. Jonathan Lurie, *Arming Military Justice*, 62–68; Ansell to Crowder, December 11, 1917; Baker to Crowder, December 28, 1917 [in Hearings I, 91–98]; Ansell to Baker, December 1, 1917; Baker to Crowder (memorandum), December 28, 1917 [NDB/1].

101. Baker to Crowder, November 13, 1917; Crowder to Baker, November 18, 1917 [EHC/R3]; Baker to Wilson, August 22, 1918 [EHC/R4]; Ansell to Baker, December 20, 1917 [NDB/1].

102. Jonathan Lurie, *Arming Military Justice*, 75–76.

103. "Judge Advocate General Opinions," *Army-Navy Times*, September 28, 1918, pp. 123–124.

104. Ansell to Baker, December 1, 1917; Baker to Crowder, December 28, 1917 [NDB/1]; General Order 169, dated December 29, 1917 [hearings, 131]; see also Attorney General Gregory to Crowder, November 17, 1917 [EHC/5]

CHAPTER 3

1. Douglas B. Craig, *Progressives at War: William G. McAdoo and Newton Baker* (Baltimore: Johns Hopkins University Press, 2003), 158–159; and Reginald C. Stuart, *Civil Military Relations During the War of 1812* (Santa Barbara, CA: Greenwood Press, 2009), 87–110. Even when Martin van Buren advocated state conscription in New York, the majority of the legislature opposed him. See Martin Van Buren, *Autobiography of Martin Van Buren* (Washington, DC: GPO, 1920), 1:55–56; and Donald P. Cole, *Martin van Buren and the American Political System* (Princeton, NJ: Princeton University Press, 1984), 37–40.

2. William Harding Carter, *The American Army* (Indianapolis: Bobbs-Merrill, 1915), 19.

3. *Jacobsen v. Massachusetts*, 197 U.S. 11 (1905); *Butler v. Perry* 240 U.S. 248 (1916).

4. WSJ to George A. Rhodes, October 15, 1915 [WS-U-Del/47 f-23]. On Dent, see Seward W. Livermore, *Politics Is Adjourned: Woodrow Wilson and the War Congress, 1916–1918* (Boston: Wesleyan University Press, 1966), 17. On Kitchin, see Claude Kitchin, *The Nation's Preparedness* (Washington, DC: GPO, 1916); George Huddleston, "Conscription Is Undemocratic: Selfishness and Deceit of Militarists Exposed," January 10, 1917 (Washington, DC: GPO, 1917); Thurston T. Hicks to Kitchin, February 23, 1917 [CK-UNC/18 f-268]; Kitchin to Mr. Bruce Cotton, April 4, 1917 CK-UNC/19 f-285]. On general discussion over the Armed Ship Bill and opposition to conscription, see e.g. Jennifer D. Keene, *Doughboys: The Great War and the Remaking of America* (Baltimore: Johns Hopkins University Press, 2001), 8–11; John Whiteclay Chambers, *To Raise an Army: The Draft Comes to Modern America*, 165; and Richard Drake, *The Education of an Anti-Imperialist: Robert La Follette and U.S. Expansion* (Madison: University of Wisconsin Press, 2013), 170.

5. Crowder to Stimson, March 26, 1917 [HL/R-48]; "Bill Authorizing the President to Increase Temporarily the Military Establishment of the United States," in Hearings Before the Committee on Military Affairs in the House of Representatives, Sixty-Fifth Congress, First Session, April 7, 14, and 17, 1917.

6. For a recent biography, see A. Scott Berg, *Wilson* (New York: G.P. Putnam's Sons, 2013), 457–458. For other biographers who omit Crowder's contribution to conscription, see Richard Striner, *Woodrow Wilson and WWI: A Burden too Great to Bear* (Lanham, MD: Rowman and Littlefield, 2014), 115; August Heckscher, *Woodrow Wilson* (New York: Scribner, 1991), 446–447; Arthur Walworth, *Woodrow Wilson* (New York: Norton, 1976), 2:105–107; and Edward Coffman, *The War to End All Wars*, 25. On Crowder's enthusiasm for a universal conscription program, see Crowder to Baker, March 25, 1916 [JD/38]; Baker to Daniels, March 27, 1916 [JD/38]; Crowder to Stimson, March 22, 1917 [HLS/R-48]; Crowder to Stimson, March 26, 1917 [HLS/R-26]; House to Baker, March 23, 1917 [EMH/9].

7. David Kinley to Newton Baker, July 26, 1917 [NDB/2]; Hugh Johnson to H. H. Sheets, September 17, 1917 [DLP-UNC]; Sanders, "Flag Day Address," June 4, 1918 [ES/4]; John Whiteclay Chambers II, *To Raise an Army: The Draft Comes to Modern America*, 180. Professor Jonathan Lurie lauded Chambers's work as comprehensive and superbly documented. I agree with his assessment. On Congress, see e.g. Carl Hayden to Hugh Scott, March 1, 1917 [HLS/28]; and Crowder to Solicitor General Davis, August 18, 1919 [JWD/8-fl1], in which Crowder conveys a note from Senator Smoot to this effect.

8. Lindley M. Garrison, *An Address by the Honorable Lindley M. Garrison, Secretary of War, at New York City*, January 17, 1916; Crowder to Garrison, December n.d., 1915 [LG/1]. On Garrison's resignation, see A. Scott Berg, *Wilson*, 390.

9. On the Philippine muster of militia to fight overseas, see Brian McAllister Linn, *The Philippine War: 1899-1902*, 11. On doubts over the Guard's effectiveness, see John Wingate Weeks to EHC, July 24, 1916 [JWW-RSC/3-f19]; also generally, Jerry Cooper, *The Rise of the National Guard: The Evolution of the American Militia, 1865-1920* (Lincoln: University of Nebraska Press, 1997), 128-152. George van Horn Moseley, diary entry for August 7, 1916 [GVM/1].

10. Allen R. Millet and Peter Maslowski, *For the Common Defense: A Military History of the United States from 1607 to 2012*, ch. 11; David F. Schmitz, *Henry L. Stimson: The First Wise Man* (Wilmington, DE: Scholarly Resources, 2001), 35-37. See also Baruch to Wood, May 4, 1916 [BB-SGM/3], and Baruch to Hagedorn, November 20, 1928 [HH/4].

11. George Chamberlain to H. H. Sheets, August 10, 1916; Root to H. H. Sheets and General S. B. Young, August 17, 1916 [NAUMT/6]; Root to H. H. Sheets and General S. B. Young, August 17, 1916 [NAUMT/6].

12. Taft to Crowder and Baker, February 6, 1917 [WWP/R88]; Taft to Crowder, September 4, 1917 [WHT/183]. Crowder also assured Taft that he would try to obtain a commission for Taft's son Charles Taft.

13. Crowder to Stimson, May 16, 1917; Crowder to Stimson, May 17, 1917 [HLS/R-49]; see Roosevelt to Crowder, August 22, 1917 [TR/R 243]; and Roosevelt to Crowder, April 14, 1918 [TR/R 402].

14. On Upton, see Stephen Ambrose, *Upton and the Army* (Baton Rouge, LA: Louisiana State University Press, 1964).

15. *Houston v. Moore*, 18 U.S. 1 (1820). This decision arose from the appeal of a Pennsylvania militia soldier who failed to muster with his unit after the state governor ordered the militia into the army.

16. Crowder to Scott, November 9, 1916 [JBS-GUSP/2 f 14]; Congressman Louis Campton to Pepper, March 5, 1915; Pepper to Congressmen Cramton, Lenroot, and McClintock, April 5, 1916 [SP/2].

17. BM Chipperfield to Peyton March, March 29, 1932 [PM/1].

18. Tillman to Lever, May 1, 1917 [FAL-STI/B3]. On Tillman's distrust of a standing army, anti-imperialism, and support for the war, see Stephen Kantrowitz, *Ben Tillman and the Reconstruction of White Supremacy* (Chapel Hill: University of North Carolina Press, 2000), 263- 305. On Vardaman, see William F. Holmes, *The White Chief: James Kimble Vardaman* (Baton Rouge: Louisiana State University Press, 1970), 81-85, 307.

19. Davis to Wallace, June 8, 1917 [JWD/10].

20. Testimony of General Scriven, *Hearings Before the Committee on Military Affairs, House of Representatives, Sixty-Fourth Congress*, 2d Sess (December 6, 1916 to January 15, 1917), 989-991.

21. Baker to Wilson, June 2, 1917 [NDB/3]; George Chamberlain, "Universal Liability to Military Service," Senate Military Affairs Committee, April 19, 1917 (DC: GPO, 1917); Daniel Beaver, *Newton Baker and the American War Effort, 1917-1919*, 32; Frank L. Paxson, "The American War Government, 1917-1918," *The American Historical Review* 26, no. 1 (October 1920): 55-76.

22. Parker to Chamberlain, April 6, 1916 [GEC-OHS/3f-1]; Chamberlain to General H. P. McCain, February 21, 1917 [GEC-OHS/6f-4]; William Gibbs McAdoo to Chamberlain, April 22, 1912 [GEC-OHS/3f-1]; Chamberlain to Baker, June 29, 1918 [NDB/5]; Newton Baker to GEC, February 23, 1917 [GEC-OHS/3f-1]; H. P. McCain, Adj Gen to Chamberlain, February 23, 1917 [GEC-OHS/3f-1]; Chamberlain to Hugh Scott, May, 5, 1917 [GEC-OHS/6 f4]; Crowder to Chamberlain, January 20, 1918 [GEC-OHS/6-f15]; Crowder to Chamberlain, July 5, 1918 [JHW-NW/48].

23. General Enoch Crowder, *Second Report of the Provost Marshal of the United States to the Secretary of War On the Operation of the Selective Service System to December 20, 1918* (Washington, DC: GPO, 1919), 199.

24. Rev E. A. Elam to Hull, July 13, 1917 [CH/R 1]; W. Stephens to Hull, July 30, 1917 [CH/R 1]; Senator McKellar to Hull, July 13, 1917 [CH/R1]; Flood to J. M. Fulwinder, March 11, 1918 [HDF/76]. On the Agricultural Exemption generally, see Gerald Shenk, *Work or Fight: Race, Gender, and the Draft in World War One* (New York: Palgrave-MacMillan, 2005), 34-38.

25. Charles Beecher Warren, circular to state governors, December 11, 1917 [CBW-DPL/6]; Baker to Wilson, September 22, 1917 [NDB/3].

26. Crowder, *Second Report of the Provost Marshal General to the Secretary of War on the Operations of the Selective Service System*, 335–336. On Fairbanks, see John Ross Delafield, Final Report on the Board of Contract Adjustment of the War Department, June 30, 1920 (Washington, DC: GPO, 1920).

27. Crowder to Glass, September 6, 1918; Glass to R. L. Jordan, September 5, 1918 [CG-UVA/111]. On the "Pals' Battalions," see Alexander Watson, *Enduring the Great War: Combat, Morale and Collapse in the German and British Armies, 1914–1918* (London: Cambridge University Press, 2008), 64; and Lawrence Sondhaus, *World War One: The Global Revolution* (London: Cambridge University Press, 2011), 179–180.

28. Ford to Warren, July 31, 1917 [CBW-DPL/7]; Warren to Ford, August 10, 1917 [CBW-DPL/7]; Baker to Crowder, November 1, 1917; Crowder to Baker, November 2, 1917 [NDB/1].

29. Lippman to Crowder, July 17, 1917 [WL-SML/R7]; Crowder to Lippman, August 10, 1917 [WL-SML/R7].

30. Knapp to Crowder, August 27, 1918; Crowder to Conkling, September 5, 1918; Conkling to A. B. Bielaski, Justice Department, Chief, Bureau of Investigation, September 5, 1918 [RG 163 Records of the Selective Service System, 1917–1919 General Files/ Box 10 F 581–600]; Crowder to Breckenridge Jones, September 17, 1918; Crowder to Bielaski [RG 163 Records of the Selective Service System, 1917–1919 General Files/ Box 10 F 601–620].

31. La Follette to Mr. D. C. Wolfe, August 20, 1917 [LFFP/I:B 111]; La Follette to Crowder, January 16, 1918 [LFFP/I:B 112]; La Follette to Pomerene, April 19, 1918 [LFFP/I:B 112].

32. Pepper diary entry for October 23, 1917 [SP-UM/1].

33. Lansing to Baker, September 3, 1918 [RG 163 Records of the Selective Service System, 1917–1919 General Files/ Box 10 F 621–640].

34. "No deferral of service for Great Lakes pilots and mariners," December 7, 1917; "Unlawful to turn away teachers who voluntarily offered to enlist," December 10, 1917; National Guardsmen are not part of the Army for the purpose of determining correct pay until specifically designated as such by the War Department, December 10, 1917; Army cannot turn away negro volunteers simply on account of their race, February 12, 1917; Deserters under the First Draft requesting attention to such deserters, July 19, 1918 [CBW-DPL/6]; Daniel to Baker, January 30, 1918 [JD/38].

35. Walsh to Crowder, April 10, 1917 [TWP/215]; McCain to Crowder, April 11, 1917 [TWP/215].

36. RG 163 [Provost Marshal General's Office: Information Files on Court Decisions B/1]; In re Calloway, n.d., unpub decision (DC AL 1918); Crowder to W. B. Wilson, September 18, 1917 [NA RG 163, Selective Service System, General File Box 10/GF 581–600].

37. Crowder to White, January 21, 1918; White to Crowder, January 14, 1918 [WHW/10]; Crowder to White, May 13, 1918 [WHW/11]; Thomas Asklov to Crowder, April 4, 1918 [NA RG 153 E 390/6 f014.31].

38. Watson, "All Aboard for the State Convention," *The Jeffersonian*, August 9, 1917, p. 8; Crowder to AG Gregory, n.d. [TWG/4].

39. See e.g. Graham Adams Jr., *Age of Industrial Violence, 1910–15: The Activities and Findings of the United States Commission on Industrial Relations* (New York: Columbia University Press, 1983); Rosemary Laughlin, *The Ludlow Massacre of 1913–14* (North Carolina: Morgan-Reynolds, 2006).

40. *Conditions in the Paint Creek District, West Virginia. United States Congress: Committee on Education and Labor*, S. Res 37, Part I (Washington, DC: GPO, 1913), 238–261.

41. Wallace provided this synopsis of his career in Wallace to Adjutant General, USA, November 10, 1916.

42. Bethel to Wallace, September 2, 1916; State of West Virginia, Military Department to Wallace, September 27, 1916; to Wallace, March 28, 1917.

43. On Wallace's work on Winthrop, see Bethel to Wallace, November 16, 1916; on the draft law, see Wallace to Ansell, December 15, 1917.

44. See Ansell to Wallace, April 18, 1916 [GWP-WVU/11]. On contemporary criticisms of Wallace and the judge advocate involvement in the Montana and Colorado strikes, see Henry Winthrop Ballantine, "Unconstitutional Claims of Military Authority," *American Journal of Criminal Law and Criminology* 5 (March 1915): 718. Ballantine was, at the time of the article's publication, the secretary of the American Society of Military Law.

45. See Gary Kaunonen, *Community in Conflict: A Working-Class History of the 1913–14 Michigan Copper Strike and the Italian Hall Tragedy* (East Lansing: Michigan State University Press, 2013); Arthur Thurner, *Rebels on the Range: The Michigan Copper Miners' Strike of 1913–1914* (Lansing, MI: John Forster Press, 1984).

46. On Pepper's role in the strike, see Ansell to Pepper, September 20, 1915; Bethel to Pepper, September 20, 1915 [SP-BHL/2]; Special Orders no. 10, September 1, 1913; Anthony J. Lucas, Prosecuting Attorney, Houghton County, Calumet to Pepper, September 22, 1913 [SP-BHL/2].

47. On Pepper's challenge to the state trial judge's contempt order, see Pepper to Major Roy Vandercook, 1914 [SP-BHL/2]; on Pepper's lobbying on behalf of immigrants serving in the National Guard, see Henry McMorran, Chairman of the Committee on Manufactures to Pepper, January 21, 1911 [SP-BHL/2]. On his attempts at protecting guardsmen from employment termination based on state guard status, see Pepper to Capt J. P. DeRight, January 19, 1915; and Pepper to state adjutant general, April 3, 1915 [SP-BHL].

48. On the court-martial, see Diary entry for September 19, 1916; Diary entry for September 29, 1916. On the state trial of the ranger, see Diary entries for September 22 and September 23 [SP-BHL/2].

49. Wallace to Ansell, June 2, 1916 [GWP-WVU/11]; Ansell to Wallace, April 18, 1916 [GWP-WVU/11].

50. On Teare, see George W. Cullum, *Biographical Register of Officers and Graduates of the United States Military Academy*, Supplement VI-A, 367.

51. On Kincaid, see NY Dept of State, *Manual for the Use of the Legislature of New York* (New York: Department of State, 1917), 524. On Stiness, see Rhode Island State Auditor, *Annual Report* (Pawtucket, RI: Pawtucket Linotyping, 1918), 77, and War Records Committee, *Brown University in the War* (Providence, RI, 1919), 47.

52. General William Johnston to Crowder, February 16, 1918 [EMP-JAGS/1]; Lt Col Herbert White to Maj McNeil, November 7, 1917 [EMP-JAGS/1].

53. McNeil to Crowder, January 2, 1918 [EMP-JAGS/1].

54. McNeil to Crowder, January 2, 1918 [EMP-JAGS/1].

55. Hoke Smith to Adjutant General, January 20, 1918 [MHS-UGA/30]; Wing to Wallace White, May 18, 1917; Wing to Wallace White, June 3, 1918; White to Crowder, May 21, 1918 [WHW/11]; Swanson to Browning, November 23, 1918 [CAB-UVA/1]; Van Devanter to Winslow, March 26, 1917 [WVD/11, p. 2]; Van Devanter to Dean Frederick S. Jones, Yale University, April 18, 1917 [WVD/11 p. 48]; Van Devanter to Judge Advocate General, November 14, 1917 [WVD/11 p. 309]; Van Devanter to Judge Advocate General, December 4, 1917 [WVD/11 p. 327]; Van Devanter to Pershing, June 22, 1919 [Van Devanter/11, p. 274]; Hayen to Tillman, June 27, 1917 [BRT-STI/Se II b58]; Glass to Mr. George O. Gregory [CG-UVA/100].

56. Wilson, Report of the Secretary of the Lexington Orphan Asylum for 1917 [SW-UK/1917]; Stanley C. Arthur, Louisiana Historical Society Chair to Wilson, December 30, 1914; R. S. Morris, president, Kentucky Society of Louisiana to Wilson, December 18, 1914 [SW-UK/1914]; Robert Thompson, President Navy League of the United States to Wilson, January 2, 1917 [SW-UK/1917]. See also E. Polk Johnson, *History of Kentucky and Kentuckians: The Leaders and Representative Men in Commerce, Industry, and Modern Activities* (Chicago: The Lewis Co., 1912), 3:1258; and G. Glenn Clift, "Samuel MacKay Wilson, 1871–1946: An Appreciation," *The Register of the Kentucky Historical Society* 45, no. 150 (January 1947): 27–38.

57. Bell to Wilson, February 19, 1898; Bell to Wilson, December 15, 1897, December 15, 1897; Bell to Wilson, February 24, 1901; Bell to Wilson, May 16, 1914; Wilson to Bell, May 20, 1914; Bell to Wilson, March 21, 1916; Bell to Wilson, April 5, 1917 [SW-UK/1897–1919 file].

58. Davis to Wilson, August 10, 1914; C. C. Calhoun to Wilson, August 19, 1914 [SW-UK/1914]; Roster of Eighth and Ninth Regiments: Fourth Military Training Camp, Plattsburg, New York [51W20].

59. Wilson Talks on Preparedness," *Lexington Leader*, February 23, 1917 [SW-UK/1917]; Wilson to Navy League, April 16, 1917 [SW-UK/1917]. Wilson to President Wilson, April 101, 1917 [SW-UK/ 1898–1917]; Tumulty to Wilson, May 7, 1917 [SW-UK/1917]; Wilson to John Shelby, March 14, 1918 [SW-UK/1918]; Wilson to Senator James, April 10, 1917 [SW-UK/1917].

60. Wilson to W. A. McDowell, May 11, 1917 [SW-UK/1917]; R. L. Northcutt to Wilson, May 7, 1917; Ernest Woodward to Wilson, May 21, 1917; Ona Abbot to Wilson, May 24, 1917 [SW-UK/1917]; Dodds to Wilson, June 9, 1917; Jno Flood to Henry Flood, September 1, 1917 [HDF/82].

61. Elmer C. Hess, *Official Congressional Directory for the Sixty-Seventh Congress* (Washington, DC: GPO, 1922), 43; "Negroes Will Still Vote in Maryland," *Baltimore Sun*, October 24, 1909; "Amendment is Full of Snakes," *Baltimore American*, October 25, 1909; "Bitter Opposition to Naming of Hill: Baltimore Attorneys Will Fight Taft Nominee for District Attorney," *Baltimore Chronicle*, March 25, 1910; "Bar Wires Protest Against Hill's Name," *Baltimore News*, March 26, 1910 [JPH/1].

62. "Honorable John Philip Hill: Former United States Attorney Enters the List as a Republican for Mayor," *The Crusader*, March 20, 1915; "Major Hill Cheered: Address Gathering in East Baltimore Hall," *Baltimore American*, March 24, 1915; "Marylanders Feel Preparedness Need: Find Great Crowd of Eminent People Urging Campaign of Security League," *Baltimore Sun*, January 21, 1916; "Fur May Fly in G.O.P.: John Philip Hill Handed 'Lemon,' Puts on War Paint," *Baltimore Sun*, April 12, 1916; "How Major Hill was Impressed: Baltimorean Calls on Republican Candidate," *Baltimore American*, June 15, 1916; "Major Hill Off Today," *Baltimore American*, September 18, 1916 [JPH/3].

63. Major John Philip Hill, "National Protection," in *National Protection: Policy, Armament, and Preparedness*, ed. John Philip Hill (Baltimore: Monumental Printing, 1916), 8–14; Major John Philip Hill, "The Autumn Manuevers of a German Army Corps," in *National Protection: Policy, Armament, and Preparedness*, 77–84; "John Philip Hill will see German Army Tactics," *Baltimore News*, September 5, 1911; "Emperor Lauds Major J. P. Hill," *Baltimore Sun*, September 29, 1911 [JPH/1].

64. Herbert White to Senator Oscar Underwood, January 14, 1918 [HDF/82].

65. Smith, Application file, 1917 [MS-USC/6]; Tillman to Smith, August 27, 1917 [BRT-STI/19].

66. Smith to Ellison Smith, October 16, 1917; Ellison Smith to Smith, October 24, 1917; Lt Col H. A. White to Ellison Smith, October 30, 1917; Lever to Smith, December 6, 1917 [MS-USC/5 671]; Ragsdale to Smith, December 15, 1917 [MS-USC/6 fl 562]; Smith to Manning, July 23, 1918 [MS-USC/6 fl 562]; Special Orders 202, July 31, 1918 [MS-USC/6 fl 564]; Smith to Major Cole, Disciplinary Branch, October 4, 1918 [MS-USC/6 fl 563]; Mendel Smith, Army medical file [MS-USC/5-655].

67. Henry Flood to John Flood, November 22, 1917; John Flood to Henry Flood, January 11, 1918; Jno Flood to Henry Flood, February 7, 1918; Ansell to Henry Flood, March 6, 1918 [HDF/82].

68. *Pennsylvania in the World War: The Twenty-Eighth Division* (Chicago and Pittsburgh: States Publication Society, 1921), 1:280–281; Philander Knox notes, n.d., 1916 [PK/28]; Moseley, diary entry for September 5, 1917 [GVM/1].

69. H. A. Frank to Walsh, August 21, 1914; Walsh to Frank, August 24, 1914 [TWP/215]. In this correspondence, Walsh conveys his discussions with Crowder to a constituent regarding Raborg.

70. J. Wilson to Crowder, July 5, 1916 [JHWP/6]; Crowder to Wilson, August 21, 1918 [JHWP/6]; Wilson to Crowder, September 30, 1918 [JHWP/6]; Crowder to Wilson, October 2, 1918 [JHWP/6].

71. Roosevelt to Crowder, July 19, 1917 [TR/R 393]; Roosevelt to Crowder, May 8, 1917 [TR/R 241]; Rand to Brandeis, July 5, 1917 [LDB/R-48]. On Rand's role in reviewing courts-martial, see "High Army Officers Contradict Watson: Weeks Gives Official Figures Showing 10 Were Put to Death for Non-Military Offenses," *New York Times*, November 2, 1921.

72. Otis B. Drake to Edward J. Walsh, April 13, 1917 [WWP/R359 C3960]; Tumulty to Crowder, May 17, 1917; Crowder to Tumulty, June 12, 1917 [WWP/R359 C3961].

73. "Captain and Civilian Arraigned on Graft Charge at Battle Creek," *New York Times*, March 20, 1918, p. 2; "Captain Pillenger to Serve Four Years," *New York Times*, August 2, 1918, p. 2. The secretary of war reduced Pillenger's sentence to four years, and the civilian was sentenced to two

years' imprisonment by the district court. For memoranda detailing Muphy's experience in the army, see Division Adjutant to 1st Lieutenant Murphy, October 9, 1918; Colonel F. C. Bolles to Murphy, January 16, 1919; Murphy to Adjutant General, USA, July 18, 1919 [FM-UMI/91]; Sidney A. Fine, *Frank Murphy in World War One* (Ann Arbor: Michigan Historical Collections, 1969), 22–41.

74. Prettyman, diary entry, April 17, 1918 [EBPP/1]. On Prettyman's wartime experiences, see also Oral interview of Prettyman, Historical Society of the District of Columbia Circuit Oral History Project [LOC/6].

75. Prettyman, Naylor file [EBPP/10].

76. Gorfinkle, Application for re-commission as a judge advocate, 1941 [BJA- BG/1].

77. Gorfinkle to his family, September 18, 1917 [BG-JA/1].

78. Smith to Commanding General, October 17, 1818 [MS-USC/570].

79. Crowder to Dunn, January 17, 1918 [SW-UK/JACM 1918]. This document was found in Samuel Wilson's papers, perhaps indicating that Crowder intended for all judge advocates to become aware of his displeasure with Dunn's advice. The document does not appear to exist in Crowder's papers and is likely misplaced in the hundreds of thousands of judge advocate documents in the National Archives.

80. Wilson to Colonel Paul A. Wolf, November 4, 1917; Wilson to Lieutenant Colonel P. W. Arnold, November 4, 1917; Wilson to Hon B. D. Warfield, November 6, 1917 [SW-UK/1917]; Wilson to John Wiley and Sons, November 10, 1917 [SW-UK/1917]; B. D. Warfield, Louisville & Nashville Railroad Co., January 3, 1918 [SW-UK/1918]; Wilson to W. T. Smith esq., January 7, 1918; Wilson to R. L. Northcutt, January 21, 1918 [SW-UK/1918]; Ernest Woodward, January 24, 1918.

81. Pepper, diary entry for October 20, 1917. On his own vaccine experience, Pepper wrote, "In the afternoon we got our shots in the arm again. By supper time I was pretty fevered up, stiffened and generally all from the same treatment, so remained in the house all night. In the morning my arm was sore and I had a high fever."

82. Smith to Crowder, November 13, 1918 [MS-USC/6-574]; *Washington Times*, October 29, 1918, p. 7; *Harrisburg Telegraph*, October 21, 1918, p. 2.

83. Smith to Division Commanding General, November 8, 1918 [MS-USC/6-574].

84. Smith to Division Commanding General, November 8, 1918 [MS-USC/6-574].

85. "Called to Active Service in Capital," *Anniston Evening Star*, August 4, 1917; "Court Martials Organized at Camp," *Anniston Star*, September 24, 1917 [JPH/3]; John Abrams Cutchins, *History of the Twenty-ninth Division, "Blue and Gray," 1917–1919* (Philadelphia: Press of MacCalla & Co., 1921), 32–52. This history was prepared under the order of the division's commander, Major General Charles G. Morton, and Hill was a contributing author to it.

86. General Court Martial Order no. 12, January 18, 1918 [RG 393 E 1594—Eastern Department]; General Court Martial Order no. 248, April 26, 1918 [RG 393 E 1594—Eastern Department].

87. NARG RG 153 General Courts-Martial Ledger Sheets, Box 2, 1917–1918.

88. Id.

89. Eastern Department, General Court Martial Order 280, May 11, 1918 [RG 393 Pt 1 E1541].

90. Smith to Judge Advocate General, June 30, 1918; Commanding General, Camp Wadsworth to Presidents of all Court-Martial and Trial Judge Advocates, July 18, 1918 [MS-USC/6 f61].

91. Crowder to all Department and Division Judge Advocates, March 7, 1918 [EG-SGM/33].

92. Winthrop, *Military Law and Precedents*, 541–542.

93. Spooner to Stimson, May 20, 1908 [HLS/R-16]; Roosevelt to Stimson, May 16, 1908 [HLS/ R-16]; see generally Hearings before the Committee on Military Affairs; John Downing Weaver, *The Brownsville Raid* (New York: W.W. Norton, 1970).

94. McNeil to Crowder, January 2, 1918 [EMP-JAGS/1]; Tillman to Crowder, March 2, 1918 [BRT-STI/SI 2].

95. Goff to Nathan Goff, n.d., 1919 [GDG-WVU/2]; Connor to father, July 24, 1919 [WCP-UVA/1-2]; Hugh Ogden to Lisbeth, February 12, 1919 [HO-SIU/III].

96. Charles L. Lumpkins, *American Pogrom: The East Saint Louis Race Riot and Black Politics* (Athens: Ohio University Press, 2008), 101–126; Ann V. Collins, *All Hell Broke Loose: American Race Riots from the Progressive Era through World War II* (Santa Barbara, CA: ABC-CLIO, 2012), 57–61; Crowder to Lowden, n.d., 1917 [CP/98].

97. Garna L. Christian, *Black Soldiers in Jim Crow Texas, 1899–1917* (College Station: Texas A & M Press, 1995), 159–163; William G. Jordan, *Black Newspapers and America's War for Democracy, 1914–1920* (Chapel Hill: University of North Carolina Press), 91–101; Mark Ellis, *Race, War and Surveillance: African Americans and the United States Government During World War I* (Bloomington: Indiana University Press, 2001), 46.

98. Ansell to Adjutant General, September 8, 1917 [NA RG 393 Southern Department Records]; Sutphin to Crowder, October 4, 1919 [NA RG 153]; Shapiro, *White Violence and Black Response: From Reconstruction to Montgomery* (Boston: University of Massachusetts Press, 1988), 108–111.

99. Ansell to Crowder, December 12, 1917 [Hearings II, 139]; Daniel R. Anthony to Baker, January 11, 1918 [NDB/5]; Arthur E. Barbeau and Florette Henry, *The Unknown Soldiers: African American Troops in World War I* (Philadelphia: Temple University Press, 1974), 30.

100. *Muskogee Times Democrat*, May 15, 1919, p. 8; "Mayor to Help Negroes on to Rockford," *The Broad Ax*, Chicago, IL, October 27, 1917; "Choctaw Indian Gets His Place: Gabe Parker to be Register of the Treasury Instead of Patterson," *Daily Ardmorite*, August 3, 1913, p. 1; "Oswald Garrison Villard, Grandson of William Lloyd Garrison Writes a Strong Article," *The Appeal*, January 3, 1914, p. 1. While there is little specifically on Patterson, see Eric Yellin, *Racism in the Nation's Service: Government Workers and the Color Line* (Chapel Hill: University of North Carolina Press, 2013), 80; and Kenneth O'Reilly, *Nixon's Piano: Presidents and Racial Politics from Washington to Clinton* (New York: Free Press, 1995), 85.

101. Biographical descriptions of these justices can be found in Walter F. Pratt, *The Supreme Court Under Edward Douglass White, 1910–1921* (Columbia: University of South Carolina Press, 1999), 1–25.

102. McReynolds to O'Laughlin, July 11, 1916 [JCO/]; Robert Lansing, *War Memoirs of Robert Lansing* (Indianapolis: Bobbs-Merrill, 1935), 274. On McReynolds, see Edward Pratt, *The Supreme Court Under Edward Douglass White,* 112–114; Gerald H. Hagar, "Judge Advocate General's Department in the American Expeditionary Forces," *California Law Review* 8, no. 5 (1920): 300–327.

103. Wigmore to Frankfurter, June 10, 1925 [JHW-NW/57]; Bliss, Memorandum of Interview with Wallace Donham, April 14, 1917 [THB/211]. For more on the Crowder-Brandeis relationship, see Melvin Urofsky, *Louis D. Brandeis: A Life*, 498.

104. Wilson to Clarke, July 18, 1916 [WW R/146]; Clarke to Wilson, December 21, 1916; Wilson to Clarke, December 21, 1916 [WW/R84]; Wilson to Clarke, August 1, 1916 [WW/R146].

105. Clarke to Wilson, April 3, 1917 [WW/R 86]; Wilson to Clarke, May 19, 1917 [WW/R150]; Wilson to Clarke, September 4, 1917 [WW/R152]. On Clarke generally, see Rebecca S. Shoemaker, *The White Court: Justices, Rulings, and Legacy* (Santa Barbara, CA: ABC-CLIO, 2004), 97–101.

106. John H. Clarke to Baker, August 5, 1917; John H. Clarke to Baker, August 30, 1917 [NDB/1]; Clarke to Wilson, September 28, 1918 [WWP/R100]; Clarke to Wilson, October 16, 1918 [WWP/R101]; Thomas R. Marshall, *Recollections*, 337.

107. "Anti-Draft Agitator Held," *New York Times*, July 17, 1917, p. 1.

108. *Goldman v. United States*, 245 U.S. 474 (1918); *Ruthenberg v. United States*, 245 U.S. 80 (1918).

109. See e.g. Leon Friedman, "Conscription and the Constitution: The Original Understanding," *Michigan Law Review* 67 (June 1969): 1493–1552; Brandeis to White, n.d., 1918 [LDB-LU/48].

110. Wigmore to Crowder, n.d., October 1917 [JHW-NW/32].

111. *Franke v. Murray*, 248 F.865 (CA 8, 1918).

112. Crowder to Wigmore, September 24, 1918 [RG 163 Records of the Selective Service System, 1917–1919 General Files/ Box 10 F 621–640]; Frankfurter to Baker, April 15, 1917 [NDB/1].

456   NOTES TO CHAPTER 4

CHAPTER 4

1. Hines to Bethel, August 7, 1917 [RG 153, PC 30 E 53 000.72/Box 1]; Adjutant General to James G. Harbord, May 26, 1917 [JGH/10]; Pershing to McCain, September 21, 1917 [JGH/11]; General Order 1, May 26, 1917 [JLH/3]. On Bethel's draft agreement with Painleve, see Bethel to Pershing, September 8, 1918, reminding Pershing on the importance of re-signing the agreement that came into effect on July 28, 1917 [NA RG PC 29 E 53 370.8/B9]. In late November, Bayne returned to France and was assigned as the assistant judge advocate to the Services of Supply.

2. Bethel to Harbord, December 1, 1917 [RG 120, E594, 250.4/7]. On venereal disease, see Bethel to Director Training Schools of Aviation, LOC and Pershing, December 6, 1918; Bethel to Pershing, January 1, 1918; Bethel to Bayne, February 18, 1918 [RG 120 E 1772 250.1/8]. On the issue of marriage, see Susan Zeiger, *Entangling Alliances: Foreign War Brides and American Soldiers in the Twentieth Century* (New York: New York University Press, 2010), 33.

3. Bethel to Bliss, December 19, 1917 [RG120, E 594 WDDS320].

4. David F. Trask, *The AEF and Coalition Warmaking, 1917-1918* (Lawrence: University Press of Kansas, 1993), 58-65.

5. Basil H. Liddell Hart, *The Real War: 1914-1918* (Boston: Little, Brown, 1930), 449-469.

6. Bethel to Secretary for the General Staff, December 1, 1917 [RG 120 3.21-4]. On the American buildup in France, see Martin Gilbert, *The First World War: A Complete History*, 340-341.

7. General Order no. 7, January 17, 1918 [RG 120 E594]; General Order no. 15, January 18, 1918 [RG 120 E594]; Crowder to All Department and Division Judge Advocates, March 7, 1918 [EG-SGM/33].

8. Pershing to Scott, February 24, 1918; Crowder to Pershing, February 23, 1918 [RG 120 E594]; Crowder to Bethel, April 5, 1918 [RG 120 E594]; Crowder to "All Judge Advocates serving with Expeditionary Forces," March 8, 1918 [EG-SGM/33]; Kreger to his wife, May 26, 1918 [EAK-DBC/1]. On Pershing's irritation with Kreger, see "Pershing Protests Curtailment of Power: War Department Denied Head of AEF Refused to Obey Order; Admits Complaint," *New York Tribune*, March 1, 1919, p. 1; and "Pershing was Obedient, War Department Says: General Merely Registered Protest against Court-Martial Order," *Philadelphia Ledger*, March 1, 1919 [EHC/1053]. On Bethel being in a subordinate position to Kreger, see Crowder, hearings, 1207.

9. On the origins of General Order 7, see, Crowder to Baker, March 26, 1919 [ECH/R5]. On Pershing's view of General Order 7, see Harbord to Bethel, March 8, 1918 [RG 120 E594] and Harbord to Pershing, December 8, 1918 [JGH/11].

10. Baker to Wilson, May 1, 1918 [NDB/6]; Clarence H. Cramer, *Newton D. Baker: A Biography*, 108; also *Official Bulletin* of May 1, 1918, reprinted in *Washington Post*, February 28, 1919 [EHC/1052].

11. Bethel to Corps and Divisional Judge Advocates, April 18, 1918 [RG 120 E594 WDDS321.4]; Bethel to Pershing, October 21, 1918 [JJP/24]. See also Clarence H. Cramer, *Newton D. Baker*, 108-109.

12. Crowder to Kreger, April 13, 1918 [EG-SGM/33].

13. Gerald H. Hagan, "Judge Advocate General's Department in the American Expeditionary Forces," 308-320.

14. Major General Ernest Hinds to Pershing, September 7, 1918; Bethel to Chief of Staff, September 10, 1918; Major C. V. Porter to Kreger, September 18, 1918; Bethel to Pershing, November 15, 1918; Major J. A. Howell to Kreger, November 23, 1918 [RG 153 PC 29 E 53 322.04/B 10].

15. Bayne, Memoirs [HAB-UNC/R-3].

16. General Court Martial Order 14, Trial of Private Frank Cadue [RG 120 B5069]; "American Soldier Hanged," *New York Times*, December 3, 1917, p. 1; "Execution of Soldier is Approved," December 3, 1917, *Evening Standard*, p. 1; and "Death Penalty is Approved," *Ogden Standard*, December 3, 1917

17. On Pershing's insistence of maximizing sentences in instances where French citizens were victims, see General Orders no. 56, April 13, 1918 [SW-UK/CM-1918]; General Court-Martial Order 14, October 8, 1917 Trial of Private McGlade, NARA RG 120 [B5069]

18. General Court-Martial Order 6, October 17, 1917 Trial of Captain Leroy Overpeck [RG 120 B5069].

19. General Court-Martial Order 2, August 17, 1917 Trial of Private Leo Renn [RG 120 B5069]; General Court-Martial Order 13, November 9, 1917 Trial of Private Norman Rhodes [RG 120 B5069]. On Patton's relationship to Pershing, see Carlo D'Este, *Patton: A Genius for War* (New York: Harper Perennial, 1995), 156–187.

20. General Court-Martial Order 16, December 18, 1917 Trial of Private Frederick Peloquin [RG 120 B5069]; General Court-Martial Order 3, October 8, 1917 Trial of Richard Prina [RG 120 B5069]; Court-Martial Order 5, October 8, 1917 Trial of Private James Mosely [RG 120 B5069].

21. Bethel to Crowder, February 6, 1918 [RG 120 E594/27]; Adjutant General to Bethel, August 8, 1918, September 18, 1918 [RG120 E802 B262—"Malingering"].

22. Bethel to Adjutant General, October 12, 1918; Special Court Martial Order 189 [NARA RG120, E594 WDDS-000.5].

23. General Court-Martial Order 21, March 27, 1919, Trial of Private Thomas P. Oates [RG120 E595, GCMO Orders 6th–77th Divisions/B1].

24. General Court-Martial Order 19, March 27, 1919, Trial of Private Charles Jensen [RG120 E595, GCMO Orders 6th–77th Divisions/B1]; General Court-Martial Order 19, March 31, 1919, Trial of Private Gus Schrader [RG120 E595, GCMO Orders 6th–77th Divisions/B1].

25. Perrot Grossard, Department of Haute Marne, Gendarmerie to American Expeditionary Forces, Deputy Adjutant General, August 18, 1918; Adjutant General to Major General Hanson E. Ely, Commander Fifth Division, AEF, October 26, 1918; Adjutant General to Ely, February 14, 1919 [RG120, E594 WDDS-000.5].

26. General Court Martial Order 293; General Walter Bethel to Pershing, March 3, 1919; C. A. Trott to Adjutant General, May 21, 1919; General Walter Bethel to Chief of French Military Mission, May 27, 1919 [RG120, E594 WDDS-000.5].

27. Lieutenant Colonel Mendel Smith, Review of record of trial by general court-martial, AEF, February 25, 1919; Concurrence, Colonel H. A. White, March 25, 1919 [RG 153 PC 29 E 53/Box 1]. These documents total twenty-seven pages.

28. Wilson to Division Adjutant, September 4, 1918; Wilson to Bethel, October 8, 1918 [SW-UK/CM-1918] [case of Private John Lucey].

29. Lieutenant Colonel Marion Howze, Review of record of trial by general court-martial, AEF, February 18, 1919; Concurrence, Colonel H. A. White, March 7, 1918 [RG 153 PC 29 E 53/Box 1]. Howze became the judge advocate for the District of Paris in late 1918; see George W. Cullum, *Biographical Register of Officers and Graduates of the United States Military Academy*, Supplement VI-A, 1023.

30. Lieutenant Colonel Marion Howze, Review of record of trial by general court-martial, AEF, March 5, 191; Concurrence, E. A. Kreger, March 7, 1919 [RG 153 PC 29 E 53/Box 1]; Lieutenant Colonel Marion Howze, Review of record of trial by general court-martial, AEF, December 18, 1918; Concurrence, E. A. Kreger, December 19, 1918 [RG 153 PC 29 E 53/Box 1].

31. Bethel to Kreger, August 27, 1918 [RG 120 E 802 NM 91 First Army Records//262]. Bethel wrote to Kreger, "It is most desirable that appointees have previous line experience. There are a number of wounded officers who are good lawyers." On Hill's relationship to Frankfurter, see Hill to Frankfurter, October 8, 1918 [FF-Harv/R-40]. Holmes congratulated Hill on leaving his legal practice to join the army; see Hill to Holmes, March 7, 1919 [OWH-UPA/33].

32. AD Hill to HH, January 7, 1918 [ADHP-PA/1]; ADH to HH, July 4, 1918 [ADHP-PA/1].

33. Charge Sheet for AD Hill, July 24, 1918 [ADHP-PA/1]. On John Albert Tiffin Hull, see *Biographical Directory of the United States Congress, 1774–2005* (Washington, DC: GPO, 2005), 1298.

34. AD Hill to AD Hill Jr., July 7, 1918; AD Hill to AD Hill Jr., November 5, 1918 [ADHP-PA/1]; Hill, Report of Investigation to Provost Marshall, September 10, 1918 [ADHP-PA/2].

35. Order draft on March 22, 1917; and March 19, 1918 [ADHP-PA/1]. Pershing was a stickler for preventing venereal disease and wanted to have soldiers court-martialed who became infected. See Mary C. Gillet, *The Army Medical Department*, 254.

36. AD Hill to AD Hill Jr., May 3, 1918 [ADHP-PA/1].

37. AD Hill to AD Hill Jr., April 6, 1918; AD Hill to AD Hill Jr., May 17, 1918; AD Hill to AD Hill Jr., July 2, 1918 [ADHP-PA/1]; AD Hill, Claim no. 706, September 3, 1918 [ADHP-PA/2].

38. AD Hill to AD Hill Jr., May 8, 1918; AD Hill to AD Hill Jr., May 18, 1918; AD Hill to AD Hill Jr., July 2, 1918; AD Hill to AD Hill Jr., April 4, 1919 [ADHP-PA/1].

39. AD Hill to Major Palmer, May 7, 1918 [ADHP-PA/2].

40. AD Hill to AD Hill Jr., August 15, 1918 [ADHP-PA/1]; AD Hill to HH Hill, July 28, 1918 [ADHP-PA/1].

41. AD Hill to AD Hill Jr., August 15, 1918 [ADHP-PA/1].

42. AD Hill to Colonel Hull, August 29, 1918 [ADHP-PA/1].

43. Pepper, diary entries for January 3, 1918, and February 26, 1919 [SP-UM/2].

44. Pepper diary entries for March 22, 23, and 27, 1918 [SP-UM/2].

45. Pepper, diary entries for April 30 and May 26 [SP-UM/2].

46. Pepper, diary entries for June 6, June 16, and June 30, 1918 [SP-UM/2].

47. Pepper, diary entries for July 27 and September 1, 1918 [SP-UM/2].

48. Cosgrave to Pearl Jane Cosgrave (daughter), June 19, 1937 [WC-NHS/1].

49. Id.; also Cosgrave, Fifth Division correspondence, April 27, 1918.

50. Cosgrave to Pearl Jane Cosgrave, July 1, 1918 [WC-NHS/1].

51. Cosgrave to Pearl Jane Cosgrave, July 1, 1918 [WC-NHS/1].

52. Cosgrave, diary entry for May 19, 1919 [WC-NHS/2].

53. Porter to Bethel, October, 1918 [NA RG 120 E 802 NM 91 Seventy-Ninth Division Records/371].

54. Ogden to his wife, June 15, 1918; Ogden to his wife, June 16, 1918 [HO-SIU.II].

55. On Ogden's biography, see Stephen Puleo, *Dark Tide: The Great Molasses Flood of 1919* (Boston: Beacon Press, 2003). On Senator Weeks's support for Ogden, see William H. Lewis to Weeks, July 20, 1917 [JWW-RSP/5-4].

56. Address by Lieutenant Colonel Hugh W. Ogden, printed in *Boston City Club Bulletin*, October 1, 1919, pp. 41–58,; Ogden to Weeks, November 22, 1917 [JWW-RSP/5-35].

57. Ogden to his wife Lisbeth, November 17, 1917 [HO-SIU/I]; Ogden to Lisbeth, undated [HO-SIU/I]; Ogden to Lisbeth, January 4, 1918 [HO-SOU/II]; Address by Lieutenant Colonel Hugh W. Ogden, 53; Ogden to John Weeks, December 24, 1917 [JWW-RSP/6-35].

58. Howze to Duncan and Bell, June 4, 1918; Duncan, approval of sentence, June 1, 1918. All information on this case is found in a file marked as "Private William A. Kerner" [SW-UK/1918].

59. Wilson to Winship, November 6, 1918 [SW-UK/1918]; Charles G. Milham, *"Atta Boy!": The Story of New York's 77th Division, U.S.A.*, (New York: Brooklyn Daily Eagle, 1919).

60. Bayne, Memoirs [HAB-UNC/R-3].

61. Dowell to Bethel, May 4, 1918 [BG-JA/2]; Gorfinkle to his mother, December 3, 1917 [BG-JA/1]; Gorfinkle to his father, December 16, 1917 [BG-JA/1].

62. Gorfinkle, diary entry for March 8, 1918 [BG-JA/2].

63. Gorfinkle, diary entry for April 24, 1918 [BG-JA/2].

64. Gorfinkle, diary entry for May 23, 1918 [BG-JA/2]. On Anderson, see Gorfinkle to "dear men," April 14, 1918 [BG-JA/1].

65. Gorfinkle to "dear men," December 18, 1917, and Gorfinkle to "dear men," January 19, 1918 [BG-JA/2]; Gorfinkle to "dear men," October 20, 1918 [BGA-JA/3].

66. Hill, Report of Twenty-Ninth Division.

67. "Harold Content Quits U.S. Attorney's Staff," *New York Tribune*, January 24, 1918, p. 14; "Federal Laws Cover a Variety of Offenses," *Columbia Daily Spectator*, October 28, 1914, p. 1; John Abrams Cutchins, *History of the Twenty-Ninth "Blue and Gray": 1917–1919*, 249.

68. John Abrams Cutchins, History of the Twenty-Ninth "Blue and Gray": 1917–1919, 144; "Wants Colonel to Run for Congress," *Baltimore American*, April 24, 1920 [JPH/3].

69. Hull to Bethel, July 17, 1918 [NA RG 153 PC 3- E 54, 000.151/1].

70. Bethel to Crowder, January 8, 1918 [NA RG 153 PC 3- E 54, 000.150/1]. It must be noted that Bethel's and Hull's memoranda to Crowder are not only located in one of the "confidential files"

but were also sealed in envelopes that had not been opened since 1919. On Bauer, see *Harvard Alumni Bulletin* 21, no. 1 (September 1918): 388.

71. A. W. Brown to Chief of Staff, First Army, December 16, 1918, and accompanying documents [RG 120 First Army Records NM 91 E 802/258].

72. Bethel to Crowder, January 6, 1918 [RG 120 E594]. For the Supreme Court decisions in 1968, see *Levy v. Louisiana*, 391 U.S. 68 (1968); *Glona v. American Guarantee and Liability Insurance Co.*, 391 U.S. 73 (1968).

73. Bethel to Winship, January 7, 1918 [RG 120 E594]; Adjutant General to Bethel, August 8, 1918, September 18, 1918 [RG120 E802 B262—"Malingering"].

74. Blanton Winship to Commanding General, First Army Corps, February 20, 1918 [RG 120 E594 250.1].

75. Bethel to Pershing, October 21, 1918 [JJP/24].

76. Liggett to Kreger, n.d., 1918; Headquarters Eastern Department, General Court-Martial, Orders no. 127 and accompanying papers, March 7, 1918 [RG 393 Pt 1, E 1593].

77. Wallace to Kreger, September 20, 1918 [GW-WVU]. In this letter, Wallace references his 1918 advice to Kreger. On British and Canadian courts-martial and the death penalty, see Ernest Thurtle, *Shootings at Dawn: The Army Death Penalty at Work* (London: Victoria House Printing, 1924); and Teresa Iocobelli, *Death or Deliverance: Canadian Courts-Martial in the Great War* (Vancouver: University of British Columbia Press, 2013), 14.

78. Pershing to Allen, October 24, 1918 [HTA/10]; "Watson Must Prove Army Hanging Story," *New York Times*, November 2, 1921, p. 1. On Watson, see C. Vann Woodward, *Tom Watson: Agrarian Rebel* (New York: Oxford University Press, 1955), 480–481.

79. Bethel to Chief of the French Military Mission, February 2, 1919, "Alleged Affray Caused by American Soldiers" [RG 120, E594 250.1]; Bethel to Chief of the French Military Mission, May 15, 1918, "Infraction of the Decree of September 5, 1897 prohibiting the use of explosives to catch fish" [RG 120, E594 250.1]; Bethel to GG HQ Base, October 4, 1917 "Damage to fruit trees of Kinsgley Nursery at Bordon Hants, England by American soldiers" [RG 120, E594 250.1]; Mayes to Captain Pingree, October 30, 1918, "Theft of Cheese" [RG 120, E594 000.6]; Bethel to Chief French Military Mission, January 23, 1918, "Theft of Mutton Carcass" [RG 120, E594 250.1].

80. Bethel to Chief of the French Military Mission, March 2, 1919, "Misbehavior of American soldiers at Esnes, Meuse" [RG 120, E594 250.1].

81. See file no. 250.21 [RG 120, E594].

82. Bayne, Memoirs [HAB-UNC/R-3].

83. Kernan Memorandum, January 10, 1918; Bethel to Pershing endorsement of the same [RG 120 E 1772 250.01/8]. Bethel appears to have adopted the language from a medical corps officer in his response to Kernan.

84. Colonel Linnard, Chief of FMM to Bethel, November 12, 1918; Bethel to Pershing, November 14, 1918 [RG 120, E594].

85. Major Charles C. Teare to Adjutant General, First Army, October 3, 1918 [RG120 E802 B263—Fourth Division Correspondence].

86. Major Hugh Ogden to Adjutant General, Frist Army, October 3, 1918 [RG120 E802 B263—Forty-Second Division Correspondence]; Ogden to his wife, June 27, 1918 [HO-SIU/II].

87. Chiperfield, returns for November 1, 1918; MacChesney to Colonel Herbert White, Kreger, and Crowder, April 26, 1919 [RG PC 29 E 53 319.1/Box8].

88. 29 Division Records [RG120 E802 B263].

89. Berntheizel to Moseley, October 24, 1918 [GVM/1].

90. *History of the Fortieth (Sunshine) Division* (Los Angeles: C. S. Hutson, 1920) , 46–48; George B. Clark, *The American Expeditionary Force in World War I: A Statistical History* (Jefferson, NC: McFarland Press, 2013), 278–281. On the Court, see *Madsen v. Kinsella*, 343 U.S. 341 (1952); Eli E. Nobleman, *Military Government Courts: Law and Justice in the American Zone of Germany, American Bar Association Journal* 33 (1947): 777, 778–779; *Reid v. Covert*, 354 U.S. 1 (1957); *Grisham v. Hagen*, 361 U.S. 278 (1960); and *United States ex rel McElroy v. Guagliardo*, 361 U.S. 281 (1960).

91. See General John J. Pershing, *My Experiences in the World War*, 2:45, 221; Gerald Astor, *The Right to Fight: A History of African Americans in the Military* (New York: Da Capo, 1998), 129–132; Arthur E. Barbeau, *The Unknown Soldiers: African-American Troops in World War I* (Philadelphia: Temple University Press, 1974), 137; Miles S. Richards, "Charles Clarendon Ballou," in *The United States in the First World War: An Encyclopedia*, ed. Anne Cipriano Venzon (New York: Garland Press, 1995), 65; Ogden to Lisbeth, February 2, 1919 [HO-SIU/III]; Chad Williams, *Torchbearers of Democracy: African American Soldiers in the World War I Era* (Chapel Hill: University of North Carolina Press, 2010), 322.

92. Sanders Marble, *Scraping the Barrel: The Military Use of Substandard Manpower* (New York: Fordham University Press, 2001), 130; William L. Chew, *National Stereotypes in Perspective: Americans in France, Frenchmen in America* (Amsterdam: Rodopi BV, 2001), 277–280.

93. Edward M. Coffman, *The War to End All Wars*, 317–320; A. W. Brown to Bethel, April 15, 1919 [RG120 E802 B263]; Howell to Bethel [RG120 E802 B263]; Blanton Winship to Bethel, April 16, 1919 [RG120 E802 B263].

94. Howell to Liggett and Adjutant General, March 21, 1919 [RG120 E802 B263]; Howell to Troop B Headquarters Commander, March 16, 1919 [RG120 E802 B263].

95. Winship to Gallogly, October 2, 1918; Gallogly to Winship, September 27, 1918 [RG120 E802 B263—First Corps Correspondence].

96. Gallogly to Kreger, October 28, 1918 [RG120 E802 B263—First Corps Correspondence]; Pepper, diary entry for November 8, 1918 [SP-UM/2]. On the "Sacred Way," see Paul Jankowski, *Verdun: The Longest Battle of the Great War* (London: Oxford University Press, 2014), 73.

97. R. C. Stewart to Winship, September 18, 1918 [NARA RG120 E802 B263—First Division Correspondence].

98. Kreger to Divisional Commanders endorsement of Liggett, August 25, 1918, First US Army JA Records [RG 120, Case 8, Box 260].

99. Wallace to Kreger, January 22, 1919 [GWP-WVA].

100. Captain V. Webb to Commanding General, First Army, December 16, 1918 [RG 120, Case 8, Box 260]; Webb to Adjutant General, October 13, 1918 [RG 120, Case 8, Box 260]; Webb to Commanding General, First Army, December 17, 1918 [RG 120, Case 8, Box 260].

CHAPTER 5

1. See General Order 2, July 4, 1919. On the judge advocate division between France and Germany, see Colonel H. A. White, Acting Judge Advocate General to Crowder, September 4, 1919 [RG120 E2215 B3]. Each commander was vested with the authority to convene general courts-martial.

2. Moore to Crowder, November 11, 1918 [JBM/38].

3. On the occupation of Germany generally, see Byron Farwell, *Over There: The United States in the Great War* (New York: W.W. Norton, 1999), 267–272; and Keith L. Nelson, *Victors Divided: America and the Allies in Germany, 1918–1923* (Los Angeles: University of California Press, 1975), 34.

4. War Department, *Annual Report, 1917* (Washington, DC: GOP, 1917), 1:240.

5. Bethel, draft, December 1, 1919 [JLH/12]. Colonel I. L. Hunt, *Report of the Officer in Charge of Civil Affairs, Third Army: American Military Government of Occupied Germany, 1918–1920* (Washington, DC: GPO, 1921, reprint 1943), 56. The transition from the Third Army to the "American Forces in Germany" occurred on July 2, 1919.

6. Winship to Judge Advocate, Department of the Philippines, April 1, 1902 [RG 395 E2246]; Rucker to Kreger, December 24, 1918 [NARA RG 120].

7. Rucker to Dickman, December 14, 1918 [RG120 E1342 B4].

8. I. L. Hunt, *American Military Government in Germany*, 20.

9. "Court Opinion on the Draft," *Army and Navy Times*, September 1, 1917, p. 11.

10. Westenhaver to Wilson, February 21, 1917; Wilson to Westenhaver, February 23, 1917 [NDB/3]; *Ex Parte Dostol on behalf of Hackenberg* , 243 Fed. Rep. 664 (ND OH, 1917); and Otto Schlobohm, "The Constitutionality of the Selective Draft Law," *Georgetown Law Journal* 6 (1917), 11–18. Westenhaver maintained a close correspondence with Baker throughout the war and encouraged Baker to consider using the army to contain Bolshevism both in Russia and in the United States; Westenhaver to Baker, August 23, 1920 [NDB/11].

11. Adjutant General to Chief of Staff, December 11, 1939—Bode case file [RG 165, E 68 B 4045].

12. "Ms. Gerrard Has the Camera's Eye," *Evening Independent*, May 27, 1919; Bode File incl. Churchill to Judge Advocate General, September 6, 1918; Ansell to Churchill, September 17, 1918 [RG 165 E 68 B 4046].

13. Churchill to Crowder, September 20, 1918; Acting Director of Military Intelligence to Adjutant General of the Army, December 6, 1918; Dunn to Churchill, December 20, 1918; DE Nolan to Chief of Staff, February 26, 1921 ; Nolan to Adj Gen, February 26, 1921 [RG 165 E 68 B 4046].

14. War Department, Special Regulations no. 62, March 28, 1917; and accompanying notes in John Davis files [JWD/7].

15. Ansell to Adjutant General, July 20, 1917; Colonel Mayes to Adjutant General, October 20, 1917 [RG 165 E310, Records of the War Department and Special Staffs—Judge Advocate Records B226]; Overman Committee Report, 3.

16. On General Order 100, see generally *John Fabian Witt, Lincoln's Code: The Laws of War in American History* (New York: Simon and Schuster, 2012). See also Brian McAlister Linn, *The Philippine War*, 9.

17. Miscellaneous no. 13, Sworn Statement by Horst von der Goltz alias Bridgeman Taylor, 1916 [BL/178].

18. Warren, meeting notes, November 1917 [CW/7]; the facts of the Navy's imprisonment and trial of the Germans are found in *United States ex rel Wessels v. McDonald*, 265 F. 754 (DCNY, 1920).

19. Report 10541-268, JAG to MID, October 24, 1918; Report 10541-268-208, MID to JAG [RG 165/E 58 B56].

20. *R. v. Governor of Lewes Prison, ex Parte Doyle* [1917] 2 KB 254; *R v. Governor of Wormwood Scrubs, ex Parte Foy* [1917] 2 KB 305. See also Keith D. Ewing and C. A. Gearty, *The Struggle for Civil Liberties, Political Freedom, and the Rule of Law in Britain* (London: Oxford University Press, 2000), 331–392.

21. Lansing to Gregory, September 21, 1916; Lansing to Gregory, September 22, 1916; Tumulty to Lansing, September 22, 1916; Lansing to Tumulty, October 2, 1916; Tumulty to Lansing, October 3, 1916 [RL/21]; Charles Warren to Lansing, December 1, 1916 [RL/22]. On senators supporting a resolution condemning the British response to the 1916 Easter Uprising, see William F. Holmes, *The White Chief: James Kimble Vardaman*, 298; Leonard Bates, *Senator Thomas Walsh of Montana: Law and Public Affairs, from TR to FDR* (Champaign: University of Illinois Press, 1999), 117–124; and Robert E. Hennings, *James D. Phelan and the Wilson Progressives of California* (New York: Garland Publishing, 1985), 117–118.

22. On the Witzke affair, see General Order 32, June 4, 1920 [copy in NA RG 153]. See also Joan Jensen, *Army Surveillance in America: 1775–1980* (New Haven, CT: Yale University Press, 1991), 177; and Roy Talbert, *Negative Intelligence: The Army and the American Left, 1917–1941* (Columbus: University of Mississippi Press, 1991), 12.

23. Bliss to Scott, April 30, 1917 [THB/212]; Davis to McCain, April 28, 1918 [JWD/7]; James Brown Scott to Lansing, April 4, 1917 [JBS-GUSC/18].

24. Headquarters, First Army, Judge Advocate Memorandum, September 20, 1918 [NA RG 120 First Army Records, B802/262]; V. Webb to Bethel, October 11, 1918; Undersecretary of State for Military Justice to Bethel, September 8, 1918 [NARA RG120 E802 B262].

25. Gorfinkle to his mother, November 17, 1917 [BG/1].

26. Pershing to Harbord, January 7, 1918 [JGH/13].

27. Bethel to Pershing, May 18, 1918, [NA RG 120 E 1772 010.2/1]; Pershing to March, September 21, 1918 [JGH/13].

28. Davis to his mother [JWD/5/fl50]; Davis to George Wallace, October 17, 1918 [JWD/5/51].

29. Gorfinkle to his mother, November 8, 1918 [BG/1].

30. Bayne, Memoirs [HAB-UNC/R-3]; Agreement Between the United States of America and Germany Concerning Prisoners of War, Sanitary Personnel, and Civil Prisoners (Washington, DC: GPO, 1918).

31. See e.g. Hays Parks, "Joint Service Shotgun Program, *Army Lawyer* (1997): 15–24; and U.S. Department of State, *Papers Relating to the Foreign Relations of the United States, 1918 Supp. 2* (Washington, DC: GPO, 1933), 785–786.

32. Bayne to Assistant Chief of Staff, G-4, May 14, 1918 [RG 120 E 1772 010.2/1].

33. Bethel, draft, December 1, 1919 [JLH/12].

34. See John Horne and Alan Kramer, *The German Atrocities of 1914: A History of Denial* (New Haven, CT: Yale University Press, 2001).

35. De Castlenau to Liggett, September 23, 1918 [RG 120, Case 8, Box 260].

36. Drum to Liggett, October 8, 1918; Liggett to Divisional Commanders, November 10, 1918 [RG 120, Case 8, Box 260].

37. Case notes on Fratel court-martial [RG 153, JAG Reports on Military Justice, E 28 P 28/ Box 15].

38. "Eurasian Doctor's Defence," *Times of London*, August 12, 1919, p. 24; "Horror at Kut," *Sydney Morning Herald*, August 11, 1919, p. 7; "Charges of Cruelty: Officer Court-Martialed—Inhuman Treatment Alleged," *Otago Daily Times*, August 11, 1919, p. 5; "Inhuman Medical Doctor," *King County Chronicle*, November 6, 1919, p. 3; "Court-Martial Sensation: Amazing Allegation against Assistant Surgeon," *Singapore Straits Times*, August 29, 1919, p. 9.

39. Bliss to Allen, November 6, 1919 [HTA/11]; Allen to Baker, March 29, 1920 [NDB/9].

40. Allen to Liggett, January 8, 1920 [HTA/12].

41. Allen to Rucker, January 26, 1921 [HTA/16].

42. Allen to Rucker, October 21, 1919; Captain Robert E. Ireton to Rucker, November 15, 1919 [RG 120 E1362].

43. IL Hunt, *American Forces in Germany*, 186–187.

44. Morrisette to Allen, June 8, 1921 [NARA RG 120, General Correspondence, 1919–1923 E1362]; Winship to Kreger, September 22, 1921 [EAK/3].

45. Morrisette to Allen, June 15, 1922; C. C. Todd to Allen, November 14, 1921, "Trial of Private Abelardo Diaz"; C. C. Todd to Allen, September 13, 1921; Rucker to Allen, June 30, 1921, "Trial of Adelard Gadbois"; Rucker to Allen, December 31, 1920 [RG 120, General Correspondence, 1919–1923 E1362]; Rucker to War Department, July 20, 1921 [RG 120, General Correspondence, 1919–1923 E1366].

46. Rucker to Allen, February 5, 1915 [HAT/16]. This document contains a copy of the Bergdoll affidavit.

47. Rucker to Allen, January 31, 1921 [HAT/16]; Colonel William H. Johnston to Allen, February 10, 1921 [HAT/16].

48. Rucker to Allen, January 31, 1921 [HAT/16]; "Judge Advocate of our Coblenz Forces Meets with Prompt Refusal," *New York Times*, January 30, 1921; Allen to Rucker, March 31, 1921 [HAT/16].

49. Ogden to Lisbeth, November 19, 1918 [HO-SIU/III].

50. I. L. Hunt, *American Forces in Germany*, 84; Ogden to Lisbeth, December 16, 1918 [HIO-SIU/III].

51. Allen to Rucker, September 21, 1919; Rucker to Allen, September 23, 1919 [NARA RG 120 E1362]; Allen to Maurice Weygand, September 16, 1919 [HTA/11].

52. Allen to Pershing, September 23, 1919 [HTA/11].

53. Johnson Hagood to Barnwell, February 8, 1919 [JH-SCHS/178-13].

54. While the Schied-Ring trial is maintained in the National Archives, it is difficult to reproduce as it consists of multiple pages of bound onion-skin paper. Nonetheless, the following is

helpful in understanding the trial: Special Order 33, February 2, 1919, "Order convening military commission"; Special Order 42, February 11, 1919, "Detail of General W. C. Neville"; "Goff to Allen, March 29, 1919, "Review of record of trial by Military Commission held on February 13, 14, and 15" [AJAGO 201-2628]; Rucker to Allen, August 11, 1919, "Disposition of Property" [NA RG120 E1363 B1].

55. Goff to Allen, March 29, 1919, "Review of record of trial by Military Commission held on February 13, 14, and 15" [AJAGO 201-2628]. On Senator McCarthy, see Frederic L. Borch, "The Malmedy Massacre Trial, the Military Court Proceedings and the Controversial Legal Aftermath," *Army Lawyer* (January 2011).

56. Rucker to Allen and Chief of Staff, January 29, 1919 [RG 120, General Correspondence— military commissions, 1919–1923 E1362]; J. Berry King, JA to Provost Marshal and Rucker, April 18, 1919; Rucker to Bethel, June 25, 1919 [RG 120 E1363].

57. Rucker to Allen, December 26, 1921; Allen to Rucker, December 26, 1921; C. C. Todd to Rucker, December 24, 1921 [NA RG 120, General Correspondence, 1919–1923 E1362].

58. Goff to Nathan Goff, April 2, 1919 [WVA-GDG].

59. Goff to Nathan Goff, April 22, 1919 [WVA-GDG]; on Holderness's court-martial, see GCMO 596, June 10, 1918, trial of Major Roy Holderness, Southern Department NA RG 393.

60. IL Hunt, American Forces in Germany, 253; Baker to Bainbridge Colby, April 6, 1920 [BC/2]. See also Keith L. Nelson, *Victors Divided: America and the Allies in Germany, 1918–1923*, 213.

61. Cosgrave to "sweetheart mama, and darling daughter," June 8, 1919 [WC-SHSN/1 F5]; Cosgrave Diary entry for May 28, 1919 [PJC—SHSN/1 F7].

62. On Goff's unsuccessful campaign for mayor of Milwaukee, see John D. Buekner, *The History of Wisconsin: Vol. 4: The Progressive Era, 1893–1914* (Madison: State Historical Society of Wisconsin, 1998), 168. On La Follette's opposition to Goff's appointment as United States attorney, see "La Follette opposes," *Milwaukee Tribune*, January 23, 1911; Lenroot to Ms. Guy D. Goff, January 9, 1933 [ILL/2].

63. On the *Los Angeles Times* bombing, see John Milton Cooper Jr., *Pivotal Decades: The United States, 1900–1920* (New York: W.W. Norton, 1990), 145.

64. Baker to Wilson, April 2, 1917 [NDB/1].

65. Goff to Nathan Goff, April 22, 1919 [WVA-GDG].

66. Goff to Crowder, May 1, 1919 [WVA-GDG].

67. Root to Lansing, November 14, 1918 [RL/40]; Lansing to Root, December 3, 1918 [RL/40].

68. Goff to Crowder, May 2, 1919 [WVA-GDG].

69. Goff to Davis, April 16, 1918 [JWD/8 fl34]; M. Cherif Bassiouni, *Introduction to International Criminal Law*, 2nd ed. (Leiden: Brill, 2001), 548.

70. Ogden to Lisbeth, December 26, 1918 [HO-SIU/III]; Root to Scott, March 15, 1920 [JBS-GUSC/7 fl 4]; Scott to Wigmore, May 14, 1919 [JBS-GUSC/9 fl 2]; "World Owes Holland a Debt of Gratitude: Lawyer Declares That Netherlands' Refusal to Surrender Former German Emperor for Trial on Political Offense Serves Justice," *Philadelphia Inquirer*, January 22, 1920 [JBS-GUSC/30 f 11].

71. J. Reuben Clark to Knox, April 4, 1921 [PKP/23].

72. Frank W. Fox and D. Michael Quinn, *J. Reuben Clark: The Public Years*, 273.

73. Moseley, diary entry for October 10, 1918 [GVM/1]; Gallogly to Winship, August 1, 1919 [RG 120 E 1772 250.4./8].

74. Winship to S. A. Cherry, DATS, October 6, 1919 [RG120 E2215, B3].

75. General Order 172, December 6, 1919; Lt Col George V. Strong to Chief of Staff, October 4, 1919; General Order 201, October 4, 1919 [RG 120 E2215, B2].

76. Bethel to Winship, July 1, 1919; Bethel to Harbord, August 19, 1919 [RG 120 E 1772 010.2/6]. On the numbers of claims, see House of Representatives Committee on Foreign Expenditures, Subcommittee on Expenditures in the War Department (hereafter EWD), Winship's testimony on September 8, 1919, p. 825.

77. Bethel to Winship, January 6, 1919; Hubert J. Turney to Winship, January 23, 1918; Bethel to Winship, January 20, 1919 [RG 120 E 1772 010.2/5]; Berntheizel to Moseley, October 24, 1918; Moseley to Berntheizel, November 11, 1918 [GVM/1].

78. Herman Decius to McCorkle, January 3, 1919; Hubert J. Turney to J. A. 91st Division, January 26, 1919 [NA RG 120 E 1772 010.2/5]. Of interest, McCorkle had a long and varied career. In 1936 he returned to the line, and in 1955 he retired as a general from the United States Air Force as a missile officer. On Lauchheimer, see "Obituary," *Report of the Annual Meeting of the Maryland Bar Association* (Baltimore, 1936), 30.

79. *Columbia Alumni News*, May 17, 1918 (New York: Columbia Alumni Federation, 1919), 1018; "Charles S. Albert Seeks to Convert Wickersham," *New York Times*, April 3, 1915; F. M. Coulter, History of Kentucky in Five Volumes, 65; "As we don't see them," *Columbia Spectator*, October 21, 1936; "Leon Fraser Is Now a Sergeant Major," *Columbia Spectator*, October 25, 1917; Bayne, Memoirs [HAB-UNC/R-3].

80. "Candidates Named for Alumni Trustee Election," *The Princeton Alumni Weekly*, February 22, 1930, 509.

81. "Many Trials, Lots of Firsts: Hebling, Long Arm of the Law," *Beaver County Times*, February 8, 1974, p. 15. On Dabney, see Frederick S. Mead, *Harvard's Military Record in World War* (Boston: Harvard Alumni Association, 1921), 241.

82. Gerald H. Hagar, "Judge Advocate General's Department in the American Expeditionary Forces," *California Law Review* 8, no. 5 (1920): 300–327. On Brinton, see Michael Haag, *Alexandria: City of Memory* (New Haven, CT: Yale University Press, 2004), 126; Bayne, Memoirs [HAB-UNC/R-3].

83. For information on the prison farm abuses, see *Hearings Before a Sub-Committee No. 3 (Foreign Expenditures) of the Select Committee on Expenditures in the War Department, House of Representatives, Sixty-Sixth Congress* (Washington, DC: GPO, 1920).

84. See "General March Tells of Cruelty in Army Prisons," *New York Times*, July 24, 1919.

85. Kincaid to Bethel, September 1, 1918; Kincaid and Lieutenant Colonel J. Mayhew Wainright to General John F. O'Ryan, December 26, 1918 [RG 120—Loose Files].

86. General Court Martial no. 324, May 19, 1919.

87. A. L. James to Wilson, December 12, 1918 [SW-UK/1918-77-1]; Bulletin No. 1, January 7, 1919; Memorandum 17, January 6, 1919 [CM 1919].

88. Wilson to John J. Davis, March n.d., 1919.

89. Memorandum, February 15, 1919.

90. See Wilson, Case file on Revnes, including Judge Advocate Review and Advice, January 26, 1919; and Major General Alexander to Wilson [SW-UK/1898–1919]. On disciplinary aspects of the "Lost Battalion," see Robert H. Ferrell, *Five Days in October: The Lost Battalion of World War I* (Columbia: University of Missouri Press, 2005), 36–37; and Alan D. Gaff, *Blood in the Argonne: The Lost Battalion of World War I* (Norman: University of Oklahoma Press, 2008), 201–271. Ferrell notes that Colonel James Mayes recommended disapproving Revenes's conviction and dismissal, but this occurred on the basis of Wilson's advice.

91. Wilson to Major General Alexander, October 1, 1918; Trial of Major Sanders, December 1, 1918.

92. Wilson to Alexander, March 18, 1919; Winship to Wilson, March 19, 1919 [SW-UK/1919].

93. Seating List, Dinner tendered to the Officers of the Seventy-Seventh Division, Waldorf Astoria: Tuesday May Sixth, 1919 [SW-UK/1918-77-1]; Bethel to Wilson, March 31, 1919; Wilson to Bethel, April 4, 1919 [SW-UK/1919] ;Wilson, telegram, May 1, 1919; Miko Kessler to Wilson, March 17, 1919; Hugh Drum to Wilson, March 16, 1919; Stephens Blakely to Wilson, March 4, 1919.

94. James Beauchamp Clark to his son James Clark, March 18, 1918 [JBC/MH]; Lewis Strauss to Frankfurter, November 18, 1918 [FF-Harv/R-15]. On Wilson's reluctance, see John Whiteclay Chambers, *The Tyranny of Change* (New Brunswick, NJ: Rutgers University Press, 1992), 260. On the formation and reasons for the expeditions, see George H. Cassar, *Lloyd George at War: 1916–1918* (London: Anthem Press, 2011), 285–286.

95. Crowder to Pershing, July 22, 1918 [JJP/14]. On Baker's disagreement with Wilson's decision to send soldiers to Russia, see Douglas B. Craig, *Progressives at War: William G. McAdoo and Newton Baker* (Baltimore: Johns Hopkins University Press, 2003), 215.

96. Wambaugh to Baker, February 12, 1919 [NDB/7]; *Collins v. McDonald*, 258 U.S. 416 (1922).

97. Fred L. Borch III, "Bolsheviks, Polar Bears, and Military Law: The Experiences of Army Lawyers in North Russia and Siberia in World War I," *Prologue* 181–191; also "Albert John Galen," *The Michigan Alumnus* 42 (1936): 512. On Stewart, see Byron Farwell, *Over There: The United States in the Great War, 1917–1918*, 278–281.

98. Trial of 2d Lieutenant John Barnes, General Court-Martial Orders no. 9, November 6, 1919; Trial of 1st Lieutenant Jesse Edward Ballou, General Court Martial Orders no. 10, November 6, 1919; Trial of 1st Lieutenant Jefferson Moffitt, General Court Martial Orders no. 8; General Court-Martial Orders no. 172, November 26, 1918 [NA RG 395 NM-94 E-6003]; Trial of Cook T. Murtaugh, General Court-Martial Orders no. 14, October 24, 1918. On the poor start to the expedition, see Carl J. Richard, *When the United States invaded Russia: Woodrow Wilson's Siberian Disaster* (Lanham, MD: Rowman and Littlefield, 2013), 56–59.

99. General Court-Martial Orders no. 35, December 19, 1919 [RG 395 NM-94 E-6003]. See also Carl J. Richard, *When the United States Invaded Russia*, 62; and Ronald E. Powaski, *The Cold War: The United States and the Soviet Union, 1917–1991* (1998), 21–23.

100. General Court-Martial Orders no. 26, January 30, 1920 [RG 395 NM-94 E-6003].

101. See Robert Willett, *Russian Sideshow: America's Undeclared War, 1918–1920* (Washington, DC: Potomac Books, 2003), 122–128; Thurston to Acting Judge Advocate General, AEF, February 28, 1919 [NA RG 153 PC 29 E 53 370.7/B9]. On the relations with the British, see Ronald Powaski, *The Cold War: The United States and the Soviet Union*, 22.

102. Charles Beecher Warren to Adjutant General, May 7, 1917 [CEL U. Mich/2]; Lt Col Edward R. Thurston to Lewis, June 14, 1919 [CEL U-Mich/2]; September 18, 1918; October 3, 1918; Death certificate. Lewis died in 1981 at the age of ninety-two.

103. Lewis to Capt D. A. Stroh, December 29, 1932 [CEL U. Mich/2].

104. Opinions of the Judge Advocate General (Washington, DC: GPO, 1919), 2:1032.

105. Ronald Powaski, *The Cold War: The United States and the Soviet Union*, 25–28.

106. Crowder to Baker , n.d., 1919 [RG, 153.2.1].

107. Morgenthau to Harbord, June 25, 1919; Harbord to Morgenthau, June 28, 1919; General Orders 87. See also Richard Hovannisian, *The Republic of Armenia: The First Year, 1918–1919* (Los Angeles: University of California Press, 1971), 1:338–339; Martin Sickler, *The Middle East in the Twentieth Century* (New York: Praeger, 2001), 122–124; Richard Hovannisian, "The Armenia Genocide and Post-War Commissions," in *America and the Armenian Genocide*, ed. Jay Winter (London: Cambridge University Press, 2004); Secil Karal Akgun, "The General Harbord Commission and the American Mandate Question," in George Sellers, *Studies in Ataturk's Turkey: The American Dimension*, 55–82.

108. Harbord, *Report of the American Military Mission to Armenia*; [RG 256, 184.021]; also, George van Horn Moseley, *Mandatory Over Armenia: Report Made to Maj Gen James G. Harbord on the Military Problem of a Mandatory over Armenia* (Washington, DC: GPO, 1920).

109. Harbord to Wadsworth, n.d., 1919; Brinton to Wadsworth, n.d., 1919 [JWW/32].

110. Moseley, diary entry for November 1, 1919 [GVM/5]; Taft to Brinton, November 23, 1923 [WHT/R-258].

111. Todd to Allen and Liggett, December 22, 1921 [RG 120, General Correspondence, 1919–1923 E1362].

CHAPTER 6

1. Williams to Tumulty, January 7, 1916 [JSW/1]; Tumulty to Williams, January 10, 1916 [JSW/1]; *Keyes v. United States*, 15 Cl. Ct. 532 (Ct. Cl. 1878); *Keyes v. United States*, 109 U.S. 336 (1883); Williams to Wilson, June 14, 1917 [JSW/2].

2. On Van Buren, see Donald P. Cole, *Martin van Buren and the American Political System* (Princeton, NJ: Princeton University Press, 1984), 37–40; Anthony J. Yanik, *The Fall and Recapture*

of Detroit: In Defense of William Hull (Detroit: Wayne State University Press, 2011), 106; Robert H. Zieger, *America's Great War: World War I and the American Experience* (Lanham, MD: Rowman and Littlefield, 2000), 58–64.

3. Wilson to Crowder, November 7, 1917 [WWP/R88].

4. Private John Kelsey to Wilson, June 4, 1917; Baker to Wilson, June 11, 1917; Wilson to Frankfurter, June 21, 1917; Frankfurter to Wilson, June 12, 1917 [WW/R88].

5. Crowder to Greene, February 11, 1914 [FLG/25]; "In Defense of the Right to Trial by Jury—Ex Parte Milligan: Extension of Remarks of Hon. William Gordon of Ohio, October 6, 1914; Section 3 of Article 110 of Section 1342, Revised Statutes, Report to accompany H.R. 8479 [FLG/25].

6. David Hilger to Walsh, May 6, 1914; Sloan to Walsh, May 28, 1914 [TWP/11]. See also Edward M. Coffman, *The Regulars: The American Army, 1898–1941*, 121–122.

7. Jones to J.W. Levy, April 3, 1913; Crowder to Jones, April 14, 1913; Jones to Garrison, April 14, 1913; Garrison to Jones, June 6, 1913; General Court Martial Orders no. 51, March 12, 1913 [WLJ-UW/152]; also John Weeks to Crowder, April 1, 1917 [JWW-RSC/4-f2].

8. Chamberlain to Wilson, June n.d; Crowder, Review of Mason Court Martial, to Garrison, June 18, 1914 [WWP/R318 C1557].

9. Crowder to Garrison, July 7, 1914; Wilson to Chamberlain, July 8, 1914 [WWP/R318 C1557].

10. Douglas B. Craig, *Progressives at War: William G. McAdoo and Newton Baker*, 190.

11. Congressman Henry Bruckner to Wilson, December 11, 1914; Herbert White to Garrison, December 11, 1914; Crowder to Garrison, December 21, 1914 [WWP R 319, C1617]; Papers associated with General Court Martial Order no. 112, January 18, 1918 [RG 393 E 1594—Eastern Department].

12. Williams to JAGO, May 1, 1917; Bethel to Williams, May 10, 1917 [JSW/26].

13. Congressman Daniel Garrett to Wilson, August 6, 1917; Ansell to Baker, August 22, 1917 [WWP R363, C4222].

14. Congressman A. S. Kreider to Wilson, May 29, 1917; Ansell to Baker, August 22, 1917 [WWP R359, C3992].

15. Hinds to Wilson, n.d.; Crowder to Baker, n.d. 1917 [WWP/R319 C1627].

16. McCain to Saulsbury, January 4, 1917; Joseph Frazier to McCain, November 17, 1916; Colonel Dickinson to Saulsbury, November 14, 1916; Conrad Bock, November 20, 1916 [WS U-Del/47 f-24].

17. P. J. Harris to Glass, September 10, 1918; General McCain to Glass, July 2, 1918; Glass to Reverend Calloway, June 29, 1918 ; J. Calloway Robertson, June 22, 1918 [CG-UVA/121].

18. Walsh to Tumulty, April 9, 1919; Benedict Crowell to Tumulty, April 10, 1919; James Gavillan to Tumulty, April 14, 1919; Kreger to Tumulty, April 15, 1919; E.B. Howard to Tumulty, August 18, 1919; E. B. Howard to Tumulty, August 28, 1919; Kreger to Tumulty, September 25, 1919 [WWP R361, C 4983].

19. Baskin to Lever, April 3, 1919 [FAL-STI/3]; Crowder to Lever, April 6, 1919 [FAL-STI/3]; Kreger to Lever, May 6, 1919 [FAL-STI/4].

20. A good judicial discussion on the difference between conscription in World War I and World War II is found in *Billings v. Truesdell*, 321 U.S. 542 (1944). On Borah, see *John Chalmers Vinson, William E. Borah and the Outlawry of War* (Athens: University of Georgia Press, 1957), 5–7.

21. Borah to Stimson, May 1, 1908; Roosevelt to Stimson, May 4, 1908; Borah to Stimson, May 8, 1908; Roosevelt to Stimson, May 16, 1908 [HLS/R-16]; Crowder to Stimson, May 17, 1917 [HLS/R-49].

22. Ralph E. Mitchell to Borah, February 10, 1919 [WEB/70]; Arnold McBride to Borah, February 12, 1919 [WEB/70].

23. Abraham Lincoln Post no. 1 to Borah, April 24, 1920 [WEB/82]; Crowder to Borah, May 6, 1920 [WEB/82]; Crowder to Borah, May 21, 1920 [WEB/82].

24. Marian J. Maynard to Borah, January 30, 1919 [WEB/70].

25. La Follette to Baker, October 1, 1919; Adjutant General, October 27, 1919 to La Follette, La Follette to Anna Snyder, October 22, 1919.

26. Cadotte to La Follette, January 10, 1920 ; JAG to La Follette, February 1, 1920 [LFFP/I:C 74].

27. General Prisoner Gonzalez to Senator La Follette, January 25, 1920, February 1, 1920 [LFFP/I:C 74].

28. A. W. O'Rourke to Miles Taylor, October 22, 1920; Walsh to General P. C. Harris, Adj Gen., October 26, 1920; General Harris, Adj Gen. to Walsh, November 1, 1920; Walsh to O'Rourke, November 2, 1920; A.O. O'Rourke to Miles Taylor, November 24, 1920 [TWP/216].

29. George Goethals, diary entry for February 21, 1918 [GG/1].

30. See "Petitions for the Pardon of Louis Gibson," May 1919 [RG E 25A/ Boxes 1-4]. On the reporting of Neville's efforts, see *North Platte Semi-Weekly*, May 23, 1919, p. 1; *Dakota County Herald*, May 22, 1919, p. 1; *Red Cloud Chief*, May 29, 1919, p. 1.

31. Guerin, draft letter for Hull, June 8, 1921; Hull to McKellar and Byrnes, July 2, 1921 [RG E12D, Papers of Colonel Mark Guerin/1].

32. Hull to McKellar and Byrnes, July 2, 1921; notations in Guerin's files [RG E12D, Papers of Colonel Mark Guerin/1].

33. Hines to Wurzbach, November 13, 1922 [JLH/6].

34. Glass to Holmes, November 7, 1918 [CG-UVA/100].

35. William Calder to James Weldon, March 10, 1919; John R. Shillady to Mr. Stanley King, January 13, 1919 ; Stanley King to Shillady, January 17, 1919; Stanley King to Shillady, January 3, 1919; General Court-Martial Orders no. 244, November 20, 1918 [NAACP/C-374].

36. Crowder to Baker, January 2, 1918 NARA.

37. Robert Wooster, *The Military and United States Indian Policy*, 1865–1903 (Lincoln: University of Nebraska Press, 1988), 67; Crowder to Garrison, June 22, 1914; B. Dively to A. Mitchell Palmer, June 16, 1914 [WWP/ R318, C1516].

38. Headquarters Eastern Department, General Court-Martial, General Orders no. 32, January 22, 1918 [RG 393 Pt 1 E1594].

39. See e.g. Walter E. Barton, *The History and Influence of the American Psychiatric Association* (New York: APA, 1987), 126; Mary C. Gillette, *The Army Medical Department, 1917-1940*, 377–380; Edgar Jones and Simon Wesley, *Military Psychiatry from 1900 to the Gulf War* (Sussex, UK: Psychiatry Press, 2005), 19–24.

40. General W. G. Haan to Pershing, November 9, 1918; Easby-Smith to Tumulty, June 18, 1919 [WWW R360, C4987].

41. John Greene to William Redfield, September 13, 1920; Henry M. Cotton, MD to Redfield, December 13, 1920; Crowder to Redfield, June 17, 1920 [WWP/R362 C 5203].

42. Crowder to Tumulty, March 8, 1920 [WWP/R362 C 5194].

43. Sanders to Chamberlain, January 2, 1920; Sanders to La Follette, January 19, 1920; Sanders to La Follette, June 15, 1920; Summerall to La Follette, July 2, 1920 [LFFP/I:C 74].

44. Sanders case file, id.

45. Hitchcock to Peyton March, June 24, 1919 [GH/1].

46. General Court Martial Orders, no. 24, March 19, 1918 [WEB/49]. There is little on Church, but see Caserne Desjardins, "The History of the 16th Engineers, First Depot Division, American Expeditionary Forces, France.

47. J. H. Gibson to Borah, April 27, 1918 [WEB/49]; American Red Cross to Borah, May 21, 1918 [WEB/49]; Gibson to Borah, June 13, 1918 [WEB/49].

48. Inspector General to War Department, conveyed to Nugent, May 25, 1918 [WEB/49].

49. Borah to Baker, June 1, 1918 [WEB/49]; Baker to Borah, June 1, 1918 [WEB/49].

50. E. G. Davis to Adjutant General, June 25, 1918 [WEB/49]; Baker to Borah, June 18, 1918 [WEB/49].

51. Anthony Babington, *Shell-Shock: A History of the Changing Attitudes to War Neurosis* (London: Pen and Sword, 1997), 89–107.

52. *Hearings Before the Committee on Military Affairs, Second Session on HR 12731,* August 19, 1918, vol. 5 (Washington, DC: GPO, 1918); American Federation of Labor to Senator Charles S. Thomas, August 10, 1918; American Federation of Labor to Frank Lester Greene, August 25, 1918 [FLG/34]; Crowder to Brandeis, March 32, 1918 [LDB-LU/60].

53. Johnson to Knox, November 16, 1917 [PKP/30]; Richard Coke Lower, *A Bloc of One: The Political Career of Hiram Johnson* (San Francisco: Stanford University Press, 1993), 106–107; Archibald M. Johnson to Philander Knox, November 16, 1917 [PKP/30]; Johnson to Wilson, August 25, 1917; Johnson to Crowder, August 22, 1917 [NDB/2].

54. Watson, "All Aboard for the State Convention," *The Jeffersonian,* August 9, 1917, p. 8.

55. Crowder to Tumulty, November 30, 1917 [JPT/10]; Poindexter to Crowder, August 26, 1917; Poindexter to Oliver Leiser, August 28, 1917; Poindexter to Leiser, September 14, 1917 [MP-UW/115/f1]; Poindexter, Speech Notes, July 25, 1917 [MP-UW/82 f9].

56. Walsh to Kalispell mayor, June 2, 1917 [TWP/268].

57. Provost Marshal Report, 62–63.

58. John Whiteclay Chambers, *The Tyranny of Change* (New Brunswick, NJ: Rutgers University Press, 1992), 240; Thomas J. Knock, *To End All Wars,* 132; and Jeremy K. Kessler, "The Administrative Origins of Modern Civil Liberties Law," *Columbia Law Review* (June 2010): 1083.

59. Frankfurter to Baker, September 18, 1917 [FF/R-92]. For further information, see H. C. Patterson and Gilbert Fite, *Opponents of the War, 1917–1918,* 124; Jeremy Kessler, "The Administrative Origins of Modern Civil Liberties Law"; and Samuel Wilson, *In Defense of American Liberties: A History of the ACLU,* 2nd ed. (London: Oxford University Press, 1990), 18.

60. David M. Kennedy, *Over Here: The First World War and American Society,* 164.

61. Jeremey Kessler, "The Administrative Origins of Modern Civil Liberties Law," 1133; Walter Guest Kellogg, *The Conscientious Objector* (New York: Boni & Liveright, 1919), 25.

62. Crowder to Walsh, July 11, 1918 [TWP/217]; Crowder to Kitchin, May 22, 1917 [CK-UNC/21 f-285]. See also Alex Matthews Arnett, *Claude Kitchen and the Wilson War Policies* (New York: Russell and Russell, 1937), 53–65.

63. Crowder to Glass, December 7, 1917; Glass to A. V. Hicks, December 17, 1917 [CG-UVA/100]. On the case of Private Robert J. Dooley, see Crowder to Glass, March 16, 1918, and Major Roscoe S. Conkling to Glass, March 19, 1918 [CG-UVA/100]; Glass to Ms. Bessie L. Stratton, September 22, 1917 [CG-UVA/100]; *Ehlert v. United States,* 402 U.S. 99 (1971).

64. Cooper to Poindexter, July 1, 1918; Poindexter to Adjutant General, July 6, 1918; Poindexter to W. W. Cooper, July 6, 1918; Adjutant General to Cooper, August 9, 1918 [MP-UW/118/2].

65. Tillman to Warren, April 25, 1918 [BRT-STI/22].

66. Baker to Walsh, October 21, 1919; "Conscientious Objector Tortured at Alcatraz Island," *St. Paul Enterprise,* October 14, 1919 [TWP/162].

67. Baker to Norris, February 2, 1920 [GWN/46]; Norris to Baker, January 23, 1920 [GWN/46].

68. Walsh to Fred Gabriel, County Attorney to Walsh, March 3, 1919; Gabriel to Walsh, March 25, 1919; Walsh to Crowder, March 31, 1919; R. O. Wilmarth to Walsh, April 3, 1919; Walsh to General P. C. Harris, Adj Gen, April 4, 1919 [TWP/217].

69. Thomas Marshall, *Recollections of Thomas Marshall,* 72.

70. J. B. Mullins to Senator Swanson, June 2, 1911; Crowder to Senator Swanson, June 11, 1920 [CAS-UVA/3].

71. Watson to Crowder, October 20, 1921 [TEW-UNC].

72. On Calley, see Telford Taylor, *Nuremberg and Vietnam: An American Tragedy* (Chicago: Quadrangle, 1976) , 138; Guenther Lewy, *America in Vietnam* (New York: Oxford University Press, 1978), 356–361; William Thomas Allison, *Military Justice in Vietnam: The Rule of Law in an American War* (Lawrence: University Press of Kansas, 2007), 93–97.

73. "Proof is Lacking: Dr. Denies Griffiths was Mentally Incapable: Court-Martial Near End," *The Morning Oregonian,* June 4, 1914; "Griffiths Admits He Was Short of Army Funds," *The Tacoma Times,* June 13, 1914, p. 2; "Griffiths Guilty," *The Morning Oregonian,* June 28, 1914; "Wilson Approves," *Honolulu Star Bulletin,* September 29, 1914, p. 6. The court-martial was also reported in

scattered fashion across the country. See e.g. "Army Officer Sentenced," *Evening Times Iowa Republican*, September 11, 1914.

74. Kreger to Watson, July 25, 1921 [TEW-UNC].

75. Hull to Watson, August 25, 1922 [TEW-UNC].

76. Court-martial record papers of Edward M. Harding [WWP R397, C4990].

77. James B. Regan to Tumulty, April 16, 1919 [WWP/R397, C4990]; Kreger to Tumulty, April 24, 1919.

78. Kreger to Lever, October 10, 1919 [FAL-STI/4].

79. For a background on Chamberlain, see Allan C. Bevilacqua, "The Strange Case of Edmund Chamberlain," *Leatherneck* 92, no. 5 (May 2009): 32–35.

80. "Doubt Story of Heroism: Court-Martial to Investigate Exploits of Captain Chamberlain," *New York Times*, March 15, 1919.

81. Auchincloss to Gregory, February 27, 1923 [TWG/10-f1].

82. See e.g. "Hero Ace," *Bismarck Tribune*, September 18, 1919; "Marine Officer Is Given High Honors," *Arizona Republican*, September 16, 1918, p. 2.

83. J. M. Salmond to Minister for Air and Judge Advocate General of the United States Navy, October 4, 1918 [TWG/10-f2]; C. N. Lowe to Air Ministry, undated [TWG/10-f2].

84. David Cronon, ed., *The Cabinet Diaries of Josephus Daniels* (Lincoln: University of Nebraska Press, 1963), entry for December 6, 1919, 467. See also "Daniels Condemns Captain Chamberlain: Approves Sentence of Dismissal by Court-Martial for False Story of Air Exploits," *New York Times*, December 9, 1919, Senate Bill 2039, 67 Cong. 1st Sess, June 10, 1921; Gregory to Sheppard, August 19, 1921 [TWG/10-f2]; "Senators Close Doors in Air Hero Inquiry," *Washington Evening Star*, June 26, 1921 p. 5.

85. Gregory to Auchincloss, February 26, 1923 [TWG/10-f1].

86. Gregory to Auchincloss, February 26, 1923 [TWG/10-f1]; Gregory to Auchincloss, March 2, 1923 [TWG/10-f1]; Edwin Chamberlain to Gregory, August 23, 1923; Edwin Chamberlain to Senator Morris Sheppard, December 3, 1923; Edwin Chamberlain to Gregory, December 11, 1924 [TWG/10-f1]; Morris Sheppard to Edwin Chamberlain, December 22, 1924.

87. Edwin Chamberlain to Gregory, December 24, 1924 [TWG/10-f1]; Gregory to Edwin Chamberlain, December 26, 1924 [TWG/10-f1]; Osborne to Chamberlain, December 28, 1924 [TWG/10-f1]; Gregory to Burkinshaw, January 8, 1925 [TWG/10-f1].

88. Gregory to Chamberlain, February 7, 1925 [TWG/10-f1].

89. Gregory to Chamberlain, January 11, 1926 [TWG/10-f1]; *Chamberlain v. United States*, 66 Ct. Cl. 317 (1928); *Chamberlain v. United States*, 279 U.S. 845 (1929)

90. R. Hawley to Ansell, December 19, 1918 [RG 165 E310, Records of the War Department and Special Staffs—Judge Advocate Records B227].

91. T. R. Hawley to Ansell, December 19, 1918 [RG 165 E310, Records of the War Department and Special Staffs—Judge Advocate Records B227]; Baker to Assistant Secretary of War, September 15, 1919 [NDB/9].

92. Carter Glass, Statement by Carter Glass, December 27, 1918 [WHW/9]; Glass to Lindsley, January 8, 1919 [CG-UVA/140].

93. La Follette to Glass, n.d. march 1918 [LFFP/I:C 74]

94. Lever to Crowder, December 1, 1918; Glass to Lever, December 27, 1918 [FAL-STI/3]; Smith to Crowder, December 27, 1918 [MHS-UGA/26].

95. See William H. White, case of Ms. Myrtle Burford, February 1, 1919. On the other cases, see files of Brannigan, Wood, Berube, Jewell, Pouliot, Woodhead, Forcier, Ricker, Jacob, Roberge, Robertson, Furbish, Connor, Glidden, Richmond, Simard, True, Bucker, et al. [WHW/9].

96. Edmund J. Arsenault files, February 15, 1919 [WHW/9].

97. Louis J. Braun to White, December 6, 1919; Adjutant General to White, December 26, 1919 [WHW/30].

98. Crowder to Adjutant General, February 1, 1918; Bulletin no. 31, Campo Upton, February 12, 1918 [SW-UK/CM-1918].

99. Lt. C. W. Fee to Poindexter, October 1, 1918; Poindexter to Baker, October 24, 1918; McAdoo to Poindexter, October 30, 1918, Chamberlain to Poindexter, November 4, 1918; Lansing to Poindexter, November 26, 1918 [MP-UW/119f4].

100. M. H. Carter to Stedman, November 12, 1917; Stedman to Crowder, November 19, 1917 [CMS-UNC/f-5].

101. Clark to Charles Warren, June 15, 1917; Breckinridge Long to Clark, June 19, 1917; Charles Warren to Lansing, June 15, 1917; Long to Attorney General Gregory, June 12, 1917; Frank Polk to Secretary of Labor, June 9, 1917; Long to Clark, June 8, 1917 [BL/25].

102. S. P. Ferguson to Flood, April 3, 1918; Flood to Crowder, April 24, 1918; Crowder to Cronkhite, April 26, 1918.

103. Kreger to Hull, August 15, 1919 [CH/R 1].

104. Crowder to Flood n.d. 1919 [HDF/82].

105. "Accuses Pershing of Ignoring Order," New York Times, February 28, 1919, p. 1; "Says Cabinet Members Kept Sons out of War," New York Times, February 16, 1919. Although Johnson convened the hearing, the congressional investigation might not have occurred at all if Congressman Frederick Dallinger, a Massachusetts Republican, had not lobbied Johnson to investigate the claims of his constituents; March's testimony begins at 164.

106. Hearings Before a Sub-Committee no. 3, 164.

107. Hearings Before a Sub-Committee no. 3, 1182.

108. Flood to Congressman W. J. Graham, July 25, 1919 [HDF/82]; Hubert F. Fisher to Flood, July 19, 1919 [HDF/82]. After Flood accused the Republican majority of relying on the testimony of convicted soldiers, two former soldiers filed suit against him. The court ultimately dismissed the lawsuit. Ira F. Morgan to Flood, January 13, 1920 [HDF/82].

CHAPTER 7

1. On Haywood, see J. Anthony Lukas, Big Trouble: A Murder in a Small Western Town Sets Off a Struggle for the Soul of America (New York: Simon and Schuster, 1997), 687–721.

2. Garrison to Crowder, June 1913 [LMGP-SGM]; Crowder to William L. Thompson, December 12, 1913 [EHC/66]; "Army Witness Found Dead," San Francisco Call, June 21, 1913, p. 14; "Army Board Sustains All Treason Charges," San Francisco Call, August 11, 1913, p. 2; Spokesman Review, June 24, 1913, p. 7; Daily Capitol Journal, June 21, 1913, p. 10; Senate Bill 4023; Philip Sheldon Foner, Militarism and Organized Labor, 1900–1914 (Minneapolis: MEP Publications, 1987), 18; "Relief for Dishonorably Discharged Soldier," Army and Navy Register, March 21, 1914, p. 364.

3. NARA RG 153, General Court Martial Offense Ledger Sheets, 1919, Box 3; John Reed, "At the Throat of the Republic," The Masses, vol. 8, no. 9 (July 1916),: 7–11.

4. Gilbert E. Roe to Borah, August 1918 [WEB/70].

5. John Chalmers Vinson, William E. Borah and the Outlawry of War, 3–4.

6. Ray Talbert, Negative Intelligence, 97.

7. Prettyman, diary entry for September 8, 1918 [EBPP/1].

8. Baker to Webb, August 11, 1916 [EYW-UNC/14].

9. Frankfurter to Baker, February 8, 1917; Baker to Frankfurter, April 3, 1917; Baker to Frankfurter, April 11, 1917 [FF-Harv/R13]; Crowder to Frankfurter, February 20, 1917 [FF-Harv/R30].

10. General Barry, memoranda of meeting, Sunday night, April 1, 1917; Barry to Baker, April 20, 1917 [NDB/1].

11. Patterson v. Colorado, 205 U.S. 454 (1907); Crowder to Clark, July 29, 1917 [RG 120, E2215, B1].

12. Ernest Freeberg, Democracy's Prisoner: Eugene V. Debs, the Great War and the Right to Dissent (Cambridge, MA: Harvard University Press, 2008), 4–30; John Whiteclay Chambers II, The Tyranny of Change (New Brunswick, NJ: Rutgers University Press, 1992), 240–246. For a discussion on

the Defense Secrets Act and the Espionage Act, see Patricia L. Bellia, "Wikileaks and the Institutional Framework for National Security Disclosures," *Yale Law Journal* 121, no. 1448 (2012): 1486–1487. For state antisyndicalism laws, see Thomas Ralph Clark, *Defending Rights: Law, Labor, and Politics in California, 1890–1920* (Detroit: Wayne State University Press, 2002), 186–189.

13. Campbell to Charles Clyne, US Attorney, January 4, 1919 [RG 165 B 4050]; Edwin P. Grosvenor, Law Officer, Negative Branch to Captain Schmuck, October 31, 1918 [RG 165 B 4050].

14. H. R. Corbin to Major General Merriam, May 31, 1899, and R. A. Alger to General Merriam, May 31, 1899 [WMK/7]; Baker to Josephus Daniels, October 24, 1919 [JD/3]; John Henry Wigmore, *A Source Book on Military Law and Wartime Legislation* (Minneapolis: West Publishing, 1919), 148–150. On the IWW and the war, see Melvin Dubofsky, *We Shall Be All: A History of the I.W.W.*, 2nd ed. (Champaign: University of Illinois Press, 1988), 356–383. On Walsh, see J. Leonard Bates, *Senator Thomas Walsh of Montana: Law and Public Affairs, from TR to FDR* (Champaign: University of Illinois Press, 1999), 148.

15. Creel to Wilson, January 25, 1918 [GC/3]; Creel to Wilson, February 12, 1918; Melvin Urofsky and Paul Finkleman, *A March of Liberty*, 2:613–614; George Creel, *The German Bolshevik Conspiracy Issued by The Committee on Public Information* (Washington, DC: War Dept, 1918).

16. John D. Inazu, *Liberty's Refuge: The Forgotten Freedom of Assembly* (New Haven, CT: Yale University Press, 2012), 46–48.

17. John Milton Cooper Jr., *Pivotal Decades: The United States, 1900–1920*, 146; Richard H. Frost, *The Mooney Case*, 66; Frankfurter to Lippman, June 21, 1917 [WL-SML/R-9]; Joan M. Jensen, *Army Surveillance in America, 1775–1980* (New Haven: Yale University Press, 1991), 172.

18. "Benedetto Brin Trial," *Army-Navy Times*, September 21, 1918, p. 90; Lawrence Sondhaus, *The Naval Policy of Austria-Hungary, 1867–1918: Navalism, Industrial Development, and the Politics of Dualism* (West Lafayette, IN: Purdue University Press, 1994), 290.

19. Frankfurter to Baker, August 7, 1918 [NDB/1]; Chief of Engineers to Bliss, June 25, 1917 [THB/214]; Bliss to bureau chiefs on document [THB/214].

20. Alistair Horne, "Petain," in Michael Carver, *The Warlords* (London: Pen and Sword, 2005), 198; Jean-Jacques Becker, "Opposition to the War in France: The Case of Clovis Andrieu," in Hugh Cecil and Peter Lidle, eds., *Facing Armageddon: The First World War Experience* (London: Pen and Sword, 1996), 677–678.

21. Leonard Smith, "Remobilizing the French Soldier through the French Mutinies of 1917," in John Horne, ed., *State, Society and Mobilization in Europe During the First World War* (London: Cambridge University Press, 1997), 144–159; also Leonard Smith, "Narrative and Identity at the Front: Theory and the Poor Bloody Infantry," in *The Great War and the Twentieth Century*, ed. Geoffrey Parker (New Haven, CT: Yale University Press, 2001), 132–166; Jere Clemens King, General and Politicians (Los Angeles: University of California Press, 1951), 202; John Terraine, *The Great War* (London: Wordsworth, 1965), 128; Gordon Wright, *Raymond Poincare and the French Presidency* (San Francisco: Stanford University Press, 1942), 184–185; Basil Liddell Hart, *The Real War, 1914–1918*, 300–303.

22. On Caillaux's political views, see, John V. F. Keiger, *France and the Origin of the First World War* (New York: St. Martin's Press, 1983), 35 and 87; Paul B. Miller, *From Revolutionaries to Citizens: Anti-Militarism in France, 1870–1914* (Durham, NC: Duke University Press, 2002), 173; and Benjamin F. Martin, *The Hypocrisy of Justice in the Belle Epoque* (Baton Rouge: Louisiana State University Press, 1984), 151–225.

23. "Arrest Bolo Pasha as a German Agent," *New York Times*, September 30, 1917; Bayne, *Memoirs*, 45.

24. Bureau of Intelligence, Synopsis to Bureau and Staff Chiefs, June 27, 1918 [NA RG 393 Pt 1. E4429 B1].

25. John H. Sherwood, *Georges Mandel and the Third Republic* (Palo Alto, CA: Stanford University Press, 1970), 20–25; Jere Clemens King, *Generals and Politicians*, 202.

26. On Frankfurter, see Frankfurter to Wilson and Crowder, June 1917 [FF-Harv/120] and Frankfurter to Baker, August 7, 1917 [NDB/1]. Frankfurter's letter to Baker was sent under seal for

both Baker's and Wilson's consideration; see Baker to Wilson, August 12, 1917 [NDB/3]. See also Richard M. Watt, *Dare Call it Treason: The True Story of the French Army Mutinies of 1917* (New York: Dorset Press, 1969), 199–224; Hunter Liggett, *The American Expeditionary Forces*, 10–11.

27. On fears of an "enemy from within," see generally Jennifer Weber, *Copperheads: The Rise and Fall of Lincoln's Opponents in the North* (New York: Oxford, 2006); and Wood Gray, *The Hidden Civil War: The Story of the Copperheads* (New York: Viking, 1942).

28. On German immigration, see Frederick Luebke, *Bonds of Loyalty: German Americans in World War I* (DeKalb: Northern Illinois University Press, 1974), 1–7.

29. Overman Committee Conclusions, 10; Robert Lansing, *War Memoirs*, 73.

30. Niall Ferguson, *The Pity of War: Explaining World War I* (New York: Basic Books, 1998), 339–366.

31. Ray Talbert, *Negative Intelligence*, 49.

32. Pomerene to Baker, January 8, 1919 [NDB8]; Frankfurter to Baker, September 4, 1917 [NDB/1]; Melvin Urofsky, *Louis Brandeis: A Life*, 498.

33. Report 10317-254, 5-6, JAG April 9, 1919 [RG 165/E 58 B56]; Report 10541-268, JAG to MID; October 24, 1918; Report 10541-268-208, MID to JAG [RG 165/E 58 B56]. Colonel R. H. Van Denman, Chief of the Military Intelligence Section to Bureau Chiefs, December 14, 1917 [RG 393 Pt 1. E4429 B1]. See also Thomas J. Knock, *To End All Wars*, 81–82.

34. "Climax to German Intrigue," *Baltimore Sun*, March 11, 1917 [JPH/3].

35. "Officers Deplore Captain Reichmann's Note," *New York Times*, November 18, 1906; "Senate Holds Up Two Generals," *New York Times*, August 18, 1917; Report Favors Reichmann," *New York Times*, September 7, 1917.

36. Poindexter to Anderson, August 14, 1917; US Senate, Memorandum, n.d.; Ms. Faison to Anderson (and Poindexter), August 27 [MP-UW/117 f11].

37. On Poindexter's political biography and early years, see, Howard W. Allen, *Poindexter of Washington: A Study in Progressive Politics* (Carbondale: Southern Illinois University Press, 1981), 1–98.

38. Howard W. Allen, *Poindexter of Washington: A Study in Progressive Politics*, 126–189.

39. Ms. Faison to Anderson (and Poindexter), August 27 [MP-UW/117 f11]; Reichmann, Appointment, Commission, and Personal Branch Files [NA RG 94, Entry 297 Reichmann files, 4119 ACP], Record Group 94, NARA I, Washington, DC.

40. Poindexter to Chamberlain, August 16, 1917; Poindexter to Anderson, September 8, 1917; Crowder to Poindexter, September 19, 1917 [MP-UW/117 f11].

41. Joan Jensen, *The Price of Vigilance* (Chicago: Rand McNally, 1969), 122; Phillip Yanella, *The Other Carl Sandburg* (Jackson: University of Mississippi Press, 1996), 116; Mark Ellis, *Race, War and Surveillance*, 271.

42. Files of Victor C. Von Unruh, Southwestern Command, April 17, 1919; Intelligence Officer, Camp Forrest, Georgia to Police Chiefs, May 7, 1918; File no. 10446-3, May 7, 1918 [RG 393 Pt 1. E4429 B1].

43. Baker to Daniels, April 18, 1917; Baker to Daniels, July 10, 1917 [JD/38].

44. Crowder to Baker, June 29, 1918 [NDB/5]; Wilson to Creel, December 29, 1917 [GC/3]; Creel to Wilson, February 26, 1918; Wilson to Creel, March 25, 1918. Wilson also noted to Creel, "The enclosed letter from the Attorney General (which I would be very much obliged if you would return to me when you have read it), puts a very different face on the case of the young Swedes about whom you spoke to me, and I thought you ought to see it."

45. Byron Farwell, *Over There*, 53.

46. Long to Crowder, November 17, 1917 [BL/187].

47. R. L. Williams to Baker [telegram], August 4, 1917 [THB/217].

48. Nigel Anthony Sellars, *Oil, Wheat, and Wobblies: The Industrial Workers of the World in Oklahoma, 1905-1930* (Norman: University of Oklahoma Press, 1998), 77–92.

49. Reports of Bolshevism in Alaska [NA RG 165 E 54 B 18].

50. Joan Jensen, *Army Surveillance in America*, 187; Crowder, memorandum n.d., 1919, 152.2.1.

51. Lynch, Assistant United States Attorney to Breckinridge Long, October 25, 1917 [BL/187].

52. Dunn to Leland Harrison, State Department, June 1, 1918; Ansell to Adjutant General, October 8, 1918; Ansell to Attorney General Gregory, October 14, 1918; Ansell to General Holbrook, October 14, 1918; Gregory to Ansell, October 21, 1918 [NARG 153 E 390/B6 f 013.1].

53. Crowder to Baker, October 29, 1917; Crowder to IL Hunt, October 30, 1917; Ansell to Colonel I. L. Hunt, November 2, 1917; General Order 265, October 1, 1864 [RG 153 E 390/ B1 f-000.2.2]; *Flower v. United States*, 407 U.S. 97 (1972); and *Greer v. Spock*, 424 U.S. 828 (1976).

54. Colonel M. Churchill to Crowder, June 26, 1918; Mayes to M. Churchill, July 11, 1918 [RG 153 E 390/B1 f 000.7]; *Coleman v. Tennessee*, 97 U.S. 509 (1878); Director Military Intelligence Division, Memorandum on "The World in Perplexity," September 18, 1918 [RG 393 Pt 1. E4429 B1].

55. Berger to House, October 2, 1917 [EMH-Yale/28]; Ernest Freeberg, *Democracy's Prisoner*, 224; Rebecca M. Shoemaker, *The White Court: Justices, Rulings, and Legacy* (Santa Barbara, CA: ABC-CLIO, 2004), 206; Thomas Healy, *The Great Dissent: How Oliver Wendell Holmes Changed his Mind—And Changed the History of Free Speech* (New York: Henry Holt, 2013), 19.

56. Berger to Judson, December 6, 1911 [WVJ-NL/1]; Berger to Judson, January 18, 1911 [WVJ-NL/1]; Judson to Burleson, June 1, 1917 [WVJ-NL/1]; Judson to Burleson, February 1, 1921 [WVJ-NL/1]; Burleson to Judson, February 3, 1917 [WVJ-NL/1]; Berger to Burleson, July 12, 1917 [AB/19].

57. Burleson to Judson, April 10, 1919 [WVJ-NL/1]; Judson to War Department, November 14, 1917 [WVJ-NL/1]. Note: Judson to War Department (Baker, but forwarded to both Crowder and Ansell). Burleson was also provided a copy of it, November 14, 1917 [for some reason the excerpt is in a file marked to Chief of MI division, November 1, 1920); Judson to Peyton C. March, May 21, 1919 [WVJ-NL/1].

58. *Berger v. United States*, 255 U.S. 22 (1921).

59. Crowder to Weeks, n.d.

60. Nina Mjagki, *Loyalty in Time of Trial: The African-American Experience During World War I* (Lanham, MD: Rowman and Littlefield, 2011); also Mark Ellis, *Race War and Surveillance*; Dubofsky, *We Shall be All: A History of the IWW*, 148–151; on Dubois, see John Whiteclay Chambers II, *To Raise an Army: The Draft Comes to Modern America*, 156.

61. Dunn to Van Deman, May 24, 1919 [NA RG 165 "Negro Subversion" M1440]; Dunn, report, February 2, 1917 [NA RG 165 "Negro Subversion" M1440].

62. Theodore Kornweibel, *Investigate Everything: Federal Efforts to Enforce Black Loyalty During World War I* (Bloomington: Indiana University Press, 2002), 76–77; M. D. Wheeler to All Intelligence Officers, Southeastern Department, April 18, 1918 [NA RG 393 Pt 1. E4429 B1]; Frankfurter to Van Deman, September 21, 1917 [NA RG 165 "Negro Subversion" M1440].

63. Van Denman to Intelligence Officer, Southeastern Department, May 21, 1918; Van Denman to Mayes, April 25, 1918 [RG 393 Pt 1. E4429 B1].

64. Frankfurter to Wilson, Baker, and Crowder, November 18, 1918 [FF-Harv/120]. On the 1945 efforts, see J. Edgar Hoover to Truman, January 9, 1946, and January 11, 1946 [HST R/21]; Robert Ferrell, *Harry S. Truman, A Life* (Columbia: University of Missouri Press, 1994), 227–228. R. Alton Lee, "The Army Mutiny of 1946," *The Journal of American History* 53, no. 3 (December 1966): 555–571. On the British 1919 mutiny, see Anthony Read, *The World on Fire: 1919 and the Battle With Bolshevism* (New York: W.W. Norton, 2008), 56–57.

65. McCain to Commanding General of all Departments and National Guard and National Army Divisions in the United States, "Subject Reports Concerning and disposition of alien enemies in the United State Army," August 3, 1917; McCain to Commanding General of all Departments and National Guard and National Army Divisions in the United States, "Discharge of Aliens Drafted into Military Service," 1918 [RG 120, E2215, B1].

66. Case file Robert H. Hall; Chief of Staff, Adj Gen, December 28, 1916 [RG 165 E 68 B 4046].

67. On the British extension of military jurisdiction over civilians, see R. v. Governor of Lewes Prison ex parte Doyle [1917] KB 254; also Keith D. Ewing and C. A. Gearty, *The Struggle for Civil Liberties: Political Freedom and the Rule of Law in Britain, 1914–1945* (London: Oxford University Press, 1999), ch 7. On trials in France, see Lawrence Sondhaus, *World War One: The Global Revolution* (New York: Cambridge University Press, 2011), 351–354; Thomas Fleming, *The Illusion of Victory: America in World War I* (New York: Basic Books, 2003), 169–172.

68. NARA RG 153, General Court Martial Offense Ledger Sheets, 1919, Box 3.

69. Report 10657-109, MIB to 10 Commander, Kelly Field, July 19, 1918; CMIB to Commander, Kelly Field, August 14, 1918 [NA RG 165/E 58 B90].

70. Report 10478-5, JAG to MIB, February 25, 1918; Report 10536-52, JAG to MIB, March 1, 1918 NA RG 165/E 58 B56.

71. Headquarters, Southern Department, General Court Martial Order no. 59, January 10, 1918 [RG 393 E 4449]; Headquarters, Southern Department, General Court Martial Order no. 617, June 14, 1918 [RG 393 E 4449].

72. Headquarters Southern Department, General Court Martial Order no. 772, July 15, 1918 [RG 393 E 4449].

73. Headquarters, Southern Department, General Court Martial Order 788, August 9, 1918 [RG 393 Pt 1 E 4449]; Headquarters, Southern Department, General Court-Martial Orders 835, August 9, 1918 [RG 393 Pt 1 E 4449].

74. Headquarters Eastern Department, General Court-Martial Order no. 85 [RG 393 Pt I, E 1593]; "Give Army Officer 25-Year Term for Aiding the Enemy," *New York Times*, February 25, 1918, p. 1; *McRae v. Henkes*, 273 F. 108 (CA 8, 1921).

75. Headquarters Eastern Department, General Court-Martial orders no. 90, February 19, 1918 [RG 393 Pt I, E1593].

76. "Accused Army Surgeon: Alleged Seditious Remarks Lead to McAllister's Arrest," *New York Times*, May 2, 1918; Eastern Department, General Court-Martial Order 289 and accompanying documents, May 17, 1918 [RG 393 Pt I, E 1594].

77. General Court Martial of Private Clarence Cotter, October 19, 1917, GCMO 525, Chicago IL [NA RG 393 E565, Central Division Records B/11]; General Court Martial of Private Joe Tomonocy, July 16, 1918, GCMO 506, Chicago IL [NA RG 393 E565, Central Division Records B/12]; General Court-Martial of Private Marcus Breitfeller, GCMO 528, July 25, 1918 Chicago IL [NA RG 393 E565, Central Division Records B/12].

78. General Court-Martial of Private Weitman, GCMO 649, September 14, 1918, Chicago IL [NA RG 393 E565, Central Division Records B/12]; General Court-Martial of Private Frank Prassel, GCMO 217, May 27, 1919, Chicago IL [NA RG 393 E565, Central Division Records B/12].

79. Smith to Ansell, November 22, 1918 [MS-USC/569].

80. General Court Martial Order no. 6, September 17, 1918; Smith to Commanding General, Camp Meade, September 17, 1918 [MS-USC/6-574].

81. Report 10424, MIB to JAG, March 27, 1918; *In re Bayles*, 156 App. Div 663 (NY 1913).

82. See "President Cheats Firing Squad of 3: Saves Soldiers Sentenced by Court-Martial," *Detroit Free Press*, March 1, 1919 [EHC/1053].

83. Wigmore to Baker, August 1918 [NDB/4]; Baker to Crowder, July 19, 1918; Wigmore to Crowder, July 22, 1918 [JHW-NW/121]; Rigby to Chamberlain, March 11, 1919, in Hearings, 911.

84. Judge Advocate General Allen W. Gullion memorandum for Chief of Staff, September 16, 1938 [RG 165/E 58 B56]; Hagood to Harbord, October 22, 1918 [JH/778-8].

85. General D. E. Nolan to commanding officer 29th Engineers, December 19, 1918 [RG 120, E193, B6291]; Nolan to Bethel, October 28, 1918 [RG 120, E193, B6291].

86. Albert E. White to CMIB, Chiperfield, January 31, 1918; Mayor J. Loyal Gilbert to Chiperfield, January 29, 1918; CMIB to G-2 / JAG, October 28, 1918; Chief Military Intelligence Branch to Asst Chief of Staff, July 31, 1918.

87. CMIB-AEF to G-2, October 10, 1918; CMIB AEF to JA, AEF, October 19, 1918 [RG 120, E193, B6291].

88. CMIB to G-2, July 23, 1918 [RG 120, E193, B6291].

89. CMIB-AEF to G-2, July 29, 1918 [RG 120, E193, B6291].

90. Captain J. C. Dooley, Div Intelligence Officer to CMIB, October 18, 1918; CMIB to JAGO, October 24, 1918 [RG 120, E193, B6291]; on Wold, see General D.E. Nolan to JAGO, October 28, 1918 [RG 120, E193, B6291].

91. General Court-Martial Orders no. 97, October 31, 1918 [SW-UK/CM-1918].

92. Report 10922-9, IO SD, February 26, 1918 [RG 165/E 58 B54]; Report 10594-2, JAG, January 26, 1918 [NA RG 165/E 58 B54]; Report 10428-94-3 [RG 165/E 58 B54].

93. Report 1059-13-1, JAG, January 8, 1918 [RG 165/E 58 B54].

94. CMIB to G-2, February 26, 1919; 1Lt Archie Palmer to CMIB, June 3, 1918 [RG 120, E193, B6291].

95. Allen to March, December 27, 1918; Allen to Beckham, December 28, 1918; Allen to Pershing, February 24, 1919 [HTA/11].

96. Bliss to Allen, October 13, 1919 [HTA/11]; Allen to Pershing, October 19, 1919 [HTA/11].

97. Goff to Nathan Goff, April 22, 1919 [WVU-GDG]; Goff to Chiperfield, November 1, 1919 [WVU-GDG]; Goff to Nathan Goff, June n.d., 1919.

98. Daniel Okrent, *Last Call: The Rise and Fall of Prohibition* (New York: Scribner, 2010), 98–108.

99. Alex Goodall, *Loyalty and Liberty: American Counter-subversion from World War I to the McCarthy Era* (Champaign: University of Illinois Press, 2013), 45–50; Anne Hagedorn, *Savage Peace: Hope and Fear in America, 1919* (New York: Simon and Schuster, 2007), 53–55; Crowder to Baker, July 18, 1918.

100. On Humes, see "U.S. Attorney Accused: Defendants in Steel Fraud Case Allege he was too Friendly with Juror," *Harrisburg Star Independent*, May 28, 1915, p. 12; "Officious Mr. Humes," *Harrisburg Telegraph*, August 9, 1917, p. 8.

101. On Nelson, see Millard L. Gieske and Steven Keillor, *Norwegian Yankee: Knute Nelson and the Failure of American Politics, 1860–1923* (Northfield, MN: The Norwegian-American Historical Association, 1995), 3–48.

102. Statement of Humes to Nelson, October 10, 1918 [KN-MHS/31]; Nelson to Humes, October 11, 1918 [KN-MHS/31].

103. *Subcommittee on Brewing and Liquor Interests, and German Propaganda and Bolshevik Propaganda* (hereafter Overman Committee), vol. 1. On Ansell's lobbying for Humes to serve on the committee, see Ansell to Nelson, September 19, 1918 [KN-MHS/31].

104. Overman Committee, vol. 2.

105. Overman Committee, vol. 2 1642–1643; Amos Pinchot to Overman, n.d., 1919 [AP/83].

106. Report 10922-17, IO SD, February 1, 1919 [NA RG 165/E 58 B54]; John Milton Cooper Jr., *Pivotal Decades: The United States, 1900–1920* (New York: W.W. Norton, 1990), 217.

107. Archibald Thacher to Moseley, January 19, 1919 [GVM/2]. On the fears of Bolshevism in the army after the Armistice, see Micheal Pearlman, *To Make Democracy Safe For America: Patricians and Preparedness in the Progressive Era* (Champaign: University of Illinois Press, 1984), 170–183.

108. Crowder to Wigmore, June 11, 1920 [JHW-NW/48]; Crowder to Wigmore, June 14, 1920 [JHW-NW/48].

109. On Crouch, see "Witness Tells of Order to Place Reds in Army," Associated Press, February 14, 1954 [PCP-Stan/8]; United States Army Surveillance of Dissidents, Report on Resistance Inside the Military, April 18, 1968 [UPA/17]. On Crouch, see also *Crouch v. United States*, 13 F.2d 348 (CA 9, 1926). See also Joseph Alsop, "The Powerful Imaginer," *Washington Post*, April 19, 1954.

CHAPTER 8

1. Taft, editorial, *Washington Times*, December 27, 1918, p. 1; see also *El Paso Times*, December 15, 1918, p. 1; "Permanent Draft for US Army Proposed," *Salt Lake Herald*, December 15, 1918, p. 1; "Volunteer Army Done," *Washington Star*, December 15, 1918, p. 1; "Permanent Draft," *Brooklyn Daily*

Eagle, December 15, 1918; "Permanent Draft," *New York Sun*, December 1, 1918, p. 1; "Crowder on Army," *New York World*, December 15, 1918, p. 2; "Draft Needed," *St. Louis Globe Democrat*, December 15, 1918, p. 1; "Draft makes transition of US industry from wartime to peacetime more predictable," *Chicago Tribune*, December 17, 1918, p. 1; *Louisville Courier-Journal*, December 17, 1918, p. 1; "Draft not synonymous with militarism," *Albany Knickerbocker Press*, December 18, 1918, p. 1.

2. Crowder lauds Kahn, Chamberlain, *Washington Star*, December 15, 1918, p. 1.

3. On Hecksher, see *Harvard Alumni Bulletin*, vol. 21, pt 1 , 436. On the board of review, see Jonathan Lurie, *Arming Military Justice*, 82.

4. Crowder to Garrison, December 18, 1918 [ECH/R4]. On the planned reduction of the army and its effect on the Judge Advocate General's Office, see Army Reorganization Hearings Before the House Committee on Military Affairs, Sixty-Fifth Congress, 3d Sess, on H.R. 14560 "To Reorganize and Increase the Efficiency of the Regular Army" (Washington, DC: GPO, 1919), p. 5.

5. Baker to Crowder, November 13, 1917; Crowder to Baker, November 18, 1917; Baker to Wilson, August 22, 1918 [EHC/R3].

6. Crowder to Baker, March 3, 1919 [JHW-NW/174]. It appears likely that Wigmore wrote this letter for Crowder to convey to Baker. See also Michael Pearlman, *To Make Democracy Safe For America: Patricians and Preparedness in the Progressive Era*, 170–183.

7. Hearings I, 164; "Ansell Back to Old Rank," Baker Says Demotion is Not Connected with Clemency Controversy," *New York Times*, March 6, 1919.

8. Bethel to Crowder, December 23, 1918 [NARA RG120, E594 321.4]; Samuel Pepper, "my impressions of military justice," n.d., 1919 [SP-UM/2].

9. General Allen to Baker, March 29, 1920 [NDB/9]; Allen to Baker, August 10, 1920 [NDB/9]; Colfelt to Summerall, December 20, 1919 [CPS/291].

10. Judson to March, May 21, 1919 [WVJ-NL/1].

11. On Dowling, see *Minnesota Law Review* 4, no. 2 (1920): 50. On Strode, see Paul Lombardo, *Three Generations: No Imbeciles* (Baltimore: Johns Hopkins University Press, 2008), 59. On Fegan, see Hugh J. Fegan, 1881–1954, "43 *Geo L. J.* 163, no. 2 (1954); on McGovern, see John D. Buekner, *The History of Wisconsin: Vol. 4: The Progressive Era, 1893–1914*, 521; on Morgan, see Roger K. Newman, *The Yale Biographical Dictionary of American Law* (New Haven, CT: Yale University Press, 2009), 389.

12. Weeks, Office Memorandum, November 13, 1918 [NA RG 153, Mark E. Guerin E12-D/1].

13. Ansell, Office Memorandum, November 6, 1918; Crowder, Office Memorandum, November 7, 1918 [NA RG 153, Mark E. Guerin E12-D/1]; Crowder, Office Order no. 18, 1919 [NA RD 152.3 E44, Office Orders /B1].

14. Weeks, Office Memorandum, December 4, 1918 [NA RG 153, Mark E. Guerin E12-D/1]. On Bailey, see Obituary, *Army Navy Journal*, April 9, 1929, p. 349.

15. *State ex rel County Attorney of Trego County v. Rea*, 104 Kan 148 (Kan 1919); Jacob C. Ruppenthal, "The German Element in Central Kansas," in *Collections of the Kansas State Historical Society*, 1913–1914 (Lawrence, KS: 1919): 513–534.

16. On Scott, see Report of the Adjutant General of Pennsylvania for the Year 1898 (Philadelphia: State Printer of Pennsylvania, 1898), 570, and Byron D. Stokes, ed., *The Sigma Chi Quarterly 1918–1919*, vol. 38 (Chicago: Ind, 1919), 50–51. On McKinney, see Edgar L. Murlin, *The New York Red Book: An Illustrated Legislative Manual* (Albany: J. B. Lyon, 1902), 82.

17. Crowder to Baker, January 4, 1918; Adjutant General to all Commanding Generals, September 22, 1917 [RG 165 E310, Records of the War Department and Special Staffs—Judge Advocate Records B225].

18. Ansell to Baker [NA RG 153, Reports on Administration of Military Justice in European Countries, 1918–1919/5].

19. Ansell to Crowder, February 10, 1919 [NDB/7]; F. Wigmore to McKellar, February 20, 1919 [JHW/172]; Frankfurter to Stimson, January 24, 1919 [FF-HARV/R-63]; Frankfurter to Stimson, February 1, 1919 [FF-HARV/R-63].

20. Brig. Gen. Ansell to Speak, *Washington Evening Star*, January 17, 1919, p. 26; "Charges Crowder Withheld Memoranda: Had to Appeal Court-Martial Sentences to President, General Ansell Says," *Washington Evening Star*, February 20, 1919.

21. Crowder, files, n.d. [EHC/6]; Brandeis to Crowder, January 12, 1919 [LDB-LU/48].

22. Baker to Wilson, May 1, 1918 [NDB/6]; Timothy D. Johnson, "Anti-War Sentiment and Representative John Lawson Burnett of Alabama," *Alabama Review* 39 (July 1986): 187–195.

23. Speech of Senator Chamberlain to the Senate, January 9, 1919 [Hearings II, 1091].

24. Crowder to Stimson, February 4, 1919 [HLS/R-51]; "Crowder to Stay in the Army," *New York Times*, May 17, 1919.

25. John Milton Cooper, *Pivotal Years*, 310; see "A Bill to provide for universal military, naval, and vocation training and for mobilization of the manhood of the United States in a national emergency." In addition to Chamberlain's, reasons are found in Wallace H. White's papers. See American Defense Society Inc to White, September 16, 1919 [WHW/31]; Military Training Camps Association of the United States to White, December 1, 1919 [WHW/32]. Chamberlain's reasons are now missing from his collections. However, he tried to enlist Republican support in the House of Representatives. H. C. Peterson and Gilbert Fite, *Opponents of War, 1917–1918*, 14; and Seward Livermore, *Politics Is Adjourned: Woodrow Wilson and the War Congress*, 81. On the Joint Committee on the Conduct of the War in the Civil War, see Louis Smith, *American Democracy and Military Power: A Study of the Civil Control of Military Power in the United States* (Chicago: University of Chicago Press, 1951), 203. On Woodrow Wilson's view of Chamberlain, see E. David Cronon, ed., *The Cabinet Diaries of Josephus Daniels*, entry for January 21, 1918, 270.

26. Maud Hanan to Chamberlain, December 31, 1917 [GEC-OHS/3 f-f]. On the large volume of letters, see GEC-OHs/3 f-2 and f-3; Chamberlain to Samuel Garland, April 11, 1918 [GEC-OHS/6f-5].

27. General Crozier to Glass, February 9, 1918; Lansing to Glass, February 18, 1918; Padgett to Glass, February 25, 1918; Vinson to Glass, February 25, 1918 [CG-UVA/128].

28. "Court-Martial Probe Provided by Johnson," *Lawrence Journal-World*, March 1, 1919; "To Seek Reforms in Courts-Martial," *New York Times*, December 28, 1918; Hoke Smith to JNO Graves, December 18, 1918 [MHS-UGA/13]; Jonathan Lurie, *Arming Military Justice*, 127.

29. Hearings I, 4–5.

30. Wigmore to McKellar, February 20, 1919 [JHW-NW/172]; Hoke Smith to Adjutant General, January 19, 1919 [MHS-UGA/30]; Hooper Alexander to Smith, November 16, 1918 [MHS-UGA/29]. The term *fully and fairly*, would become part of the military justice lexicon in 1953 when the Supreme Court decided, in *Burns v. Wilson*, that where the military court system had "fully and fairly" decided an appeal, the federal judiciary could not grant jurisdiction over the contested issue. On La Follette, see James Leonard Bates, *Senator Thomas J. Walsh of Montana*, 150; and Nancy C. Unger, *Fighting Bob La Follette: The Righteous Reformer*, 257.

31. "Wadsworth to John McAuley Palmer, January 20, 1918 [JWW/29]; Courts-Martial Called Atrocious," *New York Times*, February 14, 1919, p. 1; "Harsh Rulings at Military Trials Arouse Senate," *Washington Herald*, February 15, 1919, p. 1; Richard Coke Lower, *A Bloc of One: The Political Career of Hiram Johnson* (San Francisco: Stanford University Press, 1993), 105–114; James Leonard Bates, *Senator Thomas Walsh of Montana*, 180–181; *Fighting Bob La Follette: The Righteous Reformer* (Chapel Hill, NC: University of North Carolina Press, 2000), 257.

32. Hearings I, 10–13.

33. Hearings I, 40–44; Crowder to Baker, March 3, 1919 [JHW-NW/174].

34. Hearings I, 99–101.

35. Hearings I, 111.

36. Hearings I, 177.

37. Hearings I, 219.

38. Hearings I, 239.

39. Hearings I, 232.

40. Hearings I, 245.

41. Hearings I, 241–245.

42. Hearings I, 246.

43. Crowder to Baker, March 5, 1919 [NDB/7].

44. Ansell to Crowder, February 10, 1919; Crowder to Baker, February 15, 1919; Baker to Crowder, February 28, 1919 [NDB/7].

45. Baker to Crowder, March 1, 1919 [NDB/7]; Ansell, testimony, Hearings II, 168.

46. Crowder to Baker, March 26, 1919 [NDB/7]; "Accused Wigmore of Franking Abuse," New York Times, April 9, 1919.

47. Rigby to Crowder, March 14, 1919; Wambaugh to Crowder March 16, 1919; Crowder to Baker, March 16, 1919; Rigby to Baker, March 28, 1919; Kreger to Baker, April 2, 1919; Adjutant General to Rigby, April 4, 1919 [RG 153, JAG Reports on Military Justice, E 28 P 28/Box 15].

48. Frederick C. Giffin, "The Rudowitz Extradition Case," Journal of the Illinois State Historical Society 72 (1982): 61–72.

49. Rigby to Crowder, June 1, 1919 [EHC/17].

50. Major Calvin Wells to Rigby, May 31, 1918; Rigby to Kreger, June 3, 1919; Rigby to Kreger, June 9, 1919.

51. Rigby to Wells, July 25 1919 [EHC/4]; Childs, recorded interview, June 1, 1919 [Box 16].

52. Rigby to Crowder, May 31, 199 [EHC/16]; Rigby, interviews with Hallmin and Pressard [Box 12]. General Geraud Reveilhac ordered the executions, and this incident created a furor in France after the war. See Mark Lloyd, The Art of Military Deception (London: Pen and Sword, 2003), 177–178.

53. Rigby to Winship, May 12, 1919 [EHC/5]. On the early Soviet military, see John Erickson, The Soviet High Command: A Military-Political History, 1918–1941 (London: St. Martin's Press, 1962), 1–83; see also John Coffey, Deterrence in the 1970s (Denver: University of Denver Press, 1970); and Raymond Garthoff, Soviet Military Policy: A Historical Analysis (London: Faber and Faber, 1966). Parker v. Levy, 417 U.S. 733 (1974); and Blackmun, memorandum to the conference, undated [HAB/186]. Frederick Bernays Weiner, a military law expert who had served as a judge advocate in World War II and also in his postwar civilian practice, and prevailed over the Department of Defense in the Supreme Court on the issue of military jurisdiction over civilians residing on American posts overseas, influenced Blackmun to write about the Soviet military.

54. Proceedings and Report of Special War Department Board on Courts-Martial and Their Procedure, July 17, 1919 (Washington, DC: GPO, 1919); Gerry Oram, "The Greatest Efficiency: British and American Military Law, 1866–1918," in Barry S. Godfrey, Clive Emsley, and Graeme Dunstall, Comparative Histories of Crime (London: Routledge, 2011), 171.

55. Wilson to Bethel, December 13, 1918 [SW-UK/CM-1918].

56. Winship to Kernan, June 28, 1919; Winship to Kernan, June 28, 1919 [RG 120 E 1772 010.06/1].

57. Hayes to Hines, May 23, 1919 [JLH/6].

58. Crowder to Ansell, July 31, 1919 [NDB/7].

59. Chamberlain Raps Crowder," New York Times, March 6, 1919; "Crowder Asserts Ansell Tried to Seize His Powers," New York Times, March 9, 1919; Wigmore, Speech to New York Bar, March 8, 1919 [JHW-NW/173].

60. "Court-Martial System Declared to do Terrible Injustice," Christian Science Monitor, April 4, 1919, p. 1; Crowder to Baker, April 19, 1919; General J. W. Heard to Crowder, April 22, 1919 [NDB/7]; "Ansell blames Baker for Evils of Army System," Associated Press, April 4, 1919.

61. Jonathan Lurie, Arming Military Justice, 103–106; "Ansell Submits Reforms to Baker," New York Times, April 6, 1919; "Baker Welcomes Ansell's Reforms … But Bars Personalities," New York Times, April 8, 1919; "Siegel tells of Injustices: Asks Baker to Investigate Courts-Martial," New York Times, April 4, 1919.

62. On Crowder's reluctance, see Crowder to Baker, July 19, 1919 [NDB/7]. On President Menocal's insistence, see Bainbridge Colby to Wilson, July 28, 1920 [BC/3]. On Kreger's assignment, see Kreger to his wife, March 21, 1919 [EAK-DBC/1]; Kreger to his brother, March 21, 1919 [EAK-DBC/1];

Kreger to his wife, March 30, 1919 [EAK-DBC/1]. On Kreger's assignment being widely reported, see "Gen Kreger to Act as Judge Advocate General of the Army," *Washington Post*, March 7, 1919.

63. Henry Stimson, "A Defense of Crowder's Administration of his Office," *New York Times*, April 9, 1919; Chamberlain to Crowder, February 1, 1919 [RG 153, Reports on Administration of Military Justice in European Countries, 1918–1919/5]. Major William Rigby maintained the Ansell-Chamberlain-Chamberlain, Ansell-Crowder, and Ansell-Baker correspondence in the study files, which are now part of the Reports on Administration of Military Justice in European Countries. See also Perkins to Stimson, April 8, 1919; Keppel to Stimson, April 8, 1919; Judson to Stimson, April 8, 1919; Army Navy Journal to Stimson, April 9, 1919; Army Navy Gazette to Stimson, April 9, 1918; George Wickersham to Stimson, April 10, 1919 [HS/R-52].

64. Crowder to Stimson, April 11, 1919 [HS/R-52].

65. Arthur Train, "Military Justice in the American Army," *Colliers: The National Weekly*, April 19, 1919, 1; A. H. Robbins, "American Justice in the American Army," *Central Law Journal* 88, no. 19, p. 338; J. B. W. Gardiner, "The Court-Martial Controversy," *The National Weekly*, May 31, 1919, pp. 9–28; "Crowder answers Ansell," *Washington Post*, March 20, 1919, p. 1; George Rothwell Brown, "Ansell Reform Plan: Baker's Advice Accepted, Secretary Asked to Make Letter as Public as Crowder's," *Washington Post*, April 6, 1919, p. 1; Ex Judge Advocates Committee Says Men are Regarded as Subjects, Not Citizens: Calls Army Courts a Despotic System," *New York Times*, April 13, 1919.

66. McReynolds's papers are housed at the University of Virginia, and there are several letters between Gregory and the justice. However, none of the surviving correspondence involves courts-martial. However, the NAACP also retained Gregory to defend African Americans accused of fomenting the "Chicago Riots" in 1919. See Elliot Rudwick and Arthur Meier, "Attorneys Black and White: A Case Study of Race Relations within the NAACP," in August Meier, *Along the Color Line: Explorations in the Black Experience* (Champaign: University of Illinois Press, 2002), 128–173. On reporting on the Bar Association's investigation, see "Gregory Outlines Army Court Plans: Bar Association Committee Indicates First Views as to Course of Reforms," *New York Times*, April 25, 1919; "Wigmore Argues Against Ansell: Both Appear at American Bar Association's Hearing on Military Justice," *New York Times*, April 24, 1919; "Ansell Charges Bias in Inquiry: Tells Lawyers' Committee it is Influenced by War Department," *New York Times*, April 22, 1919.

67. Sidle to Baker, August 31, 1919 [NDB/8]; Proposed Amendment to Senate Bill 3792, n.d., 1919; Scott to H. H. Blake, March 11, 1919 [NAACP/C-374].

68. "Speech of Colonel John Henry Wigmore," in Report of the Twenty-Fourth Annual Meeting of the Maryland State Bar Association, Held at Atlantic City, N.J., June 26, 27, 28, 1919 (Annapolis, MD: Maryland State Bar Association, 1919), 183–195.

69. "Speech of Edmund M. Morgan," in Report of the Twenty-Fourth Annual Meeting of the Maryland State Bar Association, Held at Atlantic City, N.J., June 26, 27, 28, 1919 (Annapolis, MD: Maryland State Bar Association, 1919), 196–212.

70. "Columbia honors Ishii and Crowder," *New York Times*, June 2, 1919; Scott Speech, June 1, 1919 [HLS/121]; "Defends Courts-Martial: Gen Scott Says AEF Officers are Against Change," *New York Times*, June 6, 1919; "Finds Army Courts Unfair," *New York Times*, June 27, 1919.

71. Westenhaven to Baker, June 2, 1919; Westenhaver to Baker, July 22, 1919 [NDB/9]; Clarke to Baker, July 19, 1919 [NDB/7].

72. Robert K. Murray, *Red Scare: A Study in National Hysteria*, 1919–1920 (Minneapolis: University of Minnesota Press, 1955); John Milton Cooper, *Breaking the Heart of the World: Woodrow Wilson and the Fight for the League of Nations* (New York: Cambridge University Press, 2001).

73. Lenroot Speech, Superior Wisconsin, June 19120 [ILL/5].

74. Hearings II, 23–92.

75. Hearings II, 289.

76. Hearings II, 184. On the professionalization of the army's officer corps following the Civil War, see Carol Reardon, *Soldiers and Scholars: The U.S. Army and the Uses of Military History*, 1865–1920 (Lawrence: University Press of Kansas, 1990).

77. Hearings II, 120–122. Ansell also noted that one of the duties of officers assigned to posts at higher than the company level was to ensure the post housing and headquarters was properly landscaped.

78. Hearings II, 138–140. On Ogden's role in investigating the accident, see Stephen Puleo, *Dark Tide: The Great Boston Molasses Flood of 1919* (Boston: Beacon Press, 2004), 112.

79. Jonathan Lurie, *Arming Military Justice*, 79–81.

80. Hearings II, 295.

81. Hearings, II 174.

82. Hearings II, 321–361.

83. Hearings II, 1113.

84. Hearings II, 1163.

85. Hearings II, 1339–1371.

86. Jonathan Lurie, *Arming Military Justice*, 96–123.

87. On Warren, see Anne Carolyn Hansen, "The Congressional Career of Francis E. Warren from 1890 to 1902," *Annals of Wyoming* 20 (January 1948): 131–158; Robert C. Byrd, *Committee on Appropriations, United States Senate: 135th Anniversary 1867–2002* (Washington, DC: GPO, 2002), 51; C. H. Hoebeke, *The Road to Mass Democracy: Original Intent and Seventeenth Amendment* (New Brunswick, NJ: Transaction Press, 1995), 142.

88. Warren to Weaver, January 17, 1918 [FEW-AMC/V87-B16]; John Wingate Weeks to Warren, October 21, 1919 [JWW-RSP/5-3]; Warren to Weeks, September 25, 1919 [JWW-RSP/5-3].

89. Warren to Baker, October 22, 1919; Warren to Baker, October 27, 1919; Warren to Baker, October 28, 1919; Warren to Taft, November 17, 1919.

90. Warren to Pershing, August 27, 1918; Warren to Mr. Isley, August 22, 1918 [FEW-AMC/V87-B16]; Warren to Ms. Seth Scofield, January 16, 1919 [FEW-AMC/V86-B16]; Warren to Fred Warren, October 2, 1918 [FEW-AMC/V87-B16].

91. Warren to Mr. George M. Kerr, October 7, 1919; Warren to Arthur Gill, October 10, 1919; Warren to Dewey, Gould & Co, October 17, 1919; Secretary of Commerce to Warren, October 13, 1919.

92. Warren to Ms. Packard, October 16, 1919; Warren to Pershing, October 11, 1919. [In this letter Warren informed Pershing that the chairman of the Republican National Committee had approached him. Warren to Pershing, October 21, 1919.

93. Warren to General Chamberlain, October 7, 1919; Warren to Baker, October 9, 1919; Warren to Morgan, November 10, 1919 [FEW-AMC/V88-B17].

94. Warren to Gallant, October 29, 1919; Frank Palmer Sibley, *With the Yankee Division in France*. 1919. Repr., London: Forgotten Books, 2013, 146–147.

95. Hagood to Warren, October 27, 1919 [JH-SCHS/178-19]; Hagood to Kreger, July 1, 1919 [JH-SCHS/178-16]; Francis E. Warren to Hines, September 18, 1919 [JLH/1]; Warren to Hines, November 26, 1919 [FEW-AMC/V29-B16]; Allen to Baker, March 29, 1920 [NDB/9].

96. Warren to Morgan, November 14, 1919 [FEW-AMC/V29-B16]; Crowder to Bullitt, November 4, 1919 [ECH-MHS/8].

97. Warren to Crowder, October 17, 1919.

98. Warren to Lenroot, October 29, 1919.

99. "Bill Destructive of Military Discipline, Taft Avers," *Philadelphia Ledger*, September 15, 1919; "Assails Taft's Stand on Courts-martial: Chamberlain and Ansell reply to his Defense of the System," September 16, 1919.

100. Kahn to Taft, February 25, 1919 [WHT/R-205]. On Crowder's surprise with Taft's editorials, see Taft to Crowder, September 20, 1919 [WHT/R-557]. For Morgan's correspondence, see Morgan to Taft, September 19, 1919 [WHT/R-212]; Taft to Morgan, September 23, 1919 [WHT/R-557]; Morgan to Taft [WHT/R-212]. Although I have lauded Professor Lurie for his chapters on the dispute between Ansell and Crowder, he only cited Morgan's first letter to Taft and not Taft's response, or Morgan's counter-response. Taft's response details the former president's high opinion of and loyalty to Crowder and his disgust with Ansell. Morgan appears to have desired peace with

Taft not only because the two men would work together at Yale and Taft was nationally regarded as a preeminent legal scholar, but also out of deference to a former president.

101. H. F. Hodges to Taft, September 17, 1919 [WHT/R-212].

102. "Would Make Crowder Lieutenant General," September 20, 1919; "Advocate for Crowder," September 30, 1919 p. 1.

103. Flood, minority report draft to Bland, n.d., 1920 [HDF/73].

104. Flood to Kahn et al., September 19, 1919 [HDF/86].

105. Crowder to Dickman, November 5, 1920 [EHC/R7]; Nelson to Baker, August 26, 1919 [KN-MHS/43]; Crowder to Nelson, September 29, 1919 [KN-MHS/43].

106. AD Hill to AD Hill Jr., April 4, 1919 [ADHP-PA/1]; Wilson to Bethel, December 13, 1918 [SW-UK/CM-1918].

107. Goff to Coolidge, September 29, 1929 [CC/R35].

108. "Colonel Hill Marks Time," Baltimore Sun, May 14, 1919; "Hill Being Urged to run for State's Attorney," Baltimore Star, July 22, 1919; "Hypocrisy Scored by Colonel Hill," American, October 17, 1919; "Hill Responds on 'National Affairs'" American, October 25, 1919 [JPH/3]; "Poll in Maryland Favors General Wood," American, March 19, 1920; "Hill Considering Call to Congress," Baltimore Star, April 18, 1920 [JPH/3]; "John Philip Hill is Out for Wood: Makes Strong Appeal for Support of the general," Baltimore American, April 24, 1920 [JPH/3].

109. Cosgrave Diary entry for July 23, 1919 [PJC—SHSN/1 F7].

110. Address by Lieutenant Colonel Hugh W. Ogden, printed in Boston City Club Bulletin, October 1, 1919, 41–58, 53; Ogden to Weeks, October 2, 1919 [JWW-RSP/6-35].

111. Connor's biographical information is taken from: Connor to President, US Army Examining Board no. J.A. 127-E, JAG, July 6, 1920; Connor to Byrnes, July 6, 1945 [MWC-UVA/1-1]; Military Record of Major William Connor to accompany the record of application, April 21, 1919 [MWC-UVA/1]; Statement of William M. Connor, Proceedings of the Committee on Military Law of the Military Law Association, Shorthand Report, June 6, 1919 [MWC-UVA/1-1]; B. R. Tillman to Connor, July 1, 1917; Tillman to Baker, June 29, 1917; Baker to Tillman, June 30, 1917 [WCP-UVA/3]; Ansell to Connor, February 26, 1919 [MWC-UVA/1-1]; Ansell Memorandum for the Full Clemency Board, April 9, 1919; Ansell, Memorandum for Clemency Board, March 5, 1919; Ansell to Connor, March 5, 1919 [MWC-UVA/1-1].

112. Connor to Ansell, April 28, 1919 [MWC-UVA/1-1]; Major General Francis Kernan to Connor, May 20, 1919 [MWC-UVA/1-1]; Connor to Crowder, undated, 1919 [MWC-UVA/1-1].

113. Warren to FR Marshall, June 8, 1920 [FEW-AMC/V89-B17].

114. Baker to Wilson, September 19, 1919 [NDB/9].

115. Crowder to Baker [NDB/9].

116. 1920 Articles of War, in full.

CONCLUSION

1. Investigations on the National War Effort," Report of the Committee of Military Affairs, House of Representatives, Seventy-Ninth Congress, 2d Sess, June 1947, p. 18. On the court-martial controversy not becoming part of the public memory following World War I, see Johnathan Lurie, Arming Military Justice, 125.

2. On the "return to normalcy," see Brian Loverman, No Higher Law: Foreign Policy and the Western Hemisphere Since 1776 (Chapel Hill: University of North Carolina Press, 2010), 219; and Peter G. Renstrom, The Taft Court: Justices, Rulings, and Legacy (Santa Barbara CA: ABC-CLIO, 2003), 11–13.

3. Board of Review and attached documents, United States v. First Lieutenant Ewell Ledford, April 3, 1919 [NA RG 154, PC 29 E 53, 250.042/5].

4. Board of Review and attached documents, United States v. Private Basil Lambright, April 29, 1919; Board of Review and attached documents, United States v. Private Lawrence Lee, March 10, 1919 [NA RG 154, PC 29 E 53, 250.042/5].

5. *Kahn v. Anderson*, 255 U.S. 1 (1921); *Givens v. Zerbst*, 255 U.S. 11 (1921).

6. *United States v. Drum*, 107 F.2d 897 (CA 2, 1937); *United States ex rel Feld v. Bullard*, 290 F. 704 (CA 2, 1923); *McRae v. Henkes*, 273 F. 108 (CA 8, 1921).

7. *Sanford v. Robbins*, 115 F.2d 435 (CA 5, 1940).

8. *Schita v. King*, 133 F.2d 283 (CA 8, 1943).

9. *Schita v. Cox*, 139 F.2d 971 (CA 8 1944). Schita died in the federal penitentiary in 1945 at the age of eighty. According to his penitentiary medical records, Schita was a veteran of the Sudan Campaign of 1898, the Boer War, and trench warfare on the Western Front in 1915. There is no record as to how Schita came into the United States. Schita's information is found in the Missouri State Archives.

10. See e.g. Miriam Galston, "Activism and Restraint: The Evolution of Harlan Fiske Stone's Judicial Philosophy," 70 *Tulane Law Review* (1995): 131–40.

11. Crowder to Connor, March 28, 1923 [WCP-UVA/2].

12. "Harding Frees Debs and Twenty-Three Others Held for War Violations," *New York Times*, December 21, 1921; Admiral Julian L. Latimer, Judge Advocate General of the Navy to Senator Jones, April 10, 1924; Jones to J. M. Moore, April 2, 1914; Charles Lambert to Jones, March 15, 1924 [WLJ-UW/136].

13. Crowder to Pershing, November 24, 1922; Crowder to Pershing, January 18, 1923 [JJP/56].

14. Hull to Summerall, October 26, 1928 [NA RG 165/E 58 B56].

15. Adjutant General Wahl to Pershing, July 3, 1928; Pershing to Wahl, June 28, 1928; Pershing to Kreger, November 15, 1928 [JJP/113]; Kreger note to Pershing, November 1, 1927 [EAK-DBC/2]; Roscoe C. Pollock to Kreger, June 19, 1953 [EAK-DBC/1].

16. Hull to Summerall, October 26, 1928 [NA RG 165/E 58 B56]; Rigby to Blanton Winship, June 26, 1937; Rigby to Winship, Feb 18, 1942 [Rigby papers]. On Winship's recall to active duty in World War II, see Louis Fisher, *Nazi Saboteurs on Trial: A Military Tribunal and American Law* (Lawrence: University Press of Kansas, 2005), 169.

17. Holmes to Frankfurter, April 25, 1919 [OWH-UPA/26]; Moshik Temkin, *The Sacco-Vanzetti Affair: America on Trial* (New Haven, CT: Yale University Press, 2009), 198.

18. "Dumped by Young Officer, She avers," *Baltimore News*, December 2, 1920 [JPH/4]; "Hill Proposes Repeal," February 2, 1920; "Congressmen of Five States behind bill to repeal Dry Act," *Philadelphia Inquirer*, April 4, 1921; Congressional Record, April 4, 1921, p. 138 [JPH/4].

19. Frederic L. Kirgis, *The American Society of International Law's Century: 1906-2006* (New York: Brill, 2006), 111–162; Hatsue Shinohara, *US International Lawyers in the Interwar Years: A Forgotten Crusade* (New York: Cambridge University Press, 2012), 1–48.

20. On Pepper, see Sidney Fine, *Sit Down: The General Motors Strike of 1936-1937* (Ann Arbor: University of Michigan Press, 1969), 243–294. On Warren, see C. Q. Press, *Guide to Congress, 7th ed.* (Washington, DC: Sage, 2013), 353. On Warren, see Taft to Charley, March 27, 1925 [WHT/272]. Taft informed his son that he tried to warn Coolidge against nominating Warren.

21. Frankfurter to Patterson, July 5, 1932 [Patterson/10]. Frankfurter's participation in identifying persons to fill key positions in the Roosevelt administration was not limited to the War and Naval Departments. He also participated in discussions regarding the attorney general and secretary of labor. See Grenville Clark to Henry Stimson, August 11, 1941 [HLS/104]. See also Roger K. Newman, ed., *The Yale Biographical Dictionary of American Law* (New Haven, CT: Yale University Press, 2009), 369–370. On Royall, see Royall to Frankfurter, May 20, 1937 [FF]; Frankfurter to Royall, May 22, 1937 [FF]. There is no biography on Royall, but for a general outline see William S. Powell, *Dictionary of North Carolina Biography* (Chapel Hill: University of North Carolina Press, 1994), 5:260. For Frankfurter's view of Royall as "a close relation," see Joseph P. Lash, *From the Diaries of Felix Frankfurter* (New York: Norton, 1974), 171.

22. John R. Shillady, August 1, 1919; Edgar Scott to Shillady, September 17, 1919; Press Service of the NAACP, September 18, 1919 [NAACP/C-347]; *In re Information to Discipline Certain Attorneys of the Sanitary District of Chicago*, 351 IL 206 (IL 1932).

23. John Weeks to Coolidge, n.d., 1924 [CC/12].

24. George Chamberlain, "Our Military Legislation," *The Forum: A Magazine of Constructive Nationalism*, June 1918, 725–732; Ansell to Chamberlain, December 1, 1920 [GEC-OHS/5f-1]; Ansell to Chamberlain, October 25, 1920 [GEC-OHS/5 f-1]; William Ivy Hair, *The Kingfish and His Realm: The Life and Times of Huey P. Long* (Baton Rouge: Louisiana State University Press, 1991), 255–256; *Long v. Ansell*, 293 U.S. 76 (1933).

25. Kreger to Captain Rock, August 13, 1921 [RG 152.3 E47, French Files/B2]; E. A. Kreger to Crowder, October 20, 1921 [RG 152.3 E47/B2]; Colonel Frederick Brown to Spencer Gordon esq, "In re Major Wilbur Brown," November 22, 1921; Crowder to Hull, February 22, 1922, "Case of Matlock"; Colonel Brown to Solicitor General James Beck, February 14, 1922 [RG 153.2, E 47, Records Relating to the French and Creary Retirement Cases Box/1]; Vernon West, United States Attorney to Brown, April 11, 1921 [RG 152.3 E44, Office Orders /B2].

26. James W. Beck, Solicitor General to Colonel Frederick Brown, February 23, 1922; Crowder to Attorney General, "Rights of an Officer of the Army Who has Received and Accepted an Appointment to Higher Office and has Failed of Confirmation to Revert to his Former Grade," n.d., 1920; Fitzgerald to Brown/Crowder, January 9, 1922 [NA RG 153.2, E 47, Records Relating to the French and Creary Retirement Cases Box/1].

27. Cresson to Flood, August 23, 1921; Bullard to Flood, August 20, 1921; Morris Sheppard to Flood, August 27, 1921 [HDF/70]; Daugherty to Harding, May 13, 1921 [WGH/R204]; Ansell to Weinberger, July 29, 1939 [HW-SL/5]; Weinberger to Ansell, August 2, 1930 [HW-SL/5].

28. Weinberger to Arthur Capper, April 28, 1939; Weinberger to Emmanuel Celler, April 28, 1939; Weinberger to Bennett Clark, April 28, 1939; Weinberger to Clark, May 18, 1939; Celler to Weinberger, May 1, 1939; Ed Villmare to Weinberger, May 1, 1939; Weinberger to Hiram Johnson, May 26, 1939; Weinberger to Clark, June 8, 1939 [HW-SL/6]; Ansell to Weinberger, July 1, 1940 [HW-SL/6].

29. On the courts-martial trials of civilians, see *McCune v. Kilpatrick*, 53 F.Supp 80 (DC VA, 1943); and *In re Berue*, 54 F.Supp. 252 (DC Oh, 1944); *Reid v. Covert*, 354 U.S. 1 (1957).

30. On courts-martial statistics, see Jonathan Lurie, *Arming Military Justice*, 128.

Index

Adler, Leon, 130–131
African-Americans, 13, 52, 69, 116, 122, 138,
    279, 302, 319, 329
    Soldiers, War Department, and, 69, 91, 102,
        112, 138–142, 182, 187, 192, 260, 265,
        327–328, 365, 385, 411
Allen, Henry, General, 117–118, 133, 186,
    199–200, 203, 216–225, 242, 249, 337,
    344–345, 356, 399
American Expeditionary Forces
    Battles
        Cantigny, 152
        Chateau Thierry, 78, 152, 165, 190, 267
        Meuse-Argonne, 38, 117, 156, 162–163,
            164, 172, 174, 177, 179–180, 186, 189,
            190, 192, 196, 199, 224, 234, 261–262,
            269–270, 414
        St. Michel, 117
        Soissons, 153, 195, 269
    Formation of Judge Advocate General's
        Office in
    Prison scandal in France, 228–232, 289–290
Anarchists, 27–28, 31, 146, 226, 267, 307–309,
    313, 315, 324–325, 329, 356, 416
Ansell, Samuel, 29, 41, 57–58, 66, 68, 70–71, 73,
    75, 81, 86, 88, 127, 140–142, 156, 178, 189,
    197, 204–206, 209, 213–215, 226, 240, 257,
    263–264, 266, 278, 288, 290, 307, 324, 326, 331,
    334–335, 339, 347, 353, 375, 380, 382–385,
    399, 402–404, 406, 408, 415–416, 420, 422
    Appointment as Acting Judge Advocate
        General, and difficulties early in the war,
        89–92
    Early judge advocate work of, 75, 84
    Testimony to Senate Committee, 388–393
    Warren, Francis E., Senator, distrust of
        Ansell, 398
Baker, Newton's early approval of, 89
Baker, Newton's anger with, 374
Bergdoll, Grover Cleveland, 421

Carter, Glass, Congressman, distrust of
    Ansell, 258
Claims that British, Italian, and French
    courts-martial were "more just" than
    American courts-martial, 369–370, 376,
    379
Chamberlain, George Earl, Senator, 355,
    365, 419
Crowder, Enoch, initial positive opinion of
    Ansell, 74–75
Crowder, Enoch, defended to Bell, J.
    Franklin, 74
Crowder, Enoch, defended to Bliss, Tasker
    H., 75–76
Crowder, Enoch, anger with Ansell, 297–298,
    327, 372, 374, 382
Crowder, Enoch, Ansell's anger with,
    353–361, 368
Frankfurter, Felix, distrust of Ansell, 362
General Order 7, opposed, 46
Hines, John Leonard, defended in
    court-martial, 44, 52–54
        called Ansell "basest hypocrite," 44
Judson, Walter, General, fears that Ansell
    would enable "bolshevism" in the Army,
    356
Morgan, Edmund, defense of Ansell,
    386–388
Opinions of other judge advocates, 379–381,
    402–405, 416
Opposed military jurisdiction over civilians,
    31
Resigned from Army, 354
Supported military jurisdiction over civil-
    ians, 114–116, 321, 323–324
Taft, William Howard, attacks Ansell's
    motives and defends Crowder, Enoch,
    400–402
Wigmore, John Henry, Ansell's disagreement
    and anger with, 353, 375

Anti-War movements in the United States
  Industrial Workers of the World, 113
  "Green Corn Rebellion," 332
  Socialist opposition, 28, 76, 113, 277,
    324–325, 349
Armenian Genocide, 237, 241–248
Armes, George, 62–65, 288, 407
Army, United States, basic structure
  Friction between Chief of Staff and Bureaus
    and Departments, 23–24, 42
  Engineer Department, 5, 309, 326, 356
  Inspector General, 90, 271, 375
  Ordnance Bureau, 5, 40, 126
  Military Intelligence Branch, 204, 306, 312,
    325–327, 329, 331
  War College, 95, 124, 245, 315
  Irish immigrants in, 203, 343
Articles of War (in use in World War I), 43, 46,
  50, 53, 54, 55, 57, 64, 66, 134, 169, 323,
  1874 version, 20, 50
  1920 version, 406–408
  Franco-Prussian War, influence on 1874
    version, 50
  Crowder, Enoch, authorship of 1916 Articles
    of War, 20, 24
  Freedom of speech curtailed, 43
  Jefferson, Thomas, 50
  Origin of, Sweden and Britain, 50
  Winthrop, William, 71
  Double Jeopardy, 54, 61, 159, 390, 411
  "Revisory Authority," 51, 89, 91, 368, 370,
    380, 382,
  Offenses and Sentences
    Absence without leave (AWOL), 43
    Conduct Unbecoming an Officer and
      Gentleman, 54–55
    Death penalty, 46, 92
    Desertion, 18–19, 43
    Draft evasion (desertion), 105
    Fraudulent enlistment, 253
    "General Article," 54
    Insubordination, 63
    Larceny and robbery, 136
    Murder, 66

Bailey, Robert Kemper, 359 -360, 418
Barry, Thomas, General, 43, 52, 304, 335–336
Battles of World War I (without US Army
  involvement)
  "Nivelle Offensive," and French Army
    mutiny, 45, 153, 309–310, 369
  Gallipoli, 151

Kut el-Amara, 215
Lys, 169
Verdun, 44–45, 153, 165, 179, 295,
Somme, 107, 153, 169, 171, 174, 204,
Ypres (Third), 153
Baker, Newton, 11, 13, 27, 28–33, 46, 48, 54, 55,
  65, 72, 75–77, 80–81, 87, 102, 117, 122, 127,
  134, 140–141, 145, 148, 177, 186, 199, 201,
  205, 209, 212–213, 240–241, 246, 251–252,
  256–258, 261–264, 267, 270–274, 276, 280,
  291, 294, 301, 302–304, 306, 308, 314, 317,
  320–321, 325, 329, 332, 334–335, 344, 349,
  352, 354–356, 359–361, 364, 368, 380–381,
  385, 388, 393–384, 400, 406, 410, 420
  Ansell, Samuel, 89, 91–92, 361–362,
  Conscientious Objectors, 105
  Crowder, Enoch, 23–24, 50, 69, 85, 90, 100,
    106, 315, 338, 373, 375–377, 402,
  Appoints Crowder, Enoch, as Provost
    Marshal of the United States, 11
  General Order No., 7, 46–47, 154–156
  Pershing, John J., disagreement with, 156
  Selective Service, 95–97, 100, 103–104
Barnwell, Nathaniel, 222
  Seventh Division's judge advocate, 222
Baruch, Bernard, 79–82, 98, 106, 248, 360
Bauer, Frederick, Gilbert, 86, 181
Bayne, Hugh A., 86, 87, 150, 153, 159, 177–178,
  181, 187, 212,-213, 234–235, 312
Beach, Charles, 357
Belgium, 4, 92, 158, 213, 225, 228, 230, 249, 274,
  309, 340, 360,
Bell, George, General, 189
  Command of Thirty-Third Division, 189
Bell, J. Franklin, General, 37, 68, 74, 121, 324,
  329, 335, 372
  Wilson, Samuel, 121, 123, 132, 152, 177
Berger, Victor, Congressman, 166, 266, 325–327,
  387
Berntheizel, Cleon, 125–126, 190, 232, 247, 303,
  346
Bethel, Walter A., General, 29, 60–64, 80, 106,
  109, 150–152, 156, 163, 168, 171, 173,
  174–188, 202, 224–226, 232, 248, 269, 289,
  331–332, 345, 375, 384, 391, 395, 411
  Crowder, Enoch, general approval of Bethel,
    with reservations, 407
  German citizens, treatment in occupied
    Germany, 204
  Prisoners of war, treatment of, 203
  Military jurisdiction over civilians, views of,
    106–107

General Order No. 7, 149
Pershing, John J., relationship with, 142,
152
Prison scandal in France, 228
Formation of Judge Advocate General's
Office in the American Expeditionary
Forces, 142–148
War crimes trials, views of, 206
Wigmore, John Henry, relationship with,
75
Bliss, Tasker, General, 23–24, 34, 40, 77, 79,
95, 152, 205–206, 209, 216, 309, 319, 326,
344–345, 352, 389,
Ansell, Samuel relationship with and
negative opinion of, 75–76
Boer War, 74, 317, 347, 376, 412
Bolshevism, 28, 36, 69, 76, 78, 92, 196, 202,
216, 208, 220, 224–241, 244–248, 294, 301,
303, 306–307, 309–310, 313, 316, 318–334,
344–352, 356, 364, 371, 379, 384, 397, 390,
395, 399, 402–404, 416
Borah, William, Senator, 114, 113, 139,
259–261, 271–272, 300, 302, 305, 319, 364
Bourquin, Gabriel, Judge, 315, 387
Brandeis, Louis, 20, 82, 126, 143, 241–242, 277,
294, 304, 315–316, 318–319, 349, 363, 383,
402, 420
Advised Crowder on conscription and
other War Department matters, 81,
142–143, 273
Support for Samuel Wilson's commission
as Judge Advocate, 120
Brinton, Jasper, 107, 235, 246–248
British Army, 35
Military discipline in, 45–46, 142, 193,
263, 277
British Expeditionary Forces, 45, 169, 171, 174,
191, 210, 288
Military discipline in, 45, 372
Mutinies in, 151
Bryan, William Jennings, Secretary of State, 22,
49, 84, 207, 254, 318,
Burleson, Alfred, Postmaster General, 22, 114,
317, 325

Cadue, Frank, 159
Court-martial and execution, 160
Caillaux, Joseph, 311–313
Carter, Oberlin, 59–60
Court-martial of, 60
Federal appeals and Supreme Court
decisions, 60–62

Carter, William Harding, General, 94
Chamberlain, George Earle, Senator, 30, 50, 54,
91, 99, 108, 226, 247, 255, 269, 295, 299, 301,
319, 353, 359, 363–367, 381, 383, 384, 387,
391, 393, 396–397, 400, 402, 403, 407, 408, 415
Ansell, Samuel, allies with, 370, 373, 375,
380, 419
Crowder, Enoch, accuses Crowder of lying,
381,
Conscription, support for, 99, 104–15, 256
Chamberlain, George, United States Marine
Corps, court-martial of, 285–289
China, 32, 200
China Relief Expedition, 65–67, 99, 206, 242
Chiperfield, Burnett, M, 87–88, 102, 148,
340–341, 417
Thirty-Third Division, judge advocate, 189
Churchill, Marlboro, General, 204, 306
Churchill, Winston, 377–378
Clark, James "Champ," Congressman, 94, 104,
148, 241, 268, 295,
Clark, J. Reuben, 85, 229–230, 417
Clarke, John Hessin, Justice, 143, 145, 241, 305,
387
Clemenceau, Georges, French Premier, 171, 311,
331
Cleveland, Grover, President, 30, 32, 63, 173, 394
Coffman, Waldo, and the IWW mutiny
court-martial, 300–301, 319–320
Columbia University Law School, 18–19, 71, 84,
180, 198, 234, 323, 357, 386
Committee of Public Information, 307, 320
Connor, William Mellard, 140, 404–406, 414
Coolidge, Calvin, President, 179, 233, 403,
413–415, 417, 418,
Cosgrave, Partick, 158, 173–174, 197, 225, 404,
418
Ansell, Samuel, accused Ansell of "meritless
attacks," on courts-martial, 404,
Fifth Division's judge advocate, 174
Bethel, Walter A., positive view of Cosgrave,
181–182
Cleveland, Grover, presidential escort, 173
Nebraska state judge, 166, 173
Creel, George, 307–308, 321
Cresson, Charles, 117–119
Crowder, Enoch, (passim)
African American soldiers, 13
Ansell, Samuel 297–298, 327, 353–361, 368,
372, 374, 382
Baker, Newton, 23–24, 50, 69, 85, 90, 100,
106, 315, 338, 373, 375–377, 402,

Chamberlain, Senator, accuses Crowder of
    lying, 381
Bell, J. Franklin, 74
Bliss, Tasker H., 75–76
Kreger, Edward, 63, 65, 71, 206, 345, 375, 407
Pershing, John J., friendship with, 24
Taft, William Howard, 16, 18–19, 24, 27, 41,
    49, 60, 99, 352, 357
White, Wallace, Congressman, 111
Wilson, Woodrow, 18–19, 352
Appointed Provost Marshal of the United
    States, 11
Nominated as Judge Advocate General to
    replace General Davis, 1911
"Gentleman's Agreement," with Joffre, Field
    Marshal, 8, 248
On under-aged soldiers in France, 176–177
Personality of, 12–13
Lack of scholarly biography of, 12
"Shell shock" and insanity, 267–270
War Crimes, 15
Drafts order for Baker to enable officers
    to arrest civilians committing crimes
    against the military in late March 1917,
    28
Authored Selective Service Act, 97, 102–4
Russo-Japanese War, observer for War
    Department, 18, 21
Bill to promote Crowder, Enoch, to Lt
    General, 408
Cuba, 6, 18, 33, 47, 49, 65, 69, 71–75, 86, 102, 113,
    189, 200, 254, 264, 275, 334, 382–383, 420
Bolo, acting as agent of Germany in, 311
Crowder, Enoch, assisted in drafting consti-
    tution, 383, 414

De Castlenau, Noel, Field Marshal, 214
Daniels, Josephus, Secretary of the Navy, 84, 96,
    205, 286
Davis, Dwight, Secretary of War, 403
Davis Edwin, G., 46, 86, 272, 370–371
Davis, George Breckenridge, General, 17–18, 24,
    42, 57–58, 70–71, 74, 84, 139, 200, 206
Davis, John, Solicitor General, 92, 101–103,
    121–122, 148, 205, 209, 211–212, 228, 377,
    380
Day, Stephen Rufus, Justice, 141, 145
Debs, Eugene, 203, 327, 327, 385, 414
Dickman, Joseph T., General, 186, 199–202,
    220–222, 242, 402,
Dodds, Frank L., Colonel, 29, 60, 62–63, 114,
    315, 327

Advised that threat of IWW and German
    attempts to recruit African-American
    doctors did not exist, 321
Oldest judge advocate in the Judge Advocate
    General's Office, 62
Dowell, Cassius, 22, 77–78, 178–179, 293–294,
    416
Dunn, George M., 68, 69, 131–132, 141–142,
    166, 202, 205, 259, 295, 316, 328, 333,
    Crowder, Enoch, low opinion of Dunn, 69,
    142, 259

Edwards, Clarence, General, 69, 78
Espionage and other German activities in the
    United States and its territories, 25, 28, 30,
    146, 204, 208–209, 301–304, 305, 313–314,
    329, 409
Espionage Act, 305–309, 318, 321, 326–328,
    387
Courts-martial of soldiers for espionage,
    339–347
Almereyda, Miguel, 310, 313, 322
"Black Tom Island" explosion, 207, 209
Bolo, Paul, 310–313, 322
    Attempts to stoke labor unrest in
        Cuban sugar industry, 311
    Bayne, Hugh, name in Bolo's address
        book, 312
Cuba, German activities in, 311
"Hindu Plot," 199
Hill, John Philip, warns of German espio-
    nage operations, 316
Irish nationals, 208, 227
Sedition in Army, 90, 301, 330–339, 343,
Witzke, Lothar, 209–210
"Zimmerman Telegram," 317

Flood, Henry De La Warre, Congressman, 4,
    105, 122, 125, 296–298, 401–402
Foch Ferdinand, Field Marshal, 169, 171, 198,
    221
Franco-Prussian War, 35, 50, 124
Frankfurter, Felix, 12, 20, 62, 74, 79–83, 126,
    129, 143, 148, 166, 227, 241, 252, 277, 353,
    362–363, 403, 408, 419–420, 422
Ansell, Samuel, 403
Biography, 81
Brandeis, Louis, 142, 304
Conscientious objectors, 148
Crowder, special relationship with, 82, 414,
    418
Internal subversion and the Army, 309

Mutinies in French Army, 313, 329–330

Taft, William Howard, dislike of Frankfurter, 82

French Government, 20, 24, 152, 157, 168, 171, 181, 210, 222, 231, 242, 297, 309, 311, 331

War Ministry, 144, 149–151, 286, 310, 415,

French Army, 28, 35, 81, 101, 141, 150, 159, 163, 183, 188, 190, 214, 224, 242, 331, 392

Crowder, Enoch, had high opinion of early in war, 110

China Relief Expedition, 50

"Ceremonial Executions," 156

German prisoners of war, 210

Senegalese and Moroccan Soldiers in 172

Military discipline in, 44, 45–46, 142, 151, 156, 162, 171–172, 178, 181, 184, 263, 277, 369, 375, 378

Mutiny in 310, 322, 356

Punishment companies, 184

Funston, Frederick, General, 77–79, 199, 258

Gallogly, James A., 77–78, 194

Third Division's judge advocate, 78

First Army Corps' judge advocate, 194, 230

Garrison, Lindley, 7, 21–22, 32–34, 206–208, 251, 254–255, 267, 288, 301, 354

Coffman, Waldo, court-martial of, 301–302

Crowder, Enoch, 64, 81, 97–98, 253

Expansion of Judge Advocate General's Office, 80

Aligned with Crowder to defeat bill forbidding fraudulent enlistment prosecutions, 253

George, David Lloyd Prime Minister, 208, 343, 345,

Georgetown University Law School, 70, 77, 128, 134, 352, 357

George Washington University's law school, 18, 20, 64, 78

German Army, 25, 98–100, 111, 123, 134, 149, 152, 153, 188, 198–199, 204, 211, 214, 224, 227, 295, 317, 329, 334, 338, 360, 388

German Nationals in United States, 209

Glass, Carter, Senator (and Secretary of the Treasury), 41, 107, 120, 125, 258, 265, 278–279, 291–293, 346, 365, 402

Glasscock, William E, Governor, 113–114,

Goff, Guy Despard, 9, 89, 140, 166, 222–229, 304–305, 345, 403, 417, 420

African-American soldiers, Goff disparaged, 140

Goff, Nathan, Senator, 345, 394

Goodier, Lewis, 68, 70,

Gorfinkle, Bernard, 6, 129–130, 166, 178, 181, 210–212, 231, 418

Baruch, Bernard, aided by Gorfinkle, 248

Hull, John, lauded Gorfinkle, 181

Great Britain, 4, 66, 85, 93, 228, 311, 314, 343, 347, 387

Greene, Frank Lester, Congressman, 50, 253

Crowder, Enoch, congressional ally of, 50, 402

Gregory, Thomas Watts, Attorney General, 30–31, 77, 86, 92, 101, 108–109, 112, 121–123, 201, 208–209, 226, 288–289, 304, 315, 317, 322, 324–325,

Hackenberg, John, 202

Legal challenge to presidential call-up of National Guard, 202–205

Haig, Douglas, Field Marshal, 45, 191

Hand, Learned, Judge, 75, 87

Harbord, James., General, 45, 70, 155–156, 162, 167–170, 206, 201–211, 213, 232–237, 246, 298, 339,

Hull, John A. lobbied for Hull's promotion, 70

Crowder, Enoch, expressed anger at Crowder to Pershing, 155

Harding, Warren G., 209, 230, 247, 263, 288, 327, 409, 414, 421

Harvard University, Law School, 15, 20, 74, 80–84, 86, 106, 119, 122, 127, 166, 175, 181, 190, 225, 234–235, 277, 353, 417–418

Hill, Arthur Dehon, 158, 162, 166–168, 175, 181, 235, 403, 418

Bethel, Walter A., accorded Hill praise as the best judge advocate in the AEF, 181

Crowder, Enoch, defended against Ansell, 404

Services of Supply, assistant judge advocate, 167–170, 197, 234

Holmes, Oliver Wendell, jr., 166

Sacco, Niccolo and Vanzetti, Bartolomeo, represented, 167

Roosevelt, Thodore, relationship with 166

Hill, John Philip Clayton Boynton, 122, 134, 180, 189–191, 316, 403, 417

Ansell, Samuel, accused Ansell of lying to Crowder, 403, 417

Warns of German espionage in United States, 316

Twenty-Ninth Division's judge advocate, 134, 387

Conscription, advocated for in 1914, 124
Republican Party official in Maryland, 123
United States Attorney for Maryland, 122–123
Maryland National Guard's judge advocate, 123
German Army, attended maneuvers prior to the outbreak of war, 124
Injured by German gas attack, 180
Elected to Congress in 1920, 417
Hines, John Leonard, General, 44, 52, 54, 88, 150, 265, 381, 399,
Holbroke, Willard Ames, General, 333–334
Holmes, Oliver W., Justice, 57, 82, 143, 144–146, 166, 241, 403, 416
House, Edward, 20, 96, 286, 288, 325, 365
Houston Riot courts-martial, 141–143, 166, 328, 333, 379
Howard, Oliver O., 12–13
Howell, James A., 190–191
Howell, Wiley, 77, 234, 236
First Army's judge advocate, 193
Howze, Marian, 132, 165, 177
Huddleston, George, Congressman, 95
Accused Crowder, Enoch, of being a despot, 95
Humes, Edwin Lowry, 346–349
Hull, Cordell, Congressman, 105–106, 296
Hull, Harry, Congressman, 103
Hull, John A., 20, 68–70, 79, 83, 167–168, 181, 186, 264–265, 284, 339, 350, 383, 392, 399, 403
Crowder, Enoch, low opinion of Hull, 70–71, 166, 415
"Houston Riot" trials, 141–142
Services of Supply's judge advocate, 70, 168,
Hull, John A.T., Congressman, 68
Hutcheson, Grote, General, 65–66

International Committee of the Red Cross, 180, 211, 213, 233, 271,
International Workers of the World (IWW), 22, 28, 108, 113, 172, 225–226, 300, 303, 307–309 315–318, 321, 323–337, 340–342, 347, 349, 371, 395–396, 416
Influenza, 134, 245, 320
Insanity, as a legal defense in courts-martial, 19, 266, 272
Court-martial of Lieutenant Walter Church as example, 270–273
Court-martial of Private Julian Jarecky as example, 342

Ireland, 208, 314, 336, 343–344
Soldiers' sympathies for, 334–344
Italy, 28, 65, 87, 158, 198, 207, 227, 241, 287, 333,

Japan, 18, 21, 35, 65, 83, 99, 206, 245, 330, 319
Army of in WWI, 241–243
Russo-Japanese War, influence on U.S. Army, 35, 47, 317
Joffre, Joseph, Field Marshal, 144, 150, 221
"Gentleman's Agreement" with Crowder, Enoch, and Baker, Newton, 144
Johnson, Hiram, Senator, 246, 273, 274, 303, 305, 318, 321, 338, 368, 396
Crowder, Enoch, opposed Crowder's "work or fight" order, 273
Johnson, Hugh, 20, 77, 79, 87, 106
Johnson, Royal Cleves, Congressman, 297, 353, 401, 404, 417, 419
As Congressman, aligns with Samuel Ansell and Senator George Chamberlain, 353, 364, 402
Judson, William V., General, 326–327, 356–357, 383

Kahn, Julius, Congressman, 103–104, 296, 353, 364–365
Crowder, Enoch, defends Crowder during court-martial controversy, 400, 402
Kernan, Francis, General, 187, 212
"Kernan Report," 379–381, 389
Knox, Philander, Senator, 29–30, 85, 125, 229–230, 273, 367–368, 370, 387, 401,
Korn, Louis, 134
Kreger, Edward, General, 12, 60, 65–67, 149, 154–155, 178, 180–183, 187–188, 202, 209, 228, 251, 262, 269, 275–280, 315, 375, 382, 384, 390, 395, 402, 408
Ansell, Samuel, developed a negative opinion of Ansell, 361, 367
On under-aged soldiers in France, 176–177
Observed Russian Civil War, 371
Advised Pershing on reversal of courts-martial due to jurisdictional defects, 150–151
Intended appointment as Judge Advocate to the American Expeditionary Forces, 146
Appointed judge advocate for the First United States Army, 147
Crowder, Enoch, positive opinion of Kreger, 62, 63, 65, 71, 206, 345, 375, 407
Personal Representative of Crowder in France, 147
Treatment of prisoners of war, 203

Treatment of American soldiers imprisoned
in American military prisons in France,
218, 289
Intended war crimes prosecutions of
Germans, 206
Military trials of German civilians in occupied German areas, 214

La Follette, Robert, Senator, 27, 94, 108–109, 226,
261–262, 269–270, 299, 303, 318, 327, 357,
367, 387, 421
Crowder. Enoch, defended La Follette in
Senate inquiry, 281
Landis, Kenesaw, Judge, 320–321, 327
Lansing, Robert, Secretary of State, 49, 84–85,
109, 144, 201, 208–211, 225, 227–228,
246–248, 294, 365, 383,
Lenroot, Irvine Luther, Senator, 226, 387–388,
392–393, 397, 400
Lever, Francis Asbury, Congressman, 102–103,
125, 259, 285, 292, 345–346
Lieber, Francis, 74, 206
Lieber, G. Norman, 14–15, 18, 46, 61, 64, 78, 200,
307, 384 415
Liggett, Hunter, General, 46–47, 164, 182–184,
193–194, 214, 220, 242, 249, 313, 373,
Military discipline, views on, 47, 193
Lippman, Walter, 108, 309
Lodge, Henry Cabot, Senator, 247, 295–296, 306,
318, 327, 352, 387, 395

MacChesney, Nathan, 80, 85, 189, 203, 417
McAdoo, William Gibbs, 126, 290–294, 298,
311, 336,
McCain, H.P., General, 75–76, 209, 258, 330
McGovern, Francis E., 357
McNeil, Edward C., 77–78, 117–119, 416
Ninetieth Division's judge advocate, 139
McKinley, William, President, 16, 28, 32, 61, 68,
72, 84, 241, 334, 384, 395,
McReynolds, James C., Justice, 143–144, 241, 385
Mack, Julian, 148
March, Peyton, General, 12, 24, 42, 209, 211,
270, 278, 298, 328, 344, 356, 365, 396,
Mayes, James, 175, 186, 206, 312, 320, 324–325,
328
Mexico, 85, 320, 324, 330–331,
Army operations on border with United
States, 23, 43, 78, 86, 98, 112–117, 121,
124, 125, 129, 189, 202, 250, 257, 267,
298, 334, 347
German military observers in, 207, 318

Punitive Expedition, 79, 206, 316, 33
Nationals drafted into Army, 109–110, 341,
Military Affairs Committee, United States House
of Representatives, 69, 91, 95, 100, 103, 253,
273, 296, 365, 374, 408
Crowder, Enoch, testifies about conscription
at, 100
Military Affairs Committee, United States
Senate, 54, 104, 247, 301, 354–355, 364, 366,
374, 381, 294, 401
Moore, John Bassett, 16, 19, 69, 78, 180, 198
Morgan, Edmund, 357, 362, 385, 386, 392,
399–401, 408
Morgan, J.P., 311
Morrow, Henry A., 38, 68, 71–72, 78, 399
Murphy, Frank, Justice, 9, 127–129, 244, 413, 417

National Association for the Advancement of
Colored People (NAACP), 266, 328, 385,
419
Nelson, Knute, Senator, 346–347, 394
Ansell, Samuel, accuses of "Bolshevik
tendencies," 402
Norris, George, Senator, 27, 94, 263, 280,
318–319
Northwestern University Law School, 20

Ogden, Hugh, 6, 140, 166, 173, 197, 229,
379–380, 389
Ansell, Samuel, opposed courts-martial
reform efforts of, 404
Forty-Second Division's judge advocate, 171,
175–176, 181, 188–190
African-American soldiers, prejudice
against, 140
Provost Judge in Coblenz, Germany, 220
Ottoman Empire, 10, 111, 123, 215, 237, 324
Investigation in treatment of Armenians
(Armenian Genocide), 241, 246–248
Overman, Lee Slater, Senator, 30, 306, 345–347
Overman Committee, 345–347

Palmer, A. Mitchell, Attorney General, 267,
346–347, 375, 397
Palmer, John MacAuley, General, 368
Patents, 29–30, 42,
Patterson, Adam E., 142–143, 182, 192, 197, 419
Patton, George S, 262
Petain, Henri, Field Marshal, 160, 169
Pershing, John J., 11, 15, 23, 24, 27, 44, 46, 70, 73,
77, 95, 119, 149, 154, 174, 183, 186, 188, 191,
193–196, 199, 200–201, 206, 241, 319, 344,

345, 352, 363, 373, 383, 390, 394, 396–397, 400, 404, 415, 416

Bethel, Walter A., 37, 171

Crowder, Enoch, similar upbringing, 12

Crowder, Enoch, close relationship with, 21, 24, 70–71, 415

Crowder, Enoch, differences of positions regarding military discipline, 47, 155, 156, 158

Crowder, Enoch, influences the addition of officers into the Judge Advocate General's Office, 77–79, 88

Crowder, Enoch, expressed disappointment in Pershing's silence during court-martial debates, 402

American Expeditionary Forces, command over, 35–36, 40, 144, 150–151, 153, 158–163,

Allies, relationships with, 36, 45, 214

Law of war, treatment of German prisoners of war, 210–211

Command in occupied Germany, 213, 219, 235,

Prison scandal, 237

Courts-martial in the American Expeditionary Forces, oversight of, 46, 268, 271, 297, 313,

Summary punishments, 47

Pepper, Samuel, 101, 109, 115, 133, 170, 172, 197, 234, 303, 356, 417

Bethel, Walter A., positive opinion of Pepper, 181

Mexican border service, 116

Thirty-Second Division's judge advocate, 133, 171–172, 233

Opposed summary punishments, 172, 191

Philippines, 4, 21, 34–35, 44, 47, 49, 57, 65, 76, 84, 86–87, 99, 102, 112–113, 117, 121, 138, 140, 189, 199, 200, 213, 251, 275, 290, 295, 333, 370, 391, 404

Crowder, Enoch, and service in 15–18, 24

"Insurrection," 1899–1902, 15, 68, 70–73, 98, 173, 206, 254, 420

Poindexter, Miles, Senator, 275, 279, 294–296, 301, 317–319, 401

Porter, Charles V, 158, 175

Seventy-Ninth Division's judge advocate, 175, 181

Porter, John B., 68, 70

Prettyman, Elijah, Barret, 9, 127, -129, 303

Prisoners of War, 151, 167, 179, 190, 197, 202, 205, 209–212

Prohibition (liquor), 77, 176, 181, 237, 256, 346, 348, 366, 397, 400

Prostitution, 9, 118, 160, 220, 243, 284, 363

Read, Beverly A., 68, 71, 371

Reichmann Carl, 317–320

Roosevelt, Theodore, President, 5, 13, 15, 27, 32, 42, 49, 69, 72, 100, 104, 106, 126, 139, 145, 166–167, 205, 260, 302, 318, 349, 367

Root, Elihu, Secretary of War, 17, 18, 49, 68, 74, 82, 84, 86, 99–100, 227–229, 355, 362, 376, 384, 391, 402

Crowder, Enoch, 17,

Winship, Blanton, 68, 72

Rucker, Kyle, 77, 199–201, 216–229, 333

Ruckman, John, General, 132, 141, 328, 333–334

Ruppenthal, Jacob, 359–360, 418

Russia, 18, 26, 32, 36, 47, 66, 67, 92, 212, 240, 269, 294, 307, 345, 376, 402

Bolshevik Revolution, 28, 348, 357, 379, 388

Russo-Japanese War, 47

United States Army in Port Arthur, 1918–1920, 67, 241–246, 400–402

United States Army in Murmansk, 1918–1920, 241, 241–246, 400–402

Crowder, Enoch, advised that Russian nationals could not be held as prisoners of war, 245

Sanner, James Sidney, 359, 418

Saulsbury, Willard, Senator, 26

Schofield, John McAlister, 12, 62

Scott, James Brown, 80

"Shell-Shock," 175, 267–268, 272, 279

Crowder, Enoch, views of, 272

Court-martial of Private Earl Sanders as example, 269–271

Smith, M. "Hoke," Senator, 119, 263, 292, 367

Smith, Mendel, 124–125, 131, 133, 137, 164, 237, 337, 418

Socialist Party, United States, 26, 104, 146, 302, 318, 324–327

Spanish-American War, 4–5, 32, 49, 69, 71, 73, 76, 78, 84, 94, 98, 100, 112, 117, 126, 131, 166, 206, 222, 251, 292, 376, 384, 388

Speer, Emory, Judge, 112

Stimson, Henry A, 7, 22, 139, 260, 354, 362–364, 401

Crowder, Enoch, 85, 96, 99–100, 384

Court-martial controversy of 1919, 383

Frankfurter, Felix, 81–82, 419

Stone, Harlan Fiske, 71, 78, 87, 148, 180, 277, 386, 391, 413, 418
Strode, Aubrey, 357
Summerall, Charles Pelot, General, 156, 269, 356, 391
Supreme Court, 7, 8, 9, 11, 15, 19, 31, 49, 54, 58, 59, 62, 74–75, 78, 81, 83–85, 87, 94, 101–102, 103, 105, 119, 127, 143, 146, 183, 191, 203, 241–242, 249, 250, 255, 260, 278, 290, 324, 327, 357, 368, 379, 385–387, 413, 420
  Cambell, John A., Justice, 87
  Field, Stephen A., Justice, 31
  Douglas, William O., 278
  Judge advocates who later became justices, 9, 127
  Butler v. Perry, 94
  Coleman v. Tennessee, 249, 325
  Collins V. McDonald, 242
  Dynes v. Hoover, 55
  Ex Parte Mason, 6, 7
  Ex Parte Milligan, 21, 82, 102, 422
  Grafton v. United States, 59–60, 390
  Kahn v. Anderson, 410–411
  Jacobson v. Massachusetts, 94
  McClaughery v. Deming, 5, 7
  Martin v. Mott, 116
  Parker v. Levy, 379
  Patterson v. Colorado, 305
  Reeves v. Ainsworth, 421
  Runkle v. United States, 52, 59
  Selective Draft Cases (Arver v. United States), 143
  Trop v. Dulles, 255
  United States v. Hudson and Goodwin, 54, 228
  United States v. Page, 60
Sutphin, Dudley, 141, 166
  Eighty-Third Division's judge advocate, 166

Taft, William Howard, 16, 17, 32, 85, 123, 141, 166, 226, 277, 305, 360, 366, 368, 384, 400
  Ansell, Samuel, disparages Ansell's motives in court-martial controversy, 400–402
  Brandeis, Louis, dislike of, 82
  Crowder, Enoch, 18–19, 24, 27, 41, 49, 60, 99, 352, 357
  Frankfurter, Felix, dislike of, 82
  Prisoner of war, advised War Department on status of interned German nationals, 30, 212
  Selective Service, support for, 100, 106
Teare, Charles, 117, 175, 225

Fourth Division's judge advocate, 117, 165, 188, 192
Tillman, Benjamin Ryan, Senator, 102, 120, 124, 139, 143, 222, 266, 279, 282, 319, 329,
Tumulty, Joseph, 33–34, 41, 127, 208, 250, 252, 259, 268, 284,

University of California's law school, 20, 79, 120
Upton, Emory, 100, 147, 156

Van Deman, Ralph, General, 316, 329, 349, 363
Van Devanter, Willis, Justice, 119, 143
Vallandigham, Clement, 305
Venereal Disease, 151, 187, 216
Villard, Oswald Garrison, 143, 267

Wadsworth, James, Senator, 247, 295, 318, 366–370, 397, 395, 401
Wadsworth, Military Encampment, 137
Wallace, George, 22, 49, 86, 89, 103, 113, 185, 196, 211, 225, 303
  Martial law in West Virginia, 114–116
  Mexican border service, 23
  Military jurisdiction over civilians, 22, 113–114
  Soldiers and Sailors Civil Relief Act, 49–50, 87
  Suppression of newspapers, 114
Walsh, Thomas, 110–111, 126, 208, 254, 274, 280, 289, 307
Wambaugh, Eugene, 20, 80, 242, 246, 304, 354, 360, 368, 375, 417
War Risk Insurance, 42, 48, 108, 233, 261, 290–295, 357, 373, 406
Watson, Thomas, Senator, 112, 186, 274, 281, 283, 367,
Weeks, John, Senator (and later Secretary of War), 175–176, 205, 270, 283, 295, 319, 327, 350, 365, 367–368, 370, 395, 401, 403, 404, 419
Weinberger, Harry, 421
Warren, Charles, Assistant Attorney General, 207, 209
Warren, Charles Beecher, 86–87, 106–107, 110, 148, 244, 276, 279, 336, 418
  Ford, Henry, 107
Warren, Francis E. Senator, 306, 367, 371, 385, 387, 391–400, 405–406
Webb, Edwin Yates, Congressman, 29, 304, 307, 397
West, Duvall, Judge, 118, 324
Westenhaver, David, Judge, 54, 203, 387

Weygand, Maurice, Field Marshal, 221, 223,
Wheless, Joseph, 80
White, Edward Douglass, Chief Justice, 116, 143,
    146-147
White, Herbert, 68, 89, 112, 118, 125, 256, 403, 410
White, Wallace, Congressman, 111, 119, 293
Whitsett, George P., 86, 181
Wigmore, John Henry, 20, 144, 205, 227, 229,
    295, 338, 350, 367, 376, 408
    Allegations of criminal conduct by Senator
        George Chamberlain, 375
    Ansell Samuel, 353, 359
    Brandeis, Louis, 144
    Court-Martial Controversy of 1919, 382,
        384-386, 390-391, 399, 408
    Crowder, Enoch, 80-81, 85, 277
    Early military service and influence on
        military law, 83, 114
    Influence on Selective Draft Act, 105, 148
    Reactionary conservatism of, 416, 418
    Winship, Blanton, work on evidence rules
        for courts-martial in 1916, 83
Williams, John Sharp, Senator, 26, 76, 250-251
Wilson, James, Secretary of Agriculture, 68
Wilson, James Harrison, 126
Wilson, Samuel MacKay, 120-122, 132, 139, 164,
    223, 237, 239-240, 342, 380, 403
    Seventy-Seventh Division's judge advocate,
        176
    Opposed Kentucky law banning the teaching
        of children German, 238
    Wilson, Woodrow, support for judge advo-
        cate commission, 121-122
    Henry Ford, Wilson derides as a "sissy," 122
    War crimes trials, argued to prosecute Otto-
        man officials for murder of Armenians,
        247-248
Wilson, William, Secretary of Labor, 313
Wilson, Woodrow, 3, 11, 20, 25, 27, 32-36, 43, 49,
    55, 76, 79, 81-83, 87, 95-98, 101, 104, 106,
    112, 116, 123-125, 127, 141, 143-144, 156,
    159, 195, 201, 203, 206, 208-209, 226, 229,
    241-242, 247, 248, 250-258, 264, 287-288,

    291, 296, 301, 307, 317-318, 325, 327, 332,
        334, 336, 345, 357, 363-365, 367, 396, 399,
        401, 406, 409, 410, 412
    Ansell, Samuel, 382
    Armed Ship Bill, 94
    Crowder, Enoch, 18-19, 352
    Courts-martial and congressional pressure
        to overturn, 250-259, 268
    Espionage Act, 305, 307
    Fourteen Points, 213
    Houston "Riot" trials, 142
    Lack of knowledge of courts-martial, 46
    League of Nations, 92
    Object of soldier derision in sedition cases,
        332-337, 341
    Russia, decision to send soldiers into,
        241-243, 245-246
    Selective Service, 93, 96 102, 274, 277, 281
    Wilson, Samuel McKay, supported for com-
        mission as judge advocate, 121-122
Winship, Blanton, 20, 33, 57, 68, 78, 83, 127,
    164, 174-177, 183-185, 194, 195, 201, 210,
    214, 217, 230, 231-236, 240-246, 247, 286,
    297-298, 320, 350, 369, 376, 380, 416,
    Judge Advocate to First United States Army,
        72, 155
    Liggett, Hunter, General, relationship with,
        184, 193
    Prison scandal in the American Expedition-
        ary Forces, 234-236, 297
    Wigmore, John Henry, work on evidence
        rules for courts-martial in 1916, 83
    Wood, Leonard, General, positive opinion of
        Winship, 72
Winthrop, William, 57-58, 71, 83, 200, 210, 390,
    415
    Military Law and Precedents, 57, 71, 83, 114,
        132, 158, 210, 220, 240, 415
    Ansell, Samuel, blames for unfairness in
        courts-martial, 390

Yale University's law school, 70, 87, 141, 175, 357,
    384, 400-401